CompTIA CASP+ (CAS-005) Certification Guide

Expert resource for advanced cybersecurity concepts
and vulnerability assessment techniques,
with mock exams and real-world scenarios

2nd Edition

Dr. Akashdeep Bhardwaj

bpb

www.bpbonline.com

Second Revised and Updated Edition 2025

First Edition 2022

Copyright © BPB Publications, India

ISBN: 978-93-65899-870

To View Complete
BPB Publications Catalogue
Scan the QR Code:

Dedicated to

My beloved parents

Late Wg. Cdr. (Retd.) **K C Bhardwaj** *and* **Usha Bhardwaj**
and

My wife **Archana** *and my daughter* **Raavi**

About the Author

Dr. Akashdeep Bhardwaj is working as a professor at *UPES, Dehradun, India*. An eminent IT industry expert in cybersecurity, digital forensics and IT operations areas, he mentors graduate, masters and doctoral students. Additionally, as the Head of Cybersecurity (Center of Excellence), he leads several industry projects.

Dr. Akashdeep is a Post-Doctoral from Majmaah University, Saudi Arabia, and a PhD (doctoral) in computer science. He has over 150 international publications (including SCI, Scopus, WoS papers, Copyrights, Patents) and authored several books and chapters. He has also worked as a technology leader for several multinational organizations during his time in the IT industry. Dr. Akashdeep is certified in multiple technologies including compliance audits, cybersecurity, and industry certifications in Microsoft, Cisco, and VMware technologies.

Acknowledgement

There are a few people I want to thank for the continued and ongoing support they have given me during the writing of this book. First and foremost, I would like to thank my parents for continuously encouraging me to write the book. I could have never completed this book without their support.

My gratitude also goes to the team at BPB Publications for being supportive enough to provide me quite a long time to finish the first part of the book and also allow me to publish the book since the topics included are vast and it was impossible to explore different class of problems in a single book, especially by not making it too voluminous.

Preface

This book covers many different aspects of cybersecurity. Obtaining the CASP certification demonstrates proven capabilities in terms of knowledge and skills to design and maintain security services for complex, enterprise environments and large organizations to secure their valuable assets. This includes core, technical knowledge, and hands-on skills to design and implement and integrate security solutions across enterprise environments. This book will serve as a guide written to provide deep insights into the operations of IT security, risks, technical security integrations, and working of security operations at the enterprise level with real-world tasks and activities security professionals at the lead and specialist level tend to perform day-in and day-out on the security floor. This book provides added-value apart from enhancing the required technical skills in form of stories, tips, notes, and links for additional knowledge to prepare you for the certification.

Chapter 1: Introduction to CASP+ Exam- This chapter introduces the CASP exam certification is a popular security certification. There are several popular vendor-specific certifications in the IT industry but CASP is a unique, vendor-neutral certification. This certification is a stepping-stone to other specialized, vendor-specific certifications. CASP exam topics are generic and apply to several varied security technologies, irrespective of the vendors. This book has several examples associated with vendor tools, configurations, and technologies. For specific vendor products, training regarding that vendor hardware, device, or software can be found in training specific to that vendor.

Chapter 2: Bussiness and Industry Trends, Influences, and Risks- This chapter presents the business and industry, trends, influences and risks, as security and IT teams do not operate independently, the work and tasks are highly influenced by the organization's business objectives, which define the IT roadmap and decisions. However, factors outside the enterprise control, like constant attacks, technology changes, and upgrades, regulations, compliance add to the complexity of securing the organization's security ecosystem. This chapter includes the various security risks due to the influences and the global market trends affecting IT.

Chapter 3: Organization Security Policies and Documents- This chapter includes the organizational security and privacy, policies and procedures. Since IT security policy and governance procedures are implemented to secure organizational assets, this chapter presents the creation, implementation, and management of the security policy life cycle. Use of business contracts for service level agreements and project documents to support security is also covered.

Chapter 4: Risk Mitigation Strategies- This chapter presents the risk mitigation strategies and controls for security teams to ensure organizations have proper risk mitigation strategies and controls in place. Using risk management frameworks helps to identify and implement the appropriate controls. This chapter covers the steps involved in risk mitigation, which include Asset identification, CIA Triad, determination of threats, the likelihood of attacks, implementing countermeasures. Then conducting risk analysis to determine the security threshold level. This chapter also covers the best practices and scenarios to implement user authentication and authorization in organizations.

Chapter 5: Enterprise Risk Measurement and Metrics- This chapter covers the enterprise risk measurement and metrics for securing an organization and assigning the highest priority, yet the business and senior management need to be convinced to allocate budget and resources for ensuring top-notch security. Security heads need to justify implementing security controls or buying new security technologies. After the security controls have been implemented, this chapter presents the review and assessment of the effectiveness of the risk controls by gathering and analyzing the risk metrics. The results are further interpreted for future trends, existing security levels, and trends against industry standards and baselines.

Chapter 6: Components of Network Security- This chapter presents the components of network security for organizations that seek to implement secure architecture for its network and systems. The secure design needs to have an understanding of the organization services and delivery components like servers, networks to include in the secure design. To implement security features, IT teams need to account for users' ease of use, performance cost, and security standards and principles. This chapter presents the building blocks for implementing a secure architecture for enterprises and critical infrastructures, which includes physical, virtual, network and servers.

Chapter 7: Securing Networks, Hosts Systems, and Devices- This chapter includes securing host systems and devices even as securing an enterprise does not stop at network traffic monitoring, since cyberattacks are initiated to exploit servers and user systems (hosts). This chapter presents the various controls for protecting and securing servers and user systems. This includes the use of trusted OS, bootloader security, OS hardening, endpoint security, application-level vulnerabilities.

Chapter 8: Secure Storage Controls- This chapter presents the storage control security for organizations to implement network security controls and perform audits, as security assessments. If every component of the organization is not included, the assessment is incomplete and leaves the organization exposed. This chapter presents a defence-in-depth strategy that needs to be implemented which should include physical, virtual, cloud, on-premise, and user devices connecting to the office network. This chapter presents the assessment tools for performing security assessments at all levels.

Chapter 9: Securing the Internet of Things- This chapter discusses the security of the Internet of Things, after securing operating system and hardening the security assessments should mandatorily assess the smart devices inside industrial plants, homes and organizations. The chapter explains the concept to include an industrial closed loop control system in which data is collected, combined with related data, sent to an intelligent station, processed, and acted upon to change the environment. IoT is an ideal domain for not only securing devices, but also for innovations in secure system design, secure building block technologies, and secure hardware and software development practise, all of which combine to make the Internet of Things into the Secure Internet of Things.

Chapter 10: Cloud and Virtualization Security- This chapter presents cloud and virtualization security to monitor and detect cloud security incidents, and investigate and respond to them, as organizations have in-house or outsourced security operations. The incident response is a well-defined document for normal operations about actions to perform during an attack or breach. This serves as a baseline for ensuring operational recovery and back to normal activities. This helps security analysts recognize security incidents or anomalies and a process to respond. Every organization gathers the attacks and response to create a baseline over some time and measures the security operational incident response and effectiveness.

Chapter 11: Application Security Controls- This chapter discusses the different application vulnerability controls as this chapter examines some of the cyberattacks that can be launched against application, as well as the vulnerabilities that apps running on various operating systems present. It also covers safe coding techniques. Finally, the devices and services utilised to secure apps are discussed in this chapter.

Chapter 12: Security Assessments- This chapter covers the different procedures and methodologies involved in security vulnerability assessments, penetration testing, internal and external audits and colour based-team exercises.

Chapter 13: Selecting Vulnerability Assessment Tools- The chapter presents the process for selecting vulnerability assessment tools, even as most people think in terms of the network when they consider security assessments, security assessments encompass much more than this. If only network security were considered, major vulnerabilities would be left exposed. It can be argued that without sufficient physical security, network security cannot be achieved. Moreover, when exercising a defence-in-depth strategy, security must be considered at the network, host, and physical levels. This chapter looks at the tools used to perform assessments at each of these levels.

Chapter 14: Securing Communication and Collaborative Solutions- The chapter discusses securing communication and collaborative solution since increasingly, workers and the organizations for which they work are relying on new methods of communicating and working together that introduce new security concerns. As a CASP professional, you need to be familiar with these new technologies, understand the security issues they raise, and implement controls that mitigate the security issues. This chapter describes these new methods and technologies, identifies issues, and suggests methods to secure these new workflow processes.

Chapter 15: Implementing Cryptographic Techniques- This chapter discusses cryptography since this is one of the most complicated fields of security expertise. Both at rest and in transit, cryptography is a vital component of data security. It's a science that comprises hiding data or altering it to make it unreadable. Message authorship, source verification, and delivery proof are all ensured via cryptography. cryptography is concerned with confidentiality, integrity, and authentication, but not with availability. The CIA triumvirate is a basic security paradigm that includes secrecy, integrity, and availability, with cryptography addressing two of the triad's main pillars. It aids in the identification and prevention of data manipulation, deletion, and modification. Cryptography also provides non-repudiation by demonstrating a message's origin. Each of these ideas is examined in further depth in this chapter.

Chapter 16: Identification, Authentication, and Authorization- This chapter discusses identification of persons and devices, as well as determining the actions that a person or device is permitted to undertake, are at the heart of access control models. While this paradigm has stayed consistent since network computing's conception, the methodologies for conducting this key set of activities have developed tremendously and continue to do so. While simple usernames and passwords have historically served as access control, in today's world, more complicated and secure approaches are fast developing. Not only are such primitive approaches no longer secure, but today's access credential systems value convenience above everything else. Single sign-on and federated access control are two techniques for making a system as user-friendly as possible. The newest authentication and authorization approaches and processes are discussed in this chapter.

Chapter 17: Security Incidents and Response- This chapter discusses security incident analysis that involve an organisation should first capture the usual actions and performance of a system before determining if an event has happened. This serves as a benchmark against which all other activities are measured. To effectively determine when an event has happened, security professionals should ensure that the baseline is captured during periods of high and low activity. Additionally, they should collect baselines over time to ensure the best overall baseline is achieved. Following that, the company must design policies that detail how security personnel should respond to incidents.

Chapter 18: Integrating Hosts, Networks, Storage, and Applications- Organizations need to securely integrate hosts, storage, networks, and applications. It is the security practitioner's responsibility to ensure that appropriate security access controls are implemented and tested apart from several other steps. This chapter discusses integration of hosts, network, storage and applications.

Chapter 19: Security Activities across Technology Lifecycle- This chapter explores the security activities across the technology lifecycle when it comes to managing an enterprise's security, security practitioners must consider security throughout the whole technological life cycle. Security practitioners must ensure that the necessary security controls are installed as the company evolves as new devices and technologies are added, maintained, and removed. Understanding the systems and software development life cycles, adapting solutions to handle evolving risks, disruptive technologies, and security trends, and asset management are all part of providing security across the technology life cycle.

Chapter 20: CASP+ Skill Assessment Exam-I- This chapter presents the first part of the CASP+ skill assessment questions and answers.

Chapter 21: CASP+ Skill Assessment Exam-II- This chapter presents the second part of the CASP+ skill assessment questions and answers.

Code Bundle and Coloured Images

Please follow the link to download the
Code Bundle and the *Coloured Images* of the book:

https://rebrand.ly/9bc9ef

The code bundle for the book is also hosted on GitHub at
https://github.com/bpbpublications/CompTIA-CASP-Plus-CAS-005-Certification-Guide-2nd-Edition.
In case there's an update to the code, it will be updated on the existing GitHub repository.

We have code bundles from our rich catalogue of books and videos available at
https://github.com/bpbpublications. Check them out!

Errata

We take immense pride in our work at BPB Publications and follow best practices to ensure the accuracy of our content to provide with an indulging reading experience to our subscribers. Our readers are our mirrors, and we use their inputs to reflect and improve upon human errors, if any, that may have occurred during the publishing processes involved. To let us maintain the quality and help us reach out to any readers who might be having difficulties due to any unforeseen errors, please write to us at :

errata@bpbonline.com

Your support, suggestions and feedbacks are highly appreciated by the BPB Publications' Family.

Did you know that BPB offers eBook versions of every book published, with PDF and ePub files available? You can upgrade to the eBook version at www.bpbonline. com and as a print book customer, you are entitled to a discount on the eBook copy. Get in touch with us at :

business@bpbonline.com for more details.

At **www.bpbonline.com**, you can also read a collection of free technical articles, sign up for a range of free newsletters, and receive exclusive discounts and offers on BPB books and eBooks.

Piracy

If you come across any illegal copies of our works in any form on the internet, we would be grateful if you would provide us with the location address or website name. Please contact us at **business@bpbonline.com** with a link to the material.

If you are interested in becoming an author

If there is a topic that you have expertise in, and you are interested in either writing or contributing to a book, please visit **www.bpbonline.com**. We have worked with thousands of developers and tech professionals, just like you, to help them share their insights with the global tech community. You can make a general application, apply for a specific hot topic that we are recruiting an author for, or submit your own idea.

Reviews

Please leave a review. Once you have read and used this book, why not leave a review on the site that you purchased it from? Potential readers can then see and use your unbiased opinion to make purchase decisions. We at BPB can understand what you think about our products, and our authors can see your feedback on their book. Thank you!

For more information about BPB, please visit **www.bpbonline.com**.

Join our book's Discord space

Join the book's Discord Workspace for Latest updates, Offers, Tech happenings around the world, New Release and Sessions with the Authors:

https://discord.bpbonline.com

Table of Contents

CHAPTER 1
Introduction to CASP+ Exam

Introduction

The **CompTIA Advanced Security Practitioner (CASP+)** certification is a popular security certification. There are several popular vendor-specific certifications in the IT industry, but CASP is a unique, vendor-neutral certification. This certification is a stepping-stone to other specialized, vendor-specific certifications. CASP exam topics are generic and apply to several varied security technologies, irrespective of the vendors. This book has multiple examples of vendor tools, configurations, and technologies. For specific vendor products, training regarding that vendor's hardware, device, or software can be found in training specific to that vendor.

Structure

In this chapter, we will cover the following topics:

- Intended audience
- Steps to exam preparation
- Exam objectives
- Exam topics description

Objectives

The objective of this book is to understand the topics and technologies covered by the CASP blueprint from CompTIA. This book will enhance your knowledge and help you master the goal of clearing the CASP exam. To help you understand the CASP certification objectives, the chapters provide the opening topics list, which defines all the topics covered in that chapter. It also provides key topic icons to indicate important figures, tables, or information. These icons are available throughout the chapters and are also summarized in a table format at the end. Memory tables help memorize the important information for the CASP topics. Key terms are listed at the end of each chapter; try to learn and understand the definitions of each term and check your understanding of that chapter.

This book will summarize external and business influences on security, compare organizational security policies and procedures, analyze and perform risk mitigations and controls, integrate network and OS architecture to comply with security requirements, and design and select appropriate security controls.

Intended audience

Readers of this book can vary from those attempting to attain specialist or lead roles in the IT security domain to those who want to sharpen their technical skills to apply for new project roles or even go for the certification as per the organization mandate that wants them to take the new CASP exam. Those seeking to acquire additional skills and certification beyond the CASP certification, say those planning for **Certified Information Systems Security Professional (CISSP)**, **Certified Information Security Manager (CISM)** certifications, and beyond will find this book useful.

The book is designed to offer an easy transition for future certifications for experienced security architects, security specialists, technical leads, and security application engineers, who seek to enhance their skills and expertise, along with work experience, to leverage their experience and grow in the security career.

To be successful in this certification, first, you will need to bring your work experience, with a recommendation of having around 10 years of hands-on, core technical security real-world experience. The expectation is to build and use your home lab of virtual machines and tools, which will provide you with an environment to make-break and test your security skills. This would include network security, operating systems, cloud, governance, risk, and tons of security tools. The practitioners will learn to analyze a real-world scenario involving cloud, virtualization, networks, servers, applications, and end-user systems to select and implement appropriate security controls and perform assessments and recovery procedures at the enterprise level.

Steps to exam preparation

The suggested strategy while preparing for the CASP exam is to read and understand the book chapters and take down notes of key topics and concepts on a notepad or a separate paper book. It is highly advised to download the latest CASP exam objective list from the CompTIA certification site at **http://certification.comptia.org/examobjectives.aspx**.

Practice exams have been included in this book and you are recommended to attempt the practice exams, find out areas where you lack confidence, and review the specific concepts. After you review those specific areas, re-attempt the practice exams a second time to rate yourself. As you attempt the exams, you will become familiar with the terms, questions, and keywords. After a few attempts, you will feel confident in your understanding and skills. Then, schedule the CompTIA CASP exam from a center near you. Refer to *Pearson* **Virtual University Enterprises (VUE)** or any information you need when planning to register for the exam at **www.pearsonvue.com/comptia**.

Following are the exam details:

- **Maximum questions**: 90
- **Type of questions**: **Multiple-choice questions (MCQ)** and performance-based
- **Test duration**: 165 minutes
- **Recommended experience**: The following are the recommendations:
  - Minimum of ten years of general hands-on IT experience, with at least five of those years being broad hands-on IT security experience.
  - Network+, Security+, CySA+, Cloud+, and PenTest+ or equivalent certifications.
- **Pass score**: Pass or Fail only

Exam objectives

Table 1.1 lists the domains measured by this examination and the extent to which they are being represented:

Domains	Percentage %
Security Architecture	29%
Security Operations	30%
Security Engineering and Cryptography	26%
Governance, Risk, and Compliance	15%
Total coverage	**100%**

Table 1.1: Exam domains

Exam topics description

The exam chapter descriptions are mentioned in the following section, which lists the chapter names along with the objectives, descriptions, and keyword topics for each chapter.

Chapter 1: Introduction to CASP+ Exam

This chapter introduces **CompTIA Advanced Security Practitioner (CASP+)** certification, describing CASP sponsoring bodies, goals, and the value of CASP as a career and business driver. The official objectives covered on the CASP exam and steps to become CASP are explained along with the information on the CompTIA certification exam policies. This book presents the topics with detailed subject contents, including key learnings and essential keywords at the end of each chapter.

The exam topics covered are as follows:

- CASP goals
- Target audience
- Steps to CASP
- Exam topic description

Chapter 2: Business and Industry Trends, Influences, and Risks

Security and IT teams do not operate independently. The work and tasks are highly influenced by the organization's business objectives, which define the IT roadmap and decisions. However, factors outside the enterprise's control, like constant attacks, technology changes and upgrades, regulations, and compliance, add to the complexity of securing the organization's security ecosystem. This chapter includes the various security technology and market trends, influences, and global risks affecting IT security.

The exam topics covered are as follows:

- Business and industry influences
- External and internal factors
- New and changing business models or strategies
- Risk management
- Dynamic business models
- New strategies
- Security concerns during integration
- External and internal influence
- De-Perimeterization

Chapter 3: Organization Security Policies and Documents

IT security policy and governance procedures are implemented to secure organizational assets. This chapter presents the creation, implementation, and management of the security policy life cycle. Use of business contracts for service level agreements and project documents to support security are also covered.

The exam topics covered are as follows:

- Organization security policies
- Enterprise security procedures
- Security process life cycle management
- Business documents for security management
- Legal support and compliance
- Research security requirements
- Privacy principles

Chapter 4: Risk Mitigation Strategies

Security teams ensure organizations have proper risk mitigation strategies and controls in place. Using risk management frameworks helps identify and implement the appropriate controls. This chapter covers the steps involved in risk mitigation, which include asset identification, **confidentiality, integrity, and availability (CIA)** triad, determination of threats, the likelihood of attacks, implementing countermeasures, and conducting a risk analysis to determine the security threshold level.

Following are the exam topics covered:

- Asset classification
- Threat identification
- Risk determination
- Countermeasures and controls
- CIA-impact decisions
- Aggregate score for security controls
- Worst case scenario
- Technical to business risk
- Risk controls
- Business continuity planning

Chapter 5: Enterprise Risk Measurement and Metrics

Securing an organization should be assigned the highest priority, yet the business and senior management need to be convinced to allocate budget and resources for ensuring top-notch security. Security heads need to justify implementing security controls or buying new security technologies. After the security controls have been implemented, this chapter presents the review and assessment of the effectiveness of the risk controls by gathering and analyzing the risk metrics. The results are further interpreted for future trends, existing security levels, and trends against industry standards and baselines.

Following are the exam topics covered:

- Effective security control review
- Create risk metrics
- **Key performance indicators (KPI), recovery time objective (RCO), total cost of ownership (TCO)**
- Compare security baselines
- Anticipate future needs
- Risk review of controls
- Analyze metrics
- Benchmarks
- Baselines
- Data analysis and interpretation
- Judgmental solutions

Chapter 6: Components of Network Security

Any organization seeks to implement secure architecture for its network infrastructure. The secure design needs to have an understanding of the organization's services and delivery components like servers, and networks to include in the secure design. To implement security features, IT teams need to account for users' ease of use, performance cost, and security standards and principles. This chapter presents the building blocks for implementing a secure architecture for enterprises and critical infrastructures, which include physical, virtual, and network devices.

Following are the exam topics covered:

- Physical and virtual network devices
- Application-aware technologies
- Secure and complex traffic flow

- Network management
- Critical infrastructure
- Security zones
- Network components
- Complex network security
- Software-defined networks
- Critical systems

Chapter 7: Securing Networks, Host Systems, and Devices

Securing an enterprise does not stop at network traffic monitoring, since cyberattacks are initiated to exploit servers and user systems (hosts). This chapter presents the various controls for protecting and securing servers and user systems. This includes the use of trusted OS, bootloader security, OS hardening, and endpoint security vulnerabilities.

Following are the exam topics covered:

- Trusted OS
- Bootloader security
- OS hardening process
- Endpoint security
- Hardware and software vulnerabilities
- Application delivery
- Terminal services

Chapter 8: Secure Storage Controls

Most organizations implement network security controls and perform audits, as security assessments. If every component of the organization is not included, the assessment is incomplete and leaves the organization exposed. This chapter presents a defense-in-depth strategy that needs to be implemented, which should include physical, virtual, cloud, on-premise, and user devices connecting to the office network. This chapter presents the assessment tools for performing security assessments at all levels.

Following are the exam topics covered:

- Storage controls
- Cloud storage
- Geotagging

- Wearable technologies
- Encrypted and unencrypted communication
- Resource provisioning and de-provisioning
- Data flow security
- Resilience issues
- Data security considerations
- Cloud and on-premise data security

Chapter 9: Securing the Internet of Things

Disruptive new-age devices and their related technologies have changed how work is done and has created new options to use technologies in offices, homes, healthcare, manufacturing, agriculture, and other domains. While such technologies are revolutionary, they are not always secure. Security is not always the primary focus in a rush to have disruptive technology in the markets. Organizations and users adopting such cutting-edge **things on the internet** often ride on the bleeding edge of the technology.

Following are the exam topics covered:

- Internet of Things
- Insecure Internet of Things deployments
- IoT security challenges and requirements
- Managing IoT security services
- Future IoT security
- Wearable devices

Chapter 10: Cloud and Virtualization Security

The primary focus of cloud computing was to ensure resources were available via web-based data centers accessible from any location. Virtualization of servers and network devices became a key to reducing the physical footprint in data centers. This enabled software applications, hardware infrastructure, and computing environments for multi-tenants. It changed the landscape and brought about cloud and virtual server security issues.

Following are the exam topics covered:

- Cloud architecture and design
- Cloud data security
- Cloud application security
- Virtualization operations

- Technical deployment models
- Virtualization advantages and disadvantages
- Cloud-augmented security services
- Host provisioning and de-provisioning

Chapter 11: Application Security Controls

Enterprise security controls and mitigations must be assessed, upgraded, or implemented in the latest security technologies. Technology changes quickly to keep up with the new-age sophisticated attacks and risks. System applications need to be designed using secure development coding practices and design. Trained professionals must understand the new attack trends and security controls for applications. This chapter covers the security activities across IT lifecycles, including ongoing best practices to implement and mitigate application vulnerability controls.

Following are the exam topics covered:

- Application security design
- Security issues in applications
- Sandboxing
- Database security
- Firmware security
- Design considerations
- Web application firewalls
- Client-server side
- Encrypted enclaves
- Database monitoring
- OS and firmware vulnerabilities

Chapter 12: Security Assessments

Before securing an organization's infrastructure, its security weaknesses and gaps need to be analyzed. A vulnerability assessment of the current state of the infrastructure presents the existing weaknesses. To resolve these, multiple methods and assessment tools need to be used. This chapter discusses the different types of assessments and the weaknesses each is designed to reveal. The chapter also discusses methods for security weaknesses that cannot be discovered with those tools.

Following are the exam topics covered:

- Reconnaissance

- Fingerprinting
- **Open-source intelligence (OSINT)**
- Social engineering
- Malware sandboxing
- Memory dumping
- Runtime debugging
- Vulnerability scan
- Penetration testing
- Assessment methods and types

Chapter 13: Selecting Vulnerability Assessment Tools

While considering network and OS security, the hardening or rules are implemented. However, vulnerability assessments involve a lot more. It can be argued that proper security cannot be achieved without sufficient network and physical security. Moreover, a defense-in-depth strategy with layered security is often considered at the network, host, and physical levels. This chapter looks at the vulnerability assessment tools used to perform assessments at each of these levels.

Following are the exam topics covered:

- Port scanners
- Protocol analyzers
- Application interceptors
- Exploitation frameworks
- Visualization tools
- Log analysis tools
- Physical security tools
- Analysis tools

Chapter 14: Securing Communication and Collaborative Solutions

Office staff working from home or remote areas are increasingly relying on new methods of communication and collaborations to work together, even as enterprises are adopting these new technologies in the environments. This change has introduced new security concerns, and there is a high-priority focus on implementing controls and mitigating these security issues. This chapter describes these new collaborative technologies and security issues and suggests mitigation methods to secure these new workflow processes.

Following are the exam topics covered:

- Remote access
- Unified collaboration
- **Voice Over IP (VoIP)**, Web, and video integration

Chapter 15: Implementing Cryptographic Techniques

Cryptography is a crucial factor in protecting the data at rest and in transit. Cryptography concerns CIA or confidentiality, integrity, and authentication, but not availability. The security tenet covering confidentiality, integrity, and availability is the CIA triad. Cryptography includes two of these tenets and prevents fraudulent insertion, modification, or deletion of data. Cryptography also provides non-repudiation by providing proof of origin. These concepts are discussed in this chapter.

Following are the exam topics covered:

- **Secure Socket Layer (SSL)** or **transport layer security (TLS)**
- Cryptographic applications
- Hashing
- **Secure or Multipurpose Internet Mail Extension (SMIME)** or message authentication
- Code signing
- **Digital Rights Management (DRM)** watermarks
- **Public Key Infrastructure (PKI)**

Chapter 16: Identification, Authentication, and Authorization

Identifying users and devices and determining the actions permitted by a user or device form the foundation of access control models. While this paradigm has not changed since the beginning of network computing, the methods used to perform this important set of functions have changed greatly and continue to evolve. This chapter covers evolving technologies and techniques that relate to authentication and authorization.

Following are the exam topics covered:

- User identification processes

- User validation and authentication
- Authorization

Chapter 17: Security Incidents and Response

To monitor and detect security incidents, and then investigate and respond, organizations have in-house or outsourced security operations. The incident response is a well-defined document for normal operations about actions to be performed during an attack or breach. This serves as a baseline for ensuring operational recovery and back to normal activities. This helps security analysts recognize security incidents or anomalies and a process to respond. Every organization gathers the attacks and response to create a baseline over some time and measures the security operational incident response and effectiveness.

Following are the exam topics covered:

- Asset identification
- Security operations
- Data risks and breaches
- Incident response
- Post-incident recovery

Chapter 18: Integrating Hosts, Networks, Storage, and Applications

Organizations strive to integrate and secure end-user systems, hosts, networks, applications, and storage. The security practitioner ensures that the appropriate security controls are implemented. This includes secure data flows, security standards, handling the increasing reliance on technologies when integrating enterprise-level systems into networks with data storage, and enabling application integration.

Following are the exam topics covered:

- Adapt data flow security
- Interoperability issues
- Resilience and heterogeneous components
- Design considerations during M and A
- Security standards

Chapter 19: Security Activities Across Technology Lifecycle

When managing the security of an enterprise, security practitioners need to consider security across the entire technology life cycle. As the enterprise grows, new devices and technologies are introduced, maintained, or retired. Security practitioners need to ensure that the appropriate security controls are deployed. Providing security across the technology lifecycle includes understanding both the systems' development life cycle.

Following are the exam topics covered:

- System development lifecycle
- Secure software development
- Asset inventory and control
- Adopting disruptive technologies

Chapter 20: CASP+ Skill Assessment Exam-I

As a learner, this chapter presents 90-exam preparation exercises and practice questions and answers in the form of multiple-choice questions.

Following is the exam topic covered:

- MCQs for chapters one to ten with answers

Chapter 21: CASP+ Skill Assessment Exam-II

As a learner, this chapter presents 90-exam preparation exercises and practice questions and answers in the form of multiple-choice questions.

Following is the exam topic covered:

- MCQs for chapters eleven to nineteen with answers

Conclusion

This chapter introduces the CASP+ exam, covering topics like course objectives, intended audience, steps to exam preparation, exam objectives, and exam topics description. Security and IT departments cannot function in isolation and must align their operations with organizational goals.

The next chapter will focus on identifying specific security risks arising from dynamic business influences. It will outline methods to address risks associated with regulatory compliance, third-party collaborations, and technological innovations. Strategies to mitigate these risks and maintain an adaptive and resilient security framework will be discussed in detail. The additional considerations brought about by external pressures and internal dynamics demand a cohesive, policy-driven approach to security decision-making. This chapter provided an overview of how these challenges emerge and highlighted the need for integrating business objectives with security strategies to manage risks effectively.

Exercise

1. **The highest priority security-related concern for BYOD is:**
    a. The filtering of sensitive data out of data flows at geographic boundaries
    b. Removing potential bottlenecks in data transmission paths
    c. The transfer of corporate data onto the mobile corporate device
    d. The migration of data into and out of the network in an uncontrolled manner

2. **Your IT security head or the CISO is concerned that systems administrators with privileged access may be reading other users' emails. A review of a tool's output shows the administrators have used webmail to log into other users' inboxes. Which of the following tools would show this type of output?**
    a. Log analysis tool
    b. Password cracker
    c. Command-line tool
    d. File integrity monitoring tool

3. **A power outage is caused by a severe thunderstorm and a facility is on generator power. The CISO decides to activate a plan and shut down non-critical systems to reduce power consumption. Which of the following is the CISO activating to identify critical systems and the required steps?**
    a. BIA
    b. CERT
    c. IRP
    d. COOP

4. **A pharmaceutical company is considering moving its technology operations from on-premises to externally hosted to reduce costs while improving security and resiliency. These operations contain data that includes prescription records, medical doctors' notes about treatment options, and the success rates of prescribed drugs. The company wants to maintain control over its operations because many custom applications are in use. Which of the following options represents the most secure technical deployment options? (Select THREE).**

    a. Single tenancy

    b. Multi-tenancy

    c. Community

    d. Public

    e. Private

    f. Hybrid

    g. SaaS

    h. IaaS

    i. PaaS

5. **Which of the following describes a contract that is used to define the various levels of maintenance to be provided by an external business vendor in a secure environment?**

    a. NDA

    b. MOU

    c. BIA

    d. SLA

6. **During a security assessment, activities were divided into two phases, internal and external exploitation. The security assessment team set a hard time limit on external activities before moving to a compromised box within the enterprise perimeter. Which of the following methods is the assessment team most likely to employ next?**

    a. Pivoting from the compromised, moving laterally through the enterprise, and trying to exfiltrate data and compromise devices

    b. Conducting a social engineering attack attempt with the goal of accessing the compromised box physically

    c. Exfiltrating network scans from the compromised box as a precursor to social media reconnaissance

    d. Open-source intelligence gathering to identify the network perimeter and scope to enable further system compromises

7. **During the decommissioning phase of a hardware project, a security administrator is tasked with ensuring no sensitive data is released inadvertently. All paper records are scheduled to be shredded in a crosscut shredder, and the waste will be burned. The system drives and removable media have been removed before e-cycling the hardware. Which of the following would ensure no data is recovered from the system drives once they are disposed of?**

a. Overwriting all HDD blocks with an alternating series of data

b. Physically disabling the HDDs by removing the drive head

c. Demagnetizing the hard drive using a degausser

d. Deleting the UEFI boot loaders from each HDD

8. A Chief Information Security Officer (CISO) is reviewing the controls in place to support the organization's vulnerability management program. The CISO finds patching and vulnerability scanning policies and procedures are in place. However, the CISO is concerned the organization is siloed and is not maintaining awareness of new risks to the organization. The CISO determines systems administrators need to participate in industry security events. Which of the following is the CISO looking to improve?

a. Vendor diversification

b. System hardening standards

c. Bounty programs

d. Threat awareness

e. Vulnerability signatures

9. While attending a meeting with the human resources department, an organization's information security officer sees an employee using a username and password written on a memo pad to log into a specific service. When the information security officer inquires further as to why passwords are being written down, the response is that there are too many passwords to remember for all the different services the human resources department is required to use. Additionally, each password has specific complexity requirements and different expiration timeframes. Which of the following would be the BEST solution for the information security officer to recommend?

a. Utilizing MFA

b. Implementing SSO

c. Deploying 802.1XPushing SAML adoption

d. Implementing TACACS

10. A security engineer is managing operational, excess, and available equipment for a customer. Three pieces of expensive leased equipment, which are supporting a highly confidential portion of the customer network, have recently been taken out of operation. The engineer determines the equipment lease runs for another 18 months. Which of the following is the BEST course of action for the engineer to take to decommission the equipment properly?

a. Remove any labeling indicating the equipment was used to process confidential data and mark it as available for reuse.

b. Return the equipment to the leasing company and seek a refund for the unused time.

c. Redeploy the equipment to a less sensitive part of the network until the lease expires.

d. Securely wipe all device memory and store the equipment in a secure location until the end of the lease.

Answers

1. d
2. A
3. C
4. a, e, h
5. d
6. a
7. c
8. d
9. b
10. d

Join our book's Discord space

Join the book's Discord Workspace for Latest updates, Offers, Tech happenings around the world, New Release and Sessions with the Authors:

https://discord.bpbonline.com

## CHAPTER 2

Business and Industry Trends, Influences, and Risks

Introduction

In this chapter, we will learn about the challenges presented by constant yet dynamic business changes. The security and IT departments do not operate in silos. The tasks and aims are influenced by the organization's business objectives and corporate policies, which guide and alter the decisions. The job of the security and IT professionals is more difficult due to the additional considerations, either introduced by factors that are outside the enterprise or out of their control, legal regulations, partnerships, or technical concerns. Add to this, the introduction of new, untested, and unfamiliar technologies, and there is a perfect prescription for a security incident waiting to happen.

This chapter covers the security risks introduced by the dynamic business influences, along with some actions that are taken to minimize the risks.

Structure

In this chapter, we will cover the following topics:

- Risk management of new technology
- Security concerns about integrating industries
- Internal and external client requirements

- Impact of de-parameterization
- Outsourcing

Objective

After studying this chapter, you will get to understand the challenges presented by risks from new products, businesses, and technologies, along with new partnerships, outsourcing, or acquisitions and mergers. Security concerns due to cloud, internal, and external factors, along with the constantly changing edge network boundaries, are also discussed in this chapter.

Risk management of new technologies

For security experts, the list of new products, technologies, collaborations, and user behaviors is never-ending. It is neither conceivable nor advised to halt the technological tide, but it is always necessary to manage any associated hazards. Every new technology and behavior must be thoroughly examined as part of a systematic risk management procedure. The most important takeaway from this chapter is that risk management is a circular, never-ending activity. While the approach should result in a risk profile for each activity or technology, keep in mind that the elements that affect risk profiles and technology profiles are continually changing. When a company decides to implement new cutting-edge technology, there are always worries regarding the system's maintenance and support operations. This is especially true for software applications. For instance, what would happen if the software provider shuts down or goes out of business? Include a source code provision in the contract to alleviate this worry. Source code is maintained by third-party providers. If the vendor goes out of business, they are accountable for giving the client the most recent updated source code.

To improve user performance, it is important to stay on top of any changes in the tasks that users do on a daily basis. For example, if an organization's users are increasingly interested in using chat sessions rather than emails when discussing sensitive issues, secure instant messaging communications become just as important as securing email systems.

To stay up-to-date with the ever-changing work habits of users, the security teams should monitor user activity frequently to uncover new threat vectors and protect themselves from expanding and changing the risk regions. *Figure 2.1* illustrates the new trends in the IT domain. These reveal new performance-enhancing techniques used by office workers, as well as potentially dangerous habits such as writing passwords on sticky notes. Security policies and user awareness training assist in reducing, dissuading, and avoiding hazards. The aim is to proactively anticipate harmful user behaviors by monitoring emerging mobile trends, such as cloud usage. Refer to *Figure 2.1* that illustrates the upcoming technology trends:

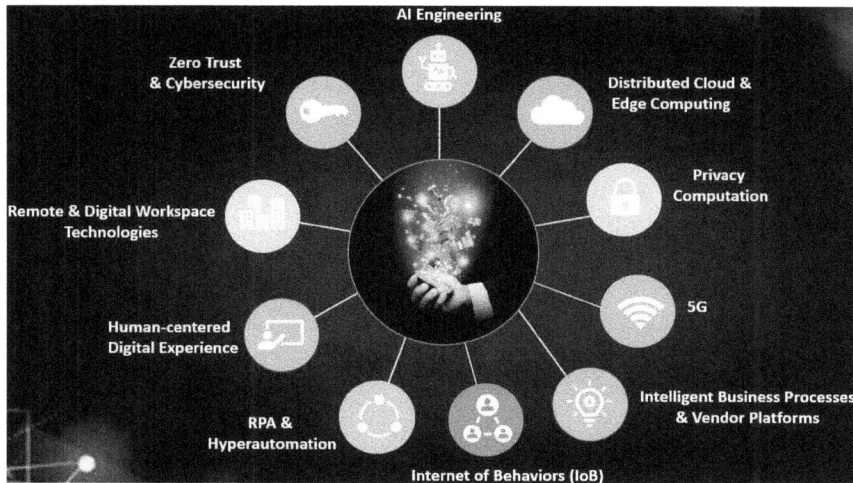

Figure 2.1: *Upcoming technology trends*

Changing business models

The way an organization does business with others is the major cause for a change in the organization's risk profile associated with a process or a specific activity. The organization's security is influenced in some manner as new partnerships and collaborations are created, new assets are added or lost, and new technologies are introduced as a result of mergers or demergers. Establishing official or informal connections with other organizations necessitates the interchange of sensitive data and information. This inevitably results in new security concerns. The security procedures that must be followed while managing sensitive data sent between the two parties are spelled out in a **third-party connection agreement (TCA)** document. This agreement is used whenever the relationship necessitates relying on another organization to protect corporate data. Organizational collaborations do not always entail the exchange of sensitive information, but rather the provision of a shared service. These can be created between comparable company organizations in the same industry or with third-party affiliates. The TCA agreement defines the parties' duties for securing data, connections, and sensitive information, regardless of the nature of the partnership. Learners should conduct research and study the following security organizations, which have adjusted their business models in response to the shifting trends:

- Clear biometrics **https://www.clearme.com/**
- Onfido **https://onfido.com/**
- Stanley security **https://www.stanleysecurity.com/**
- Telstra **https://www.telstra.com.au/**
- **Transportation Security Administration (TSA) https://www.tsa.gov/**

Outsourcing and partnerships

Outsourcing labor to third-party providers introduces liability, which many firms overlook when doing risk assessments. Outsourcing agreements must guarantee that the information entrusted to third parties is constantly secured by appropriate security procedures that meet legal and regulatory standards. *Figure 2.2* presents the IT outsourcing contract and procurement processes, like third-party outsourcing agreements, that must be codified. Contract and procurement management processes should be established by organizations to guarantee that regulatory and legal obligations are satisfied. Periodic audits confirm that the contractual vendor organizations are adhering to the contract's terms. Refer to *Figure 2.2* that illustrates the IT outsourcing models:

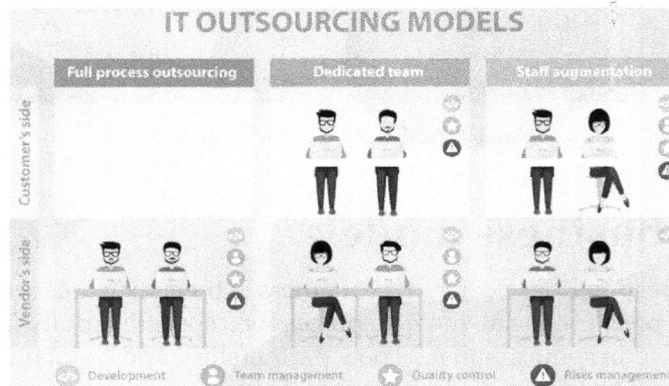

Figure 2.2: IT outsourcing models

When a vendor subcontracts a function to another third party, outsourcing can become a problem for a corporation. In that instance, the firm that owns the data should immediately cancel the contract with the vendor if the vendor cannot show an agreement with the third party that assures the appropriate security for any data handled by the third party. When functions are distributed among numerous providers, the risks associated with outsourcing might be exacerbated. The separation of tasks amongst providers has a negative influence on strategic architecture. Vendor management expenses rise, limiting the organization's ability to respond to the changing market conditions. Internal IT system expertise is dwindling, limiting future platform development. This is because security restrictions and upgrades must be implemented across different borders, it takes longer. Finally, when outsourcing crosses national borders, other challenges emerge. The laws of certain countries are more stringent than those of others.

Cloud computing trends

The regulations of many countries or regulatory organizations must be addressed when it comes to cloud computing trends and cloud security in terms of data origin and storage. This is because the laws in other nations are less stringent, businesses may be hesitant to do business with anyone. Regulatory compliance and security levels of environments, such as restrictions with credit and debit cards handled by shared hosting providers or outside the nation that do not follow **Payment Card Industry Data Security Standard (PCI DSS)**, impede the use of the public cloud. Refer to *Figure 2.3* that illustrates the cloud computing trends:

U.S. cloud computing market size, by end use, 2016 - 2027 (USD Billion)

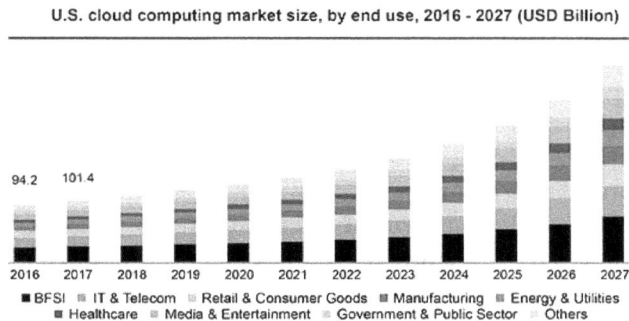

Figure 2.3: Cloud computing trends

Instead, a private cloud hosted on-site within the firm should be explored. Security concerns, cloud benefits, and drawbacks must be outlined in relation to the options, and a path forward should be recommended. Elasticity is a feature of cloud deployments since virtual resources are commissioned and decommissioned on the fly over a shared resource pool. The hardware platforms utilized are not disclosed to the organizations. Another risk is that data may be scraped from decommissioned hardware for a period of time after it has been stored on that platform. Hybrid clouds combine public and private environments that are separate but interconnected. An organization's data might be stored on a private cloud that links to a public cloud-based business intelligence platform. In the event that massive demand exceeds the capacity of the private cloud, organizations may use a public cloud provider to access the services. A third-party or cross-company team serves as the supplier for community clouds shared by enterprises with a common objective to address. When a community cloud is set up, it may be beneficial to everyone because the overall cost is split among the participating organizations.

Merger and acquisition influences

Networks are joined, server systems and applications are integrated, and new infrastructures are occasionally created during mergers and acquisitions. Such conditions offer an opportunity to reconsider the idea of safeguarding the linked infrastructures. However, if one business uses hardware manufacturers, network designs, or rules and processes different from those of the others, things get difficult. During the integration planning and talks, all parties must consider security issues. This is known as the due diligence phase, which allows you to analyze and comprehend every area of the other company's activities. Then, with a thorough understanding of the integrated infrastructure environment ahead of time to assure security, a suitable merger or acquisition is achievable.

Penetration testing on both sides is required prior to merging the networks. Both businesses will have a comprehensive grasp of the current and future hazards as a result of this. An **Interconnection Security Agreement (ISA)** that includes a full risk analysis of the acquired organization's whole operating ecosystem is recommended. Systems and equipment that do not meet the requirements for compliance and security must be removed, changed, or rebuilt.

When a corporation splits or demerges sections of itself, a spin-off is executed, with the demerger resembling a divorce. The impacted parties or agencies must agree upon which entity's assets, services, and infrastructure will be used. This normally entails removing all data from systems and reviewing security measures on both sides in preparation for the upgraded architecture. When components of an organization are sold to another firm, the parent company should verify that just the necessary data is transmitted to the acquiring company and nothing else. The hazard of integrated networks during the transition phase is the greatest risk faced by an organization selling a unit to another firm or acquiring from another company. It is vital to identify the data flow between the companies involved, and any data flow that is not required should be avoided. To achieve secure mergers or de-mergers, a due diligence team made up of professionals from both firms must be formed. This group is in charge of establishing a strategy for assessing current security measures as well as monitoring the process at each stage. The team also looks for security overlaps and gaps between the two integrating units. For each identified risk, risk profiles should be built, which includes transferring data and prioritizing procedures to identify those that require immediate attention. Auditors and compliance teams must ensure that security procedures and frameworks are in sync.

Data ownership

A changing company model has an impact on data ownership. Management must make judgments about data ownership based on the business model being used. Security experts must assess if data will stay as independent ownership or be integrated as part of a corporate purchase or merger. If a data merging is to take place, a strategy detailing the actions involved in the data merge should be created. Management must select which organization will control the data in a corporate sale or demerger. To guarantee that the required data is collected effectively, detailed plans and processes must be created.

Data reclassification

Security professionals need to examine the data classification model when an acquisition, merger divestiture, or demerger occurs. In the case of an acquisition or merger, the security professionals must decide whether to keep the data separate or merge the data into a single entity. In the case of a divestiture or demerger, security professionals must ensure that legally protected data is not given to an entity that is not covered under the same laws, regulations, or standards. Laws, regulations, and standards governing the two organizations must be considered. It may be necessary for the organization to carefully design the new data classification model and define the procedures for data reclassification. The laws, rules, and standards that regulate the organizations must be considered. When it comes to weather data, whether it is being integrated, kept distinct, or split based on ownership, enterprises must make sure data security is a top concern. Assume a healthcare organization has decided to sell an application it has built. Management must collaborate with security experts to guarantee that all application data, source code, development plans, and marketing and sales data are supplied to the acquiring business. Management must guarantee that no confidential healthcare data is included in the data that will be taken as part of the divestiture by accident.

Security concerns about integrating industries

In many situations nowadays, businesses are combining business models that are vastly different from one another. Organizations are sometimes venturing into new domains with vastly diverse cultures, geographic locations, and regulatory regimes. This can lead to new business opportunities, but it can also lead to security flaws. The following sections provide an overview of some of the concerns that must be examined. When it comes to merging different industries, the problem is to strike a balance in terms of rules. While uniformity across all aspects of a company is a noble objective, imposing an unfamiliar set of regulations on one element of the company may result in resistance and morale issues.

A long-standing culture in one unit may be one of trusting users to administer their computers, which may include local administrator powers, but another unit may be hostile to allowing users such access. While standardizing regulations throughout a company may become necessary, it should not be done without first assessing the advantages and downsides. The advantages should be weighed against any opposition that may arise, as well as any potential productivity losses. However, due to localized concerns, it may be essential to have a few alternative regulations. This decision should be made by top management in collaboration with the security specialists.

This is because policies are less likely to prescribe precise answers, they may be easier to standardize than the rules or regulations. Many rules use ambiguous terminology, such as **the utmost feasible data protection must be provided for data believed to be secret**. This terminology gives each department the freedom to decide what is and is not a secret. However, when a business acquires or merges, its rules should be thoroughly examined to ensure that they are current, offer adequate security precautions, and are not unduly onerous to any unit within the firm. Government bodies such as the **Department of Homeland Security (DHS), Federal Communications Commission (FCC),** and **Department of Telecom (DOT)** frequently adopt regulations to guarantee that specific areas of the sector are controlled. When corporations from severely regulated sectors are joined with companies from less heavily regulated industries, the degrees of regulation within each business unit will be vastly different. In many circumstances, this scenario should be recognized as usual, rather than being viewed as lacking standards.

Export controls

The laws and regulations that regulate the transfer or transmission of commodities from one nation to another are known as export controls. This includes the disclosure of technical data transfers to individuals outside the nation. Exports are governed by rules and regulations in both the United States and the European Union. Concerns about exports emerge for three main reasons such as, the item's qualities, the item's intended destination, and the item's probable final use. Export controls are in place to safeguard national security, carry out foreign policy, and retain the military and economic advantage. Governing organizations, such as those in the United States and the EU, publish lists of restricted items. Entity lists, disbarred parties, denied people, and embargoed states are common. While the export rules include exceptions, firms should consult with legal counsel before exporting any entities. Failure to follow export control laws can result in criminal charges, monetary penalties, damage to one's reputation, and the loss of export control licenses. Organizations with issues about export controls in the United States should contact the North-Western University's office for export controls' compliance.

Legal requirements

Any organization's security approach must include legal compliance. Organizations must understand the regulations that apply to their business to achieve legal compliance. Financial, healthcare, and industrial production are examples of industries with numerous federal, state, and municipal rules to consider. The following sections highlight a few of the laws and rules that organizations must consider. You do not need to remember the rules and regulations presented in these sections; nonetheless, you should have a broad understanding of how they influence businesses in order to analyze the scenarios you may experience on the CASP test.

Sarbanes oxley act

The **Sarbanes-Oxley (SOX)** Act, also known as the Public Company Accounting Reform and Investor Protection Act of 2002, impacts any company that is publicly traded in the United States. It governs the accounting practices and financial reporting for businesses, as well as imposing penalties and even jail time on senior officials. Significant modifications to the existing securities legislation are required, as well as harsh new punishments for violators. This legislation was enacted in reaction to the financial crises involving publicly listed corporations such as Enron Corporation, Tyco International plc, and WorldCom in the early 2000s.

HIPAA

The Kennedy-Kassebaum Act, often known as the **Health Insurance Portability and Accountability Act (HIPAA)**, applies to all healthcare institutions, health insurance companies, and healthcare clearinghouses. The Office of Civil Rights of the Department of

Health and Human Services is in charge of enforcing it. It establishes rules and processes for the storage, use, and transmission of medical and healthcare data. Unless the state laws are tougher, HIPAA takes precedence. All covered businesses must perform the following to comply with the HIPAA security rule:

- Ensure the confidentiality, integrity, and availability of all electronically protected health information.
- Detect and protect against any risks to the information's security.
- Protect against anticipated, impermissible uses or disclosures.
- Certify compliance by their workforce

Gramm Leach Bliley act

All financial institutions are affected by the **Gramm-Leach-Bliley Act (GLBA)**, including banks, lending firms, insurance companies, investment organizations, and credit card companies. It establishes security requirements for all financial data and forbids the sharing of financial data with third parties. This legislation has a direct impact on the protection of **personally identifiable information (PII).**

PIPEDA

The **Personal Information Protection and Electronic Documents Act (PIPEDA)** governs how private-sector businesses in Canada gather, use, and disclose personal data in the course of doing business. The legislation was enacted in response to EU concerns regarding the security of PII in Canada. The legislation requires companies to acquire consent before collecting, using, or disclosing personal information, as well as to establish clear, intelligible, and easily accessible personal information policies.

PCI DSS

The PCI DSS applies to all businesses that handle cardholder data for the main credit card issuers. PCI DSS version 3.2 is the most recent. An organization's compliance with the standard must be verified at least once a year. Despite the fact that the PCI DSS is not a law, it has influenced the implementation of various state legislation. Refer to *Figure 2.4*, that illustrates the PCI DSS framework:

Figure 2.4: PCI DSS framework

Federal information security management act

Every federal agency, as well as suppliers and service providers, is affected by the FISM of 2002. It mandates that each federal agency establish, publish, and implement an information security program for the whole organization. FISMA mandates that federal entities create an effective risk management program for information security. The **National Institute of Standards and Technology (NIST)** provides detailed recommendations for compliance with FISMA. This strategy produces formal advice that helps agencies meet their cyber security standards while emphasizing the risk-based approach, which builds a program that is fit for purpose based on the circumstances while putting a special emphasis on cost-effective protection.

USA Patriot Act

The USA Patriot Act of 2001 has an impact on the US law enforcement and intelligence institutions. Its goal is to improve law enforcement's investigative capabilities, such as email communications, phone records, Internet communications, medical records, and financial information. The Foreign Intelligence Surveillance Act and the Electronic Communications Privacy Act were both altered by this statute when it was passed. Although the **USA Patriot Act** does not prohibit private citizens from using investigative tools, there are some exceptions, for example, if a private citizen is acting as a government agent—even if not formally employed, if the private citizen conducts a search that would require law enforcement to obtain a warrant, if the government is aware of the private citizen's search, or if the private citizen is performing a search to assist the government.

The purpose of the USA Patriot Act is to deter and punish terrorist acts in the United States and around the world, to enhance law enforcement investigatory tools, and other purposes, some of which include the following:

- To strengthen U.S. measures to prevent, detect, and prosecute international money laundering and financing of terrorism

- To subject to special scrutiny foreign jurisdictions, foreign financial institutions, and classes of international transactions or types of accounts that are susceptible to criminal abuse

- To require all appropriate elements of the financial services industry to report potential money laundering

- To strengthen measures to prevent the use of the U.S. financial system for personal gain by corrupt foreign officials and facilitate the repatriation of stolen assets to the citizens of countries to whom such assets belong

European Union laws and regulations

Several legislation and regulations affecting security and privacy have been established by the EU. The EU privacy principles contain strong legislation to protect personal data. The

EU's Data Protection Directive outlines how to comply with the requirements contained in the principles. The safe harbor privacy principles were designed by the EU to assist U.S. firms in complying with the EU privacy principles. Some of the guidelines include the following:

- Data should be collected following the law.

- Information collected about an individual cannot be shared with other organizations unless the individual gives explicit permission for such sharing.

- The information transferred to other organizations can be transferred only if the sharing organization has adequate security in place.

- Data should be used only for the purpose for which it was collected.

- Data should be used only for a reasonable period.

A safe harbor, according to the EU, is an entity that complies with all of the EU privacy principles. A data haven is a jurisdiction that does not safeguard personal data legally, with the primary goal of attracting data-gathering firms. Electronic signature principles are defined in the EU Electronic Security Directive. A signature must be uniquely connected to the signer and the data to which it refers according to this guideline, so that any future data modification may be detected. The signer's signature must be able to identify him or her.

Geography

Geographical differences have a significant influence on ensuring that a merger or demerger goes as smoothly as feasible. Aside from any language obstacles that may exist, the kind of technology accessible in different regions of the world might vary dramatically. While an organization may have rules in place requiring the use of specific technologies to secure data, the hardware and software necessary to implement these policies may be unavailable in other nations or areas, such as Africa or the Middle East. As a result, it may be required to implement policy changes and exclusions. If that is not acceptable, the organization may be forced to find alternative means to fulfill the long-term aim, such as prohibiting the transmission of particular types of data from a place where the requisite technologies are not accessible. Another difficulty is that legal and regulatory standards vary by country. While one jurisdiction may have stringent data archival and security regulations, another may have almost none. The question is once again whether cross-national standards make sense. In certain cases, the expense of standardization may be greater than the benefits gained. It may also be required for the business to opt not to keep data with greater security needs in countries that lack the relevant policies or laws to secure the data.

Data sovereignty

Data sovereignty refers to the idea that digital data is subject to the laws of the nation in which it is housed. The many privacy rules and regulations enacted by nations and governing bodies have an impact on this idea. The deployment of cloud technologies further complicates this paradigm. Many nations have passed laws requiring that customer data be stored in the country where the client resides. When engaging with service providers and other third parties, however, companies are finding it more difficult to confirm that this is the case. To ensure compliance, organizations should check the service-level agreements with these suppliers.

However, keep in mind that the legislation of several nations may have an impact on the facts. Consider the case where a corporation in the United States uses a data center in the United States, but the data center is managed by a company in France. US and EU rules and regulations would apply to the data. Another consideration is the type of data being saved, as various data types are governed differently. The regulations governing the transit and storage of data for healthcare and consumer data are substantially different. The following questions should be answered by a security specialist:

- Where is the data stored?
- Who has access to the data?
- Where is the data backed up?
- How is the data encrypted?

The answers to these four questions will assist security professionals in developing a governance policy for their company that will help them solve any data sovereignty risks.

Note: Both the entity that owns the data and the vendor providing the data storage service, if any, are responsible for adhering to data rules.

Jurisdictions

A jurisdiction is a geographical area or territory that is subject to governmental authority. Jurisdictions, on the other hand, are frequently flexible, owing to reciprocity agreements between various jurisdictions. For example, the United States has signed mutual legal aid accords with several nations, allowing information to flow freely between jurisdictions. As a result, businesses may not just need to be familiar with the rules and regulations that apply to a particular nation or regulatory agency. This is because many nations have begun to address data residency and sovereignty issues, and security professionals must keep track of the jurisdictions that may have an impact on corporate data.

Internal and external influences

Security rules are not born out of thin air. Without the impact of opposing constituencies, balancing security, performance, and usability is tough enough. Internal and external pressures must be considered and resolved in some way. The following sections go through the various sorts of impacts and how they might affect the formulation and execution of security policies.

Competitors

When it comes to security, businesses should constantly be looking at what their rivals are doing. While each company's security requirements are distinct, maintaining one's reputation is a worry shared by everyone. Almost every day, we hear about corporations whose digital reputations have been harmed by security breaches. Proclaiming a company's network security has virtually become another commercial distinction. While increasing network security is clearly a good aim, security experts must guarantee that no superfluous steps are performed. In virtually all circumstances, ineffective security measures degrade network performance or make the network less usable for users. While businesses should strive to improve their security to outperform their rivals, security professionals should properly investigate any new measures they want to adopt to verify that the benefits exceed the risks.

Auditors or audit findings

Without a record of actions and an assessment of those activities, accountability is impossible. The degree and scope of auditing should correspond to the company's security policy. Self-audits or audits by a third party are also options. Self-audits are always fraught with the risk of subjectivity creeping into the procedure. The outcomes of audits or tests, regardless of how they are conducted, are meaningless unless they are incorporated into a revision of present policies and processes. Internal audits are conducted on a regular basis throughout the year, while external audits are conducted once a year. The **International Organization for Standardization (ISO)**, also known as the **International Standards Organization**, collaborated with the **International Electro-Technical Commission (IEC)** to standardize **British Standard 7799 (BS7799)** into the ISO/IEC 27000 family of worldwide standards.

Regulatory entities

Many businesses operate in a highly regulated environment. Two examples are banking and healthcare. Regulations have a different impact on security. A third party verifies that a company is adhering to industry or government norms and laws. This third party examines organizational activities as well as any other area specified by the certifying or regulatory body. The third party informs the certifying or regulatory body of all of its findings. Any discoveries or conclusions shall be conveyed solely to the analyzing organization and the regulatory organization, according to the contract with the third party. This procedure should be overseen by a member of top management, who will grant access to the third party as needed. A third party may be required to provide an onsite assessment, document exchange, or process/policy review as part of this study. A third-party team conducts an onsite examination. This team needs unrestricted access to all elements of the company. Observing personnel execute their daily responsibilities, examining records, evaluating paperwork, and other tasks may be included in this evaluation. To establish solid control of the process, the management should appoint a member of management to whom the team may make formal requests.

This testing might encompass both vulnerability and penetration testing, and it would be carried out by a team made up of both employees and hired third parties. A document exchange/review entails sending a group of papers to a third party for evaluation. On both sides of the transaction, the document exchange procedure must be secure. This is achieved by employing an encryption level that represents the sensitivity of the material in question, or, in certain situations, the level mandated by law or recognized industry standards. A process or policy review examines a specific process or policy inside an organization to ensure that it complies with the rules.

Internal and external client requirements

The security relationship that must be established with both internal and external customers can also play a part in defining the types of security to be employed. When we talk about customers, we are referring to people who need to engage with the network in some manner. Internal customers, who operate within the **local area network (LAN)**, and external customers, who operate outside the LAN, must communicate with the network. For example, while uploading data, connecting to a VPN, or downloading data, the sensitivity of the activities and the data they are handling determines which security measures should be used. It is common knowledge that security measures have an impact on network performance as well as user ease of use. It is critical to distinguish between instances when certain security measures (such as encryption) are. Unnecessary procedures can improve the network speed while also reducing user complexity. While installing access control lists on a router can improve security, keep in mind that the processing consumes router CPU cycles and reduces the router's capacity to accomplish its primary duty of routing. When there is an excessive reliance on such protection, when it is not necessary, the network's performance will be slowed needlessly.

Top level management

While senior management often brings the least amount of security knowledge to the table, these executives have a disproportionate amount of influence over security choices. They make judgments based on company needs, not on their infatuation with the latest security gadgets or their security fears. Most executives consider security only in the event of an emergency. While senior management's role is to split the budgetary pie in the most cost-effective way possible, an IT security professional's responsibility is to make the case for security solutions that add value to the firm. This entails showing that the money saved by avoiding data breaches and losses outweighs the cost of a certain security measure. Accepted risk management techniques must be used to present and assess the specified measures.

Impact of de-parameterization

This has to do with the fact that network boundaries are continually shifting. Security experts used to approach security by hardening the network's edges, or the network's entrances and exits. The location of a network's edges has shifted as a result of new working methods. Furthermore, most corporate networks' interiors are now separated into smaller portions, with control points in between. With the advent of wireless networks, portable network devices, virtualization, and cloud service providers, the network barrier and attack surface have become increasingly permeable. Security architecture progress has resulted in improved security capabilities, the same number of security threats, a higher total cost of ownership, and, on average, a smaller corporate data center. In conclusion, the game has altered as a result of de-parameterization, or the continual shifting of network boundaries.

Telecommuting

Telecommuting is becoming more popular for a variety of reasons. It saves money on petrol, and time spent commuting and is environmentally friendly because it minimizes the amount of hydrocarbons emitted into the atmosphere. Despite its many benefits, telecommuting did not gain widespread acceptance until the technology to protect it was established. Secure VPN connections may now be provided to telecommuters, allowing them to access resources and work as if they were in the office, except for coffee and lunch. Telecommuting involves several security implications. For example, the **network access control (NAC)** technology may be required to guarantee that machines not under the direct supervision of the IT department are examined and remedied if necessary before being allowed access to the LAN to avoid virus introduction.

Mobile threats

The introduction of mobile devices such as cell phones, tablets, and USB flash drives to an organization's network poses a number of risks, which are as follows:

- Insecure web browsing
- Insecure Wi-Fi connectivity
- Lost or stolen devices holding company data
- Corrupt application downloads and installations
- Missing security patches
- Constant upgrading of personal devices
- Use of location services
- Insecure data storage

While corporate emails and company contact information are the most common types of corporate information stored on mobile devices, it is alarming to note that nearly half of these devices also contain customer data, network login credentials, and corporate data accessed through business applications. The growing usage of mobile devices, along with the reality that many of these devices connect to public networks with little or no protection, poses new problems for security experts. Educating users about the dangers of mobile devices and ensuring that they utilize suitable security measures will help protect them from the hazards that these devices pose.

Implementing a device-locking PIN, employing device encryption, adopting GPS location, and implementing remote wiping are some of the suggestions that should be presented to mobile device users. Users should also be wary about installing programs without first verifying that they are from a trusted source. **mobile device management (MDM)** and **mobile application management (MAM)** technologies have been increasingly popular in businesses in recent years. They are used to guarantee that an organization can control the settings, programs, and other aspects of mobile devices while they are connected to the network.

Bring your own device

Users' urge to use personal computing devices in the workplace, such as cellphones, tablets, and laptops, is similar to the pressure to utilize wireless networks in the company. The **bring your own device (BYOD)** genie is officially out of the bottle, despite the fact that the concept gives security experts nightmares. The impact on security is similar to that of telecommuting in that technologies like NAC may be required to ensure that personal devices that are not under the direct control of the IT department can be scanned and remedied if necessary before being allowed access to the LAN to prevent malware from being introduced. It should be noted that government restrictions that pertain to medical, financial, and other sorts of PII apply to the data, not to specific devices. This implies that the obligation to secure data that lives on personal devices brought into the network as part of a BYOD program remains the same. Keep in mind that while typical business images and software installation limitations may provide some data security, they do not cover all risks. An employee may, for example, use a business FTP tool to move customer lists and other proprietary material to an external computer and then sell them to a rival.

This is because they are not limiting enough, BYOD programs fail. Non-company endpoint devices are not allowed on the business network, thus some firms have had to rethink and revise their rules. It could also be a good idea to create security-focused standard operating environments for all essential operating systems and make sure that each business unit's demands are addressed. When it comes to supporting a BYOD program as a security expert, you should keep in mind that you have more to worry from users' negligence than from hackers. Users are not just slackers when it comes to applying security updates and fixes to their devices. Not only are users less than diligent in maintaining security updates and patches on devices, but they also buy new devices as often as they change clothes. These factors make it difficult to maintain control over the security of the networks in which these devices are allowed to operate.

Centralized MDM technologies are quickly becoming the most popular option for both business and personal needs. Some solutions make use of the message server's administration features, while others are third-party programs that can handle several device brands. Cisco Systems Manager is an example of a product that works with Cisco Meraki cloud services. Apple configurator is a good example for iOS devices. One of the difficulties in putting such a system in place is that not all personal devices offer native encryption and management. In most cases, centralized MDM technologies differentiate between company-issued and personal mobile devices. A client application oversees the setup and security of the complete device for organization-issued devices. If the device is a personal device, the application normally only maintains the setup and security of itself and its data if it is part of a BYOD program. The application and its data are isolated from the rest of the system. As a consequence, if the device is taken, the organization's data is safeguarded, but the privacy of the user's data is also protected. Regardless of whether a centralized MDM tool is in use, a BYOD policy should add the following to the security policy of the organization:

- Identify the allowed uses of personal devices on the corporate network.

- Create a list of allowed applications on the devices and design a method of preventing the installation of applications not on the list (for example, software restriction policies).

- Ensure that high levels of management are on board and supportive.

- Train users in the new policies.

In the process of deploying and supporting a mobile solution, the following guidelines must be implemented:

- Ensure that the selected solution supports applying security controls remotely.

- Ensure that the selected vendor has a good track record of publicizing and correcting security flaws.

- Make the deployment of an MDM tool a top priority.

- In the absence of an MDM system, design a process to ensure that all devices are kept up-to-date on security patches.

- Update the policy as technology and behaviors change.

- Require all employees to agree to allow remote wiping of any stolen or lost devices.

- Strictly forbid rooted (Android) or jailbroken (iOS) devices from accessing the network.

If possible, choose a product that supports the following:

- Encrypting the **solid-state drive** (**SSD**) and non-volatile
- RAM

- Requiring a PIN to access the device
- Locking the device when a specific number of incorrect PINs are attempted

Outsourcing

The link between the firms becomes a component of the perimeter when data is transferred to a third party. As a result, the connection's security is crucial. With outsourcing, security protections like ISAs and contract language that clearly describe essential security implementations have become even more important. Finally, outsourcing procedures to a third party that handles sensitive information or personal information protected by a regulatory body would almost certainly have an impact on security. Outsourcing to third parties is a risk that many companies overlook while doing risk assessments. Any outsourcing agreement must guarantee that the information transferred to the other business is safeguarded by appropriate security measures in order to meet all regulatory and legal requirements.

Assuring that a third party has the necessary level of data security downstream liability is the debt incurred by a company as a result of its relationships with other businesses and customers. Consider if a hired third party has the necessary procedures in place to ensure that a company's firewall receives the necessary security upgrades. Customers can sue the company for negligence if hackers enter the network through a security flaw and steal data and identities. Liability issues that an organization must consider include third-party outsourcing and contracts and procurements.

Due diligence and due care

These are two words that have to do with liability. Due diligence indicates that a company is aware of the security threats it confronts and has taken reasonable steps to mitigate those threats. Due care refers to an organization's taking all reasonable steps to prevent security concerns or minimize the consequences of security breaches. Due care and due diligence are sometimes used interchangeably, but they must be understood independently before being evaluated together. Gathering information is at the heart of due diligence. Organizations must put in place the necessary procedures to evaluate potential dangers to their assets.

Due diligence gives you the knowledge you need to make sure your company is taking proper precautions. Due care cannot be taken without proper due diligence. It is all about taking action when it comes to taking proper care. All organizational assets, particularly intellectual property, must be protected, and processes must be implemented. Failure to fulfill minimal standards and procedures is deemed negligent when done with appropriate care. An organization is negligent if it fails to take activities that a reasonable person would have taken in identical circumstances. Due diligence and due care, as you can see, have a symbiotic connection. Organizations detect areas of risk when they do due diligence.

A company may discover, for example, that normal employees are unaware of fundamental security concerns, that printed material is not properly disposed of, and that employees have access to files to which they should not have access. Organizations consider the areas of recognized risk and take measures to defend against the risks when necessary care is taken. Due care would entail offering employees security awareness training, putting processes in place for the correct destruction of printed material, and installing suitable access restrictions for all files for the due diligence instances just described. When working with other parties, it is critical to make sure that the third party delivers the level of security that the data necessitates. There are several ways to facilitate this, which are as follows:

- Include contract clauses that detail exactly the security measures that are expected of the third party.

- Periodically audit and test the security provided to ensure compliance.

- Consider executing an ISA, which may be required in some areas (for example, healthcare).

Conclusion

While engaging third parties can help meet time-to-market demands, a third party should be contractually obligated to perform adequate security activities, and evidence of those activities should be confirmed by the company prior to the launch of any third party-engaged products or services. The contract should also state that the corporation has the authority to audit the third party at any moment.

In the next chapter, we will cover the organization's security policies and documents.

Exercise

1. **What is the primary step in managing risks associated with new technology adoption?**
   a. Ignoring emerging threats
   b. Conducting a risk assessment
   c. Implementing new technology immediately
   d. Eliminating all associated risks

2. **What is a significant security concern when integrating industries through digital systems?**
   a. Enhanced system redundancy
   b. Improved operational efficiency
   c. Increased exposure to cyber threats
   d. Reduction in data privacy compliance

3. **What is essential to address both internal and external client security requirements?**

    a. Limiting communication with clients

    b. Establishing a clear Service Level Agreement (SLA)

    c. Ignoring external client audits

    d. Using outdated security standards

4. **What is the primary security challenge associated with de-parameterization?**

    a. Increased reliance on physical barriers

    b. Difficulty in implementing network segmentation

    c. Greater reliance on endpoint security and identity management

    d. Decreased need for zero-trust model

5. **Which of the following is a critical risk in outsourcing IT services?**

    a. Enhanced organizational flexibility

    b. Loss of control over sensitive data

    c. Reduced operational costs

    d. Access to advanced technologies

Answers

1. b
2. c
3. b
4. c
5. b

Join our book's Discord space

Join the book's Discord Workspace for Latest updates, Offers, Tech happenings around the world, New Release and Sessions with the Authors:

https://discord.bpbonline.com

CHAPTER 3

Organization Security Policies and Documents

Introduction

In *Chapter 2, Business and Industry Trends, Influences, and Risks,* we learned about business influences on security. IT governance documents should be implemented to ensure that organizational assets are protected as much as possible. This chapter explains how the process and policy life cycles are managed and how to support legal compliance. It discusses business documents and contracts that are commonly used to support security. It also covers general privacy principles. Finally, it discusses the development of policies containing standard security practices.

Structure

In this chapter, we will cover the following topics:

- Process life cycle management
- New business and technologies
- Environmental changes
- Regulatory requirements
- Emerging risks
- Legal compliance and advocacy

- Business documents to support security
- Agreements or contract
- Security requirements for contracts
- Privacy principles for sensitive information
- Incident response
- Information classification and life cycle
- Design secure system principles

Objectives

This chapter will discuss the IT security policy and governance procedures that are implemented to secure organizational assets. This chapter will present the creation, implementation, and management of the security policy life cycle. The use of business contracts for **service level agreements (SLAs)** and project documents to support security will also be covered. Business documents supporting security are deliberated, which include risk assessments, **business impact analysis (BIA)**, agreements, MoU, and SLA among others. This chapter also presents the standard security practices of separation of duties, job rotation, least privileged, incident response, and other procedures.

Process life cycle management

Management initiates, supports, and drives the security program in a top-down approach. Staff employees build a security program before getting instruction and assistance from management in a bottom-up manner. This is because management's support is one of the most critical components of a security program, a top-down strategy is significantly more efficient than a bottom-up approach. The top-down method can assist in guaranteeing that a company's policies are in line with its strategic objectives. A policy is a course or principle of action set by an organization in the context of organizational security, while a process is a sequence of actions conducted to attain a certain goal. A process is a set of actions carried out in a specific order or a specific manner. All important decisions and activities inside an organization are determined by policies, procedures, and processes, and all organizational tasks work within the bounds imposed by policies, procedures, and processes. The policies are developed initially to guide the construction of procedures and processes in order to comprehend the link between the three. The high-level perspective of tasks inside the processes is provided by processes. Procedures are step-by-step instructions for completing a task, as illustrated in *Figure 3.1*.

Consider the following scenario, assume that a company has a certain procedure for handling accounts payable. Receiving the bill, entering the bill, authorizing the payment, printing the check, signing the check, and mailing the check are all examples of high-level actions that must be completed as part of the process developed around this policy. Each step involved in each task in the process would be documented in the procedures. Policies, as depicted in *Figure 3.1*, should be written based on the following life cycle:

1. Develop or design the policy.
2. Perform modeling and quality control.
3. Obtain approval for executing the policy.
4. Publish or execute the policy and perform periodic monitoring and checks.
5. Review for optimization and archive the policy, if it is no longer needed or applicable.

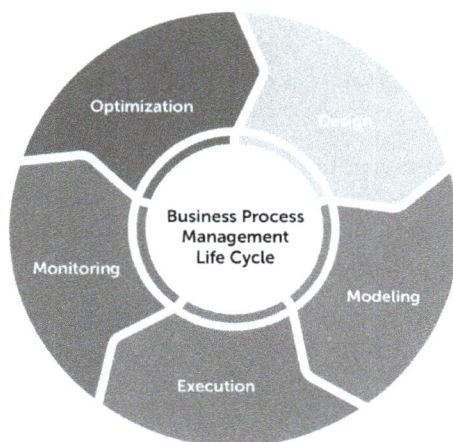

Figure 3.1: Process life cycle

Changes in the company, technology, risk, and environment constantly need a policy review, such as the adoption of new technology, mergers, or the discovery of new attack methods. If workers want to access business email and shared drives from home, or remote access has never been given but is suddenly required because of the need to boost productivity and respond quickly to consumer requests, the company should assess the requirement to see if it is legitimate. If a company decides to enable remote access, security experts should plan and design security policies based on the presumption that external environments are hostile. A quality check should be performed before approval to ensure that the policy complies with all applicable laws, regulations, and standards. When the policy is finalized, the company must make certain that all affected workers are properly notified. The new policy should be included in any training that this person gets. If policies need to be changed, version control should be used to ensure that the most recent version is used throughout the company. A policy should be archived if it is no longer applicable. Policies should be reviewed at least once a year and on a frequent basis.

The first phase in this life cycle is to study the policy, and the second is to build the process based on the policy. All staff engaged in the process should be informed of how the new process works after it is deployed. The method should be reviewed on a regular basis and tweaked if concerns occur or the main policy is revised. Keep in mind that policies guide the creation of procedures. A new process is required whenever a new policy is implemented. If a policy is revised or retired, the policy's procedure should be revised or retired as well. Procedures must be written once the policy and associated processes have been documented.

Procedures are the closest to computers and other devices and contain all the particular activities that workers are expected to follow. Step-by-step listings of how policies and processes are executed are common in procedures. After an organization has assessed business, technological, risk, and environmental changes to build and update policies, it must next design and update its processes and procedures to reflect the new or updated policies, as well as the environment and business changes. If the business changes to the newest version of the backup software it employs, for example, the procedures may need to be adjusted.

The majority of software updates entail examining present methods and deciding on how they should be altered. As an example, suppose the management wishes to hire more outside contractors to finish the job. It is possible that the company will need to implement a new method for evaluating the quality of the outside contractor's work.

As the last example, assume a company wishes to replace its present Microsoft file servers with numerous Linux servers. While the high-level policies will stay the same, the methods for implementing those rules will need to be revised. If a company's marketing department needs to provide more real-time interaction with its partners and customers and decides to establish a presence on multiple social networking sites to share information, the company will need to appoint a group of trained individuals to release information on the company's behalf and train other employees on how to share the information. Change management, configuration management, network access procedures, wireless access procedures, and database administration procedures are just a few processes and procedures to think about.

However, keep in mind that procedures and processes should only be developed or modified once the relevant policies have been accepted. Processes and procedures will be developed in accordance with the policies. Internal organizational drives serve as the foundation for developing rules and procedures. When a new business or business change occurs, new technologies are launched, environmental changes occur, or regulatory requirements alter, organizations should ensure that policies and processes are developed or evaluated.

New business and technologies

When a company starts or buys a new line of business, it is referred to as a new business. Consumer expectations frequently drive business changes governed by the nature of an organization's company. When a change happens, an organization must ensure that it is aware of the change and its implications for the business's security posture. When it comes to these developments and difficulties, businesses should be proactive. Anticipate the changes and use mitigation strategies to assist you in avoiding them. Assume a company chooses to begin a new venture in which consumers may now acquire things that were previously only available through huge retail locations. A new business policy based on this new model will need to be created, as well as a new procedure to manage the new business. Security specialists are essential to every project involving the start-up of a new firm or changes to an existing business because they guarantee that security measures are considered. All risks related to the new business or business shift should be documented, examined, and reported to management by security specialists. They must also disclose any security procedures they propose to address these risks.

New technologies

New technical breakthroughs require enterprises to embrace new technologies, which drive technology transformations. Organizations must once again ensure that they are aware of the developments and their consequences for their security posture. Assume a company decides to enable employees to implement a BYOD policy. The security professionals should strive to ensure that the policy establishes the boundaries within which BYOD will be permitted or prohibited. Furthermore, the procedure will need to be formalized and will most likely comprise gaining official permission for a device, analyzing the device's security posture, and allowing full or limited access to the device based on the device's security posture. Security specialists are essential in the adoption or use of new technologies because they guarantee that security measures are taken into account. All hazards related to new technology should be documented, examined, and reported to management by security specialists. To reduce these risks, they must also advise and record security procedures.

Environmental changes

Environmental changes are separated into two categories, those prompted by an organization's culture and those motivated by the industry's environment. Organizations must ensure that they understand the changes and their consequences for their security posture, just as they do with new businesses or technology. Assume a company chooses to introduce a new policy that requires each of its facilities to include a particular quantity of green space. Management would have to devise a method for completing and maintaining these green places. It would most likely entail acquiring the property, creating a plan for the area, putting the new green space in place, and keeping the green space up to date.

Regulatory requirements

Regulatory requirements are any legal or regulatory requirements that must be documented and obeyed. Standards can be utilized as part of a regulatory framework, although they are not enforced as tightly as laws and regulations. Organizations must ensure that they understand the legislation and its consequences for the security posture of the company, just as they do with new business, technological, or environmental developments. The **International Organization for Standardization (ISO)** has created a set of guidelines to assist enterprises in developing security strategies. Local, state, federal, and other government entities are among the other regulating bodies.

Consider the following scenario, assume an organization is updating its security rules and has come to a standstill because the management feels the company's key vendors have a strong grip on compliance and regulatory standards. Executive-level managers are enabling suppliers to have a big say in how the organization's policies are written. While vendor support is crucial, the IT director thinks that the firm must design the policy objectively since the suppliers may not always put the organization's interests first. The IT director should make the following recommendations to the senior staff:

- Consult legal and regulatory requirements.
- Draft a general organizational policy.
- Specify functional implementation policies.
- Establish necessary standards, procedures, baselines, and guidelines.

As this example demonstrates, you do not need to memorize the exact conditions. You must, however, understand how they are utilized in enterprises, how they are modified, and how they may be adjusted to match the company's needs.

Emerging risks

Emerging hazards are any threats that have arisen as a result of the recent security environment. Dangers in new technologies, gadgets, and apps are usually not discovered until after they have been deployed. According to the policies and procedures created by organizations, security specialists should conduct an extensive study to identify emerging threats. Patch management is extremely crucial when there are new issues to deal with. Vendors usually strive to provide security upgrades as quickly as feasible in response to emerging risks. Assume a corporation wants to introduce a new **Internet of Things (IoT)** device. After a few weeks, the vendor finds a security flaw that allows attackers to take over the device's functionality. As a result, they have published a security patch to address the issue. If the necessary processes are in place, the organization's security experts should monitor the vendor for patch management announcements and implement the update after it has been adequately tested.

Legal compliance and advocacy

A company's human resources department, legal department or legal counsel, senior management, and other internal and external entities should all be included in its legal compliance and advocacy program. A company's legal compliance ensures that it follows all applicable laws, regulations, and business practices. By or for an organization, legal advocacy is the practice of influencing public policy and resource allocation decisions in political, economic, and social systems and organizations. Human resources involvement ensures that the firm follows all labor laws and regulations in order to protect its employees. Human resources professionals may help guide a company's security policy to ensure that individual rights are preserved while corporate assets and liabilities are safeguarded. To prevent legal issues, an organization should ensure that the users are informed of the employer's rights to monitor, seize, and search organizational devices when they log in. If a technician is needed to take an employee's workstation into custody as part of an investigation, the firm is protected. HR and legal departments should be involved in the development of the statement that will be delivered to guarantee that it has all relevant information.

Business documents to support security

Security professionals need to use many common business documents to support the implementation and management of organizational security. Understanding these business documents helps ensure that all areas of security risk are addressed and the appropriate policies, procedures, and processes are developed.

Risk assessment

Risk assessment is a risk management tool that is used to discover vulnerabilities and threats, assess the consequences of those vulnerabilities and threats, and decide which controls to install. Risk assessment or analysis has the following three main steps, as illustrated in *Figure 3.2:*

1. Identify hazards, vulnerabilities, and threats.
2. Identify assets and the asset value at risk.
3. Calculate threat probability and business impact.

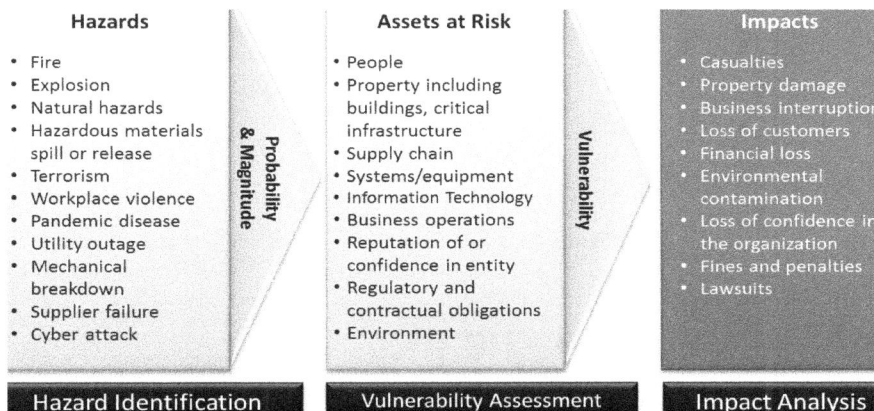

Figure 3.2: Risk assessment

The management and the risk assessment team must first decide which assets and threats to evaluate before beginning the risk assessment. This step entails establishing the project's scope. After that, the risk assessment team must provide a report to the management detailing the worth of the assets under consideration. The asset list is then reviewed and finalized, with the management adding and deleting assets as needed, before determining the risk assessment project's budget. A risk assessment will not be successful unless it is endorsed and led by the high management. The aim and scope of a risk assessment must be defined by the management, who must then assign personnel, time, and financial resources to the project. The **Statement of Applicability (SOA)** outlines and explains the controls that an organization has selected, as well as how and why they are applicable. The SOA is obtained from the risk assessment's result. If ISO 27001 compliance is critical to a company, the SOA must link the chosen controls to the risks they are supposed to manage. The SOA should relate to the rules, procedures, additional documents, or systems that will be used to implement the specified control. It's also a good idea to keep track of why certain controls were left out.

Business impact analysis

A BIA, as shown in *Figure 3.3,* is a type of functional analysis used in business continuity and catastrophe recovery. A detailed BIA will aid the business units in comprehending the impact of a disaster. BIA produces a document that specifies the important and necessary business functions, as well as their resource requirements and criticality to the broader company. Refer to *Figure 3.3,* that illustrates the BIA:

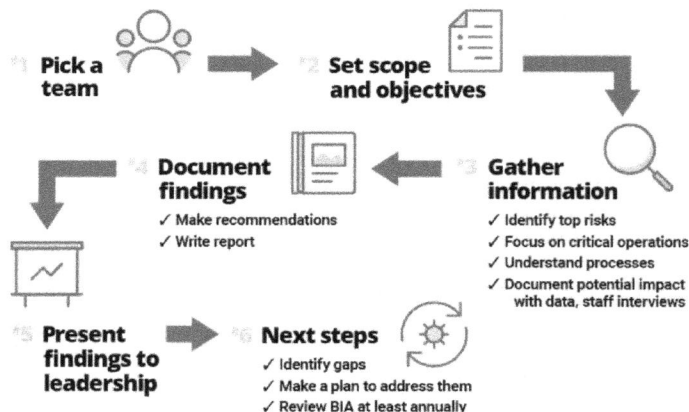

Figure 3.3: Business impact analysis

Interoperability agreement

An **interoperability agreement (IA)** is a contract between two or more entities to collaborate in order to exchange information. These agreements are most commonly used between sister firms that are controlled by the same major organization. Despite the fact that the businesses are built and operated differently, they may share systems, telecommunications, software, and data to enable resource consolidation and improved use. IAs are legally enforceable contracts. An IA is not the same as a reciprocal agreement. A reciprocal agreement is an agreement between two organizations that have comparable technology demands and infrastructures, whereas an IA covers routine operations. In a reciprocal agreement, one organization undertakes to operate as an alternate venue for the other if one of the **organization's** principal facilities becomes unavailable. Unfortunately, in the vast majority of circumstances, these agreements are not legally enforceable.

Interconnection security agreement

An **interconnection security agreement** (**ISA**) is a contract that documents the technical requirements of a connection between two entities that own and run linked IT systems. In most circumstances, each organization's security control requirements are stated in the agreement to avoid any misunderstandings. The ISA also encourages the groups to sign a memorandum of understanding. For example, if a company has completed the connection of its network to a national high-speed network and local businesses in the area are seeking sponsorship to connect to the high-speed network by connecting directly through the company's network, an ISA would be the best way to document the connection's technical requirements.

Memorandum of understanding

A **memorandum of understanding** (**MOU**) is a document that defines a shared course of action between two or more organizations. MOUs are frequently utilized when the parties do not have a legal commitment or when they are unable to reach a legally binding agreement. It's also known as a letter of intent in some circumstances.

Service level agreement

A SLA is a contract that specifies how quickly the support system will respond to problems while maintaining a specified level of service. Internal SLAs between departments or external SLAs with a service provider are also possible. Agreeing on the speed with which certain problems are treated brings some predictability to the reaction to problems, which in turn helps maintain resource access. An SLA is often included with most service contracts, and it may contain security priorities, duties, guarantees, and warranties. When a new third-party vendor, such as a cloud computing provider, is chosen to maintain and administer an organization's systems, an SLA is the best option. When an organization needs 24-hour assistance for specific internal services and wishes to utilize a third-party provider for shifts where the business does not have internal staff on duty, an SLA is a smart alternative.

Operating level agreement

An **operating level agreement** (**OLA**) is a document that specifies the relationships that exist across departments to support business activity. SLAs are frequently used with OLAs. An OLA is a contract between the IT department and the accounting department in which the IT department agrees to be responsible for the accounting server's backup services while the accounting employees are accountable for the server's day-to-day operations.

Non-disclosure agreement

A **non-disclosure agreement** (**NDA**) is a contract between two parties that specifies what information is secret and cannot be discussed with anyone else. An organization can use NDAs with its employees to protect its intellectual property. When two companies collaborate to create a new product, NDAs might be employed. NDAs are signed to ensure that each partner's data is secured because some information must be disclosed for the partnership to succeed. While the NDA cannot guarantee that sensitive information is not released, it does contain information on the consequences for the offender, including fines, jail terms, and the loss of rights.

When a business wishes to legally assure that no sensitive information is compromised through a project with a third party or in a cloud-computing environment, for example, it should establish an NDA. The NDA you sign before taking the CompTIA Advanced Security Practitioner test is an example of one in use. You must digitally sign an NDA that explicitly indicates that you are not permitted to discuss any information about the exam's contents other than what is officially stated in the CompTIA blueprint, which is published on the company's website. If you do not follow the terms of this NDA, you risk losing your CompTIA certification and being barred from taking future CompTIA examinations.

Business partnership agreement

A **business partnership agreement** (**BPA**) is a contract between two or more company partners that spells out the terms of their cooperation. The obligations of each partner, profit or loss sharing specifics, resource sharing information, and data sharing details are commonly included in a BPA. For example, if an organization enters into a marketing agreement with a marketing firm in which the organization will share some of its customer information with the marketing firm, the terms of the agreement should be spelled out in a BPA, along with any contract boundaries, such as allowing the marketing firm to only contact customers who have explicitly agreed to be contacted by third parties. Any organizational policies that may influence the partner and its employees should be included in BPAs. Any BPAs with partners who may have staff working onsite should contain the details of your organization's USB flash drive security policy.

Master service agreement

A **master service agreement** (**MSA**) is a contract between two parties in which the majority of the parameters that will control future transactions or agreements are agreed upon by both parties. If a company will have a long-term connection with a vendor or a supplier, this agreement is excellent. For the term of each contract, MSA offers a risk allocation plan that describes the risks and duties of contractors and employees included in the agreement. It also includes indemnity, which permits one party to hold another party blameless or protect them from current or future damages. Regardless of who is at blame, the indemnifying party undertakes to pay for damages it has caused or may cause in the future; these losses include legal expenses and litigation costs. A **statement of work** (**SOW**) is frequently included in an MSA, and it specifies the precise work that the vendor will perform for the customer. It outlines the tasks to be completed, as well as the deliverables and a timetable for completion.

Security requirements for contracts

Contracts with third parties are a common occurrence in the industry. Contracts now include provisions that expressly outline the vendor's security requirements, as security has become a priority for most enterprises and government institutions. Organizations should engage in legal advice to ensure that the contracts they execute have the required security criteria to meet not just their own demands but also any applicable government rules and laws. An organization may want to consider including provisions such as the following as part of any contract:

- Required policies, practices, and procedures related to handling organizational data
- Training or certification requirements for any third-party personnel
- Background investigation or security clearance requirements for any third-party personnel
- Required security reviews of third-party devices
- Physical security requirements for any third-party personnel
- Laws and regulations that will affect the contract
- Security professionals should research security requirements for contracts, including **request for proposals (RFPs)**, **request for quotes (RFQs)**, **request for informations (RFIs)**, and other agreements

Figure 3.4 illustrates the three security requirements for contracts:

Figure 3.4: *RFI, RFQ and RFP*

These are further explained in the following paragraphs.

Request for information

An RFI is a document used in the bidding process to gather written information on the capabilities of potential vendors. If necessary, an RFI can be used before an RFP or RFQ, but it can also be used thereafter if the RFP or RFQ fails to acquire sufficient specification information. Assume a major private firm's security administrator is studying and putting up a proposal to acquire an **intrusion prevention system (IPS)**. This is because no single IPS type has been chosen, the security administrator will need to gather information from multiple suppliers before deciding on a solution. An RFI would aid in the selection of a certain brand and model. Now, consider a case in which the RFI follows the RFP or RFQ. Assume that three senior executives have been collaborating to request bids for a series of firewall solutions for a big installation at the firm's new office. The three managers have not received any meaningful data on the specs of any of the solutions after examining RFQs aquired from three suppliers, and they require that data before the procurement continues. To bring the procurement process back on track, the managers should call the three submitting vendor businesses and request that they file the supporting RFIs with more extensive information about their product solutions.

Request for quote

An invitation for bid, often known as an RFQ, is a bidding process document that encourages vendors to submit bids on specified items or services. RFQs are useful for procuring items that are standardized or produced in large quantities, such as desktop computers, RAM modules, or other devices because they generally include item or service requirements. Assume a small private firm's security administrator is studying and putting up a proposal to acquire an IPS. The security administrator has to acquire cost information for a certain brand and model that has been chosen. To conduct a cost analysis report, the security administrator should write an RFQ. Payment terms, for example, would be included in the RFQ.

Request for proposal

An RFP is a document used in the bidding process that describes a commodity, a service, or an asset that the organization wants to buy. The RFP is used as a framework for presenting a formal bid by potential providers. After three suppliers deliver their requested documents, two members of senior management believe they have a better understanding of what each vendor does and what solutions they can supply. However, the executives now want to understand the complexities of how these solutions might meet the firm's needs. To gather this information, the managers should issue an RFP to the three submitting businesses.

Agreement or contract

Organizations employ a variety of third-party agreements in addition to the ones mentioned. Even though many of these agreements are not as formal as RFPs, RFQs, or RFIs, it is nevertheless critical for an organization to address any security needs in an agreement so that the third party is aware of them. This comprises purchase orders, sales agreements, manufacturing agreements, and other sorts of contracts that an organization employs to do business.

Privacy principles for sensitive information

When it comes to technology and how it is used nowadays, consumers' privacy is a key worry. This privacy problem generally revolves around three areas such as whether personal information may be shared with whom, whether messages can be transmitted privately, and whether and how a user can send messages anonymously. Privacy is an important aspect of a company's security measures. **Personal identifiable information** (**PII**) must be understood, identified, and secured as part of the security measures that companies must take to preserve privacy. Any piece of data that may be used alone or in combination with other information to identify a specific individual is referred to as PII. Any PII that an organization acquires must be safeguarded to the greatest extent practicable. Full name, identification numbers such as driver's license and social security numbers, date of birth, place of birth, biometric data, financial account numbers such as bank account and credit card numbers, and digital identities such as social media names and tags are all examples of personally identifiable information.

It is important to remember that various nations and levels of government may use different criteria to identify PII. Security experts must ensure that they are familiar with PII rules and legislation at the international, national, state, and local levels. As the theft of this data grows more common, you may expect additional regulations affecting your profession to be implemented. Encourage the creation of policies that include standard security practices. To support all areas of security, organizational policies must be developed. Separation of duties, job rotation, mandatory vacation, least privilege, incident response, forensic tasks, employment and termination procedures, continuous monitoring, training and awareness for users, and auditing requirements and frequency should all be included in organizational security policies, according to experienced security professionals.

Separation of duties

When creating an organization's authentication and authorization procedures, keep the separation of roles in mind as a preventative administrative control, as presented in *Figure 3.5*. By spreading tasks and their accompanying rights and privileges across users, the separation of responsibilities prevents fraud. This helps prevent fraud and collusion because if a company adopts proper separation of functions, fraud against the organization would need collaboration between two or more employees. Authorizing one person to control the backup operations and another to manage and restore procedures is an excellent illustration of splitting roles. Refer to *Figure 3.5* that illustrates the separation of duties:

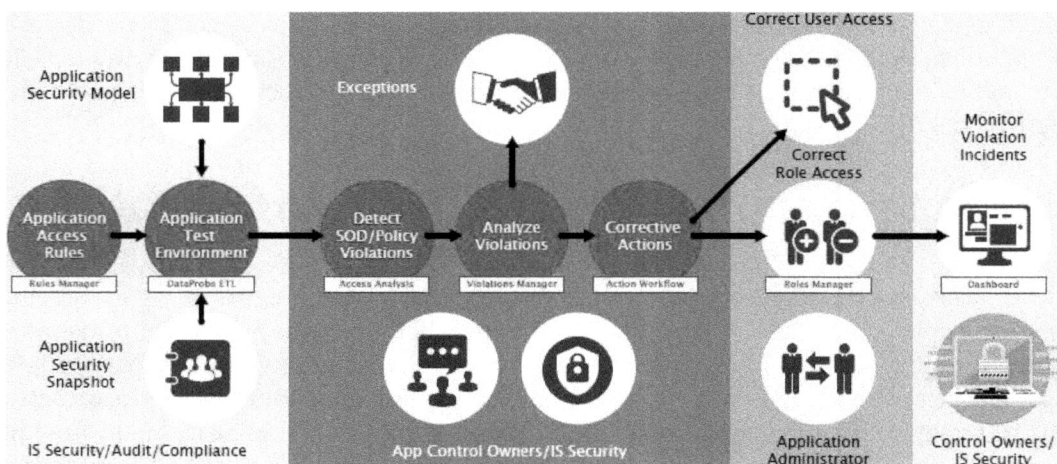

Figure 3.5: Separation of duties

Dual controls and divided knowledge are linked to the separation of responsibilities. Two or more people are permitted and needed to conduct particular operations with dual controllers. A retail firm, for example, could require two supervisors to unlock the safe. Split knowledge guarantees that no single person has access to all of the information required to complete a job. Split knowledge is demonstrated by the military's need for two people to input a different combination to approve missile fire. Separation of responsibilities, as shown in *Figure 3.6*, assures that no single individual is capable of jeopardizing the organization's security. Any high-risk activity should be broken down into discrete tasks, which may then be assigned to various people or departments. The separation of roles is the guiding concept when an organization establishes a policy stating that the systems administrator cannot be present during a system audit.

Refer to *Figure 3.6* that illustrates segregated and non-segregated separation of duties:

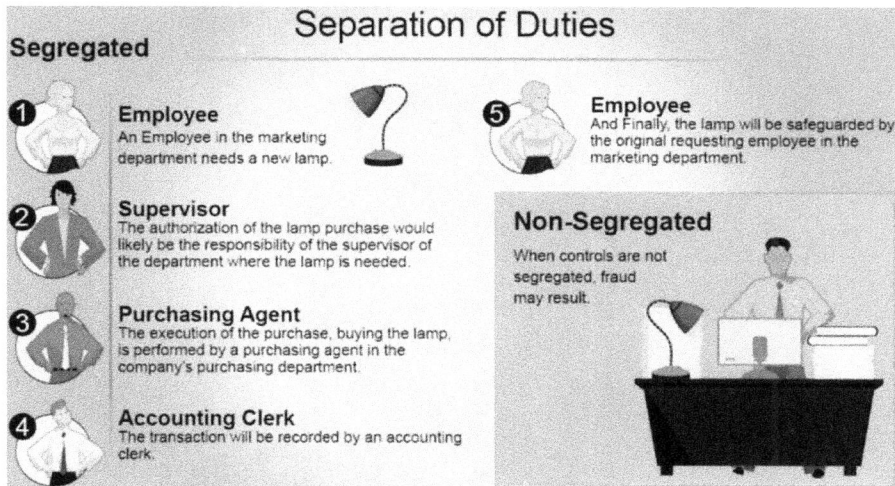

Figure 3.6: Separation of duties (segregated and non-segregated)

Consider the following example of a breach of the division of roles, assume that an organization's internal audit department is looking into a probable security breach. One of the auditors interviews three employees, a clerk in charge of inputting data into the financial system at the accounts receivable office, an administrative assistant in charge of purchasing orders approval at the accounts payable office, and the financial department manager, who may work as a clerk and an administrative assistant at the same time. To prevent future security breaches, the auditor should recommend that the manager's role be limited to data assessment and approval of purchase orders.

Job rotation

Job rotation, as depicted in *Figure 3.7*, from a security standpoint, refers to the investigative administrative control in which numerous users are taught to fulfill the functions of a position in order to assist in preventing fraud by any single employee. The premise is that by familiarizing several persons with the lawful tasks of the job, the probability of odd behavior by any one person being observed increases. Job rotation is frequently combined with required vacations. Beyond the security aspects of job rotation, additional benefits include the following:

- Trained backup in case of emergencies
- Protection against fraud
- Cross-training of employees
- Mandatory vacation

Refer to *Figure 3.7* that illustrates job rotation:

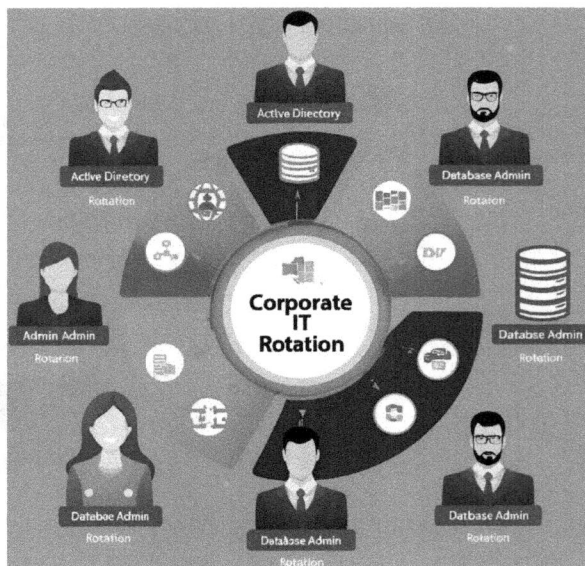

Figure 3.7: *Job rotation*

Mandatory vacations require all employees to take time off, enabling other employees to fill in for them while they are away. This investigative administrative control improves the chances of uncovering odd conduct. Some of the security benefits of using mandatory vacations include having the replacement employee perform the following tasks:

- Run the same applications as the vacationing employee.
- Perform tasks in a different order from the vacationing employee.
- Perform the job from a different workstation than the vacationing employee.

Employees who are filling in for a vacationing employee should avoid running scripts that were written by the vacationing employee. A substitute employee should either write their own script or execute the duties in the script manually.

Least privilege

The idea of least privilege states that a user or process should only have the access privileges necessary to complete a job. This principle's major goal is to guarantee that users only have access to the resources they require and are permitted to execute just the jobs they require. Organizations must identify all users' occupations and restrict users to only the rights indicated to fully execute the least privilege concept. The idea of least privilege is intimately linked to the need-to-know principle. The need-to-know concept sets the minimums for each profession or company function, despite the fact that least privilege attempts to minimize access to a bare minimum.

When a user has more rights, privileges, and permissions than he needs to execute his job, this becomes an issue. In corporate contexts, excessive rights are difficult to manage. When a systems administrator is given both an administrative-level account and a regular user account, this is a frequent application of the least privileged and need-to-know concepts. Administrators should often utilize a regular user account. The administrative-level account should be used by systems administrators for perfoming administrative-level duties. When administrators undertake everyday operations using administrative-level accounts, they risk jeopardizing system security and user accountability. Organizational rules that support the principle of least privilege include the following:

- Keep the number of administrative accounts to a minimum.

- Administrators should use normal user accounts when performing routine operations.

- Permissions on tools that are likely to be used by attackers should be as restrictive as possible.

Users should be separated into groups to make confining knowledge to a specific group or region easier to support the least privileged and need-to-know principles. The term for this procedure is compartmentalization. No access should be the default level of access. Users should only have access to the resources they need to execute their work, and that access should be granted manually after a supervisor has validated the necessity. User systems need to know and include discretionary access control and role-based access control. To ensure the least amount of privilege, the user's work must be recognized, and each user must be given the lowest level of clearance necessary for his or her responsibilities. The implementation of views in a database is another example. The operator must have the bare minimum of understanding of the system in order to complete his or her duty. If an administrator examines a recent security audit and discovers that two financial users also have access to human resource data, this might be a breach of the principle of least privilege if one of the identified users exclusively works in finance. Users should only have access to the data they need to fulfill their tasks. While certain users may need data from outside their department, this is not the norm and should always be thoroughly scrutinized.

Incident response

Security-related incidents are unavoidable. The organization's response to a catastrophe has a significant influence on how harmful the event will be. Policies for incident response should be properly defined, clearly communicated, and adhered to. They should pay special attention to cyber-attacks on a company's IT infrastructure. The steps in the incident response system (refer to *Figure 3.8*) can include the following:

1. **Detection**: The first step is to find out what happened. This feature is included in all investigative controls, such as auditing. An event that goes unreported is the worst kind.

2. **Respond**: The incident should be responded to in a manner that is suitable for the kind of occurrence. DoS assaults on a web server would necessitate a more immediate and distinct reaction than a lost mouse in the server room. An organization should establish standard responses and response times ahead of time.

3. **Report**: All incidences should be reported within a reasonable time period, taking into account the severity of the situation. Creating a list of event categories and who to call when each sort of incident happens is beneficial in many circumstances. At this early stage, when time-sensitive information is still accessible, meticulous attention to detail is essential.

4. **Recover**: Recovering entails taking steps to restore the network or system's functionality. What that entails depends on the circumstances and the recovery options available. If fault tolerance is in place, for example, the recovery may be as simple as enabling one server in a cluster to fail over to another. In other circumstances, restoring the server from a recent backup may be necessary. The major purpose of this stage is to re-establish access to all resources.

5. **Remediate**: This step entails removing any lingering threat or network harm that may still persist. For example, in the event of a viral epidemic, scanning systems to find any further infected devices might be necessary. When time permits, these approaches will be used to provide more extensive mitigation.

6. **Recap**: The third stage is to go through each episode again to see what lessons may be learned. Changes to processes may be required in order to communicate lessons gained with all workers who may be involved in a similar occurrence in the future.

During the reaction, report, and recovery processes, the real investigation of an event takes place. During an investigation, following proper forensic and digital investigative protocols may assist in guaranteeing that the evidence is maintained. Refer to *Figure 3.8,* which illustrates the incident response steps:

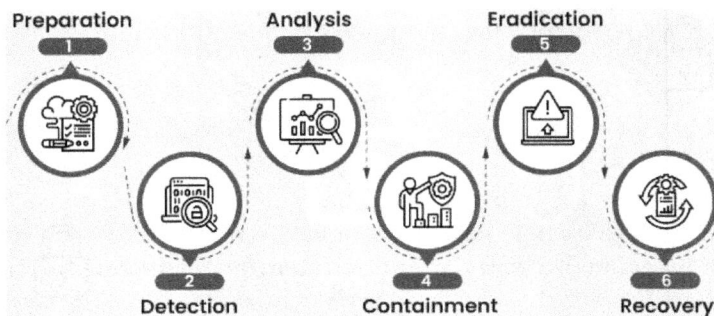

Figure 3.8: Incident response steps

Every firm must have an incident response plan in place to guarantee that any security issues are recognized, contained, and investigated. Any inquiry begins with an incident reaction. Issue response employees carry out particular activities when an incident has been found. Throughout the event response, the incident response team must ensure that the right protocols are followed in order to preserve evidence. Security personnel must know the distinction between events and occurrences while responding to issues. The incident response team must have adequate incident response protocols in place to ensure that an event is handled properly, but the processes must not obstruct any forensic investigations that may be required to hold parties accountable for any illegal conduct. Any incident investigation requires security experts to grasp the rules of engagement, as well as the authority and scope of the inquiry.

Events versus incidents

There is a fundamental distinction between events and incidents when it comes to incident response. A change of status is referred to as an event. Whereas events may be both good and bad, incident response is mainly focused on negative occurrences, those that have been determined to have a detrimental impact on the company. An incident is a set of events that have a negative influence on the operations and security of a company. An attempt to connect to the server, for example, is an event. An incident occurs when a system is breached as a result of a series of failed attempts to connect to the server. These are illustrated in *Figure 3.9*:

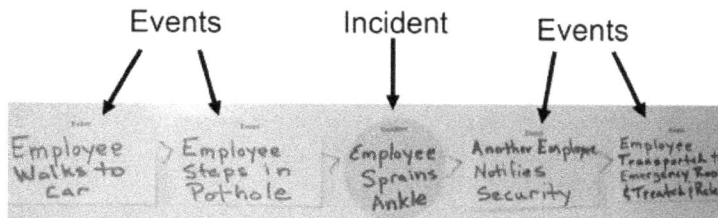

Figure 3.9: Events and incidents

Only if a company has developed sufficient auditing and security procedures to monitor activities, may the events be discovered. It is possible that a single bad occurrence will occur. An incorrect login attempt, for example, may be recorded in the auditing log. This login attempt is not a security risk on its own. However, if a large number of incorrect login attempts occur in a short period of time, the organization may be under assault. The first invalid login attempt is considered an event, but a succession of invalid login attempts over a period of hours would be termed an incident, especially if the incorrect login attempts all came from the same IP address.

Rules of engagement, authorization, and scope

The incident response team's rules of engagement, authorization, and scope should all be documented. If an event has happened, the rules of engagement establish which acts are allowed and which are not. The authorization and scope give the incident response team the power to conduct an investigation as well as the extent of any investigation that the team is required to conduct. The incident response team's rules of engagement serve as a guide to ensure that they do not cross the line from enticement to entrapment. Enticement happens when the attacker is offered the option to engage in illicit behavior (luring), but the attacker chooses to act on his own. Entrapment is the act of persuading someone to commit a crime that they had no intention of doing. Although the incentive is legal, it raises ethical concerns and may not be admissible in court. Entrapment is a crime.

Forensic tasks

This is because the time constraint for the investigator is constricted, and an expert may be necessary to assist in the investigation, computer investigations involve different processes than ordinary investigations. Furthermore, because computer data is intangible, extra caution is typically required to guarantee that the data is preserved in its original format. Finally, obtaining evidence of a digital crime might be challenging. After a decision has been made to investigate a computer crime, you should follow standardized procedures, including the following:

- Identify what type of system is to be seized.
- Identify the search and seizure team members.
- Determine the risk of the suspect destroying evidence.

The investigator's limits of the organization are raised if law enforcement is notified of a computer crime. It may be essential to turn the inquiry over to law enforcement to guarantee that the evidence is properly maintained. Evidentiary rules must be followed while investigating a computer crime. Computer evidence must show a fact that is relevant to the case and be trustworthy. It is crucial to keep the chain of custody intact. If the procedure for creating computer evidence has not been recorded, it is less likely to be allowed in court as evidence. The forensic investigation involves the following steps:

1. Identification
2. Preservation
3. Collection
4. Examination
5. Analysis
6. Presentation
7. Decision

Employment and termination procedures

The vast majority of security vulnerabilities inside a business are caused by employees. As a result, an organization's people security rules must be implemented. Screening, hiring, and firing rules should all be included in an organization's people security policy. A criminal background check, job history, background investigations, credit history, driving records, substance-abuse tests, and education and license verification should all be done before an offer of employment is made. Screening requirements should be developed depending on the organization's requirements and the degree of employment held by the potential recruit. Signing all applicable paperwork, including government-required documentation, no expectation of privacy declarations, and NDAs, should be part of the employment process.

New workers are given a copy of the personnel handbook as well as other employment material. After a formal verification that the employee has finished all of the training, IDs and passwords should be provided. Depending on whether the termination is pleasant or unfriendly, it must be addressed accordingly. Human resources procedures may guarantee that organizational property is returned, user access is terminated when it is no longer needed, and departure interviews are done. When it comes to unfavorable terminations, organizational processes must be proactive in order to protect the company's assets. As a result, unfavorable termination processes should involve the cessation of system and facility access before notifying employees of their termination, as well as security escort from the premises.

During employment, management must also guarantee that adequate security rules are in place. Some roles may necessitate employment agreements in order to preserve the business and its assets even after the employee has left. NDAs, non-compete provisions, and code of conduct and ethics agreements are examples of these agreements.

Continuous monitoring

An organization's operating baselines must be captured before continuous monitoring may be successful. After all, if an organization does not know what **normal** is, it will not be able to spot aberrant patterns of behavior. These baselines should be checked on a regular basis to confirm that they have not been altered. A new performance baseline should be acquired if a single web server is upgraded to a web server farm, for example. The organization's security posture must be maintained at all times, according to security specialists. This needs constant monitoring. On a regular basis, auditing and security logs should be inspected. Baselines should be compared against performance measurements. Even simple actions like user login and logout timings should be tracked. If a user starts logging in and out at odd times, the user's supervisor should be notified to make sure the user is permitted. Organizations must maintain constant vigilance over their enterprise's security.

Training and awareness for users

Security awareness training, security training, and security education are all phrases that are frequently used interchangeably, but they are not interchangeable. The need to employ security measures to preserve precious resources is reinforced through awareness training. Personnel are taught the skills they need to execute their professions safely during security training. Security awareness training, which combines awareness and security training, promotes user security awareness and guarantees that users may be held accountable for their activities. Security education is more self-contained and geared at security professionals who need security knowledge to manage security programs in-house. As a result, awareness training focuses on what, security training on how, and security education on why. The audience should be considered while developing security awareness training. Trainers must also be aware of the business culture and how it influences security. In a small customer-focused bank, for example, bank workers may be encouraged to form connections with bank customers. In this scenario, security awareness training must take into account the hazards associated with close client connections.

High-level management, middle management, technical professionals, and other staff are among the audiences to consider while developing training. Security awareness training for high-level management must include a thorough grasp of potential risks and threats, the impact of security concerns on the organization's reputation and financial position, and any applicable rules and regulations that apply to the security program. Policies, standards, baselines, guidelines, and procedures, as well as how these components relate to different departments, should be discussed during middle management training. Middle management must also be aware of their security duties.

Technical employees should be trained on how to configure and maintain security safeguards, as well as how to spot an attack when it happens. Furthermore, technical employees should be pushed to earn industry certifications and advanced degrees. Other employees must be aware of their security obligations in order to carry out their daily activities safely. Using real-life examples to stress adequate security practices is helpful for this team. Targeted security training is necessary to ensure that users at all levels of the company are aware of their security responsibilities. Assume the manager is in a training session that lasts all day. He is behind inputting bonus and payroll information for subordinates; he believes that logging into the payroll system and activating desktop sharing with a trusted subordinate is the best method to get the updates in. The manager hands over control of the desktop to the subordinate, giving him or her complete access to the payroll system. The subordinate lacks the necessary permissions to access the payroll system. Another employee reported the event to the security staff. The most effective way to deal with this problem is to give targeted security awareness training and fire repeat offenders.

Employees should sign a paper attesting to the fact that they have finished the training and comprehended all of the themes. Although initial security awareness training should take place when someone is employed, it should be regarded as an ongoing process, with future training sessions occurring at least once a year. It is critical for businesses to ensure that processes are followed correctly at all times. If a business detects that employees are not adhering to proper processes of any type, the procedures should be reviewed to ensure that they are right. The workers should then be provided the necessary training to ensure that the correct processes are followed.

For example, if a recent security breach resulted in the disclosure of sensitive customer information, the firm must ensure that employees are properly taught to improve security and limit the risk of data disclosure. In this situation, the privacy compliance training program should primarily focus on explaining to employees how customer data is collected, utilized, released, and maintained. It's also critical to conduct security audits on a regular basis. Consider the case where a security audit discovered a lack of security controls relating to employee account management. The audit indicates that accounts are not deactivated immediately once an employee leaves the company. According to corporate policy, an employee's account should be disabled within eight hours of termination. However, according to the audit, 10% of the accounts were not blocked until seven days after a terminated employee had left. In addition, 5% of the accounts are still active. To guarantee fast reporting of employee terminations, security professionals should discuss the termination policy with the organization's managers. To guarantee that accounts are disabled when necessary, it may be important to develop a systematic mechanism for reporting terminations.

Auditing requirements and frequency

You must first recognize typical patterns of conduct before you can detect aberrant patterns of behavior. You should also define a clipping level, which is a threshold over which infractions will be reported. Three failed login attempts are a commonly used clipping level. Any unsuccessful login attempt that exceeds the three-time limit is deemed malicious. After this clipping threshold is achieved, most lockout policies will lock out a user's account. Users are held accountable for their behavior through auditing and reporting. However, an auditing system can only report on occurrences that it is equipped to monitor.

Organizations must find a balance between checking essential events and processes while also ensuring device performance is adequate. Organizations must also ensure that any monitoring they do is compliant with all applicable laws. Audit trails are used to identify computer breaches because they uncover behaviors that suggest abuse. Security experts should evaluate patterns of access to specific assets using audit trails.

Information classification and life cycle

The importance of data to the organization and its sensitivity to disclosure should be considered when classifying it. As previously stated in this chapter, assigning a value to data helps an organization identify the resources that should be spent to safeguard the data. Personnel resources, monetary resources, and access control resources are all employed to safeguard data. Data classification based on **confidentiality, integrity, and availability (CIA)** allows you to employ various safeguards. After the data has been categorized, it can be split according to the level of protection required. Data is handled and safeguarded in the most cost-effective way possible, thanks to the categorization levels. The categorization levels that an organization utilizes should be determined based on the needs of the organization. Commercial information categories, as well as military and government information classifications, are widely employed. The classification of the data should also be used to guide the information life cycle. According to municipal, state, and federal rules and regulations, businesses are obligated to save certain information, notably financial data.

Commercial business classifications

Commercial businesses usually classify data using the four main classification levels, listed as follows, from the highest sensitivity level to the lowest:

- Confidential
- Private
- Sensitive
- Public

Trade secrets, intellectual property, application programming code, and other private information might have major consequences for the firm if it was leaked. Only employees in the organization whose job is related to the data subject would have access to this level of data. Each access to private data normally necessitates authorization. The Freedom of Information Act protects confidential information from dissemination. External entities can only have permitted access to secret data after signing a confidentiality agreement and complying with a court order in most situations. In the context of a government project or a contract procurement agreement, any information on employees, such as human resources records, medical records, and wage information, that is utilized solely within the firm is considered private data. Sensitive data, such as corporate financial information, needs additional safeguarding to ensure its CIA and correctness. The term **public data** refers to information that would not be harmful to the company.

Military and government classifications

Military and government entities usually classify data using the five main classification levels, listed as follows, from the highest sensitivity level to the lowest:

- Top secret
- Secret
- Confidential
- Sensitive but unclassified
- Unclassified

Weapons designs, technical specifications, spy satellite intelligence, and other military data classified as top secret might jeopardize national security if revealed. Secret data contains deployment plans, missile locations, and other information that, if revealed, may jeopardize national security. Patents, trade secrets, and other proprietary information may have major consequences for the government if it is released without permission. Medical or other personal data that may not pose a severe threat to national security, but may cause individuals to question the government's reputation, are examples of sensitive but unclassified data. Unclassified military and government material that does not fall into any of the other four categories must normally be released to the public under the Freedom of Information Act.

Information life cycle

Data retention and deletion protocols must be in place in all enterprises. All local, state, and federal requirements and laws must be followed while retaining and destroying data. Documenting the right processes guarantees that information is kept for the length of time necessary, avoiding financial penalties and possible imprisonment of high-ranking organizational executives. Both the retention term, including prolonged retention periods for legal holds, and the disposal process must be included in these protocols.

Design secure system principles

Following are the use cases:

- **Use case 1**: Design and implement a secure SDLC for developing and deploying containerized applications on a Kubernetes cluster as per the following steps:

    1. **Define security requirements:** To establish a robust foundation for securing the SDLC, it is critical to define and document security requirements that align with the organization's risk posture and compliance obligations:

        a. **Threat modeling**: Conduct a threat modeling exercise (for example, STRIDE, DREAD) to identify potential vulnerabilities at each stage of the SDLC.

        b. **Security goals**: Clearly define security goals, such as confidentiality, integrity, availability, and compliance with relevant regulations (for example, SOC 2, ISO 27001).

    2. **Secure coding practices:** Adopting secure coding practices ensures that security vulnerabilities are identified and mitigated during the development process, reducing risks before deployment:

        a. **Code reviews**: Implement mandatory code reviews by experienced security engineers to identify and address vulnerabilities early in the development process.

        b. **Static and dynamic analysis**: Integrate **Static and Dynamic application security testing (SAST and DAST)** tools into the CI and CD pipeline to automatically scan code for vulnerabilities.

   c. **Secure coding standards**: Enforce secure coding standards and best practices through automated linting tools and code style checkers.

3. **Infrastructure as Code (IaC):** Leveraging IaC ensures consistent, secure configurations for Kubernetes clusters and containerized environments, minimizing human error:

   a. **Secure infrastructure configuration**: Define and enforce security configurations for Kubernetes clusters and container images using IaC tools like Terraform, Ansible, or Pulumi.

   b. **Least privilege**: Implement the principle of least privilege by granting containers only the necessary permissions to perform their functions.

4. **Runtime security:** Maintaining runtime security involves protecting Kubernetes clusters from threats by implementing real-time controls and monitoring mechanisms:

   a. **Network policies**: Define and enforce network policies within the Kubernetes cluster to control inter-pod communication and isolate critical services.

   b. **Intrusion detection**: Deploy and configure security monitoring tools (for example, Falco, Sysdig) to detect and respond to malicious activity within the Kubernetes environment.

5. **Continuous monitoring and improvement:** Ensuring the security of containerized applications is an ongoing process that requires regular monitoring, auditing, and updating of the environment:

   a. **Security audits**: Regularly conduct security audits and penetration tests to identify and address any remaining vulnerabilities.

   b. **Vulnerability management**: Implement a vulnerability management program to track and remediate vulnerabilities in a timely manner.

- **Use case 2**: Design and implement a zero trust architecture for an organization with a hybrid cloud environment (on-premises data centers and multiple cloud providers).

Following are the hands-on steps:

1. **Micro-segmentation:** Begin by isolating critical systems and resources within the hybrid cloud environment to reduce the attack surface and prevent lateral movement:

   a. **Network segmentation**: Divide the network into smaller, isolated segments based on business needs and security requirements.

   b. **Software-defined perimeter (SDP)**: Implement SDP solutions to create secure access paths to applications and data, regardless of location.

2. **Identity and access management (IAM):** Implement robust IAM controls to enforce strong authentication and access policies for users and devices:

   a. **Least privilege**: Implement least privilege access controls for all users and devices, granting only the necessary permissions to access resources.

   b. **Multi-factor authentication (MFA)**: Enforce MFA for all users and devices accessing sensitive resources.

   c. **Identity federation**: Implement identity federation solutions (for example, SAML, OAuth) to enable secure access across different cloud environments and on-premises systems.

3. **Data protection:** Safeguard sensitive organizational data by implementing encryption and access control measures:

   a. **Data loss prevention (DLP):** Implement DLP solutions to prevent sensitive data from leaving the organization's control.

   b. **Data encryption:** Encrypt data both at rest and in transit using strong encryption algorithms.

4. **Threat detection and response:** Enhance the security posture by proactively detecting and responding to threats in real-time:

   a. **Security information and event management (SIEM):** Implement an SIEM system to collect and analyze security logs from various sources.

   b. **Security orchestration, automation, and response (SOAR):** Implement SOAR tools to automate security responses to incidents.

5. **Continuous monitoring and improvement:** Regularly evaluate and enhance the security framework to adapt to emerging threats and vulnerabilities:

   a. **Security posture management**: Regularly assess and improve the security posture of the hybrid cloud environment.

   b. **Incident response testing**: Conduct regular incident response drills to test and improve the organization's ability to respond to security incidents.

- **Use case 3:** Design and implement a secure system for deploying and managing a fleet of IoT devices (for example, smart sensors, industrial control systems).

Following are the hands-on steps:

1. **Device onboarding:** Establish secure mechanisms to validate and connect IoT devices to the network:

   a. **Secure boot**: Implement secure boot mechanisms to ensure that only trusted firmware and software are loaded onto the devices.

    b. **Device identity and attestation**: Establish and verify the identity and authenticity of each device before allowing it to join the network.

2. **Secure communication:** Protect data integrity and confidentiality in device-to-cloud communication:

    a. **Encryption**: Encrypt all communication between devices and the cloud using strong encryption protocols (for example, TLS or SSL).

    b. **Authentication**: Implement mutual authentication between devices and the cloud to prevent unauthorized access.

3. **Firmware updates:** Maintain device integrity by securely updating firmware:

    a. **Secure firmware updates**: Implement secure firmware update mechanisms to ensure the integrity and authenticity of firmware updates.

    b. **Over-the-air (OTA) updates**: Utilize OTA update mechanisms to efficiently and securely update firmware on deployed devices.

4. **Device monitoring and management:** Enable efficient oversight and control of IoT devices through secure platforms and algorithms:

    a. **Anomaly detection**: Implement anomaly detection algorithms to identify and respond to suspicious device behavior.

    b. **Remote device management**: Implement a secure remote device management platform to configure, monitor, and troubleshoot devices.

5. **Security audits and compliance:** Continuously evaluate the security of the IoT ecosystem to address vulnerabilities and meet standards:

    a. **Regular security audits**: Conduct regular security audits to identify and address vulnerabilities in the IoT ecosystem.

    b. **Compliance with standards**: Ensure compliance with relevant industry standards and regulations (for example, IEC 62443).

Conclusion

This chapter discussed the impact of new business, technologies, and business and environmental changes on security policies and processes. Legal compliance aspects for human resources, staff, and management were also discussed. Business documents supporting security are deliberated which include risk assessments, BIA, agreements, MoU, and SLA among others. This chapter also argued on the standard security practices of separation of duties, job rotation, least privileged, incident response, and other procedures. Security professionals must help the organizations they work for to put in place the proper risk mitigation strategies and controls.

The next chapter covers the risk management and risk mitigation strategies.

Exercise

1. **What is the primary objective of process life cycle management?**

    a. To create a backup of data

    b. To ensure the continuous improvement of business processes

    c. To minimize employee turnover

    d. To manage software licenses

2. **Which technology is most associated with enabling real-time analytics in businesses?**

    a. Cloud computing

    b. Blockchain

    c. Internet of Things (IoT)

    d. Big Data

3. **Which of the following is an example of an environmental change affecting businesses?**

    a. A new company policy

    b. Fluctuations in currency exchange rates

    c. Introduction of a carbon tax

    d. Changes in the organizational hierarchy

4. **Which regulation is focused on data protection and privacy for all individuals within the European Union?**

    a. SOX

    b. HIPAA

    c. GDPR

    d. PCI-DSS

5. **Which of the following is considered an emerging risk in cybersecurity?**

    a. Traditional malware attacks

    b. Social engineering techniques

    c. Quantum computing-enabled attacks

    d. Natural disasters

6. **What is the purpose of legal compliance in an organization?**

   a. To maximize profits

   b. To ensure adherence to laws and regulations

   c. To develop new products

   d. To reduce employee turnover

7. **Which document outlines an organization's approach to identifying and managing security risks?**

   a. Incident Response Plan

   b. Risk Management Policy

   c. Vendor Agreement

   d. Non-Disclosure Agreement (NDA)

8. **What is a primary purpose of a Service Level Agreement (SLA)?**

   a. To define the scope of financial audits

   b. To establish employee responsibilities

   c. To specify performance metrics between service provider and client

   d. To document intellectual property ownership

9. **Which clause in a contract ensures that a vendor complies with cybersecurity policies?**

   a. Confidentiality clause

   b. Security requirements clause

   c. Indemnification clause

   d. Non-compete clause

10. **Which principle emphasizes collecting only the data required for a specific purpose?**

    a. Transparency

    b. Data minimization

    c. Integrity

    d. Accountability

11. **What is the first step in the incident response process?**

    a. Containment

    b. Recovery

    c. Identification

    d. Post-incident analysis

12. Which is the correct sequence of phases in the information life cycle?

    a. Creation, storage, sharing, disposal

    b. Storage, creation, sharing, disposal

    c. Creation, disposal, sharing, storage

    d. Sharing, creation, storage, disposa

13. What is the main goal of applying engineering principles to secure system design?

    a. Reducing costs

    b. Enhancing usability]

    c. Minimizing security risks

    d. Ensuring compliance with HR policies

Answers

1. b
2. d
3. c
4. c
5. c
6. b
7. b
8. c
9. b
10. b
11. c
12. a
13. c

Join our book's Discord space

Join the book's Discord Workspace for Latest updates, Offers, Tech happenings around the world, New Release and Sessions with the Authors:

https://discord.bpbonline.com

## CHAPTER 4

Risk Mitigation Strategies

Introduction

Security professionals play a crucial role in guiding organizations to establish effective risk mitigation strategies and controls. This chapter explores the implementation of a robust risk management framework to ensure risks are accurately identified and managed. Key topics include data classification by impact levels based on **confidentiality, integrity, and availability (CIA)**, incorporating stakeholder input into CIA impact-level decisions, and calculating aggregate CIA scores to determine the minimum required security controls. It discusses implementing controls aligned with CIA requirements, planning for extreme scenarios, and conducting system-specific risk analyses. The chapter emphasizes translating technical risks into business terms to align with organizational goals and highlights the importance of defining a risk appetite strategy. Additionally, it examines essential risk management processes, **business continuity planning** (**BCP**) to ensure operational resilience, and IT governance as a cornerstone for managing risks effectively. This chapter aims to equip security professionals with the tools and strategies to align risk management practices with organizational objectives, ensuring informed decision-making and sustained security posture in an increasingly complex threat landscape.

Structure

In this chapter, we will cover all the tasks involved in risk mitigation, including the following:

- Data classification by impact levels based on CIA
- Incorporate stakeholder input into CIA decisions
- Determine the aggregate CIA score
- Minimum required security controls
- Implement controls based on CIA requirements
- Extreme scenario planning or worst-case scenario
- Conduct system-specific risk analysis
- Risk determination using known metrics
- Translate technical risks into business terms
- Risk appetite strategy
- Risk management processes
- Business continuity planning
- IT governance

Objectives

Security teams ensure organizations have proper risk mitigation strategies and controls in place. Using risk management frameworks helps identify and implement the appropriate controls. This chapter covers the steps involved in risk mitigation, which include asset identification, CIA triad, determination of threats, the likelihood of attacks, implementing countermeasures, and conducting a risk analysis to determine the security threshold level.

Data classification by impact levels based on CIA

CIA are the three cornerstones of security. Most security concerns arise in a breach of at least one CIA triad aspect. Understanding these three security principles will aid security professionals in ensuring that at least one of these principles is protected by the security controls and processes in place. You must avoid disclosing data or information to unauthorized parties in order to maintain confidentiality. Before any access restrictions are put in place, the sensitivity level of data must be evaluated as part of confidentiality. Access controls will be in place for data with a greater sensitivity level than the data with a lower sensitivity level.

Disclosure is the polar opposite of secrecy. Confidentiality is something that most security experts think about when it comes to data on a network or device. Data, on the other hand, may be printed. Data on a network should be safeguarded with appropriate controls, but data in its printed form must also be protected, which necessitates the implementation of data disposal rules. Encryption, steganography, **access control lists** (**ACLs**), and data classifications are examples of restrictions that promote secrecy.

The second component of the CIA trinity, integrity, guarantees that data is safe from unwanted change or corruption. The purpose of data integrity is to keep the data consistent. Corruption is the polar opposite of honesty. Many people believe that data integrity is less essential than data confidentiality. Data alteration or corruption, on the other hand, may be just as damaging to a business because the original data is lost. Digital signatures, checksums, and hashes are examples of integrity-enhancing measures.

Finally, availability refers to the capacity to obtain data when it is required. Only those with a legitimate need for data should have access to it. The opposite of destruction or isolation is availability. While many people believe this to be the least critical of the three tenets, an availability failure will have the greatest impact on end-users and customers. Consider a **denial-of-service** (**DoS**) assault on a web server that serves customers. Load balancing, hot sites, and RAID are examples of measures that increase availability. DoS attacks have an impact on availability.

Every security control implemented by an organization satisfies at least one of the CIA triad's security principles. It is just as crucial to know how to get around these security principles as it is to know how to offer them. When security measures are introduced, a balanced security approach should be used to guarantee that all three aspects are taken into account. You should determine the aspect that the control targets before implementing it. Data availability is addressed by RAID, data integrity is addressed by file hashes, and data secrecy is addressed by encryption.

No aspect of the CIA trifecta is overlooked with a balanced approach. FIPS 199 (Government Information Processing Standard Publication 199) establishes security classification rules for federal information systems. This US government standard specifies security categories for federal government information systems. FIPS 199 mandates that federal agencies evaluate their information systems in terms of confidentiality, integrity, and availability, assigning a low, moderate, or high impact rating to each system in each area. The overall security category of an information system receives the highest grade of any category.

If the loss of any CIA tenet is projected to have a modest negative impact on organizational operations, organizational assets, or personnel, the prospective impact is low. This happens when an organization can accomplish its core role, but not as well as it might. Only minimal damage, financial loss, or injury is included in this category.

If the loss of any CIA tenet is projected to have a severe negative impact on organizational operations, organizational assets, or personnel, the potential impact is moderate. This occurs when the organization's ability to accomplish its principal function effectively is considerably decreased. This category involves significant damage, financial loss, or harm.

If the loss of any CIA tenet is projected to have a significant or catastrophic unfavorable effect on organizational operations, organizational assets, or personnel, the potential impact is considerable. This happens when a company is unable to fulfill one or more of its core activities. Major damage, financial loss, or serious injury fall under this category. It is also critical for security professionals and businesses to understand the categorization and life cycle of information. Depending on whether the organization is a commercial enterprise or a military/government body, classification differs.

Incorporate stakeholder input into CIA decisions

CIA levels for business information assets are sometimes difficult to evaluate by security experts alone. Security experts should seek opinions from asset stakeholders to know which level should be ascribed to each tenet for an information asset. However, keep in mind that all stakeholders must be consulted. While the department heads should be contacted since they have the most impact on CIA decisions concerning departmental assets, other stakeholders within the department and organization should also be consulted. This guideline applies to every security endeavor a company conducts. Stakeholder involvement should be sought early on in the project to ensure that stakeholder demands are captured and that project buy-in is obtained. If difficulties with the security project occur later and adjustments are required, the project team should consult with project stakeholders before approving or implementing any project changes. Any input should be documented and integrated with the security professional's evaluation in order to calculate the CIA levels.

Determine the aggregate CIA score

FIPS 199 establishes three effects (low, moderate, and high) for the three security pillars. However, the organization must define the levels that are given to organizational entities since only the organization can judge if a particular loss is limited, serious, or severe. The security category of an identifiable entity conveys the three tenets with their values for an organizational entity, according to FIPS 199. After that, the values are utilized to decide which security restrictions should be put in place. If an asset is made up of numerous entities, the security category for that asset must be calculated based on the entities that make it up.

Minimum required security controls

For all organizational assets, suitable security procedures must be applied. Based on the aggregate CIA score outlined previously in this chapter, the security policies that need to be applied are identified. It is critical for security professionals to understand the different types of coverage given by the various security measures that might be used. Security experts should define a minimal set of security measures that must be applied as the study progresses.

Implement controls based on CIA requirements

For organizational assets to be secured, security experts must ensure that the right measures are adopted and executed. The controls that are chosen and implemented should be based on the CIA's needs as well as the organization's rules. Following the implementation of controls, a gap analysis may be required to establish where the security holes still exist so that more security controls may be introduced. The many types and categories of access restrictions that might be imposed should be recognizable to the security experts.

Access control categories

As a countermeasure to the discovered vulnerabilities, security engineers create access controls. Any access control put in place will fall into one or more of these categories. There are seven different types of access control techniques that are utilized, which are as follows:

- Compensative
- Corrective
- Detective
- Deterrent
- Directive
- Preventive
- Recovery

Compensative

Compensative controls are in place to lessen risks in the absence of primary access control. You can minimize the risk to a more reasonable level by employing compensatory measures. Compensatory measures include needing two authorized signatures to disclose sensitive or secret information and requiring two keys to unlock a safe deposit box maintained by separate people.

Corrective

Corrective measures have been put in place to lessen the impact of an assault or other unfavorable occurrence. Corrective controls can be used to repair or restore the entity that has been attacked. Installing fire extinguishers, isolating or terminating a connection, creating new firewall rules, and employing server images to restore to a prior state are all examples of corrective measures. After an event has occurred, corrective controls are important.

Detective

There are detective measures in place to identify an assault in progress and inform the proper individuals. Motion detectors, **intrusion detection systems (IDSs)**, logs, guards, investigations, auditing, and job rotation are all examples of detective controls. During an event, detective controls are important.

Deterrent

An attacker is deterred or discouraged by deterrent measures. Attacks can be detected early in the process, thanks to deterrent controls. Preventive and corrective controls are frequently triggered by deterrent controls. User identity and authentication, fencing, lights, and corporate security rules, such as non-disclosure agreements, are examples of deterrent controls (NDAs).

Directive

Within an organization, directive controls define what is and is not acceptable. They exist to establish an organization's security mandate, which is primarily directed at its personnel. An **Acceptable Usage Policy (AUP)**, which outlines correct processes and behaviors that employees must follow, is the most common directive control (and is often an example of improper procedures). This access control category generally includes any organizational security rules or processes. Keep in mind that directive controls are only effective if there is a specified penalty for failing to obey the organization's instructions.

Preventive

Preventive measures keep an assault from occurring in the first place. Locks, badges, biometric systems, encryption, **intrusion prevention systems (IPSs)**, antivirus software, personnel security, security guards, passwords, and security awareness training are examples of preventative controls. Preventive measures are beneficial prior to an occurrence.

Recovery

After an assault, recovery controls are used to restore a system or device. The restoration of resources is the major purpose of recovery controls. Disaster recovery plans, data backups, and remote facilities are examples of recovery measures. After an attack, recovery controls are used to restore a system or device. The restoration of resources is the major purpose of recovery controls. Disaster recovery plans, data backups, and remote facilities are examples of recovery measures. Effective recovery also involves validating the integrity of restored systems to ensure they are free of residual malware or vulnerabilities. For instance, after a ransomware attack, a recovery plan might include restoring data from secure backups and conducting a thorough audit of the system to identify and patch exploited vulnerabilities. Additionally, organizations may utilize failover systems, such as cloud-based infrastructure, to maintain continuity while primary systems are being restored.

Access control types

Access control necessitates the employment of all three types of access controls in any organization where defense in depth is a concern. You cannot fully secure the environment without logical controls, even if you use the toughest physical and administrative controls. Access control types are divided based on their method of implementation. There are three types of access controls, which are as follows:

- Administrative (management) controls
- Logical (technical) controls
- Physical controls

Administrative management controls

Security policies, procedures, standards, baselines, and guidelines developed by the management are used to administrate the organization's assets and workers. Soft controls are the term for these kinds of controls. Personnel controls, data categorization, data labeling, security awareness training, and supervision are just a few examples. Training in security awareness is a crucial administrative control. Its goal is to change the organization's attitude toward data security. Security awareness training has several advantages, including a decrease in the frequency and severity of mistakes and omissions, a better knowledge of the value of information, and improved administrator notice of unauthorized infiltration attempts. Creating an award or recognition program is a cost-effective strategy to ensure that the staff takes security awareness seriously.

Logical technical controls

Logical controls, also known as technical controls, are software or hardware components that are used to limit access. Firewalls, IDSs, IPSs, encryption, authentication systems, protocols, auditing and monitoring, biometrics, smart cards, and passwords are all examples of logical controls. Adopting a new security policy that prohibits workers from remotely setting up the email server from a third-party location during business hours is an example of putting in place technological control. Despite the fact that auditing and monitoring are logical controls and are frequently included together, they are two distinct controls. Auditing is a one-time or ongoing process for assessing security. Monitoring is a continuous process that checks the system or the users.

Physical controls

Physical controls are put in place to safeguard an organization's assets and workers. Considerations about personnel should take precedence above all other concerns.

Perimeter security, badges, swipe cards, guards, dogs, mantraps, biometrics, and cabling are all types of physical controls. For instance, implementing biometric access systems, such as fingerprint or iris scanners, can ensure that only authorized personnel access sensitive areas. Additionally, mantraps, which require individuals to pass through two interlocking doors, are effective in high-security environments to prevent unauthorized tailgating. Combining these measures with regular security audits helps identify potential vulnerabilities in the physical infrastructure and address them promptly.

Security control frameworks

To assist security professionals, several firms have established security management frameworks and approaches. Security program development standards, enterprise and security architect development frameworks, security controls, development techniques, corporate governance methods, and process management methods are just a few of the frameworks and methodologies available. This is because frameworks, standards, and techniques are all connected, they are discussed together.

Standards are considered the best practices, whereas frameworks are commonly used practices. Frameworks are generic, whereas standards are specialized.

A methodology is a set of practices, techniques, processes, and regulations that are followed by persons who operate in a certain field. Based on the demands of the stakeholders, the organizations should choose the framework, standard, and technique that best reflects the organization.

ISO/IEC 27000 series

ISO 27000 is a security program development standard on how to create and maintain an information security management system, albeit it is not exactly a framework (ISMS). The 27000 series consists of several standards, each of which focuses on a different component of ISMS. These guidelines have either been published or are in the works, as shown in *Figure 4.1:*

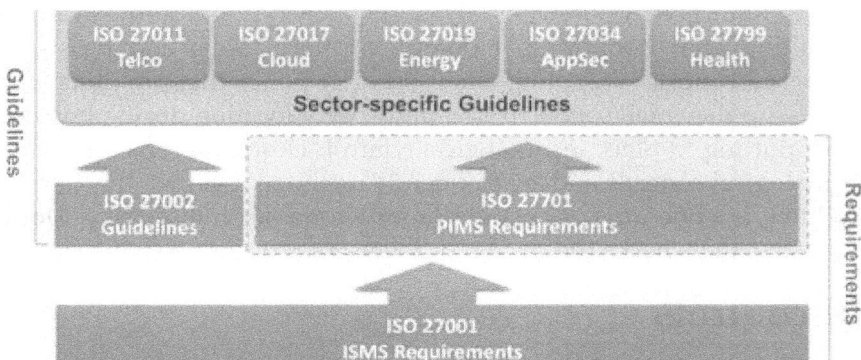

Figure 4.1: ISO 27000 series

Zachman Framework

The Zachman Framework is a two-dimensional categorization system based on six communication questions (what, where, when, why, who, and how), is an enterprise architectural framework that collides with diverse points of view (executive, business management, architect, engineer, technician, and enterprise). This approach enables an organization's analysis to be delivered to various groups within the organization in ways that are relevant to their responsibilities. Even though this framework is not security-oriented, it might assist you in relaying information to workers in the language and format that they prefer.

Open group architecture framework

Another enterprise architectural framework, **The Open Group Architecture Framework (TOGAF)**, assists businesses in the design, planning, implementation, and governance of an enterprise information architecture. TOGAF is made up of four areas that are all interconnected, such as technology, applications, data, and business, as shown in *Figure 4.2:*

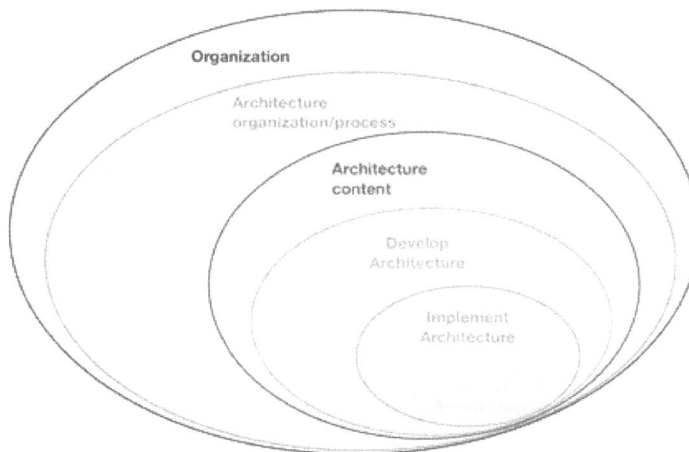

Figure 4.2: TOGAF

CIS critical security controls

Critical security controls, published by the **Center for Internet Security (CIS)**, is a list of 18 controls. These propose concrete and effective solutions to stop today's most ubiquitous and serious assaults by recommending a set of cyber security procedures. **SysAdmin, Audit, Network and Security (SANS)** provides training, research, and certification to support the CIS Controls. Backward compatibility with earlier versions is also provided, as well as a migration path enabling users of previous versions to upgrade to v8, as shown in *Figure 4.3:*

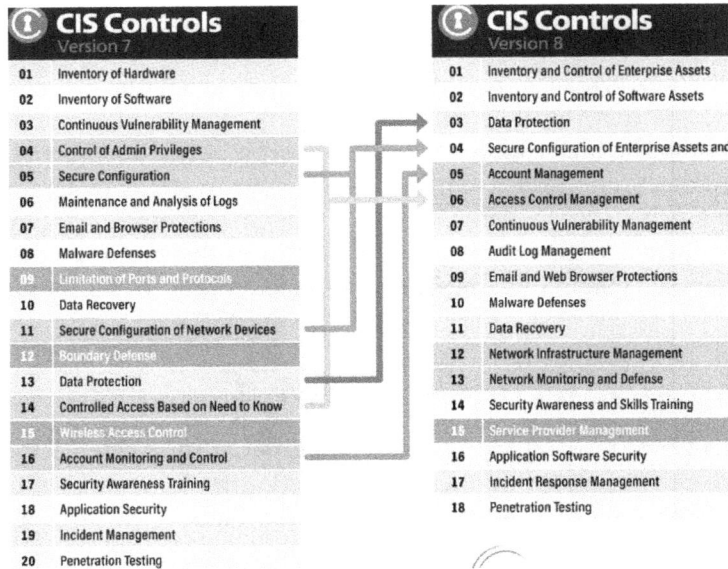

Figure 4.3: CIS version 8

Information Technology Infrastructure Library

The Office of Management and Budget created the **Information Technology Infrastructure Library (ITIL)** as a process management development standard in OMB Circular A-130. *ITIL Service Strategy, ITIL Service Design, ITIL Service Transition, ITIL Service Operation, and ITIL Continual Service Improvement* are the five fundamental ITIL books. There are 26 processes in these five key articles. Although ITIL has a security component, it is primarily focused on establishing **service-level agreements** (**SLAs**) between a company's IT department and its clients, as shown in *Figure 4.4*:

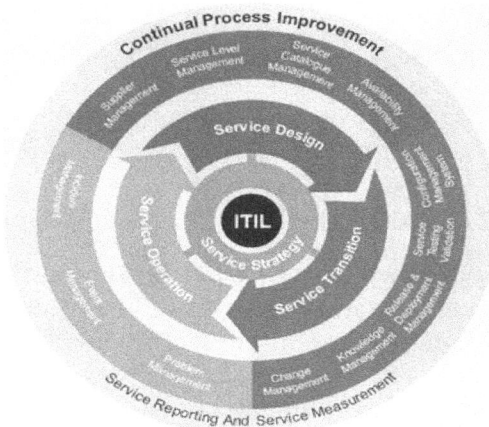

Figure 4.4: ITIL framework

Six Sigma

Six Sigma is a process improvement standard that incorporates two project techniques based on the Plan–Do–Check–Act cycle developed by *W. Edwards Deming*. Six Sigma was created to find and eliminate errors in the manufacturing processes, but it can be used for a variety of company tasks, including security. The following two Six Sigma project methodologies are illustrated in *Figure 4.5*:

- **DMAIC**: Define, Measure, Analyze, Improve, and Control
- **DMADV**: Define, Measure, Analyze, Design, and Verify

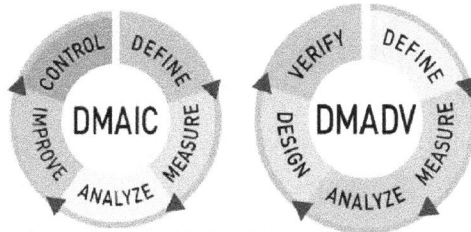

Figure 4.5: *DMAIC v/s DMADV*

Capability maturity model integration

Capability maturity model integration (CMMI) is a method for improving processes in three areas such as product and service development (CMMI for development), service establishment and administration (CMMI for services), and product service and acquisition (CMMI for product service and acquisition) (CMMI for acquisitions). All processes within each level of interest are assigned one of the following five levels of maturity:

- **Level 1**: Initial
- **Level 2:** Managed
- **Level 3:** Defined
- **Level 4:** Quantitatively managed
- **Level 5:** Optimizing

Extreme scenario planning or worst-case scenario

A company must do extreme scenario or worst-case scenario preparation as part of any security strategy. This planning guarantees that an organization can predict catastrophes and put in place adequate preparations before they happen. The first stage in the worst-case scenario planning is to assess all hazards and identify all players that offer a major risk to the company. The examples of the threat actors include the following:

- **Internal actors**: Reckless, untrained, or disgruntled employees, internal or government spies, vendors, and thieves.

- **External actors**: Anarchist, competitor, data miner, irrational individual, legal adversary, mobster, activist, terrorist, vandal.

Non-hostile and aggressive actors can be split into two types. Three actors in the preceding categories are often regarded as non-hostile, the careless employee, the inexperienced employee, and the partners. All other players should be regarded as adversarial. The company must next assess each of these threat actors against a set of criteria. To assist in selecting which threat danger actors will be studied, each threat actor should be assigned a ranking. Some of the most commonly used criteria include the following:

- **Skill level**: None, minimal, operational, adept

- **Resources**: Individual, team, organization, government

- **Limits**: Code of conduct, legal, extra-legal (minor), extra-legal (major)

- **Visibility**: Overt, covert, clandestine, do not care

- **Objective**: Copy, destroy, injure, take, do not care

- **Outcome**: Theft, business advantage, damage, embarrassment, technical advantage

The organization must then decide which of the actors it wishes to investigate using these criteria. For example, the organization may decide to examine all hostile actors with an adept skill level, the organization's or government's resources, and the organization's or government's extra-legal (minor) or extra-legal (major) constraints (major). The list is then whittled down to only the threat actors that meet all these requirements. The business must next establish what it truly cares about safeguarding. This judgment is frequently made using the FIPS 199 approach or a business impact study. Using the objective and outcome values from the threat actor analysis, as well as the **asset value** (**AV**) and business effect information from the impact analysis, the company should pick the scenarios that might have a catastrophic impact on the firm. Scenarios must then be created in order to thoroughly assess them.

For example, a company could decide to investigate a situation in which a hacktivist group conducts long-term DoS assaults, producing long-term disruptions that harm the company's reputation. Then, for each scenario, a risk assessment should be made. After all of the situations have been defined, the organization must create an attack tree for each one. This attack tree should contain all of the phases and criteria that must be met for the attack to succeed. The security controls must then be mapped to the attack trees by the organization. An organization would need to consult industry standards, such as NIST SP 800-53, to establish the security measures that may be implemented. Finally, the controls would be mapped back into the attack tree to ensure that they are used at as many levels as feasible during the attack. As you can see, the worst-case scenario planning is an art that takes a lot of practice and works to master. Candidates should concentrate on the procedure and actions necessary for the CASP test, rather than on how to execute the analysis and prepare the scenario documentation.

Conduct system specific risk analysis

A risk assessment is a risk management tool that identifies vulnerabilities and threats, assesses their effect, and determines which controls to adopt. Risk assessment or analysis has four main goals, which are as follows:

- Identify assets and AV
- Identify vulnerabilities and threats
- Calculate threat probability and business impact
- Balance threat impact with countermeasure cost

Management and the risk assessment team must first decide which assets and threats to evaluate before beginning the risk assessment. The scale of the project is determined by this method. After that, the risk assessment team must provide a report to the management detailing the worth of the assets under consideration. After that, the management may evaluate and complete the asset list, add and eliminate assets as needed, and decide the risk assessment project's budget.

For instance, to boost efficiency, the sales division decides to use touchscreen technology and tablet PCs. A new sales application that works with the new technology will be built as part of this new initiative. The **chief security officer** (**CSO**) sought to halt the deployment from the start since the technology was not supported in the organization. The deployment was approved by the upper management. The CSO should collaborate with the sales division and other stakeholders to adequately document the risk associated with the new deployment's complete life cycle and to apply suitable controls and tactics during deployment. Before any mergers and acquisitions, or the deployment of new technology and applications, a risk assessment should be conducted. A risk assessment will not be successful unless it is endorsed and led by high management. The aim and scope of a risk assessment must be defined by management, who must then assign personnel, time, and financial resources to the project.

Risk determination using known metrics

To make a risk determination, an organization must perform a formal risk analysis. Formal risk analysis often asks questions such as the following:

- What corporate assets need to be protected?
- What are the business needs of the organization?
- What outside threats are most likely to compromise network security?

Different types of risk analysis, including qualitative risk analysis and quantitative risk analysis, should be used to ensure that the data obtained is maximized.

Qualitative risk analysis

All aspects of the risk analysis process are not assigned monetary and mathematical values in the qualitative risk analysis. Intuition, experience, and best practice procedures, such as brainstorming, focus groups, surveys, questionnaires, meetings, interviews, and Delphi, are all examples of qualitative risk analysis methodologies. The Delphi method is a method for calculating the probability and outcome of future occurrences. Despite the fact that any of these strategies may be employed, most companies will choose the best one(s) based on the threats to be assessed. There is a need for experience and education about the hazards.

Each member of the group, who has been chosen to participate in the qualitative risk analysis, ranks the likelihood of each danger and the potential damage it may do based on his or her own experience. The data is compiled in a report to provide to the management after each group member ranks the threat likelihood, loss potential, and safeguard benefit. Qualitative risk analysis has two advantages over quantitative risk analysis. It prioritizes risks and finds opportunities for quick improvement in managing threats. These are some of the disadvantages of qualitative risk analysis such as all of the outcomes are subjective, and no monetary value is given for cost or benefit analysis or budgeting purposes. These are some of the disadvantages of qualitative risk analysis such as all outcomes are subjective, and no cash value is supplied for cost or benefit analysis or budgeting.

Quantitative risk analysis

All aspects of the risk analysis process, including AV, threat frequency, vulnerability severity, impact, and safeguard costs, are assigned monetary and mathematical values in quantitative risk analysis. Total and residual hazards are calculated using equations. Quantitative risk analysis has the benefit of requiring less guessing than qualitative risk analysis. The intricacy of the calculations, the time and effort required to conduct the analysis, and the amount of data that must be obtained for the study are all disadvantages of quantitative risk analysis. The majority of risk assessments incorporate a mix of quantitative and qualitative risk assessments. Quantitative risk analysis is preferred by most businesses for tangible assets, whereas qualitative risk analysis is preferred for intangible assets. Keep in mind that, while quantitative risk analysis includes numeric values, a totally quantitative analysis is impossible to obtain since data always contains some element of subjectivity. Historical data, industry experience, and expert opinion should all be used to make this sort of assessment.

Magnitude of impact based on ALE and SLE

Risk impact, also known as the magnitude of impact, is a calculation of how much harm a negative risk can do or the possible opportunity cost if a positive risk occurs. Risk effect can be calculated in monetary terms (quantitative) or on a subjective scale (qualitative). Risks are often graded on a scale devised by the organization. Low-level risks result in small losses, whereas high-level risks result in considerable losses. When the scale of an influence can be described in monetary terms, using monetary value to quantify, the magnitude has the advantage of being simple to understand by the employees. Long-term expenses in operations and support, loss of market share, short-term costs in more effort, or opportunity costs might all have a financial impact. When calculating the amount of effect, two calculations are used such as **single loss expectancy** (**SLE**) and **annualized loss expectancy** (**ALE**).

Single loss expectancy

The monetary effect of each danger occurrence is referred to as SLE. You will need to know the AV and the exposure factor to calculate the SLE (EF). The EF is the percentage of an asset's value or functionality that will be lost if a threat event happens. The following is the formula for calculating the SLE:

$$SLE = AV \times EF$$

Imagine a company that owns a web server farm with a value of $20,000 in AV. If a power outage is judged to be a danger agent for the web server farm by the risk assessment, and the exposure factor for a power outage is 25%, the SLE for this event is $5,000.

Annualized loss expectancy

An annual threat event's estimated risk factor is known as ALE. You'll need to know the SLE and the **annualized rate of occurrence** (**ARO**) to calculate the ALE The following is the formula for calculating the ALE:

$$ALE = SLE \times ARO$$

Using the previously described example, if the risk assessment determines that the ARO for a web server farm power outage is 50%, the ALE for this event is $2,500. The company can use the ALE to determine whether or not to establish controls. If the yearly cost of a web server farm protection control exceeds the ALE, the organization might simply opt to accept the risk by not deploying the control. If the annual cost of the control to protect the web server farm is less than the ALE, the organization should consider implementing the control.

Likelihood of threat

The likelihood of threat is a calculation of the possibility that a certain risk occurrence will have an impact on the company. The loss potential for each vulnerability and danger must be calculated once they have been discovered. This loss potential is calculated by combining the probability of an occurrence with the impact that such an event would have. An occurrence with a high probability and significant impact would be prioritized over the one with a low probability and low impact. Natural catastrophes will have varying degrees of probability depending on where you live. Human-made hazards, on the other hand, are more dependent on organizational characteristics such as visibility, location, and technology footprint. The levels used for threat likelihood are usually high, moderate, and low. The motive, source, ARO, and trend analysis are commonly used to determine the chance of an event occurring.

Motivation

Organizations and their attackers are influenced by motivation. Not all risks identified by a company will be motivated. Natural catastrophes, for example, have no purpose or cause for occurring other than climatic or other natural circumstances that are conducive to their occurrence. Most human-made attacks, on the other hand, have motives. Understanding the motivations behind these risks is critical in selecting which risk management technique your company should use. If your organization identifies any risks that are due to the actions of other people or organizations, these risks are usually motivated by the following:

- Acquisition or theft
- Business advantage
- Damage
- Embarrassment
- Technical advantage

Total cost of ownership

Organizational risks abound, ranging from easily insurable property hazards to risks that are difficult to predict and quantify, such as the loss of a key employee. The **total cost of ownership** (**TCO**) of risk is a metric that reflects the whole expenses of running an organization's risk management process, including insurance premiums, financing charges, administrative costs, and any losses. This figure should be weighed against the company's entire revenue and asset base. TCO is a method of determining how an organization's risk-related expenditures are changing in comparison to the overall growth rate. TCO can also be compared to industry benchmarks provided by trade associations and industry organizations. Working with appropriate businesses and industry specialists ensures that the company obtains comparable and relevant risk data. A financial organization's risk TCO should not be compared to the TCOs of healthcare firms. There are several benefits to calculating risk TCO. It can assist companies in identifying anomalies in their risk management strategy. It can also spot situations where risk management is overly aggressive in comparison to similar risks addressed elsewhere. Risk TCO may potentially save money in the long run by revealing inefficient risk management processes. Comparable risk TCO, on the other hand, is sometimes difficult to come by since many direct rivals guard this sensitive information. Using trade associations and industry standards organizations may frequently solve this challenge. Also, keep in mind the possibility that TCO will be perceived as a cost-cutting exercise, resulting in a lack of complete buy-in from employees. When assessing risk TCO, a business should keep the following principles in mind:

- Determine a framework that will be used to break down costs into categories, including risk financing, risk administration, risk compliance costs, and self-insured losses

- Identify the category costs by expressing them as a percentage of overall organizational revenue

- Employ any data from trade bodies for comparison with each category's figures

- Analyze any differences between your organization's numbers and industry figures for reasons of occurrence

- Set future targets for each category

    When calculating and analyzing risk TCO, you should remember the following basic rules:

- Industry benchmarks may not always be truly comparable to your organization's data.

- Cover some minor risks within the organization.

- Employ risk management software to aid in decision-making because of the complex nature of risk management.

- Remember the value of risk management when budgeting. It is not merely a cost.

- Risk TCO does not immediately lead to cost savings. Savings occur over time.

- Not all possible solutions will rest within the organization. External specialists and insurance brokers may be needed.

Translate technical risks in business terms

Nontechnical workers are frequently misinformed about technical cybersecurity threats. Security experts must close the knowledge gap in a way that stakeholders can comprehend. To effectively explain technical hazards, security professionals must first understand their target audience and then be able to convert those risks into commercial language that the target audience understands. Semi-technical audiences, nontechnical leadership, the board of directors and executives, and regulators are among the people who need to know about technical hazards. The semi-technical audience is aware of the challenges of security operations, and thus, it frequently includes significant friends. Typically, this audience needs a data-driven, high-level message based on verifiable facts and trends. The non-technical leadership audience needs the message to be put in context with their responsibilities. This audience needs the cost of cybersecurity expenditures to be tied to business performance. Security professionals should present metrics that show how cyber risk is trending without using popular jargon. The board of directors and executives are primarily concerned with business risk management and managing return on assets. The message to this group should translate technical risk into common business terms and present metrics about cybersecurity risk and performance.

Finally, it is critical to be comprehensive and upfront when engaging with regulators. Additionally, before an audit, companies may choose to hire a third party to do a gap analysis. This allows the third party to speak on behalf of the security program and will assist security experts in identifying and remediating problems prior to the audit. Security experts should focus on business interruption, regulatory difficulties, and negative press to translate technical dangers into business terms for these audiences. A severe interruption of business operations occurs when a company's database is breached, and the website is unable to offer items to customers. A regulatory issue has developed if an occurrence happens that results in a regulatory inquiry and penalty. Negative publicity can result in lost revenue as well as expenditures to rebuild the company's reputation. Risk metrics must be understood by security professionals, as well as the expenses associated with each statistic. Although security professionals may not be able to predict the **return on investment** (**ROI**), they should consider the frequency of security incidents at the company and assign costs in terms of risk exposure to each risk. To ensure that the organization's investment is safeguarding the most important assets, it will also be beneficial to match the risks with the assets safeguarded.

Risk appetite strategy

The process of changing parts of an organization in response to risk analysis is known as **risk reduction**. After determining the ROI and TCO, an organization must decide on how to handle risk, which is dependent on the company's risk appetite, or how much risk it can take on its own. Avoid, transfer, mitigate, and accept are the four key tactics you must know for the CASP test.

Avoid

The avoid approach entails stopping a dangerous activity or adopting a less risky option. Regrettably, this strategy cannot be utilized to counteract all risks. Organizations that use alternate data centers in separate geographic regions to avoid natural disasters hitting both facilities are an example of avoidance. It is nearly impossible to avoid danger in many situations. Avoiding the danger, for example, is difficult if a CEO acquires a new mobile device and demands that he be provided internal network access via this device. You would have to find a means to reduce and transfer the risk in this scenario.

Consider the following case:

A firm is in discussions to purchase another company for $1,000,000. Due diligence investigations revealed widespread security problems in the company's flagship product. This is because of the security vulnerabilities; a complete product rebuild is anticipated to cost $1,500,000. The corporation should not purchase the other company in this situation since the acquisition would cost $2,500,000 in total.

Transfer

The risk is transferred to a third party, such as an insurance company, as part of the transfer plan. Outsourcing specific activities to a supplier, for example, frequently involves a third-party SLA. However, depending on the contract's terms, the risk may still be borne by the original company. Legal counsel should verify that the contract offers the amount of protection required if your business intends to adopt this strategy. Consider the following case:

A tiny firm has opted to boost its earnings by selling to the general public via an internet system. This will be a short-term experiment at first. If the system proves to be successful, it will be enlarged and integrated into daily operations. The following two main business risks for the initial trial have been raised:

- Internal IT staff have no experience with secure online credit card processing.

- An internal credit card processing system will expose the business to additional compliance requirements.

In this situation, it is best to transfer the initial risks by outsourcing the payment processing to a third-party service provider.

Mitigate

The mitigate strategy entails determining the organization's acceptable risk threshold and reducing the risk to that level. This is the most widely used approach. Implementing security measures such as IDSs, IPSs, firewalls, and so on is part of this strategy. Consider the following case:

Three times a year, your firm's web server has a security issue, which costs the organization $1,500 in downtime each time. The web server will be deactivated in five years and will only be used for archival access. The initial cost of putting software in place to avoid this catastrophe would be $15,000, plus $1,000 each year in upkeep. The cost of the security incident is calculated as follows:

$$(\$1,500 \text{ per occurrence} \times 3 \text{ per year}) \times 5 \text{ years} = \$22,500$$

The cost to prevent the problem is calculated as follows:

$$\$15,000 \text{ software cost} + (\$1,000 \text{ maintenance} \times 5 \text{ years}) = \$20,000$$

In this situation, mitigation (implementing the software) is cheaper than accepting the risk.

Accept

Understanding and accepting the amount of risk as well as the cost of potential losses is part of the accepted approach. This method is typically employed to protect against residual risk. It is often used for assets with low exposure or value. However, an organization may be forced to accept risks if the funding set aside for establishing measures to defend against risks has been spent. Accepting risk is acceptable if the risks and assets are low-profile. However, if they are deemed high-profile hazards, the management should be notified that more funding is required to minimize the risks.

Risk management processes

Automated risk assessment tools, questionnaires, interviews, and policy document reviews, according to NIST SP 800-30 Rev. 1, are standard information-gathering strategies used in risk analysis. When determining the risks associated with a particular asset, keep in mind that several sources should be used. NIST SP 800-30 identifies the following steps in the risk assessment process:

1. Prepare for the assessment.
2. Conduct the assessment.
   a. Identify threat sources and events.
   b. Identify vulnerabilities and predisposing conditions.
   c. Determine the likelihood of occurrence.
   d. Determine the magnitude of the impact.
   e. Determine risk as a combination of likelihood and impact.
3. Communicate the results.
4. Maintain the assessment.

Asset appraisal, vulnerability identification, and threat identification are all part of the risk management process. Exemptions, deterrents, inherent risk, and residual risk must all be understood by security experts.

Information and asset value and costs

As previously said, identifying assets and determining asset valuations is the first stage in any risk assessment. Both tangible and intangible assets exist. Computers, facilities, materials, and staff are examples of tangible assets. Intellectual property, data, and corporate reputation are examples of intangible assets. The asset's worth should be assessed in light of the asset owner's perspective. The following six considerations can be used to determine an asset's value:

- Value to owner
- Work required to develop or obtain the asset
- Costs to maintain the asset
- Damage that would result if the asset were lost

- The cost that competitors would pay for the asset
- Penalties that would result if the asset were lost

After determining the value of the assets, you should determine the vulnerabilities and threats to each asset.

Vulnerabilities and threats identification

When determining vulnerabilities and threats to an asset, considering the threat agents first is often the easiest. Threat agents can be grouped into the following six categories:

- **Human**: This category includes both malicious and non-malicious insiders and outsiders, terrorists, spies, and terminated personnel.

- **Natural**: This category includes floods, fires, tornadoes, hurricanes, earthquakes, and other natural disasters or weather events.

- **Technical**: This category includes hardware and software failure, malicious code, and new technologies.

- **Physical**: This category includes CCTV issues, perimeter measures failure, and biometric failure.

- **Environmental**: This category includes power and other utility failures, traffic issues, biological warfare, and hazardous material issues (such as spillage).

- **Operational**: This category includes any process or procedure that can affect the CIA.

Exemptions

While most businesses should conduct a full risk assessment and take steps to mitigate all threats, certain organizations are excluded from some risks owing to the nature of their operations or government regulations. The **Environmental Protection Agency** (**EPA**) in the United States, for example, has restrictions governing the use and storage of specific chemicals like ammonia and propane. Organizations that keep these substances in quantities greater than a specific threshold must adhere to the EPA's accidental release prevention requirements and risk management program standards. These laws, however, do not apply to most farmers who use ammonia as a soil fertilizer or use of propane in data distribution centers. In most circumstances, businesses should get legal advice to ensure that they are aware of any exclusions that may apply to them.

Deterrence

The use of the threat of punishment to dissuade people from doing specific tasks is known as **deterrence**. Many government entities utilize this risk management strategy by publishing legal declarations that threaten unauthorized users with fines and jail if they obtain access to their network or systems. When accessing mail systems, eCommerce systems, or other systems that may include private data, organizations use comparable procedures that incorporate warnings.

Inherent

As it is nearly difficult to prevent, inherent risk has no mitigating measures or therapies applied to it. Consider a determined attacker with the ability to physically gain entry to an organization's facilities. While numerous measures may be established to safeguard against this hazard, such as guards, CCTV, fences, locks, and biometrics, an organization cannot completely promise that this risk will never occur if the attacker has the necessary capabilities. This is not to say that these measures, which are considered baseline controls, should not be implemented. When possible, inherent risks should be identified for the following reasons:

- Knowing the risks helps identify critical controls.
- Audits can then be focused on critical controls.

Risks that are inherent but might have catastrophic repercussions can be exposed to more rigorous scenario testing. Risks that might have catastrophic implications can be made known to the organization's board of directors and management.

Residual

It is difficult to completely avoid all dangers, no matter how cautious a company is. The degree of risk that remains after safeguards or controls have been introduced is known as residual risk. The following equation is used to represent residual risk:

$$Residual\ risk = Total\ risk - Countermeasures$$

This equation is thought to be more conceptual than practical for actual calculations.

Continuous improvement or monitoring

Any organization's risk management must be constantly improved and monitored. All changes to the enterprise must be tracked in order for security specialists to analyze the dangers that such changes pose. Security measures should be altered to handle the modifications as soon as feasible after they are deployed. If your company wishes to upgrade a vendor program, for example, security experts must examine the application to determine how it affects enterprise security. Certain aspects of the organization, including audit log collecting and analysis, antivirus and malware detection upgrades, and application and operating system updates, should be automated to aid in continual improvement and monitoring. Change management, configuration management, control monitoring, and status reporting are all part of continuous monitoring. Security experts should examine enterprise security measures on a regular basis to ensure that modifications do not have a detrimental impact on the business. Management should establish a consistent risk lexicon and convey expectations effectively. Employees, particularly new recruits, must also get training to ensure that they understand risk in the context of the company.

Business continuity planning

Continuity planning entails determining the impact of a disaster and putting in place a workable recovery strategy for each function and system. Its main focus is on how to carry out organizational operations in the event of a disruption. BCP takes into account all elements of a disaster's impact, including functions, systems, employees, and facilities. It identifies and prioritizes the services that are required, with a focus on telecommunications and information technology. Developing a BCP is critical to ensure that the company can recover from a disaster or disruptive incident. For business continuity, several organizations have set standards and best practices. Many common components and actions are included in these standards and best practices. The people components, project scope, and business continuity tasks that must be accomplished are covered in the following areas.

Personnel components

The most significant people in the growth of the BCP are senior management. The overarching organizational view of the process is driven by senior management support for business continuity and catastrophe recovery. This procedure will fail if the high management does not support it. The overall goals of business continuity and catastrophe recovery are determined by the senior management. The BCP committee should be led by a business continuity coordinator appointed by senior management. The BCP and disaster recovery plan are developed, implemented, and tested by the committee (DRP). Each business unit should have a representative on the BCP committee. This committee should include at least one member of senior management. Furthermore, because of the critical responsibilities that the IT department, legal department, security department, and communications department play during and after a crisis, the business should guarantee that they are represented. The BCP committee must engage with business units under management's supervision to define the business continuity and catastrophe recovery priorities. Time-critical systems must be identified and prioritized by senior business unit managers. Following the completion of all components of the plans, the BCP committee should be entrusted with evaluating them on a regular basis to ensure that they stay current and sustainable. All business continuity measures should be actively monitored and controlled by senior management, and any accomplishments should be publicly praised. Other teams are involved when an organization begins catastrophe recovery planning.

Project scope

Senior management must establish the BCP scope for the BCP development to be effective. A business continuity project with an unbounded scope is frequently too big for the BCP committee to handle properly. As a result, the senior management may need to divide the business continuity project into smaller, easier-to-manage chunks. When it comes to dividing the BCP into portions, an organization may decide to do so depending on the geographic location or facility. However, an enterprise-wide BCP should be developed to ensure the compatibility of the individual plans.

The following list summarizes the BCP steps:

1. Develop a contingency planning policy.
2. Conduct **business impact analysis (BIA)**.
3. Identify preventive controls.
4. Create contingency strategies.
5. Develop an information system contingency plan.
6. Test, train, and exercise.
7. Maintain the plan.

Conduct the business impact analysis

The goal of the BIA is to link the system to the important mission/business activities and services it provides and then define the repercussions of a disruption based on that knowledge. The BIA is the most important factor in the construction of a BCP. The BIA assists an organization in determining the impact of a disruptive event on the organization. It is a management-level examination that determines the impact of a company's resources being lost. The four main steps of the BIA are as follows:

1. Identify critical processes and resources.
2. Identify outage impacts and estimate downtime.
3. Identify resource requirements.
4. Identify recovery priorities.

Any vulnerability analysis and risk assessment that has been conducted is extensively relied upon by BIA. The BCP committee or a separately constituted risk assessment team can conduct the vulnerability analysis and risk assessment. As part of determining how critical an asset is, you need to understand the following terms:

- **Maximum Tolerable Downtime (MTD):** The maximum amount of time that an organization can tolerate a single resource or function being down. This is also referred to as the **Maximum Period Time of Disruption (MPTD)**.

- **Mean Time To Repair (MTTR):** The average time required to repair a single resource or function when a disaster or disruption occurs.

- **Mean Time Between Failures (MTBF):** The estimated amount of time a device will operate before a failure occurs. This amount is calculated by the device vendor. System reliability is increased by a higher MTBF and lower MTTR.

- **Recovery Time Objective (RTO):** The shortest time period after a disaster or disruptive event within which a resource or function must be restored to avoid unacceptable consequences. RTO assumes that an acceptable period of downtime exists. RTO should be smaller than MTD.

- **Work Recovery Time (WRT):** The difference between RTO and MTD, which is the remaining time that is left over after the RTO before reaching the maximum tolerable.

- **Recovery Point Objective (RPO):** The point in time to which the disrupted resource or function must be returned.

IT governance

Information security governance is made up of numerous components that work together to provide comprehensive security management within a company. Data and other assets should be safeguarded primarily on the basis of their monetary value and sensitivity. Long-term security actions (3–5 years or more) are guided by strategic plans. Tactical plans accomplish the strategic plan's objectives in a shorter period of time (6–18 months). Management consent must be gained early in the process of establishing and adopting an information security policy since the management is the most crucial link in the computer security chain. Senior management must take the following measures prior to the development of any organizational security policy:

- Define the scope of the security program.

- Identify all the assets that need protection.

- Determine the level of protection that each asset needs.

- Determine personnel responsibilities.

- Develop consequences for noncompliance with the security policy.

Senior management assumes responsibility for an organization's security by fully embracing an organizational security policy. Senior management's intention to assist security is expressed through high-level policies. The first stage in developing an information security program is to adopt an organizational information security statement after receiving approval from top management. The security planning process must specify how security will be managed, who will be in charge of setting up and monitoring compliance, how security measures will be evaluated for effectiveness, who will be engaged in defining the security policy, and where the security policy will be developed. Risk management frameworks must be understood by security experts, and companies must follow the right risk management frameworks. They must also comprehend the components of organizational governance and how they interact to ensure governance. To create a complete security plan, security professionals must understand how the information security components interact. Information security governance components include the following:

- Policies
- Processes
- Procedures
- Standards
- Guidelines
- Baselines

Policies

A security policy specifies the function of security as determined by the senior management and is strategic in nature, that is, it specifies the security outcome. Policies are classified according to two factors such as the organizational level at which they are implemented and the category to which they apply. Policies must be broad in scope, that is, they must not be tied to a single technology or security solution. Policies define objectives but do not provide details on how to achieve them. Each policy must have an exception section to guarantee that the management can handle scenarios that may need exceptions.

Policies are broad in scope and serve as the foundation for the establishment of security standards, baselines, guidelines, and procedures. Administrative, technological, and physical access restrictions complete the security program's security and structure. Organizational security policies, system-specific security policies, and issue-specific security policies are the policy layers used in information security. Regulatory security policies, advisory security policies, and informational security policies are the three types of policies employed in information security. An organization's highest-level security policy is called an **organizational security policy**. The organizational security policy is guided by business objectives, contains general directions, and should have the following components:

- Define the overall goals of the security policy.
- Define the overall steps and the importance of security.
- Define a security framework to meet the business goals.

Processes

A process is a set of actions or processes taken to accomplish a certain goal. Individual processes and their interrelationships are defined by organizations. An organization may, for example, design a process for how consumers place online purchases, how payments are handled, and how items are delivered once payments are completed. While each of these processes is distinct and has its own set of responsibilities to perform, they all rely on one another to get the job done. A procedure outlines how to accomplish a goal or finish a task. Procedures are created as a result of processes.

Procedures

Procedures are the closest to the computers and other devices and contain all the particular activities that workers are expected to follow. Step-by-step listings describing how rules, processes, standards, and recommendations that are applied are common in procedures which are essential in ensuring that the organization's security policies are consistently followed by all employees and stakeholders. They are the closest to the computers and other devices and contain all the activities that workers are expected to follow. Step-by-step listings describing how rules, processes, standards, and recommendations that are applied are common in procedures. These procedures serve as a clear roadmap for employees to handle specific tasks or respond to situations in a standardized way, reducing the potential for human error and improving overall efficiency. For example, an incident response procedure may detail the specific steps an employee should take when a security breach is detected, from isolating the affected system to reporting the incident to the security team.

Well-documented procedures also help ensure compliance with regulations, providing a traceable record of actions taken. In cybersecurity, procedures might include regular software updates, password management, data backup, and access control processes. They are frequently reviewed and updated to adapt to new threats, technological advancements, and changes in regulatory requirements. Additionally, procedures provide a reference point for training new employees, ensuring that they understand and can follow the necessary steps to maintain organizational security standards effectively. The thoroughness and clarity of procedures play a critical role in the resilience and security posture of an organization.

Standards

The implementation of policies inside an organization is described by standards. They are tactically oriented, mandated acts or regulations that give the procedures the essentials to accomplish security. Standards, like rules, should be evaluated and amended on a regular basis. The implementation of policies inside an organization is described by standards. They are tactically oriented, mandated acts or regulations that give the procedures the essentials to accomplish security. Standards, like rules, should be evaluated and amended on a regular basis. These standards provide clear guidelines on how specific security practices should be executed to ensure consistent and effective protection of the organization's assets. For example, a password policy standard may dictate minimum password length, complexity, and expiration periods to enforce secure access controls. In addition to internal standards, organizations often align with industry-wide or international standards, such as ISO/IEC 27001 or NIST SP 800-53, which provide a framework for establishing robust security controls. Regularly updating standards is crucial in adapting to evolving threats, new technologies, and changing compliance requirements. This ensures that the organization's security practices remain relevant and effective in mitigating emerging risks. Additionally, standards help to create a baseline for employees and third parties to follow, reducing ambiguity and enhancing compliance across all levels of the organization.

Guidelines

Guidelines are suggestions for activities that are far more flexible than standards, allowing for unforeseen scenarios. When standards are not applicable, guidelines give direction. Guidelines serve as flexible recommendations designed to offer direction in various activities, especially in situations where rigid standards may not apply. Unlike standards, which are typically set rules or criteria that must be followed, guidelines are intended to provide a framework that can adapt to unforeseen or unique scenarios. These suggestions help professionals navigate complex situations where standardized approaches might not be sufficient or relevant. For example, in cybersecurity, guidelines might offer best practices for responding to emerging threats or vulnerabilities that do not yet have established standards.

While guidelines are not mandatory, they offer valuable insights and recommendations to ensure decisions align with organizational goals, industry best practices, or legal requirements. They are particularly useful when dealing with new technologies, evolving risks, or situations that require a nuanced approach. In some cases, guidelines also serve as a bridge between rigid standards and highly dynamic environments, allowing decision-makers to apply discretion and make informed choices while still maintaining a level of consistency with broader goals. Ultimately, guidelines allow for more innovation and adaptability in processes, ensuring that organizations can respond effectively to challenges while mitigating potential risks.

Baselines

A baseline is a determined and recorded reference point that will be used as a future reference point. While it is critical to capture baselines, it is also critical to use baselines to assess the security condition. Even the most thorough baselines are worthless if they are never used. It is also crucial to take a baseline measurement at the right moment. When a system has been properly configured and upgraded, baselines should be taken. When new baselines are created, they should be compared to the existing baselines. Adopting new baselines based on the most recent data may be essential at that time.

Conclusion

In this chapter, you learned about categorizing data types based on CIA and incorporating stakeholder input into CIA impact-level decisions. The process of selecting and implementing CIA-based controls and security control frameworks was also discussed. This chapter discussed and analyzed risks based on systems and their attributes for security professionals to determine and communicate the identified risks in business terms.

In the next chapter, we will discuss solutions to decide upon the security controls to deploy for securing the organization.

Exercise

1. **When classifying data based on its impact level, which of the following is NOT typically considered in the CIA triad?**

   a. Confidentiality

   b. Integrity

   c. Availability

   d. Cost

2. **Why is it important to involve stakeholders in determining the CIA impact levels for data?**

   a. To ensure the organization's compliance with regulations

   b. To gather insights on business priorities and potential risks

   c. To streamline the decision-making process

   d. To avoid the need for data encryption

3. **How is the aggregate CIA score typically determined for an asset?**

   a. By averaging the individual CIA ratings for confidentiality, integrity, and availability

   b. By assigning equal weight to each CIA element regardless of context

   c. By multiplying the confidentiality, integrity, and availability ratings

   d. By considering only the availability rating of the asset

4. **What is the purpose of determining the minimum required security controls based on the aggregate CIA score?**

   a. To calculate the potential cost of implementing security measures

   b. To ensure that controls are implemented based on the data's overall risk profile

   c. To avoid unnecessary investments in security technologies

   d. To determine the exact number of personnel required to maintain security

5. **Which of the following is a critical factor when implementing controls based on CIA requirements?**

   a. The number of employees available for deployment

   b. The cost-benefit analysis of control implementation

   c. The specific needs of confidentiality, integrity, and availability for each asset

   d. The legal restrictions on data access

6. **What is the primary objective of extreme scenario planning in cybersecurity?**

   a. To prevent all security incidents from occurring

   b. To prepare for the most severe risks and minimize their impact

   c. To ensure that security controls are not too costly

   d. To identify vulnerabilities in the organization's financial systems

7. **When conducting a system-specific risk analysis, what should be the main focus?**

   a. Assessing the security measures of all company departments

   b. Identifying vulnerabilities and potential risks specific to that system

   c. Evaluating the physical security of the organization's infrastructure

   d. Determining the overall market conditions affecting the system

8. **What role do known metrics play in determining risk in cybersecurity?**

   a. They provide a subjective estimate of risk based on historical incidents

   b. They help quantify and evaluate risks based on past data, incidents, and trends

   c. They eliminate the need for any further risk analysis

   d. They solely focus on compliance with industry regulations

9. **Why is it important to translate technical risks into business terms for non-technical stakeholders?**

   a. To ensure the technical team can focus solely on security measures

   b. To help decision-makers understand the business impact of cybersecurity risks

   c. To reduce the need for external audits and compliance checks

   d. To increase the budget for cybersecurity investments

10. **What does a risk appetite strategy help an organization determine?**

    a. The maximum amount of risk the organization is willing to accept in pursuit of its objectives

    b. The budget available for implementing security controls

    c. The legal and regulatory requirements the organization must meet

    d. The level of insurance coverage required for cybersecurity incidents

11. **Which of the following is a critical component of an effective risk management process?**

a. Implementing controls without assessing the risk

b. Continuously monitoring, assessing, and adjusting risk management strategies

c. Focusing solely on external threats while ignoring internal vulnerabilities

d. Avoiding the involvement of stakeholders in risk decision-making

12. **What is the primary goal of business continuity planning?**

a. To ensure that the organization operates at a minimal level of risk

b. To minimize downtime and ensure continued operations in the event of a disruption

c. To eliminate all potential risks from affecting business operations

d. To focus solely on data protection and compliance

13. **In the context of IT governance, what is the role of aligning IT strategies with business objectives?**

a. To focus exclusively on compliance with industry regulations

b. To ensure that IT investments and initiatives support the overall business goals

c. To restrict IT infrastructure to legacy systems

d. To increase IT spending for innovation without regard for business goals

Answers

1. d
2. b
3. a
4. b
5. c
6. b
7. b
8. b
9. b
10. a
11. b
12. b
13. b

Join our book's Discord space

Join the book's Discord Workspace for Latest updates, Offers, Tech happenings around the world, New Release and Sessions with the Authors:

https://discord.bpbonline.com

## CHAPTER 5

Enterprise Risk Measurement and Metrics

Introduction

Securing an enterprise is very important. Security should be a top priority for any organization, but often, it can be difficult to convince the senior management to provide the funds for the security endeavors you wish to use. As a security professional, you need to provide justification for any security technology and control you want to implement.

Structure

In this chapter, we will cover the following topics:

- Review the effectiveness of existing security controls
- Reverse engineer or deconstruct existing solutions
- Creation, collection, and analysis metrics
- Prototype and test multiple solutions
- Create benchmarks and compare baselines
- Analyze trends and data
- Analyze security solution metrics and attributes
- Judgment to solve problems
- Analyze security requirements

Objectives

This chapter explains the effectiveness of security controls, gap analysis, and after-actions. The use of reverse engineering and deconstructing existing controls helps gather sensitive information about the organization's controls as well as create, gather, and analyze metrics, including **key performance indicators (KPIs)** and **key risk indicators (KRIs)**. This chapter explains solutions to decide upon the security controls to deploy for securing the organization. As a CASP+ security professional, you need to provide justification for any security technology and control you want to implement.

Review effectiveness of existing security controls

Organizations should evaluate the efficacy of current security procedures on a regular basis. All areas of security, including security training, device configuration (router, firewall, IDS, IPS, and so on), and policies and procedures, should be reviewed by security specialists. Vulnerability and penetration testing should also be performed. These audits must be carried out at least once a year. A review of the effectiveness of security controls should include answering the following questions:

- Which security controls are we using?
- How can these controls be improved?
- Are these controls necessary?
- Have any new issues arise?
- Which security controls can be deployed to address the new issues?

To aid in the review of existing security controls, security administrators should perform a gap analysis and document the lessons learned in an after-action report.

Gap analysis

An information security gap study compares the security program of a company to industry best practices. Security experts can identify vulnerabilities and dangers by comparing these recommended practices to real practices. An information security gap analysis includes the following five steps:

1. Select an industry-standard framework.

2. Examine the individuals and procedures involved. Collect information on the IT environment, application inventories, organizational charts, rules and practices, and other important elements.

3. Collect information and technology. This stage assists a company in determining how well its present security program functions inside the technological

architecture. Comparing best practice controls or relevant requirements to organizational controls, sampling network devices, servers, and applications to validate gaps and weaknesses, reviewing automated security controls, and reviewing incident response processes, communications protocols, and log files are all examples of this.

4. Analyze or compare the information acquired. This step entails using the information gathered to conduct an analysis of the organization's security program, as well as correlating the findings and results across all factors to create a clear and concise picture of the organization's IT security profile, including strengths and areas for improvement.

5. Gap analysis is finally performed. Gap analysis is a complex, in-depth procedure that necessitates a full understanding of security best practices as well as a complete understanding of security threats, controls, and operational difficulties. While doing a gap analysis does not ensure 100 percent security, it does go a long way toward ensuring that the organization's network, staff, and security policies are solid, effective, and cost-effective.

Refer to *Figure 5.1,* that illustrates the gap analysis steps:

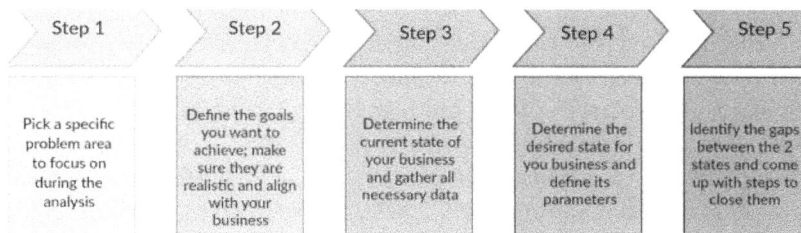

Step 1	Step 2	Step 3	Step 4	Step 5
Pick a specific problem area to focus on during the analysis	Define the goals you want to achieve; make sure they are realistic and align with your business	Determine the current state of your business and gather all necessary data	Determine the desired state for you business and define its parameters	Identify the gaps between the 2 states and come up with steps to close them

Figure 5.1: Gap analysis steps

Lessons learned and after-action reports

When a problem emerges, security experts are generally focused on addressing the problem, implementing a new security control, or upgrading an existing security control. The lessons learned or after-action evaluation should be filed after the immediate crisis has passed. Personnel describes the issue facts, the cause of the issue, why the issue happened, feasible strategies to prevent the issue in the future, and improvement ideas in case the issue arises again in this report. Anyone who was engaged in finding or fixing the problem should be included in the review. Because specifics are sometimes lost over time, reviews should be held as soon as feasible after the issue has been resolved.

It is ideal to format the official review document such that it follows the incident in chronological order. The investigation should include as many details regarding the occurrence as feasible. Remember that lessons learned or follow-up reviews may be used for any major organizational project, such as operating system updates, new server deployments, firewall upgrades, and so on.

Reverse engineer or deconstruct existing solutions

An organization's security measures are only effective until the hacker figures out how to breach or bypass a control. As a result, a security professional's ability to think like a hacker and reverse engineer or disassemble the existing security systems is critical. Each security solution should be examined independently by a security expert. When examining each solution, you should consider what the security solution performs, which systems it is supposed to protect, how the solution affects the company, and what information it discloses about itself. Keep in mind that the goal of reverse engineering is to learn as much as possible about your company in order to find a method to get into it. Physical entry to the building is sometimes overlooked by security specialists. Physical security controls, on the other hand, are just as critical as any other control. If an attacker can enter your facility and connect a rogue access point or protocol analyzer to the enterprise, it does not matter how many security safeguards you have in place.

Creation, collection, and analysis of metrics

Metrics should be checked on a regular basis. Furthermore, measurements should be examined as quickly as possible after they are gathered to see if any modifications are required. Metrics that are properly created, collected, and analyzed, help a company forecast future demands far before an issue emerges. The organization's security budget is prepared by the **chief security officer** (**CSO**) or another designated high-level management, who also defines the security metrics and reports on the security program's efficacy. This officer must collaborate with **subject matter experts** (**SMEs**) to ensure that all security expenses, including development, testing, implementation, maintenance, staff, and equipment, are accounted for. The budgeting process necessitates a thorough analysis of all risks and guarantees that the most cost-effective security initiatives are performed. Long-term and strategic projects, which take more than 12 to 18 months to complete, require additional resources and finance. Both short- and long-term patterns may be found in security measurements. A security expert can calculate the daily workload by collecting these variables and comparing them on a day-to-day basis. The trends that emerge when the indicators are evaluated over a longer period of time might help determine future security programs and expenditures.

For assistance in building metrics rules and processes, security professionals could examine information security governance frameworks, notably ISO/IEC 27004 and NIST 800-55. Metrics, on the other hand, are not simply for live events. You may also use the generated data to examine the effects of security policies in a virtual environment that simulates the real world. Then, you may utilize the simulated data to see if the security controls should be implemented in the real world.

Assume a security administrator is attempting to establish a body of knowledge to allow heuristic and behavior-based security event monitoring of global network operations. The instrumentation is chosen to enable network monitoring and measurement. Modeling the network in a series of **virtual machines** (**VMs**), implementing systems to record comprehensive metrics, running a large volume of simulated data through the model, recording and analyzing results, and documenting expected future behavior is the best methodology to use in establishing this baseline. The security administrator would be able to determine how the new monitoring would operate using this complete way.

Although the security team should examine metrics on a daily basis, a third-party study of the metrics on a regular basis may assure the security metrics' accuracy and efficacy by confirming the internal team's results. The data from the third party should subsequently be used to improve the security program and security metrics procedure. The two types of metrics that are generated, gathered, and assessed are **KPIs** and **KRIs**. **Information Security Forum** (**ISF**) recommends the following 14-step approach to KPIs and KRIs to support informed decision-making:

1. Understand the business context.

2. Identify audiences and collaborators.

3. Determine common interests.

4. Identify the key information security priorities.

5. Design KPI or KRI combinations.

6. Test and confirm KPI or KRI combinations.

7. Gather data.

8. Produce and calibrate KPI or KRI combinations.

9. Interpret KPI or KRI combinations to develop insights.

10. Agree to conclusions, proposals, and recommendations.

11. Produce reports and presentations.

12. Prepare to present and distribute reports.

13. Present and agree on the next steps.

14. Develop learning and improvement plans.

Security experts must lead their organization in monitoring KPIs and KRIs using this method. A performance indicator is a measure that tells you how well your company is performing. It instructs you on what to do and how to proceed. Measures, which are observed values at a certain point in time, are used to create metrics. Metrics are ratios, averages, percentages, or rates produced from measures, whereas measures are raw numbers and data points.

Key performance indicators

KPIs monitor factors that are directly related to individual actions or activities, rather than the end outcome. Profit, expenses, and the number of accounts should not be utilized as **KPIs**. They are the consequence of a variety of activities; hence, they do not provide specific measures to perform. KPIs that organizations need to capture include the following:

- Increase or decrease in reported incidents
- Number of large and small security incidents
- Cost per incident
- Amount of time for incident resolution
- Downtime during an incident

Refer to *Figure 5.2,* that illustrates a sample KPI report:

Figure 5.2: *Sample KPI report*

Let us look at an example. Suppose an organization's IT department reported a significant decrease in the reported incidents over the past quarter. Some questions that the management may need to look into include the following:

- Were new security controls put into place during the quarter that possibly caused this significant decrease?
- Was there an actual decrease in incidents or just a failure to discover or report incidents?
- What are the operational differences (for example, system upgrades, new tools, heavily attacked systems that have been patched, removed, or replaced) between the last quarterly report and this quarterly report?

KRIs are used in management to indicate how risky an activity is or how likely a risk is to occur. Organizations use them as early signals that particular risks may occur. KRIs that organizations need to capture include the following:

- **Acceleration of high-severity events**: Are more severe events showing up on your systems in a shorter amount of time?

- **Handle time**: How long does it take for you to identify a threat-pattern change and eliminate the cause of that threat?

- **Attack surface area**: How many hosts are involved in a security event? How many hosts are included in an attack?

Refer to *Figure 5.3,* that illustrates a sample KPI risk report:

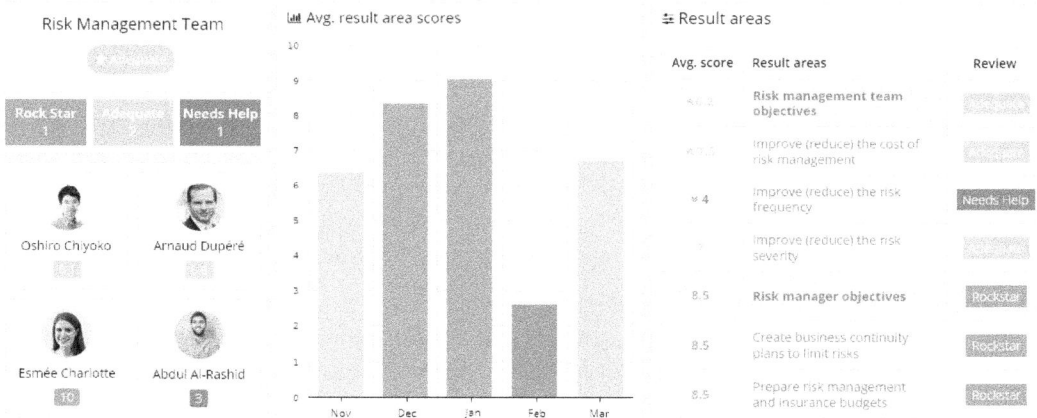

Figure 5.3: Sample KPI risk report

Consider the following scenario:

Let us say a company is concerned about its security awareness training. Examining the pass or fail metrics for the security awareness training is a KRI for this. If the failure rate is high, the organization's training practices must be improved, particularly the amount of time spent on training each year and the employee engagement index for the training. The pass or fail rate for security awareness training will be directly affected by the amount of time spent training and the amount of training delivered to personnel. In this case, the company may opt to require additional security awareness training for employees.

Prototype and test multiple solutions

Once a security specialist has determined that a device or technology has a definite problem, he or she should consider viable remedies. Hardware improvements, new device or technology purchases, and configuration adjustments are all possible remedies. The security professional should then prototype or test the solutions. Any prototyping or testing should preferably be done in a lab environment to evaluate the impact of any deployed solution. Prototypes also assist in ensuring that the tested solutions are satisfactory to the company before they are launched into production. Virtualization technologies have made creating and testing solutions in a virtual **live** environment a lot easier. Make sure that any testing is done in a vacuum, with no other solutions implemented, to ensure that the impacts of that particular solution are completely understood. After you have figured out what each solution does, you may prototype or test various solutions to see whether it is better to apply numerous solutions to your company's problem.

Let us say you uncover a web server that is not performing well. Deploying a second web server and putting both servers in a load-balancing environment is one method being examined. Upgrades to the hard disc and RAM of the concerned server might also be an option. Of course, an even better method would be to improve the original web server, deploy a second web server, and load-balance both servers. Budget restrictions, on the other hand, frequently hinder the adoption of many solutions. Testing may demonstrate that upgrading the web server's hardware is sufficient. A hardware upgrade may be the best short-term answer until the funds for deploying a second web server become available. You may test the solution in the live environment once you have prototyped or tested it in the lab and cut down your solution options. Keep in mind that such solutions are generally best implemented during times of low traffic. Always make a complete backup of the device you are upgrading before proceeding with the upgrade.

Also, keep in mind that monitoring performance and recording baselines and benchmarks will have an impact on the performance of the systems being watched. It is critical to capture both a baseline and a benchmark at the right moment. When a system has been properly configured and upgraded, baselines should be taken. In addition, rather than a day or an hour, baselines should be measured over a longer period of time, such as a week or a month. When new baselines are created, they should be compared to the existing baselines. It may be required to adopt new baselines based on the most recent data at that time.

Create benchmarks and compare baselines

A baseline is a predetermined and documented reference point that will be utilized as a future benchmark. It is important to acquire baselines, but it is even more important to utilize baselines to analyze the security situation. Even the most detailed baselines are useless unless they are used. However, baselines will not help you if you do not have current standards to compare to. A benchmark is a point of reference that captures the same data as a baseline and may even be used as a new baseline, if necessary. It is then utilized for comparison. A benchmark is compared to the baseline to check whether there are any security or performance flaws.

The sales team's visit on Thursday explains the rise in authentication volume. On the other side, if you detect an increase in VPN traffic on Thursdays, you should be concerned since the sales staff will not be utilizing the VPN because they will be at the office. Understanding baselines and benchmarks also entails comprehending thresholds, which ensure that security risks do not escalate beyond a certain level. If the system administrators must be notified before a security event occurs, the ideal technique is to arrange the program to send an alert, alarm, or email message when certain occurrences reach the threshold. To ensure that they can appropriately notice when potential concerns emerge, security experts should collect baselines at different times of the day and on different days of the week. Furthermore, security experts must ensure that benchmarks are being compared to the correct baseline. Comparing a Monday 9 a.m. benchmark to a Saturday 9 a.m. baseline may not allow you to adequately analyze the issue. You should design a feasible remedy to every issue you uncover once you have identified the trouble areas.

Analyze trends and data

Analyzing and understanding trend data to predict cyber protection needs is a crucial step in safeguarding a company. Security specialists should be able to predict where and when defenses will need to be strengthened using trend data.

Consider the following scenario:

Let us say you discover that the user accounts are getting locked out at an increasing rate over time. Several users claim that they are not responsible for their accounts being locked out. You think a hacker has gotten a list of user account names after analyzing the server and audit logs. Furthermore, you learn that the attacker is attempting to connect from the same IP or MAC address over and over. You may wish to adjust the firewall that safeguards your network to prohibit any connections from the attacker's IP or MAC address after the analysis is complete. Changing all usernames is another viable security measure. Changing the user account names, on the other hand, might have ramifications for other services, such as email. As a result, the company could be ready to disregard the possibility that an attacker knows all the user account names.

Let us have a look at a more complicated scenario. Assume a security administrator has discovered a slew of network issues plaguing the proxy server. The administrator observes that the firewall is being attacked with multiple web assaults at the same time that the network difficulties are occurring when analyzing the logs. Deploying a protocol analyzer on the switch span port, adjusting the external-facing IPS, reconfiguring the firewall ACLs to block unnecessary ports, verifying that the proxy server is configured correctly and hardened, and continuing to monitor the network is the most effective way to conduct an in-depth problem assessment and remediation.

It is critical to keep track of such patterns so that the right security measures may be implemented before they turn into genuine concerns. Furthermore, tracking these trends might help you predict resource requirements before they become urgent. For example, if you detect that web server traffic is rising at a specific pace each month, you may plan for upgrades before the traffic reaches a point where the server becomes obsolete and can no longer process client requests.

Analyze security solution metrics and attributes

Security solutions are used to keep a company safe. When security experts install security solutions, they must first define a specific business requirement that the solution addresses. Performance, latency, scalability, capability, usability, maintainability, availability, recoverability, and cost or benefit analysis are the essential business needs to grasp for the CASP test.

Performance

The way in which or the efficiency with which a product or technology reacts or performs its intended goal is referred to as performance. The performance level that should be maintained on each device and throughout the enterprise as a whole should be determined by the company. Any security solutions that are installed should meet the performance criteria that have been defined. Performance criteria should consider both present and future requirements. For example, if a company wants to install an authentication server, the solution it chooses should meet the company's present authentication needs as well as any future authentication requirements. Deploying a solution that gives even higher performance than required will allow the solution to be used for longer than expected.

Latency

Latency refers to the time it takes for network data to be processed. A low-latency network connection has relatively short delay periods, whereas a high-latency network connection has very large delays (refer to *Figure 5.4*). Many security measures have the potential to increase latency. Routers, for example, take a certain amount of time to analyze and forward data. Configuring extra rules on a router often increases latency, consequently resulting in lengthier delays. This is because of the detrimental consequences of network latency, an organization may opt not to use certain security measures. Auditing is an excellent example of a security solution that has a negative impact on latency and performance. When auditing is enabled, it logs certain activities as they happen. The latency and performance may be affected by the recording of these actions. Refer to *Figure 5.4*, that illustrates network latency:

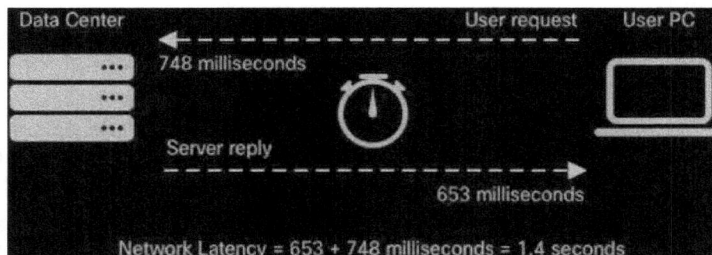

Figure 5.4: Network latency

Scalability

Scalability is a feature of a device or security solution that specifies its capacity to cope with and function under a growing workload. Time factors are commonly used to describe scalability. In order to determine scalability, it is necessary to assess the existing and future demands. Scalability also refers to a system's capacity to expand in response to changing requirements. Refer to *Figure 5.5,* that illustrates the non-scalable setup:

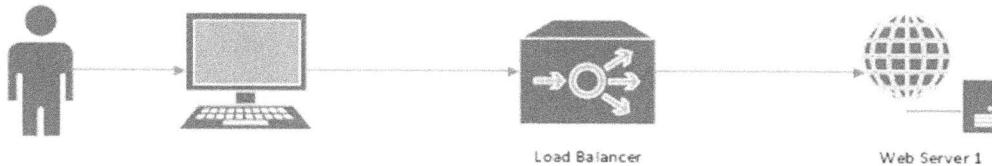

Non Scalable: Single Server serving all the users. If the server cannot handle large number of users, it will not be able serve the subsiquent requests.

Load Balancer   Web Server 1

Figure 5.5: *Non-scalable setup*

To improve performance, a scalable system can be enlarged, load-balanced, or clustered. Let us say a company has to set up a new web server. An older system is found that can be converted to function as the new web server by a systems administrator. Following an assessment of the organization's requirements, it is concluded that the web server will meet the organization's present requirements. It will, however, be unable to meet the estimated demands in six months. If the expenses of the upgrade are not prohibitive, upgrading the server to boost scalability may be an alternative. The cost of the update and the new scalability value should be compared to the cost and scalability of a completely new system. Refer to *Figure 5.6,* that illustrates scalable setup:

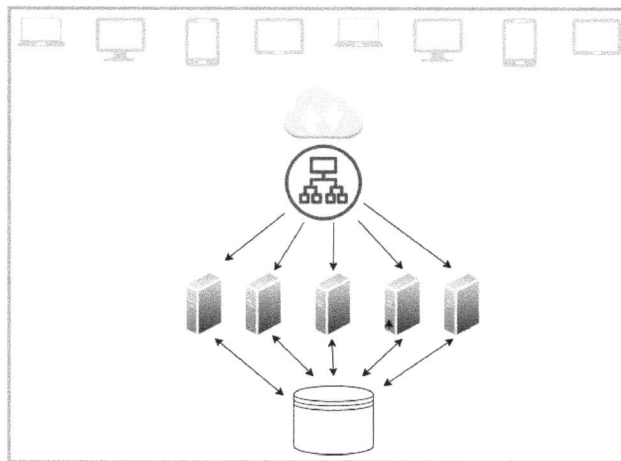

Figure 5.6: *Scalable setup*

Capability

The activity that a solution is capable of performing is referred to as its capacity. An **intrusion detection system (IDS)**, for example, detects invasions, whereas an **intrusion prevention system (IPS)** prevents them. The mechanism by which a solution performs its functions, as well as any solution capabilities that the organization does not require, should be understood. Often, security solutions come with more features at a higher cost.

Usability

Making a security system or device easier to use and aligning it more closely to organizational objectives and requirements are referred to as usability. It is critical to ensure that your organization's employees can adopt and manage a new security system. When calculating **return on investment (ROI)** and total cost of ownership, all staff training expenditures must be included in the solution's costs (TCO). This is because of their usability, even the finest security systems may be eliminated as options.

Maintainability

The frequency with which a security system or device must be updated, as well as the length of time it takes to do so, is referred to as maintainability. Patching, cleaning logs, and updating software are all part of this process. When assessing maintainability, an organization should examine how much maintenance is necessary, how long it takes to complete, and how frequently maintenance is typically performed. Any projected future changes should also be factored into the maintenance concerns.

Availability

The length of time a computer system is available for usage, expressed as a percentage, is known as availability. The words **maximum acceptable downtime (MTD)**, **mean time to repair (MTTR)**, and **mean time between failures (MTBF)** are frequently used when determining availability, as presented in *Figure 5.7*. You must be able to determine when new devices or technologies are being installed to boost data availability in order to pass the CASP test. Consider the following scenario:

Assume a small business uses a single host to host many virtualized client servers. To form a cluster, the organization is contemplating adding a new host. Although the new host's hardware and operating system will differ from the original, the underlying virtualization technology will remain compatible. A shared iSCSI storage solution will be used by both hosts. Customers' data will be more accessible, thanks to the iSCSI storage solution. The best way to assess availability is to look at the component of the security system that is most likely to fail. Knowing how long a solution will be unavailable, how long it will take to fix it, and how long it will take between failures are all critical factors in evaluating availability. Refer to *Figure 5.7,* that illustrates the system downtime availability:

Total downtime per year	Availability
36.5 days	1 nine (90%)
3.6 days	2 nines (99%)
8.7 hours	3 nines (99.9%)
52 minutes	4 nines (99.99%)
5 minutes	5 nines (99.999%)
30 seconds	6 nines (99.9999%)
3 seconds	7 nines (99.99999%)
0.3 seconds	8 nines (99.999999%)

Figure 5.7: System downtime availability

Recoverability

The likelihood that a failed security solution or device may be restored to its normal operational state within a certain time frame utilizing the defined practices and procedures is known as **recoverability**. The phrases **recovery time objective** (**RTO**), **work recovery time** (**WRT**), and **recovery point goal** (**RPO**) are frequently used when assessing recoverability. Researching the activities that will need to be conducted if a partial or complete recovery of the security solution or device is necessary is the best way to assess recoverability. When deciding between different security systems or devices, knowing how long it would take to recover is critical.

Cost or benefit analysis

Before introducing any security solutions to the organization, a cost-benefit analysis is conducted (*Figure 5.8*). This form of analysis compares the expenses of implementing a solution with the advantages that will be realized as a result of its implementation. For the most part, an organization should only deploy a solution if the advantages of doing so outweigh the expenses of doing so. Refer to *Figure 5.8* that illustrates the cost-benefit analysis:

Cost Benefit Analysis
Purchase of New Stamping Machine

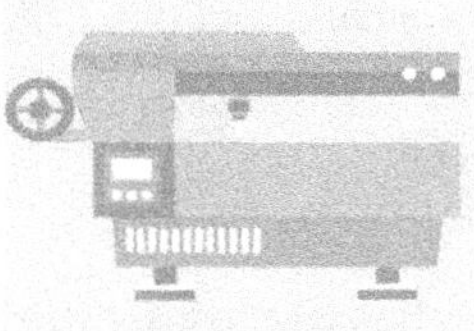

	Benefits	Costs
•	Purchase of Machine	- $20,000
•	Installation of Machine	- 3,125
•	Increased Revenue	27,520
•	Quality Increase Revenue	358
•	Reduced material costs	1,128
•	Reduced Labor Costs	18,585
•	New Operator	- 8,321
•	Utilities	- 250
•	Insurance	- 180
•	Square footage	0

Figure 5.8: Cost-benefit analysis

Cost-benefit analysis is a key decision-making tool that helps determine whether a planned action or expenditure is literally worth the price. The analysis can be used to help decide almost any course of action, but its most common use is to decide whether to proceed with a major expenditure. Since it is based on adding positive factors and subtracting negative ones to get a net result, it is also known as **running the numbers**. Refer to *Figure 5.9,* that illustrates the project-wise cost-benefit analysis:

Cost Benefit Analysis Examples

Project 1

Project 2

- Total Cost = $8000
- Earning Total Benefits = $12000
- Cost Benefit Ratio = ($8000/$12000) i.e **1.5**

- Total Cost = $11000
- Earning Total Benefits = $20000
- Cost Benefit Ratio = ($11000/$20000) i.e **1.81**

So, Project 2 is feasible having high Cost-Benefit Ratio

Figure 5.9: Project wise cost-benefit analysis

Return on investment

Return on investment (**ROI**) refers to the money gained or lost after an organization makes an investment. ROI is a necessary metric for evaluating security investments, as shown in *Figure 5.10*:

Return on Investment Formula $=$ $\dfrac{\text{Net Profit}}{\text{Cost of Investment}}$ $\times$ 100

Figure 5.10: Return on investment

Total cost of ownership

The **total cost of ownership** (**TCO**) measures the overall costs associated with securing the organization, including insurance premiums, finance costs, administrative costs, and any losses incurred. This value should be compared to the overall company revenues and asset base. Refer to *Figure 5.11,* that illustrates the TCO:

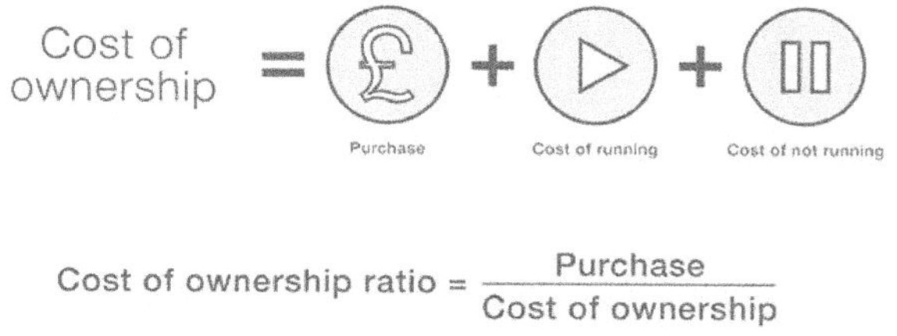

Figure 5.11: *Total cost of ownership*

Judgment to solve problems

You will frequently be asked for your input as a security professional. There is no actual right or wrong answer in these situations, and you will have to apply your judgment to tackle complex challenges when the most secure option is not practicable or if there is no optimum solution. The greatest thing you can do in this situation is to conduct a study. Use all of the resources at your disposal to learn more about the issue, including visiting vendor websites, polling your peers, and getting third-party comparative studies. Understanding why the most secure solution is not possible will help you choose a different one. Due to cost, time, or scope restrictions, the most secure solution may not be possible. Whatever the limitation, security experts must assist in the development of solutions to minimize the problem. As your expertise and knowledge grow, you will be better equipped to make these decisions based on that experience and knowledge while still conducting some research. Making excellent judgments requires information. Pose questions and receive responses. Then, balance each of your responses to evaluate any solutions found. You will have to decide and live with it in the end. Making an informed decision, on the other hand, is always the better option.

Analyze security requirements

In today's interconnected world, organizations face a constantly evolving threat landscape. From sophisticated cyberattacks to internal threats and regulatory compliance mandates, ensuring the security of critical systems and data is paramount. CompTIA CASP+ (now SecurityX) certification provides a robust foundation for understanding and addressing these challenges. This section discusses the critical aspects of analyzing security requirements and implementing effective security controls to manage risk in complex environments. The cornerstone of any effective security program lies in a thorough risk assessment. This process involves identifying, analyzing, and prioritizing potential threats and vulnerabilities that could impact an organization's assets. A comprehensive risk assessment typically involves the following steps:

1. **Asset identification**: The first step is to identify all critical assets within the organization. This includes hardware (servers, workstations, mobile devices), software (applications, databases, operating systems), data (customer information, financial records, intellectual property), and personnel.

2. **Threat identification**: Once assets are identified, potential threats are determined. These can include:

   a. **Internal threats:** Malicious or negligent actions by employees, such as accidental data breaches, insider attacks, and social engineering.

   b. **External threats:** Cyberattacks from malicious actors, such as malware, phishing, ransomware, and denial-of-service attacks.

   c. **Natural disasters:** Events like earthquakes, floods, and fires that can disrupt operations and damage equipment.

3. **Vulnerability assessment:** After identifying threats, vulnerabilities within the organization are assessed. Vulnerabilities are weaknesses that can be exploited by threats. Common vulnerabilities include:

   a. **Software vulnerabilities:** Bugs and flaws in software that can be exploited by attackers.

   b. **Hardware vulnerabilities:** Weaknesses in hardware devices that can be exploited.

   c. **Configuration issues:** Incorrectly configured systems or devices that create security holes.

4. **Threat modeling:** Threat modeling involves analyzing how threats could exploit vulnerabilities to impact assets. This often involves creating threat scenarios and identifying potential attack vectors.

5. **Risk analysis:** Once threats and vulnerabilities are identified, the potential impact of each risk is assessed. This involves considering the likelihood of a threat occurring and the potential consequences if it does.

6. **Risk prioritization:** Based on the risk analysis, risks are prioritized. High-priority risks require immediate attention and mitigation efforts.

Once risks are identified and prioritized, appropriate security controls can be implemented to mitigate them. Security controls are safeguards put in place to protect systems and data from threats. They can be categorized into three main types:

- **Preventive controls**: These controls aim to prevent security incidents from occurring in the first place. Examples include:

  o **Access control:** Implementing strong authentication mechanisms (for example, multi-factor authentication) and authorization policies to restrict access to sensitive resources.

  o **Intrusion prevention systems (IPS):** Deploying IPS devices to monitor network traffic for malicious activity and block attacks in real-time.

  o **Firewalls:** Implementing firewalls to filter network traffic and prevent unauthorized access to internal systems.

- o **Data loss prevention (DLP):** Implementing DLP solutions to prevent sensitive data from leaving the organization's network.

- **Detective controls:** These controls aim to detect security incidents that have already occurred. Examples include:

  - o **Intrusion detection systems (IDS):** Deploying IDS systems to monitor network traffic for suspicious activity and generate alerts.

  - o **Log management:** Implementing log management systems to collect and analyze security logs from various sources to identify and investigate security incidents.

  - o **Security information and event management (SIEM):** Deploying SIEM solutions to collect, analyze, and correlate security logs from multiple sources to provide a comprehensive view of security events.

- **Corrective controls:** These controls aim to mitigate the impact of security incidents that have already occurred. Examples include:

  - o **Incident response plans:** Developing and implementing incident response plans to guide the organization's response to security incidents.

  - o **Data recovery plans:** Implementing data recovery plans to ensure that critical data can be restored in the event of a data breach or other disaster.

  - o **Disaster recovery plans:** Developing and implementing disaster recovery plans to ensure that business operations can continue in the event of a disaster.

Several key security concepts are crucial for effectively analyzing security requirements and implementing security controls:

- **Defense in depth:** Employing multiple layers of security controls to protect systems and data. This creates a more robust defense by making it more difficult for attackers to compromise the system.

- **Least privilege:** Granting users only the minimum necessary privileges to perform their job duties. This helps to limit the potential damage that can be caused by malicious or accidental actions.

- **Separation of duties:** Distributing critical tasks among multiple individuals to prevent fraud and collusion.

- **Principle of least astonishment:** Designing systems and controls that behave in a predictable and expected manner. This helps to reduce user confusion and errors.

Example scenario

In a healthcare organization, where the safety and privacy of patient data are paramount, understanding and addressing the security requirements is critical to maintaining trust and compliance. A thorough analysis of security requirements helps in identifying valuable assets, potential threats, and existing vulnerabilities that could compromise the organization's operations and sensitive health data. This analysis ensures that security controls are tailored to protect against the unique challenges faced by healthcare organizations. Let us consider a hypothetical scenario: a healthcare organization with a complex IT infrastructure, including **electronic health records (EHRs)**, patient databases, and remote access for medical professionals:

- **Security requirements analysis**: Once the security requirements are clearly defined, the next step is to implement appropriate security controls that can effectively mitigate identified risks. These controls are categorized into preventive, detective, and corrective measures, each designed to protect sensitive data, detect potential breaches, and restore operations in the event of a security incident. By taking a layered approach, the organization can ensure robust protection for its IT infrastructure and patient data against evolving threats:

  o **Asset identification:** Critical assets include EHR systems, patient databases, medical devices, workstations, servers, and the organization's network infrastructure.

  o **Threat identification:** Potential threats include:

    ▪ **Cyberattacks:** Ransomware attacks targeting EHR systems, phishing attacks targeting employees, and data breaches from unauthorized access.

    ▪ **Internal threats:** Accidental or intentional data breaches by employees, such as sharing patient information without authorization.

    ▪ **Compliance violations:** Non-compliance with healthcare regulations such as **Health Insurance Portability and Accountability Act (HIPAA)**.

  o **Vulnerability assessment:** A comprehensive vulnerability assessment is essential for identifying weaknesses within an organization's IT infrastructure that could be exploited by attackers. By systematically evaluating the software, hardware, and security policies in place, healthcare organizations can uncover critical vulnerabilities—whether they are outdated software, weak authentication practices, or unencrypted sensitive data. This proactive approach allows organizations to prioritize and address these vulnerabilities before they can be leveraged in a cyberattack, ensuring a more secure environment for both patient data and medical operations:

    ▪ **Software vulnerabilities:** Outdated software on medical devices and workstations.

    ▪ **Weak passwords:** Employees using weak or easily guessable passwords.

    ▪ **Lack of encryption:** Sensitive patient data stored without encryption.

- **Security control implementation**: After identifying security risks and vulnerabilities, it is crucial to implement effective security controls to protect the organization from potential threats. Security controls are designed to prevent, detect, and respond to incidents, ensuring that sensitive data and critical systems are well-defended against cyberattacks, internal breaches, and compliance violations. A multi-layered approach that incorporates preventive, detective, and corrective measures will strengthen the organization's security posture, safeguard patient information, and ensure business continuity in the face of evolving threats:

  o **Preventive controls:** Preventive controls are the first line of defense in securing an organization's IT infrastructure and sensitive data. By implementing measures that proactively block potential threats, such as strong authentication mechanisms, firewalls, and encryption, healthcare organizations can minimize the likelihood of successful attacks. These controls are designed to prevent unauthorized access, reduce the risk of data breaches, and ensure that sensitive health information remains protected from both internal and external threats. Implementing effective preventive controls is a crucial step in creating a resilient security posture:

    ▪ **Implement strong authentication:** Require multi-factor authentication for all users, especially those accessing sensitive data.

    ▪ **Deploy firewalls:** Implement firewalls to filter network traffic and prevent unauthorized access to the organization's network.

    ▪ **Implement IPS:** Deploy IPS devices to monitor network traffic for malicious activity and block attacks in real-time.

    ▪ **Encrypt sensitive data:** Encrypt all sensitive data both in transit and at rest.

    ▪ **Conduct regular security awareness training:** Educate employees about security best practices, such as recognizing phishing emails and avoiding social engineering attacks.

  o **Detective controls:** Detective controls play a crucial role in identifying and responding to security incidents in real time. These controls are designed to continuously monitor the organization's network and systems for suspicious activities, unauthorized access, and potential security breaches. By implementing tools such as intrusion detection systems, log management solutions, and regular security audits, healthcare organizations can swiftly detect and assess threats, enabling them to take immediate action to mitigate damage and protect sensitive patient data from emerging risks:

    ▪ **Implement intrusion detection systems:** Deploy IDS systems to monitor network traffic for suspicious activity and generate alerts.

    ▪ **Implement log management:** Collect and analyze security logs from various sources to identify and investigate security incidents.

- ▪ **Conduct regular security audits:** Conduct regular security audits to identify and address any security gaps.

- ○ **Corrective controls:** Corrective controls are essential for restoring and improving security after an incident has occurred. These measures focus on not only addressing the immediate damage but also on mitigating future risks by refining processes and enhancing defenses. In the context of a healthcare organization, corrective controls ensure that in the event of a security breach or system failure, there are clear, actionable steps to recover lost data, resume normal operations, and prevent similar incidents from reoccurring. This ongoing improvement is vital for maintaining long-term security and compliance in a constantly evolving threat landscape:

  - ▪ **Develop and implement incident response plans:** Define clear procedures for responding to security incidents, such as data breaches and ransomware attacks.

  - ▪ **Develop and implement data recovery plans:** Ensure that critical data can be restored in the event of a data breach or other disaster.

- • **Ongoing monitoring and maintenance:** Security is an ongoing process, not a one-time event. Organizations must continuously monitor their security posture, adapt to new threats, and update their security controls accordingly. This includes:

  - ○ **Regularly reviewing and updating security policies:** Ensure that security policies are up-to-date and aligned with the latest threats and best practices.

  - ○ **Conducting regular vulnerability scans and penetration testing:** Identify and address vulnerabilities in systems and applications.

  - ○ **Monitoring security logs and alerts:** Investigate and respond to security incidents promptly.

  - ○ **Staying informed about the latest security threats and vulnerabilities:** Keep up-to-date on the latest security threats and vulnerabilities through industry news, security advisories, and training.

Thus, analyzing security requirements and implementing effective security controls is critical for protecting organizations from the ever-evolving threat landscape. By following a structured risk assessment process and implementing a layered defense-in-depth strategy, organizations can significantly reduce their exposure to cyberattacks and other security threats. The CompTIA CASP+ (now SecurityX) certification provides a valuable framework for understanding and applying these principles, enabling IT professionals to build and maintain secure and resilient systems.

Conclusion

This chapter explains the review of the effectiveness of security controls to determine new control deployment or deconstruct existing solutions to simulate attackers. The collection and analysis of metrics to use for determining which security control needs to be deployed are also discussed in this chapter. Interpreting data to anticipate defense needs and take decisions is also discussed.

In the next chapter, we will discuss network security as the building block to implementing a secure architecture.

Exercise

1. **Which of the following is the primary purpose of reviewing the effectiveness of existing security controls?**

    a.   To increase the complexity of security policies

    b.   To determine if security controls are achieving their intended outcomes

    c.   To decrease the overall cost of security measures

    d.   To bypass unnecessary controls

2. **What is the main goal of reverse engineering or deconstructing an existing security solution?**

    a.   To integrate the solution with unrelated systems

    b.   To understand its design and identify potential weaknesses or flaws

    c.   To create new features for the solution

    d.   To duplicate the solution for use in other applications

3. **What is the primary purpose of creating and collecting security metrics?**

    a.   To track the overall performance of the organization's IT infrastructure

    b.   To gauge the effectiveness of security measures and guide improvements

    c.   To reduce the number of security incidents in the organization

    d.   To improve employee performance in the security department

4. **Why is it important to prototype and test multiple security solutions?**

    a.   To find the least expensive solution

    b.   To determine the most suitable solution based on performance, cost, and risk factors

    c.   To reduce the time spent on security testing

    d.   To identify which solution requires the least maintenance

5. **What is the purpose of creating benchmarks and comparing them to security baselines?**

    a.   To measure the maximum acceptable risk level

    b.   To identify deviations from the desired security state

    c. To justify the use of advanced security technologies

    d. To reduce the overall spending on security solutions

6. **What is the primary reason for analyzing security trends and data over time?**

    a. To predict future security incidents and adjust strategies accordingly

    b. To monitor the performance of new security software

    c. To identify the most cost-effective security solutions

    d. To evaluate employee security awareness levels

7. **When analyzing security solution metrics and attributes, what is the key factor to consider?**

    a. The number of systems protected by the solution

    b. The effectiveness of the solution in reducing vulnerabilities and risks

    c. The amount of time the solution has been in operation

    d. The number of security incidents in the last year

8. **When faced with a security problem, what role does judgment play in solving it?**

    a. Judgment allows the quick implementation of any solution without review

    b. Judgment helps evaluate the risks, resources, and potential outcomes before choosing the best solution

    c. Judgment limits the available solutions based on historical data

    d. Judgment relies solely on past experiences, ignoring the current context

Answers

1. b
2. b
3. b
4. b
5. b
6. a
7. b
8. b

## CHAPTER 6

Components of Network Security

Introduction

A secure network design cannot be achieved without an understanding of the components that must be included and the concepts of secure design that must be followed. While it is true that many security features come at the cost of performance or ease of use, these are costs that most enterprises will be willing to incur if they understand some important security principles. This chapter discusses the building blocks of a secure architecture. To implement a secure network, you need to understand the available security devices and their respective capabilities. The following sections discuss a variety of devices, both hardware and software-based.

Structure

In this chapter, we will cover the following topics:

- Unified threat management
- Application-and protocol-aware technologies
- Secure socket layer or transport layer security
- Network intrusion prevention system
- Security information and event management

- Software-defined networking
- Endpoint and network security

Objective

Any organization seeks to implement secure architecture for its network infrastructure. The secure design needs to have an understanding of the organization's services and delivery components like servers and networks to include in the secure design. To implement security features, IT teams need to account for the users' ease of use, performance cost, and security standards and principles. This chapter presents the building blocks for implementing a secure architecture for enterprises and critical infrastructures, which includes physical, virtual, and network devices.

Unified threat management

Unified threat management (**UTM**) is a method of executing numerous security duties on a single device or appliance; these capabilities are sometimes referred to as **next-generation firewalls** (**NGFW**) (refer to *Figure 6.1*). These combine many security features and services into a single network device or service, allowing consumers to be protected from security risks in a more straightforward manner. NGFW may include the following functions:

- Network firewalling
- Network intrusion prevention
- Gateway antivirus
- Gateway antispam
- **Virtual private network** (**VPN**)
- Content filtering
- Load balancing
- Data leak prevention
- On-appliance reporting

UTM eliminates the need to manage several systems. Some security experts, on the other hand, believe that UTM provides a single point of failure and that establishing numerous layers of devices is a more safe method, as presented in *Figure 6.1*:

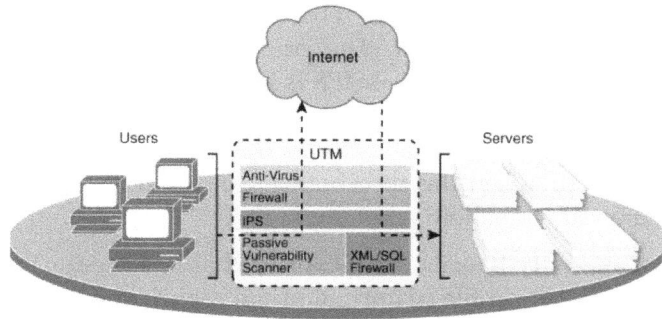

Figure 6.1: *Unified Threat Management deployment*

IDS or IPS

An **intrusion detection system** (**IDS**) is a system that monitors systems and networks for unwanted access or assaults. Threats from the outside and inside the network may be verified, itemized, and classified. In most cases, IDS are pre-programmed to respond in specified ways in specific scenarios. An IDS relies heavily on event notification and alarms. When assaults are discovered, they notify administrators and security specialists. An **intrusion prevention system (IPS)** is a system that guards against assaults. An IS is a system that detects and prevents attacks. When an attack starts, an IPS takes steps to stop and confine it. An IPS, like an IDS, can be network or host-based (refer to *Figure 6.2*). IDS or IPS implementations are further divided into the following categories:

- **Signature-based**: This sort of IDS or IPS examines traffic and compares it to attack or state patterns stored in the IDS database, known as **signatures**. A misuse-detection system is another name for it. Despite its popularity, this form of IDS can only distinguish attacks when compared to its database and is only as effective as the signatures given. Updates are required on a regular basis. The two main types of signature-based IDSs or IPSs are as follows:

  - **Pattern matching**: The IDS or IPS compares traffic to a database of attack patterns. The IDS carries out specific steps when it detects traffic that matches an attack pattern.

  - **Stateful matching**: The IDS or IPS records the initial operating system state. Any changes to the system state that specifically violate the defined rules result in an alert or a notification being sent.

- **Anomaly-based**: This form of IDS or IPS examines traffic and compares it to typical traffic in order to determine if it is a danger. It's also known as a profile-based or behavior-based system. The difficulty with this sort of system is that it reports any traffic that deviates from the expected norms, resulting in a higher number of false positives than signature-based systems. There are three main types of anomaly-based IDSs, which are as follows:

o **Statistical anomaly-based**: To record actions, the IDS or IPS takes samples from the live environment. The profile that is developed becomes more accurate, the longer the IDS or IPS is in operation. Developing a profile with a low number of false positives, on the other hand, can be challenging and time-consuming. In this ID, activity deviation thresholds are crucial. False positives occur when the threshold is set too low, whereas false negatives occur when the threshold is set too high.

o **Protocol anomaly-based**: The IDS or IPS has knowledge of the protocols that it will monitor. A profile of normal usage is built and compared to activity.

o **Traffic anomaly-based**: The IDS or IPS tracks traffic pattern changes. All future traffic patterns are compared to the sample. Changing the threshold reduces the number of false positives or negatives. This type of filter is excellent for detecting unknown attacks, but user activity might not be static enough to effectively implement this system.

- **Rule or heuristic-based**: An expert system with a knowledge base, an inference engine, and rule-based programming is what this form of IDS or IPS is. The knowledge is organized as a set of rules. Data and traffic are assessed, and the rules are applied to the traffic that has been studied. To learn, the inference engine employs clever software. If an attack's criteria are satisfied, alarms or notifications are triggered. This is also known as an if/then system or an expert system.

The most common way to classify an IPS or IDS is based on its information source, such as network-based or host-based. Refer to *Figure 6.2* that illustrates IPS vs IDS:

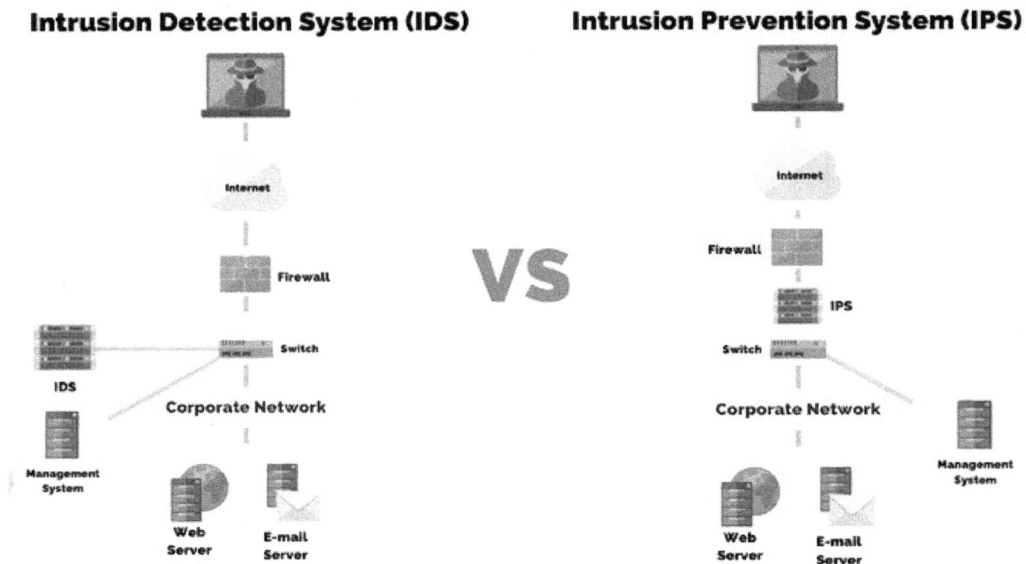

Figure 6.2: *IDS vs IPS*

HIDS or HIPS

The traffic on a single system is monitored using a **host-based IDS (HIDS)** or **host-based IPS (HIPS)**. Its main function is to safeguard the system on which it is installed. The information from the operating system audit trails and system logs is used by a HIDS or HIPS. The completeness of audit logs and system logs limits the detection capabilities of a HIDS. A customized IDS or IPS that analyzes transaction log files for a specific application is known as an application-based IDS or IPS. This form of IPS/IDS is normally included with a program or can be purchased separately.

Network intrusion prevention system

A **network intrusion prevention system** (**NIPS**) monitors network traffic for signals of malicious activity and then takes action to avoid it. A NIPS is a network monitoring system that keeps track of the whole network. You must be cautious when using a NIPS filter to ensure that false positives and false negatives are kept to a minimum. A false positive is an alarm that is not warranted, whereas a false negative is a traffic that is bothersome but does not trigger an alarm.

Network IDS

A **network IDS** (**NIDS**) is the most popular IDS, and it analyses network traffic on a local network segment. The **network interface card** (**NIC**) must be in promiscuous mode to monitor traffic on the network segment. NIDS can only monitor network traffic, it cannot monitor any internal system activity, such as an attack carried out via logging into the system's local terminal. A switched network has an impact on NIDS since most NIDS monitor only a single network segment. *Figure 6.3* illustrates the network and host-based IDS:

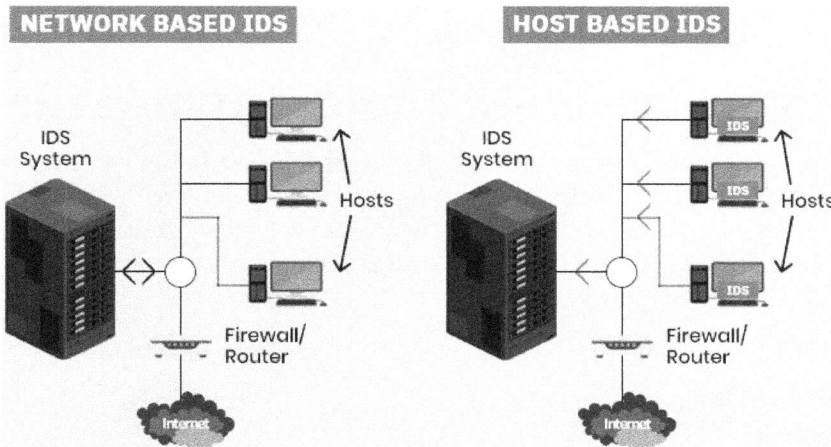

Figure 6.3: NIDS vs HIDS

Network access control

When initiating remote access or VPN connection to the network, **network access control (NAC)** is a service that goes beyond user authentication and involves a review of the status of the machine the user is introducing to the network (*Figure 6.4*). These services are referred to as **network admission control (NAC)** services by Cisco and **network access protection (NAP)** services by Microsoft. Regardless of the terminology used, the features' aims are the same that is to scan any device seeking network access for malware, missing security updates, and any other security vulnerabilities that the devices could contribute to the network. Refer to *Figure 6.4* that illustrates NAC:

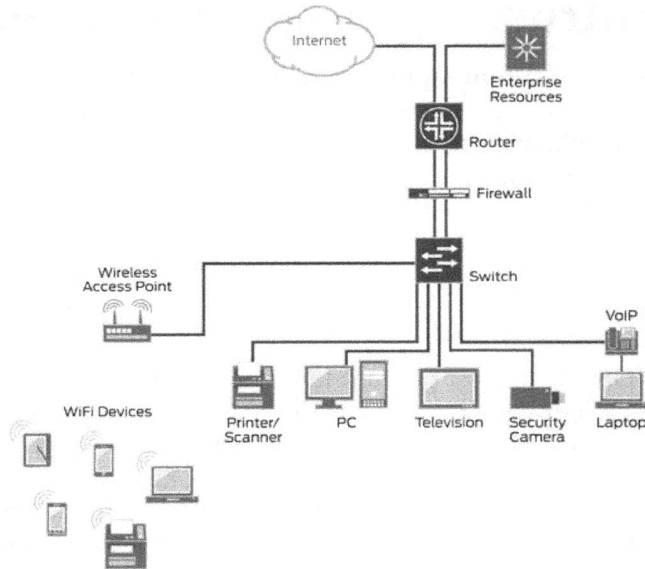

Figure 6.4: Network access control

Security information and event management

Security information and event management (SIEM) solutions collect data from crucial system log files and centralize the collection and analysis (*Figure 6.5*). SIEM technology combines two technologies that are closely related to **security information management (SIM)** and **security event management (SEM)**. Log sources for SIEM can include the following:

- Application logs
- Antivirus logs
- Operating system logs
- Malware detection logs

Refer to *Figure 6.5* that illustrates SIEM:

Figure 6.5: *SIEM*

When dealing with a SIEM system, one thing to remember is to keep the quantity of data collected to a minimum. Furthermore, you must guarantee that sufficient resources are accessible to ensure that good performance is achieved. *Figure 6.6* illustrates the SIEM log flow from initial logs received to the final tickets:

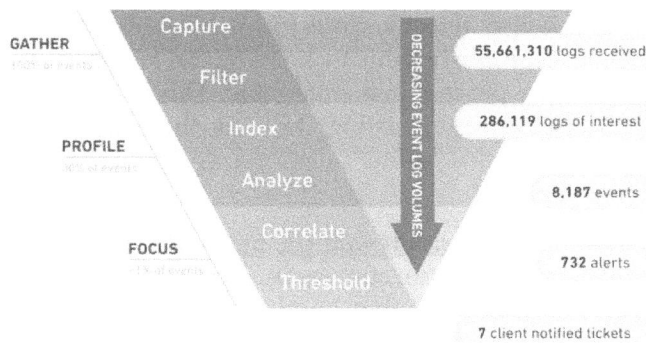

Figure 6.6: *SIEM log flow*

An organization should implement a SIEM system when the following is required:

- More visibility into network events is desired
- Faster correlation of events is required
- Compliance issues require reporting to be streamlined and automated
- Needs help prioritizing security issues

Firewall

The firewall is the network equipment that is most closely associated with the concept of security. A firewall can be a piece of software that runs on top of a server or client operating system, or it can be a standalone device with its own operating system. In any scenario, a firewall's role is to inspect and limit the types of communications that are permitted. When we look at firewalls, we pay attention to the distinctions in how they work. The following are the types of firewalls:

- **Packet-filtering firewalls**: These firewalls have the least impact on performance since they merely look for approved IP addresses or port numbers in the packet header. While this function delays traffic, it just requires a fast check at the beginning of the packet and a choice to allow or disallow. While packet-filtering firewalls are useful, they cannot protect against all forms of attacks. They cannot stop IP spoofing, application-specific attacks, attacks that rely on packet fragmentation, or attacks that take advantage of the TCP handshake. To thwart these assaults, more complex inspection firewall types are necessary.

- **Stateful firewalls**: These firewalls are aware of how the TCP handshake works, maintain track of the state of all connections in relation to it and can detect when packets attempting to join the network do not make sense in the context of the TCP handshake. A packet with both the SYN and ACK flags set should never arrive at a firewall for delivery unless it is part of an established handshake procedure; it should also be in response to a packet received from inside the network with the SYN flag set. This is the kind of packet that the stateful firewall won't let through. A stateful firewall can also detect various forms of attacks that try to take advantage of this process. It accomplishes this by keeping track of all current connections and where they are in the process in a state table. This enables it to detect any traffic that is inconsistent with the existing status of the connections. Maintaining and referring to this table has a greater performance impact on this firewall type than a packet-filtering firewall.

- **Proxy firewalls**: This form of firewall sits between the internal and external sides of an internal-to-external connection and connects the endpoints on their behalf. A forward proxy is a firewall that is utilized in this manner. There is no direct connection with a proxy firewall; rather, the proxy firewall functions as a relay between the two destinations. Proxy firewalls can operate at two different layers of the **Open System Interconnection (OSI)** model, which are as follows:

  o **Circuit-level proxies**: These proxies work at the OSI model's session layer (layer 5). The protocol header and session layer information are used by this sort of proxy to make judgments. This proxy is deemed application-agnostic and may be used for a wide range of layer 7 protocols since it does not do deep packet inspection (at layer 7, or the application layer). A circuit-level firewall is an example of a SOCKS firewall. It necessitates the installation of a SOCKS client on the machines. To make using this form of firewall easier, many companies have linked their software with SOCKS.

  o **Application-level proxies**: Deep packet inspection is performed by these proxies (inspection up to layer 7). This form of firewall comprehends the application's layer 7 communication mechanism in depth. Each protocol has its own proxy function in an application-level firewall. The proxy, for example, may read and filter HTTP traffic depending on HTTP instructions. This is because operating at this layer necessitates the entire opening and closing of each packet, this firewall has the largest influence on performance.

o **Dynamic packet filtering**: Although dynamic packet filtering is not technically a form of firewall, it is a process that a firewall may or may not be able to manage, therefore it is worth mentioning here. When internal computers try to establish a connection with a distant computer, the packet contains both the source and destination port numbers. If a computer requests a secure web server, for example, the destination will be port 443 because HTTP uses port 443 by default.

o **Kernel proxy firewalls**: A fifth-generation firewall is an example of this sort of firewall. It inspects a packet at each layer of the OSI model, but because it does it at the kernel layer, it does not have the same performance hit as an application-layer firewall. It also uses the proxy paradigm, in which it acts as a middleman between two systems, establishing connections on their behalf.

• **Next-generation firewalls (NGFWs)** are a type of device that attempts to solve the inadequacies of a typical stateful firewall in terms of traffic inspection and application awareness without sacrificing speed. Although UTM systems strive to solve these challenges, they employ distinct internal engines to conduct various security duties. Refer to *Figure 6.7* that illustrates the NGFWs:

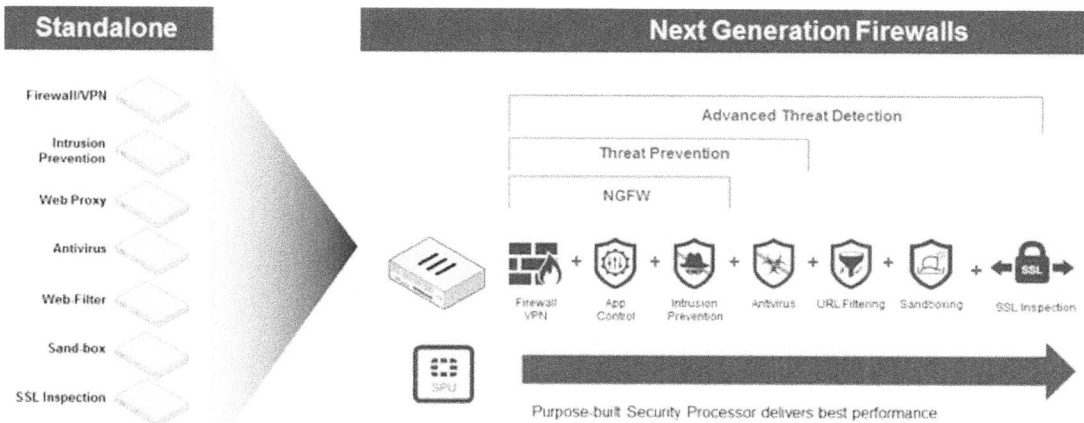

Figure 6.7: *Next-generation firewall*

This implies that a packet may be evaluated by various engines many times before being permitted into the network. NGFWs are application-aware, meaning they can discriminate between certain apps rather than allowing all traffic to come in over standard web ports. Furthermore, during the deep packet inspection step, they only analyze packets once (which is required to detect malware and anomalies). The following are the features provided by NGFWs:

o Non-disruptive in-line configuration, which has little impact on network performance

o Standard first-generation FW capabilities, such as network address translation, stateful protocol inspection, and virtual private networking

o Integrated signature-based IPS engine

o Application awareness, full-stack visibility, and granular control

o Ability to incorporate information from outside the firewall, such as directory-based policy, blacklists, and whitelists

o Upgrade path to include future information feeds and security threats and **secure sockets layer (SSL)** decryption to enable identifying undesirable encrypted applications

Switches

These are intelligent devices that function at the OSI layer 2 level. They map to this layer because MAC addresses, which are stored at layer 2, are used to make switching decisions. This is known as **transparent bridging**. Switches are more efficient than hubs because they prevent accidents. Each switch port has its own collision domain, however, all hub ports share one collision domain. Switches are safer from a security viewpoint since a sniffer attached to a single port can only collect communications destined for or originating from that port. Some switches, on the other hand, may function as both routers and switches. Layer 3 switches are devices that can both route and switch data. When utilizing switches, keep in mind that while redundant connections between switches are good, they can cause switching loops, which can be disastrous to the network. To avoid switching loops, most switches use the **Spanning Tree Protocol** (**STP**). You should check to see whether a switch does this and if it is turned on.

Router

If we are only talking about the routing function, we may claim that routers work at layer 3. Some routing devices can integrate routing, switching, and layer 4 filtering into one device. Routing, on the other hand, is a layer 3 function since it makes decisions based on layer 3 information (IP addresses). Routing tables are used by routers to instruct them on which way to deliver traffic destined for a certain network (*Figure 6.8*). Although routers may be set to direct to specific computers, they are usually designed to route to networks rather than specific computers. When a packet arrives at a router that is directly linked to the target network, the router does an ARP broadcast to determine the computer's MAC address before sending the packet as a frame at layer 2. Routers serve an essential security purpose by allowing **access control lists (ACLs)** to be established. ACLs are a collection of rules that determine which traffic is allowed or refused to utilize a certain path via the router. These rules can function at the layer 3 level, making judgments based on IP addresses, or at the layer 4 level, allowing only particular types of traffic. An ACL usually refers to a service or application's port number that is authorized or disallowed. Refer to *Figure 6.8* that illustrates the network routing and switching:

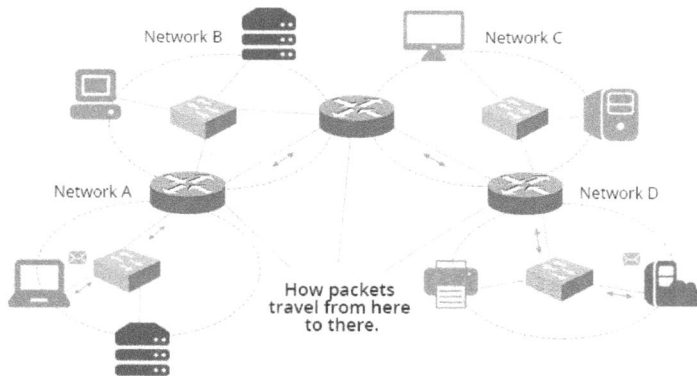

Figure 6.8: Network routing and switching

To secure a router, you need to ensure that the following settings are in place:

- Configure authentication between the routers to prevent them from performing routing updates with rogue routers.
- Secure the management interfaces with strong passwords.
- Manage routers with SSH rather than Telnet.

Proxy

Proxy servers can be hardware or software that runs on a server's operating system. These servers work in the same way as proxy firewalls, in that, they establish web connections between computers on their behalf, however, they can usually accept and restrict traffic on a more detailed level. A proxy server, for example, may allow the sales group to access particular websites while denying the data entry group access to the same sites. The capability goes beyond HTTP to include other forms of communication, such as FTP. Proxy servers can also perform a useful service known as **web caching**. When a proxy server is set up to enable web caching, it keeps a copy of every web page served to an internal computer in a web cache. If another user requests the same page later, the proxy server already has a local copy and does not need to go to the trouble of retrieving it from the internet. This significantly enhances the performance of frequently visited pages on the web.

Load balancer

Load balancers are hardware or software solutions that balance network traffic. The same methods are supported by **application delivery controllers** (**ADCs**), but they additionally utilize complicated number-crunching procedures to balance the load, such as per-server CPU and memory usage, quickest response times, and so on. Server farms or pools are terms used to describe load-balancing technologies, as shown in *Figure 6.9*:

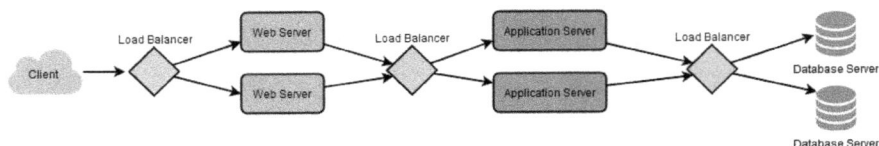

Figure 6.9: Load Balancer locations

Hardware security module

A **hardware security module** (**HSM**) is an appliance that safeguards and manages digital keys used with strong authentication and provides crypto processing. The following are among the functions of an HSM:

- Onboard secure cryptographic key generation

- Onboard secure cryptographic key storage and management

- Use of cryptographic and sensitive data material

- Offloading of application servers for complete asymmetric and symmetric cryptography

Figure 6.10 illustrates the connections directly to a computer or server:

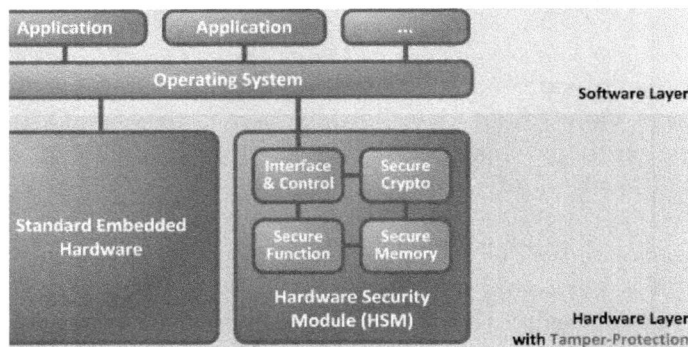

Figure 6.10: Hardware security module in infrastructure

HSM devices can be used in a variety of scenarios, like the following:

- **Public key infrastructure (PKI)** environment to generate, store, and manage key pairs in card payment systems to encrypt PINs and to load keys into protected memory

- To perform the processing for applications that use SSL

- In **Domain Name System (DNS) Security Extensions (DNSSEC)** is a secure form of DNS that protects the integrity of zone files to store the keys used to sign the zone file

Refer to *Figure 6.11* that illustrates HSM key storage and acceleration:

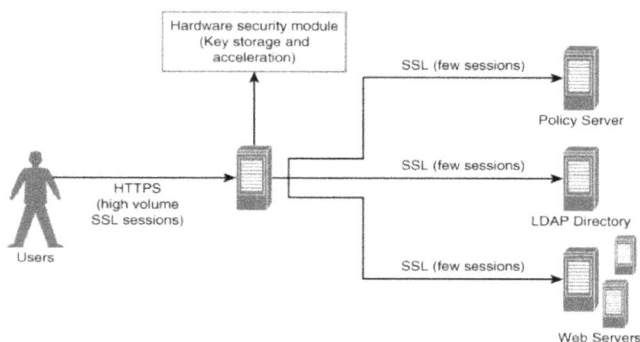

Figure 6.11: HSM Key Storage & Acceleration

Application and protocol-aware technologies

Technologies that are application- and protocol-aware keep track of current information about apps and the protocols that link to them. These intelligent technologies make use of this data to improve the protocols, and consequently, the application's performance.

Web application firewall

An HTTP interaction is routed through a **web application firewall (WAF)**, which applies rule sets to it (*Figure 6.12*). These rule sets address the most prevalent forms of attacks that these session types are vulnerable to. Cross-site scripting and SQL injections are two of the most prevalent attacks they handle. WAF can be installed as a standalone device or as a server plug-in. While most solutions route all traffic in-line via the device, others monitor a port and work out-of-band, allowing them to be deployed directly on web servers. Refer to *Figure 6.12* that illustrates the WAF:

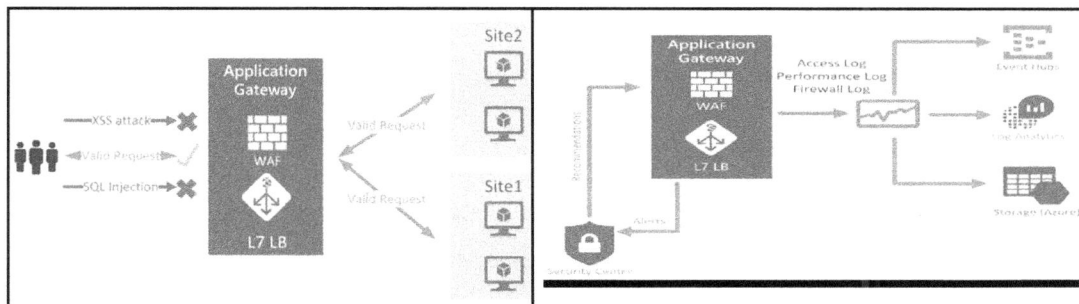

Figure 6.12: Web application firewall

Passive vulnerability scanners

Vulnerability scanners are programs or utilities that are used to investigate and disclose security flaws in a network. To detect topology, services, and vulnerabilities, a **passive vulnerability scanner** (**PVS**) examines network traffic at the packet layer (*Figure 6.13*). By actively scanning for vulnerabilities, it eliminates the instability that can be caused to a system. PVS tools examine the packet stream and conduct direct analysis to check for vulnerabilities. They are used in the same way as the network IDSs or packet analyzers are used. A PVS can choose a network session that is directed towards a protected server and monitor it as needed. The capacity of a PVS to do this without affecting the monitored network is its most significant advantage. Refer to *Figure 6.13* that illustrates PVS:

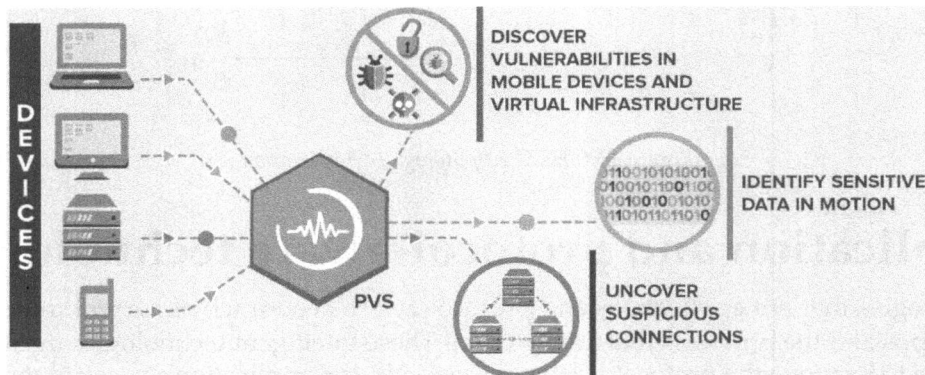

Figure 6.13: Passive vulnerability scanner

Active vulnerability scanners

Active scanners, as opposed to passive scanners, can take action to prevent attacks, such as banning problematic IP addresses. They can also be used to test readiness by simulating an assault. They function by sending signals to nodes and analyzing the answers, which might cause network traffic to be disrupted.

Virtual private network

The information is protected by robust authentication procedures and encryption techniques over a VPN connection that uses an untrusted carrier network. While we usually pick the most untrustworthy network—the internet—VPNs do travel over the internet. A VPN may also be used to safeguard traffic on an internal network. In VPN operations, entire protocols wrap around other protocols which include the following:

- **Required**: LAN and remote access or line protocol
- **Optional**: Authentication and encryption protocol

Refer to *Figure 6.14* that illustrates VPN:

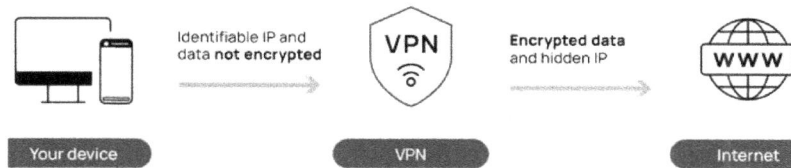

Figure 6.14: *Virtual private network*

VPN concentrators are devices that terminate numerous VPN connections and use the most powerful encryption and authentication procedures available. If the ISP also uses **virtual local area networks** (**VLAN**) in their internal network, VLANs in a VPN solution may not be supported by the ISP in some cases. Customers can create VLANs to other sites by choosing a supplier that offers **multiprotocol label switching** (**MPLS**) connections. VPN services with address and route isolation between VPNs are provided by MPLS. VPN connections come in the following two flavors:

- **Remote access VPNs**: A remote-access VPN can be used to provide remote access to teleworkers or traveling users. The tunnel that is created has, as its endpoints, the user's computer and the VPN concentrator. In this case, only the traffic traveling from the user's computer to the VPN concentrator uses this tunnel.

- **Site-to-site VPNs**: VPN connections can be used to securely connect two locations. In this type of VPN, called a site-to-site VPN, the tunnel endpoints are the two VPN routers, one in each office. With this configuration, all traffic that goes between the offices will use the tunnel, regardless of the source or destination. The endpoints are defined during the creation of the VPN connection and thus must be set correctly, according to the type of remote access link being used.

Internet Protocol Security

Several remote access or line protocols (tunneling protocols) are used to create VPN connections, which include the following:

- **Point-to-Point Tunneling Protocol** (**PPTP**): PPTP is a Microsoft protocol based on PPP. It uses built-in Microsoft Point-to-Point encryption and can use several authentication methods, including CHAP, MS-CHAP, and EAP-TLS. One shortcoming of PPTP is that it only works on IP-based networks, as illustrated in *Figure 6.15* and *Figure 6.16*. If a WAN connection that is not IP-based is in use, L2TP must be used. When using PPTP, the encryption is included, and the only remaining choice to be made is the authentication protocol.

- **Layer 2 Tunneling Protocol** (**L2TP**): L2TP is a newer protocol that operates at layer 2 of the OSI model. Like PPTP, L2TP can use various authentication mechanisms; however, L2TP does not provide any encryption. It is typically used with **Internet Protocol Security** (**IPsec**), which is a very strong encryption mechanism. When using L2TP, both encryption and authentication protocols, if desired, must be added. IPsec can provide encryption, data integrity, and system-based authentication, which makes it a flexible and capable option.

Figure 6.15 illustrates the IPsec in tunnel mode:

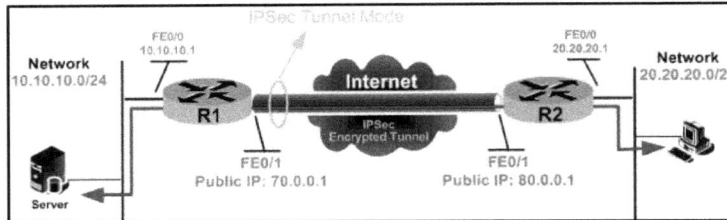

Figure 6.15: IPsec in tunnel mode

By implementing certain parts of the IPsec suite, you can choose or not choose to use these features. IPsec is actually a suite of protocols, much like TCP/IP. It includes the following components:

- **Authentication Header (AH)**: AH provides data integrity, data origin authentication, and protection from replay attacks.

- **Encapsulating Security Payload (ESP)**: ESP provides all that AH does, as well as data confidentiality.

- **Internet Security Association and Key Management Protocol (ISAKMP)**: ISAKMP handles the creation of a security association for the session and the exchange of keys.

- **Internet Key Exchange (IKE)**: Also sometimes referred to as IPsec Key Exchange, IKE provides the authentication material used to create the keys exchanged by ISAKMP during peer authentication.

Figure 6.16 illustrates IPsec in transport mode:

Figure 6.16: IPsec in transport mode

IPsec is a framework, which means it does not specify many of the components used with it. These components must be identified in the configuration, and they must match in order for the two ends to successfully create the required security association that must be in place before any data is transferred.

Secure sockets layer or transport layer security

Another alternative for establishing secure connections to servers is SSL. It operates at the OSI model's application layer. It is mostly used to secure HTTP traffic and web servers. Most browsers have it built-in, and using it usually doesn't need any activity on the user's behalf. *Figure 6.17* illustrates SSL Communication:

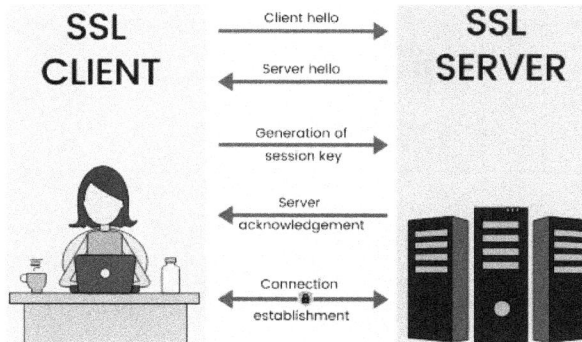

Figure 6.17: SSL Communication

SSL is widely and frequently used to secure other protocols. For example, the **Secure Copy Protocol** (**SCP**) employs SSL to encrypt file transfers between servers. When deciding where to install the SSL gateway, you must weigh the following factors such as the closer the gateway is to the network edge, the less encryption is required in the LAN (and the less performance loss), but the closer it is to the network edge, the more traffic flows in the clear through the LAN. It all boils down to how much faith you have in your own network. This is used to secure Internet transactions and can be implemented in the following two ways:

- **SSL portal VPN**: In this case, a user has a single SSL connection for accessing multiple services on the web server. Once authenticated, the user is provided a page that acts as a portal to other services.

- **SSL tunnel VPN**: A user may use an SSL tunnel to access services on a server that is not a web server. This solution uses custom programming to provide access to non-web services through a web browser.

TLS and SSL are very similar but not the same. When configuring SSL, a session key length must be designated. The two options are 40-bit and 128-bit keys. Using self-signed certificates to authenticate the server's public key prevents man-in-the-middle attacks.

Transport layer security

The current version of the **transport layer security** (**TLS**) protocol, version 1.3, provides an encrypted connection between two computers connected to the Internet. It confirms the server's identity and protects data from being intercepted by hackers. When a user attempts to connect to a server, the server provides its TLS certificate to the user. To create a secure connection, the user checks the server's certificate using CA certificates on the user's device. To confirm the CA signed the certificate, this verification method employs public-key cryptography such as **Rivest, Adi Shamir (RSA)** or **elliptical curve cryptography (ECC)**. As long as you trust the CA, this demonstrates you are communicating with the server certificate's subject. *Figure 6.18* illustrates this TLS 1.3 process:

Figure 6.18: TLS 1.3 process

This maintains data integrity while also providing anonymity between the various data transfer destinations. Digital certificates are also used to validate the validity of servers. TLS certificates are the most frequent name for these certificates. The public key cryptography is used to authenticate these certificates. This is based on key pairs, which are made up of a public and private key. Only when both the public and private keys are present, can the encrypted data be decrypted. TLS certificates employ public key authentication to ensure that only the intended receiver has access to the contents.

Secure shell

Administrators or network professionals are frequently required to manage and configure network devices remotely. Technicians can use protocols like Telnet to connect to equipment like routers, switches, and wireless access points and administer them from the command line. Telnet, on the other hand, sends data in cleartext, which is a security risk. To offer an encrypted means of executing these tasks, **Secure Shell (SSH)** was invented. It links a server and a client running SSH server and SSH client applications, respectively, over a secure channel and an unsafe network. It is a popular alternative to Telnet and should be taken into account while doing remote management from the command line. Several steps can be taken to enhance the security of an SSH implementation, which are as follows:

1. Change the port number in use from the default 22 to something above 1024.

2. Use only version 2, which corrects many vulnerabilities that exist in earlier versions.

3. Disable root login to devices that have a root account (in Linux or UNIX).

4. Control access to any SSH-enabled devices by using ACLs, IP tables, or TCP wrappers.

Remote desktop protocol

Remote desktop protocol (**RDP**) is a Microsoft-developed proprietary protocol that allows you to connect to another computer through a network connection using a graphical interface. RDP allows you to operate on a remote computer as if you were sitting at its terminal, unlike Telnet and SSH, which only allow you to work from the command line. RDP sessions employ native RDP encryption, however, the session host server is not authenticated. SSL can be used for server authentication and to encrypt RDP session host server interactions to help prevent this. This necessitates the use of a certificate. You can use an existing certificate or the self-signed certificate that comes with Windows. RDP may be used to connect users to a **virtual desktop infrastructure** (**VDI**) as well as remote access to a workstation. This allows the user to operate from a virtual desktop from any location. Each user may have their own **virtual machine** (**VM**) image, or several users may share the same VM image.

Reverse proxy

A reverse proxy is a sort of proxy server that receives resources from one or more internal servers on behalf of external clients. The client is then given these resources as though they came directly from the web server. Unlike a forward proxy, which allows internal clients to communicate with external servers, a reverse proxy allows external clients to communicate with inside servers. Popular web servers frequently employ reverse proxy capability to protect application frameworks from HTTP limitations.

Network authentication methods

One of the protocol choices that must be made in creating a remote access solution is the authentication protocol. The following are some of the most important of those protocols:

- **Password Authentication Protocol** (**PAP**): PAP provides authentication, but the credentials are sent in cleartext and can be read with a sniffer.

- **Challenge Handshake Authentication Protocol** (**CHAP**): CHAP solves the clear text problem by operating without sending the credentials across the link. The server sends the client a set of random text called a **challenge**. The client encrypts the text with the password and sends it back. The server then decrypts it with the same password and compares the result with what was sent originally. If the results match, the server can be assured that the user or system possesses the correct password without ever needing to send it across the untrusted network. Microsoft has created its own variant of CHAP, as follows:

- o **MS-CHAP v1**: This is the first version of a variant of CHAP by Microsoft. This protocol works only with Microsoft devices, and while it stores the password more securely than CHAP, like any other password-based system, it is susceptible to brute-force and dictionary attacks.

- o **MS-CHAP v2**: This update to MS-CHAP provides stronger encryption keys and mutual authentication, and it uses different keys for sending and receiving.

- **Extensible Authentication Protocol (EAP)**: EAP is not a single protocol but a framework for port-based access control that uses the same three components that are used in RADIUS. A wide variety of EAP implementations can use all sorts of authentication mechanisms, including certificates, a PKI, and even simple passwords, as follows:

  - o **EAP-MD5-CHAP**: This variant of EAP uses the CHAP challenge process, but the challenges and responses are sent as EAP messages. It allows the use of passwords.

  - o **EAP-TLS**: This form of EAP requires a PKI because it requires certificates on both the server and clients. It is, however, immune to password-based attacks as it does not use passwords.

  - o **EAP-TTLS**: This form of EAP requires a certificate on the server only. The client uses a password, but the password is sent within a protected EAP message. It is, however, susceptible to password-based attacks.

802.1x

802.1x is a standard that defines a framework for centralized port-based authentication (*Figure 6.19*). It can be applied to both wireless and wired networks and uses the following three components:

- **Supplicant**: The user or device requesting access to the network.

- **Authenticator**: The device through which the supplicant is attempting to access the network.

- **Authentication server**: The centralized device that performs authentication.

A wide range of network access devices, including remote access servers (both dial-up and VPN), switches, and wireless access points, can function as authenticators. A **Remote Authentication Dial-in User Service (RADIUS)** or **Terminal Access Controller Access-Control System Plus (TACACS+)** server can function as the authentication server. The authenticator obtains credentials from the supplicant and sends them to the authentication server for validation. The authenticator is told that the supplicant's port has been successfully verified, allowing network access. *Figure 6.19* illustrates 802.1x components:

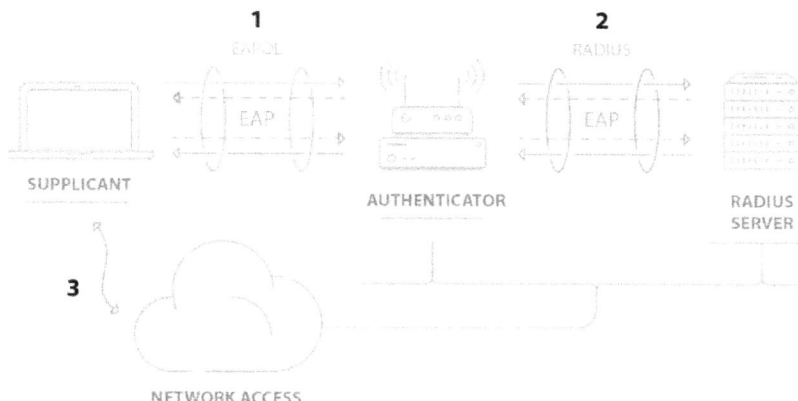

Figure 6.19: *802.1x components*

RADIUS and TACACS+ both perform the same functions; however, they have distinct properties. These distinctions must be taken into account while selecting a method.

Note: Whereas RADIUS is a standard, TACACS+ is a Cisco-only product. Many security experts believe that activating 802.1x authentication on all devices is the finest network security you can give.

Software-defined networking

The separation of the control plane from the data plane in networking is what **software-defined networking (SDN)** is traditionally characterized as. These planes are implemented in the firmware of routers and switches in a traditional network. The control plane is implemented in software in SDN, allowing programmatic access to it. It has the advantage of allowing highly precise access to and control over network parts. It enables IT businesses to replace manual interfaces with programmatic ones, allowing configuration and policy administration to be automated. The use of software to centralize the control planes of several switches that would otherwise function independently is an example of SDN in action. Normally, the control plane is implemented in hardware; however, with SDN, it is implemented in software. SDN provides variety, speed, and agility in deployment, as well as the ability to mix and match solutions from various suppliers. SDN has a number of drawbacks. When the controller loses connectivity, the entire network goes down, and SDN might theoretically allow assaults on the controller. *Figure 6.20* illustrates the SDN architecture:

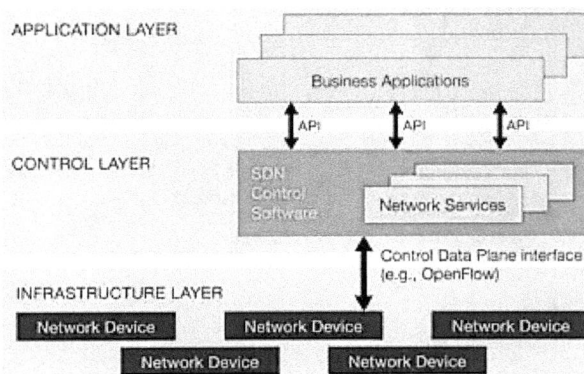

Figure 6.20: SDN architecture

Endpoint and network security

This section delves into the practical implementation of advanced endpoint and network security solutions. By implementing these advanced endpoint and network security solutions, organizations can significantly enhance their security posture, mitigate risks, and protect their valuable assets from cyber threats. We explore three real-world use cases, providing step-by-step instructions and insights:

- **Use case 1:** Implementing a Zero Trust framework

  The scenario, a mid-sized organization is transitioning to a remote work model, increasing the attack surface and necessitating a more robust security posture. The objective is to implement a Zero Trust framework to enhance security and mitigate risks associated with remote work.

  Following is the step-by-step instructions:

  1. **Define the scope:** Identify critical assets, users, and data to be protected within the Zero Trust model.

  2. **Implement multi-factor authentication (MFA):** Enforce MFA for all user access, regardless of location. This can be achieved through:

     a. **Time-based one-time passwords (TOTP):** Using authenticator apps like Google Authenticator or Authy.

     b. **Hardware tokens:** Providing physical tokens for enhanced security.

     c. **Biometric authentication:** Utilizing fingerprint or facial recognition for added convenience.

  3. **Implement least privilege access control:** Grant users only the necessary permissions to perform their job functions. Regularly review and adjust access rights based on roles and responsibilities.

4. **Deploy Endpoint Detection and Response (EDR) solutions:** Implement EDR solutions to monitor endpoint behavior, detect threats, and respond to incidents in real-time.

5. **Implement network segmentation:** Isolate critical networks and systems, limiting lateral movement in case of a breach.

6. **Conduct regular security audits and penetration testing:** Continuously assess the effectiveness of the Zero Trust implementation and identify areas for improvement.

- **Use case 2:** Securing **Internet of Things (IoT)** devices

The scenario, a manufacturing company is increasingly reliant on IoT devices, introducing new vulnerabilities and attack vectors. The objective is to secure IoT devices and their communication channels to prevent unauthorized access and data breaches.

Following is the step-by-step instructions:

1. **Inventory IoT devices:** Identify and catalog all IoT devices connected to the network.

2. **Segment IoT networks:** Create a dedicated network segment for IoT devices, isolating them from critical business systems.

3. **Implement secure protocols:** Enforce secure communication protocols like HTTPS and TLS for all IoT device traffic.

4. **Update firmware regularly:** Keep IoT device firmware up-to-date to patch vulnerabilities and improve security.

5. **Implement NAC:** Enforce device and user authentication before granting access to the network.

6. **Monitor IoT traffic:** Utilize network traffic analysis tools to detect and respond to malicious activity targeting IoT devices.

- **Use case 3**: Implementing advanced threat hunting

The scenario, a cybersecurity team needs to proactively identify and respond to advanced threats that may have evaded traditional defences. Objective is to implement an advanced threat hunting program to detect and respond to sophisticated attacks.

Following is the step-by-step instructions:

1. **Establish a threat hunting team:** Assemble a team of skilled cybersecurity professionals with expertise in threat intelligence, network analysis, and incident response.

2. **Develop a threat hunting framework:** Define clear objectives, methodologies, and processes for threat hunting activities.

3. **Utilize threat intelligence:** Leverage threat intelligence feeds and data sources to identify potential threats and vulnerabilities.

4. **Conduct regular threat hunting exercises:** Perform regular hunts for specific threat actors, techniques, and **indicators of compromise (IOCs).**

5. **Analyze security logs and events:** Utilize SIEM systems to analyze logs and identify suspicious activity.

6. **Develop and test incident response plans:** Create and regularly test incident response plans to ensure effective and timely response to detected threats.

Conclusion

This chapter discussed security and network devices such as UTM, IDS/IPD, NIDS, NIPS, NAC, SIEM, routers, switches, load balancers, and HSM. Hardware and software firewalls, WAF, and Vulnerability Scanners were also discussed. Identifying secure methods with an emphasis on baselining was also covered.

In the next chapter, we will look at securing host machines and devices, along with issues to protect the systems.

Exercise

1. **Which of the following best describes Unified Threat Management (UTM)?**
   a. System that provides only antivirus protection
   b. Comprehensive security solution integrating multiple security services in one device
   c. Software used solely for intrusion detection
   d. Cloud-based storage solution for security logs

2. **What is the primary function of application- and protocol-aware technologies?**
   a. Monitoring and blocking malware in emails
   b. Understanding and analyzing application-level data for security and performance
   c. Encrypting data at rest
   d. Providing backup for critical business data

3. **Which of the following is a key feature of TLS over SSL?**
   a. TLS is more secure and supports stronger encryption algorithms than SSL
   b. SSL provides better performance than TLS

    c. SSL is more compatible with modern applications than TLS

    d. TLS does not support digital certificates

4. What is the main function of a Network Intrusion Prevention System (NIPS)?

    a. Encrypting network traffic

    b. Blocking malicious activities based on network traffic patterns in real time

    c. Performing regular system backups

    d. Scanning emails for spam

5. What is a primary feature of a SIEM solution?

    a. Backup of system logs to external storage

    b. Real-time analysis of security alerts generated by network hardware and applications

    c. Blocking unauthorized access to wireless networks

    d. Securing mobile endpoints against malware

6. What is a key benefit of software-defined networking (SDN)?

    a. Static configuration of network devices

    b. Centralized control of network traffic using programmable controllers

    c. Improved hardware compatibility between routers

    d. Decentralized network management

7. What is the primary focus of endpoint security?

    a. Protecting individual devices like desktops, laptops, and mobile devices from cyber threats

    b. Monitoring traffic at the network perimeter

    c. Backing up data stored on the endpoint devices

    d. Encrypting data during transit across networks

Answers

1. b

2. b

3. a

4. b

5. b

6. b

7. a

Join our book's Discord space

Join the book's Discord Workspace for Latest updates, Offers, Tech happenings around the world, New Release and Sessions with the Authors:

https://discord.bpbonline.com

CHAPTER 7

Securing Networks, Hosts Systems, and Devices

Introduction

In an interconnected world where cyber threats evolve daily, securing hosts and devices is paramount to safeguarding networked systems. While network traffic monitoring and control are crucial, they alone cannot thwart sophisticated attacks targeting individual hosts. Cyber adversaries exploit vulnerabilities in hosts and devices, making a multi-layered security strategy essential. This chapter delves into the comprehensive measures needed to protect hosts from diverse threats and addresses the challenges posed by both software and hardware vulnerabilities. The key topics covered in this chapter include the role of trusted **operating systems (OS)** in establishing foundational security and the significance of bootloader security in preventing unauthorized modifications during system startup. The chapter explores the OS hardening process, which involves eliminating unnecessary features and applying stringent policies to fortify the operating environment. It also examines endpoint security software designed to detect and neutralize malware and intrusions.

Hardware vulnerabilities are scrutinized alongside software loopholes, highlighting their interplay in modern attacks. Application delivery methods and terminal services are discussed, emphasizing secure deployment and access mechanisms. The chapter investigates the **Trusted Platform Module (TPM)** and its contributions to hardware-level encryption and authentication. Additional focus is given to network security as an overarching framework supporting secure host operations. Finally, the text addresses application vulnerabilities, interoperability challenges, and integration issues, recognizing the complexities of maintaining a cohesive and secure system. By exploring these elements, this chapter equips readers with the knowledge to enhance host and device security in dynamic and hostile environments.

Structure

In this chapter, we will cover the following topics:

- Trusted OS
- Bootloader protection
- Endpoint security software
- Vulnerabilities associated with hardware
- Application whitelisting and blacklisting
- Trusted Platform Module

Objectives

Securing an enterprise does not stop at network traffic monitoring, since cyberattacks are initiated to exploit servers and user systems (hosts). This chapter presents the various controls for protecting and securing servers and user systems. This includes the use of trusted OS, bootloader security, OS hardening, and endpoint security vulnerabilities.

Trusted operating system

A trusted operating system is one that supports multilayer security and can demonstrate that it meets a certain set of government standards. Where the secure boot leaves off, the trusted boot takes over. Before installing the Windows 10 kernel, the bootloader checks its digital signature. The Windows 10 kernel, in turn, checks the boot drivers, startup files, and **Early Launch Anti-Malware (ELAM)** components of the Windows start-up process. The bootloader recognizes the error and refuses to load the faulty component if a file has been edited. Often, Windows can repair the faulty component automatically, restoring Windows' integrity and allowing the PC to start properly.

The **Trusted Computer System Evaluation Criteria (TCSEC)** was the first to propose the objective of classifying operating systems as trusted. The TCSEC was created by the **National Computer Security Center (NCSC)** to help the US **Department of Defense (DoD)** evaluate products. TCSEC published the **Rainbow Series** of publications, which focus on computer systems and the networks in which they function. TCSEC's **Orange Book** is a set of criteria based on the **Bell-LaPadula** model for grading or rating the level of security provided by a computer system product. Covert channel analysis, trusted facility management, and trusted recovery are among the subjects covered in **The Orange Book**.

TCSEC was superseded by the worldwide **Common Criteria (CC)** standard, which was developed through a collaborative effort. The CC rates systems using **Evaluation Assurance Levels (EALs),** with different EALs signifying varying levels of system security testing and design. The resultant score reflects the system's ability to offer security. It is assumed that the customer would configure all security solutions effectively. To allow the consumer to completely attain the rating, the vendors must supply adequate paperwork. The International Organization for Standardization's version of CC is ISO or IEC 15408-1:2009. CC offers seven assurance levels, ranging from EAL1 (lowest) to EAL7 (highest), which includes functionality testing as well as detailed testing and verification of the system design, as follows:

- **EAL1**: Functionally tested
- **EAL2**: Structurally tested
- **EAL3**: Methodically tested and checked
- **EAL4**: Methodically designed, tested, and reviewed
- **EAL5**: Semi-formally designed and tested
- **EAL6**: Semi-formally verified, designed, and tested
- **EAL7**: Formally verified, designed, and tested

Some examples of trusted OS and the EAL levels they provide are as follows:

- Mac OS X 10.6 (rated EAL 3+)
- HP-UX 11i v3 (rated EAL 4+)
- Some Linux distributions (rated up to EAL 4+)
- Microsoft Windows 7 (rated EAL 4+)

In any case where security is critical, such as in government agencies, while working as a contractor for the DoD, or when putting up a web server that will be linked to sensitive networks or hold sensitive data, trusted OS should be utilized. However, because these operating systems are often more difficult to understand and operate, there may be a learning curve while utilizing them. Three trustworthy operating systems are discussed in the *SELinux, SEAndroid, and TrustedSolaris* sections.

Security Enhanced Linux

Security-Enhanced Linux (SELinux) is a security module for the Linux kernel that isolates the enforcement of security choices from the security policy itself, reducing the amount of software required to implement security policies (*Figure 7.1*). SELinux additionally implements obligatory access control restrictions that limit access to files and network resources, also restricting user programs and system servers. It does not have the concept of a **root** superuser and does not have the well-known flaws in the typical Linux security methods. In high-security scenarios, where the sandboxing of the root account is beneficial, the SELinux system should be chosen over the regular versions of Linux. *Figure 7.1* illustrates the SELinux decision process:

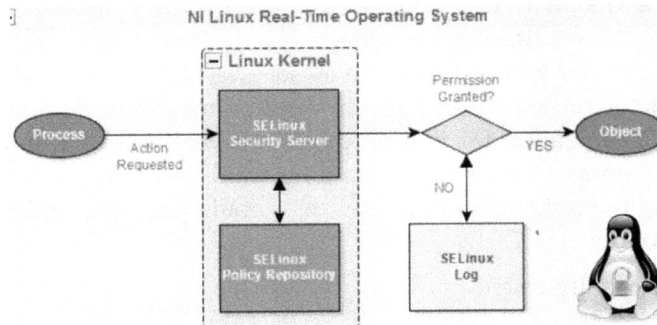

Figure 7.1: Security-enhanced Linux decision process

SEAndroid

SEAndroid is a version of SELinux for Android smartphones. Building on the permissive release of SEAndroid 4.3 and the partial enforcement of Android 4.4, the SEAndroid 5.0 release progressed to full SELinux enforcement. SEAndroid software operates with just the rights required to function successfully (helping to limit the harm that malware can cause), yet it can occasionally prohibit programs or functionalities that workers require. You will need a shell and root access to the Android devices to manage the default SEAndroid behavior. SSHDroid is a **Secure Shell (SSH)** program that lets you access Android devices from a computer. The **Android Debug Bridge (adb)** command, which is part of the Android **Software Development Kit (SDK)**, may be used to get root access, or you can root the device to gain complete access. This is because device vendors do not enable rooting, this method is not for everyone.

TrustedSolaris

TrustedSolaris is a set of security extensions incorporated in the Solaris 10 trusted OS. Solaris 10 5/09 is a common criterion certified at EAL4. Enhancements include the following:

- Accounting
- Role-based access control
- Auditing
- Device allocation
- Mandatory access control labeling

The TrustedSolaris environment allows the security administrator role to extend the list of trusted directories, as shown in *Figure 7.2:*

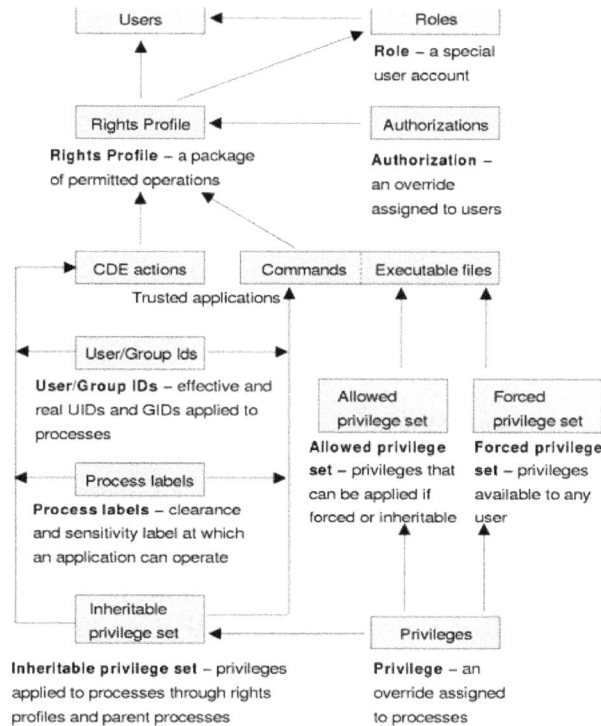

Figure 7.2: Trusted Solaris environment

The method is different in the TrustedSolaris 8 environment than in the previous releases.

Least functionality

The principle of least functionality calls for an organization to configure information systems to provide only essential capabilities, and specifically prohibits and restricts the use of other functions.

Endpoint security software

An endpoint is any device that connects to the corporate network from outside its firewall. Examples of endpoint devices include laptops, the **Internet of Things (IoT)**, **Point-of-Sale (POS)** systems, tablets, mobiles, switches, digital printers, and any devices that communicate with the central network. Endpoint security is accomplished by ensuring that every computing device on a network meets security standards. Endpoint security or endpoint protection is the process of protection from malicious threats in the different endpoints on a network through end-user devices, such as desktops, laptops, mobile devices, as well as network servers, in a data center considered endpoints, as illustrated in *Figure 7.3*:

Figure 7.3: End point security functionalities

Every device remotely connecting to the client devices is a possible entry point for security threats. Endpoint security is designed to defend each endpoint on the network created by these devices. Endpoint security tools help monitor, detect, and block malicious attacks. Endpoint security solutions streamline security measures with multi-layer protection at the point of entry for many attacks as well as the point of existence for sensitive data.

An endpoint security strategy is essential because every remote endpoint can be the entry point for an attack, and the number of endpoints is only increasing with the rapid pandemic-related shift to remote work. According to a *Gallup Poll*, a majority of US workers worked remotely in 2020, with 51% still working remotely as of April 2021.

The risks posed by endpoints and their sensitive data are a challenge that's not going away. The endpoint landscape is constantly changing, and businesses of all sizes are attractive targets for cyberattacks. This is common knowledge, even among small businesses. According to a study conducted by *Connectwise* in 2020, 77% of 700 SMB decision-makers surveyed worry they will be the target of an attack in the next six months. Last year, according to the FBI's Internet Crime Report, they received an increase of 300,000 complaints in 2019, with reported losses of over $4.2 billion. The *Verizon 2021 Data Breach Investigations Report* found **Servers are still dominating the asset landscape due to the prevalence of web apps and mail services involved in incidents. As social attacks continue to compromise people (they have now pulled past user devices), we begin to see the domination of phishing emails and websites delivering malware used for fraud or espionage.**

Each data breach costs, on average, $3.86 million globally, with the United States averaging at $8.65 million per data breach, according to *Ponemon's Cost of a Data Breach Report 2020* (Commissioned by IMB). The study identified the biggest financial impact of a breach, **lost business**, was making up almost 40% of the data breach average cost. Protecting against endpoint attacks is challenging because endpoints exist where humans and machines intersect. Businesses struggle to protect their systems without interfering with the legitimate activities of their employees. While technological solutions can be highly effective, the chances of an employee succumbing to a social engineering attack can be mitigated but never entirely prevented.

Endpoint protection working

The terms endpoint protection, **Endpoint Protection Platforms (EPP)**, and endpoint security are all used interchangeably to describe the centrally managed security solutions that organizations leverage to protect endpoints like servers, workstations, mobile devices, and workloads from cybersecurity threats. Endpoint protection solutions work by examining files, processes, and system activity for suspicious or malicious indicators. Endpoint protection solutions offer a centralized management console (*Figure 7.4*) from which administrators can connect to their enterprise network to monitor, protect, investigate, and respond to incidents. This is accomplished by leveraging either an on-premise, hybrid, or cloud approach.

The **traditional or legacy** approach is often used to describe an on-premise security posture that is reliant on a locally hosted data center from which security is delivered. The data center acts as the hub for the management console to reach out to the endpoints through an agent to provide security. The hub and spoke model can create security silos since administrators can typically only manage endpoints within their perimeter.

With the pandemic-driven work from home shift, many organizations have pivoted to laptops and **Bring Your Own Device (BYOD)** instead of desktop devices. This, along with the globalization of workforces, highlights the limitations of the on-premise approach. Some endpoint protection solution vendors have, in recent years, shifted to a hybrid approach, taking a legacy architecture design and retrofitting it for the cloud to gain some cloud capabilities. *Figure 7.4* illustrates the endpoint security dashboard:

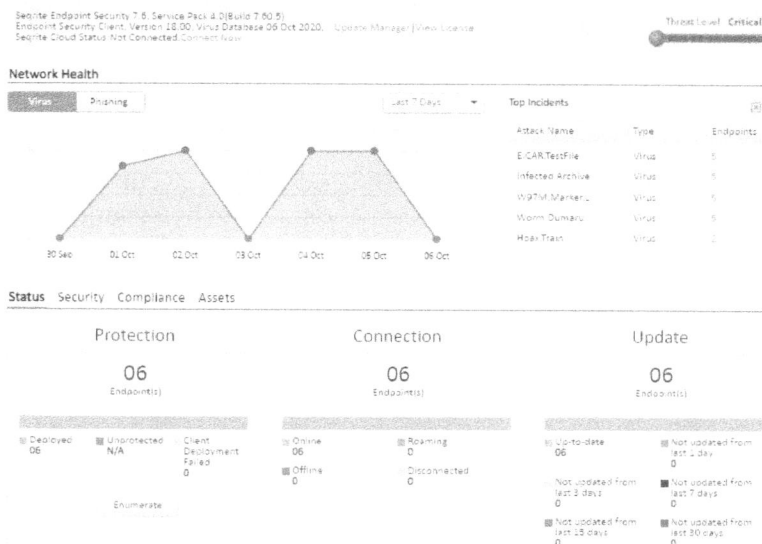

Figure 7.4: Endpoint security dashboard

The third approach is a built-in **cloud-native** solution for the cloud. Administrators can remotely monitor and manage endpoints through a centralized management console that lives in the cloud and connects to devices remotely through an agent on the endpoint. The agent can work with others or independently provide security for the endpoint, in case it does not have internet connectivity. These solutions leverage cloud controls and policies to maximize security performance beyond the traditional perimeter, removing silos and expanding administrator reach.

Endpoint protection versus antivirus software

Endpoint security software protects endpoints from being breached no matter if they are physical or virtual, on- or off-premises, in data centers, or in the cloud. It is installed on laptops, desktops, servers, virtual machines, as well as remote endpoints themselves.

Antivirus is often part of an endpoint security solution and is generally regarded as one of the more basic forms of endpoint protection. Instead of using advanced techniques and practices, such as threat hunting and **Endpoint Detection and Response (EDR)**, antivirus simply finds and removes known viruses and other types of malware. Traditional antivirus runs in the background, periodically scanning a device's content for patterns that match a database of virus signatures. Antivirus is installed on individual devices inside and outside the firewall.

Endpoint security tools that provide continuous breach prevention must integrate the following fundamental elements:

- **Prevention NGAV**: Traditional antivirus solutions detect less than half of all attacks. They function by comparing malicious signatures, or bits of code, to a database that is updated by contributors whenever a new malware signature is identified. The problem is that malware that has not yet been identified, or unknown malware, is not in the database. There is a gap between the time it takes for a piece of malware to be released into the world and the time it takes to become identifiable by traditional antivirus solutions. **Next-Generation Antivirus (NGAV)** closes that gap by using more advanced endpoint protection technologies, such as AI and machine learning, to identify new malware by examining more elements, such as file hashes, URLs, and IP addresses.

- **Detection EDR**: Prevention is not enough. No defenses are perfect, and some attacks will always make it through defenses and successfully penetrate the network. Conventional security cannot see when this happens, leaving attackers free to dwell in the environment for days, weeks, or months. Businesses need to stop these **silent failures** by finding and removing attackers quickly. To prevent silent failures, an EDR solution needs to provide continuous and comprehensive visibility into what is happening on endpoints in real-time. Businesses should look for solutions that offer advanced threat detection, investigation, and response capabilities, including incident data search and investigation, alert triage, suspicious activity validation, threat hunting, and malicious activity detection and containment.

- **Managed threat hunting**: Not all attacks can be detected by automation alone. The expertise of security professionals is essential to detect today's sophisticated attacks. Managed threat hunting is conducted by elite teams that learn from incidents that have already occurred, aggregate crowdsourced data, and provide guidance on how best to respond when malicious activity is detected.

- **Threat intelligence integration**: To stay ahead of attackers, businesses need to understand threats as they evolve. Sophisticated adversaries and **advanced persistent threats (APTs)** can move quickly and stealthily, and security teams need up-to-date and accurate intelligence to ensure defenses are automatically and precisely tuned. A threat intelligence integration solution should incorporate automation to investigate all incidents and gain knowledge in minutes, not hours. It should generate custom **indicators of compromises (IoCs)** directly from the endpoints to enable a proactive defense against future attacks. There should be a human element as well, comprised of expert security researchers, threat analysts, cultural experts, and linguists, who can make sense of emerging threats in a variety of contexts.

Endpoint detection response

EDR is a proactive endpoint security approach designed to supplement existing defenses. This advanced endpoint approach shifts security from a reactive threat approach to one that can detect and prevent threats before they reach the organization. It focuses on three essential elements for effective threat prevention: automation, adaptability, and continuous monitoring. Some examples of EDR products are as follows:

- FireEye endpoint security
- Carbon black Cb response
- Guidance EnCase endpoint security
- Cybereason enterprise protection
- Symantec endpoint protection
- **Rivest-Shamir-Adleman (RSA)** NetWitness endpoint

The advantage of EDR systems is that they provide continuous monitoring. The disadvantage is that the software's use of resources could impact the performance of the device.

Patch management

Software patches are updates released by vendors that either fix functional issues or close security loopholes in operating systems, applications, and versions of firmware that run on network devices. To ensure that all devices have the latest patches installed, a formal system should be deployed to ensure that all systems receive the latest updates after thorough testing in a non-production environment. It is impossible for the vendor to anticipate every possible impact that a change may have on business-critical systems in the network. It is the responsibility of the enterprise to ensure that patches do not adversely impact operations. *Figure 7.5* illustrates patch management:

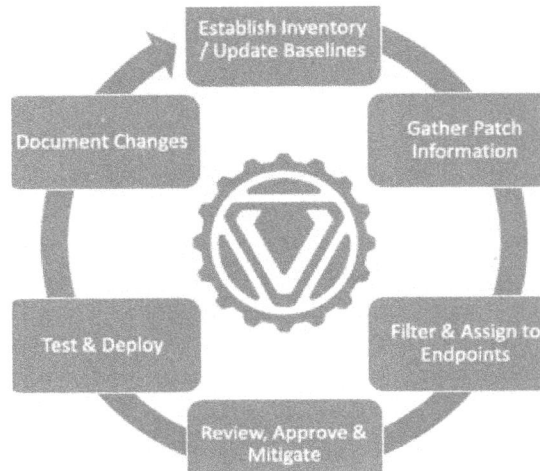

Figure 7.5: Patch management

Vendors generally make several types of patches available, which are as follows:

- **Hot fixes**: A hot fix is an update that solves a security issue and should be applied immediately if the issue it resolves is relevant to the system.

- **Updates**: An update solves a functionality issue rather than a security issue.

- **Service packs**: A service pack includes all updates and hot fixes since the release of the operating system.

Manual patch management

While manual patch management requires more administrative effort than an automated system (discussed in the following section), it can be done, using the following steps:

1. Determine the priority of the patches.

2. Test the patches prior to deployment to ensure that they work properly and do not cause system or security issues.

3. Install the patches in the live environment.

4. After patches are deployed, ensure that they work properly.

Automated patch management

Most organizations manage patches through a centralized update solution such as **Windows Server Update Services (WSUS)**. With such services, organizations can deploy updates in a controlled yet automatic fashion. WSUS server downloads the updates, which are applied locally from the WSUS server. Group policy is also used in this scenario to configure the location of the server holding the updates. Scripts can also be used to automate the patch process. This may offer more flexibility and control of the process than using automated tools. A deeper knowledge of scripting might be required, however. In some cases, geographically dispersed servers may be used to provide the patches referenced in the scripts. In that case, proper replication must be set up to ensure that all patches are available on all patch servers. Windows PowerShell commands are increasingly being used to automate Windows functions. In the Linux environment, Linux shell scripting is used for this. *Figure 7.6* illustrates the automated patch management process:

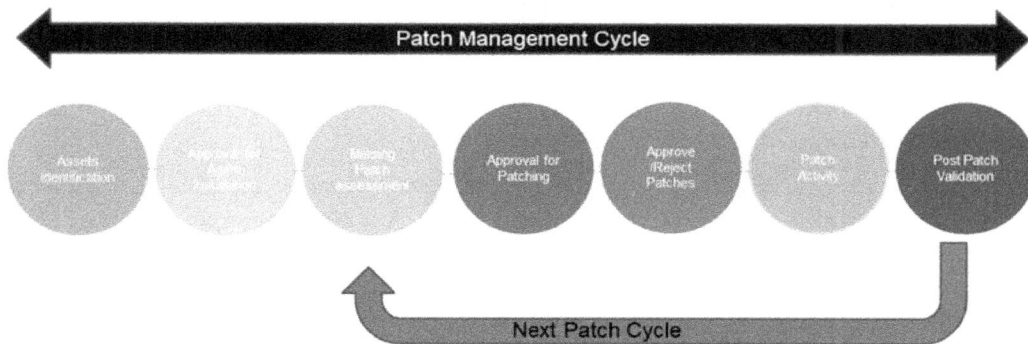

Figure 7.6: Automated patch management process

Data loss prevention

Data leakage occurs when sensitive data is disclosed to unauthorized personnel either intentionally or inadvertently. **Data loss prevention (DLP)** is a collection of technologies and tools that monitor and protect business data from unauthorized access. When DLP technology is implemented, it protects data in three places, in use by authorized personnel, in motion (being transferred via the intranet), or at rest (on a file server or in a database). For example, DLP software can stop users from copying data to move it outside a company's network. At the center of all DLP software is content inspection, which is the software looking at pieces of data as they move on a network, evaluating the type of file that contains them, and determining whether the data is where it should be and whether it is being used for its intended purposes. Accidental exposure or nefarious activity can put sensitive data in jeopardy, which is why DLP security is important to organizations that need to protect their data assets. *Figure 7.7* illustrates the benefits of implementing DLP in an organization:

Figure 7.7: DLP benefits

Working of data loss prevention

DLP software is based on content inspection, which uses a series of methods to catch policy violations, as follows:

- First, content inspection is based on rule-based expressions that are detected by DLP software and lead to subsequent actions. A typical example is that of 16-digit credit card numbers. Organizations can create rules that state if you try to email a credit card number (that starts with a 4, 5, or 6), especially with the 3-digit security code and expiration date, the DLP software will block the email from sending or automating encryption.

- Next, there is exact file matching. This identifies files in use, in motion, or at rest whose content matches exactly that of an indexed file. This is also called **data fingerprinting**.

- Third is the content analysis within DLP solutions that uses conceptual or lexicon analysis. This level of analysis uses a compilation of dictionaries or other lists and rules to identify unwanted behavior, such as specific internet searches, or sharing trade secrets with those outside the network.

- Finally, content analysis can incorporate sophisticated statistical analysis techniques. Statistical methods use machine learning to protect specific pieces of information. When the machine learns what the data should look like, it constantly looks for anomalous data that doesn't match the given pattern.

When looking at how to prevent data loss, technology is often the last line of defense. Its role is to apply the organization's data security policies consistently over all egress points, identify possible violations, and take the appropriate remedial actions. Traditional DLP solutions are inflexible in the way they operate, making them difficult to configure and implement. Typically, the solutions **stop and block** any action deemed to have risk implications, often incorrectly mistaking legitimate daily actions as an exfiltration or data loss threat. This generates large numbers of **false positives** that can easily overwhelm the IT security staff who need to action the alerts and frustrate users who cannot work productively.

Log monitoring

Computers, their operating systems, and the firewalls that may be present on them generate system information that is stored in log files. You should monitor network events, system events, application events, and user events. Keep in mind that any auditing activity will impact the performance of the system being monitored. Organizations must find a balance between auditing important events and activities and ensuring that device performance is maintained at an acceptable level. *Figure 7.8* illustrates the log management dashboard:

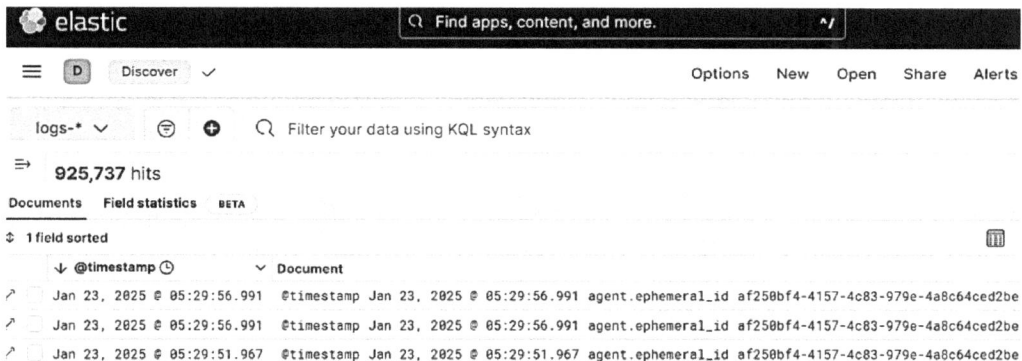

Figure 7.8: Log management dashboard

When designing an auditing mechanism, security professionals should remember the following guidelines:

- Develop an audit log management plan that includes mechanisms to control the log size, backup processes, and periodic review plans.

- Ensure that the ability to delete an audit log is a two-person control that must be completed by administrators.

- Monitor all high-privilege accounts (including all root users and administrative-level accounts).

- Ensure that the audit trail includes who processed a transaction, when the transaction occurred (date and time), where the transaction occurred (which system), and whether the transaction was successful.

- Ensure that deleting the log and deleting data within the logs cannot occur.

Audit trails detect computer penetrations and reveal actions that identify misuse. As a security professional, you should use audit trails to review patterns of access to individual objects. To identify abnormal patterns of behavior, you should first identify normal patterns of behavior. Also, you should establish the clipping level, which is a baseline of user errors above which violations will be recorded. For example, your organization may choose to ignore the first invalid login attempt, knowing that initial invalid login attempts are often due to user error. Any invalid login after the first one, however, would be recorded because it could be a sign of an attack. Audit trails deter attackers' attempts to bypass the protection mechanisms that are configured on a system or device. As a security professional, you should specifically configure the audit trails to track system or device rights or privileges being granted to a user and data additions, deletions, or modifications. You can use group policy in a Windows environment to create and apply audit policies to computers.

Finally, audit trails must be monitored, and automatic notifications should be configured. If no one monitors the audit trail, the data recorded in the audit trail is useless. Certain actions should be configured to trigger automatic notifications. For example, you may want to configure an email alert to occur after a certain number of invalid login attempts because invalid login attempts may be a sign that a password attack is occurring.

Host hardening

Another of the ongoing goals of operations security is to ensure that all systems have been hardened to the extent that is possible while still providing functionality. The hardening can be accomplished both on a physical and logical basis. From a logical perspective, the following should be implemented:

- Unnecessary applications should be removed.
- Unnecessary services should be disabled.
- Unrequired ports should be blocked.
- External storage devices and media should be tightly controlled if allowed at all.
- Unnecessary accounts should be disabled.
- Default accounts should be renamed, if possible.
- Default passwords for default accounts should be changed.

Standard environment or configuration baselining

One practice that can make maintaining security simpler is to create and deploy standard images that have been secured with security baselines. A security baseline is a set of configuration settings that provide a floor of minimum security in the image being deployed. Security baselines can be controlled through the use of group policy in Windows. These policy settings can be made in the image and applied to both users and computers. These settings are refreshed periodically through a connection to a domain controller and cannot be altered by the user. It is also quite common for the deployment image to include all of the most current operating system updates and patches as well. When a network makes use of these types of technologies, the administrators have created a standard operating environment. The advantages of such an environment are more consistent behavior of the network and simpler support issues. Scans should be performed on the systems weekly to detect changes to the baseline. Virtual machine images can also be used for this purpose.

Application whitelisting and blacklisting

Application whitelists are lists of allowed applications (with all others excluded), and blacklists are lists of prohibited applications (with all others allowed). It is important to control the types of applications that users can install on their computers. Some application types can create support issues, and others can introduce malware. It is possible to use Windows group policy to restrict the installation of software on network computers. Using Windows group policy is only one option, and each organization should select a technology to control application installation and usage in the network.

Security or group policy implementation

One of the most widely used methods of enforcing a standard operating environment is using group policy in Windows. In an active directory environment, any users and computers that are members of a domain can be provided a collection of settings that comprise a security baseline. (It is also possible to use local security policy settings on non-domain members, but this requires more administrative effort.) Group policy leverages the hierarchical structure of an active directory to provide a common group of settings, called **Group Policy Objects (GPOs)**, to all systems in the domain while adding or subtracting specific settings to certain subgroups of users or computers, called containers. An additional benefit of using group policy is that an administrator can make changes to the existing policies by using the **Group Policy Management Console (GPMC)**. Affected users and computers will download and implement any changes when they refresh the policy, which occurs at startup, shutdown, logon, and logoff. It is also possible for the administrator to force a refresh when time is of the essence. The following are some of the advantages provided by the granular control available in the GPMC:

- Ability to allow or disallow the inheritance of a policy from one container in an active directory to one of its child containers.

- Ability to filter out specific users or computers from a policy's effect.

- Ability to delegate administration of any part of the active directory namespace to an administrator.

- Ability to use **Windows Management Instrumentation** (WMI) filters to exempt computers of a certain hardware type from a policy.

The following are some of the notable policies that relate to security:

- **Account policies**: These policies include password policies, account lockout policies, and Kerberos authentication policies.

- **Local policies**: These policies include audit, security, and user rights policies that affect the local computer.

- **Event log**: This policy controls the behavior of the event log.

- **Restricted groups**: This is used to control the membership of sensitive groups.

- **Systems services**: This is used to control the access to and behavior of system services.

- **Registry**: This is used to control access to the registry.

- **File system**: This includes security for files and folders and controls security auditing of files and folders.

- **Public key policies**: This is used to control the behavior of a **Public Key Infrastructure (PKI)**.

- **Internet Protocol Security policies on active directory**: This is used to create IPsec policies for servers.

Command shell restrictions

While Windows is known for its **graphical user interface (GUI)**, it is possible to perform anything that can be done in the GUI at the command line. Moreover, many administrative tasks can be done only at the command line, and some of those tasks can be harmful and destructive to the system when their impact is not well understood. Administrators of other operating systems, such as Linux or UNIX, make even more use of a command line in day-to-day operations. Administrators of routers and switches make almost exclusive use of a command-line when managing those devices.

With the risk of mistakes, coupled with the possibility of those with malicious intent playing havoc at the command line, it is advisable in some cases to implement command shell restrictions. A restricted command shell is a command-line interface where only certain commands are available. In Linux and UNIX, a number of command-line shells are available, and they differ in terms of the power of the commands they allow.

In Cisco IOS, the commands that are available depend on the mode in which the command-line interface ID is operating. You start out in user mode, where very few things can be done (and none of them are very significant), and then progress to privileged mode, where more commands are available. However, you can place a password on the device, which the user will be prompted to do when moving from user mode to privileged mode. For more granular control of administrative access, user accounts can be created on the device, and privilege levels can be assigned to control what technicians can do, based on their accounts.

Configuring dedicated interfaces

Not all interfaces are created equal. Some, especially those connected to infrastructure devices and servers, need to be more tightly controlled and monitored due to the information assets to which they lead. Some of the ways sensitive interfaces and devices can be monitored and controlled are presented in the following section.

Out-of-band management

An interface that is **out-of-band (OOB)** is connected to a separate and isolated network that is not accessible from the local area network or the outside world. These interfaces are also typically live even when the device is off. OOB interfaces can be ethernet or serial. Guidelines to follow when configuring OOB interfaces include the following:

1. Place all OOB interfaces in a separate subnet from the data network.

2. Create a separate **Virtual LAN (VLAN)** on the switches for this subnet.

3. When crossing **Wide Area Network (WAN)** connections, use a separate internet connection for the production network.

4. Use **Quality of Service (QoS)** to ensure that the management traffic does not affect production performance.

5. To help get more returns for the investment in additional technology, consider using the same management network for backups.

6. If the **Network Interface Cards (NICs)** support it, use Wake on LAN to make systems available even when they are shut down.

Some newer computers that have the Intel vPro chipset and a version of **Intel Active Management Technology (Intel AMT)** can be managed OOB even when the system is off. When this functionality is coupled with the OOB management feature in System Center 2016 R2 Configuration Manager, you can perform the following tasks:

- Power on one or many computers (for example, for maintenance on computers outside business hours).

- Power off one or many computers (for example, if the operating system stops responding).

- Restart a nonfunctioning computer or boot from a locally connected device or known good boot image file.

- Re-image a computer by booting from a boot image file that is located on the network or by using a **Preboot Execution Environment (PXE)** server.

- Reconfigure the **Basic Input Output System (BIOS)** settings on a selected computer (and bypass the BIOS password if this is supported by the BIOS manufacturer).

- Boot to a command-based operating system to run commands, repair tools, or diagnostic applications (for example, upgrading the firmware or running a disk repair tool).

- Configure scheduled software deployments to wake up computers before the computers are running.

Management interfaces

These are used for accessing devices remotely. Typically, a management interface is disconnected from the in-band network and is connected to the device's internal network. Through a management interface, you can access the device over the network by using utilities such as SSH and Telnet. **Simple Network Management Protocol (SNMP)** can use a management interface to gather statistics from a device. In some cases, the interface is an actual physical port labeled as a management port; in other cases, it is a port that is logically separated from the network (for example, in a private VLAN). The point is to keep these interfaces used for remotely managing the device separate from the regular network traffic the device may encounter.

There are no disadvantages to using a management interface, but it is important to secure management interfaces. Cisco devices have dedicated terminal lines for remote management, called **Virtual Teletype (VTY)** ports. A VTY port should be configured with a password. To secure the 16 VTY lines on some Cisco switches, use the following command set to set the password to Cisco:

```
Switch001>enable
Switch001#configure terminal
Switch001(config)#line vty 0 15
Switch001(config-line)#password Ci$c0
Switch001(config-line)#login
```

Data interface

Data interfaces are used to pass regular data traffic and are not used for either local or remote management. The interfaces may operate at either layer two or layer three, depending on the type of device (router or switch). These interfaces can also have **Access Control Lists (ALC)** defined at either layer. On routers, we call them access lists, and on switches, we call them concept port security. Some networking devices, such as routers and switches, can also have logical or software interfaces. An example is a loopback interface. This is an interface on a Cisco device that can be given an IP address, and it will function the same as a hardware interface. Why would you use such an interface? Well, unlike hardware interfaces, loopback interfaces never go down. This means that as long as any of the hardware interfaces are functioning on the device, you will be able to reach the loopback interface. This makes a loopback interface a good candidate for making the VTY connection, which can be targeted at any IP address on the device.

Creating a loopback interface is simple. The commands are as follows:

```
Switch001>enable
Switch001#configure terminal
Switch001(config)#interface Loopback0
Switch001(config-if)#ip address 192.168.15.15 255.255.255.0
```

Bluetooth

Bluetooth is a wireless technology that is used to create **personal area networks (PANs)**, which are short-range connections between devices and peripherals, such as headphones. It operates in the 2.4 GHz frequency at speeds of 1 to 3 Mbps and over a distance of up to 10 meters. Several attacks can take advantage of Bluetooth technology. With Bluejacking, an unsolicited message is sent to a Bluetooth-enabled device, often for the purpose of adding a business card to the victim's contact list. This type of attack can be prevented by placing the device in non-discoverable mode.

Bluesnarfing involves unauthorized access to a device using a Bluetooth connection. In this case, the attacker is trying to access information on the device rather than sending messages to the device. The use of Bluetooth can be controlled, and such control should be considered in high-security environments. Increasingly, organizations are being pushed to allow corporate network access to personal mobile devices. This creates a nightmare for security administrators. **Mobile device management (MDM)** solutions attempt to secure these devices. These solutions include a server component, which sends management commands to the devices. There are a number of open specifications, such as **Open Mobile Alliance (OMA)** device management, but there is no real standard as yet. Among the technologies, these solutions may control the Bluetooth settings and wireless settings.

File and disk encryption

While largely the same in concept, file and disk encryption are different from one another. Disk encryption occurs at the hardware level. File encryption, on the other hand, is a software process. Another difference is that disk encryption is effective when the device is off, while file encryption provides security while the device is on. The following sections look at both types.

Trusted Platform Module

While it can be helpful to control network access to devices, in many cases, devices such as laptops, tablets, and smartphones leave your network and also leave behind all the measures you have taken to protect the network. There is also a risk of these devices being stolen or lost. For these situations, the best measure to take is full disk encryption. The best implementation of full-disk encryption requires and makes use of a TPM chip. A TPM chip is a security chip installed on a computer's motherboard that is responsible for protecting symmetric and asymmetric keys, hashes, and digital certificates. This chip provides services to protect passwords and encrypt drives and digital rights, making it much harder for attackers to gain access to the computers that have TPM chips enabled.

Two particularly popular uses of TPM are binding and sealing. Binding actually **binds** the hard drive through encryption to a particular computer. Because the decryption key is stored in the TPM chip, the hard drive's contents are available only when the drive is connected to the original computer. Keep in mind that all the contents are at risk if the TPM chip fails and a backup of the key does not exist. Sealing, on the other hand, **seals** the system state to a particular hardware and software configuration. This prevents attackers from making any changes to the system. However, it can also make installing a new piece of hardware or a new operating system much harder. The system can only boot after the TPM chip verifies system integrity by comparing the original computed hash value of the system's configuration to the hash value of its configuration at boot time. TPM chip consists of both static memory and versatile memory that is used to retain important information when the computer is turned off, as follows:

- **Endorsement Key (EK)**: The EK is persistent memory installed by the manufacturer that contains a public or private key pair.

- **Storage Root Key (SRK)**: The SRK is persistent memory that secures the keys stored in the TPM.

- **Attestation Identity Key (AIK)**: The AIK is versatile memory that ensures the integrity of the EK.

- **Platform Configuration Register (PCR) hash**: A PCR hash is a versatile memory that stores data hashes for the sealing function.

- **Storage keys**: A storage key is a versatile memory that contains the keys used to encrypt the computer's storage, including hard drives, USB flash drives, and so on.

BitLocker and BitLocker to Go by Microsoft are well-known full disk encryption products. The former is used to encrypt hard drives, including operating system drives, and the latter is used to encrypt information on portable devices such as USB devices. However, there are other options. Additional whole disk encryption products include the following:

- PGP whole disk encryption

- Secure star DriveCrypt

- Sophos SafeGuard

- MobileArmor data armor

Virtual Trusted Platform Module

A **Virtual TPM (VTPM)** chip is a software object that performs the functions of a TPM chip. It is a system that enables trusted computing for an unlimited number of virtual machines on a single hardware platform. VTPM makes secure storage and cryptographic functions available to operating systems and applications running in virtual machines.

Firmware updates

The firmware includes any type of instruction stored in non-volatile memory devices such as **Read-Only Memory (ROM)**, **Electrically Erasable Programmable Read-Only Memory (EPROM)**, or flash memory. BIOS and **Unified Extensible Firmware Interface (UEFI)** code are the most common examples of firmware. Computer BIOS does not go bad, however, it can become out of date or contain bugs. In the case of a bug, an upgrade will correct the problem. An upgrade may also be indicated when the BIOS does not support some component that you would like to install, such as a larger hard drive or a different type of processor. Today's BIOS is typically written to an EEPROM chip and can be updated through the use of the software. Each manufacturer has its own method for accomplishing this. Check out the manufacturer's documentation for complete details. Regardless of the exact procedure used, the update process is referred to as flashing the BIOS. This means that the old instructions are erased from the EEPROM chip, and the new instructions are written to the chip. Firmware can be updated by using an update utility from the motherboard vendor. In many cases, the steps are as follows:

1. Download the update file to a flash drive.
2. Insert the flash drive and reboot the machine.
3. Use the specified key sequence to enter the UEFI or BIOS setup.
4. If necessary, disable secure boot.
5. Save the changes and reboot again.
6. Re-enter the **Complementary Metal-Oxide-Semiconductor (CMOS)** settings again.
7. Choose the boot options and boot from the flash drive.
8. Follow specific update directions to locate the upgrade file on the flash drive.
9. Execute the file (usually by typing flash).
10. While the update is completed, ensure that you maintain power to the device.

Bootloader protections

When a system is booting up, there is a window of opportunity for breaking into the system. For example, when physical access is possible, you could set a system to boot to other boot media and then access the hard drive. For this reason, bootloader protection mechanisms should be utilized, as discussed in the following sections.

Secure boot

Secure boot is a term that applies to several technologies that follow the secure boot standard. Its implementations include Windows secure boot, measured launch, and **integrity measurement architecture (IMA)**, step for which are mentioned below:

1. The firmware verifies all UEFI executable files and OS loader to be sure they are trusted.

2. Windows boot components verifies the signature on each component to be loaded. Any non-trusted components will not be loaded and will trigger remediation.

3. The signatures on all boot-critical drivers are checked as part of secure boot verification in **Windows Boot Loader** (**Winload**) and by the ELAM driver.

The disadvantage is that systems that ship with UEFI secure boot enabled, do not allow the installation of any other operating system. This prevents installing any other operating systems or running any live Linux media.

Measured launch

A measured launch is a launch in which the software and platform components have been identified, or **measured**, using cryptographic techniques. The resulting values are used at each boot to verify trust in those components. A measured launch is designed to prevent attacks on these components (system and BIOS code) or at least to identify when these components have been compromised. It is part of the **Intel Trusted Execution Technology (Intel TXT)**. TXT functionality is leveraged by software vendors, including HyTrust, PrivateCore, Citrix, and VMware.

An application of measured launch is Measured Boot by Microsoft in Windows 10 and Windows Server 2016. It creates a detailed log of all components that are loaded before the anti-malware. This log can be used to both identify malware on the computer and maintain evidence of boot component tampering. One possible disadvantage of measured launch is the potential slowing of the boot process.

Integrity measurement architecture

Another approach that attempts to create and measure the runtime environment is an open-source trusted computing component called IMA. IMA creates a list of components and anchors the list to the TPM chip. It can use the list to attest to the system's runtime integrity. Anchoring the list to the TPM chip in hardware prevents its compromise.

BIOS or UEFI

UEFI is an alternative to using BIOS to interface between software and firmware of a system. Most images that support UEFI also support legacy BIOS services. Some of its advantages are as follows:

- Ability to boot from large disks (over 2 TB) with a GUID partition table
- CPU-independent architecture
- CPU-independent drivers
- Flexible pre-OS environment, including network capability
- Modular design

Attestation services

Attestation services allow an authorized party to detect changes to an operating system. These services involve generating a certificate for the hardware that states what software is currently running. The computer can use this certificate to attest that unaltered software is currently executing. Windows operating systems have been capable of remote attestation since Windows 8.

Vulnerabilities associated with hardware

While security professionals devote a lot of time to chasing software vulnerabilities, they often forget about hardware vulnerabilities. Remember that one of the most well-known hacks, like the **Target hack,** took advantage of a hardware encryption flaw. Another example of a hardware vulnerability is the hacking of a car system and the subsequent takeover of the control system using **Radio Frequency Identification (RFID)**. Hackers use hardware attacks because of the difficulty in detecting them, but the compromising of hardware goes beyond backdoors. Vulnerabilities also include the following:

- Backdoors that affect embedded RFID chips and memory
- Eavesdropping through protected memory without any other hardware being opened
- Faults induced to interrupt normal behavior
- Hardware modification tampering with hardware or jailbroken software
- Backdoors or hidden methods for bypassing normal computer authentication systems
- Counterfeit products made to gain malicious access to systems

The only assured way of preventing such vulnerabilities is to tightly control the manufacturing process for all products. DoD uses the Trusted Foundry Program to validate all vendors in this regard. No longer can organizations simply purchase the cheapest devices from Asia, they must now begin to grapple with the creation of their own programs that emulate the Trusted Foundry Program.

Conclusion

This chapter defines the concepts of trusted OS and ways of improving system security. This includes antivirus, antimalware, antispyware and spam filters, patch management, and DLP, along with endpoint monitoring and response. Concepts for host hardening, boot loader protection, and hardware vulnerabilities are also discussed. This chapter also includes security recommendations and measures when using terminal and application delivery services.

In the next chapter, we will discuss challenges and measures for implementing secure storage controls.

Exercise

1. **What is a primary feature of a Trusted Operating System (Trusted OS)?**
   a. Enhanced graphical user interface
   b. Built-in antivirus software
   c. Enforced access control policies
   d. Support for multiple users

2. **Which method is commonly used to secure a bootloader against unauthorized modifications?**
   a. Encrypting the bootloader code
   b. Verifying digital signatures of boot components
   c. Disabling BIOS updates
   d. Replacing the bootloader with third-party software

3. **What is the primary function of endpoint security software?**
   a. Manage network bandwidth usage
   b. Detect and mitigate threats on individual devices
   c. Facilitate faster application updates]
   d. Monitor cloud infrastructure performance

4. **Which of the following is a common hardware vulnerability?**
   a. SQL Injection
   b. Spectre and Meltdown attacks
   c. Cross-Site Scripting (XSS)
   d. Man-in-the-middle attacks

5. **What is the primary difference between application whitelisting and blacklisting?**

    a. Whitelisting blocks all applications by default, while blacklisting blocks specific applications.

    b. Blacklisting blocks all applications by default, while whitelisting allows specific applications.

    c. Whitelisting only works for cloud applications, while blacklisting works for local applications.

    d. Blacklisting is more secure than whitelisting in all cases.

6. **What is the primary function of a Trusted Platform Module (TPM)?**

    a. Enhance graphical processing speed

    b. Store cryptographic keys securely

    c. Optimize memory usage during runtime

    d. Improve network bandwidth

Answers

1. c
2. b
3. b
4. b
5. a
6. b

Join our book's Discord space

Join the book's Discord Workspace for Latest updates, Offers, Tech happenings around the world, New Release and Sessions with the Authors:

https://discord.bpbonline.com

CHAPTER 8
Secure Storage Controls

Introduction

Many organizations face challenges in implementing robust data security measures that go beyond regulatory compliance. Security professionals must protect applications, computing, and network environments, while audit professionals verify these efforts. Storage security often gets overlooked due to limited familiarity with the technology, leaving storage managers and administrators grappling with these issues for the first time. This chapter discusses key business drivers for data security, outlines threats and attacks, and emphasizes the importance of storage security in safeguarding information. Organizations heavily rely on digital information processed electronically and transmitted over local and public networks. Many critical tasks are entirely dependent on **information and communications technology (ICT)**, making ICT failures potentially catastrophic for enterprises and society. Among ICT components, storage systems are pivotal, serving as repositories and the last line of defense against adversaries. However, this requires storage managers to implement and activate appropriate security controls. Despite the growing value of data as a critical asset for organizations and individuals, global or national standards to classify data sensitivity and value remain absent. Data categories include personal information (for example, PII), business information, and national security data (classified or unclassified). Strengthening storage security is essential to address these gaps and protect digital assets effectively.

Structure

In this chapter, we will cover the following topics:

- Data classification
- Business drivers
- Information assurance
- Security implications or privacy concerns
- Cloud storage
- Data security considerations
- Security and privacy consideration of storage

Objectives

Most organizations implement network security controls and perform audits, as security assessments. If every component of the organization is not included, the assessment is incomplete and leaves the organization exposed. This chapter presents a defense-in-depth strategy that needs to be implemented, which should include physical, virtual, cloud, on-premise, and user devices connecting to the office network. This chapter presents the assessment tools for performing security assessments at all levels.

Data classification

Data classification is a scheme by which the organization assigns a level of sensitivity to each piece of information that it owns and maintains. Although the existence of and adherence to a formal data classification scheme is one of the foundational elements of an information security program, many organizations, even those that profess a strong commitment to protecting the company and customer information, fail to implement data classification. Common reasons include waiting for a scheme that is perfect in theory (but not practical), cost, and lack of organizational will to drive a data classification program through to full implementation. Properly valuing data and categorizing based on sensitivity helps avoid both under and over-protection. Overprotection increases costs without accompanying value, while under protection increases the likelihood of loss or compromise, which can impact both overall profitability as well as competitiveness, protecting the following types of data:

- One that is worthy of protection
- One that is proportional to its value
- One that is only useful for its lifetime

As an example, consider the following data security classification scheme:

- **Public**: Minimally sensitive data that is useful to corporate affiliates and the general public on a need-to-know basis; the protection of data is at the discretion of the custodian (per corporate policy). Examples include building maps and business contact data in a directory.

- **Sensitive**: Moderately sensitive data that is useful to corporate employees and non-employees with a business need to know; the protection of data is covered by corporate policy and contracts. Examples include information in non-disclosure agreements, research details, and most financial transactions.

- **Restricted**: Highly sensitive data that is available for approval only by individuals with designated access rights and signed non-disclosure agreements; the protection of data is covered by the law. Examples include medical records, non-public research data, most PII, and contracts.

It is important to use only a few data security classifications in order to keep the classification process manageable. Also, an organization can ease into its security classification activity by starting with the **most sensitive** and **highest value**. Finally, a good data classification scheme should include a time element, to allow a piece of information to change its status on a certain date (for example, when data becomes public).

Business drivers

Organizations that proactively address their data protection and data security needs can realize tangible benefits in the form of increased customer trust, reduced losses due to fraud and theft, and competitive advantage, while competitors are distracted with their own reactive security initiatives. Unfortunately, data security is not viewed as a business enabling capability by most organizations. Instead, it is viewed similarly to insurance, that is, something an organization must have in order to preserve its viability. Consequently, the business drivers for data security tend to be defensive and reactive in nature. The following business drivers are associated with data security:

- **Theft prevention**: Threats of insider larceny, industrial espionage, and organized crime exploitation are on the rise. Perpetrators are often faced with poor defenses, potentially high rewards, and light penalties if caught. Increasingly, perpetrators target specific victims, as noted by the 2008 CSI or FBI report1. Data security may provide enough of a deterrent that it prevents the crime altogether or makes it less rewarding.

- **Prevention of unauthorized disclosure**: Increasingly, data protection and privacy regulations are holding firms accountable for safeguarding their data. The unauthorized (whether intentional or accidental) disclosure of regulated data (customer records, trade secrets, business information) has resulted in serious embarrassment, significant inconveniences, and harsh penalties for organizations that do not exercise appropriate due diligence and care. This trend is expected to continue with increasingly severe penalties and expand the scope of the types of data that are explicitly regulated.

- **Prevention of data tampering**: Whether for purposes of theft, blackmail, deception, or malicious destruction, unauthorized modifications to data can lead to substantial financial losses and criminal prosecution under laws such as the **Sarbanes-Oxley Act (SOX)** if it involves financial information. An equally insidious possibility occurs in the form of a successful attack with inconclusive evidence of tampering (data may or may not have been modified) that erodes confidence in the integrity of the data.

- **Prevention of accidental corruption or destruction**: Increased complexity within ICT, flat or declining budgets, expanding workloads, limited expertise, and inadequate training combine to increase the likelihood of human error. Something as simple as adding a switch to a live storage network could result in a complete network outage or corruption of data in-flight if the appropriate precautions have not been taken. Mistakes within storage ecosystems can have catastrophic impacts because this is where data resides.

- **Accountability**: Corporate officers are being held to higher standards of accountability. For example, the SOX in the U.S. makes these executives explicitly responsible for establishing, evaluating, and monitoring the effectiveness of internal controls over financial reporting. ICT lies at the foundation of an effective system of internal controls over the data used in financial reporting. These controls should include separation of duties and enforcement of least privilege policies.

- **Authenticity**: As more and more digital records are created, modified, processed, archived, and ultimately destroyed, there is a need to demonstrate the authenticity of some of this data at each stage in its lifecycle. To establish the authenticity of data, additional information metadata such as cryptographic hashes and secure timestamps, as well as data provenance information like transaction/change logs and conversion records, must be maintained.

- **Verifiable transactions**: While identification, authentication, and authorization are usually considered to be technologies primarily directed at controlling who can do what to which data, they can also play a role in tracing responsibility for transactions that change sensitive data values. To fulfill this role, technologies, and procedures must be strengthened to assure adequate traceability and non-repudiation of transactions. The associated records should meet the standards required for acceptance as evidence in legal proceedings.

- **Business continuity**: For many organizations, the availability of business-critical data, along with the applications and services they support, is of paramount importance. Thus, substantial resources have been dedicated to ensuring the continuity of business operations in the face of limited disruption events (system failures, hacker attacks, denial of service attacks, and operator errors) and **smoking**

crater events. Storage technology already figures heavily in these solutions and is expected to play an even more dominant role in the future.

- **Regulatory and legal compliance**: At a basic level, compliance is the state of being in accordance with specified requirements, and for many organizations, compliance is the top business driver for data and ICT infrastructure security investments. However, regulatory and legal requirements rarely include enough specificity to determine whether the data handling and ICT infrastructure operations and outcomes are compliant without some degree of interpretation and **reading between the lines**. For example, new requirements for the retention of electronic records have been mandated in both statutory and regulatory law during the last decade. The preservation of legal, medical, and enterprise data in digital form, previously a concern in sound administration of the business, has become a legal necessity that confronts the networked storage industry with both challenges and rich opportunities.

Information assurance

Information assurance defines and applies a collection of policies, standards, methodologies, services, and mechanisms to maintain mission integrity with respect to people, processes, technology, information, and supporting infrastructure (*Figure 8.1*). Information assurance includes the following core principles:

- **Confidentiality**: Ensures the disclosure of information only to those persons with authority to see it.

- **Integrity**: Ensures that information remains in its original form; the information remains true to the creator's intent.

- **Availability**: Information or information resource is ready for use within the stated operational parameters.

- **Possession**: Information or information resource remains in the custody of authorized personnel.

- **Authenticity**: Information or information resources conform to reality; it is not misrepresented as something it is not.

- **Utility**: Information is fit for a purpose and in a usable state.

- **Privacy**: Ensures the protection of personal information from observation or intrusion as well as adherence to relevant privacy compliances.

- **Authorized use**: Ensures cost-incurring services are available only to authorized personnel.

- **Nonrepudiation**: Ensures the originator of a message or transaction may not later deny action.

Figure 8.1 illustrates information assurance:

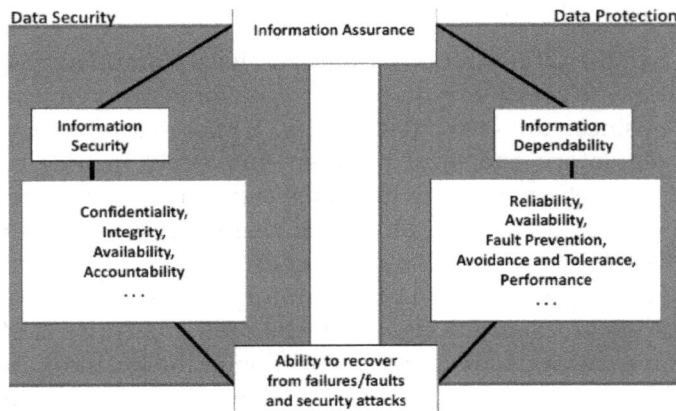

Figure 8.1: *Information assurance*

When some form of data protection or data security is required, a range of security services can be brought to bear. The **National Security Agency's (NSA) Information Assurance Technical Framework (IATF)** identifies the following as the primary security service areas:

- **Access control**: Assuring that networked resources and data are usable only by authorized entities and that data is protected from unauthorized disclosure or modification. It also includes resource control, for example, preventing logon to local workstation equipment or limiting the use of remote access. Access control mechanisms are fundamental measures that may be used by other security services (for example, confidentiality, integrity, availability, and limiting the use of network resources all depend on limiting the ability of an unauthorized entity to access an item or service). The key elements of access control include the following:

  - **Identification**: A process or measure used to recognize an entity (a user, a process, or a role associated with multiple users).

  - **Authentication**: A process or measure for determining whether something or someone is who or what it is declared to be, with some level of assurance (an authenticated identity).

  - **Authorization**: A process or measure for determining the access rights of an entity, also with some level of assurance.

  - **Enforcement**: A process or measure for actual enforcement of the access control decision; this is what actually provides protection against attacks. The concept of enforcing an access control decision is separate from the decision itself.

  - **Confidentiality**: Assuring that data (both at rest and in-flight) is available only to authorized entities. Confidentiality services will prevent disclosure of data while in storage, transiting a local network, or flowing over the public

Internet. The provision of the confidentiality security service depends on several variables to determine the protection needs, such as location(s) of the data, type of data, amounts or parts of user data, and value of data. The key elements of confidentiality include the following:

- **Data protection**: A process or measure that invokes mechanisms that act directly on the data (or act in response to characteristics of the data) rather than responding to an entity's attempt to access data. The most common method for providing confidentiality by data protection is to encrypt the appropriate data.

- **Data separation**: Data separation traditionally refers to the concept of providing for separate paths (for example, Red or Black7) or process separation (computer security techniques). Data separation mechanisms provide confidentiality by preventing data from reaching a location or destination where it could be disclosed to unauthorized entities (for example, servers containing sensitive HR information are inaccessible from the public internet). The primary variable in the level of assurance provided by a data separation mechanism is the level of trust associated with the process or machine implementing the mechanism.

- **Traffic flow protection**: Important information can be observed or inferred from traffic characteristics such as frequency, quantity, and destination of communications. Measures that add superfluous (usually random) data and hide network layer addresses can obfuscate this kind of information.

- **Integrity**: Guarding against improper modification or destruction of information as well as assuring non-repudiation and authenticity. It includes prevention of unauthorized modification of data (both stored and communicated), detection and notification of unauthorized modification of data, and logging of all changes to data. Integrity can be applied to a single data unit (protocol data unit, database element, file, etc.) or to a stream of data units (for example, all protocol data units exchanged in a connection).

- **Availability**: Assuring timely and reliable access to and use of data and information services for authorized users. A loss of availability is the disruption of access or use of information or an information system. It includes protection from attacks, unauthorized use, and resilience to routine failures.

- **Nonrepudiation**: Repudiation is denial by one of the entities involved in a transaction that it participated in that transaction. The nonrepudiation security service provides the ability to prove to a third party that the entity did indeed participate in the transaction.

The manner in which these services are implemented is also important. Conventional wisdom within the security community suggests the use of a defense in depth strategy, in which an organization uses multiple security techniques to help mitigate the risk accruing from compromise or circumvention of one component of the defense being compromised or circumvented. Different security products from multiple vendors are sometimes deployed to defend different potential attack vectors, helping prevent a shortfall in any one defense, leading to a wider failure.

The secure administration of storage systems has the following benefits:

- Centrally manages, records, and audits admin actions for storage of **command line interface (CLI)** and **graphical user interface (GUI)** sessions with real-time monitoring.

- Ensures that the storage administrator has no control over the audit logging to prevent tampering.

- Eliminates the need to share privileged administrative credentials (like the root user password on Linux) that are required for some **software-defined storage (SDS)** products.

- Provides time-bound privilege storage admin sessions and remote termination of storage admin sessions.

- Supports multi-factor authentication for the users accessing storage admin sessions.

- Can capture keystrokes, process activity, and programs that are running (useful in some SDS offerings).

- Manages and audits privileged storage accounts and authentication secrets, such as passwords and **Secure Shell (SSH)** keys.

Secure remote support is managed by the customer, and it has the following benefits:

- Provides time-bound audited access to the service, maintenance, or support teams.

- Supports a custom approval workflow (multi-level approval) for each access session.

- Records and audits all activity that is performed in support or service sessions.

Use case examples

This chapter demonstrates the integration of the IBM spectrum scale with the verify privilege vault. The concept can be extended and applied to other IBM storage systems. IBM® Security™ verify privilege vault on-premises (verify privilege vault), formerly known as IBM Security™ secret server, is the next-generation privileged account management that integrates with IBM storage to ensure that access to IBM storage administration sessions is secure and monitored in real-time with required recording for audit and compliance. Privilege access to storage administration sessions is centrally managed, and each session can be time-bound with remote monitoring.

IBM spectrum scale

IBM spectrum scale is a scalable, high-performance file system that is suitable for various use cases (*Figure 8.2*). It provides world-class storage management with scalability, flash-accelerated performance, and automatic storage tier capabilities. IBM spectrum scale reduces storage costs while improving security and management efficiency in the cloud, big data, and analytics environments. In a nutshell, IBM spectrum scale provides the following benefits:

- Virtually limitless scaling to nine quintillion files and yottabytes of data.

- High performance and simultaneous access to a common set of shared data.

- Integrated **Information Lifecycle Management (ILM)** functions to automatically move data between storage tiers, including flash, disk, tape, and object storage (public and private cloud). ILM can reduce operational costs because fewer administrators can manage larger storage infrastructures.

With SDS, you can build your infrastructure solution with the following characteristics:

- Easy to scale with relatively inexpensive commodity hardware while maintaining world-class storage management capabilities.

- Deployable on **Amazon Web Services** (**AWS**) and IBM Cloud. A cross-platform solution that is available on IBM AIX®, Linux, and Windows server nodes, or a mix of all three. IBM spectrum scale is also available for IBM Z.

- Available as the prepackaged storage solution that is named IBM **Elastic Storage System (ESS)** with de-clustered RAID included.

- Global data access across geographic distances and unreliable **wide area network (WAN)** connections.

- Multi-site support to connect a local IBM spectrum scale cluster to remote clusters, which provides greater administrative flexibility and control.

- Proven reliability across multiple sites, and support for concurrent hardware and software upgrades.

- State-of-the-art protocol access methods for managing files and objects under the same global namespace, which make more efficient use of storage space and avoid data islands. The supported protocols include **Network File System (NFS)**, **Server Message Block (SMB)**, **Portable Operating System Interface (POSIX)**, OpenStack Swift, and S3.

- Seamless integration for Hadoop applications through the **Hadoop Distributed File System (HDFS)** transparency feature.

- Proven security features to ensure data privacy, authenticity, and auditability.

- File-level encryption for data at rest and secure erase.

- Policy-driven compression to reduce the size of data at rest and increase storage efficiency.

- Can be used as persistent storage for containers.

- Includes a GUI to simplify storage administration tasks and monitor many aspects of the system.

Figure 8.2 illustrates the IBM spectrum scale:

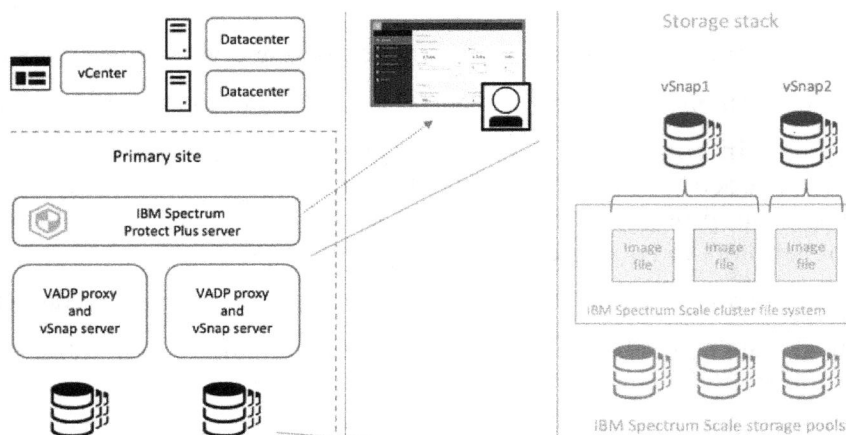

Figure 8.2: *IBM spectrum scale*

IBM spectrum scale is often used in high-performance and computationally demanding environments across different areas, such as banking, financial, healthcare, oil and gas, and automotive industries. It is most common use cases are in AI and deep learning, big data analytics, content repository, private cloud, and compute clusters. It is also commonly used for data optimization and resiliency for archives, high-speed backup, and disaster recovery, and ILM.

IBM spectrum scale supports various deployment models, and one of them is IBM ESS, which is a modern hardware-based implementation. IBM ESS is available as IBM ESS 3000 (high-density storage) and IBM ESS 5000 (high-capacity and high-performance storage).

Verify privilege vault

IBM security verify privilege provides on-premises and cloud offerings. Verify privilege vault (*Figure 8.3*) is a cloud-based solution, for which organizations do not need to worry about any hardware or software requirements. However, IBM security verification privilege on-premises requires a dedicated server for installation and an SQL database to store details. Based on the requirements, features, and architecture, your organization can decide which offering to select. In this chapter, we refer to verifying privilege vault on-premises, although the information in this paper can be extended to the cloud offering with relevant and required changes. **Privileged Access Management (PAM)** is the route to an organization's most valuable information. As a result, implementing PAM has become a top priority. Verify privilege vault is a full-featured PAM solution that is available both on-premises and in the cloud, and it is ready to empower your security and IT ops team to secure and manage all types of privileged accounts quickly and easily. With verify privilege vault, you can do the following:

- Establish a secure vault.

- Discover privileges.

- Protect passwords.

- Meet compliance requirements.

- Control sessions.

Verify privilege vault is fast to deploy, easy to use, and scalable for the enterprise. It integrates with the larger IBM security portfolio for key use cases, such as identity governance and multi-factor authentication. *Figure 8.3* illustrates the IBM privilege vault:

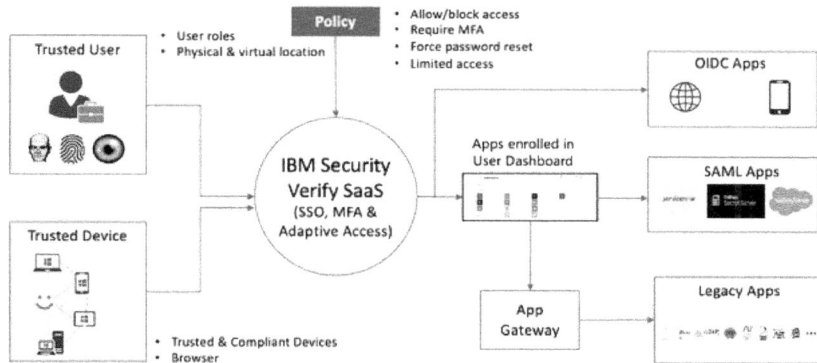

Figure 8.3: *IBM privilege vault*

The following list describes the architecture that is shown in the preceding figure:

- The left side of the architecture represents different mediums through which verify privilege vault can be accessed. The right side represents the high-level internal working.

- Verify privilege vault requires an SQL server for its configuration and data management. You can configure the setup for high availability as needed.

- Verify privilege vault provides session launchers that are tailored to start specific applications based on triggers in a secret template. For example, for the Windows platform, the remote desktop connection application is invoked when trying to access a Windows account secret. Similarly, for the UNIX or Linux platforms, the PuTTY application is triggered when using a UNIX or Linux account secret.

- A distributed engine is used for remote password changing and the discovery of new accounts.

Security implications or privacy concerns

One of the biggest obstacles presented by BYOD or COPE initiatives is the security issues that are inherent with mobile devices. Many of these vulnerabilities revolve around storage devices. Let us look at a few. Unauthorized access to sensitive data can occur if devices are lost, stolen, or accessed by unauthorized users due to insufficient security controls. Malware or malicious applications can exploit vulnerabilities in mobile operating systems, potentially compromising stored data or enabling unauthorized access. Data leakage risks increase when personal and corporate data coexist on the same device, especially without clear segregation or encryption policies.

Data storage

While protecting data on a mobile device is always a good idea, in many cases, an organization must comply with an external standard regarding the minimum protection provided to the data on the storage device. For example, the **Payment Card Industry Data Security Standard (PCI DSS)** enumerates requirements that payment card industry players should meet to secure and monitor their networks, protect cardholder data, manage vulnerabilities, implement strong access controls, and maintain security policies. The different storage types share certain issues and present issues unique to each type.

Non-removable storage

The storage that is built into a device may not suffer all the vulnerabilities shared by other forms, but it is still data at risk. One tool at our disposal with this form of storage that is not available to others is the ability to remotely wipe the data if the device is stolen. At any rate, the data should be encrypted with AES-128 or AES-256 encryption. Also, a backup copy of the data should be stored in a secure location.

Removable storage

While removable storage may be desirable in that it may not be stolen if the device is stolen, it still can be lost and stolen itself. Removable storage of any type represents one of the primary ways data exfiltration occurs. If removable storage is in use, the data should be encrypted with AES-128 or AES-256 encryption.

Cloud storage

While cloud storage may seem like a great idea, it presents many unique issues. Among them are the following:

- **Data breaches**: Cloud providers may include safeguards in **service level agreements (SLAs)**, but ultimately the organization is responsible for protecting its own data, regardless of where it is located. When this data is not in your hands, and you may not even know where it is physically located at any point in time, protecting your data is difficult.

- **Authentication system failures**: These failures allow malicious individuals into the cloud. This issue is sometimes made worse by the organization itself when developers embed credentials and cryptographic keys in source code and leave them in public-facing repositories.

- **Weak interfaces and APIs**: Interfaces and **application programming interfaces (APIs)** tend to be the most exposed parts of a system because they are usually accessible from the open internet.

Transfer or backup data to uncontrolled storage

In some cases, users store sensitive data in cloud storage that is outside the control of the organization, using sites such as Dropbox. These storage providers have had their share of data loss issues as well. Policies should address and forbid this type of storage of data from mobile devices.

Improper storage of sensitive data

Sensitive information in this discussion includes usernames, passwords, encryption keys, and paths that applications need to function, but that which would cause harm if discovered. Determining the proper method of securing this information is critical and not easy. It is a generally accepted rule not to hard-code passwords, although this was not always considered a best practice. Instead, passwords should be protected using encryption when they are included in the application code. This makes them difficult to change, reverse, or discover. Storing this type of sensitive information in a configuration file also presents problems. Such files are usually discoverable, and even if hidden, they can be discovered by using a demo version of the software if it is a standard or default location. Whatever the method used, significant thought should be given to protecting these sensitive forms of data. To prevent disclosure of sensitive information from storage, the following measures can be implemented:

- Ensure that memory locations where this data is stored are locked memory.

- Ensure that ACLs attached to sensitive data are properly configured.

- Implement an appropriate level of encryption.

Data recovery and storage

In most organizations, data is one of the most critical assets when recovering from a disaster. However, an operations team must determine which data is backed up, how often the data is backed up, and the method of backup used. An organization must also determine how data is stored, including data in use and data that is backed up. While data owners are responsible for determining data access rules, data life cycle, and data usage, they must also ensure that data is backed up and stored in alternate locations to ensure that it can be restored.

Let us look at an example. Suppose that an organization's security administrator has received a subpoena for the release of all the emails received and sent by the company's **Chief Executive Officer (CEO)** for the past three years. If the security administrator is only able to find one year's worth of email records on the server, they should check the organization's backup logs and archives before responding to the request. Failure to produce all the requested data could possibly have legal implications. The security administrator should restore the CEO's email from an email server backup and provide whatever is available up to the last three years from the subpoena date. Keep in mind, however, that the organization should provide all the data that it has regarding the CEO's emails. If the security administrator is able to recover the past five years' worth of the CEO's email, the security administrator should notify the appropriate authorities and give them access to all five years' data.

As a rule of thumb, in a subpoena situation, you should always provide all the available data, regardless of whether it exceeds the requested amount or any internal data retention policies. For example, if users are not to exceed 500 MB of storage, but you find that a user has more than 3 GB of data, you should provide all that data in response to any legal requests. Otherwise, you and the organization could be held responsible for withholding evidence.

Data ownership

The main responsibility of a data, or the information owner, is to determine the classification level of the information she owns and protect the data for which she is responsible. This role approves or denies access rights to the data. However, the data owner usually does not handle the implementation of the data access controls. The data owner role is usually filled by an individual who understands the data best through membership in a particular business unit. Each business unit should have a data owner. For example, a human resources department employee better understands the human resources data than does an accounting department employee. The data custodian implements the information classification and controls after they are determined by the data owner. Whereas the data owner is usually an individual who understands the data, the data custodian does not need any knowledge of the data beyond its classification levels. Although a human resources manager should be the data owner for the human resources data, an IT department member could act as the data custodian for the data. This would ensure the separation of duties. The data owner makes the decisions on access, while the data custodian configures the access permissions established by the data owner. During a specific incident response and recovery process action, the response team should first speak to the data owner, the person ultimately responsible for the data.

Data handling

The appropriate policies must be in place for data handling. When data is stored on servers and is actively being used, data access is usually controlled by using **access control lists (ACLs)** and implementing group policies and other data security measures, such as **data loss prevention (DLP)**. However, once data is archived to backup media, data handling policies are just as critical. Enterprise data archiving is usually managed using a media library. All media should be properly labeled to ensure that those responsible for recovery can determine the contents of the media. Enterprises should accurately maintain media library logs to keep track of the history of the media. This is important because all media types have a maximum number of times they can safely be used. A media librarian should keep a log that tracks all media (backup and other types, such as operating system installation discs).

During media disposal, you must ensure that no data remains on the media. The most reliable, secure means of removing data from magnetic storage media, such as a magnetic tape cassette, is through degaussing, which involves exposing the media to a powerful, alternating magnetic field. It removes any previously written data, leaving the media in a magnetically randomized (blank) state. Some other disposal terms and concepts with which you should be familiar are as follows:

- **Data purging**: This involves using a method such as degaussing to make the old data unavailable even with forensics. Purging renders information unrecoverable against laboratory attacks (forensics).

- **Data clearing**: This involves rendering information unrecoverable by a keyboard.

- **Remanence**: This term refers to any data left after the media has been erased. This is also referred to as data remnants or remnant magnetization.

Data security considerations

The security of the data processed by any new system is perhaps one of the most important considerations during an integration. Data security must be considered during every stage of the data life cycle. This section discusses issues surrounding data security during integration.

Data remnants

Data remnants are data that is left behind on a computer or another resource when that resource is no longer used. If resources, especially hard drives, are reused frequently, an unauthorized user can access data remnants. The best way to protect this data is to employ some sort of data encryption. If data is encrypted, it cannot be recovered without the original encryption key. Administrators must understand the kind of data that is stored on physical drives so they can determine whether data remnants should be a concern.

If the data stored on a drive is not private or confidential, the organization may not be concerned about data remnants. However, if the data stored on the drive is private or confidential, the organization may want to implement asset reuse and disposal policies. Whenever data is erased or removed from storage media, residual data can be left behind. The data may be able to be reconstructed when the organization disposes of the media, resulting in unauthorized individuals or groups gaining access to it. Security professionals must consider media such as magnetic hard disk drives, solid-state drives, magnetic tapes, and optical media, such as CDs and DVDs. When considering data remanence, security professionals must understand the following three countermeasures:

- **Clearing**: This includes removing data from the media so that it cannot be reconstructed using normal file recovery techniques and tools. With this method, the data can be recoverable only using special forensic techniques.

- **Purging**: Also referred to as sanitization, purging makes the data unreadable even with advanced forensic techniques. When this technique is used, data should be unrecoverable.

- **Destruction**: Destruction involves destroying the media on which the data resides. Overwriting is a destruction technique that writes data patterns over the entire media, thereby eliminating any trace data.

  o Degaussing, another destruction technique, involves exposing the media to a powerful, alternating magnetic field to remove any previously written data and leave the media in a magnetically randomized (blank) state. Encryption scrambles the data on the media, thereby rendering it unreadable without the encryption key.

  o Physical destruction involves physically breaking the media apart or chemically altering it. For magnetic media, physical destruction can also involve exposure to high temperatures. The majority of these countermeasures work for magnetic media. However, solid-state drives present unique challenges because they cannot be overwritten. Most solid-state drive vendors provide sanitization commands that can be used to erase the data on the drive. Security professionals should research these commands to ensure that they are effective. Another option for these drives is to erase the cryptographic key.

Often a combination of these methods must be used to fully ensure that the data is removed.

Data remanence is also a consideration when using any cloud-based solution for an organization. Security professionals should be involved in negotiating any contract with a cloud-based provider to ensure that the contract covers data remanence issues, although it is difficult to determine that the data is properly removed. Using data encryption is a great way to ensure that data remanence is not a concern when dealing with the cloud.

Data aggregation

Data aggregation allows data from multiple resources to be queried and compiled together into a summary report. The account used to access the data needs to have appropriate permissions on all of the domains and servers involved. In most cases, these types of deployments incorporate a centralized data warehousing and mining solution on a dedicated server. Security threats to databases usually revolve around unwanted access to data. Two security threats that exist in managing databases are the processes of aggregation and inference. Aggregation is the act of combining information from various sources. This can become a security issue with databases when a user does not have access to a given set of data objects but does have access to them individually or at least has access to some of them and is able to piece together the information to which he or she should not have access. The process of piecing together the information is called inference. Two types of access measures can be put in place to help prevent access to inferable information, which are as follows:

- **Content-dependent access control**: With this type of measure, access is based on the sensitivity of the data. For example, a department manager might have access to the salaries of the employees in his or her department but not to the salaries of employees in other departments. The cost of this measure is increased processing overhead.

- **Context-dependent access control**: With this type of measure, access is based on multiple factors to help prevent inference. Access control can be a function of factors such as location, time of day, and previous access history.

Data isolation

Data isolation in databases prevents data from being corrupted by two concurrent operations. Data isolation is used in cloud computing to ensure that tenant data in a multitenant solution is isolated from other tenants' data, using tenant IDs in the data labels. Trusted login services are usually used as well. In both of these deployments, data isolation should be monitored to ensure that data is not corrupted. In most cases, some sort of transaction rollback should be employed to ensure that proper recovery can be made.

Data ownership

While most of the data an organization possesses may be created in-house, some of it is not. In many cases, organizations acquire data from others who generate such data as their business. These entities may retain ownership of the data and only license its use. When integrated systems make use of such data, consideration must be given to any obligations surrounding this acquired data. **Service-level agreements (SLAs)** that specify particular types of treatment or protection of the data should be followed. The main responsibility of a data or information owner is to determine the classification level of the information she owns and to protect the data for which she is responsible. This role approves or denies access rights to the data. However, the data owner usually does not handle the implementation of the data access controls.

The data owner's role is usually filled by an individual who understands the data best through membership in a particular business unit. Each business unit should have a data owner. For example, a human resources department employee better understands the human resources data than an accounting department employee.

The data custodian implements the information classification and controls after they are determined by the data owner. Whereas the data owner is usually an individual who understands the data, the data custodian does not need any knowledge of the data beyond its classification levels. Although a human resources manager should be the data owner for the human resources data, an IT department member could act as the data custodian for the data.

Data sovereignty

Information that has been converted and stored in binary digital form is subject to the laws of the country in which it is located. This concept is called **data sovereignty**. When an organization operates globally, data sovereignty must be considered. It can affect security issues such as the selection of controls and ultimately could lead to a decision to locate all data centrally in the home country. No organization operates within a bubble. All organizations are affected by laws, regulations, and compliance requirements. Organizations must ensure that they comply with all contracts, laws, industry standards, and regulations. Security professionals must understand the laws and regulations of the country or countries they are working in and the industry within which they operate. In many cases, laws and regulations are written in a manner whereby specific actions must be taken. However, in some cases, laws and regulations leave it up to the organization to determine how to comply.

The United States and the European Union both have established laws and regulations that affect organizations that do business within their area of governance. While security professionals should strive to understand laws and regulations, security professionals may not have the level of knowledge and background to fully interpret these laws and regulations to protect their organization. In these cases, security professionals should work with legal representation regarding legislative or regulatory compliance.

Data volume

Organizations should strive to minimize the amount of data they hold. More data means a larger attack surface. Data retention policies should be created that prescribe the destruction of data when it is no longer of use to the organization. Keep in mind that the creation of such policies should be driven by legal and regulatory requirements for the retention of data that might be relevant to the industry in which the enterprise operates.

Security and privacy considerations of storage

When integrating storage solutions into an enterprise, security practitioners should be involved in the design and deployment to ensure that security issues are considered. The following are some of the security considerations for storage:

- Limit physical access to the storage solution.
- Create a private network to manage the storage solution.
- Implement ACLs for all data, paths, subnets, and networks.
- Implement ACLs at the port level, if possible.
- Implement multi-factor authentication.

Security practitioners should ensure that an organization adopts appropriate security policies for storage solutions to ensure that storage administrators prioritize the security of the storage solutions.

Conclusion

When integrating storage systems and solutions into an enterprise's infrastructure, security practitioners are constantly involved in the design and deployment to ensure any storage security risks and issues are considered and mitigated. Storage security engineers need to ensure organizations adopt appropriate security policies for secure cloud, and on-premise storage, and the stakeholders prioritize the security of storage solutions. This chapter presents the concepts for encrypted and clear text communications and data flow security.

In the next chapter, we will discuss the new-age disruptive technology and devices, commonly termed as **Internet of Things**.

Exercise

1. **Which of the following is NOT a typical data classification category?**
   a. Public
   b. Confidential
   c. Immutable
   d. Restricted

2. **Which of the following is a common business driver for implementing cybersecurity measures?**

   a. Regulatory compliance

   b. Profit maximization without investment

   c. Ignoring security breaches

   d. Reducing IT costs at any expense

3. **What is the primary goal of information assurance?**

   a. To enforce strict network policies

   b. To ensure the availability, integrity, and confidentiality of information

   c. To protect physical assets only

   d. To provide free access to all data

4. **What is a significant privacy concern related to data collection by online platforms?**

   a. Limited storage capacity

   b. Unauthorized surveillance and misuse of personal data

   c. High cost of data processing

   d. Poor user interface

5. **Which of the following is a key advantage of cloud storage?**

   a. Unlimited security without additional cost

   b. Accessibility from anywhere with an internet connection

   c. Zero risk of data breaches

   d. No dependency on service providers

6. **Which of the following is a critical consideration for ensuring data security?**

   a. Reducing encryption to save costs

   b. Storing all data without backup

   c. Implementing access controls and encryption

   d. Sharing sensitive information openly

7. **What is an important privacy consideration for selecting a storage solution?**

   a. Low subscription costs

   b. Availability of a large number of features

   c. Compliance with data protection regulations such as GDPR

   d. Ability to share data without authentication

Answers

1. c
2. a
3. b
4. b
5. b
6. c
7. c

Join our book's Discord space

Join the book's Discord Workspace for Latest updates, Offers, Tech happenings around the world, New Release and Sessions with the Authors:

https://discord.bpbonline.com

CHAPTER 9
Securing the Internet of Things

Introduction

The **Internet of Things (IoT)** is a broad phrase that refers to any device that collects data from the world around us and then sends it over the Internet to be intelligently analyzed and used to give information and services (*Figure 9.1*). This concept was expanded to include an industrial closed-loop control system in which data is collected, combined with related data, sent to an intelligent station, processed, and acted upon to change the environment. The IoT is an ideal domain for not only securing devices, but also for innovations in secure system design, secure building block technologies, and secure hardware and software development practices, all of which combine to make the IoT into secure IoT. *Figure 9.1* illustrates the IoT:

Structure

In this chapter, we will cover the following topics:

- Internet of Things device lifecycle
- Trusted execution environment
- Software security
- Containers

- Secure device onboarding
- Security objectives and requirements

Objectives

Disruptive new-age devices and their related technologies have changed the way work is done and have created new options to use technologies in offices, homes, healthcare, manufacturing, agriculture, and other domains. While such technologies are revolutionary, they are not always secure. In the rush to have disruptive technology in the markets, security is not always the primary focus. Organizations and users adopting such cutting-edge **things on the internet** often walk on the bleeding edge of technology.

Internet of Things device lifecycle

The security of IoT devices is challenging since security is present at every stage of the device's lifespan, as illustrated in *Figure 9.1*. The security SDK or API is crucial for simplifying the device development during the build process. Provisioning and configuring the IoT device would need technologies that could scale across multiple CPU families and include giving a persona to the device. For easy deployment and potential anonymity, the deployment phase should be flexible. The security requirements and specifications for the connectivity should be followed.

Figure 9.1: Internet of Things

Confidentiality (encryption or decryption) and integrity (sign or verify) properties are used to illustrate a typical flow (for a sensing application).

To provide secure services for devices, confidentiality establishes a secure connection with the Gateway or cloud (could be one-time or periodic, depending upon the policy enforcement). This interacts with smart and dumb sensors and actuators, collects data, and regulates and drives the sensors and actuators and performs local analytics and, if desired, encrypts the data. This encrypts or signs (or both) the data and transmits it to Gateway, depending on the policy.

For Gateway security, confidentiality encrypts and authenticates the data before doing some local analytics. This includes encrypting or signing the data before sending it to the fog or cloud.

For securing the cloud, data is decrypted or authenticated by the fog or cloud instance, and cloud applications do analytics. Data is encrypted or signed and stored in databases by cloud applications.

Device identity, protected boot, protected storage, trusted execution environment, and containers are the five buckets of capabilities that security essentials focus on. *Figure 9.2* illustrates the IoT device lifecycle:

Figure 9.2: IoT device lifecycle

Device identity

A platform's hardware identity is an immutable, unique identifier. The platform and the persona must be inextricably linked. A hardware root of trust, also known as a hardware embedded cryptographic key, can be a useful device identifier. As part of the **Trusted Platform Module (TPM)** specification, the **Trusted Computing Group (TCG)** specifies hardware-roots-of-trust. For storage, all TPM manufacturers must implement a hardware root of trust. Intel® **Platform Trust Technology (PTT)** integrates a security engine into several of its **Security Operations Center (SOC)** devices to achieve TPM capabilities. A distributed group of IoT nodes may be trusted by using an IoT system that imposes a common and confirmed safe boot policy. The establishment of a secure IoT network necessitates distributed trust.

Protected boot

This functionality protects against sophisticated Bootkits and rootkits that have been shown to sit in very early boot code and are capable of launching a range of assaults on the system. These attacks take place without the awareness of the **operating system** (**OS**), making them immune to detection by anti-malware software. TCG establishes a

Root-of-Trust-for-Measurement (RTM) requirement for secure platform boot, requiring the platform to offer a secure platform reset and first boot executive that is implemented in hardware. TCG did not go into detail about a specific implementation. The hardware-based root of trust for the system boot process is Intel Boot Guard. It enforces the **original equipment manufacturer (OEM)** boot regulations architecturally and protects the initial measurement and verification of the first OEM component. OEM boot policy is stored in the OEM-programmed **field programable fuse (FPF)** file.

Protected storage

Protected storage is a basic security capability that is necessary to support a variety of additional security features. The TPM supports safe storage primitives for cryptographic keys, configuration registers, and whitelist values, among other security objects. Protected storage has the following characteristics:

- **Data confidentiality**: Unauthorized entities cannot read the data.

- **Data integrity**: Unauthorized entities cannot modify the data, or unauthorized data modification can be detected.

- **Anti-replay protection**: Unauthorized entities cannot replay or reuse stale data for storage.

PTT is an implementation of the TCG, TPM specification in an SoC that depends on hardware separation of flash and other memory to restrict access outside of the TCG specified interfaces. Intel® **QuickAssist Technology (QAT)** is a hardware data encryption accelerator with built-in key storage security. Bulk data encryptions, which enable cypher texts to be stored on regular storage media but encryption keys to be kept in hardware, are a frequent way to construct safe storage for data that surpasses the capacity of hardened secure storage resources.

Hardware security

Platform attacks have historically progressed from application-level **software (SW)** through user-mode SW, kernel-mode SW, **firmware (FW)**, and now **hardware (HW)**. From 2003 to 2021, the incidence of HW and FW level vulnerabilities rose significantly, reinforcing the necessity for HW-based security to harden the platform. The technologies involved in securing an IoT device anchored to a **hardware root of trust (HW RoT)** and eventually booting into a **trusted execution environment (TEE)** are described in this chapter. In an IoT setting, there are four main areas of concern for security, that are the device, user identification, data, and security at runtime.

Trusted execution environment

TEE is a separate execution environment from the general-purpose execution environment (*Figure 9.3*). A security coprocessor, for example, is an isolated environment, whereas the core CPU is a general-purpose execution environment. HW, SW, or FW that creates an isolated environment may be included in TEEs. The TEE can have strong guarantees for the safe and reliable execution of TEE workloads by carefully regulating the infrastructure that creates the HW, FW, or SW that implements it. A TEE is often used for workloads that need the usage of cryptographic keys to secure the confidentiality and integrity of data as it is translated to and from the ciphertext.

Figure 9.3 illustrates the TEE:

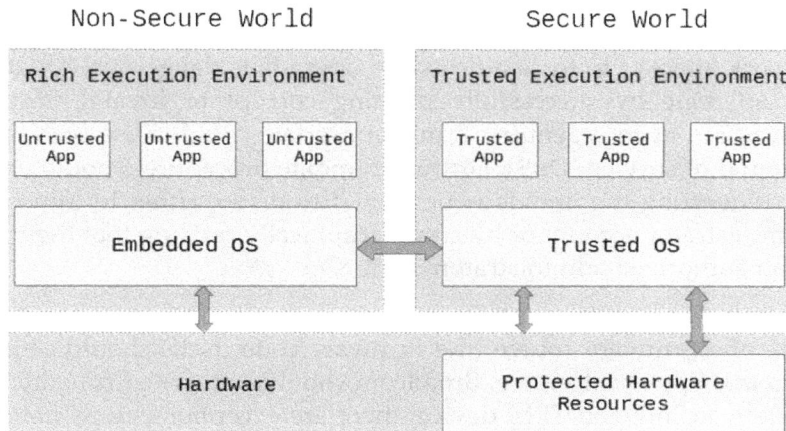

Figure 9.3: *Trusted execution environment*

Built-in security

Built-in security features are critical for a platform's security to be protected, detected, and corrected. These characteristics allow for the protection of the platforms' identity and data assets against assaults, as well as the detection of attacks and the deployment of remedial steps to make the platforms more robust.

Threats to firmware

An Internet Engineering Task Force working group named **Software Upgrades for Internet of Things (SUITS)** is addressing firmware updates for IoT systems. SUITS is a working group that established a thorough list of dangers and requirements that systems adopting updates should comply with:

- **Malicious or modified firmware updates:** When upgrading firmware, the first hazard to consider is corrupted or deliberately changed software. If an attacker can edit the firmware as it is being sent to the platform, or even while it is being updated, the attacker can insert features into the device. Accidental corruption is equally as harmful, as it might compromise a machine if the firmware is corrupted during the update process (causing the system to be permanently broken).

- **Rollback to old (vulnerable) firmware**: The second most prevalent hazard to the firmware is rolling back to a previous version. An attacker who can compel a system to reload an older version of firmware may be able to reintroduce a previous vulnerability, allowing them to seize control of the platform. This is particularly risky since the platform owner may mistakenly assume that they are immune to that vulnerability and may not be looking for signs of compromise for that specific assault.

- **Unauthorized update request**: The person or entity allowed to update firmware on the platform often neglected danger to firmware and RoT upgrades. Allowing a network attacker to force a firmware upgrade is dangerous. An attacker might cause an issue by successfully pushing corrupt or invalid firmware onto a platform, but even a genuine firmware update could cause platform instability or a **denial of service (DoS)**. Firmware update procedures should ensure that the entity requesting the update is permitted to do so, either by functioning under an administrator account or by cryptographically proving that their request came from an authorized administrator.

- **Unknown firmware source**: Even if an authorized entity requests a firmware update, the firmware source (the firmware code itself) should originate from a known and approved source. Broadcom should not write firmware that is meant to update an Infineon TPM device; there are exceptions, most notably when an OEM repackages an update for their device (that is, HP repackaging a TPM update for the devices they manufacture).

- **Incorrect firmware application**: Finally, firmware must be compatible with the system model and version of the hardware on which it runs. Hardware components can come in a variety of revisions, and software for one component may not work properly on a different stepping or version.

Software security

The OS should be the primary concern when evaluating software security on any platform. The OS is the most fundamental level of software on any computer. It regulates which hardware is turned on and what other applications may perform. The OS provides a foundation for all other software on the platform. If the OS lacks a basic capability or if other software is unable to manage or access any aspect of the system (hardware or software), no other component of the platform can compensate. If the OS lacks any security features, the remainder of the software on the platform is likely to be more vulnerable. Some essential elements of OSs are discussed, as well as how the OS should contribute to the platform's security. A basic set of security services that an OS should provide is as follows:

- **Execution separation**: Provides structures and procedures for separating distinct execution units of programs so that they don't interfere with the execution of other programs; this separation includes processes, threads, **Interrupt Service Routines (ISRs)**, and critical sections.

- **Memory separation**: Provides mechanisms for separating the various types of memory used by running applications, such as process memory, thread-only stacks, shared memory, and memory-mapped I or O.

- **Privilege levels**: Provides structures to separate executing programs into different privilege levels; this separation includes task identifiers for executing programs, user and group identities to own executing programs, and administrator versus the user privilege levels.

- **System authorization**: Provides structures and mechanisms to assign rights to objects and verify the privilege level of execution units against those rights; this includes setting the default privilege level assigned to programs and then enforcing those privileges when programs access system resources, by permitting or restricting certain operations. The least privilege principle may be implemented using this system authorization technique. This includes user authentication and the granting of rights to programs under the user's control in systems with human users.

- **Error protection in programming**: Provides structures and techniques that prevent attackers from manipulating mistakes in running programs and taking control of the platform; they generally include stack overflow protection, heap corruption detection and prevention, and control flow redirection limitation. Software attacks come from these errors, allowing a hacker to inject arbitrary code and seize control of a device. **Return-oriented programming (ROP)** and **jump-oriented programming (JOP)** are two types of control flow safeguards.

Access-controlled secure storage is a means for storing program secrets and preventing unauthorized users or programs, including the administrator, from accessing those secrets; the system typically provides this using hardware-backed secure storage.

OSs have the greatest degree of power on a platform, allowing them access to practically everything. An attacker who successfully attacks an OS can gain the entire control of the platform and privileged access to other platforms on the same network. The following five components describe popular exploitation attack patterns:

- **Fault injection:** A fault injection causes an execution fault in a process or thread, while part of the blame for this threat lies with the applications. Fault injection is the first step toward defeating the OS, so the OS must take some responsibility to protect against the vulnerabilities that cause this threat. The OS employs containment to keep these risks from becoming bigger problems for the platform, although it normally lets the error stop the attacked process or thread from running. The OS employs programming error safeguards, such as control flow prevention, as part of a basic set of security services. The OS includes programming error safeguards, such as control flow protections and stack smashing protections, to counter this danger, according to our basic list of security services.

- **Arbitrary code execution (ACE):** It is the injection of an attacker's code into a platform process or thread, forcing the injected code to run in place of the current process or thread, essentially assuming the identity and authorizations of that process or thread. ACE not only violates execution separation by enabling unauthorized code to corrupt an execution unit, but it also violates an OS's memory separation promise by allowing data to corrupt the platform's code. If fault injection succeeds, either because the application mitigations were ineffective or because the OS did not offer any fault injection safeguards, ACE is the usual escalation of fault injection. An attacker inserts code into the data used to cause the problem and uses fault injection to have the injected code execute or redirect as part of the fault. Attackers frequently utilize buffer overflows and heap corruption to construct ACE attacks.

- **Code in one execution:** This is the unit for viewing or interacting with code or data in another execution unit is referred to as a breach of containment. After gaining ACE, an attacker can use that power to extract data or corrupt other execution flows on the platform. Attackers frequently utilize side-channel assaults to obtain data and watch program execution. Because side channels allow a lower-privileged execution unit to monitor a higher-privileged execution unit, they can possibly retrieve secrets such as passwords and cryptographic keys from the other execution units. These attacks violate memory separation by allowing one program to observe or infer data from another; frequently, attacks on the execution separation are used to breach memory separation. Speculative branch prediction is a frequent example of this execution separation breach, but there are others as well.

- **Escalation of privilege**: Escalation of privilege refers to circumventing the OS's permission systems or code in order to gain access to a level of privilege that should not have been granted. An attacker can use the secrets extracted from other execution units to assume a higher privilege level after breaching confinement and obtaining secrets from other execution units. In rare situations, the attacker can inject a flaw into the OS itself, forcing it to provide a privilege to the attacker's code unit that should not have been granted. In both circumstances, the attacker has increased the privileges granted to the attacker's process by the OS. This escalation deviates from the system authorization procedures' intended behavior.

- **Rootkit**: A rootkit is a type of malware that infiltrates the OS and takes over part of its functions. Following arbitrary code injection, an attacker can use a chain of arbitrary code injections, containment flaws, and escalation of privilege attacks to finally inject the attacker's code into the OS. The attack may be a simple one-two chain in some circumstances or a sequence of more sophisticated acts in others. If the attacker can edit the OS code on disc or in flash, he or she can stay on the device indefinitely. Once an attacker has gained this degree of access to a system, removing the attacker from the system frequently necessitates a complete rebuild of both the software and firmware on the device. With rootkit access, an adversary may generally bypass the platform's access-controlled secrets safeguards, allowing the attacker to alter all secrets and execution units on the device. By altering access control decisions, concealing execution units, and decreasing or eliminating memory protections across various execution units through modifications to page table allocations, a rootkit can affect the behavior of the OS.

Containers

Containers are a sort of software separation technique that enables one or more programs, as well as their associated libraries, packages, and services, to operate in a namespace provided by the OS (*Figure 9.4*). Certain resources in an OS are arranged into namespaces. For example, all users are contained under a namespace, which implies there can only be one root user and one dave user (users are actually based on numeric identifiers, but the concept still holds). If two users have the same name, they are the same person. Devices, file paths, and some logical resources, such as network ports and process IDs, all use the same namespace notion. The OS within a container assigns the container its own namespace for some kind of resources. So, one container can open port 443 for a web server to wait for incoming traffic, while another container may do the same, and there will be no conflict. To distinguish the two network traffic flows outside the container, some sort of mapping must be performed. In our user identity example, two containers may both have the user dave, but they would not be associated with the same user; consequently, there would be no conflict between the containers and no privilege leakages or access overlaps between the containers' apps.

Figure 9.4 illustrates the containers:

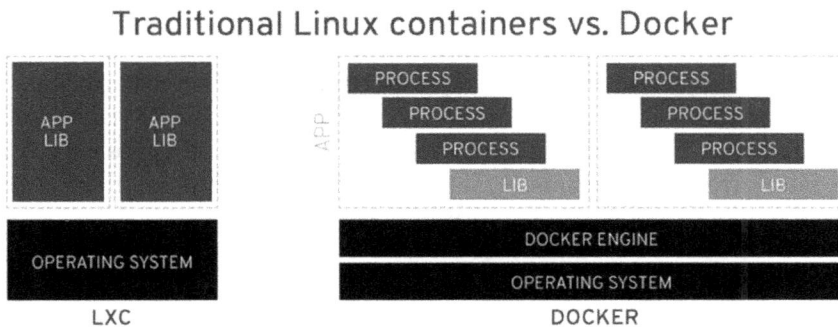

Figure 9.4: *Containers*

Containers also take advantage of a kernel feature known as **cgroups**. Cgroups define a kernel structure that restricts the amount of memory and CPU processing accessible to group programs. This may be used to make sure that a cgroup's processes do not starve out other groups. This guarantees that all containers receive an equal amount of processing time and that no one container may monopolize the CPU and prevent other containers' programs from running. Different containerization engines package these capabilities in different ways to enable the creation and management of an environment that allows for the separation of software for applications. Although all of them are referred to as containers, the attributes and controls of different containerization engines may differ somewhat.

The following is the most common types of IoT attacks:

- **Denial of service:** It attack causes a VM to stall or produce such a significant VM abort that the hypervisor refuses to let the VM continue to run. A more serious DoS might harm a platform device, prohibiting all VMs from accessing it until the platform is restarted, thereby breaking device mediation. Attacks on a virtualized hardware device that cause a DoS are a breach of execution separation. Another sort of DoS attack depletes resources, such as network socket handles, preventing other VMs from acquiring the resources required to perform a function.

- **Stack overflow and ACE**: Vulnerabilities like stack smashing, heap smashing, and use-after-free allow an attacker to run their own code on the platform. This form of attack can allow the rights of code to be escalated, making it a privileged user. This might lead the VM to misbehave and breach the hypervisor's trust in the VM, resulting in an execution or memory separation violation in para-virtualized systems (prevent abuses from direct execution of commands from guest VMs).

- **Obtain information**: An out-of-bounds read vulnerability allows a **virtual machine (VM)** to acquire memory that is not in its logical memory region. These flaws are frequent in virtualized drivers and VM software. A memory separation violation is represented as a gain information vulnerability.

- **Gain privileges**: Add-ons, such as tools and plugins, are commonly used to carry out gain privilege assaults. The CVE-2017-4943 vulnerability, for example, enables a show log plugin to obtain root access to the platform management VM, which handles network settings, system updates, health monitoring, and device management. This is because root on a para-virtualized VM allows the attacker to easily break the implicit para-virtualized cooperation agreement, gaining root on a para-virtualized system is comparable to compromising the hypervisor itself (Management of hypervisor platform).

Security management

During the installation, configuration, operation, and decommissioning of systems, security management is the combination of active processes and executed procedures that ensure the confidentiality, integrity, and availability of those system and network resources for the organization's approved mission(s).

Secure device onboarding

Device provisioning, or how to provide devices so they can connect to the relevant back-end cloud system or device management system, is the first issue that requires a solution in an IoT system. Pre-provisioning devices to connect to a certain cloud agent during manufacture is a typical technique. This is how Microsoft Azure Sphere works. While it works, the solution binds the device to a single cloud, and the technique has the potential to disrupt high-speed production.

Figure 9.5 illustrates **secure device onboarding** (**SDO**):

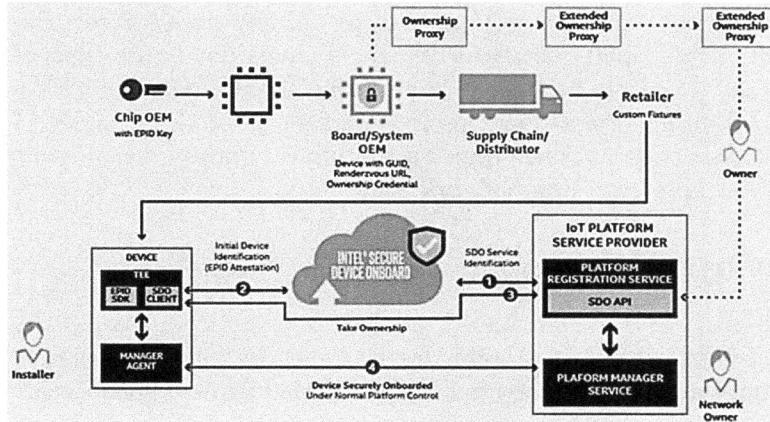

Figure 9.5: *Secure device onboarding*

SDO utilizes a few hardware security features to construct this high-level service, including the following:

- Platform's root of trust, which contains an identification key; an **enhanced privacy ID (EPID)** group signature key is preferable for device installation privacy, although the **Rivest-Shamir-Adleman (RSA)** or **Elliptical Curve Digital Signature Algorithm (ECDSA)** key may also be utilized.

- Intel SDO client firmware running on a TEE, SDO presently utilizes the **Converged Security and Management Engine (CSME)**, but **Software Guard Extensions (SGX)** or Trusty are other options.

- The manufacturer's public key, a GUID, and an ownership credential are stored securely on the device.

Platform integrity

Maintaining the integrity of the platform software once a device has been supplied is critical to keeping an IoT system running. Platform integrity refers to verifying that a device has booted the system's proper platform software and that the platform firmware, boot loader, and OS have not been corrupted. Device management software may check the integrity condition of the platform to see if anything needs to be updated or fixed. However, some software must exist on the device in order to compute platform integrity and then transmit it in a meaningful fashion to the device management software.

Network defense

This is because IoT systems are all about communication, they would be obvious targets for network attackers if they did not have some kind of protective measures in place. Firewalls and intrusion detection software are common network defensive features that should be included in each IoT device. This is because certain devices are so little and have so few resources, no attempt is made to install any network security. Limiting the apps and services that open ports to listen for connections is the first step in network protection. In fact, if your IoT device is so resource-constrained that you are considering disabling network protections, then listening services should be disabled as well, leaving just outbound connections. Firewalling, on the other hand, is the most basic defense, a software that intercepts incoming network traffic.

Platform monitoring

In the event that a network attacker is able to defeat the device's network defenses, security management comprises monitoring the device and its workload for irregularities. The monitoring features are integrated with the platform's device management agent, allowing issues to be notified to the management servers.

McAfee embedded control

In security management, there is one last software capability worth mentioning that gives some unique system authorization capabilities. **McAfee embedded control (MEC)** is a software tool that gives IoT systems more access control and integrity. MEC safeguards both executable and data files on a platform, guaranteeing that they are not altered inadvertently or maliciously, even by a user with administrator privileges. On the platform, MEC establishes a new privileged user that can only access the MEC admin interface and administers a database of integrity checksums for directories and files specified by the MEC admin. MEC establishes a robust security mechanism for IoT devices and performs exceptionally well when the platform's software and configuration do not change frequently. MEC is simple to incorporate into McAfee's **e-Policy Orchestrator (ePO)** device management package.

Security objectives and requirements

Assets in a retail IoT device include the following:

- Cardholder data and transactional information at rest and in transit.
- **Consumer identity**: **Personally identifiable information** (**PII**) should be kept under rigorous access control, preferably with data-at-rest encryption.
- **POS device identity**: Device credentials are required to protect against remote hacker assaults and maintain a stable connection to the device cloud infrastructure.

- **Hardware components**: During production and deployment, the HW BOM list in the platform must always be safeguarded via a transparent supply chain and guarded in the field as needed.

- **Firmware, including pre-OS boot loader**: The platform's firmware is a valuable asset.

- OS kernel and User-mode SW components such as apps, are all valuable assets.

Following are the threats involved on retail IoT devices:

- **Threat #1:** Allows a hacker to easily compromise the boot firmware and OS image's integrity. The hacker gains access to the system by disrupting the execution flow. Implementing Boot Guard to construct a chain of trust based on an HW Root of Trust is the mitigation. When the firmware is tampered with and an attempt is made to boot with this unsigned firmware, the Boot Guard detects this and resets the device to avoid future breaches of critical assets.

- **Threat #2:** Unauthorized actors might configure devices according to their preferences, such as usernames, passwords, and password reminders. The Intel SDO technology might be used to supply the device persona and require users to change their default passwords to more secure ones, as well as provide strong password reminders and two-factor authentication.

- **Threat #3:** Logging transaction data to a POS server. This is a serious danger in which an attack might breach the PCI DSS's P2PE rules, allowing hackers on the network to get cardholder data. To ensure secrecy, Intel AES technology in the CPU may be utilized to encrypt the cardholder's information. The encryption procedure can be done inside an SG enclave to defend against ring 0 or rootkit assaults, increasing the robustness of this aspect of the solution.

- **Threat #4:** Allows the cryptographic keys needed to secure platform and owner secrets to be readily retrieved or stored. Protecting the keys used to encrypt the cardholders' data by keeping them in a PTT or TPM so that they are never exposed to hackers is once again a significant duty.

Conclusion

This chapter focusses on IoT security for safeguarding things on the Internet as connected devices and network infrastructure of the IoT. IoT provides Internet connectivity to systems, embedded devices, sensors that are interrelated computing devices, mechanical and digital machines, objects, animals and people. Each such thing is provided with a unique identifier and the ability to automatically transfer data over a network. Allowing these devices to connect to the internet opens them up to a number of serious vulnerabilities if they are not properly protected.

In the next chapter, we will discuss cloud and virtualization technology and security issues around this domain.

Exercise

1. Scenario: A company deploys a fleet of IoT devices for smart home automation. Over time, some devices become outdated and need to be decommissioned securely. What is the best approach to securely retire these devices?

    a. Physically destroy the devices without deleting stored data

    b. Reset the device to factory settings and remove cryptographic keys

    c. Keep the device running indefinitely to avoid security risk

    d. Transfer device ownership without resetting security credentials

2. An industrial IoT system requires strong authentication mechanisms to verify the identity of connected devices. Which method provides the highest level of assurance for device identity?

    a. Assigning a static IP address to each device

    b. Using pre-shared symmetric keys stored in software

    c. Leveraging unique hardware-based cryptographic identities

    d. Authenticating devices based on their MAC address

3. A medical IoT device manufacturer wants to ensure that only authorized firmware is executed during the device startup process. What is the most effective security mechanism to achieve this?

    a. Implementing a software-only authentication mechanism

    b. Using a signed bootloader that verifies firmware integrity before execution

    c. Allowing firmware updates without authentication to simplify management.

    d. Encrypting firmware updates but skipping signature verification

4. A smart meter collects sensitive energy consumption data. To prevent unauthorized access, how should the device securely store this data?

    a. Encrypt data using a **Hardware Security Module (HSM)**

    b. Store data in plain text for easy retrieval

    c. Use software-based encryption without hardware support

    d. Store the encryption key on external flash memory

5. A manufacturer wants to protect an IoT device from physical attacks that aim to extract cryptographic keys. Which security feature would best mitigate this risk?

    a. Using a TEE to store secrets

    b. Relying on software-based encryption alone

    c. Storing cryptographic keys in application memory

    d. Disabling encryption to reduce processing overhead

6. **A financial services company deploys IoT payment terminals that require secure processing of transactions. How does a TEE enhance security in this context?**

    a. By allowing any application to access sensitive data

    b. By isolating critical operations from the main OS

    c. By storing transaction logs in external memory

    d. By providing only software-based encryption for data protection

7. **A manufacturer is designing an IoT device and wants to ensure security is embedded from the start. What is an example of built-in security?**

    a. Implementing security patches after deployment

    b. Designing the device with a secure boot and hardware-based encryption

    c. Relying on end-users to configure security settings

    d. Avoiding encryption to improve device performance

8. **A hacker attempts to modify an IoT device's firmware to introduce malicious functionality. Which security measure is most effective in preventing this attack?**

    a. Implementing firmware signing and verification

    b. Allowing unrestricted firmware updates for easy maintenance

    c. Storing firmware in unprotected flash memory

    d. Using default credentials to simplify updates

9. **A company manages thousands of IoT devices and wants to ensure timely updates and patching. What is the best approach for effective security management?**

    a. Rely on users to manually install updates

    b. Implement an automated **Over-the-Air (OTA)** update system

    c. Update only devices that report security issues

    d. Disable updates to maintain stability

10. **A smart home device manufacturer wants to ensure SDO without requiring manual configuration. What is the best approach to achieve this?**

    a. Using an automated provisioning system with device certificates

    b. Requiring users to manually enter security credentials for each device

    c. Using a shared default password for all devices

    d. Allowing anonymous connections for quick onboarding

Answers

1. b
2. c
3. b
4. a
5. a
6. b
7. b
8. a
9. b
10. a

Join our book's Discord space

Join the book's Discord Workspace for Latest updates, Offers, Tech happenings around the world, New Release and Sessions with the Authors:

https://discord.bpbonline.com

CHAPTER 10
Cloud and Virtualization Security

Introduction

The primary idea behind cloud computing is to place resources in a web-based data center that can be accessed from anywhere. A public cloud solution is when a firm pays another organization to host and administer this sort of environment. A private cloud solution is one in which the firm hosts the environment itself. In most cases, virtualization is at the heart of cloud computing. Virtualization of servers has become a critical component in reducing the data center's physical footprint. The advantages include reduced overall use of power in the data center, dynamic allocation of memory and CPU resources to the servers and high availability provided by the ability to quickly bring up a replica server in the event of loss of the primary server. This chapter looks at cloud computing and virtualization security and how these features are changing the network landscape.

Structure

In this chapter, we will cover the following topics:

- Cloud and virtualization considerations
- Cloud deployment and service models
- Virtualization security
- Hyper converged infrastructure

- Vulnerability scanning
- Sandboxing
- Secure network environments

Objective

The basic focus of cloud computing was to ensure resources are available via web-based data centers accessible from any location. Virtualization of servers and network devices became a key to reducing the physical footprint in data centers. This enabled software applications, hardware infrastructure, and computing environments for multi-tenants. It changed the landscape and brought about cloud and virtual server security issues.

Cloud deployment and service models

Any business can employ a variety of technological deployment strategies, such as outsourcing, insourcing, managed services, and partnerships, to combine hosts, storage systems, networks, and applications into a secure enterprise. Cloud deployment and service models are foundational to modern IT ecosystems, offering scalability, flexibility, and cost-effectiveness. These models include public, private, hybrid, and community cloud infrastructures, each tailored to specific organizational needs. Public clouds offer shared resources, while private clouds ensure exclusive access and enhanced security. Hybrid clouds bridge the two, balancing performance and cost, and community clouds focus on shared goals among organizations. Service models like, **Infrastructure as a Service (IaaS), Platform as a Service (PaaS)**, and **Software as a Service (SaaS)** allow businesses to offload varying levels of operational responsibilities, enabling efficient resource management and innovation without significant upfront investments.

Cloud and virtualization concerns and hosting alternatives, virtual machine vulnerabilities, safe usage of on-demand or elastic cloud computing, data remains, data aggregation, and data separation are all covered in the following sections.

Cloud and virtualization considerations

Enterprise assets may be distributed using cloud computing without the end-user knowing where the physical assets are located or how they are configured. Virtualization entails the creation of a virtual device on a physical resource, which can host several virtual devices. On a Windows computer, for example, you can run many **virtual machines** (**VMs**). However, keep in mind that each virtual machine will take some of the host computer's resources, and the virtual machine's configuration cannot exceed the host machine's resources.

You must become familiar with public, private, hybrid, community, multitenancy, and single-tenancy cloud choices in order to pass the CASP test.

Public

The basic cloud computing paradigm is a public cloud, in which a service provider makes resources available to the general public over the internet. Public cloud services can be provided for free or on a pay-per-use basis. A business or technical liaison who is responsible for maintaining the vendor relationship is required, but a cloud deployment specialist is not required. Amazon, IBM, Google, Microsoft, and a slew of other companies provide public cloud solutions. Subscribers to a public cloud model can add and remove resources as needed, depending on their subscription.

Private

A private cloud is a cloud computing concept in which a private corporation builds a cloud within its own enterprise and makes it available to its workers and partners. Private cloud services necessitate the hiring of a cloud deployment expert to administer the private cloud.

Hybrid

A hybrid cloud is a cloud computing paradigm in which a company controls and offers some resources in-house while outsourcing others to a public cloud. This strategy necessitates both a service provider connection and an in-house cloud deployment professional. To guarantee that a hybrid cloud is effectively deployed, rules must be created. Confidential data should only be stored in a private cloud.

Community

A community cloud is a cloud computing paradigm in which the cloud infrastructure is shared among a group of enterprises with similar processing requirements. The security policies that will be in place to secure the data of each company engaging in the community cloud, as well as how the cloud will be administered and maintained, should be specifically defined in this model, as illustrated in *Figure 10.1*:

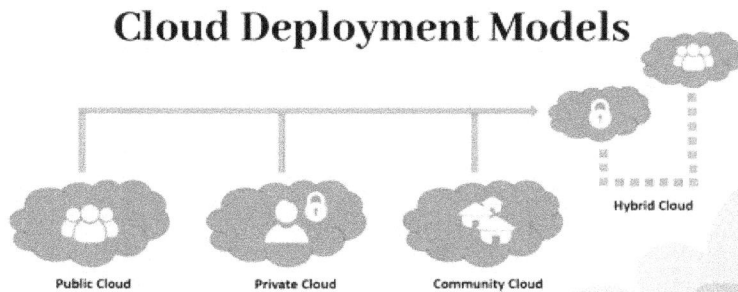

Figure 10.1: Cloud deployment models

Multitenancy

A multitenancy model is a cloud computing approach in which resources are shared by many businesses. This concept enables service providers to control resource use better. Companies should adopt this approach to guarantee that their data is safeguarded against unwanted access by other organizations or people. Furthermore, companies should ensure that the service provider has the resources to meet the organization's future demands. If multitenancy models are not effectively managed, one entity might consume more resources than its fair share, putting the other firms in the tenancy at risk.

Single tenancy

A cloud computing approach in which a single tenant accesses a resource is known as a single-tenancy model. This architecture ensures that the data of the tenant organization is kept safe from outsiders. This model, however, is costlier than the multitenancy paradigm. *Figure 10.2* presents the single and multiple tenancies on cloud systems:

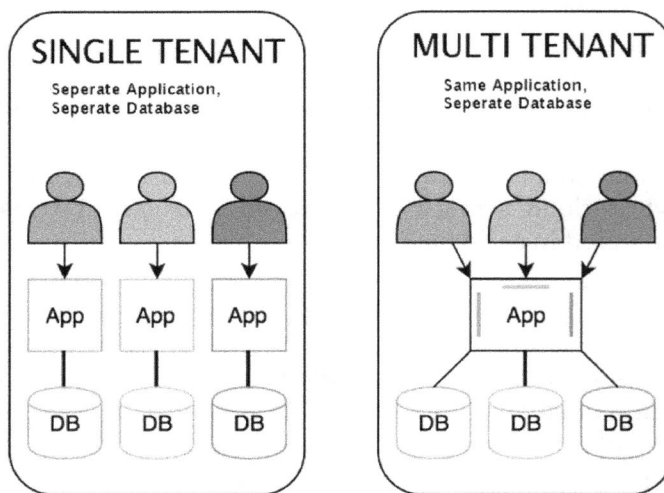

Figure 10.2: Single and multi-tenancy

On premise versus hosted

The trend toward virtualization is being accompanied by a shift toward on-premise vs hosted resource allocation. An on-premise cloud solution makes use of resources that are already on the company's network or are hosted in the company's data center. A hosted environment is one that is offered by a third party and is hosted on their physical resources. The security implications of these two approaches must be understood by security experts, especially if the cloud deployment will be hosted on third-party resources under a shared tenancy, as presented in *Figure 10.3:*

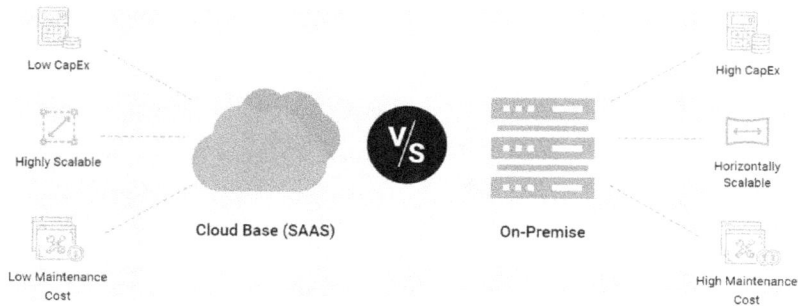

Figure 10.3: Cloud-based v/s on-premise

Cloud service models

When choosing between architectures, there are trade-offs to consider. A private solution gives you the most control over the security of your data, but it also necessitates the resources and expertise to build, maintain, and secure it. A public cloud places your data's security in the hands of a third party, but that third party is more adept and informed about data security and cloud management. Various degrees of service can be purchased with a public solution. *Figure 10.4* presents and discusses the cloud service models, as follows:

- **Software as a Service**: It is a model in which a provider delivers the full solution, including the operating system, infrastructure software, and application. The vendor may, for example, supply an email system that hosts and controls everything for the contracting firm. A firm that contracts to use Salesforce or Intuit QuickBooks through a browser rather than installing the program on every workstation is an example of this. This relieves the customer organization of the responsibility for application upgrades and other maintenance services.

- **Infrastructure as a Service**: With IaaS, the provider supplies the hardware platform or data center, while the company installs and administers its own operating and application systems. The vendor merely grants access to the data center and ensures that access is maintained. A corporation that hosts all of its web servers with a third-party provider is one example of this. Customers, who use IaaS benefit from the dynamic allocation of more resources during peak activity, while those same resources are scaled back when not in use, saving money.

- **Platform as a Service**: With PaaS, the vendor offers the physical platform or data center, as well as the software that runs on it, such as operating systems and infrastructure software. The corporation is still in charge of the system's administration. A corporation that engages a third party to provide a development platform for internal developers to utilize for development and testing is an example of this. *Figure 10.4* illustrates the cloud service models:

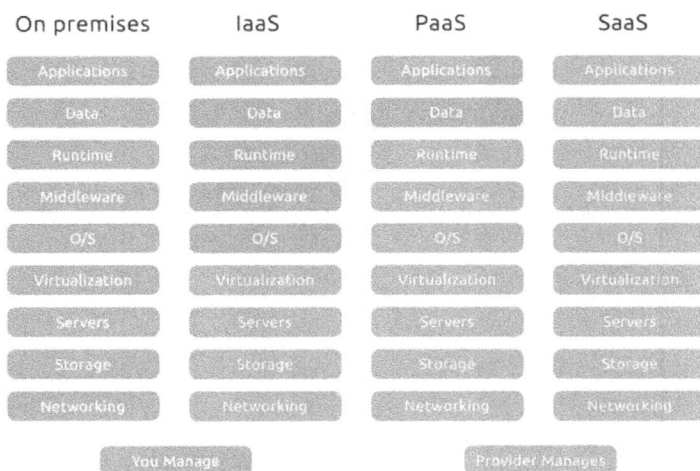

Figure 10.4: Cloud service models

Virtualization security

Virtualization of servers has become an important aspect of lowering the data center's physical footprint. The advantages include the following:

- Reduced overall use of power in the data center.

- Dynamic allocation of memory and CPU resources to the servers.

- High availability provided by the ability to quickly bring up a replica server in the event of loss of the primary server.

However, in the virtual network, most of the same security vulnerabilities that must be handled in the physical environment must also be addressed. VMs are instances of an operating system in a virtual environment. A host system can support a large number of VMs. The VMs resources (CPU, memory, and disc) are distributed by the hypervisor, as illustrated in *Figure 10.5*.

> **Note: Each virtual server housed on a physical server must be configured with its own security methods in any virtual environment.**

Antivirus and anti-malware software, as well as all the latest service packs and security updates for all the software housed on the virtual machine, are among these techniques. Also, keep in mind that all virtual servers share the actual device's resources. Any sensitive applications that must be installed on the host should be put in a chroot environment when virtualization is hosted on a Linux machine. On a UNIX-based operating system, a chroot is an operation that alters the currently running processes and its children's root directory. A program running in such a changed environment is unable to name (and so access) files outside of the allocated directory tree. *Figure 10.5* illustrates the VM architecture:

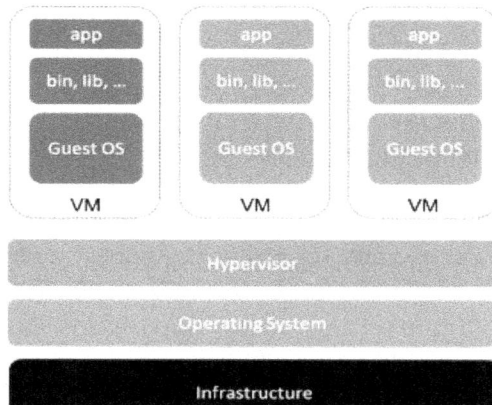

Figure 10.5: Virtual machine architecture

Type 1 versus type 2 hypervisors

Hypervisors are divided into two categories (refer to *Figure 10.6* for different types of Hypervisors). Let us look at the distinctions between them, as follows:

- **Type 1 hypervisor**: Either a type 1 or type 2 hypervisor handles the distribution of the physical server's resources. A guest operating system operates above the hypervisor on a different level. Citrix XenServer, Microsoft Hyper-V, and VMware vSphere are examples of type 1 hypervisors.

- **Type 2 hypervisor**: This operates on top of a traditional operating system. Guest operating systems run at the third level above the hardware, with the hypervisor layer as a unique second software layer. Type 2 hypervisors include VMware workstations and VirtualBox.

Figure 10.6 illustrates the type 1 and type 2 hypervisors:

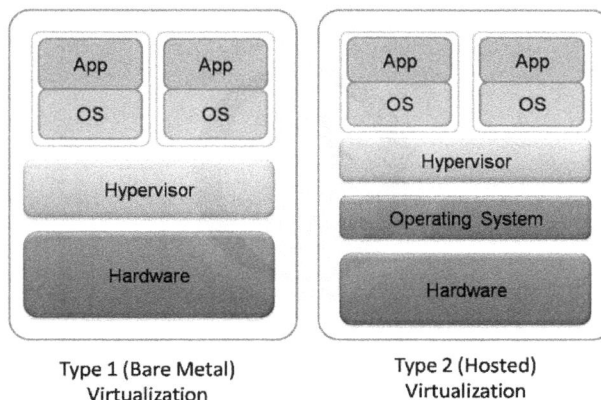

Type 1 (Bare Metal)
Virtualization

Type 2 (Hosted)
Virtualization

Figure 10.6: Type 1 and type 2 hypervisors

Container-based

Container-based virtualization, often known as operating system virtualization, is a modern method of virtualization. This type of server virtualization makes use of the kernel's ability to support many separate user-space instances. Containers, virtual private servers, and virtual environments are all terms used to describe the instances. The hypervisor is replaced in this approach by operating system-level virtualization, in which an operating system's kernel permits several separate user areas or containers. A virtual machine is not a full instance of an operating system, but rather a subset of the same operating system. Container-based virtualization is widely utilized in Linux systems, with commercial Virtuozzo and the free source OpenVZ project as examples.

Hyper converged infrastructure

Converged infrastructure is one in which the vendor combines all storage, networking, and computing equipment into a single physical box, making data center deployment easier (*Figure 10.7*). For these resources, it provides a single administration interface. The Dell system managed system is an example of this. Without requiring any hardware modifications, hyper-convergence performs this integration with software. It also makes use of virtualization. It connects a number of services and allows them to be managed through a single interface. While this technique enables growth by simply adding additional hardware without regard to the vendor, the business becomes somewhat reliant on a single hyper-convergence provider's solution. *Figure 10.7* illustrates hyper-converged infrastructure:

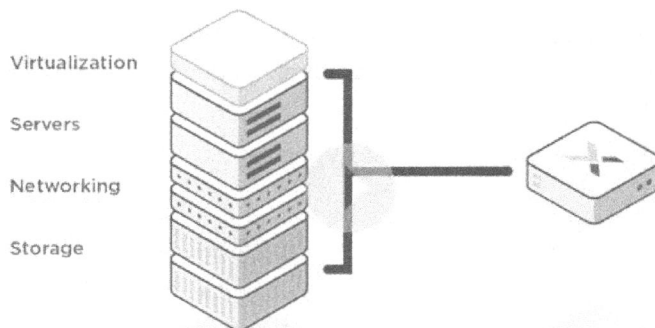

Figure 10.7: Hyper-converged infrastructure

Virtual desktop infrastructure

Virtual desktop infrastructure (VDI) is a centralized server that runs desktop operating systems in a virtual environment. The desktops are accessed and executed from the server by the users. Instead of running on local machines, the desktop environments are stored and managed on the central infrastructure, providing users with secure and consistent access to their personalized desktop experience. VDI supports various devices, including thin clients, laptops, tablets, and even smartphones, ensuring flexibility in access. A key advantage of VDI is its ability to streamline IT management by enabling centralized control over desktop provisioning, updates, and security policies. This reduces administrative overhead and enhances security since sensitive data remains within the server infrastructure and is not stored locally. VDI also improves scalability, making it ideal for organizations with fluctuating workforce sizes, such as seasonal or remote employees.

With advancements in virtualization technologies, VDI solutions now support high-performance computing and multimedia-intensive applications, addressing traditional concerns about performance latency. It also enables a seamless disaster recovery process by ensuring quick restoration of virtual desktops from secure backups. As a result, VDI offers a robust framework for organizations seeking to modernize their IT infrastructure, improve user productivity, and ensure compliance with stringent data protection regulations.

Secure enclaves and volumes

The purpose of both secure enclaves and secure volumes is to reduce the length of time-critical data that is unencrypted while in use. Secure enclaves are processors that work with data that has been encrypted. This implies that even individuals with access to the virtual environment's underlying hardware are unable to access the data. Windows Azure supports secure enclaves, and a secure processor stops the main processor from accessing data. In a different approach, secure volumes achieve this purpose. Unmount and hide a secure volume until it is needed. After that, it is mounted and decrypted. The disc is encrypted and unmounted after the modifications are finished.

Cloud augmented security services

Cloud computing is all the craze these days, and everyone is scrambling to get their data **on the cloud**. However, doing so raises security concerns. What is the physical location of your data? Is it mixed together with other people's data? Is it safe to use? It's terrifying to entrust your data's security to others. The sections that follow examine cloud security concerns.

Hash matching

A process known as hash matching, or hash spoofing, has been used to steal data from cloud infrastructure. The attack on Dropbox, a cloud vendor, is a good example of this vulnerability. As part of the data deduplication process, Dropbox used hashes to identify blocks of data stored by users in the cloud. When a user connects, these hashes, which are values derived from the data and used to uniquely identify the data, are used to determine whether data has changed, indicating whether a synchronization process is required. Spoofing hashes were used in the attack to gain access to arbitrary pieces of other customers' data.

The customer whose files were being distributed was unaware of the unauthorized access because it was granted from the cloud. Dropbox has addressed the issue since it was discovered by using stronger hashing algorithms, but hash matching can still be a problem with any private, public, or hybrid cloud solution. The forces of good can use hashing as well. Hashing is a technique used by antivirus software to identify malware. When looking for malware, signature-based antivirus products look for hashes that match. The problem is that malware has evolved to the point where it can now change itself, changing its hash value. As a result, fuzzy hashing is becoming more popular. Unlike traditional hashing, which requires an exact match, fuzzy hashing looks for hashes that are close but not identical.

Vulnerability scanning

A good example of SaaS is cloud-based vulnerability scanning, which is a service that is performed from the vendor's cloud, as presented in *Figure 10.8*. The benefits are the same as any other SaaS offering, no subscriber equipment is required, and there is no footprint in the local network. The vulnerability scanners and associated components are entirely installed on the client's premises, whereas the vulnerability management platform is hosted in the cloud using the cloud-based approach. External vulnerability assessments are performed using vulnerability scanners located at the solution provider's location, with additional scanners on the premises. The following are some of the benefits of a cloud-based approach:

- Installation costs are low because the client does not have to complete any installation or configuration.

- Maintenance costs are low because there is only one centralized component to maintain, which the vendor does (not the end client).

- Upgrades are included in the price of your subscription.

- Costs are shared between all customers.

- The client is not required to provide any onsite equipment.

Figure 10.8 illustrates the vulnerability scanning dashboard:

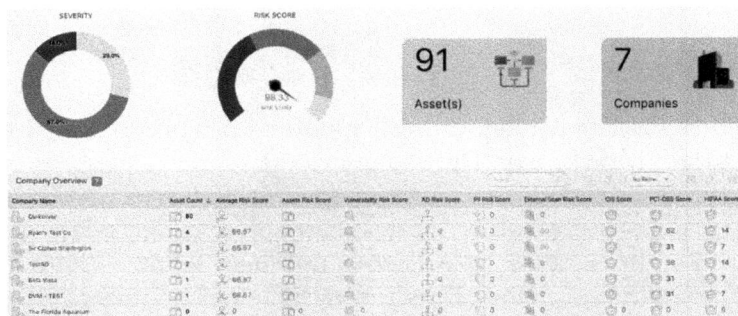

Figure 10.8: Vulnerability scanning dashboard

However, there is a significant drawback. In contrast to premise-based deployments, which store data findings on the organization's premises, cloud-based deployments keep the data on the provider's servers. This implies that the customer is reliant on the provider to keep the vulnerability data secure.

Sandboxing

Sandboxing refers to the separation of virtual environments for the purposes of security (*Figure 10.9*). Sandboxed appliances have previously been used to supplement a network's security features. In a secure environment, these appliances are used to test suspicious files. Sandboxing in the cloud has some advantages over sandboxing on-premises, as follows:

- It has no hardware limitations, making it scalable and elastic; it can track malware for hours or days.

- It can be updated with any operating system type and version, and it is not geographically restricted.

The potential drawback is that many sandboxing products are incompatible with a wide range of applications and utilities, including antivirus software.

Figure 10.9 illustrates sandboxing behavior:

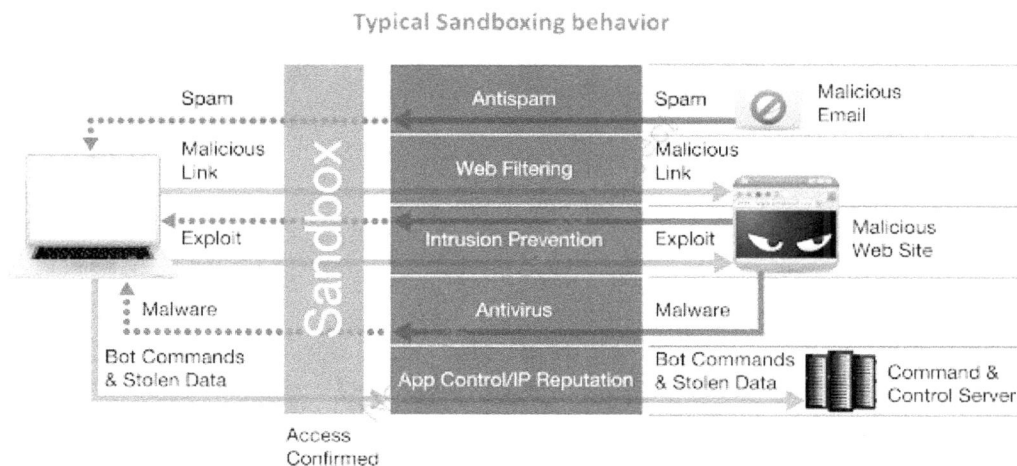

Figure 10.9: *Sandboxing behavior*

Content filtering

Web content filtering can be provided as a cloud-based service. In this case, all content is examined by the providers. The advantages are the same for all cloud solutions, equipment savings, and support for the content filtering process while maintaining process control.

Cloud security broker

A cloud security broker, also known as a **cloud access security broker (CASB)**, is a software layer that acts as a gatekeeper between an organization's on-premise network and the cloud environment of the provider. This strategic location, it can provide a wide range of services. Skyhigh Networks and Netskope are two vendors in the cloud access security space. *Figure 10.10* illustrates the cloud security broker:

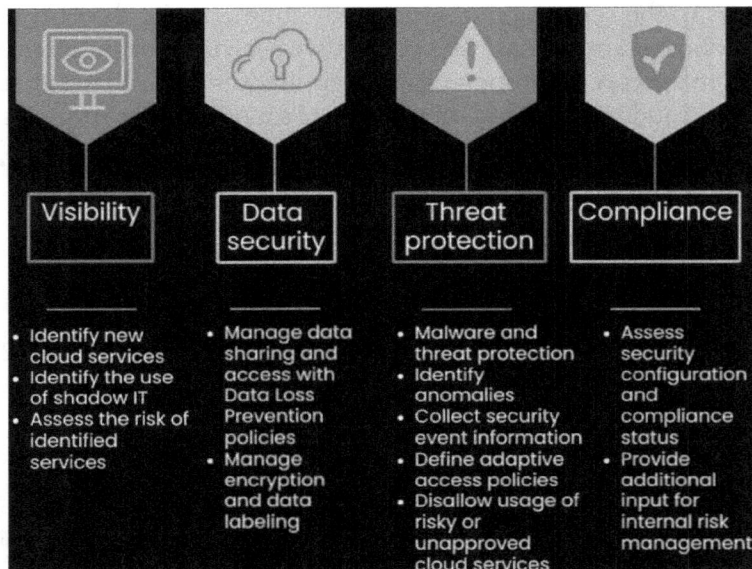

Figure 10.10: Cloud Security Broker

Security as a service

Security as a service (SecaaS) is another cloud-based service. Many businesses lack the necessary skill sets to provide the required security services, and it is not cost-effective to acquire them. It may make sense for these businesses to hire a security firm that can provide the following advantages:

- Cost savings
- Consistent and uniform protection
- Virus definition updates on a regular basis
- More security expertise
- Quicker user provisioning
- Administrative tasks outsourced
- Intuitive administrative interface

Managed security service providers

Managed security service providers (MSSPs) take the concept of SecaaS a step further by offering the option of fully outsourcing all information assurance to a third party. If a company decides to use a third-party identity service, such as cloud computing, security experts must be involved in the implementation's integration with internal services and resources. This integration can be difficult, especially if the provider's solution is incompatible with internal systems. Cloud identity, directory synchronization, and federated identity are all features that most third-party identity services offer. **Amazon Web Services (AWS), AWS Identity and Access Management (IAM)** service, and oracle identity management are examples of these services.

Vulnerabilities associated with hosts

When virtualized, guest systems may share a common host machine. Security issues can arise when this happens, and the systems sharing the host have different security requirements. The sections that follow examine some of these issues as well as some preventative measures that can be taken.

VMEscape

The attacker **breaks out** of a VM's normally isolated state and interacts directly with the hypervisor in a VMEscape attack. This is because VMs frequently share physical resources, an attacker who can figure out how his VM's virtual resources map to the physical resources will be able to attack the real physical resources directly. The attacker can affect all the VMs, the hypervisor, and possibly other programs on that machine if he can modify his virtual memory in a way that exploits how the physical resources are mapped to each VM. Virtual servers should only be on the same physical server as others in their network segment to help mitigate a VMEscape attack.

Privilege elevation

The risks of privilege elevation, or escalation, in a virtualized environment, may be equal to or greater than in a physical environment in some cases. Any flaws introduced to those calls by the hypervisor while handling calls between the guest operating system and the hardware could allow an attacker to escalate privileges in the guest operating system. A recent vulnerability in VMware's **Elastic Sky X (ESX)** server, workstation, fusion, and view products could have resulted in host escalation. VMware quickly issued a security update to address the flaw. To avoid privilege escalation, make sure all virtualization products have the most recent updates and patches.

Live virtual machine migration

One of the benefits of a virtualized environment is the system's ability to migrate a virtual machine from one host to another as needed. This is referred to as a **live migration**.

Attackers can exploit a network vulnerability to gain unauthorized access to VMs when they are on the network between secured perimeters. With access to VM images, attackers can embed malicious code to launch attacks on the data centers where VMs travel. This is because the protocols used for migration are frequently not encrypted. A man-in-the-middle attack on the VM while it is in transit is possible. The encryption of the images where they are stored is the key to preventing man-in-the-middle attacks.

Data remnants

Protect sensitive data that has been inadvertently replicated in VMs as a result of cloud maintenance functions or remnant data left in terminated VMs. Furthermore, if data is moved, residual data may be left behind, making it accessible to unauthorized users. Any remaining data in the old location should be shredded, but data remnants may persist depending on security practices. With confidential data in private clouds and any sensitive data in public clouds, this can be a problem. Commercial products, such as those made by Blancco, are available to permanently erase data from computers, servers, data center equipment, and smartphones. Any existing technology cannot recover data erased by Blancco. Blancco also generates a report for each erasure to ensure compliance.

Data security considerations

Multiple customers' VMs can be hosted on a single server or platform in a cloud deployment. If not handled properly in either case, security vulnerabilities may arise. Let us take a look at these concerns.

Vulnerabilities with single server hosting

This situation allows a company to avoid a large investment in computing resources that will be used for only a short time. Assuming that the provisioned resources are dedicated to a single company, the main vulnerability associated with on-demand provisioning is traces of proprietary data that can remain on the virtual machine and may be exploited.

Let's look at an example. Say that a security architect is seeking to outsource company server resources to a commercial cloud service provider. The provider under consideration has a reputation for poorly controlling physical access to data centers and has been the victim of social engineering attacks. The service provider regularly assigns VMs from multiple clients to the same physical resource. When conducting the final risk assessment, the security architect should take into consideration the likelihood that a malicious user will obtain proprietary information by gaining local access to the hypervisor platform. VMs from multiple organizations are hosted on a physical server in virtualization deployments. The resources of a single physical computer are shared by all VMs hosted on that physical server. All organizations with VMs on that physical server are affected if the physical server crashes or is compromised. User access to VMs should be configured, managed, and audited properly. To ensure that each VM is properly protected, appropriate security controls, such as anti-virus/malware, access control lists, and auditing must be implemented on each one. Physical server resource depletion, network resource performance, and traffic filtering between VMs are all risks to consider.

Multiple VMs and multiple data types or owners

In some virtualization deployments, a single platform hosts the VMs of multiple organizations. If all of the servers hosting VMs use the same platform, attackers will have an easier time attacking the other host servers once the platform has been discovered. If all physical servers use VMware to host VMs, any vulnerabilities found in that platform could be exploited on all host computers. Misconfigured platforms, separation of duties, and the application of security policy to network interfaces are all risks to consider. If a company's web servers, application servers, and database servers are to be virtualized, the virtual host machines should be secured by only allowing access through a secure management interface and restricting physical and network access to the host console.

Resources provisioning and de-provisioning

Virtual solution deployment and decommissioning should follow certain best practices, just like physical resource deployment and decommissioning. The process of provisioning is the addition of a resource for use, and the process of de-provisioning is the removal of a resource from use. In both virtualization and cloud environments, provisioning and de-provisioning are critical, especially if the enterprise is paying per resource or based on resource uptime. The proper provisioning and de-provisioning procedures should be documented and followed by security professionals.

Virtual devices

When virtual devices are provisioned in a cloud environment, some method of securing access to the resource (such as VMs) should be in place to ensure that the provider no longer has direct access. Only the customer should have access, and it should be secured with some sort of identifying key or ID number. To ensure that this occurs, SLAs should be scrutinized. *Figure 10.11* presents the Virtual devices to choose, using the portal:

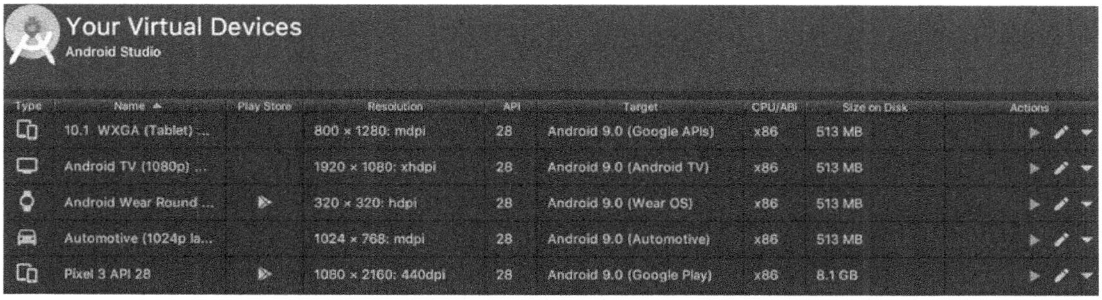

Your Virtual Devices
Android Studio

Type	Name ▲	Play Store	Resolution	API	Target	CPU/ABI	Size on Disk	Actions
	10.1. WXGA (Tablet) ...		800 × 1280: mdpi	28	Android 9.0 (Google APIs)	x86	513 MB	▶ ✎ ▾
	Android TV (1080p) ...		1920 × 1080: xhdpi	28	Android 9.0 (Android TV)	x86	513 MB	▶ ✎ ▾
	Android Wear Round ...	▷	320 × 320: hdpi	28	Android 9.0 (Wear OS)	x86	513 MB	▶ ✎ ▾
	Automotive (1024p la...		1024 × 768: mdpi	28	Android 9.0 (Automotive)	x86	513 MB	▶ ✎ ▾
	Pixel 3 API 28	▷	1080 × 2160: 440dpi	28	Android 9.0 (Google Play)	x86	8.1 GB	▶ ✎ ▾

Figure 10.11: Virtual devices

Figure 10.12 presents the choice of hardware to select as a virtual server that says an application developer may want to use for testing his or her application on a mobile platform:

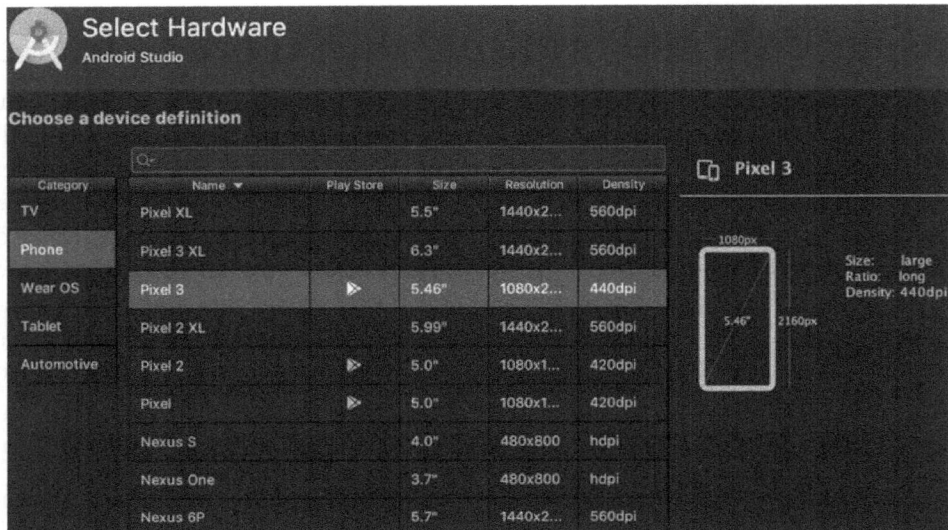

Figure 10.12: *Virtual device hardware selection*

Data remnants

When a computer or another resource is no longer in use, data remnants are data that is left behind. The best way to protect this information is to use data encryption. Without the original encryption key, data that has been encrypted cannot be recovered. An unauthorized user can access data remnants if resources, particularly hard drives, are reused frequently. Administrators must be familiar with the types of data stored on physical drives. This aids them in determining whether or not data remnants are a concern. The organization may not be concerned about data remnants if the data stored on a drive is not private or confidential. If the data on the drive is private or confidential, however, the organization should consider asset reuse and disposal policies. Data remnants must be destroyed using a method commensurate with the sensitivity of the data, or the data must be permanently encrypted and the key destroyed, according to cloud provider SLAs.

Secure network environments

The following are the use cases:

- **Use case 1:** Securing virtualized environments in multi-tenant cloud platforms

  In modern organizations, virtualization is a cornerstone of scalable infrastructure. A large e-commerce company hosts its operations on a multi-tenant cloud platform using VMs) and containers. Ensuring the security of these virtualized resources is paramount to protecting sensitive customer data.

Following are the practical implications:

o **Network isolation:** Network isolation in virtualized environments ensures that each VM or container operates within its own secure network, preventing unauthorized access or data leakage between different workloads. By segmenting the network, organizations can reduce the risk of lateral movement by attackers, limiting the impact of potential breaches. This approach enhances security by enforcing strict boundaries, controlling traffic flow, and applying tailored security policies for each isolated network segment:

   ▪ Set up **virtual private clouds (VPCs)** with strict subnet segregation for public and private workloads. Tools like AWS VPC or Azure Virtual Network can be used to establish segmentation.

   ▪ Configure security groups and **network access control lists (NACLs)** to permit only necessary traffic between VMs.

o **Hardening hypervisors and hosts:** To ensure the security of virtualized environments, it is essential to focus on hardening hypervisors and hosts. These foundational components manage and control the VMs, and their integrity is critical for protecting the entire infrastructure from potential vulnerabilities and attacks.

   ▪ Apply security patches and updates to the hypervisor (for example, VMware ESXi, KVM, or Hyper-V).

   ▪ Enable secure boot and **kernel-based virtual machine (KVM)** protection to prevent unauthorized changes.

o **Monitoring and threat detection:** Effective monitoring and threat detection are critical components of a robust cybersecurity strategy, enabling organizations to identify and respond to potential risks before they escalate into significant security incidents. By continuously tracking system activity, network traffic, and user behavior, businesses can proactively detect anomalies, mitigate threats, and safeguard their digital infrastructure.

   ▪ Deploy **intrusion detection system (IDS)** and **intrusion prevention system (IPS)** like snort or Suricata within the virtual environment.

   ▪ Enable hypervisor-level monitoring for anomalies such as memory overcommitment or unusual CPU spikes.

o **Encryption and key management:** Encryption and key management are fundamental to protecting sensitive data, ensuring that information remains secure both at rest and in transit. By utilizing advanced encryption techniques and robust key management practices, organizations can safeguard their data from unauthorized access while maintaining compliance with industry regulations and standards. Properly implemented encryption and key management ensure that only authorized parties can decrypt and access critical business and customer information.

- Encrypt VM disk images and backup files using tools like BitLocker or **Linux Unified Key Setup (LUKS).**

- Implement centralized key management via AWS **Key Management Server (KMS)** or HashiCorp vault to control encryption keys.

For example, configure VMware NSX to create micro-segments for individual VMs. Apply distributed firewalls to enforce granular security policies across applications.

- **Use case 2**: Securing distributed network architectures across geographic locations.

A global healthcare organization operates multiple clinics and data centers connected via a **wide-area network (WAN)**. Securing communication and ensuring data integrity across these distributed networks is crucial for regulatory compliance.

Following are the practical implementation

o **Set up secure tunnels:** Setting up secure tunnels is a critical approach for ensuring protected communication across distributed networks, particularly for organizations like healthcare providers that handle sensitive patient data. By establishing encrypted tunnels, such as **virtual private networks (VPNs)** or secure site-to-site connections, the organization can safeguard data in transit and maintain confidentiality, integrity, and regulatory compliance across its global network.

- Use VPNs like OpenVPN or WireGuard to encrypt communication between branch offices and central servers.

- Implement **multiprotocol label switching (MPLS)** with IPsec to secure data transport across the WAN.

o **Zero trust network architecture (ZTNA):** In a distributed network environment like that of a global healthcare organization, implementing a Zero Trust security model and robust network architecture is essential to ensure that all communications are secure and data integrity is maintained. By verifying every user, device, and network request, regardless of location, Zero Trust eliminates trust assumptions and enforces strict access controls, which are critical for maintaining regulatory compliance and safeguarding sensitive health data.

- Apply a zero-trust model using identity-based segmentation. Tools like Zscaler or Palo Alto Prisma Access can enforce authentication for every access request.

- Integrate **endpoint detection and response (EDR)** solutions to secure devices across the distributed environment.

o **Monitoring and anomaly detection:** Monitoring and anomaly detection are essential for safeguarding communication and data integrity across distributed healthcare networks. By continuously analyzing network traffic and system activity, organizations can identify unusual patterns that may indicate potential security breaches, unauthorized access, or data tampering. This proactive approach helps ensure compliance with regulatory standards while maintaining the confidentiality and availability of sensitive healthcare data:

- Use **security information and event management (SIEM)** solutions such as Splunk or QRadar to analyze logs from multiple locations.

- Deploy **network traffic analysis (NTA)** tools like Zeek (formerly Bro) to identify unusual patterns.

o **Redundancy and resilience:** Redundancy and resilience are critical for ensuring continuous and secure communication across a distributed network, particularly in industries like healthcare where data availability and integrity are paramount. By implementing redundant systems and network paths, organizations can minimize the risk of downtime or data loss, ensuring that critical operations remain unaffected during network failures or disruptions. These measures help maintain the reliability and performance of the network, supporting both regulatory compliance and operational continuity:

- Implement redundant links and failover mechanisms using **border gateway protocol (BGP)** to prevent outages.

- Conduct simulated disaster recovery drills to validate backup and recovery plans.

For example, set up WireGuard VPN for secure communication between distributed clinics. Configure each node to verify traffic signatures and enforce strict access rules.

- **Use case 3:** Securing hybrid networks with on-premises and cloud integration

A financial institution has adopted a hybrid model, integrating its legacy on-premises data centers with public cloud services for scalability. This setup introduces challenges in managing security consistently across environments.

Following are the practical implementation:

o **Identity and access management (IAM):** IAM is essential in ensuring secure and consistent access controls across both on-premises data centers and public cloud environments. By implementing IAM, financial institutions can effectively manage user identities, authenticate access, and enforce policies that govern who can access sensitive data and resources. This helps to mitigate security risks, ensure regulatory compliance, and maintain a unified approach to protecting assets across hybrid infrastructures:

- Synchronize on-premises **Active Directory (AD)** with cloud directories using Azure AD Connect or AWS Directory Service.

- Enforce **multi-factor authentication (MFA)** for administrative accounts across both environments.

o **Unified security policies:** Unified security policies are essential for maintaining consistent protection across hybrid IT environments, where organizations leverage both on-premises data centers and public cloud services. By establishing a centralized framework for security controls, businesses can ensure that all systems, regardless of location, adhere to the same standards and compliance requirements. This approach simplifies management, reduces security gaps, and enhances the overall security posture, ensuring that sensitive financial data remains protected across diverse infrastructure landscapes:

- Use hybrid firewalls like Palo Alto Networks or Fortinet to apply consistent policies to both on-premises and cloud environments.

- Deploy **software-defined WAN (SD-WAN)** solutions to dynamically route traffic based on security policies.

o **Data protection and compliance:** Data protection and compliance are essential for maintaining the confidentiality, integrity, and availability of sensitive financial information in a hybrid environment. As organizations integrate on-premises data centers with public cloud services, ensuring consistent security controls and adhering to regulatory requirements across both environments becomes a complex but crucial task. By implementing robust data protection strategies and aligning with industry standards, financial institutions can safeguard their assets while meeting stringent compliance obligations:

- Encrypt data in transit between environments using IPsec VPNs.

- Monitor data flows for compliance violations with tools like Microsoft Defender for Cloud or AWS Macie.

o **Security posture management:** Security posture management is essential for organizations leveraging hybrid environments, as it enables consistent visibility and control over security across both on-premises data centers and public cloud services. By continuously assessing and optimizing security configurations, organizations can identify vulnerabilities, ensure compliance, and proactively mitigate risks, maintaining a unified security strategy across all platforms. This approach helps financial institutions safeguard sensitive data and maintain a strong security posture despite the complexity of managing multiple environments:

- Regularly assess configurations with tools like Microsoft Azure Security Center or AWS Security Hub.

- Automate security posture management using **infrastructure as code (IaC)** and tools like Terraform to enforce secure templates.

For example, deploy AWS Direct Connect to establish a private link between the cloud and on-premises data centers. Use Azure Arc to manage security policies for both environments from a centralized console.

Conclusion

This chapter covers cloud and virtualization concepts and considerations for hosting on cloud v/s on-premise, and discusses the cloud deployment models and hypervisors along with hyper-converged infrastructure. This chapter also describes the vulnerabilities associated with a single server hosting multiple apps and data as well as the vulnerabilities associated with a single platform hosting multiple VMs.

In the next chapter, we will discuss about the controls for application vulnerabilities.

Exercise

1. **What is a primary consideration when integrating cloud and virtualization technologies in an enterprise environment?**
   a. Redundant hardware setup
   b. Data backup frequency
   c. Compatibility with legacy systems
   d. Physical location of the data center

2. **Which cloud service model provides the highest level of control over infrastructure to the end user?**
   a. Software as a Service (SaaS)
   b. Platform as a Service (PaaS)
   c. Infrastructure as a Service (IaaS)
   d. Function as a Service (FaaS)

3. **What is a major security concern when using virtualization technology?**
   a. Data encryption overhead
   b. Virtual machine escape
   c. Network bottlenecks
   d. Slow disk I/O

4. **Which of the following is a key feature of Hyper Converged Infrastructure (HCI)?**

    a. Centralized management of network components

    b. Integration of compute, storage, and networking in a single appliance

    c. Decoupling storage and compute resources

    d. Exclusive use of physical servers for higher security

5. **What is the primary purpose of vulnerability scanning in an IT environment?**

    a. To identify missing patches and security updates

    b. To monitor network traffic for performance issues

    c. To optimize storage usage

    d. To assess user compliance with security policies

6. **What is the main purpose of using a sandbox in cybersecurity?**

    a. To improve system performance by isolating resources

    b. To run untrusted code or programs in isolation to prevent harm to the host system

    c. To optimize database queries for better performance

    d. To ensure compliance with regulatory standards

7. **Which security measure is critical for ensuring secure communication in hybrid network environments?**

    a. Implementing network segmentation and isolation

    b. Increasing server physical security

    c. Relying solely on traditional firewalls

    d. Limiting the number of virtual machines deployed

Answers

1. c
2. c
3. b
4. b
5. a
6. b
7. a

CHAPTER 11
Application Security Controls

Introduction

Hardening the operating system should not be the only place where security efforts are performed. Every application has its own set of vulnerabilities. This chapter examines some of the cyberattacks that can be launched against applications, as well as the vulnerabilities that apps running on various operating systems present. It also covers safe coding techniques. Finally, the devices and services utilized to secure apps are discussed in this chapter.

Structure

In this chapter, we will discuss the following topics:

- Application security design considerations
- Application security issues
- Improper error and exception handling
- Secure cookie storage and transmission
- Application sandboxing
- Web application firewalls
- Client-side and server-side processing
- Firmware and OS vulnerabilities

Objectives

This chapter covers application security design concepts, including security-by-design, security-by-default, and security-by-deployment. Application issues such as session management, XSS, CSRF, clickjacking, input validation, SQL injections, exception handling, and privileged escalation are also discussed. The chapter also presents the use of sandboxing during application security analysis, along with issues involved with encrypting information and database security monitoring and the use of web application firewalls. The chapter also compares the client-side and server-side processing, including browser extensions, ActiveX, Java, HTML, AJAX, SOAP and JavaScript. The chapter discusses firmware and operating system related vulnerabilities.

Application security design considerations

Web-based applications are everywhere; these are designed to use web servers as a platform and to respond and communicate with the browsers of the users. Because they are widely used, they are also widely attacked. **Open Web Application Security Project (OWASP)** maintains a list of the top 10 errors found in web applications. The challenge is that those who write the code that makes applications work often do not have security as their main goal. Many times, there is a rush to deliver the application to the market. The following section looks at the concepts of security-by-design, security-by-default, and security-by-deployment.

Security by design, default, and deployment

An application should be secure by design, by default, and by deployment, which is discussed as follows:

- **Security by design**: This means the application was designed with security in mind rather than as an afterthought. An application is truly secure if you give someone the details of the application's security system, and the person still cannot defeat the security. An application should not rely on the lack of knowledge on the part of the hacker.

- **Security by default**: This means that without changes to any default settings, the application is secure. For example, some server products have certain security capabilities, but those services must be enabled in order to function so that the service is not available to a hacker. A product that requires the enabling of the security functions is not secure by default.

- **Security by deployment**: This means the environment into which the application is introduced was considered from a security standpoint. For example, it may be advisable to disable all unused interfaces on one server, while that may not be critical on another server.

Application security issues

To understand how to secure applications, you need to understand what you are up against. You need to know about a number of specific security issues and attacks. The following sections survey some of them.

Insecure direct object reference

Applications frequently use the actual name or key of an object when generating web pages. Applications do not always verify that a user is authorized for the target object. This results in an insecure direct object reference flaw. Such an attack can come from an authorized user, meaning that the user has permission to use the application but is accessing information to which she should not have access. To prevent this problem, each direct object reference should undergo an access check, as illustrated in *Figure 11.1* (Code review of the application with this specific issue in mind is also recommended.):

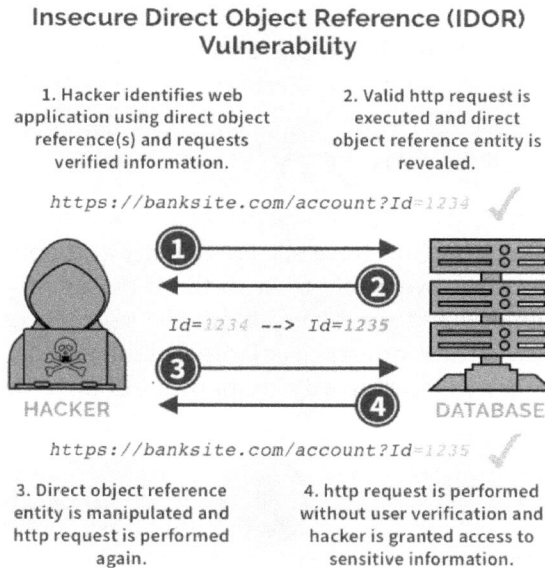

Insecure Direct Object Reference (IDOR) Vulnerability

1. Hacker identifies web application using direct object reference(s) and requests verified information.

2. Valid http request is executed and direct object reference entity is revealed.

`https://banksite.com/account?Id=1234` ✓

`Id=1234 --> Id=1235`

HACKER   DATABASE

`https://banksite.com/account?Id=1235` ✓

3. Direct object reference entity is manipulated and http request is performed again.

4. http request is performed without user verification and hacker is granted access to sensitive information.

Figure 11.1: Insecure direct object reference

Cross-site scripting

Cross-site scripting (**XSS**) occurs when an attacker locates a website vulnerability and injects malicious code into the web application. Many websites allow and even incorporate user input into a web page to customize the page. If a web application does not properly validate this input, one of two things could happen, either the text will be rendered on the page, or a script may be executed when others visit the web page. *Figure 11.2* displays an XSS attack:

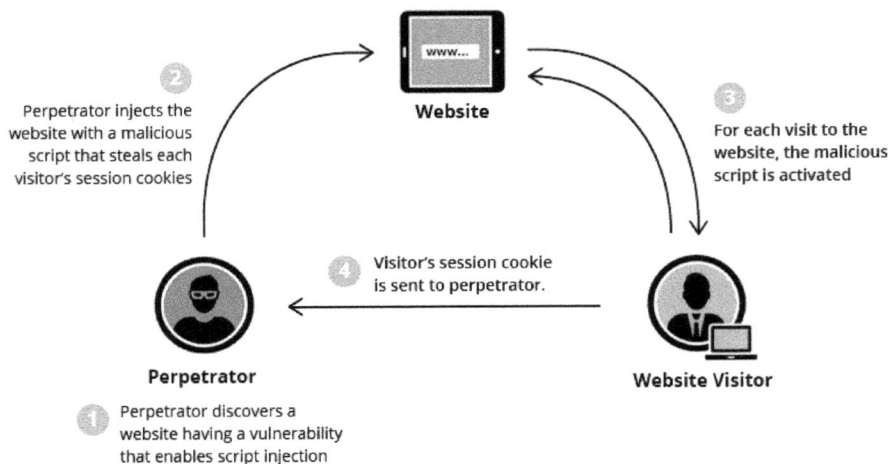

Figure 11.2: XSS attack

Proper validation of all input should be performed to prevent this type of attack. This involves identifying all user-supplied input and testing all output.

Cross-site request forgery

Cross-site request forgery (**CSRF**) is an attack that causes an end user to execute unwanted actions on a web application in which he or she is currently authenticated. Unlike XSS, with CSRF, the attacker exploits the website's trust in the browser rather than the other way around. The website thinks the request came from the user's browser and was actually made by the user. However, the request was planted in the user's browser. It usually gets there by a user following a URL that already contains the code to be injected, as illustrated in *Figure 11.3*:

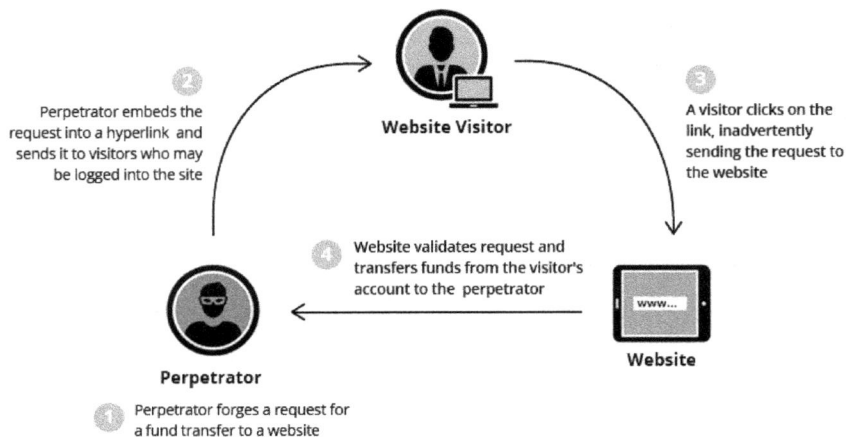

Figure 11.3: CSRF

The following measures help prevent CSRF vulnerabilities in web applications:

- Using techniques like URLEncode and HTMLEncode, encode all output based on input parameters for special characters to prevent malicious scripts from executing.

- Filter input parameters based on special characters (those that enable malicious scripts to execute).

- Filter output based on input parameters for special characters.

Clickjacking

A hacker using a click-jack attack crafts a transparent page or frame over a legitimate-looking page that entices the user to click on something. When he does, he is really clicking on a different URL. In many cases, the site or application may entice the user to enter credentials that could be used later by the attacker, as shown in *Figure 11.4*. The most responsibility for preventing click-jacking rests with the site owner. When designing website applications, the X-FRAME-OPTIONS header is used to control the embedding of a site within a frame. This option should be set to DENY, which virtually ensures that click-jacking attacks fail. Also, the SAMEORIGIN option of X-FRAME can be used to restrict the site to be framed only in web pages from the same origin. *Figure 11.4* illustrates click-jacking:

1	2	3	4	5
USER SEES AN AD FOR A PRODUCT OR SERVICE ON SOCIAL MEDIA OR EMAIL.	USER CLICKS THE LINK. "PHISH" IS SUCCESSFUL.	USER ENTERS PERSONAL INFORMATION VIA FAKE WEBSITE OR OVERLAID LOGIN FORM IMPOSED BY FRAUDSTER.	USING LOGIN DATA, ITEMS CAN BE PURCHASED. MALWARE INSTALLED, AND USER DATA CAN BE SOLD FOR FURTHER CRIMES.	COMPROMISED SYSTEM CAN ALSO GIVE HACKERS ACCESS TO LOCATION DATA, HARDWARE, AND MORE.

Figure 11.4: Click-jacking

Session management

Session management involves taking measures to protect against session hijacking. This can occur when a hacker is able to identify the unique session ID assigned to an authenticated user. It is important that the process used by the webserver to generate these IDs be truly random. The hacker would need to identify or discover the session ID of the authenticated user and could do so using several methods. A session hijacking attack is presented below and illustrated in *Figure 11.5*:

- **Guessing the session ID**: This involves gathering samples of session IDs and guessing a valid ID assigned to another user's session.

- **Stolen session ID**: Although SSL connections hide these IDs, many sites do not require an SSL connection using session ID cookies.

- **Steal cookie:** These can be stolen through XSS attacks and by gaining physical access to the cookie stored on a user's computer.

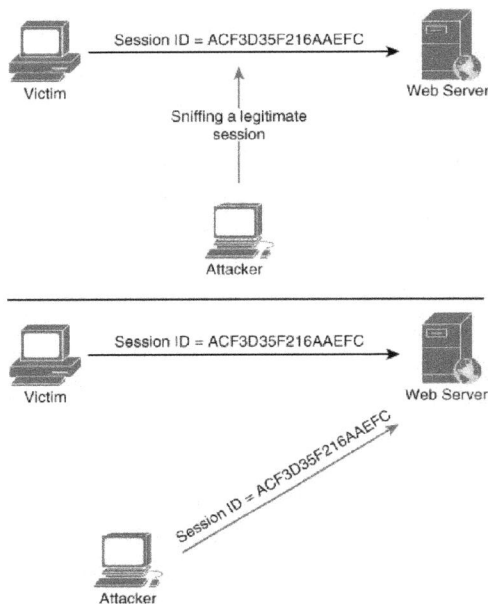

Figure 11.5: *Session hijacking*

The following measures help prevent session hijacking:

- Encode heuristic information, such as IP addresses, into session IDs.

- Use SecureSessionModule. It modifies each session ID by appending a hash to the ID. The hash or MAC is generated from the session ID, the network portion of the IP address, the UserAgent header in the request, and a secret key stored on the server. SecureSessionModule uses this value to validate each request for a session cookie.

Input validation

Many of the attacks discussed in this section arise because the web application has not validated the data entered by the user (or hacker). Input validation is the process of checking all input for things such as proper format and proper length. In many cases, these validators use either the blacklisting of characters or patterns or the whitelisting of characters or patterns. Blacklisting involves looking for characters or patterns to block. It can be prone to preventing legitimate requests. Whitelisting involves looking for allowable characters or patterns and allowing only those. The length of the input should also be checked and verified to prevent buffer overflows.

SQL injection

SQL injection attack inserts, or **injects**, an SQL query as the input data from the client to the application. This type of attack can result in reading sensitive data from a database, modifying database data, executing administrative operations on the database, recovering the content of a given file, and even issuing commands to the operating system. *Figure 11.6* shows how regular users might request information from a database attached to a web server and also how a hacker might ask for the same information and get usernames and passwords by changing the command; it also displays how the attack is prevented by the security rules:

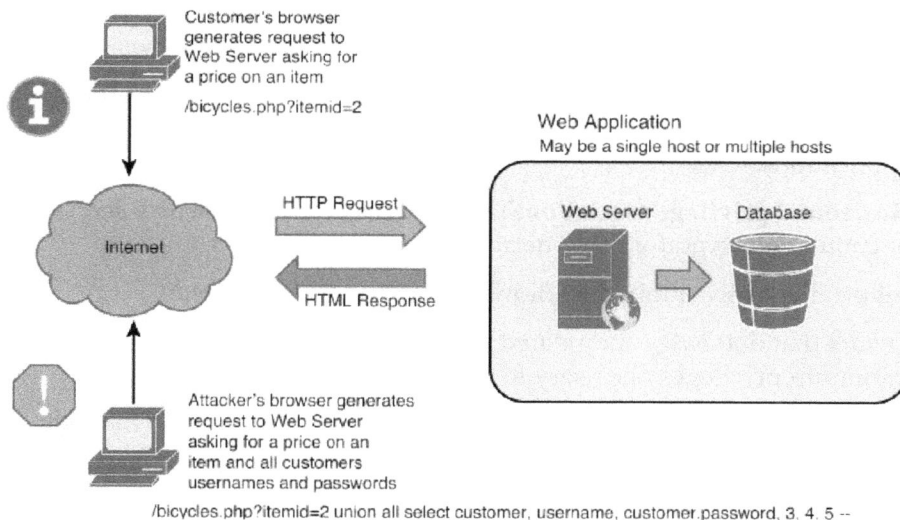

Figure 11.6: *SQL injection*

The job of identifying SQL injection attacks in logs can be made easier by using commercial tools such as Log Parser by Microsoft. This command-line utility, which uses SQL-like commands, can be used to search for and locate errors of a specific type. For example, a 500 error (internal server error) often indicates a SQL injection. To prevent these types of attacks, the following must be implemented:

- Use proper input validation.

- Use blacklisting or whitelisting of special characters.

- Use parameterized queries in ASP.Net and prepared statements in Java to perform the escaping of dangerous characters before the SQL statement is passed to the database.

Improper error and exception handling

Web applications, like all other applications, suffer from errors and exceptions, and such problems are to be expected. However, the manner in which an application reacts to errors and exceptions determines whether security can be compromised. One of the issues is that an error message may reveal information about the system that a hacker may find useful. For this reason, when applications are developed, all error messages describing problems should be kept as generic as possible. Also, you can use tools such as the OWASP's WebScarab to try to make applications generate errors.

Privilege escalation

Privilege escalation is the process of exploiting a bug or weakness in an operating system to allow a user to receive privileges to which they are not entitled. These privileges can be used to delete files, view private information, or install unwanted programs, such as viruses. There are two types of privilege escalation, which are as follows:

- **Vertical privilege escalation**: This occurs when a lower-privilege user or application accesses functions or content reserved for higher privilege users or applications.

- **Horizontal privilege escalation**: This occurs when a normal user accesses functions or content reserved for other normal users.

To prevent privilege escalation, the following must be implemented:

- Ensure that databases and related systems and applications are operating with the minimum privileges necessary to function.

- Verify that users are given the minimum access required to do their job.

- Ensure that databases do not run with root, administrator, or other privileged account permissions, if possible.

Improper storage of sensitive data

Sensitive information in this discussion includes usernames, passwords, encryption keys, and paths that applications need to function, but that would cause harm if discovered. Determining the proper method of securing this information is critical and not easy. It is a generally accepted rule not to hard-code passwords, although this was not always considered a best practice. Instead, passwords should be protected using encryption when they are included in the application code. This makes them difficult to change, reverse, or discover. Storing this type of sensitive information in a configuration file also presents problems. Such files are usually discoverable, and, even if hidden, they can be discovered by using a demo version of the software if it is a standard or default location. Whatever the method used, significant thought should be given to protecting these sensitive forms of data. To prevent disclosure of sensitive information from storage, the following must be implemented:

- Ensure that memory locations where this data is stored are locked memory.

- Ensure that **access control lists (ACL)** attached to sensitive data are properly configured.

- Implement an appropriate level of encryption.

Fuzzing or fault injection

Fuzz testing, or fuzzing, involves injecting invalid or unexpected input (sometimes called **faults**) into an application to test how the application reacts. It is usually done with a software tool that automates the process. Inputs can include environment variables, keyboard and mouse events, and sequences of API calls. *Figure 11.7* shows the logic of the fuzzing process:

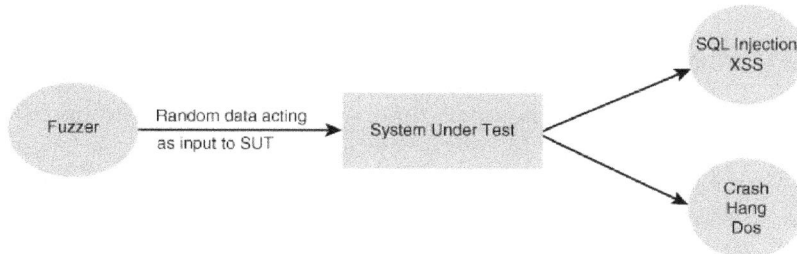

Figure 11.7: *Fuzzing*

Two types of fuzzing can be used to identify susceptibility to a fault injection attack, which are as follows:

- **Mutation fuzzing**: This type involves changing the existing input values (blindly).
- **Generation-based fuzzing**: This type involves generating the inputs from scratch, based on the specification or format.

To prevent fault injection attacks, the following must be implemented:

- Implement fuzz testing to help identify problems.
- Adhere to safe coding and project management practices.
- Deploy application-level firewalls.

Secure cookie storage and transmission

Cookies are text files that are stored on a user's hard drive or in a user's memory. These files store information on the user's Internet habits, including browsing and spending information. This is because a website's servers actually determine how cookies are used, malicious sites can use cookies to discover a large amount of information about a user. While the information retained in cookies on a hard drive usually does not include any confidential information, attackers can use those cookies to obtain information about users that can help them develop better-targeted attacks. For example, if the cookies reveal to an attacker that a user accesses a particular bank's public website on a daily basis, that action can indicate that a user has an account at that bank, and the attacker may attempt a phishing attack using an email that appears to come from the user's legitimate bank.

Many antivirus and anti-malware applications include functionality that allows you to limit the type of cookies downloaded and to hide **personally identifiable information (PII)**, such as email addresses. Often these types of safeguards end up being more trouble than they are worth because they often affect legitimate Internet communication. When creating web applications, thought should be given to the secure storage of cookies. Cookies should be encrypted. Also, cookies to be stored on the client should not contain essential information. Any cookie that does should be stored on the server, and a pointer should be provided to the client to the cookie on the server.

Buffer overflow

Buffers are portions of system memory that are used to store information. A buffer overflow is an attack that occurs when the amount of data that is submitted to data is larger than the buffer can handle. Typically, this type of attack is possible because of poorly written application or operating system code. This can result in an injection of malicious code, primarily either a **denial-of-service (DoS)** attack or an SQL injection. To protect against this issue, organizations should ensure that all operating systems and applications are updated with the latest service packs and patches. In addition, programmers should properly test all applications to check for overflow conditions.

Hackers can take advantage of this phenomenon by submitting too much data, which can cause an error or, in some cases, execute commands on the machine if the hacker can locate an area where commands can be executed. Not all attacks are designed to execute commands. An attack may just lock the computer as a DoS attack. A packet containing a long string of **no-operation (NOP)** instructions followed by a command usually indicates a type of buffer overflow attack called an NOP slide. The purpose of this type of attack is to get the CPU to locate where a command can be executed.

With proper input validation, a buffer overflow attack causes an access violation. Without proper input validation, the allocated space is exceeded, and the data at the bottom of the memory stack is overwritten. The key to preventing many buffer overflow attacks is input validation, in which any input is checked for format and length before it is used. Buffer overflows and boundary errors (when the input exceeds the boundaries allotted for the input) are a family of error conditions called **input validation errors**.

Memory leaks

Applications use memory to store resources, objects, and variables. When an application mismanages the memories it has been assigned by the operating system, several things can occur. One is that over time, by not returning the allocated memory to the operating system, memory is exhausted. In addition, objects that have been stored in memory may become inaccessible to the application. Fixing a memory leak usually involves adding or replacing some code to free the memory in the questionable code path.

Integer overflows

The integer overflow occurs when math operations try to create a numeric value that is too large for the available space. The register width of a processor determines the range of values that can be represented. Moreover, a program may assume that a variable always contains a positive value. If the variable has a signed integer type, an overflow can cause its value to wrap and become negative. This may lead to unintended behavior. Similarly, subtracting from a small unsigned value may cause it to wrap to a large positive value, which may also be an unexpected behavior. Mitigate integer overflow attacks by implementing the following:

- Using strict input validation.

- Using a language or compiler that performs automatic bounds checks.

- Choosing an integer type that contains all possible values of a calculation. This reduces the need for integer type casting (changing an entity of one data type into another), which is a major source of defects.

Race conditions

A race condition is an attack in which the hacker inserts himself between instructions, introduces changes, and alters the order of execution of the instructions, thereby altering the outcome. This condition occurs when multiple processes or threads attempt to access shared resources concurrently, leading to unpredictable or unintended outcomes. This happens when the system does not properly synchronize access to critical data, allowing attackers or even legitimate processes to manipulate the sequence in which operations are executed. Exploiting this vulnerability can lead to data corruption, privilege escalation, or unauthorized access. Race conditions are particularly dangerous in multi-threaded applications and can be difficult to detect and resolve due to their intermittent nature. Proper synchronization mechanisms, such as locks and semaphores, are essential to mitigate such risks.

Time of check or time of use

A type of race condition is time of check to time of use. In this attack, a system is changed between a condition check and the display of the check's results. For example, consider the following scenario:

At 10:00 a.m., a hacker was able to obtain a valid authentication token that allowed read or write access to the database. At 10:15 a.m., the security administrator received alerts from the **intrusion detection system** (**IDS**) about a database administrator performing unusual transactions. At 10:25 a.m., the security administrator reset the database administrator's password. At 11:30 a.m., the security administrator was still receiving alerts from the IDS about unusual transactions from the same user. In this case, a race condition was created by the hacker, disturbing the normal process of authentication. The hacker remained logged in with the old password and was still able to change data. Countermeasures to these attacks include the following:

- Make critical sets of instructions to either execute in order and in entirety or roll back or prevent the changes.
- Have the system lock access to certain items it will access when carrying out these sets of instructions.

Resource exhaustion

Resource exhaustion occurs when a computer is out of memory or CPU cycles. Memory leaks are an example of resource exhaustion, in that, eventually memory is insufficient to perform tasks. Resource exhaustion is also the goal of DoS attacks. In these attacks, the target is asked to perform some function so many times that it is overwhelmed and has no memory or CPU cycles left to perform normal activities. To prevent or minimize the effects of attacks that attempt to exhaust resources, the following must be implemented:

- Harden client machines that may be recruited for attacks that exhaust resources (for example, **distributed DoS** (**DDoS**) attacks).
- Ensure that all machines are up-to-date on security patches.
- Regularly scan machines to detect anomalous behavior.

Geotagging

Geotagging is the process of adding geographic metadata to various media, including photographs, videos, websites, **short message service (SMS)** or **really simple syndication (RSS)** feeds. This data usually consists of latitude and longitude coordinates, though it can also include altitude, bearing, distance, accuracy data, and place names. Some consider geotagging a security risk because of the information it can disclose when geotagged files are uploaded, especially to social media. In some cases, information such as the location, time of day, and where you live may be included. Measures you can take to reduce the security risk of geotagging are as follows:

- Disable geotagging on smartphones.

- Double-check and tighten security settings on social media sites.

- If possible, use geotag-specific security software to manage your multimedia.

- Remove geotagging from photos you've already uploaded.

Data remnants

A data remnant is a residual information left on a drive after a delete process. A data remnant can cause inadvertent disclosure of sensitive information. Simple deletion and formatting do not remove this data. During media disposal, you must ensure that no data remains on the media. The most reliable, secure means of removing data from magnetic storage media, such as a magnetic tape or cassette, is through degaussing, which exposes the media to a powerful, alternating magnetic field. It removes any previously written data, leaving the media in a magnetically randomized (blank) state. Some other disposal methods are as follows:

- **Data purging**: You can use a method such as degaussing to make the old data unavailable, even with forensics. Purging renders information unrecoverable against laboratory attacks (forensics).

- **Data clearing**: This type of disposal renders information unrecoverable by a keyboard. Clearing extracts information from data storage media by executing software utilities, keystrokes, or other system resources executed from a keyboard.

Use of third-party libraries

It has been estimated that 90% of software components are downloaded from code repositories. These repositories hold code that can be reused. Using these repositories speeds up software development because it eliminates the time it would take to create these components from scratch. Organizations might have their own repositories for in-house code that has been developed. In other cases, developers may use a third-party repository in which the components are sold. Vulnerabilities exist in much of the code found in these repositories. Many have been documented and disclosed as **common vulnerabilities and exposures** (**CVEs**). In many cases, these vulnerabilities have been addressed, and updates have been uploaded to the repository. The problem is that far too many have not been addressed, and even in cases where they have been addressed, developers continue to use the component they have without downloading the new version. When third-party repositories must be used, developers can no longer afford to use third-party libraries without also keeping track of the libraries' updates and security profiles.

Code reuse

Not all code reuse happens with third parties. In some cases, organizations maintain internal code repositories. The Financial Services Information Sharing and Analysis

Center, an industry forum for collaboration on critical security threats facing the global financial services sector, recommends the following measures to reduce the risk of reusing components in general:

- Ensure that developers must apply policy controls during the acquisition process as the most proactive type of control for addressing the security vulnerabilities in open-source libraries.

- Manage risks by using controlled internal repositories to provision open-source components and block the ability to download components directly from the internet.

Application sandboxing

Sandboxing an application means limiting the parts of the operating system, and user files the application is allowed to interact with. This prevents the code from making permanent changes to the OS kernel and other data on the host machine. This concept is illustrated in *Figure 11.8*:

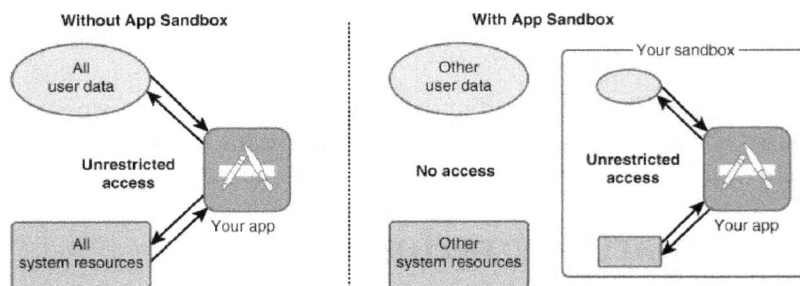

Figure 11.8: Sandboxing

The sandbox has to contain all the files the application needs to execute, which can create problems between applications that need to interact with one another. This is because of this, sandboxing can sometimes create more problems than it solves. Sandboxing is most often implemented by creating a **virtual machine** (**VM**) that is disconnected from the physical network.

Secure encrypted enclaves

A secure enclave is a part of an operating system that cannot be compromised even when the operating system kernel is compromised because the enclave has its own CPU and is separated from the rest of the system. This means security functions remain intact even when someone has gained control of the OS. Secure enclaves are a relatively recent technology being developed to provide additional security. Cisco, Microsoft, and Apple all have implementations of secure enclaves that differ in implementation but all share the same goal of creating an area that cannot be compromised even when the OS is.

Database activity monitor

Database activity monitoring (DAM) involves monitoring transactions and the activity of database services. DAM can be used for monitoring unauthorized access and fraudulent activities as well as for compliance auditing. DAM refers to the process of continuously observing and analyzing database operations to detect, alert, and respond to potential threats or policy violations. It helps organizations track user interactions with databases, including read, write, and administrative actions, providing real-time visibility into database activity. DAM solutions are essential for identifying unauthorized access attempts, data exfiltration, and suspicious behavior, thereby enhancing data security. Additionally, DAM plays a crucial role in maintaining regulatory compliance by ensuring that all database transactions are properly logged and can be audited. By implementing DAM, businesses can proactively safeguard sensitive information and meet industry standards.

Web application firewalls

Web Application Firewall (WAF) applies rule sets to an HTTP conversation. These sets cover common attack types to which these session types are susceptible. Without customization, a WAF protects against SQL injection, DOM-based XSS, and HTTP exhaustion attacks. A WAF is a security solution designed to protect web applications from a wide range of attacks by filtering and monitoring incoming HTTP/HTTPS traffic. It sits between the user and the web server, analyzing the requests to identify and block malicious activities. WAFs use predefined and customizable rule sets to prevent attacks such as XSS, SQL injection, file inclusion, and bot attacks. In addition to protecting against known threats, WAFs can be configured to detect and mitigate zero-day vulnerabilities, offering a critical layer of defense for safeguarding web applications from evolving cyber threats.

Client-side versus server-side processing

When a web application is developed, one of the decisions to be made is what information will be processed on the server and what will be processed on the browser of the client. Many web designers like processing to occur on the client side, which taxes the web server less and allows it to serve more users. Others shudder at the idea of sending to the client all the processing code, and possibly information that could be useful in attacking the server. Modern web development should be concerned with finding the right balance between server-side and client-side implementation. *Figure 11.9* shows client and server-side script processing:

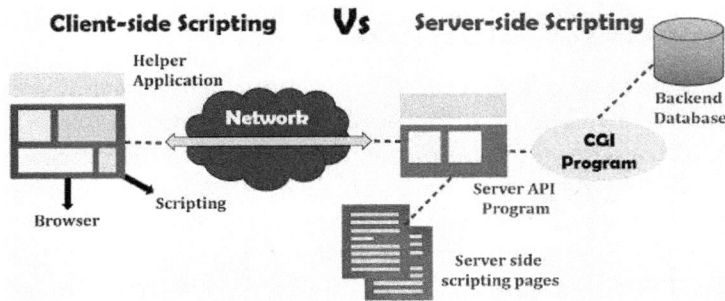

Figure 11.9: Client and server-side processing

JSON or REST

Representational State Transfer (REST) is a client or server model for interacting with content on remote systems, typically using HTTP. It involves accessing and modifying existing content and also adding content to a system in a particular way. REST does not require a specific message format during HTTP resource exchanges. It is up to a RESTful web service to choose which formats are supported. RESTful services are services that do not violate the required restraints. XML and **JavaScript Object Notation (JSON)** are two of the most popular formats used by RESTful web services.

JSON is a simple text-based message format that is often used with RESTful web services. Like XML, it is designed to be readable, and this can help when debugging and testing. JSON is derived from JavaScript and, therefore, is very popular as a data format in web applications. REST or JSON has several advantages over SOAP or XML, which are as follows:

- **Size**: REST or JSON is a lot smaller and less bloated than SOAP or XML. Therefore, much less data is passed over the network, which is particularly important for mobile devices.

- **Efficiency**: REST or JSON makes it easier to parse data, thereby making it easier to extract and convert the data. As a result, it requires much less from the client's CPU.

- **Caching**: REST or JSON provides improved response times and server loading due to support from caching.

- **Implementation**: REST or JSON interfaces are much easier than SOAP/XML to design and implement. SOAP or XML is generally preferred in transactional services such as banking services.

Browser extensions

Browser extensions, or add-ons as they are sometimes called, are small programs or scripts that increase the functionality of a website. The following sections look at some of the most popular technologies used for browser extensions. Browser extensions are lightweight software components designed to enhance or modify the functionality of web browsers. These extensions can add features, improve user experience, or enable seamless integration with third-party services, such as password managers, ad blockers, or security tools. Extensions are typically built using web technologies like HTML, JavaScript, and CSS, allowing developers to create highly customizable solutions. While browser extensions offer convenience and productivity benefits, they can also introduce security risks if not properly vetted. Malicious extensions may compromise user privacy or inject harmful code into web pages, which is why careful scrutiny is essential when installing them.

ActiveX

ActiveX is a server-side Microsoft technology that uses **object-oriented programming (OOP)** and is based on the **component object model (COM)** and the **distributed component object model (DCOM)**. COM enables software components to communicate. DCOM provides the same functionality to software components distributed across networked computers. Self-sufficient programs called controls become a part of the operating system once downloaded. The problem is that these controls execute under the security context of the current user, who, in many cases, has administrator rights. This means that a malicious ActiveX control could do some serious damage. ActiveX uses Authenticode technology to digitally sign controls. This system has been shown to have significant flaws, and ActiveX controls are generally regarded with more suspicion than Java applets.

Java applets

A Java applet is a small server-side component created using Java that runs in a web browser. It is platform-independent and creates intermediate code called **byte code** that is not processor-specific. When a Java applet is downloaded to a computer, the **Java Virtual Machine (JVM)**, which must be present on the destination computer, converts the byte code to machine code. The JVM executes the applet in a protected environment called a **sandbox**. This critical security feature, called the **Java Security Model (JSM)**, helps mitigate the damage that could be caused by malicious code. However, it does not eliminate the problem with hostile applets (also called **active content modules**), so Java applets should still be regarded with suspicion as they may launch intentional attacks after being downloaded from the internet.

Hypertext markup language 5

HTML5 is the latest version of **hypertext markup language (HTML)**. It has been improved to support the latest multimedia (which is why it is considered a likely successor to Flash). Some of the security issues of HTML4 and JavaScript remain in HTML5, and hackers who spread malware and steal user information on the Web will continue to seek new ways of doing so in HTML5. As they investigate HTML5, they are likely to find new ways of tricking users, spreading malware, and stealing clicks.

Asynchronous JavaScript and XML

Asynchronous JavaScript and XML (AJAX) is a group of interrelated web development techniques used on the client-side to create asynchronous web applications. AJAX uses a security feature called the same-origin policy that can prevent some techniques from functioning across domains. This policy permits scripts running on pages originating from the same site, a combination of scheme, hostname, and port number—to access each other's DOM with no specific restrictions, but it prevents access to DOM on different sites. An AJAX application introduces an intermediary, the AJAX engine between the user and the server. Instead of loading a web page, at the start of the session, the browser loads an AJAX engine. The AJAX engine allows the user's interaction with the application to happen asynchronously (that is, independently of communication with the server). *Figure 11.10* compares the AJAX process and that of a traditional web application:

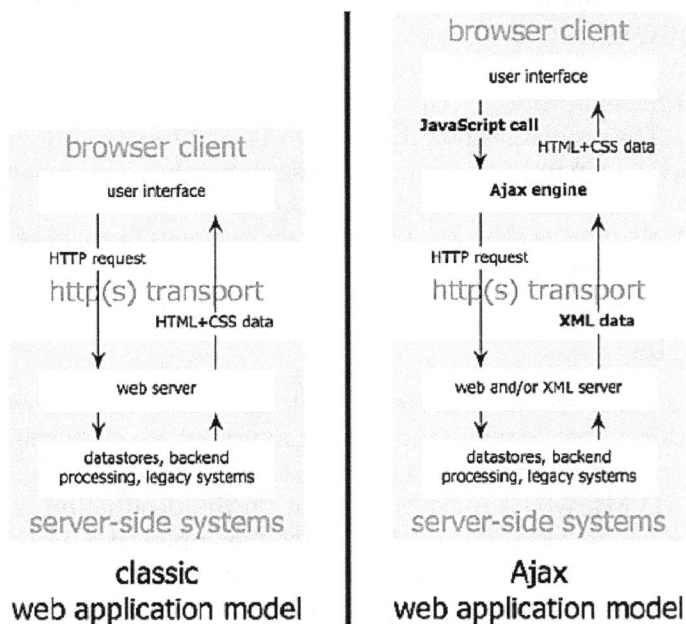

Figure 11.10: Classic and AJAX models

Simple object access protocol

Simple object access protocol (SOAP) is a protocol specification for exchanging structured information in the implementation of web services in computer networks. The SOAP specification defines a messaging framework which consists of the following:

- **SOAP processing model**: Defines the rules for processing a SOAP message
- **SOAP extensibility model**: Defines the concepts of SOAP features and SOAP modules

- **SOAP binding framework**: Describes the rules for defining a binding to an underlying protocol that can be used for exchanging SOAP messages between SOAP nodes
- **SOAP message**: Defines the structure of a SOAP message

One of the disadvantages of SOAP is the verbosity of its operation. This has led many developers to use the REST architecture instead. From a security perspective, while the SOAP body can be partially or completely encrypted, the SOAP header is not encrypted and allows intermediaries to view the header data.

State management

In the context of web applications, state management refers to the process of making an application remember the interactions the user has had with the application. Because the Web itself is stateless (that is, pages previously accessed are not remembered), this management is provided externally in some way. There are a number of ways in which this can be done. One is to use cookies to track past interactions. The advantage of this method is that it reduces the burden on the webserver. Another method is to have the server store this information. This requires local storage for the information, and it can cause problems in load balancing of fault-tolerant configurations. Another method is to store this information in RAM rather than in long-term storage. In any case, the server-side approach places a load on the server.

JavaScript

In its most common form, JavaScript resides inside HTML documents and can provide levels of interactivity to web pages that are not achievable with simple HTML. JavaScript is a text that is fed into a browser that can interpret it and then is enacted by the browser. JavaScript's main benefit is that it can be understood by the common human. JavaScript commands are known as event handlers, and they can be embedded right into the existing HTML commands.

Operating system vulnerabilities

As many of the traditional operating system vulnerabilities have been addressed, many attacks have moved up the OSI model to the application layer. Operating system vulnerabilities still pose a big issue because, as we have seen, compromising the OS leads to a compromise of everything on the system. Some of the attacks that we still see in the OS are as follows:

- **Drive-by download attacks**: These attacks involve using exploit kits to redirect users in order to enable malware installation. In this scenario, hackers can compromise a legitimate website by introducing malicious content that redirects users onto a landing page where exploits are present.

- **Local privilege escalation (LPE) attacks**: With these attacks, the malicious individuals are able to execute exploits and payloads that they would be unable to execute otherwise.

Surprisingly, and despite earlier (and somewhat undeserved) reputations for being so secure, Apple, iOS, and Linux now have vulnerabilities just like Windows. On the other hand, Internet Explorer continues to be the most vulnerable browser.

Firmware and OS vulnerabilities

Firmware updates might be some of the more neglected but important tasks that technicians perform. Many subscribe to the principle **if it is not broken, do not fix it**. The problem with this approach is that, in many cases, firmware updates are not designed to add functionality or fix something that does not work exactly right; rather, in many cases, they address security issues. Computers contain a lot of firmware, all of which is potentially vulnerable to hacking everything from USB keyboards and webcams to graphics and sound cards. Even computer batteries have firmware. A simple Google search for firmware vulnerabilities turns up pages and pages of results that detail various vulnerabilities too numerous to mention, as illustrated in *Figure 11.11*.

Firmware vulnerabilities

- Intel SA-00191. ...
- Thunderstrike. ...
- MergePoint EMS command injection. ...
- ROCA. ...
- Windows Error Reporting CVE-2019-0863.
- Intel NUC Kit buffer overflow. ...
- Key Reinstallation Attacks (KRACK) ...
- QualPwn CVE-2019-10540.

Figure 11.11: Firmware vulnerabilities

While it is not important to understand each and every firmware vulnerability, it is important to realize that firmware attacks are on the new frontier, and the only way to protect yourself is to keep up with the updates.

Conclusion

This chapter presented a brief on web application security designs and the issues related to web apps. The chapter also presented sandboxing for application security analysis and the use of web application firewalls. This chapter compared the client-side and server-side processing and discussed firmware and operating system related vulnerabilities.

In the next chapter, we will cover the various methodologies and procedures that are involved during penetration testing, vulnerability assessment scans, internal and external audits and security teaming exercises.

Exercise

1. **What is a key consideration when designing secure applications?**

    a. Use of static passwords for authentication

    b. Minimizing data exposure through encryption

    c. Storing sensitive data in plain text

    d. Allowing unrestricted user access for flexibility

2. **Which of the following is a common security issue in web applications?**

    a. Proper use of encryption for data transmission

    b. Lack of input validation leading to SQL injection

    c. Ensuring regular software updates

    d. Using multi-factor authentication

3. **What is a potential risk of improper error and exception handling in an application?**

    a. Increased system uptime

    b. Exposure of sensitive data in error messages

    c. Improved user experience

    d. Optimized resource management

4. **Which of the following ensures secure transmission of cookies?**

    a. Using the **HttpOnly** and **Secure** flags

    b. Storing cookies in plain text

    c. Allowing cookies to be accessed by JavaScript

    d. Not using any encryption for cookies

5. **What is the primary purpose of application sandboxing?**

    a. To run applications with unlimited access to system resources

    b. To isolate an application from the rest of the system for security

    c. To improve application performance by sharing resources

    d. To enable applications to freely interact with each other

6. **A WAF primarily protects against which type of threat?**

    a. Phishing attacks

    b. DoS attacks

    c. Attacks targeting web application vulnerabilities like SQL injection

    d. Insider threats

7. **Which of the following tasks is typically handled by server-side processing?**

    a. Form validation

    b. Rendering dynamic content

    c. User interface design

    d. Client-side scripting

8. **What is a common security risk associated with outdated firmware and operating systems?**

    a. Increased system efficiency

    b. Exploitation of unpatched vulnerabilities by attackers

    c. Better resource utilization

    d. Improved system speed and responsiveness

Answers

1. b

2. b

3. b

4. a

5. b

6. c

7. b

8. b

CHAPTER 12
Security Assessments

Introduction

In *Chapter 11, Application Security Controls*, we learned the application vulnerability controls and their importance in security domains. This chapter will cover the different procedures and methodologies involved in security vulnerability assessments, penetration testing, internal and external audits, and color-team exercises.

Structure

In this chapter, we will discuss the following topics:

- Vulnerability assessment methodology
- Penetration test
- Governance, risk, and compliance

Objective

Before an organization's IT security team secures a network, it must first evaluate where the security flaws exist. The only way to do so is to conduct an honest evaluation of the network's current status. Multiple techniques of evaluation should be utilized to account for the many types of vulnerabilities that might occur in a network. This chapter goes through many of the types of security vulnerability assessments and the flaws that each one is expected to discover. The chapter also covers ways to detect various types of security flaws that do not get discovered by those tools.

Vulnerability assessment methodology

To discover security flaws, a number of evaluation methodologies can be implemented. While some are responsible for finding network flaws, many others are focused on the vulnerable web server and application deployments. The following sections focus on the evaluation methodologies rather than the particular devices, with an emphasis on a conceptual approach.

Malware sandboxing

Malware sandboxing is a technique for detecting malware by running it on a computer and analysing it for signs of infection. One of its objectives is to detect zero-day malware, which is malware that has not yet been recognised by commercial anti-malware systems, and for which, no treatment exists. Cuckoo, an open-source automated malware analysis system, is an example of a commercial malware sandboxing technology. Seculert's Elastic Sandbox is an example of a cloud-based solution. Customers, partners, vendors, and Seculert's malware specialists use a web platform or application programming interface to upload suspicious executables to the Elastic Sandbox (API). The behaviour of the code is investigated in the sandbox, including network communications, metadata in network traffic, and host runtime modifications. All relevant information is evaluated using analytics to assess whether the code under investigation is malicious. *Figure 12.1* depicts the Elastic Sandboxing process, which is only one example of how malware sandboxing works; this sandbox environment may be used by vendors and customers to test malware and benefit from the results of the analysis:

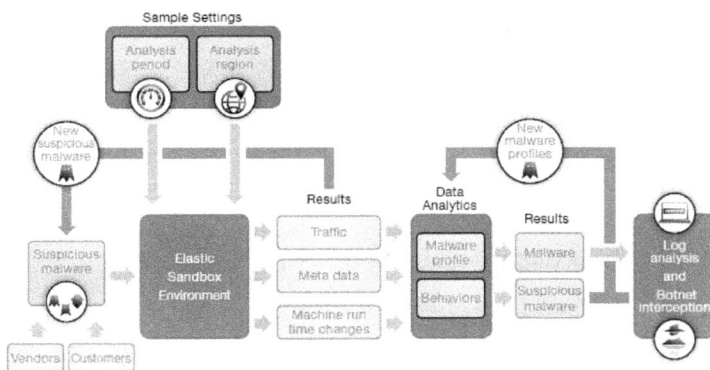

Figure 12.1: Seculert Elastic Sandbox

Malware sandboxing may be used to investigate and detect malware that has eluded the attention of the big commercial anti-malware vendors.

Memory dumping, runtime debugging

A core dump, also known as a memory dump, is performed by many penetration testing tools. Information such as sensitive data, passwords, usernames, and encryption keys are stored in memory by applications. Memory-reading tools can be used by hackers to examine all of an application's memory information. Any vulnerability testing should take this into consideration and use the same methods to detect any vulnerabilities in an application's memory. Examples of memory-reading tools are as follows:

- **Memdump**: This free tool runs on Windows, Linux, and Solaris. It simply creates a bit-by-bit copy of the volatile memory on a system.

- **KnTTools**: This memory acquisition and analysis tool used with Windows systems captures physical memory and stores it to a removable drive or sends it over the network to be archived on a separate machine.

- **FATKit**: This popular memory forensics tool automates the process of extracting interesting data from volatile memory. FATKit helps an analyst visualize the objects it finds to help in understanding the data that the tool was able to find.

Runtime debugging, on the other hand, is the process of applying a programming tool to find faults in code that might lead to memory leaks and buffer overflows in addition to identifying syntactic problems. The allocation of RAM is analyzed and monitored using runtime debugging tools. These tools are unique to the programming language used to create the code.

If a hacker is able to induce a memory dump, memory dumping can help evaluate what a hacker might be able to discover. Runtime debugging is the best way to find syntax errors in an application's code, as well as unexpected issues like memory leaks and potential buffer overflows.

Reconnaissance

Reconnaissance is a step of information gathering that usually precedes a network attack. To identify targets and piece together useful information that may make a target simpler to attack, both technical and non-technical ways might be utilized. This part of the hacking procedure is similar to a bank robber scouting a bank before conducting an attack.

Fingerprinting

Fingerprinting application scans a network, identifies hosts, and determines which services and applications are available on those hosts. They assist a hacker in sifting through the network's mundane stuff to discover what is actually of interest. A hacker can discover vulnerabilities that may work on a host by fingerprinting or identifying its operating system. There are two forms of fingerprinting, which are as follows:

- **Active**: To gather information about a target, active fingerprinting techniques send the packet to remote hosts and analyze the responses for clues about the responding system, such as using NMAP ping sweep or the traceroute command. A ping scan is usually performed first to identify all of the hosts on the network. The outcome of the nmap scan is shown in *Figure 12.2*:

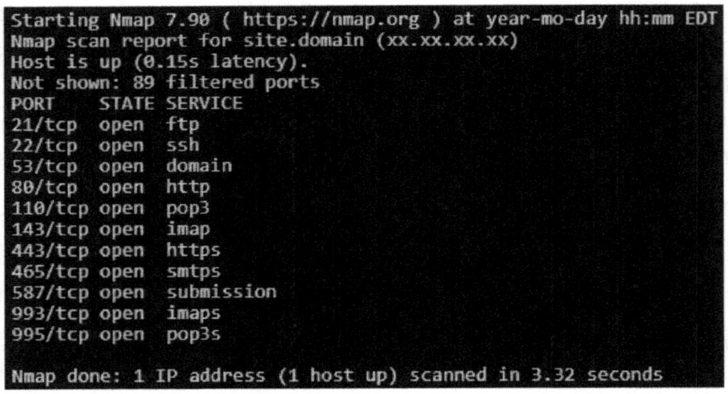

```
Starting Nmap 7.90 ( https://nmap.org ) at year-mo-day hh:mm EDT
Nmap scan report for site.domain (xx.xx.xx.xx)
Host is up (0.15s latency).
Not shown: 89 filtered ports
PORT      STATE SERVICE
21/tcp    open  ftp
22/tcp    open  ssh
53/tcp    open  domain
80/tcp    open  http
110/tcp   open  pop3
143/tcp   open  imap
443/tcp   open  https
465/tcp   open  smtps
587/tcp   open  submission
993/tcp   open  imaps
995/tcp   open  pop3s

Nmap done: 1 IP address (1 host up) scanned in 3.32 seconds
```

Figure 12.2: NMAP scan

If you examine the output in *Figure 12.2*, you can see their ports (21 – FTP, 22 – SSH, 53 – Domain, 80 – HTTP, 110 – POP3,143 – IMAP, 443 – HTTPS, 465 – SMTPS, 587 – Submission, 993 – IMPAS and 995 – POP3) along with their state (Open/Closed), and the services running on those ports. Using this information, the hacker would perform a port and services scan of the machines of interest.

- **Passive**: Rather than sending packets across a network, it is possible to simply collect and analyze them. A passive fingerprinting tool like NetworkMiner is one example. The output in *Figure 12.3* identifies the operating system, and you can view greater information by expanding the host; passive scanning is used to collect all of this data:

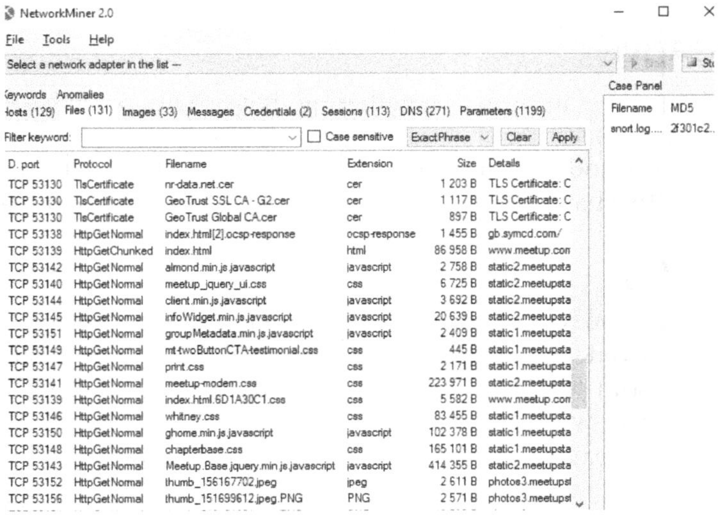

Figure 12.3: NetworkMiner

Figure 12.3 lists 129 systems or hosts that were discovered by NetworkMiner, along with 131 files that may contain anomalies or abnormalities. By tunneling into the details of each machine, you can see the IP address, MAC address, hostname, operating system, and other sensitive information such as images, credentials, sessions in progress, and **domain name server (DNS)** and porta parameters used to communicate with the users.

Code review

The systematic analysis of the code for security and functional issues is known as code review. It can take many different forms, ranging from informal peer review to rigorous code review. Code review may be divided into two categories, which are as follows:

- **Formal review**: This is a very detailed, line-by-line inspection that is usually done by various individuals throughout many phases. This is the most time-consuming sort of code review, but it is also the most effective in terms of detecting bugs.

- **Lightweight review**: This type of code review is much more cursory than a formal review. It is usually done as a normal part of the development process. It can happen in several forms, which are listed as follows:

  o **Pair programming**: Two coders work side-by-side, checking each other's work as they go.

  o **Email review**: Code is emailed around to colleagues for them to review when time permits.

  o **Over the shoulder**: Co-workers review the code while the author explains his or her reasoning.

  o **Tool-assisted**: Perhaps the most efficient method, this method involves using automated testing tools.

While code review is most commonly conducted on internal applications, it may also be necessary for other situations. Suppose you are engaged with a third party to design a web application that will process credit cards. Given the sensitive nature of the application, it is not unusual for you to request your own code review in order to check the product's security. Multiple tools should be utilized to test an application in various scenarios. For example, an online banking application that has had its source code updated should be subjected to both penetration testing and a code review of the important models to confirm that no errors are detected.

Social engineering

Attackers employ credible language and user gullibility to get user passwords or other confidential information in social engineering assaults. Phishing or pharming, shoulder surfing, identity theft, and dumpster diving are examples of social engineering hazards to be aware of. Providing user security awareness training is the safest way to combat social engineering risks. Because social engineering tactics are always evolving, this training should be required and repeated on a regular basis.

Phishing

Phishing is a type of social engineering attack in which the attacker attempts to get personal information such as credit card numbers and financial information. This sort of attack is generally carried out by creating a fake website that seems almost identical to the real thing. On the malicious website, users enter information, including credentials, allowing the attackers to capture any information entered. Spear phishing is a type of phishing attack that focuses on learning about a single target's patterns and lifestyle. This is because of the information that must be gathered, spear-phishing attacks take longer to carry out than phishing attacks. Pharming is similar to phishing, except it entails compromising a computer's DNS cache so that queries for a valid site are sent to another site. Users should be warned not to click on any links included in email messages, even if the message appears to be from a trustworthy source. Users should also verify the URL bar when they visit a site that requires personal information to confirm that the site is correct and that SSL is in use.

Shoulder surfing

Shoulder surfing happens when a user submits login or other private information while still being monitored by an attacker. Users should be encouraged to be aware of who is watching their activity at all instances. The use of privacy screens ensures that data entry is not logged.

Identity theft

Identity theft occurs when someone acquires personal information such as a driver's license number, bank account number, or social security number and uses it to impersonate the person whose information was taken. The attack can continue in any way after the identity has been assumed. The majority of times, attackers set up financial accounts in the user's identity. Attackers can also acquire access to a user's legitimate accounts.

Dumpster diving

In order to gain sensitive information, attackers examine the contents of physical garbage cans or recycle bins, such as personnel information, account login information, network diagrams, and corporate financial data. Shredding protocols for papers containing this information should be implemented by corporations.

Pivoting

Pivoting is a method used by both hackers and pen testers to go from one compromised site to another on the same network. It enables pen test tools installed on the compromised system to route traffic through other hosts on the subnet, potentially allowing access to other networks. One set of steps that could potentially illustrate pivoting is the following:

1. Compromise a client.

2. Open Metasploit.

3. Choose an exploit.

4. Get meterpreter and type meterpreter | ipconfig.

5. Scan the network you find.

6. Run scans using tools like Nmap, Msfconsole, and others.

7. Add a route from the default gateway to the compromised system so that all traffic from the default gateway must be routed through the compromised machine.

Open-source intelligence

The data obtained from publicly available sources is referred to as **open-source intelligence (OSINT)**. In many circumstances, the information obtained from these sources allows for an assault to be carried out. The sections that follow examine some of the sites where hackers hunt for information that can be used in an attack.

Social media

Organizations are increasingly turning to social media to communicate with consumers and the broader public. While using social media platforms such as Twitter, Facebook, LinkedIn, and others to connect with consumers, create brands, and disseminate information to the rest of the world can be beneficial, they can also mistakenly reveal confidential information. The following are some of the risks associated with using social media:

- **Mobile apps for business devices**: Although we can't entirely blame social media for the usage of mobile apps on corporate devices, the simplicity with which social media and other forms of mobile apps may be downloaded and installed has increased the risk of infection.

- **Unrealistic confidence in social media**: Proprietary information and business strategies may be accidentally divulged to a friend under the false assumption of secrecy. This is complicated by social networking sites' security and privacy settings, which are often misinterpreted and changed regularly.

- Malicious code may be hidden behind adverts and third-party programs on social networking platforms. Hackers profit from the way consumers repost links since it allows them to automate the dissemination process.

- **Lack of policies**: Every company should have a social media policy that specifically states how employees can use social media. A social media director or coordinator should be appointed, and appropriate training should be provided that spells out what users are permitted to say on behalf of the organization.

Adopting a social media strategy that outlines what users are authorized to say on behalf of the firm in social media postings is the best method to prevent information breaches that may be used to attack your network.

Whois

Whois is a protocol for locating private **Border Gateway Protocol (BGP)** networks on the Internet by querying databases that provide information on the owners of Internet resources such as domain names, IP address blocks, and **autonomous system (AS)** numbers. This data is a gold mine of information that may be used to improve network assaults. Whois was initially a command-line interface program, but it is now available via web-based solutions as well. Despite the fact that law enforcement agencies in the United States claim that Whois is an important tool for investigating spamming and vishing, the **Internet Corporation for Assigned Names and Numbers (ICANN)** has called for its replacement with a system that keeps information hidden from most Internet users and only discloses it for **permissible** reasons.

To erase their information from the Whois database, several corporations employ third-party privacy services. Although this is possible, the general public may be left wondering what an organization is hiding. People may be less likely to conduct business with the company as a result. Therefore, you should weigh the benefits and drawbacks while weighing your selections. *Figure 12.4* is a portion of the Whois output from a domain name search; as you can see, this tool may provide you with a wealth of information about a company:

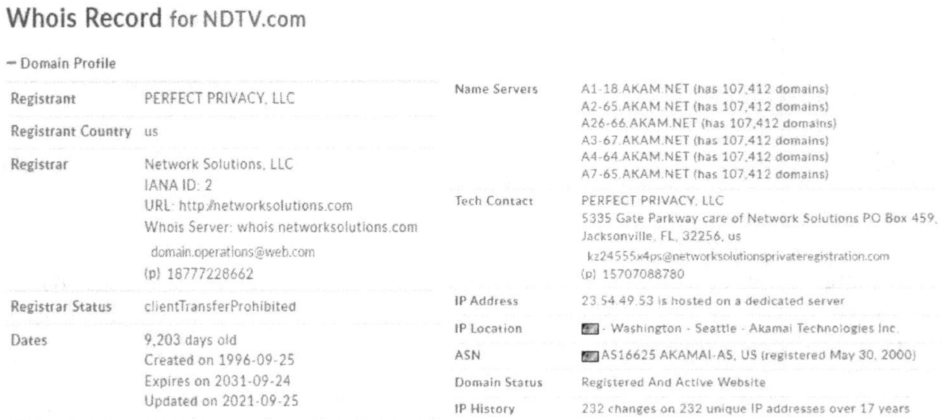

Whois Record for NDTV.com

— Domain Profile

Registrant	PERFECT PRIVACY, LLC	
Registrant Country	us	
Registrar	Network Solutions, LLC IANA ID: 2 URL: http://networksolutions.com Whois Server: whois.networksolutions.com domain.operations@web.com (p) 18777228662	
Registrar Status	clientTransferProhibited	
Dates	9,203 days old Created on 1996-09-25 Expires on 2031-09-24 Updated on 2021-09-25	

Name Servers
A1-18.AKAM.NET (has 107,412 domains)
A2-65.AKAM.NET (has 107,412 domains)
A26-66.AKAM.NET (has 107,412 domains)
A3-67.AKAM.NET (has 107,412 domains)
A4-64.AKAM.NET (has 107,412 domains)
A7-65.AKAM.NET (has 107,412 domains)

Tech Contact
PERFECT PRIVACY, LLC
5335 Gate Parkway care of Network Solutions PO Box 459,
Jacksonville, FL, 32256, us
kz24555x4ps@networksolutionsprivateregistration.com
(p) 15707088780

IP Address   23.54.49.53 is hosted on a dedicated server
IP Location   Washington - Seattle - Akamai Technologies Inc.
ASN   AS16625 AKAMAI-AS, US (registered May 30, 2000)
Domain Status Registered And Active Website
IP History   232 changes on 232 unique IP addresses over 17 years

Figure 12.4: Whois

Routing tables

The OSI model's layer 3 is where the routing takes place. This is also the layer where IP functions and packets are routed with their source and destination IP addresses. Routers are devices that send and receive data between systems on various IP networks. When computers are connected to multiple IP networks, they cannot interact unless a router is present to route messages to the appropriate networks. Routing tables are used by routers to store information about pathways to other networks. There are numerous ways to populate these tables, administrators can manually enter these routes, or routers can exchange routing tables and information via dynamic routing protocols.

Manual setup, also known as static routing, has the benefit of eliminating the extra traffic generated by dynamic routing protocols and allowing for fine control of routing behavior; nevertheless, it necessitates manual intervention when links fail. Dynamic routing protocols generate traffic, but they may also respond to connection failures and redirect traffic without the need for manual intervention. In terms of security, routing protocols present the risk of routing update traffic being intercepted, allowing a hacker to gather vital knowledge about the network's topology. Furthermore, Cisco equipment (possibly the most extensively used networking devices) employs a proprietary layer 2 protocol called **Cisco Discovery Protocol (CDP)** by default, which allows them to communicate with one another about their capabilities.

Additional information may be gathered by capturing CDP packets, which might be useful in mapping the network in advance for an attack. Hackers can also bring rogue routers onto a network and update or replace a legal enterprise router's routing table. This might be done by a hacker to understand the network's routes and basic topology, as well as to contaminate the routing table with wrong routes that could aid in an assault. The following is a sample of a routing table before it is compromised:

Source Network Next Hop Exit interface
• 10.110.0.0 [110/5] via 10.120.254.6, 0:01:00, Ethernet2
• 10.67.10.0 [110/128] via 10.120.254.244, 0:02:22, Ethernet2
• 10.68.132.0 [110/5] via 10.120.254.6, 0:00:59, Ethernet2
• 10.130.0.0 [110/5] via 10.120.254.6, 0:00:59, Ethernet2
• 10.128.0.0 [110/128] via 10.120.254.244, 0:02:22, Ethernet2
• 10.129.0.0 [110/129] via 10.120.254.240, 0:02:22, Ethernet2

Table 12.1: Routing information

The routing table displays the router's routes to external networks. The source of the routing information is shown in the first column of this example. The router, in this situation, sees the first column and is aware of the networks thanks to the **Open Shortest Path First (OSPF)** protocol. The distant network is shown in the second column, the next-hop IP address to access that network (another router) is listed in the third column, and the local exit interface on the router is listed in the fourth column. The routing table looks like the following after the hacker has persuaded the local router to share the routing information and polluted the local routing table:

- 10.110.0.0 [110/5] via 10.120.254.6, 0:01:00, Ethernet2
- 10.67.10.0 [110/128] via 10.120.254.244, 0:02:22, Ethernet2
- 10.68.132.0 [110/5] via 10.120.254.6, 0:00:59, Ethernet2
- 10.130.0.0 [110/5] via 10.120.254.6, 0:00:59, Ethernet2
- 10.128.0.0 [110/128] via 10.120.254.244, 0:02:22, Ethernet2
- 10.129.0.0 [110/129] via 10.120.254.178, 0:02:22, Ethernet2

Table 12.2: Compromised routing table

Take a look at the 10.129.0.0 network's path. It is now routing to the IP address 10.120.254.178, which is the hacker's router address. The hacker can then redirect all traffic meant for a safe server at 10.120.154.180 to a server they control at 10.120.154.181. After that, the hacker can gather names and passwords for the genuine secure server.

Routers should be set with authentication to identify and authenticate any routers with whom they communicate information to prevent such attacks. If the connection between them is configured to employ **Point to Point Protocol (PPP)** encapsulation, routers can be configured to authenticate one another. PPP is a layer 2 protocol that may be easily enabled with the command encapsulation ppp on a router interface. It uses two forms of authentication once it is enabled such as PAP and CHAP. **Password Authentication Protocol (PAP)** is a protocol that sends a credential in clear text. **Challenge-Handshake Authentication Protocol (CHAP)** is a superior option since it never sends credentials across the network. The CHAP process is as follows:

1. The local router sends a challenge message to the remote router.

2. The remote node responds with a value calculated using an MD5 hash salted with the password.

3. The local router verifies the hash value with the same password, thus ensuring that the remote router knows the password without sending the password.

Domain name server records

It is because DNS records identify each device on a network by name and IP address, they are immensely important to an attacker. This is because it is feasible to discover the network ID of the network in which each device lives and, thus, which devices are grouped into common subnets, the IP addresses may also indicate how the devices are organized. Types of DNS records are grouped. The most popular DNS record types are shown in *Figure 12.5*:

Record	Description
A	Address record (IPv4)
AAAA	Address record (IPv6)
CNAME	Canonical Name record
MX	Mail Exchanger record
NS	Nameserver record
PTR	Pointer record
SOA	Start of Authority record
SRV	Service Location record
TXT	Text record

Figure 12.5: DNS record types

DNS harvesting is the process of obtaining an organization's DNS records for use in network mapping. DNS harvesting is most easily accomplished through illegal zone transfers. However, using the tracert tool on Windows or the traceroute utility on UNIX is one method a hostile user might be able to retrieve a few records. These tools follow a packet's journey from its origin to its destination. The final few devices on tracert's list of hops or routers through which the packet has passed are usually inside the organization's network. If tracert displays the names of those devices, the hacker has access to them. The tracert output is shown in *Figure 12.6*. Tracert was able to resolve the names of some of the routers in this case, but not the last two. The last few hops frequently time out because the destination network operators have configured the routers to ignore ICMP packets. Refer to *Figure 12.6* that displays this:

```
Command Prompt

C:\>tracert mediacollege.com

Tracing route to mediacollege.com [66.246.3.197]
over a maximum of 30 hops:

  1    <10 ms    <10 ms    <10 ms  192.168.1.1
  2    240 ms    421 ms     70 ms  219-88-164-1.jetstream.xtra.co.nz [219.88.164.1]
  3     20 ms     30 ms     30 ms  210.55.205.123
  4      *         *         *     Request timed out.
  5     30 ms     30 ms     40 ms  202.50.245.197
  6     30 ms     40 ms     40 ms  g2-0-3.tkbr3.global-gateway.net.nz [202.37.245.140]
  7     30 ms     30 ms     40 ms  so-1-2-1-0.akbr3.global-gateway.net.nz [202.50.116.161]
  8    160 ms    161 ms    160 ms  p1-3.sjbr1.global-gateway.net.nz [202.50.116.178]
  9    160 ms    171 ms    160 ms  so-1-3-0-0.pabr3.global-gateway.net.nz [202.37.245.230]
 10    160 ms    161 ms    170 ms  pao1-br1-g2-1-101.gnaps.net [198.32.176.165]
 11    180 ms    181 ms    180 ms  lax1-br1-p2-1.gnaps.net [199.232.44.5]
 12    170 ms    170 ms    171 ms  lax1-br1-ge-0-1-0.gnaps.net [199.232.44.50]
 13    240 ms    241 ms    240 ms  nyc-m20-ge2-2-0.gnaps.net [199.232.44.21]
 14    240 ms    251 ms    250 ms  ash-m20-ge1-0-0.gnaps.net [199.232.131.36]
 15    241 ms    240 ms    250 ms  0503.ge-0-0-0.gbr1.ash.nac.net [207.99.39.157]
 16    251 ms    260 ms    250 ms  0.so-2-2-0.gbr2.nwr.nac.net [209.123.11.29]
 17    250 ms    260 ms    261 ms  0.so-0-3-0.gbr1.oct.nac.net [209.123.11.233]
 18    250 ms    260 ms    261 ms  209.123.182.243
 19    250 ms    260 ms    261 ms  sol.yourhost.co.nz [66.246.3.197]

Trace complete.

C:\>
```

Figure 12.6: Tracert

Another method of DNS harvesting is to persuade an organization's DNS server to transfer a zone to the attacker. While this used to be fairly straightforward, it is now a little more complicated if the organization has elected to designate the DNS servers via which zone transfers can be accomplished. You should double-check that you've completed this step before attempting a DNS zone transfer from an unauthorized DNS server. A dialogue box from a Microsoft DNS server is shown in *Figure 12.7*; you can define the only servers to which zone transfers may occur on the zone transfers tab of the DNS server's properties:

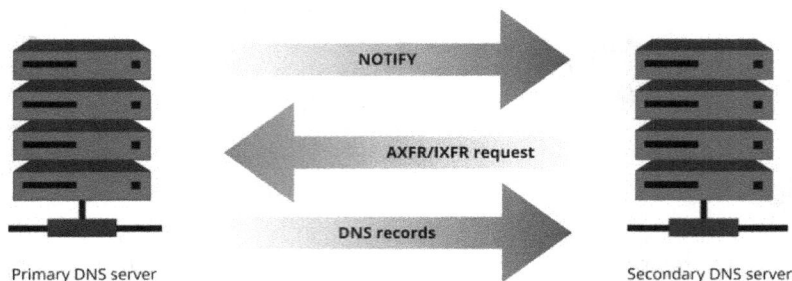

Figure 12.7: DNS zone transfers

The **nslookup** command is a command-line utility for diagnosing and testing DNS servers. It has two modes of operation such as interactive and noninteractive. Interactive mode allows you to query for either an IP address for a name or a name for an IP address without leaving 'nslookup' mode. The noninteractive mode is ideal when only a single piece of data has to be returned. As an example of 'nslookup' for a domain, refer to *Figure 12.8*. Nslookup finds the IP address and name of the DNS server that the local system is set to use, if one exists, and then returns to the command prompt. You can input an IP address or a name at this prompt, and the system will try to resolve the IP address to a name or the name to an IP address. *Figure 12.8* displays this:

```
C:\Users\Abhardwaj>nslookup
Default Server:  UnKnown
Address:  10.2.1.60

> ndtv.com
Server:  UnKnown
Address:  10.2.1.60

Non-authoritative answer:
Name:    ndtv.com
Addresses:  2600:140f:4:588::24e8
            2600:140f:4:5ab::24e8
            72.247.54.47
```

Figure 12.8: NSlookup domain

Search engines

For acquiring reconnaissance information, search engines such as Google, Yahoo, and Bing can be employed. The use of sophisticated operator-based searching to locate exploitable targets and sensitive data through search engines is known as **search engine hacking**. Some examples of hacker-friendly search engines are as follows:

- Shodan
- IVRE
- ZoonEye
- Censys
- Test Types

While maintaining network security may appear to be a daunting task, there are several technologies available to assist you. Unfortunately, every instrument with a legal application can also be used for nefarious purposes. These tools are used by hackers to identify, infiltrate, and manage networks, but you may use them to prevent assaults from succeeding. The parts that follow go through some of the most frequent assessment tools.

Penetration testing

A penetration test (also known as a pen test) is a type of security test that simulates an attack on a system, network, or application. Its importance stems from its ability to uncover security flaws that could otherwise go unreported. It varies from a vulnerability test in that it tries to exploit rather than just discover problems. Nothing draws attention to a software flaw like the disclosure of sensitive data as a result of the flaw. One of the most useful pieces of knowledge gleaned from these testing is the discovery of single actions that, although benign on their own, cause security issues when employed together. When using a framework like Metasploit or Canvas, these tests may be made more effective.

Penetration testing should be carried out on a regular basis, with the frequency defined by the sensitivity of the information on the network. *Figure 12.9* illustrates an example of Retina, a vulnerability tool that may be combined with Metasploit, a penetration testing tool. The test discovered eight major flaws (shown by upward-pointing arrows) in this output – inadequate encryption in terminal services, six Oracle vulnerabilities, and one vulnerability connected to Oracle VirtualBox, a virtualization software on the computer. *Figure 12.9* displays the Retina penetration tester:

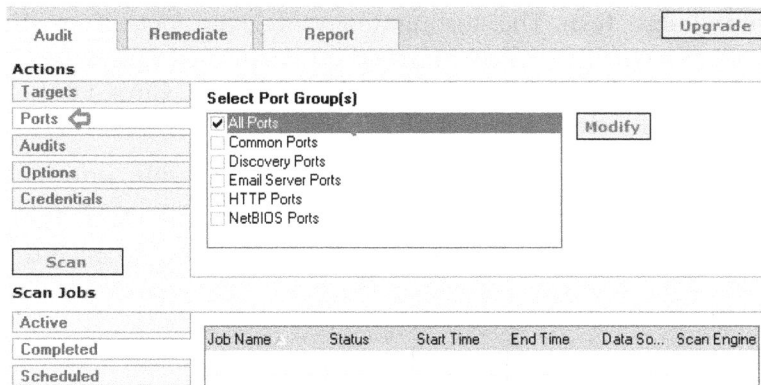

Figure 12.9: *Retina penetration tester*

The steps in performing a penetration test are as follows:

1. Document information about the target system or device.

2. Gather information about attack methods against the target system or device.

3. Identify the known vulnerabilities of the target system or device.

4. Execute attacks against the target system or device to gain user and privileged access.

5. Document the results of the penetration test and report the findings to management, with suggestions for remedial action.

Internal and exterior testing should both be carried out. Internal tests are conducted within the network, whereas external tests are conducted outside the network and are directed at publicly exposed servers and devices. Penetration testing strategies are dependent on the organization's established testing objectives. As a candidate for CASP, you should be conversant with the following strategies:

- **Blind test**: The testing team is given little knowledge of the network systems and devices and is only given publicly accessible information to execute the test. The security staff at the company is aware that an attack is imminent. This test necessitates extra work on the part of the testing team.

- **Double-blind test**: This test is similar to a blind test, except that the organization's security personnel is unaware of the impending assault. This test generally necessitates a joint effort from the testing team and the security team of the firm.

- **Target test**: The testing team and the organization's security team are both provided with as much information as possible about the network and the sort of test that will be conducted. This is the simplest sort of test to perform, but it does not offer a complete picture of the security of the company.

Penetration testing is also classified according to the quantity of data supplied to the testing team. The following are the primary categories that you should be familiar with:

- **Zero-knowledge test**: The testing team is given no information about the company's network. To collect information about the organization's network, the testing team can utilize any method available to them. Closed or black-box testing is another term for this.

- **Partial-knowledge test**: The testing team is given public information about the company's network. For this sort of test, boundaries can be established.

- **Full-knowledge test**: The testing team is given access to all information about the organization's network. This test focuses on the types of assaults that can be carried out.

Black box

Penetration testing may be classified into many types based on the quantity of data that has to be collected. In black-box testing, also known as **zero-knowledge testing**, the team is given no information about the organization's network. To collect knowledge about the organization's network, the team can employ any tool at its disposal. Closed testing is another term for this.

White box

A team begins the white-box testing procedure with a thorough grasp of the application or system. The team uses this information to create test cases that simulate each path, input field, and processing method. The team would have access to all network information in the case of a network, which they could use and leverage in the test.

Gray box

The team is given more information in gray-box testing than in black-box testing, but not as much as in white-box testing. Gray-box testing offers the benefit of being non-intrusive while keeping the developer-tester separation. On the other side, it could disclose some of the issues that white-box testing might miss. *Figure 12.10* compares the three testing methods:

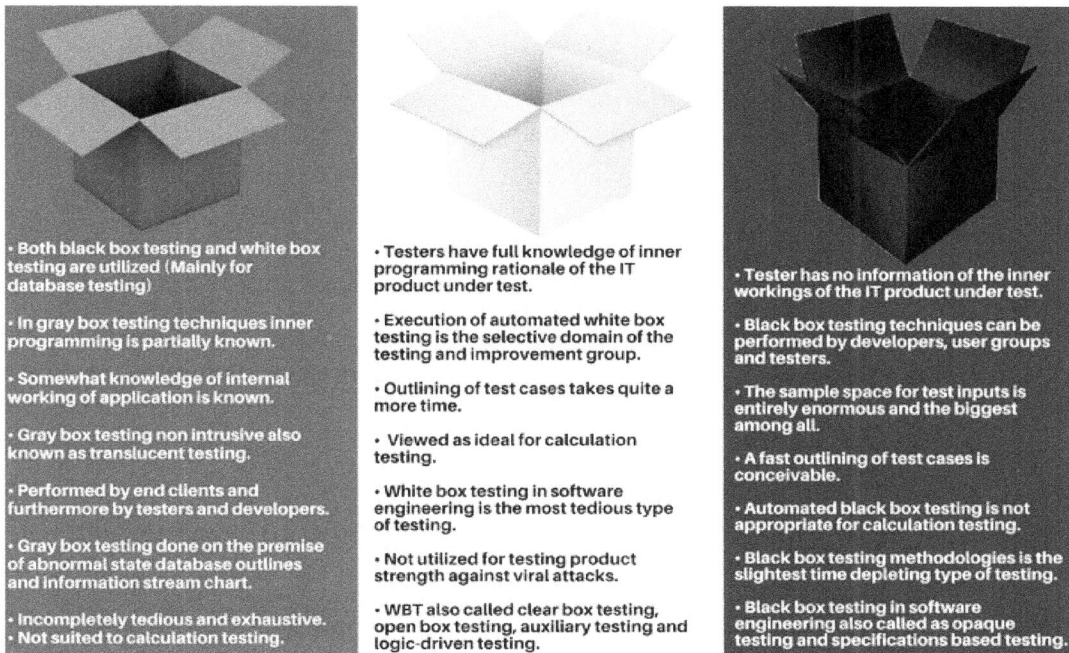

- Both black box testing and white box testing are utilized (Mainly for database testing)

- In gray box testing techniques inner programming is partially known.

- Somewhat knowledge of internal working of application is known.

- Gray box testing non intrusive also known as translucent testing.

- Performed by end clients and furthermore by testers and developers.

- Gray box testing done on the premise of abnormal state database outlines and information stream chart.

- Incompletely tedious and exhaustive.
- Not suited to calculation testing.

- Testers have full knowledge of inner programming rationale of the IT product under test.

- Execution of automated white box testing is the selective domain of the testing and improvement group.

- Outlining of test cases takes quite a more time.

- Viewed as ideal for calculation testing.

- White box testing in software engineering is the most tedious type of testing.

- Not utilized for testing product strength against viral attacks.

- WBT also called clear box testing, open box testing, auxiliary testing and logic-driven testing.

- Tester has no information of the inner workings of the IT product under test.

- Black box testing techniques can be performed by developers, user groups and testers.

- The sample space for test inputs is entirely enormous and the biggest among all.

- A fast outlining of test cases is conceivable.

- Automated black box testing is not appropriate for calculation testing.

- Black box testing methodologies is the slightest time depleting type of testing.

- Black box testing in software engineering also called as opaque testing and specifications based testing.

Figure 12.10: Testing methods

Consider the security implications of each while deciding between black, white, and gray-box testing. Because white-box testing exposes the code to the testers, it should only be done by extremely trusted individuals, such as internal testers. Untrusted entities, such as third-party testers, might benefit from black-box testing. Black-box testing should be performed by a third party with sufficient resources to run as many test cases as necessary and examine all code paths. You should also think about the sort of malevolent activity you're attempting to predict.

For example, if you want to see if an attack from outside the network is likely, you should perform a black-box test, because anyone trying it is unlikely to have any internal knowledge of the application. On the other hand, if you're more interested in the sort of assaults that may come from your own employees, gray-box testing, in which the attacker has some knowledge of the system, might be a good fit.

Finally, you should think about how the testing approach will affect the network. White-box testing has a minimal chance of affecting system stability, but black-box testing has a larger risk of causing system instability.

Vulnerability assessment

Irrespective of the elements under investigation (network, application, database, etc.), the aim of any vulnerability assessment is to identify problems before they are exploited to compromise the component, either intentionally or accidentally. The evaluation process's design has a significant influence on its performance. Prior to an assessment process being developed, the following goals of the assessment need to be identified:

- The relative worth of the information that may be obtained by compromising the components under consideration, aids in determining the quantity and kind of resources that should be allocated to the problem.

- Threats specific to the component; for example, due to the differences in their operation and locations on the network, a web application might not be vulnerable to similar issues and threats as compared to the network traffic on a firewall.

- Mitigation methods that may be used to address concerns that are discovered, such as identifying common tactics, may reveal difficulties that were not initially expected. When doing a vulnerability test on your standard network operating system image, for example, you should anticipate vulnerabilities and determine how you will resolve them.

A security analyst undertaking a vulnerability assessment must be familiar with the network's systems and devices, as well as the duties they perform. The analyst will be able to analyze the vulnerabilities of the systems and devices based on the known and possible threats to the systems and devices with this knowledge. Security analysts should look at the controls that are already in place and see if there are any dangers to them. After that, the security analyst will utilize all of the data acquired to decide which automated tools to employ to look for vulnerabilities. When the vulnerability analysis is completed, the security analyst should double-check the results to make sure they're correct, then present the findings to management with recommendations on how to fix the problem. Threat modeling should be carried out using this information to determine the dangers that might negatively affect systems and devices, as well as the attack techniques that could be deployed.

A vulnerability management system may be necessary in specific cases. A vulnerability management system is software that centralizes and automates the process of continuously monitoring and testing the network for vulnerabilities to some extent. Without human assistance, such a system can scan the network for vulnerabilities, report them, and, in many circumstances, fix the problem. While a vulnerability management system is a useful tool to have, no system can replace vulnerability and penetration testing done by skilled specialists, no matter how advanced it is. Keep in mind that the results of a vulnerability assessment are only a snapshot. Even if no vulnerabilities are discovered, the simplest way to summarize the situation is that there are currently no known vulnerabilities. It is hard to predict whether or not a flaw will be identified in the future.

Self-assessment

While many businesses opt to have third-party vulnerability and penetration testing conducted, organizations should conduct self-assessments in between these examinations. Conducting tabletop exercises is one of the most frequent approaches for this procedure.

Tabletop exercises

Before going on to higher-level testing, a tabletop exercise is the most cost-effective and efficient approach to uncovering areas of risk. A tabletop exercise is a casual brainstorming session in which corporate executives and other important personnel are encouraged to participate. In a tabletop exercise, participants agree on a specific assault scenario on which they will concentrate.

Internal and external audits

Internal and external audits should be conducted as part of any security evaluation and testing plan. All security mechanisms that are currently in place should be tested during an audit. The following are some suggestions to consider as part of a solid security audit plan:

- At a minimum, perform annual audits to establish a security baseline.
- Determine your organization's objectives for the audit and share them with the auditors.
- Set the ground rules for the audit before the audit starts, including the audit dates/ times.

- Choose auditors who have security experience.

- Involve business unit managers early in the process.

- Ensure that auditors rely on experience, not just checklists.

- Ensure that an auditor's report reflects risks that your organization has identified.

- Ensure that the audit is conducted properly.

- Ensure that the audit covers all systems and all policies and procedures.

- Examine the report when the audit is complete.

Audits are now required by several rules. Previously, organizations relied on **Statement on Auditing Standards (SAS)** 70, which provided auditors with information and verification concerning data center controls and processes linked to data center users and financial reporting. An SAS 70 audit was utilized to ensure that the data center's rules and processes were really followed. The **Statements on Standards for Attestation Engagement (SSAE)** Number 16 is a new standard that verifies controls and processes while also requiring a written claim about the controls' design and operational performance. A **Service Organization Control (SOC)** 1 report is the result of an SSAE 16 audit. Internal controls over financial reporting are the topic of this study. There are two types of SOC 1 reports, which are as follows:

- **SOC 1 type 1 report**: This type of report focuses on the auditors' opinion of the accuracy and completeness of the data center management's design of controls, systems, and/or services.

- **SOC 1 type 2 report**: This type of report includes the Type 1 report as well as an audit on the effectiveness of controls over a certain time period, normally between six months and a year.

SOC 2 and SOC 3 are two further report kinds available. Both of these audits serve as standards for controls relating to a system's security, availability, processing integrity, confidentiality, and privacy. A SOC 2 report includes service auditor testing and outcomes, whereas a SOC 3 report just includes a system description and the auditor's judgment. A SOC 3 report, which is intended for general use, is a level of certification for data center operators that guarantees facility security, high availability, and process integrity to data center customers.

Color team exercises

To respond to security incidents in the most orderly and effective manner, security analysts must practice reacting to them. There are a few tried-and-true approaches to this. This section examines how analyst teams, both internal and external, might be formed, as well as some well-known names for these groups. War game exercises, in which one party assaults the network while the other seeks to protect it, are commonly used to assess security posture. These games typically have some implementation of the following teams:

- **Red team**: The attackers are represented by the red team. It usually conducts penetration testing by acquiring information about the network, scanning the network for vulnerabilities, and attempting to exploit the weaknesses. The rules of engagement specify the activities that this team can perform ahead of time. These are frequently third-party contractors who have no prior understanding of the network. This allows them to practice assaults that aren't carried out by insiders.

- **Blue team**: This group is in charge of network defense. The red team's attempted attack puts the blue team's ability to respond to the attack to the test. It can also be used as a warm-up for a true attack. This involves looking at log files, employing a **security information and event management (SIEM)** system, gathering intelligence, and analyzing traffic and data flow.

- **White team**: This squad of technicians is in charge of officiating the match between the red and blue teams. One of the white team's responsibilities might include enforcing the rules of engagement, as well as monitoring the blue team's response to the attack, and taking note of the red team's specific tactics.

Governance, risk, and compliance

The following use cases demonstrate how advanced GRC concepts can be applied to address the unique challenges faced by healthcare organizations in securing their data and complying with regulations. By implementing a comprehensive GRC framework, healthcare providers can protect patient data, mitigate risks, and ensure business continuity:

- **Use case 1: Implementing a zero trust model**

  Consider the following scenario, a large healthcare organization is transitioning its data center to a cloud-based infrastructure to improve scalability and efficiency. This migration involves hosting sensitive patient data and critical medical applications.

  Following are the challenges faced:

  o **Data security**: Ensuring the confidentiality, integrity, and availability of sensitive patient data in a dynamic cloud environment.

  o **Compliance**: Adhering to strict regulations like HIPAA and HITECH, which mandate robust data protection measures.

  o **Risk management**: Mitigating threats from both internal and external sources, including insider threats, ransomware attacks, and data breaches.

  The solutions is to adopt and implement **zero trust model** with a *never trust, always verify* approach to security. This involves:

  o **Micro-segmentation**: Isolate applications and data within the cloud environment using **virtual private clouds (VPCs)** and network segmentation.3

o **Least privilege access**: Grant users and applications only the necessary permissions to access specific resources.

o **Multi-factor authentication (MFA):** Implement MFA for all users and devices accessing the cloud environment.

o **Continuous monitoring and threat detection**: Utilize advanced security analytics and threat intelligence to detect and respond to threats in real-time.

This will provide is with benefits like the following:

o Enhanced data security and compliance with HIPAA and HITECH.

o Reduced risk of data breaches and cyberattacks.

o Improved operational efficiency and agility.

- **Use case 2**: **Implementing a data loss prevention (DLP) solution**

Consider the following scenario, a mid-sized healthcare provider is experiencing an increasing number of data breaches due to accidental or malicious data exfiltration.

Following are the challenges:

o **Data leakage:** Preventing sensitive patient data from being shared or accessed by unauthorized individuals.

o **Compliance:** Meeting regulatory requirements for data protection and privacy.

o **Risk management:** Mitigating the risk of reputational damage and financial penalties resulting from data breaches.

The solution is to deploy DLP solution to monitor and control the movement of sensitive data within and outside the organization. This involves:

o **Data classification:** Classify data based on sensitivity levels (e.g., confidential, private, public).

o **Content inspection:** Monitor data in transit and at rest for sensitive information.

o **Anomaly detection:** Identify unusual patterns of data access and usage.

o **Real-time alerts and remediation:** Trigger alerts and automatically block suspicious activities.

The benefits of this solution are the following:

- Reduced risk of data breaches and data leakage.
- Improved compliance with data protection regulations.
- Enhanced visibility into data usage and access patterns.

- Improved incident response capabilities.
- Implement and assess policies, frameworks, and security controls

Following is the policy development and framework selection

- **Identify relevant frameworks:** To effectively develop a comprehensive security policy, it is crucial to select the appropriate frameworks that align with both regulatory requirements and best practices. The following outlines key frameworks to consider, each providing a structured approach to managing data protection, cybersecurity risks, and information security management within organizations, particularly in sensitive sectors such as healthcare. These frameworks offer a roadmap for establishing robust security measures, ensuring compliance, and mitigating potential risks like:

  o **HIPAA or HITECH:** Core regulatory framework for healthcare data protection in the US.

  o **NIST Cybersecurity Framework:** Provides a voluntary framework for managing cybersecurity risk across the enterprise.

  o **HITRUST CSF:** A comprehensive framework specifically designed for the healthcare industry.

  o **ISO 27001/27002:** International standards for information security management systems.

- **Develop organizational policies**: To ensure the security and integrity of sensitive healthcare data, organizations must develop comprehensive policies that address various aspects of data management and protection. These policies provide a structured approach to safeguarding information, managing access, and preparing for potential security incidents. The following policies should be prioritized to establish a robust security framework:

  o **Data classification policy:** Define sensitivity levels for different types of healthcare data (for example, PHI, PII, etc.).

  o **Access control policy:** Outline rules for user authentication, authorization, and least privilege access.

  o **Data security policy:** Cover encryption, data masking, secure storage, and data destruction practices.

  o **Incident response plan:** Define procedures for detecting, containing, and responding to security incidents.

  o **Business continuity and disaster recovery plan:** Ensure the availability of critical services in case of disruptions.

These policies collectively work to mitigate risks, ensure regulatory compliance, and maintain operational resilience in the face of potential security threats.

- **Zero trust model:** This security framework operates on the principle of **never trust, always verify**. It assumes that threats may exist both inside and outside the network, requiring continuous validation of users, devices, and applications. To implement a robust zero trust architecture, organizations should focus on the following key components: Network segmentation, **identity and access management (IAM)**, and DLP. These strategies work together to ensure that only authenticated and authorized users and devices can access sensitive resources, while closely monitoring and controlling the movement of critical data within the network.

  o **Network segmentation:** Implement micro-segmentation using firewalls, VPCs, and **software-defined networking (SDN)**.

  o **Identity and access management (IAM):** Implement strong authentication (MFA), **role-based access control (RBAC)**, and continuous monitoring of user activity.

  o **Data loss prevention (DLP):** Deploy DLP solutions to monitor and control the movement of sensitive data.

- **Data protection:** This is critical to safeguarding sensitive information from unauthorized access, loss, or corruption. Implementing a multi-layered approach ensures that data remains secure throughout its lifecycle. This includes methods such as encryption, where data is encrypted both at rest and in transit using strong algorithms like AES-256 to prevent unauthorized interception. Data masking is another essential practice, especially in non-production environments, where sensitive data is obscured to protect privacy. Finally, utilizing secure storage solutions, such as cloud-based object storage with robust access controls, ensures that data is securely stored and only accessible to authorized users.

  o **Encryption:** Encrypt data at rest and in transit using strong encryption algorithms (e.g., AES-256).

  o **Data masking:** Mask sensitive data in non-production environments to protect privacy.

  o **Secure storage:** Utilize secure storage solutions like cloud-based object storage with robust access controls.

- **Threat detection and response:** Effective threat detection and response are essential for identifying, mitigating, and responding to cybersecurity threats in a timely manner. By implementing a combination of proactive tools and well-trained personnel, organizations can significantly reduce the risk of a security breach. Key components of a robust threat detection and response strategy include deploying **Intrusion Detection and Prevention Systems (IDPS)** to monitor for and block malicious activity, utilizing SIEM solutions for real-time analysis of security events, conducting vulnerability management through regular scans and penetration tests, and establishing a skilled incident response team to swiftly address and resolve security incidents.

- o **Intrusion Detection and Prevention Systems (IDPS):** Deploy network-based and host-based IDPS to detect and prevent malicious activity.

- o **Security information and event management (SIEM):** Implement a SIEM solution to collect, analyze, and correlate security logs from various sources.

- o **Vulnerability management:** Conduct regular vulnerability scans and penetration tests to identify and remediate security weaknesses.

- o **Incident response team:** Establish and train an incident response team to handle security incidents effectively.

Following is the ongoing monitoring and assessment:

- **Regular security audits:** Conduct internal and external audits to assess the effectiveness of security controls.

- **Vulnerability scans:** Perform regular vulnerability scans to identify and remediate security weaknesses.

- **Penetration testing:** Conduct periodic penetration tests to simulate real-world attacks.

- **Compliance reviews:** Conduct regular compliance reviews to ensure adherence to HIPAA, HITECH, and other relevant regulations.

- **Continuous monitoring:** Utilize security analytics and threat intelligence to detect and respond to threats in real-time.

Following are the continuous improvement:

- Regularly review and update policies, procedures, and security controls based on the results of assessments, threat intelligence, and industry best practices.

- Provide ongoing security awareness training to employees to educate them about security threats and best practices.

- Continuously monitor and improve the effectiveness of security controls based on performance metrics and **key performance indicators (KPIs).**

Following are the key considerations:

- **Risk assessment:** Conduct a thorough risk assessment to identify and prioritize the most critical security risks.

- **Budget and resources:** Allocate adequate budget and resources for the implementation and maintenance of security controls.

- **Third-party risk management:** Manage the security risks associated with third-party vendors and service providers.

- **Communication and collaboration:** Foster strong communication and collaboration between IT, security, and compliance teams.

By following these steps, healthcare organizations can implement and assess effective security controls that align with their organizational objectives, mitigate risks, and ensure compliance with relevant regulations.

Risk assessments and compliance

To conduct risk assessment ensuring compliance, the scope, and objectives:

- **Define scope**: Clearly outline the systems, data, and processes included in the risk assessment.

- **Identify objectives**: Determine the specific compliance requirements (for example, HIPAA Security Rule, GDPR Article 32) and the overall goals of the risk assessment (for example, identify vulnerabilities, prioritize risks, demonstrate compliance).

- **Data inventory and mapping**: To effectively manage and protect sensitive information, organizations must establish a comprehensive approach to data inventory and mapping. This involves systematically identifying and cataloging all information assets, understanding how data flows within the organization, and classifying data based on its sensitivity. By following these key steps, organizations can ensure that appropriate security measures are in place to safeguard valuable and sensitive data throughout its lifecycle.

  o **Identify assets:** Catalog all information assets, including patient data, employee data, and other sensitive information.

  o **Data flow mapping:** Map the flow of data within the organization, including data sources, processing locations, and destinations.

  o **Data classification:** Classify data based on sensitivity levels (for example, confidential, private, public) to determine the appropriate level of protection.

- **Threat identification and vulnerability analysis:** Effective threat identification and vulnerability analysis are essential components of any robust cybersecurity strategy. By proactively identifying potential threats to the confidentiality, integrity, and availability of data, organizations can better understand and mitigate risks. This process involves conducting thorough vulnerability assessments through techniques such as vulnerability scans, penetration tests, and security audits to pinpoint weaknesses in systems, networks, and applications. Additionally, threat modeling plays a crucial role in analyzing potential attack vectors, evaluating the likelihood and impact of successful attacks, and ensuring that security measures are in place to protect against both internal and external threats.

  o **Identify threats:** Identify potential threats to the confidentiality, integrity, and availability of data, such as cyberattacks, natural disasters, and human error.[4]

- o **Vulnerability assessment:** Conduct vulnerability scans, penetration tests, and other assessments to identify weaknesses in systems, networks, and applications.[5]

- o **Threat modeling:** Analyze potential attack vectors and the impact of successful attacks on the organization.

- **Risk assessment and prioritization:** In the process of managing cybersecurity threats, risk assessment and prioritization are critical steps that help organizations allocate resources effectively and mitigate potential damage. Risk assessment involves evaluating the likelihood and impact of each identified risk using various methodologies, such as qualitative, quantitative, or hybrid approaches. Once the risks have been assessed, risk prioritization is performed to focus on the most significant risks, those that pose the greatest threat based on their potential impact and likelihood of occurrence. This ensures that high-risk areas are addressed promptly, reducing the potential for severe consequences.

  - o **Risk assessment:** Evaluate the likelihood and impact of each identified risk using a risk assessment methodology (for example, qualitative, quantitative, or hybrid).

  - o **Risk prioritization:** Prioritize risks based on their potential impact and likelihood of occurrence.[6] Focus on high-risk areas that require immediate attention.

- **Risk treatment and mitigation:** Effective risk treatment and mitigation are essential components of a comprehensive risk management strategy. Once risks have been identified and assessed, organizations must develop and implement appropriate strategies to address them. These strategies can vary depending on the nature of the risk, the organization's risk appetite, and available resources. The four primary risk treatment strategies are risk avoidance, risk mitigation, risk acceptance, and risk transfer, each offering a different approach to managing potential threats and vulnerabilities. Properly selecting and applying these strategies ensures that an organization can minimize its exposure while maintaining operational effectiveness.

  - o **Develop mitigation strategies:** Develop and implement appropriate risk treatment strategies, such as:

    - ▪ **Risk avoidance:** Eliminate or avoid the risk altogether.

    - ▪ **Risk mitigation:** Reduce the likelihood or impact of the risk.

    - ▪ **Risk acceptance:** Accept the risk and its potential consequences.

    - ▪ **Risk transfer:** Transfer the risk to a third party (for example., through insurance).

  - o **Implement Controls:** Implement security controls to mitigate identified risks, such as:

- **Technical controls:** Encryption, firewalls, intrusion detection systems, access controls.

- **Administrative controls:** Policies, procedures, training, awareness programs.

- **Physical controls:** Physical security measures and environmental controls.

- **Monitoring and review:** Effective risk management is a dynamic process that requires constant attention and adaptation to evolving threats and vulnerabilities. The key components of monitoring and review ensure that security measures remain effective, risks are proactively identified, and the organization's response to incidents is well-coordinated. This involves ongoing monitoring, regular reviews, and the development of a robust incident response plan to address security challenges as they arise, ensuring the organization's resilience against both current and future risks.

  o **Ongoing monitoring:** Continuously monitor the effectiveness of implemented controls and identify new or emerging risks.

  o **Regular reviews:** Conduct periodic reviews of the risk assessment process and update the risk register as needed.

  o **Incident response:** Develop and implement an incident response plan to address security incidents effectively.

- **Documentation and reporting:** Effective documentation and reporting are crucial components of the risk assessment process. Proper documentation ensures that all findings, assessments, and decisions are accurately recorded, providing a clear audit trail. Preparing comprehensive reports helps communicate risk assessment results and recommendations to management, enabling informed decision-making. Additionally, maintaining thorough records of risk assessments, implemented controls, and compliance activities ensures continuity and accountability, facilitating future reviews and audits. These practices not only enhance transparency but also support ongoing risk management efforts and regulatory compliance.

  o **Document findings:** Document all findings, assessments, and decisions related to the risk assessment process.

  o **Prepare reports:** Prepare reports summarizing the risk assessment findings and recommendations for management.

  o **Maintain records:** Maintain records of all risk assessments, controls, and compliance activities.

The following are the outcomes:

- **Reduced risk:** Mitigated risks to the confidentiality, integrity, and availability of data.[12]

- **Improved security posture:** Enhanced security posture and reduced vulnerability to cyberattacks.[13]

- **Enhanced compliance:** Demonstrated compliance with relevant regulations (for example, ISO, GDPR, CCPA, HIPAA).

- **Improved business continuity:** Enhanced ability to recover from security incidents and maintain business operations.

- **Enhanced reputation:** Improved reputation and trust with customers and stakeholders.

Manage security governance programs

To effectively manage cybersecurity risks, organizations must integrate security governance into their strategic decision-making. A well-defined governance framework ensures alignment between business objectives and security initiatives while fostering a proactive security culture. The following key steps outline the foundation for a structured and resilient security governance program:

- **Define business objectives and risk appetite:**

  o **Collaborate:** Work closely with business leaders to understand their strategic goals, priorities, and risk tolerance. For example, for the healthcare provider in the data breach scenario, a business objective might be to **maintain patient trust and avoid reputational damage**.

  o **Document:** Clearly document these objectives and the organization's willingness to accept certain levels of risk.

- **Develop a security governance framework:**

  o **Select a framework:** Choose a suitable framework like NIST Cybersecurity Framework, ISO 27001, or COBIT.

  o **Tailor to business:** Adapt the framework to align with the organization's specific needs, risk appetite, and regulatory requirements.

  o **Key components:**

    ▪ **Governance:** Establish clear roles and responsibilities for security governance, including a **chief information security officer** (**CISO**) and relevant committees.

    ▪ **Risk management:** Implement a robust risk management process, including threat identification, vulnerability assessment, risk assessment, and treatment.

    ▪ **Compliance:** Ensure compliance with all relevant regulations (HIPAA, GDPR, etc.) and industry standards.

- **Communication and reporting:** Establish clear communication channels and reporting mechanisms to keep stakeholders informed about security risks and incidents.

- **Integrate security into business processes:**

  o **Embed security in decision-making:** Ensure security considerations are integrated into all business decisions, from product development to mergers and acquisitions.

  o **Security awareness training:** Conduct regular security awareness training for all employees to foster a security-conscious culture.

  o **Incident response:** Develop and test an incident response plan to effectively handle security incidents.

- **Continuous monitoring and improvement:**

  o **Regular reviews:** Conduct regular reviews of the security governance program to assess its effectiveness and identify areas for improvement.

  o **Key performance indicators:** Define and track KPIs to measure the effectiveness of security controls and the overall security posture.

  o **Adapt and evolve:** Continuously adapt the security governance program to address emerging threats and changing business needs.

- **Alignment with specific scenarios:**

  o **Zero trust:** Align security governance with the principle of "never trust, always verify." This may involve implementing strong access controls, micro-segmentation, and continuous monitoring of user activity.

  o **DLP:** Ensure the DLP solution aligns with business needs and regulatory requirements. This may involve conducting data classification exercises, defining acceptable use policies, and providing employee training on data handling practices.

- **Key considerations:**

  o **Leadership support:** Obtain strong support from senior management for the security governance program.

  o **Resource allocation:** Allocate adequate budget and resources for the implementation and maintenance of security controls.

  o **Communication and collaboration:** Foster strong communication and collaboration between IT, security, and business teams.

  o **Culture of security:** Cultivate a culture of security awareness and responsibility throughout the organization.

By following these steps, organizations can establish effective security governance programs that align with business objectives, mitigate risks, and ensure compliance with relevant regulations.

Conclusion

Malware sandboxing, memory dumping, runtime debugging, reconnaissance, fingerprinting, code review, social engineering, pivoting, and open-source intelligence were among the processes addressed in this chapter. It also covered the approaches used in security vulnerability assessments, penetration testing, internal and external audits, and color-team exercises.

In the next chapter, we will discuss the selection of vulnerability assessment tools.

Exercise

1. **A security team conducts a vulnerability assessment on a company's internal network. During the scan, they identify multiple unpatched services but notice a critical system with no detected vulnerabilities. However, the system is outdated and lacks vendor support. What is the BEST course of action?**

   a. Ignore the system, as no vulnerabilities were detected, and focus on patching other systems.

   b. Classify the system as low risk, since no vulnerabilities were identified, and document the findings.

   c. Flag the system as a high-risk asset due to its end-of-life status and recommend mitigation strategies.

   d. Re-run the vulnerability scan with a different tool to confirm the absence of vulnerabilities.

2. **During a black-box penetration test, the tester successfully exploits a remote command execution (RCE) vulnerability on a web application, gaining shell access to the underlying server. What should the tester do NEXT to align with ethical penetration testing standards?**

   a. Exfiltrate sample-sensitive data to demonstrate impact on the client.

   b. Escalate privileges and attempt to pivot to other internal systems.

   c. Document the vulnerability with proof of exploitation and report it immediately.

   d. Deploy a backdoor for later access to continue testing after the engagement ends.

3. **A multinational financial institution is developing its cybersecurity risk management strategy. Which of the following BEST ensures that security risk is managed in alignment with business objectives and regulatory requirements?**

    a. Using a globally recognized cybersecurity framework like NIST CSF or ISO 27001.

    b. Relying on periodic vulnerability scans and penetration tests to mitigate security risks.

    c. Assigning IT teams full responsibility for risk management without business involvement.

    d. Focusing exclusively on regulatory compliance, as meeting compliance means the organization is secure.

4. **An organization is preparing for a compliance audit and needs to demonstrate an effective risk management process. Which of the following elements is MOST critical to provide evidence of a well-established risk management program?**

    a. A list of all past security incidents and breaches.

    b. A documented risk register with identified threats, impact assessments, and mitigation strategies.

    c. A single-point risk assessment was performed during the initial compliance certification.

    d. A comprehensive antivirus deployment across all endpoints.

Answers

1. c
2. c
3. a
4. b

Join our book's Discord space

Join the book's Discord Workspace for Latest updates, Offers, Tech happenings around the world, New Release and Sessions with the Authors:

https://discord.bpbonline.com

CHAPTER 13
Selecting Vulnerability Assessment Tools

Introduction

While most people think in terms of the network when they consider security assessments, security assessments encompass much more than this. If only network security were considered, major vulnerabilities would be left exposed. It can be argued that without sufficient physical security, network security cannot be achieved. Moreover, when exercising a defense-in-depth strategy, security must be considered at the network, host, and physical levels. This chapter looks at the tools used to perform assessments at each of these levels.

Structure

In this chapter, we will discuss the following types of assessment tools:

- Network tool types
- Exploitation tools and frameworks
- Host tools types
- Physical security tools

Objectives

By the end of the chapter, you will be able to understand the types of tools used to perform security assessments of networks, including port scanners, vulnerability scanners, protocol analyzers, SCAP scanners, network enumerators, fuzzers, HTTP interceptors, exploitation tools and frameworks, visualization tools, and log reduction and analysis tools. This section describes the tools used to assess vulnerabilities that might be present on an individual host. These types of tools include password crackers, vulnerability scanners, command-line tools, local exploitation tools and frameworks, SCAP tools, file integrity monitoring utilities, log analysis tools, antivirus, and reverse engineering tools. This chapter covers devices used to assess the physical security of an environment, including lock picks, RFID tools, and IR cameras.

Network tool types

An enterprise must first establish where the security flaws exist before it can secure a network. The only way to do so is to conduct an honest assessment of the network's current state. Multiple techniques of assessment should be utilized to account for the many sorts of weaknesses that can occur in a network. This chapter goes over the various assessment techniques and the flaws that each one is supposed to disclose.

Port scanners

A network can be scanned for open ports using **Internet Control Message Protocol (ICMP)** messages. Services that are operating and listening on a device that is vulnerable to attack are indicated by open ports. An ICMP attack, also known as a port scanning attack, pings every address and port number combination on each device and keeps note of which ports are open on each device, as the pings are responded by open ports with listening services and not by closed ports. **Network Mapper (Nmap)**, a free and open-source program for network discovery and security auditing, is one of the most extensively used port scanners. *Figure 13.1* displays the results of a scan for many hosts using Zenmap, an Nmap security scanner GUI:

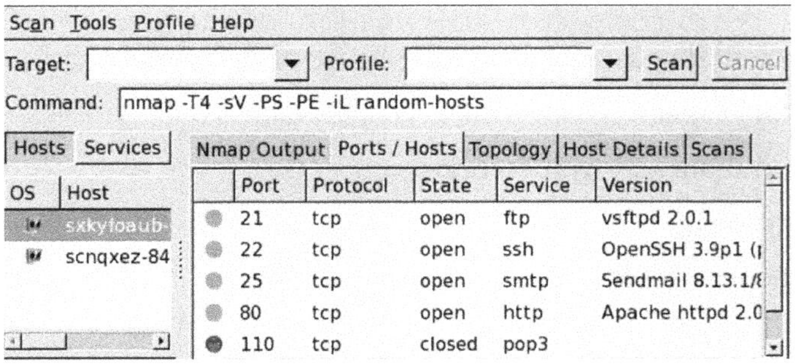

Figure 13.1: Zenmap port scan output

Figure 13.2 shows the output from the command-line version of Nmap. You can see in this figure that a ping scan of an entire network has just been completed. From it, you can see that the domain **scanme.nmap.org** has four ports open – 22, 80, 9929, and 31337:

```
C:\>nmap scanme.nmap.org
Starting Nmap 7.70 ( https://nmap.org ) at 2018-07-21 10:05 GMT Summer Time
Nmap scan report for scanme.nmap.org (45.33.32.156)
Host is up (0.17s latency).
Not shown: 996 closed ports
PORT       STATE SERVICE
22/tcp     open  ssh
80/tcp     open  http
9929/tcp   open  nping-echo
31337/tcp  open  Elite

Nmap done: 1 IP address (1 host up) scanned in 22.31 seconds

C:\>
```

Figure 13.2: Nmap port scan output

In a scenario where you need to determine what applications and services are running on the devices in your network, a port scanner would be appropriate.

Network vulnerability scanners

A vulnerability scanner, unlike a port scanner, can search for a variety of security flaws, such as misconfigurations, out-of-date software, missing patches, and open ports. Scanners for network vulnerabilities scan the entire network. Nessus, a proprietary program developed by Tenable Network Security, is one of the most extensively used vulnerability scanners. It is available for personal use in a non-commercial setting at no cost. By default, Nessus starts by listing the issues detected on a host that is ranked as the most serious at the top of the output. Vulnerability ranking of Nessus is shown in *Figure 13.3*:

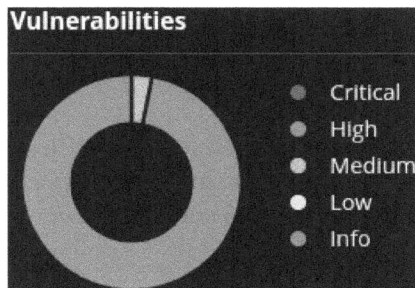

Figure 13.3: Vulnerability Raking

Figure 13.4 displays the Nessus scan output revealing one high-severity vulnerability (CVSS 8.4) related to Pandas, indicating a critical security risk that requires immediate remediation. Additionally, the report includes two vulnerabilities of mixed severities, necessitating further assessment based on their impact and exploitability. It is recommended to prioritize patching or applying mitigation measures to reduce the organization's risk exposure.

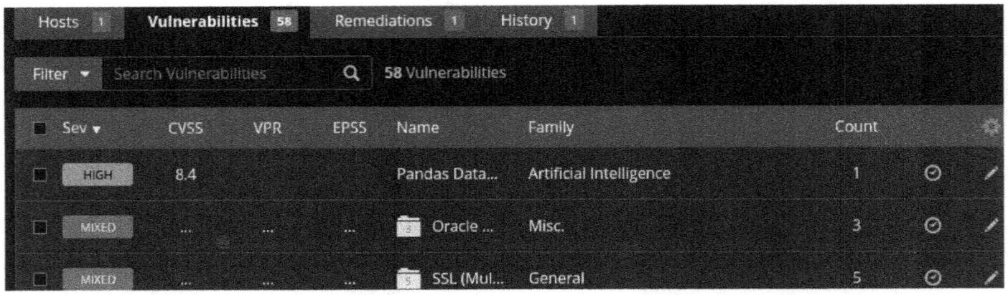

Figure 13.4: Nessus scan output

There is one high-severity issue (the default password for a Firebird database on the host) and five medium-severity concerns, including two **Secure Socket Layer (SSL)** certificates that cannot be trusted and a remote desktop man-in-the-middle attack vulnerability. When a network's security flaws extend beyond open ports, such as weak passwords, misconfigurations, and missing updates, a vulnerability scanner is the best tool to use.

Protocol analyzer

Sniffing is the process of collecting packets for examination; eavesdropping is sniffing done maliciously. Sniffing happens when an attacker adds or inserts a device or program into a communication medium in order to gather all of the data sent through it. Both respectable security experts and attackers utilize sniffers, also known as protocol analyzers, to capture raw packets from the network. When a sniffer is used lawfully, the fact that it does not send any data to the network is a benefit; when it is used against you, it is a drawback (because you cannot tell you are being sniffed). Sniffers should be monitored, and their use must be limited by the organizations. Wherever practicable, you should encrypt all network traffic.

Wired

One of the most widely used sniffers is Wireshark. It captures raw packets off the interface on which it is configured and allows you to examine each packet. If the data is unencrypted, you will be able to read the data. *Figure 13.5* shows an example of Wireshark in use:

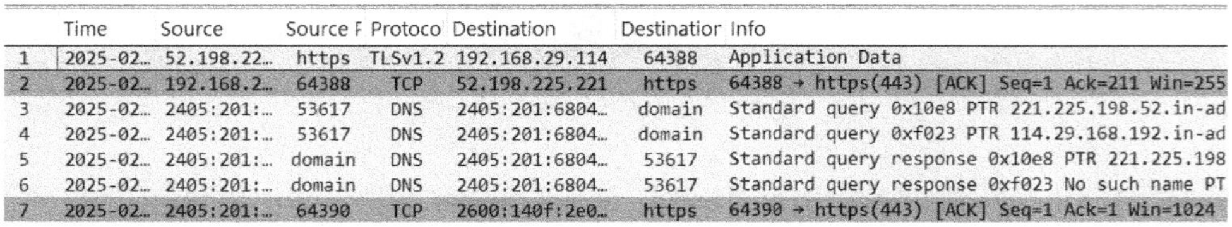

Figure 13.5: Wireshark output

Figure 13.4 shows the result, with each line representing a packet intercepted on the network. The source IP address, the destination IP address, the protocol in use, and the data in the packet are all visible. For example, line 16 displays a transmission with **transmission control protocol (TCP)** from 192.168.0.1 to 192.168.0.2. When utilizing a display filter, the capture file retains all packets. The display filter affects just the appearance of the capture file, not its content. Following that, the server sends synchronous and acknowledgment packets. You can click on a single packet to try and read it. You would be able to read and evaluate the data if it were clear language. As a result, it is easy to understand how an attacker may obtain credentials and other sensitive data. Protocol analyzers are handy when you need to observe what is going on in your network. Assume that you have a security policy mandating that certain types of traffic be encrypted. However, you are unsure if everyone is adhering to the policy. You might detect if users are complying by collecting and inspecting raw packets on the network.

Wireless analyzers

Protocol analyzers can also capture and analyze wireless frames. *Figure 13.6* shows the process of a device sending a probe request packet to find an **access point (AP)**, the AP responding with a probe response (frames 798 and 799), the device attempting authentication and association with the AP (frames 804–8010), and the AP requesting user credentials as an EAP message (frames 811 and 812):

Time	Source	Source F	Protoco	Destination	Destinatior	Info
2025-02…	2600:140f…	https	TLSv1.2	2405:201:6804…	64390	Application Data
2025-02…	2405:201:…	64390	TCP	2600:140f:2e0…	https	64390 → https(443) [ACK] Seq=9921 Ack=36 Win=?
2025-02…	2405:201:…	53617	DNS	2405:201:6804…	domain	Standard query 0x1226 PTR b.f.1.d.e.7.6.a.5.b.
2025-02…	2405:201:…	53617	DNS	2405:201:6804…	domain	Standard query 0xd365 PTR 1.0.d.1.8.a.0.c.0.0.
2025-02…	2405:201:…	53617	DNS	2405:201:6804…	domain	Standard query 0x4673 PTR 1.5.0.7.6.5.8.b.0.0.
2025-02…	2405:201:…	domain	DNS	2405:201:6804…	53617	Standard query response 0xd365 PTR 1.0.d.1.8.a
2025-02…	2405:201:…	domain	DNS	2405:201:6804…	53617	Standard query response 0x4673 PTR 1.5.0.7.6.5
2025-02…	2405:201:…	domain	DNS	2405:201:6804…	53617	Standard query response 0x1226 No such name PT
2025-02…	2600:140f…	https	TLSv1.2	2405:201:6804…	64390	Application Data
2025-02…	2600:140f…	https	TLSv1.2	2405:201:6804…	64390	Application Data
2025-02…	2405:201:…	64390	TCP	2600:140f:2e0…	https	64390 → https(443) [ACK] Seq=9921 Ack=408 Win?
2025-02…	2405:201:…	64310	TCP	2603:1046:c04…	https	64310 → https(443) [FIN, ACK] Seq=1 Ack=1 Win?
2025-02…	2405:201:…	56890	DNS	2405:201:6804…	domain	Standard query 0x6864 A ab.chatgpt.com
2025-02…	2405:201:…	53607	DNS	2405:201:6804…	domain	Standard query 0x995a HTTPS ab.chatgpt.com
2025-02…	2405:201:…	65316	DNS	2405:201:6804…	domain	Standard query 0x719b AAAA ab.chatgpt.com

Figure 13.6: *Wireshark frame list*

We know this is 802.11 traffic because there are many frame types not found in wired networks, such as the probe request and probe response frames.

Security content automation protocol scanner

Security content automation protocol (SCAP) is a security automation standard for identifying software defects and configuration concerns. The terminology and forms were standardized. A security automation product provider can acquire SCAP validation, proving that it will work with other scanners and represent scan findings in a consistent manner. Understanding the operation of SCAP requires an understanding of its components, which are as follows:

- **Common Configuration Enumeration (CCE):** These are configuration best practice statements maintained by the **National Institute of Standards and Technology (NIST)**.

- **Common Platform Enumeration (CPE):** These are methods for describing and classifying operating systems, applications, and hardware devices.

- **Common Weakness Enumeration (CWE):** These are design flaws in the development of software that can lead to vulnerabilities.

- **Common Vulnerabilities and Exposures (CVE):** These are vulnerabilities in published operating systems and applications software. The **Common Vulnerability Scoring System (CVSS)** is a system of ranking vulnerabilities that are discovered based on predefined metrics. This system ensures that the most critical vulnerabilities can be easily identified and addressed after a vulnerability test is met. Scores are awarded on a scale of 0 to 10, with the values having the following ranks:

  o **0:** No issues

  o **to 3.9:** Low

  o **4.0 to 6.9:** Medium

  o **7.0 to 8.9:** High

  o **9.0 to 10.0:** Critical

CVSS is composed of the following three metric groups:

- **Base:** Characteristics of a vulnerability that are constant over time and across user environments

- **Temporal:** Characteristics of a vulnerability that change over time but not among user environments

- **Environmental:** Characteristics of a vulnerability that are relevant and unique to a particular user's environment

The base metric group includes the following metrics:

- **Access vector (AV):** AV describes how the attacker would exploit the vulnerability and has the following three possible values:

  o **L:** Stands for local and means that the attacker must have physical or logical access to the affected system.

  o **A:** Stands for adjacent network and means that the attacker must be on the local network.

  o **N:** Stands for network and means that the attacker can cause the vulnerability from any network.

- **Access complexity (AC)**: AC describes the difficulty of exploiting the vulnerability and has the following three possible values:

  o **H**: Stands for high and means that the vulnerability requires special conditions that are hard to find.

  o **M**: Stands for medium and means that the vulnerability requires somewhat special conditions.

  o **L**: Stands for low and means that the vulnerability does not require special conditions.

- **Authentication (Au)**: The Au metric describes the authentication an attacker would need to get through to exploit the vulnerability and has the following three possible values:

  o **M**: Stands for multiple and means that the attacker would need to get through two or more authentication mechanisms.

  o **S**: Stands for single and means that the attacker would need to get through one authentication mechanism.

  o **N**: Stands for none and means that no authentication mechanisms are in place to stop the exploitation of the vulnerability.

- **Availability (A)**: The A metric describes the disruption that might occur if the vulnerability is exploited and has the following three possible values:

  o **N**: Stands for none and means that there is no availability impact.

  o **P**: Stands for partial and means that system performance is degraded.

  o **C**: Stands for complete and means that the system is completely shut down.

- **Confidentiality (C)**: The C metric describes the information disclosure that may occur if the vulnerability is exploited and has the following three possible values:

  o **N**: Stands for none and means that there is no confidentiality impact.

  o **P**: Stands for partial and means some access to information would occur.

  o **C**: Stands for complete and means all information on the system could be compromised.

- **Integrity (I)**: The I metric describes the type of data alteration that might occur and has the following three possible values:

  o **N**: Stands for none and means that there is no integrity impact.

  o **P**: Stands for partial and means that some information modification would occur.

  o **C**: Stands for complete and means that all information on the system could be compromised.

The CVSS vector looks something like the following:

CVSS2#AV:L/AC:H/Au:M/C:P/I:N/A:N

This vector is read as follows:

- **AV:L**: Access vector, where L stands for local and means that the attacker must have physical or logical access to the affected system.

- **AC:H**: Access complexity, where H stands for high and means that the vulnerability requires special conditions that are hard to find.

- **Au:M**: Authentication, where M stands for multiple and means that the attacker would need to get through two or more authentication mechanisms.

- **C:P**: Confidentiality, where P stands for partial and means that some access to information would occur.

- **I:N**: Integrity, where N stands for none and means that there is no integrity impact.

- **A:N**: Availability, where N stands for none and means that there is no availability impact.

Permissions and access

Access to scanning tools must be closely controlled because scanning devices without being authorized to do so is a crime. The group of users allowed to use these tools should be as small as possible. The use of these tools should also be audited to ensure that the tools are being used in accordance with the rules of engagement.

Execute scanning

Configuring a scan is somewhat specific to the scanning product, but the following are some general recommendations with respect to conducting a scan:

1. Test the scanner for the environment and tackle the scan surgically rather than using a shotgun, all-at-once approach.

2. Critical business traffic and traffic patterns need to be factored into vulnerability scans because a scan itself adds to network traffic.

3. Give some thought to what time scans will be run and also to the time zones in which affected businesses operate.

The following are the high-level steps in conducting a scan:

1. Add IP addresses or domain names to the scan.

2. Choose scanner appliances (hardware or software sensors).

3. Select the scan option. For example, in Nessus, under **Advanced Settings**, you can use custom policy settings to alter the operation of the scan. The following are some selected examples:

    a. global.max_hosts: Maximum number of simultaneous checks against each host tested.

    b. auto_update_delay: Number of hours to wait between two updates. Four hours is the minimum allowed interval.

    c. global.max_simult_tcp_sessions: Maximum number of simultaneous TCP sessions between all scans.

    d. max_hosts: Maximum number of hosts checked at one time during a scan.

4. Start the scan.

5. View the scan status and results.

Figure 13.7 shows vulnerability detail reported by Nessus.

Figure 13.7: *Vulnerability information Nessus*

Network enumerator

Network enumerators scan the network and collect information on visible users, groups, shares, and services, a process known as device fingerprinting. Network enumerators collect data using protocols like ICMP and SNMP. *Figure 13.8* shows an example of WhatsUp Gold, which not only detects problems with hosts and other network devices but also allows you to categorize and explore them by the problem. Currently, it is configured to show all devices. Select the devices without credentials folder in the tree view to see all devices that are lacking credentials. You may use a network enumerator to locate and arrange the information on the security posture of all machines in the network without having to physically visit each one. Refer to *Figure 13.8* for WhatsUp Gold output:

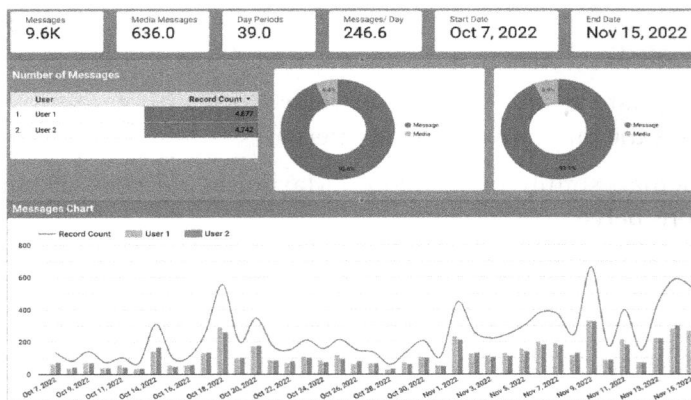

Figure 13.8: WhatsUp gold output

Fuzzer

Fuzzers are software tools that, through a process known as fuzzing, detect and exploit flaws in online applications. They work by inserting semi-random data into the program stack and then looking for problems. They are simple to use, but one of their drawbacks is that they are more likely to identify basic faults than more sophisticated ones. JBroFuzz and WSFuzzer are two tools recommended by the **Open Web Application Security Project (OWASP)**, an organization dedicated to enhancing software security. WSFuzzer is primarily interested in HTTP-based **Simple Object Access Protocol (SOAP)** services.

During the development of a web application that would manage sensitive data, fuzzer can be employed. The fuzzer will assist you in determining whether the program is processing error exceptions correctly. For example, you may notice that if you mistype your credentials on the application's login page, the software crashes and you are provided with a command prompt. If you wanted to explore the problem, you could use an online fuzzer to simulate the login screen. The output of a fuzzer named Peach is seen in *Figure 13.9*. It fuzzes the program with a mutator named StringMutator, which changes the input repeatedly. Some input to the tool has caused a crash, as you can see in this output. Peach has confirmed the error by duplicating it. It will send extra information to a log, which you may study to figure out which string value caused the crash. Refer to *Figure 13.9* for Peach Fuzzer output:

Figure 13.9: Peach Fuzzer output

HTTP interceptor

Web communication between a browser and a website is intercepted by HTTP interceptors. They allow you to do things that your browser would not. For example, an HTTP interceptor may accept 300 characters of input but the browser may only allow 50. These tools allow you to simulate what would happen if a hacker managed to get around the browser's restriction. An HTTP interceptor works similarly to a web proxy in that it monitors both channels of traffic. Burp Suite and Fiddler are two examples of HTTP interceptors. *Figure 13.10* shows how Fiddler, a Windows application, may be used to assess the performance of a website:

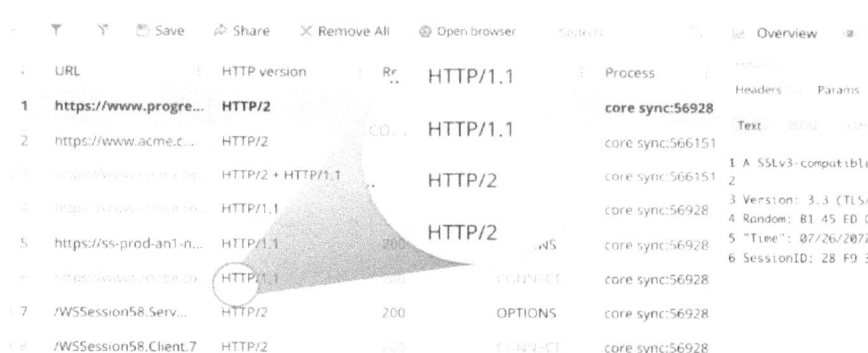

Figure 13.10: Fiddler

HTTP interceptors and fuzzers should both be used for testing web applications. They can also be used to test the proper validation of input.

Exploitation tools and frameworks

Exploitation tools, also known as exploit kits, are a collection of tools used to find and exploit security flaws. They are designed to be used in a wide range of situations. These tools target an application in the same way that a hacker would, allowing them to be used for both good and evil. Some are completely free, while others, like core impact, are incredibly costly. An exploit framework creates a consistent environment in which exploit code may be written and executed against a target. The three most widely used frameworks are as follows:

- **Metasploit**: This is an open-source framework that ships with hundreds of exploits and payloads as well as many auxiliary modules.

- **CANVAS**: Sold on a subscription model, CANVAS ships with more than 400 exploits.

- **IMPACT**: This commercially available tool uses agent technology that helps an attacker gather information on the target.

Metasploit's web interface is seen in *Figure 13.11*. The attacker (or tester) chooses an exploit from the top panel, followed by a payload from the bottom panel. The tester can utilize the console to interface with the host once the attack has been initiated. Testing programs for security flaws should include using these exploitation frameworks. Refer to *Figure 13.11* for Metasploit's web interface:

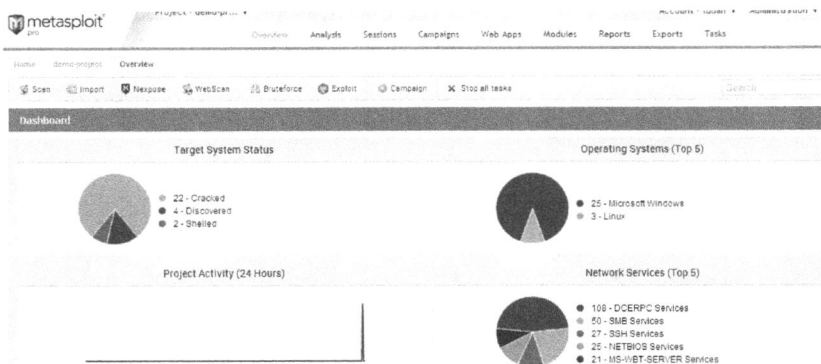

Figure 13.11: Metasploit web interface

Visualization tools

The sheer volume of security data created by the many devices scattered across our environments makes it impossible to determine what is going on in many circumstances. When the same raw data is given to us in a visual style, it becomes a little simpler to spot patterns and trends. It is much simpler to notice a pattern when the data is aggregated and graphed. Let us imagine you wanted to understand the relative split of security incidents between your Windows and Linux machines. Most tools for this purpose can not only collect all occurrences of a certain category but also graph them over time. Examples of such graphs may be seen in *Figure 13.12*; many of the tools mentioned in this section are considered visualization tools since they aid in the display and interpretation of raw data:

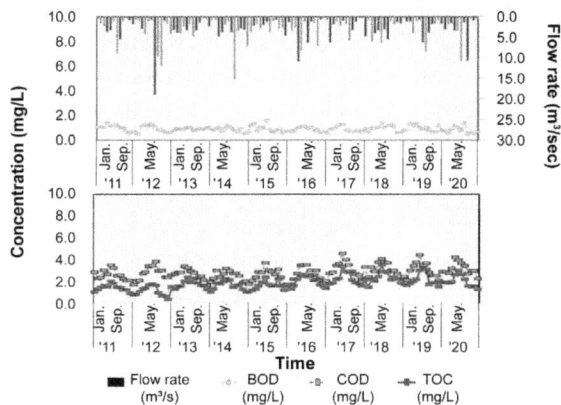

Figure 13.12: Trend analysis

Log reduction and analysis tools

Audit reduction tools are pre-processors that are meant to minimize the number of audit records so that human review may be done more quickly. These technologies can delete numerous audit data that are recognized to have minimal security value before a security assessment. These utilities usually delete records that are created by specific types of events, such as nightly backups. Scripts are used by certain technicians for this reason. Many Linux techs use a Perl script called **Simple WATCHer** (**swatch**). The amount of log data that has to be analyzed in large organizations might be fairly significant. As a result, many businesses use a SIEM system, which provides an automated method for analyzing events and determining where the attention should be focused. Most SIEM products support two ways of collecting logs from log generators, which are as follows:

- **Agentless**: With this type of collection, the SIEM server receives data from the individual hosts without needing to have any special software installed on those hosts. Some servers pull logs from the hosts, which is usually done by having the server authenticate to each host and retrieve its logs regularly. In other cases, the hosts push their logs to the server, which usually involves each host authenticating to the server and transferring its logs regularly. Regardless of whether the logs are pushed or pulled, the server then performs event filtering and aggregation and log normalization and analysis on the collected logs.

- **Agent-based**: With this type of collection, an agent program is installed on the host to perform event filtering and aggregation, and log normalization for a particular type of log. The host then transmits the normalized log data to a SIEM server, usually on a real-time or near-real-time basis, for analysis and storage. Multiple agents may need to be installed if a host has multiple types of logs of interest.

- **Some security incident and event management (SIEM):** The products also offer agents for generic formats such as Syslog and SNMP. A generic agent is used primarily to get log data from a source for which a format-specific agent and an agentless method are not available. Some products also allow administrators to create custom agents to handle unsupported log sources.

Each approach has its own set of benefits and drawbacks. The key benefit of the agentless technique is that it eliminates the need to install, configure, and maintain agents on each logging host. The main downside is the lack of filtering and aggregation at the individual host level, which can result in much higher volumes of data being carried over networks and a longer time to filter and analyze logs. Another drawback of the agentless approach is that the SIEM server may require credentials to authenticate with each logging host. In certain circumstances, only one of the two techniques is viable; for example, there may be no way to gather logs from a specific server without putting an agent on it. SIEM software often supports a wide range of log sources, including operating systems, security software, application servers (such as web servers and email servers), and even physical security control devices like badge scanners. Except for general formats like Syslog, SIEM solutions normally know how to identify the most essential reported information for each supported log source type. This greatly enhances log data standardization, analysis, and correlation over software that has a broader awareness of specific log sources and formats. In addition, the SIEM software may conduct event reduction by ignoring data fields that are irrelevant to computer security, possibly lowering the SIEM program's network traffic and data storage requirements. *Figure 13.13* shows the output from a SIEM system; notice the various types of events that have been recorded:

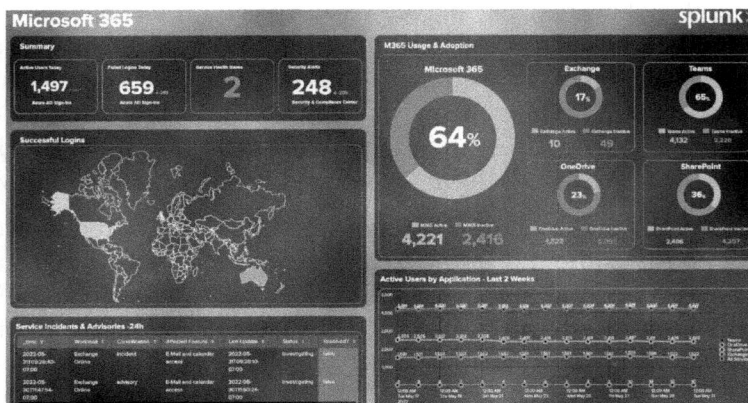

Figure 13.13: SIEM output

Host tool types

In some cases, you are concerned with assessing the security of a single host rather than the network in general. This section looks at tools that are appropriate for assessing host security and issues for which they might be indicated.

Password cracker

Password crackers are programs that do what their name implies. They attempt to identify passwords. These programs can be used to mount several types of password attacks, including dictionary attacks and Bruteforce attacks, which are explained as follows:

- In a dictionary attack, an attacker uses a dictionary of common words to discover passwords. An automated program uses the hash of the dictionary word and compares this hash value to entries in the system password file. While the program comes with a dictionary, attackers also use extra dictionaries that are found on the Internet. To protect against these attacks, you should implement a security rule which says that a password must not be a word found in the dictionary.

- Brute-force attacks are more difficult to perform because they work through all possible combinations of numbers and characters. These attacks are also very time-consuming. The best countermeasures against password threats are to implement complex password policies, have users change passwords on a regular basis, employ account lockout policies, encrypt password files, and use password-cracking tools to discover weak passwords.

Cain and Abel is a well-known password-cracking program that sniffs the network, cracks encrypted passwords using the dictionary, brute-force, and cryptanalysis attacks, records VoIP conversations, decodes scrambled passwords, reveals password boxes, uncovers cached passwords, and analyses routing protocols. *Figure 13.14* illustrates the Cain and Abel output:

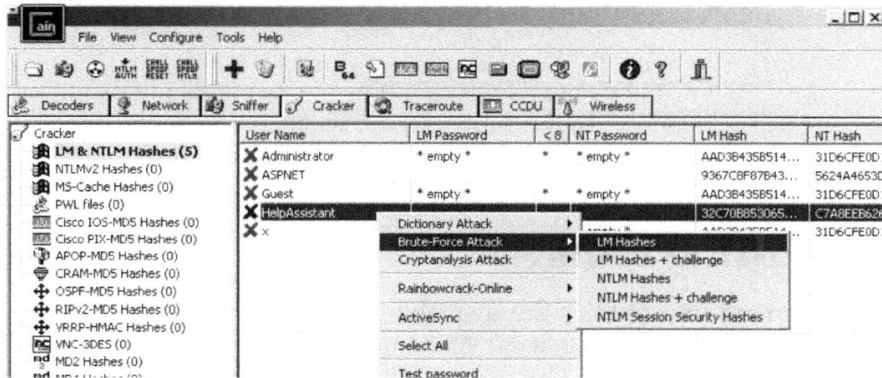

Figure 13.14: Cain and Abel output

As you can see, each account can be subjected to a variety of attacks. This example illustrates a search of the local system for user accounts, and the software finds three such as Admin, Sharpy, and JSmith. You may use the application to execute a brute-force attack or a variety of different attacks on that account.

John the Ripper is another example of a password cracker. It identifies weak UNIX passwords, but it also supports hashes for a variety of other platforms. There are three versions of John the Ripper such as a free official version, a community improved version (with numerous contributed patches but less quality assurance), and a cheap pro version. If you are having trouble enforcing strong or complicated passwords and need to uncover weak passwords on your network, you may use a password cracker to determine which ones are weak and perhaps crack them. If assessing password security is time-sensitive, save the password file to one of your more powerful PCs (a cluster is even better) and execute the password cracker on that platform. This way, you will be able to use the extra resources to complete the audit more rapidly.

Host vulnerability scanners

Like network vulnerability scanners, host scanners scan for vulnerabilities, but only on the host on which the tool is installed. Many scanners can do both. The **Microsoft Baseline Security Analyzer** is a host scanner that can also scan multiple hosts at once. It returns a clean list of all vulnerabilities and prioritizes them, as shown in *Figure 13.15*:

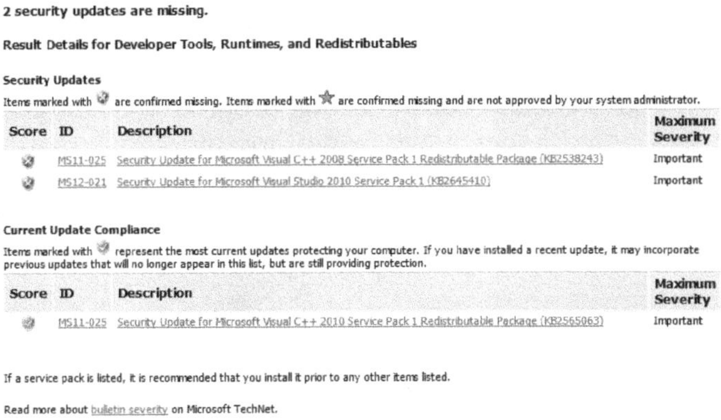

2 security updates are missing.

Result Details for Developer Tools, Runtimes, and Redistributables

Security Updates

Items marked with 🏆 are confirmed missing. Items marked with 🌟 are confirmed missing and are not approved by your system administrator.

Score	ID	Description	Maximum Severity
🏆	MS11-025	Security Update for Microsoft Visual C++ 2008 Service Pack 1 Redistributable Package (KB2538243)	Important
🏆	MS12-021	Security Update for Microsoft Visual Studio 2010 Service Pack 1 (KB2645410)	Important

Current Update Compliance

Items marked with 🏆 represent the most current updates protecting your computer. If you have installed a recent update, it may incorporate previous updates that will no longer appear in this list, but are still providing protection.

Score	ID	Description	Maximum Severity
🏆	MS11-025	Security Update for Microsoft Visual C++ 2010 Service Pack 1 Redistributable Package (KB2565063)	Important

If a service pack is listed, it is recommended that you install it prior to any other items listed.

Read more about bulletin severity on Microsoft TechNet.

Figure 13.15: *Microsoft Baseline Security Analyzer output*

Command-line tools

Many local command-line utilities are available in both Windows and Linux or UNIX for making security assessments as well. While not as user-friendly as some of the more automated tools, they are preferred by many of the more experienced in the field for their flexibility, as they do require more knowledge and background. The following sections discuss several security-related command line tools.

Netstat

On a TCP or IP-based system, the **netstat** (network status) command is used to see what ports are listening. The **-a** option displays all ports, whereas **/?** displays what additional choices are available. (The possibilities vary depending on the operating system.) The current connections are displayed when the program is run without any switches, as shown in *Figure 13.16*. Netstat can help you figure out which ports are open and which services or protocols are using them. These open ports might put the host's security at risk. Refer to *Figure 13.16* for the Netstat output:

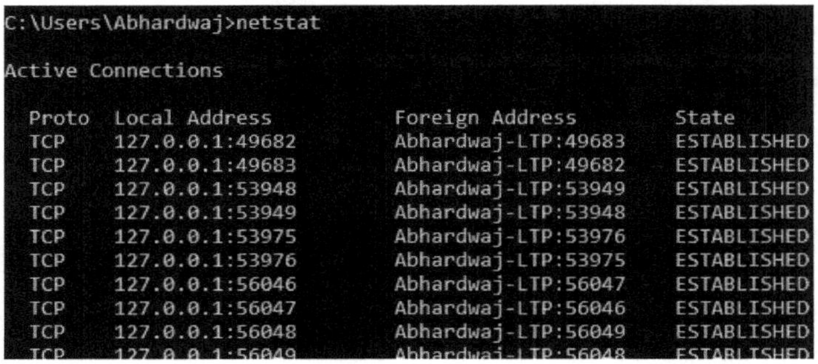

```
C:\Users\Abhardwaj>netstat

Active Connections

  Proto  Local Address          Foreign Address        State
  TCP    127.0.0.1:49682        Abhardwaj-LTP:49683    ESTABLISHED
  TCP    127.0.0.1:49683        Abhardwaj-LTP:49682    ESTABLISHED
  TCP    127.0.0.1:53948        Abhardwaj-LTP:53949    ESTABLISHED
  TCP    127.0.0.1:53949        Abhardwaj-LTP:53948    ESTABLISHED
  TCP    127.0.0.1:53975        Abhardwaj-LTP:53976    ESTABLISHED
  TCP    127.0.0.1:53976        Abhardwaj-LTP:53975    ESTABLISHED
  TCP    127.0.0.1:56046        Abhardwaj-LTP:56047    ESTABLISHED
  TCP    127.0.0.1:56047        Abhardwaj-LTP:56046    ESTABLISHED
  TCP    127.0.0.1:56048        Abhardwaj-LTP:56049    ESTABLISHED
  TCP    127.0.0.1:56049        Abhardwaj-LTP:56048    ESTABLISHED
```

Figure 13.16: *Netstat output*

Each line of Netstat output lists the source IP address and port number, the destination IP address or hostname, and the state of the connection. The following are the possible states:

- **LISTEN**: Represents waiting for a connection request from any remote TCP connection and port.

- **SYN-SENT**: Represents waiting for a matching connection request after having sent a connection request.

- **SYN-RECEIVED**: Represents waiting for a confirming connection request acknowledgment after having both received and sent a connection request.

- **ESTABLISHED**: Represents an open connection, and the data received can be delivered to the user. This is the normal state for the data transfer phase of the connection.

- **FIN-WAIT-1**: Represents waiting for a connection termination request from the remote TCP connection or an acknowledgment of the connection termination request previously sent.

- **FIN-WAIT-2**: Represents waiting for a connection termination request from the remote TCP connection.

- **CLOSE-WAIT**: Represents waiting for a connection termination request from the local user.

- **CLOSING**: Represents waiting for a connection termination request acknowledgment from the remote TCP connection.

- **LAST-ACK**: Represents waiting for an acknowledgment of the connection termination request previously sent to the remote TCP connection (which includes an acknowledgment of its connection termination request).

Ping

To verify the connection between two devices, the ping command uses the ICMP protocol. The TCP/IP protocol's **ping** command is one of the most helpful. It transmits a sequence of packets to another system, which responds with a response of its own. When troubleshooting difficulties with distant hosts, the **ping** command may be incredibly beneficial. The **ping** command shows whether or not the host can be contacted and how long it takes for the host to respond. The time on a LAN is displayed as less than 10 milliseconds. However, on WAN networks, this figure can be significantly higher. Ping also tries to resolve the hostname associated with the IP address when the **-a** parameter is used. A successful ping is shown in *Figure 13.17*:

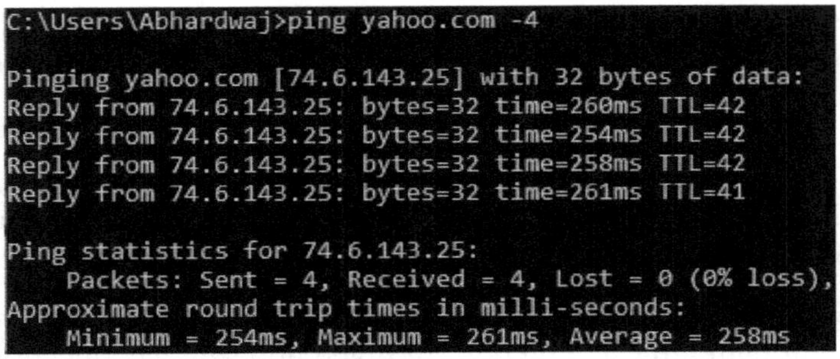

```
C:\Users\Abhardwaj>ping yahoo.com -4

Pinging yahoo.com [74.6.143.25] with 32 bytes of data:
Reply from 74.6.143.25: bytes=32 time=260ms TTL=42
Reply from 74.6.143.25: bytes=32 time=254ms TTL=42
Reply from 74.6.143.25: bytes=32 time=258ms TTL=42
Reply from 74.6.143.25: bytes=32 time=261ms TTL=41

Ping statistics for 74.6.143.25:
    Packets: Sent = 4, Received = 4, Lost = 0 (0% loss),
Approximate round trip times in milli-seconds:
    Minimum = 254ms, Maximum = 261ms, Average = 258ms
```

Figure 13.17: Successful ping

Figure 13.17 shows an unsuccessful ping. In this case, the request timed out, which typically means the host is off or disconnected from the network. When the destination cannot be reached, an error code is displayed. Refer to *Figure 13.8* for failed ping:

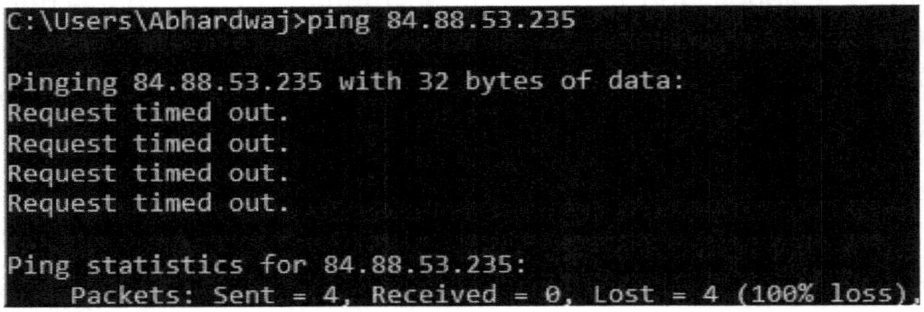

```
C:\Users\Abhardwaj>ping 84.88.53.235

Pinging 84.88.53.235 with 32 bytes of data:
Request timed out.
Request timed out.
Request timed out.
Request timed out.

Ping statistics for 84.88.53.235:
    Packets: Sent = 4, Received = 0, Lost = 4 (100% loss),
```

Figure 13.18: Failed ping

The most common of these codes are as follows:

- **Destination unreachable**: This indicates that the IP datagram could not be forwarded. This also includes an error code (number) that indicates more detail. For example, that there is no routing table entry or the destination is reachable but did not respond to ARP.

- **Request timed out**: This indicates that the TTL of the datagram was exceeded. This means you did not even get a response from a router. This can occur if the router is configured to not respond to ICMP, which is not uncommon. This is the situation in *Figure 13.18*.

Although there are easier ways to do this with other tools, such as Nmap, you can perform a ping sweep by creating a simple batch file, as follows:

```
for /l %i in(1,1,254) do ping -n 1 -w 100 <first three octets of host
network>.%i
```

For example, to sweep the **192.168.1.0** network, you can use the following command:

```
for /l %i in(1,1,254) do ping -n 1 -w 100 192.168.1.%i
```

Tracert or traceroute

The traceroute command (in Linux and UNIX) is used to trace a packet's journey via the network. Its most useful purpose is determining where a packet is lost in the network. It displays each hop (router) that the packet passes through, as well as the time it takes to do so. A traced route to **www.nascar.com** is shown in part in *Figure 13.19*. This command may also be used to record the route to a target and show it visually from within Nmap (Zenmap); graphical results are often simpler to interpret than command-line output. Each line indicates a hop, or a network that the communication passed through (that is, a router). Many times, these routes cannot be completely mapped because ICMP is blocked at the edge of the network in which the destination resides. Refer to *Figure 13.19*, which illustrates the Tracert output:

```
C:\Users\Abhardwaj>tracert www.nascar.com

Tracing route to e7436.g.akamaiedge.net [23.74.249.211]
over a maximum of 30 hops:

  1     5 ms     1 ms     2 ms  reliance.reliance [192.168.29.1]
  2     7 ms     3 ms     6 ms  10.35.168.1
  3   109 ms    99 ms    53 ms  172.16.28.1
  4    35 ms    97 ms    98 ms  192.168.97.36
  5    23 ms   131 ms    96 ms  172.26.109.117
  6   131 ms    99 ms    98 ms  172.26.109.98
  7   131 ms    69 ms    23 ms  192.168.41.72
  8    46 ms    99 ms   100 ms  192.168.41.73
  9   116 ms   100 ms    98 ms  172.16.28.2
 10   120 ms   100 ms    99 ms  172.16.0.39
 11   138 ms    99 ms    98 ms  172.25.41.167
 12   160 ms    99 ms    99 ms  49.45.4.251
 13   147 ms    99 ms   200 ms  103.198.140.207
 14   136 ms   201 ms   201 ms  snge-b3-link.ip.twelve99.net [62.115.11.246]
 15     *         *         *    Request timed out.
 16   260 ms   200 ms   305 ms  hnk-b1-link.ip.twelve99.net [62.115.135.142]
 17     *         *       271 ms  akamai-svc073290-lag003543.ip.twelve99-cust.net [62.115.153.82]
 18   374 ms   509 ms   409 ms  ae1.r01.hkg02.icn.netarch.akamai.com [23.56.133.34]
 19   307 ms   304 ms   306 ms  ae3.r01.hkg03.icn.netarch.akamai.com [23.215.54.133]
 20   308 ms   304 ms   302 ms  ae11.r01.hkg03.ien.netarch.akamai.com [23.56.143.43]
 21     *         *      2081 ms  ae3.pccw-hkg4.netarch.akamai.com [23.56.143.131]
 22   291 ms   224 ms   282 ms  a23-74-249-211.deploy.static.akamaitechnologies.com [23.74.249.211]

Trace complete.
```

Figure 13.19: Tracert output

Ipconfig or ifconfig

The ipconfig command is used to view the IP configuration of a device and, when combined with certain switches or parameters, can be used to release and renew the lease of an IP address obtained from a DHCP server and to flush the DNS resolver cache. Its most common use is to view the current configuration. *Figure 13.20* shows its execution with **/all** switch, which results in a display of a wealth of information about the IP configuration:

```
C:\Users\abhardwaj>ipconfig /all

Windows IP Configuration

    Host Name . . . . . . . . . . . . : ABHARDWAJ_LTP
    Primary Dns Suffix  . . . . . . . : DDN.UPES.AC.IN
    Node Type . . . . . . . . . . . . : Hybrid
    IP Routing Enabled. . . . . . . . : No
    WINS Proxy Enabled. . . . . . . . : No
    DNS Suffix Search List. . . . . . : DDN.UPES.AC.IN

Ethernet adapter Ethernet:

    Media State . . . . . . . . . . . : Media disconnected
    Connection-specific DNS Suffix  . : ddn.upes.ac.in
    Description . . . . . . . . . . . : Intel(R) Ethernet Connection (13) I219-V
    Physical Address. . . . . . . . . : 08-92-04-07-7A-6F
    DHCP Enabled. . . . . . . . . . . : Yes
    Autoconfiguration Enabled . . . . : Yes

Wireless LAN adapter Local Area Connection* 1:

    Media State . . . . . . . . . . . : Media disconnected
    Connection-specific DNS Suffix  . :
    Description . . . . . . . . . . . : Microsoft Wi-Fi Direct Virtual Adapter
    Physical Address. . . . . . . . . : CA-94-02-1C-38-8B
    DHCP Enabled. . . . . . . . . . . : Yes
    Autoconfiguration Enabled . . . . : Yes
```

Figure 13.20: Ipconfig output

Ipconfig may be used to release and renew a DHCP server configuration by executing the **ipconfig /release** command first, then the **ipconfig /renew** command. It is also good to note that after fixing a configuration issue (such as an IP address) on a target device, you should use the **ipconfig /registerdns** command to make sure that the device registers its new IP address with the DNS server. It may also be essential to remove any remaining inaccurate IP address-to-hostname mappings on the devices attempting to reach the destination device. This may be done with the **ipconfig /flushdns** command. The command to use on a Linux or UNIX system is **ifconfig**, not ipconfig. *Figure 13.21* shows an example of the command and its output for Linux OS; the **ifconfig** command with **-a** option shows all network interface information, even if the network interface is down:

```
┌──(kali㉿kali)-[~]
└─$ ifconfig
docker0: flags=4099<UP,BROADCAST,MULTICAST>  mtu 1500
        inet 172.17.0.1  netmask 255.255.0.0  broadcast 172.17.255.255
        ether 02:42:26:37:d3:bf  txqueuelen 0  (Ethernet)
        RX packets 0  bytes 0 (0.0 B)
        RX errors 0  dropped 0  overruns 0  frame 0
        TX packets 0  bytes 0 (0.0 B)
        TX errors 0  dropped 6 overruns 0  carrier 0  collisions 0

eth0: flags=4163<UP,BROADCAST,RUNNING,MULTICAST>  mtu 1500
        inet 192.168.119.151  netmask 255.255.255.0  broadcast 192.168.119.255
        inet6 fe80::a511:9b46:c66d:3a75  prefixlen 64  scopeid 0x20<link>
        ether 00:0c:29:17:43:2b  txqueuelen 1000  (Ethernet)
        RX packets 1  bytes 342 (342.0 B)
        RX errors 0  dropped 0  overruns 0  frame 0
        TX packets 23  bytes 3090 (3.0 KiB)
        TX errors 0  dropped 0 overruns 0  carrier 0  collisions 0

lo: flags=73<UP,LOOPBACK,RUNNING>  mtu 65536
        inet 127.0.0.1  netmask 255.0.0.0
        inet6 ::1  prefixlen 128  scopeid 0x10<host>
        loop  txqueuelen 1000  (Local Loopback)
        RX packets 8  bytes 480 (480.0 B)
        RX errors 0  dropped 0  overruns 0  frame 0
        TX packets 8  bytes 480 (480.0 B)
        TX errors 0  dropped 0 overruns 0  carrier 0  collisions 0
```

Figure 13.21: ifconfig output

Nslookup or dig

These tools allow us to interact with the DNS server and even exchange and update records with the server (if allowed), they can be used to verify that such an exchange is not possible. Allowing such updates would allow DNS pollution, which can lead to users being directed to phishing sites.

Sysinternals

Sysinternals is a collection of more than 70 Windows tools that can be used for both troubleshooting and security issues. Some of the utilities contained in Sysinternals are listed in *Figure 13.22*:

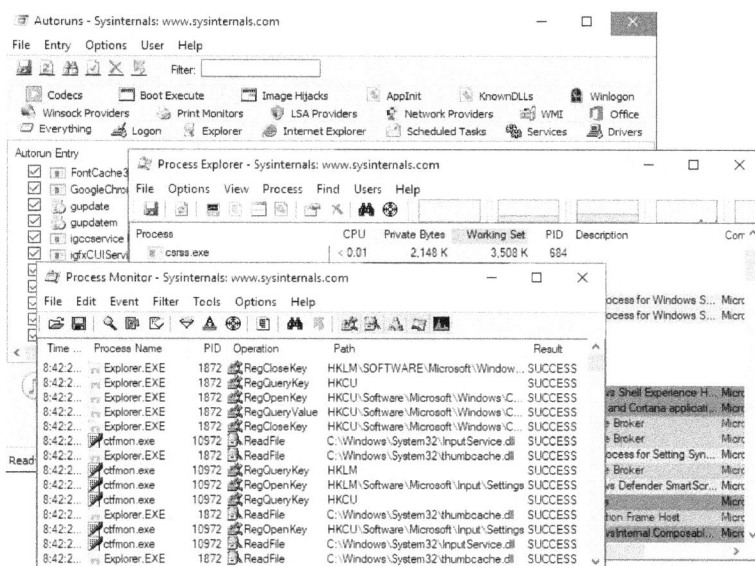

Figure 13.22: Sysinternals security utilities

OpenSSL

OpenSSL is a library of software functions that support the use of the **secure sockets layer/ transport layer security** (**SSL/TLS**) protocol. Once OpenSSL is installed, a set of commands becomes available. OpenSSL is open-source and written in C. The following are some of the functions you can perform with this tool:

- Generate a certificate request
- Generate a self-signed certificate
- Generate a self-signed key
- Test an SSL server

Local exploitation tools or frameworks

Exploitation tools and the frameworks in which they operate are effective tools for detecting security flaws. Since the targets are known to not be present in the environment, certain attacks may be excluded in a local exploit. If you don't have any Mac machines, for example, you may leave out Mac vulnerabilities. In another example, you may write an exploit for an application that you built yourself.

SCAP tool

SCAP is a standard used by the security automation industry to identify software flaws and configuration concerns. Programs and applications are beginning to adopt SCAP's terminology and formats as the computer industry accepts the standard. The Window System Centre Configuration Manager Extensions for SCAP is a good example of this. It transforms SCAP data files to **Desired Configuration Management** (**DCM**) configuration packs and DCM reports to SCAP format.

File integrity monitoring

Criminal software and malicious persons frequently alter files without permission. These files are frequently data files, but they can also be system files. Modifications to data files are unpleasant, but changes to system files can put a whole system at risk. File integrity software is the solution, which creates a hash value for each system file and validates it at regular intervals. This entire procedure is automated, and if a faulty system file is identified, it will be automatically replaced. Tripwire is a third-party application that does this, and Windows has a utility called **System File Checker** (**SFC**) that does the same thing. SFC is a command-line application for checking and verifying system file versions on a computer. If system files are corrupted, the SFC will replace the corrupted files with the correct versions. The switches vary a bit between different versions of Windows. The syntax for the SFC command is SFC [switch].

Log analysis tools

You learned how to use both scripts and filters to remove the clutter in network device logs so that you can focus on series events earlier in this chapter. Most local audit logs, on the other hand, include built-in filters that may be used to zero in on more critical incidents. These filters can be configured as either display or capture filters. Consider the situation when you suspect a user of stealing another user's password and you want to know if the suspect has used the password from his or her workstation. It might be tough to find what you are searching for in the midst of all the security happenings. Only successful login events might be filtered. For example, as shown in *Figure 13.23*, the Windows Log is filtering to show only the audit success events:

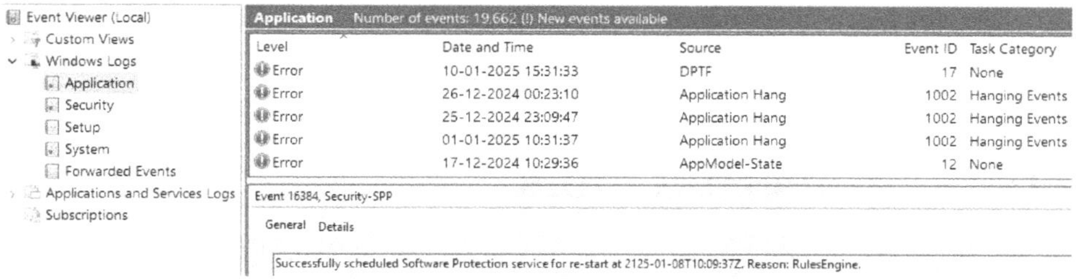

Figure 13.23: Windows Log

Some good examples of log analysis tools are as follows:

- **Loggly**: This tool has both free and paid plans per month. It makes it easy to weed out the noise and perform full-text searches.

- **Logentries**: This cloud-based system also comes in both free and paid plans. You can filter logs in real-time and can tag important events, so you can return at a later time.

- **GoAccess**: This terminal-based tool is open source and free to use. You can generate the report in HTML or CSV format. This tool has both free and paid (per month) plans. You can filter by application or use custom parameters.

- **Graylog**: This open-source tool has many large customers, such as Cisco. It makes it easy to parse logs from any data source, and it can search terabytes of data almost instantly.

Antivirus

While many scenarios that we face are new, one is not – the ever-present danger from malware. While many are still fighting this battle using traditional premises-based anti-malware tools, new approaches have emerged. Cloud antivirus products run not on the local computer but in the cloud, creating a smaller footprint on the client and utilizing the processing power in the cloud. They have the following advantages:

- They allow access to the latest malware data within minutes of the cloud antivirus service learning about it.

- They eliminate the need to continually update the antivirus software.

- The client is small, and it requires little processing power.

Cloud antivirus products have the following disadvantages:

- There is a client-to-cloud relationship, which means these products cannot run in the background.

- They may scan only the core Windows files for viruses and not the whole computer.

- They are highly dependent on an Internet connection.

Anti-spam services can also be offered from the cloud. Vendors such as Postini and Mimecast scan your email and then store anything identified as problematic on their server, where you can look through the spam to verify that it is, in fact, spam.

Reverse engineering tools

Reverse engineering may be used to solve a variety of security problems. When a host is breached, reverse engineering techniques may be used to determine the facts of the breach, including how the attacker gained access to the system and the measures taken to breach the system. When used to malware, reverse engineering may also refer to the use of tools to break down malware in order to understand its purpose and how to destroy it; when applied to malware, reverse engineering is done in a sandbox environment to prevent the virus from spreading. Reverse engineering tools are recommended for analyzing *zero-day malware* and sandboxing it, as well as when a host has been hacked and safely isolated, and you want to uncover specifics of the breach to be better prepared for the future. The *Infosec Institute* recommends the following as the top reverse engineering tools for cybersecurity professionals:

- **Apktool**: This third-party tool for reverse engineering can decode resources to their nearly original form and re-create them after making some adjustments.

- **dex2jar**: This lightweight API is designed to read the Dalvik Executable (`.dex`/`.odex`) format. It is used with Android and Java .class files.

- **diStorm3**: This tool is lightweight, easy to use, and has a fast decomposer library. It disassembles instructions in 16-, 32-, and 64-bit modes. It is also the fastest disassembler library. The source code is very clean, readable, portable, and platform-independent.

- **edb-debugger**: This is the Linux equivalent of the famous Olly debugger on the Windows platform. One of the main goals of this debugger is modularity.

- **Jad debugger**: This is the most popular Java decompiler ever written. It is a command-line utility written in C++.

- **Javasnoop**: This Aspect Security tool allows security testers to test the security of Java applications easily.

- **OllyDbg**: This is a 32-bit, assembler-level analyzing debugger for Microsoft Windows. Emphasis on binary code analysis makes it useful in cases where the source is unavailable.

- **Valgrind**: This suite is for debugging and profiling Linux programs.

Physical security tools

As stated earlier in this chapter, without physical security, other forms of security are useless. Physical security tools are essential for protecting the physical infrastructure that houses critical systems and data. These tools include surveillance cameras, motion detectors, biometric access controls, and alarm systems, all of which help prevent unauthorized access and detect potential breaches. Additionally, smart locks and RFID-based access cards provide controlled entry to secure areas, while physical barriers such as fences and locked doors further enhance protection. Intrusion detection systems, coupled with environmental sensors (temperature, humidity), ensure that servers and devices remain safe from external threats or hazardous conditions. Implementing a robust physical security system is crucial for maintaining overall cybersecurity effectiveness.

We end this chapter with several host physical security assessment tools.

Lock picks

Lock picks are tools used to test the ability of your physical locks to withstand someone picking them. These are the same tools used by a professional locksmith to open a lock when hired to do so and one of the reasons many organizations have moved away from using physical locks. *Figure 13.24* shows examples of some lock picks; if a facility uses physical locks, the locks should be checked to see if they are susceptible to these tools; it may even be advisable to hire a locksmith to attempt to open them:

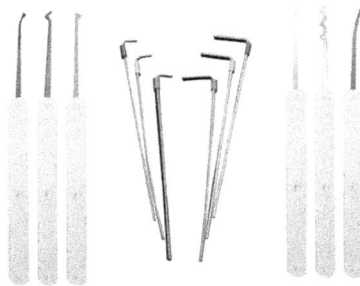

Figure 13.24: Lock picks

Locks

Door locks can be either mechanical or electronic. Electric locks, or cipher locks, use a keypad that requires the correct code to open the lock. These are programmable, and organizations that use them should change the codes frequently. Another type of door security system is a proximity authentication device, with which a programmable card is used to deliver an access code to the device either by swiping the card or, in some cases, by just being in the vicinity of the reader. These devices typically contain the following **electronic access control (EAC)** components:

- An electromagnetic lock
- A credential reader
- A closed-door sensor

Locks are also used in places other than doors, such as protecting cabinets and securing devices. The types of mechanical locks with which you should be familiar are as follows:

- **Warded locks**: This type of lock has a spring-loaded bolt with a notch in it. The lock has wards, or metal projections, inside the lock with which the key will match to enable opening the lock. A warded lock design is shown in *Figure 13.25*:

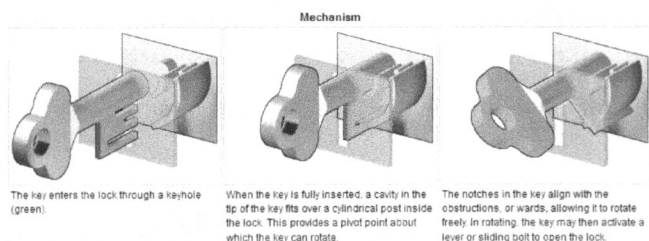

The key enters the lock through a keyhole (green).

When the key is fully inserted, a cavity in the tip of the key fits over a cylindrical post inside the lock. This provides a pivot point about which the key can rotate.

The notches in the key align with the obstructions, or wards, allowing it to rotate freely. In rotating, the key may then activate a lever or sliding bolt to open the lock.

Figure 13.25: Warded lock

- **Tumbler locks**: This type of lock has more moving parts than the warded lock, and the key raises the lock metal piece to the correct height. A tumbler lock design is shown in *Figure 13.26*:

Figure 13.26: Tumbler lock

- **Combination locks**: This type of lock requires rotating the lock in a pattern that, if correct, lines the tumblers up, opening the lock. A combination lock design is shown in *Figure 13.27*:

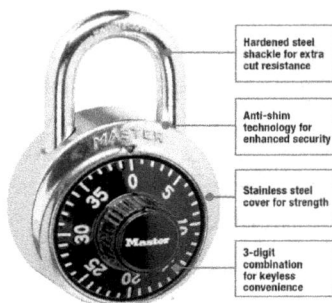

Hardened steel shackle for extra cut resistance

Anti-shim technology for enhanced security

Stainless steel cover for strength

3-digit combination for keyless convenience

Figure 13.27: Combination lock

In the case of device locks, laptops are the main item that must be protected because they are so easy to steal. Laptops should never be left in the open without being secured to something solid with a cable lock a vinyl-coated steel cable that connects to the laptop and locks around an object.

RFID tools

Malicious individuals use **radio-frequency identification** (**RFID**) tools to steal the proximity badge information from an unsuspecting employee who physically walks near the concealed device. One example is the Tastic RFID Thief by Bishop Fox. Specifically, it targets 125 KHz, low-frequency RFID badge systems used for physical security, such as those used in HID Prox and Indala proximity products. Alternatively, it could be used to weaponize a 13.56 MHz, high-frequency RFID reader, like those for HID iCLASS access control systems. When RFID systems are in use, penetration tests should include testing the vulnerability of systems to the capture of such RFID credentials, as their capture could lead to serious physical security issues.

IR camera

An infrared camera is a camera that forms an image using infrared radiation and can capture images in the dark. These cameras can also detect motion in the area, making them a great choice. When physical security assessments are performed, these devices should be fully tested to ensure that they capture all intrusion attempts.

Conclusion

This chapter discussed various tools, related to the security assessment of network tools. This chapter presented a brief on the different host related tools to assess vulnerabilities that might be present on an individual host. Such tools include password crackers, vulnerability scanners, command-line tools, local exploitation tools and frameworks, SCAP tools, file integrity monitoring utilities, log analysis tools, antivirus, and reverse engineering tools. Physical security tools and devices to assess the security of an environment, including lock picks, RFID tools, and IR cameras, were discussed.

In the next chapter, we will discuss remote access and unified collaboration.

Exercise

1. **Which of the following tools is primarily used to monitor network traffic and detect potential security issues?**

   a. Wireshark

   b. Metasploit

    c. Nessus

    d. OpenVAS

2. **Which tool is commonly used for vulnerability scanning and patch management on host systems?**

    a. NetFlow

    b. Nmap

    c. Nexpose

    d. Snort

3. **Which of the following is a physical security tool that helps ensure only authorized personnel can access a secure area?**

    a. CCTV surveillance

    b. Intrusion detection system

    c. Biometric access control system

    d. Firewall

4. **Which of these are commonly used to prevent unauthorized physical access to critical devices in a data center?**

    a. Antivirus software

    b. Security guards

    c. Smart locks

    d. VPN

Answers

    1. a

    2. c

    3. c

    4. c

## CHAPTER 14

Securing Communication and Collaborative Solutions

Introduction

Increasingly, workers and the organizations for which they work are relying on new methods of communicating and working together that introduce new security concerns. As a CASP candidate, you need to be familiar with these new technologies, understand the security issues they raise, and implement controls that mitigate the security issues. This chapter describes these new methods and technologies, identifies issues, and suggests methods to secure these new workflow processes.

Structure

In this chapter, we will discuss the following topics:

- Remote access
- Virtual private network
- Tools for unified collaboration
- Emailing
- Phishing
- Collaboration in the cloud
- Research collaboration

Objectives

After studying this chapter, you will gain an understanding of secure remote access, including the measures necessary to protect remote resources and services, facilitate desktop and application sharing, and provide remote assistance. Additionally, you will explore unified collaboration tools, which encompass web conferencing, video conferencing, and audio conferencing, along with storage and document collaboration. The chapter also delves into unified communication by covering instant messaging, presence, email, telephony, VoIP integration, and collaboration sites, ensuring a comprehensive understanding of modern collaborative technologies.

Remote access

Users may connect to an organization's resources through remote access using remote access software. These distant connections may be dial-in connections, but they are increasingly leveraging the Internet as the data transmission network. If an organization enables remote access to internal resources, the data must be encrypted when it is sent between the remote access client and the remote access server. Remote access servers may demand encrypted connections from remote access clients, which means that any attempt to connect without encryption would be rejected. Remote access to the business network is a well-established technology with well-defined security safeguards. *Figure 14.1* illustrates remote access:

Figure 14.1: Remote access

Dial-up

The **public switched telephone network (PSTN)** is used for dial-up connections. If the connection is established via an analog phone line, it will need a modem on the sending end to convert the digital data to analog, and a modem on the receiving end to convert it back to digital. These lines have a maximum speed of 56 kbps. Layer two protocols for dial-up connections include **Serial Line Internet Protocol (SLIP)** and **Point-to-Point Protocol (PPP)**. SLIP is an ancient protocol that has been superseded by PPP. Authentication and multilink capabilities are provided via PPP. The remote access server verifies the caller's identity. A **Terminal Access Control Access Control Server Plus (TACACS+)** or a **Remote Authentication Dial-in User Service (RADIUS)** server may be used to centralize the authentication process. Some basic measures that should be in place when using dial-up are as follows:

- Have the remote access server call the original caller back at a pre-determined number. Allowing call forwarding, which may be exploited to circumvent this security feature, is not allowed.

- To prevent war dialers, configure modems to respond after a certain number of rings (automated programs that dial numbers until a modem signal is detected).

- For physical security, gather all modems in one location and turn off those that aren't in use.

- Make use of the most robust authentication techniques feasible.

Virtual private network

The information is protected by robust authentication procedures and encryption techniques over a **virtual private network** (**VPN**) connection that utilizes an untrusted carrier network. While we often utilize the **Internet** as the most untrustworthy network, and most VPNs do go over the Internet, they may also be used with internal networks where traffic has to be secured from prying eyes, as shown in *Figure 14.2*:

Figure 14.2: VPN

Resource and services

Telecommuting has grown increasingly frequent in today's environment, necessitating the deployment of remote access solutions to guarantee that employees have access to company resources and services. The remote access role on Windows servers, the remote desktop service on Windows clients and servers, **virtual network computing (VNC)** or **ssh** on Linux, and a variety of other techniques may be used to offer remote access resources and services, depending on the deployment strategy. Security experts should collaborate with management to define the organization's remote access requirements and implement the right solution and controls to meet those requirements while ensuring the security of remote access transactions.

Desktop and application sharing

Desktop sharing is a collection of related technologies that enable remote login to a computer as well as real-time collaboration on a distant user's desktop. A graphical terminal emulator is used in both functions. Some of these solutions are incorporated into operating systems, such as Microsoft's Remote Desktop technology, while others, such as LogMeIn and GoToMyPC, are third-party programs. Distant administration software is one of the most popular attack vectors used by hackers. While these solutions make controlling remote machines and users simpler, they are also one of the most common attack vectors used by hackers.

Remote assistance

Remote help is a function that is often based on the same technology that is used for desktop sharing. One of its advantages is the ability for a technician to share a user's desktop with the user for the purpose of either teaching the user something or resolving a problem. Naturally, some of the same problems that plague desktop sharing software also plague remote support sessions.

- For starters, the screen data passed back and forth between the user and the technician is usually in common formats, making it simple to reconstruct a recorded picture. Many products use proprietary encryption, although this form of encryption may be illegal in regulated businesses. Always employ the encryption level mandated by your industry, such as **Advanced Encryption Standard (AES)**.

- Second, many remote help platforms lack adequate auditing features, which are crucial in areas like banking and healthcare. If auditing is a problem in your sector, look for a tool that can capture the level of data you need for legal reasons.

Many tools have limited access restrictions. When a technician connects to a remote computer, he has complete control over the system, just as if he were sitting at the console. A breach of the **Health Insurance Portability and Accountability Act (HIPAA)** arises if he views patient information at any time. You should choose a solution that enables you to control precisely what remote technicians can see and do. If any information is lost or if another issue emerges that seems to be the technician's responsibility, the technician may be held liable. Consider creating a standard statement that a user sees and must accept before enabling the connection, outlining your level of responsibility for any difficulties that happen after the remote session.

Tools for unified collaboration

New challenges for security experts are being introduced by two overlapping developments. People are collaborating or increasingly working together while also becoming more mobile and working in non-traditional ways, such as from home. This means sensitive information is being exchanged in ways we have never had to safeguard before. The parts that follow go through the unique security concerns that different collaboration tools and approaches pose, as well as the controls that need to be implemented to keep these solutions safe.

Web-based video conferencing

Companies have been able to save money on travel while maintaining real-time touch with conference attendees because of web conferencing. Web conferencing services and software often provide extensive meeting facilities, such as the ability to communicate, share documents, and observe the presenter's screen. Many of them also have video capabilities. When the information and documents you are discussing are of a sensitive nature, security concerns emerge, and you should exercise extra caution throughout the web conference, as shown in *Figure 14.3*:

Figure 14.3: *Web communication*

Some of the security concerns are as follows:

- **Data leakage**: It is because web conference data is often stored on a shared server for a short period of time, there is always the risk of the data falling into the wrong hands.

- **Unauthorized visitors**: It is because most systems rely on a basic conference code for entry, there's always the chance that uninvited people may show up.

- **Data collection en route**: There is a good chance that information will be collected en route. This may be avoided by using encryption technology.

- **Denial of service (DoS) attack**: When a web conferencing solution is linked with current applications, there is a risk of DoS assaults on local servers.

To deal with these problems, you should implement the following:

- Take charge of the web conferencing solution selection process. Other departments often choose a product, and IT and security teams are left to deal with whatever flaws the solution may have.

- Choose products that employ standard security and networking components, such as SSL, to ensure interoperability with all devices in your network.

- Make sure the underlying network is safe.

- Establish a method for choosing and using the product. The following four stages must be carried out:

  1. Define the solution's permitted applications.

  2. Determine your security requirements before deciding on a product.

  3. Make sure the request for proposal includes use scenarios and security requirements (RFP).

  4. Involve security professionals in planning and decision-making.

- If the product supports it, disable or heavily audit read or write desktop mode. Other meeting attendees may access the host desktop in this mode.

- Sign non-disclosure agreements for conferences that include the revealing of sensitive information or intellectual property.

- Create unique passwords for each conference to prevent passwords from being reused for unauthorized conference attendance.

To attend conferences, consider needing a VPN connection to the workplace network. By disabling split tunneling on the VPN concentrator, you may give better performance to the participants if this strategy is used. While split tunneling permits simultaneous access to the LAN and the Internet, it does so at the expense of each session's bandwidth.

Video conferencing

While most, if not all, video conferencing devices released in the last decade employ 128-bit AES encryption, it is vital to realize that no security solution is perfect. The **National Security Agency (NSA)** of the United States was recently accused of breaking military-grade encryption (greater than AES 128) in order to eavesdrop on a United Nations video conference. According to the same source, the NSA determined that the Chinese were working to break the encryption as well. While it is still unclear if the NSA or the Chinese were successful, this tale underlines the dangers that are present at all times. However, on high-security networks (such as those used by the US Department of Defense, Homeland Security, and others), when video conferencing is used, extra security steps are often employed to supplement the solution. The following are a few examples:

- Physical encryption keys at the device level must be input each time the system is used and are normally swapped every 30 days.

- Additional password keys that restrict access to the operations and systems of a device.

- Session keys are produced at the beginning of each session and are automatically altered during the session.

- Data is sent across secure data networks that use modern encryption techniques.

Since 128-bit AES encryption is safe, video conferencing systems are often secure right out of the box. Extending the H.323 standard to allow DES encryption is a non-proprietary technique to safeguard video conferencing and VoIP data. H.323 is an audiovisual communications standard that includes web conferencing, video conferences, and VoIP. H.235 extensions may offer security for these sessions. The ability to negotiate services and functionality in a generic way is included in H.235. It permits both conventional and custom encryption techniques to be used. It uses a security profile that consists of either a password, digital certificates, or both to identify a person rather than a device. Most security vulnerabilities aren't caused by flaws in contemporary goods but rather by the following:

- Encryption is not enabled.

- Using antiquated video systems that lack encryption.

- Failure to keep linked software on video systems and other devices up to date.

- The system's connected devices (such as gateways and video bridges) do not support encryption or have encryption turned off.

- Using software solutions or services that don't encrypt data or use weaker encryption.

- Ineffective password management.

Creating and implementing a method for choosing and utilizing the product may help avoid these problems.

Conferencing via audio

The majority of today's video collaboration platforms may be used just to offer audio capability. However, in high-security networks that produce and retain audio data (for example, the Department of Defense and the Department of Homeland Security), extra security steps are often employed to supplement the solution. The following are a few examples:

- Encrypting audio files at the file level to guarantee that only authorized users may access and listen to them.

- Using multi-factor authentication on the systems that hold the files.
- Collaboration and document storage tools.

Teams and whole enterprises may exchange documents using storage and document collaboration solutions, regardless of where team members or people are working. Popular examples of this sort of technology are Google Drive and Microsoft SharePoint. These technologies, in most instances, provide real-time updates to all users who are reading the papers, as well as capabilities that enable users to remark on particular sections of the text. The following are some of the security issues associated with these tools:

- **Breach of login credentials**: The username/password paradigm is used by the majority of tools. If attackers gain credentials, they will have access to whatever information that the user has access to. **Single sign-on** (**SSO**) may assist in guaranteeing that login credentials for collaboration tools are consistent with business login credentials.

- **Web-based dangers**: Malware and illegal tracking are examples of web-based threats. Many of these concerns may be avoided by using a VPN to connect to the collaborative platform.

- **Issues with URLs**: Default site names and other default settings make it easier for attackers to find a site. Furthermore, metadata in the site URL may disclose sensitive information.

- **Reports or summaries**: While reports and summaries are useful for rapidly determining the status of documents, they may also endanger data if they are sent by email or other insecure ways. The practice of sending these reports by email should be avoided.

- **No or limited encryption**: Carefully check the encryption provided by a tool. Encryption isn't always complete in certain tools.

Furthermore, most instruments are designed to be one-size-fits-all. If your company is required to comply with rules or legislation that require encryption or other restrictions, be sure the tool you choose gives the coverage you need. Before choosing a tool, security experts should collaborate with others in their business to verify that the products have been thoroughly examined. Furthermore, any known concerns should be investigated to see if there are any mitigating measures that can be introduced to reduce the effect of the issues.

Unified communication

Voice, video, email, instant messaging, personal assistant, and other communication functions are often combined in unified communication platforms. Document collaboration is included in some of the newer systems. Individually customizable modules are often bought with these tools. If your firm does not need the personal assistant function, for example, that module might be turned off. You should look at the following security risks:

- Datacenter vendor security is at a bare minimum.

- Insufficient data encryption.

- Internet connection's inability to meet demand at peak hours.

- Inadequate access or security controls.

- On-demand account management is neither automated nor is only partially automated.

- Experience as a vendor.

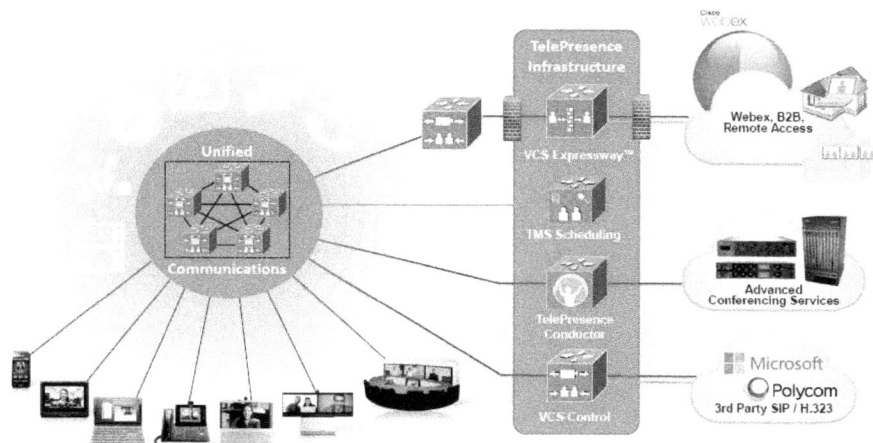

Figure 14.4: *Video conferencing*

While unified communication solutions may seem to be a fantastic way to connect all business activities, their installation and data integration might be a headache. Management should be aware of the difficulty of installing and safeguarding these technologies, according to security specialists.

Instant messaging

When talking with colleagues, **instant messaging (IM)** has grown so popular that many users prefer it over email. Many email services, such as Google Mail, have incorporated IM systems since it is so popular. Users expect it, therefore security experts must understand how to protect it. To show a user's availability, several collaboration platforms incorporate presence functionality. A presence-based system informs other users if a person is online, busy, in a meeting, and so on. When enabled across several communication tools, such as instant messaging, phone, email, and video conferencing, it may also help detect which communication channel the user is presently using and, as a result, which channel has the highest chance of receiving a rapid answer. While the information in a presence system about each person is necessary for the system to work, it is also information that may be misused. The following are some of the specific issues:

- During the status update procedure, systems that do not verify presence sources.

- Systems that do not need recipients of presence information to be authenticated (also called subscribers, or watchers).

- Systems that do not ensure the security and integrity of presence data.

- Systems that rely on insecure techniques to verify a user's identity.

Implement the following principles when choosing a presence product or analyzing a system with a presence feature:

- Choose a product with a secure protocol. **Extensible Messaging and Presence Protocol (XMPP)** over TLS and **Session Initiation Protocol for Instant Messaging and Presence Leveraging Extensions (SIMPLE)** are two examples.

- Choose a product that authenticates with your company's **public key infrastructure (PKI)**. When feasible, using certificate-based authentication is the best option.

- Encrypt internal communications as well as conversations via the Internet.

- Check to see whether the product authenticates both presence sources and subscribers.

- Use grouping to regulate the display of presence information among groups if the system enables it.

Emailing

Without question, email is the most extensively utilized mode of communication in the workplace. As shown in *Figure 14.5*, it employs three conventional communications protocols. To construct a secure communication channel, each of them may be operated over SSL. The port numbers used when they are executed over SSL are different. The following sections go through these procedures in detail. Refer to *Figure 14.5* which illustrates the email process:

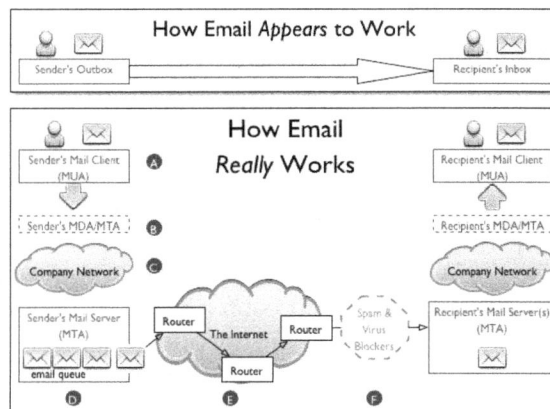

Figure 14.5: Email process

Internet message access protocol

Internet message access protocol (IMAP) is an application layer protocol for retrieving email from a server on a client. IMAP4 is the most recent version. Unlike POP3 (described in the following section), which can only get messages from the server, IMAP4 enables the user to download a copy and leave a copy on the server. Port 143 is used by IMAP4. IMAPS (IMAP over SSL) is a secure version that utilizes port 993.

Post office mechanism

Post office mechanism (POP) is an email retrieval protocol at the application layer. The most recent version is POP3. It just enables you to download messages and does not allow you to use IMAP4's extra features. Port 110 is used by POP3. There is also a secure version that operates over SSL and utilizes a port.

Simple Mail Transfer Protocol

When email servers talk to each other, they use **Simple Mail Transfer Protocol (SMTP)**, a standard application layer protocol. POP and IMAP are client email protocols for retrieving email, but when email servers talk to each other, they use SMTP, a standard application layer protocol. Clients utilize this protocol to send emails as well. When using SSL, SMTP utilizes port 465 instead of port 25. Unfortunately, persons with bad intent may use email to launch a variety of attacks. This is because many of these attacks are based on poor security practices among users, user training and awareness are usually the greatest method for avoiding them.

Email spoofing

The technique of sending an email that appears to originate from one source but really comes from another is known as email spoofing. It is accomplished by changing email header fields like From, Return Path, and Reply-To. Its goal is to persuade the recipient to trust the message and respond with sensitive information that they would not reveal to an untrustworthy source. Email spoofing is often used as part of an attempt to get usernames and passwords for banking or financial websites. There are numerous methods to protect yourself from such assaults. One option is to activate SMTP authentication, which prevents users who are unable to authenticate with the sending server from sending emails. Implementing the **Sender Policy Framework (SPF)** is another viable mitigating strategy. SPF is an email validation method that uses the **Domain Name System (DNS)** to detect whether an email has been sent by a host that has been sanctioned by the domain's administrator. It is not transmitted to the recipient's inbox if it cannot be authenticated.

Phishing

Phishing is a social engineering assault in which a receiver is persuaded to follow a link in an email that appears to go to a trustworthy website but really leads to a hacker's website. The purpose of these attacks is to collect usernames and passwords. Spear phishing is when a phishing assault is directed at a single individual rather than a group of people at random. Details about the individual gathered via social media might be used to make the assault more credible. To combat spear phishing, you may take the following steps:

1. Implement a system that validates the security of all email links. Invincea FreeSpace is an example of this, since it opens all links and attachments in a safe virtual container, protecting users' PCs from damage.

2. Teach people to be wary of all emails, even if they seem to be from friends.

Whaling

Whaling is a subset of spear phishing, just as spear phishing is a subset of phishing. The person targeted in whaling is someone of prominence or importance. For example, it might be a CEO, COO, or CTO. The assault is predicated on the presumption that these individuals are in possession of more sensitive information, *Figure 14.6* illustrates steps to identify whaling.

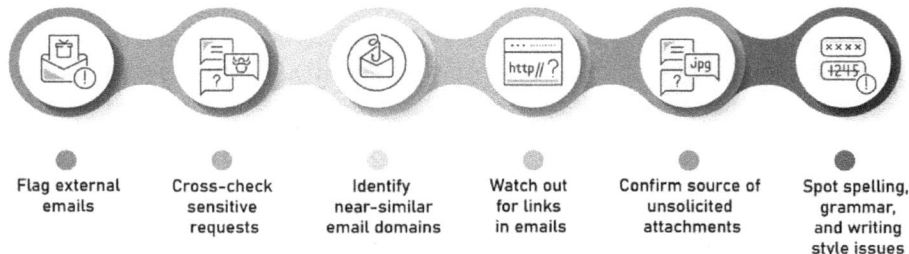

| Flag external emails | Cross-check sensitive requests | Identify near-similar email domains | Watch out for links in emails | Confirm source of unsolicited attachments | Spot spelling, grammar, and writing style issues |

Figure 14.6: Whaling Phishing

Spam

You undoubtedly do not enjoy how your inbox fills up with unwanted emails every day, many of which are attempting to sell you something. When you purchase anything or visit a website, you often cause yourself to get this email by not paying careful attention to all of the facts. Spam is defined as an email that is sent to a large number of people without their permission. Spam is more than an irritation; it may jam inboxes and force email servers to expend resources to transmit it. This is because sending spam is against the law, many spammers attempt to disguise their origins by relaying over the email servers of other businesses. This not only conceals the real source but also puts the relaying firm in jeopardy. Today's email servers may refuse to relay to any email servers that you have not specified. This may help prevent your email system from being used for spam. On your email servers, this form of relaying should be prohibited. Spam filtering should also be installed on all email servers.

Capturing messages

A protocol analyzer may collect email traffic in its raw form, just like any other sort of communication. It is possible to read an email if it is written in plain text. As a result, every email that contains critical information should be encrypted. While this may be done using the intended recipient's digital certificate, it is usually only practicable if the receiver is a member of your organization and your firm has a PKI. Many email clients come with built-in support for digital signatures and message encryption utilizing digital certificates. While email encryption applications such as **Pretty Good Privacy (PGP)** are available, many users find it difficult to utilize them appropriately without training. Encryption equipment or service that automates email encryption is another alternative. Regardless of the method used, the only way to prevent information from being leaked from captured packets is to encrypt communications.

Information disclosure

Information is sometimes leaked not because an unencrypted communication is intercepted but because the email is exchanged with people who are not always trustworthy. Even if a policy for information sharing exists, it may not be implemented by all employees. You may sanitize all outgoing material for sorts of information that should not be revealed and have it deleted to avoid this type of exposure. Axway MailGate is one example of a product that can achieve this. For international organizations or corporations with hundreds of thousands of users, MailGate can safeguard email systems against virus assaults, botnets, spam, or denial-of-service attacks. MailGate helps filter out up to 90% of unwanted emails before they reach corporate email infrastructure, preventing **accidents** or even deliberate data leakage that could harm a person's reputation or violate intellectual property laws, as shown in *Figure 14.7*:

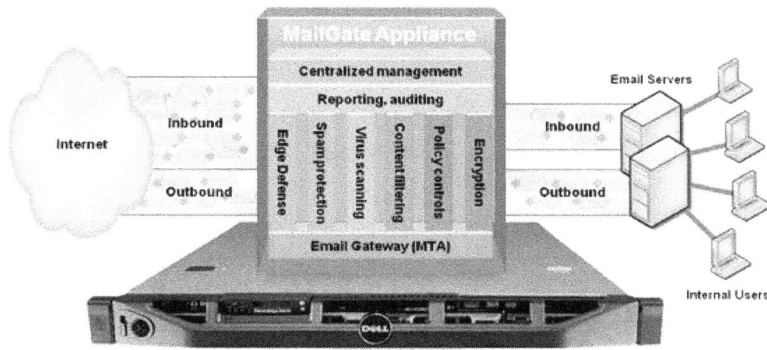

Figure 14.7: Axway MailGate

Malware

Email is a popular carrier of malware; in fact, email is the most prevalent way for malware to infect computers. Malware scanning software should be installed on both the client PCs and the email server. Malware may still get through despite these precautions; therefore, it is critical to educate consumers on how to handle emails safely (such as not opening attachments from unknown sources).

Integration of telephony and VoIP

Traditional analog phone lines and digital, or **Voice over IP** (**VoIP**), telephony systems are also available. Analog phones link to a **private branch exchange** (**PBX**) system in conventional telephony. The organization's IP data network is independent of the phone network. While analog phone networks may seem to have some security advantages, the US **Federal Communications Commission** (**FCC**) is in the process of deconstructing the analog phone infrastructure that has existed since the days of Bell Labs. While there is no specific date for definitive discontinuance, it seems silly to implement a system that will soon be outdated, no matter how safe it is. Furthermore, as stated in the following section, many of the security vulnerabilities with VoIP seem to be being addressed. *Figure 14.8* showcases the SIP protocol for VoIP:

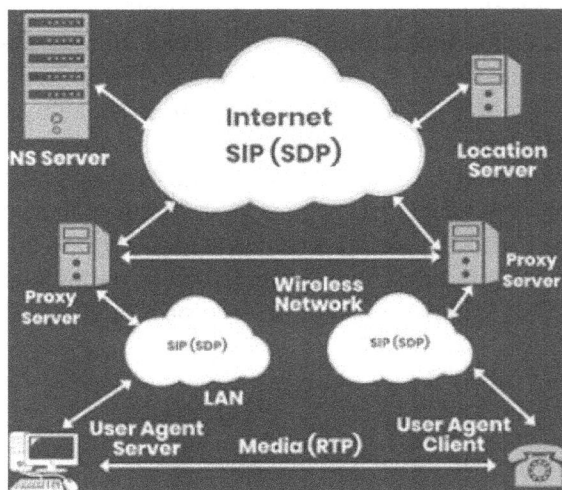

Figure 14.8: SIP Protocol for VoIP

VoIP phone systems have several benefits, but they also pose a security risk. VoIP spam, often known as **Spam over Internet Telephony** (**SPIT**), is one sort of assault. Unsolicited pre-recorded phone messages are sent in this form of assault. The only way to detect these assaults is to analyze **Session Initiation Protocol** (**SIP**) traffic on a regular basis. For call setup and teardown, SIP is utilized. If you are utilizing **Secure Real-Time Transport Protocol** (**SRTP**), encryption, integrity, and anti-replay protocol for **Real-Time Transport**

Protocol (**RTP**) communication, you should do an SRTP traffic analysis as well. RTP is used to carry audio and video communication. Some protocol analyzers, such as GL Communications' PacketScan, are specifically designed for these protocols. This kind of analysis may aid in the detection of SPIT attacks.

While the danger of spying, service theft, and denial-of-service assaults is greater with VoIP than with classic analog, there are steps that can be implemented to alleviate the concerns and lower the risks; these steps are as follows:

1. Separate the phone and data networks physically.

2. On infrastructure equipment, secure all management interfaces (for example, switches, routers, and gateways).

3. In high-security environments, use a secure phone of some kind (to provide end-to-end encryption).

4. Use **network address translation** (**NAT**) to mask the phones' genuine IP addresses.

5. Keep your operating system and VoIP software up to date with the latest updates.

6. Turn off any services or features that you don't need.

7. Use 802.11e to provide **quality of service** (**QoS**) for VoIP packets when they transit a wireless segment, just as you would for all wired segments, to avoid performance difficulties, particularly during DoS assaults on the network.

8. Use a firewall to protect the SIP servers, which are the servers responsible for generating voice and video sessions.

Sites for collaboration

Users are increasingly collaborating on cloud-based technologies employing web technology. Organizations are also using social media to communicate with consumers and share information with the rest of the world. While both social media and cloud-based collaboration have their advantages, they also have their drawbacks. The sections that follow examine these challenges and mitigating measures, as well as provide advice for responsible usage of social media and cloud-based collaboration.

Social media

While the words **social media** may bring up images of Facebook and Twitter, the usage of both public and private social media poses significant security risks. Although the security risks of public social media are more obvious than those of private social media sites, the fact that most enterprise social media tools allow for tight integration with public social media means that many of the issues that plague public social media can easily become your problem if you have an enterprise social media site. Several scenarios highlighting the security challenges and risks of social media in the workplace are divided into two categories, the publication of critical company information and the introduction of malware. Allowing corporate devices carrying sensitive data to access social media sites is one method an organization might use to become vulnerable to a disclosure event in terms of information disclosure. For further information on integration and cooperation, refer to *Figure 14.9*:

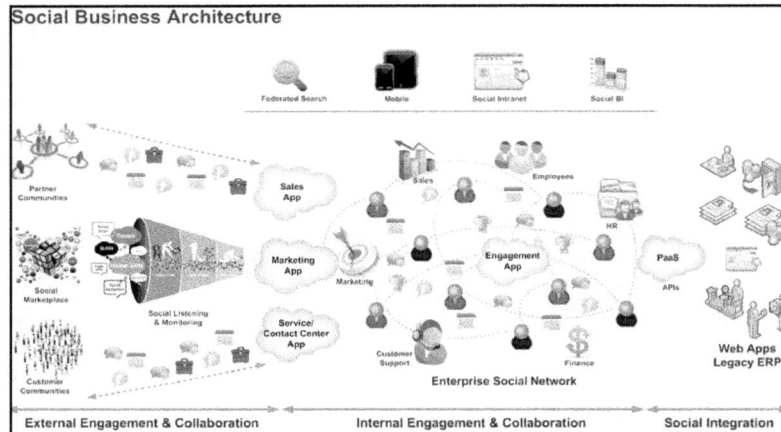

Figure 14.9: *Business and social media integration*

Collaboration in the cloud

Figure 14.10 illustrates that cloud-based collaboration is largely utilized by companies and small teams to store documents, communicate, and share project updates:

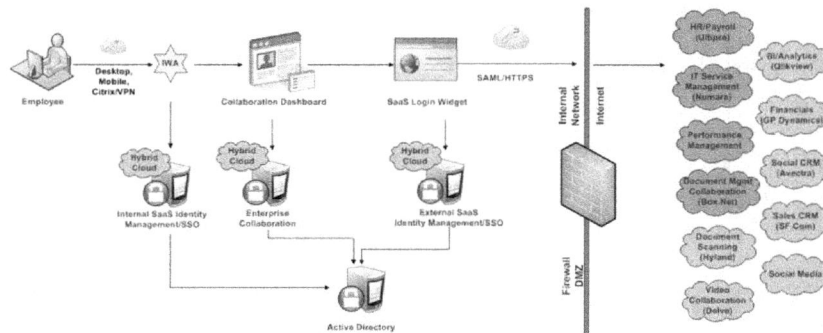

Figure 14.10: *Collaborations in the cloud*

The following are some of the advantages:

- Allows you to pay based on how much you use it
- Increases the speed with which new tools, apps, and services are deployed to employees

- Can be absorbed as a cost of operations rather than a capital expenditure
- Increases the rate of innovation
- Boosts productivity
- Improves operational effectiveness

The following are some of the concerns or obstacles that come with switching to a cloud-based collaboration system rather than a premise-based solution:

- Networks may need to be redesigned to accommodate cloud services
- Concerns about data security
- Security rules are difficult to enforce
- Issues in providing an audit trail
- Complying with legal regulations

For many highly regulated businesses, such as banking and healthcare, cloud-based collaboration is not the optimal answer due to these considerations. Information of the following sorts should not be kept in a public cloud-based solution:

- Information about credit cards
- Business secrets
- Financial information
- Medical records
- Secrets of the state and federal governments
- Confidential or proprietary information
- Information that may be used to identify you

When a cloud-based collaboration solution is acceptable, the following security steps should be taken:

1. Make sure you understand the vendor's and your organization's respective security obligations.

2. If you're dealing with sensitive data, be sure the vendor offers encryption or that you pass data via an encryption proxy before sending it to the provider.

3. On the collaborative site, need robust authentication.

4. If the vendor offers **data loss prevention** (**DLP**) services, you should seriously consider employing them.

5. If you're using databases, consider incorporating **database activity monitoring** (**DAM**).

Research collaboration

In an era of rapidly evolving cyber threats, interdisciplinary research collaboration plays a pivotal role in advancing cybersecurity defenses. By leveraging collective expertise, researchers can tackle complex security challenges and drive innovation. This chapter explores collaborative research in two transformative domains—Quantum Computing and Cybersecurity, which examines the impact of quantum technologies on cryptographic security, and AI & ML in Cybersecurity, which focuses on harnessing artificial intelligence and machine learning to enhance threat detection, prevention, and response. Through these collaborations, the cybersecurity landscape is poised for groundbreaking advancements that redefine digital security:

- **Use case 1**: Quantum computing and cybersecurity

  The emergence of quantum computing poses a significant threat to the existing cybersecurity landscape. Quantum computers, with their unparalleled processing power, have the potential to break many of the encryption algorithms currently used to secure sensitive data. Algorithms like **Rivest-Shamir-Adleman (RSA)** and **elliptic curve cryptography (ECC)**, which underpin much of modern cryptography, rely on mathematical problems that are incredibly difficult for classical computers to solve. However, quantum computers, leveraging principles like Shor's algorithm, could efficiently solve these problems, rendering these encryption methods obsolete.

  This presents a critical challenge for organizations and individuals alike. Data encrypted today could be vulnerable to decryption once sufficiently powerful quantum computers become available. To mitigate this risk, cybersecurity researchers, developers, and practitioners are actively engaged in developing **post-quantum cryptography (PQC)** solutions. PQC encompasses a range of cryptographic algorithms that are believed to be resistant to attacks from even the most powerful quantum computers. These include lattice-based cryptography, code-based cryptography, and multivariate cryptography. Collaboration between academia, industry, and government agencies is crucial to standardize and implement these new technologies. This involves researching and developing new PQC algorithms, conducting rigorous security evaluations, and developing and deploying standards and guidelines for their use. By proactively addressing this emerging threat, we can ensure the continued security of our digital infrastructure in the face of quantum computing advancements.

- **Use case 2**: AI and ML in cybersecurity

  AI and ML are rapidly transforming the cybersecurity landscape, offering both significant opportunities and new challenges. These technologies can be leveraged to enhance threat detection and response capabilities in several ways. For example, ML algorithms can be trained on massive datasets of network traffic, malware samples, and other threat intelligence to identify malicious patterns and anomalies. This enables the automated detection of threats that may be difficult for human analysts to spot, such as zero-day exploits and sophisticated phishing campaigns. AI and ML can be used to automate security tasks, such as incident response and threat hunting. AI-powered security orchestration and automation platforms can analyze security alerts, prioritize incidents based on severity, and even automate certain response actions, such as isolating infected systems or quarantining malicious files. This can significantly improve the speed and efficiency of security operations, allowing security teams to respond to threats more quickly and effectively.

However, AI and ML also present new challenges for cybersecurity. Attackers can leverage these technologies to launch more sophisticated and targeted attacks. For example, AI can be used to generate highly convincing phishing emails or to create new and more evasive malware variants. Additionally, AI and ML models themselves can be vulnerable to attacks, such as adversarial attacks that aim to manipulate or poison the training data, leading to inaccurate or biased results. To address these challenges, it is crucial to develop robust defenses against AI-powered attacks. This includes developing AI-based threat detection systems that can identify and mitigate AI-powered attacks, implementing secure machine learning practices to prevent the manipulation of AI models, and ensuring the trustworthiness and transparency of AI systems used in security contexts. Collaboration between cybersecurity researchers, AI/ML experts, and policymakers is essential to develop and implement effective AI-based security solutions that can address both the opportunities and challenges presented by these technologies.

Cross-discipline solutions

As cybersecurity challenges grow more complex, solutions increasingly require expertise from multiple disciplines. This chapter explores how cross-discipline approaches drive innovation and resilience in two critical areas. Securing **industrial control systems (ICS)** necessitates collaboration between cybersecurity experts, engineers, and **operational technology (OT)** specialists to protect critical infrastructure from cyber threats. Similarly, addressing the cybersecurity skills shortage involves integrating insights from education, workforce development, and policymaking to bridge the talent gap and build a robust cybersecurity workforce. By leveraging interdisciplinary strategies, organizations can enhance security, mitigate risks, and future-proof their systems against evolving threats:

- **Use case 1:** Securing ICS

  Securing ICS requires a multi-faceted approach that transcends traditional cybersecurity boundaries. These systems, which control critical infrastructure like power grids, water treatment plants, and manufacturing facilities, often operate on legacy hardware and software, making them vulnerable to cyberattacks. To address this, cybersecurity experts must collaborate closely with engineers, operations technicians, and domain specialists.

Following are the technical and practical details:

o **Network segmentation:** Cybersecurity experts work with network engineers to implement robust network segmentation. This involves dividing the ICS network into smaller, isolated zones, limiting the impact of a potential breach. For example, separating business networks from OT networks and further segmenting OT networks based on criticality.

o **Protocol hardening:** Collaboration with engineers and technicians is crucial to harden industrial protocols like Modbus, DNP3, and OPC UA. This involves configuring protocols with secure settings, implementing authentication and encryption mechanisms, and minimizing the attack surface by disabling unnecessary functions.

o **Threat intelligence sharing:** Cybersecurity experts leverage threat intelligence feeds from various sources, including government agencies and industry-specific **Information Sharing and Analysis Centers (ISACs)**. This intelligence helps identify emerging threats and vulnerabilities specific to the ICS environment, allowing for proactive mitigation measures.

o **Incident response planning:** Collaboration with operations teams is essential to develop and test incident response plans. This includes defining roles and responsibilities, establishing communication channels, and conducting tabletop exercises to simulate real-world cyberattacks. This ensures a coordinated and effective response to incidents, minimizing downtime and potential damage.

• **Use case 2:** Addressing the cybersecurity skills shortage

The cybersecurity industry faces a critical shortage of skilled professionals. To bridge this gap, collaboration between academia, industry, and government is essential.

Following are the technical and practical details:

o **Developing and implementing effective cybersecurity education and training programs:** Universities and colleges, in collaboration with industry partners, can develop and deliver curriculum that aligns with the evolving needs of the cybersecurity workforce. This includes hands-on training in emerging technologies like cloud security, threat intelligence analysis, and incident response.

o **Promoting cybersecurity careers:** Industry organizations and government agencies can collaborate to promote cybersecurity as an attractive and rewarding career path. This involves organizing career fairs, mentorship programs, and public awareness campaigns to highlight the importance of cybersecurity and the diverse opportunities available in the field.

o **Fostering diversity and inclusion:** Collaboration among stakeholders can help create a more inclusive cybersecurity workforce by addressing barriers to entry for underrepresented groups. This includes initiatives to increase diversity in cybersecurity education and training programs, as well as mentorship programs to support the career development of women and minority cybersecurity professionals.

o **Developing and implementing cybersecurity certifications:** Industry organizations and certification bodies can collaborate to develop and maintain rigorous cybersecurity certifications that validate the skills and knowledge of cybersecurity professionals. This provides a standardized framework for assessing and recognizing cybersecurity expertise, enhancing the credibility and professionalism of the field.

By fostering collaboration and cross-disciplinary partnerships, we can effectively address the cybersecurity challenges of today and ensure a secure and resilient future.

Emerging technologies and strategies

As the digital landscape continues to evolve, emerging technologies are reshaping the way we approach cybersecurity. This chapter explores cutting-edge advancements and strategic approaches in two critical areas. Quantum computing and PQC examine the potential threats posed by quantum computers to classical encryption methods and the development of quantum-resistant cryptographic solutions. AI and ML in cybersecurity focus on leveraging artificial intelligence and machine learning to enhance threat intelligence, automate threat detection, and improve incident response. By understanding these transformative technologies and strategies, organizations can proactively strengthen their cybersecurity posture against future threats:

- **Use case 1:** Quantum computing and PQC

  Quantum computing's potential to break existing encryption algorithms like RSA and ECC poses a significant threat to cybersecurity. To stay ahead of this emerging technology, organizations must:

  o **Research and implement PQC:** PQC algorithms, such as lattice-based, code-based, and multivariate cryptography, are designed to be resistant to attacks from even the most powerful quantum computers. Organizations should research and evaluate PQC solutions to ensure their data remains secure in the post-quantum era.

  o **Develop Quantum Key Distribution (QKD) strategies:** QKD provides a secure method for exchanging cryptographic keys using the principles of quantum mechanics. Implementing QKD can enhance the security of communication channels and protect sensitive data from quantum-based attacks.

For example, a financial institution can implement PQC algorithms to secure its online banking platform and protect customer data from potential future quantum-based attacks. They can also collaborate with telecommunications providers to implement QKD for secure key exchange between their data centers.

- **Use case 2:** AI and ML in cybersecurity

    AI and ML are revolutionizing cybersecurity by enabling faster and more accurate threat detection and response. To leverage these technologies effectively:

    o **Develop and deploy AI/ML-powered security tools:** Organizations can utilize AI/ML-powered **Security Information and Event Management (SIEM)** systems, **intrusion detection systems (IDS),** and **endpoint detection and response (EDR)** solutions to analyze large volumes of data and identify sophisticated threats.

    o **Train and educate security personnel:** Security teams need to be trained on how to effectively use AI/ML-powered tools and interpret the insights they provide. This includes understanding the limitations of AI/ML and the potential for adversarial attacks.

    For example, a healthcare provider can use AI/ML to analyze patient data and identify potential insider threats, such as unauthorized access to sensitive medical records. They can also use AI/ML-powered security tools to detect and respond to ransomware attacks in real-time, minimizing the impact on patient care.

Conclusion

In this chapter, we discussed remote access measures and services for desktop and application sharing along with unified collaboration tools such as Web, video, and audio conferencing, document collaboration, and unified communication. Instant messaging, email, telephony, and VoIP integration were also discussed.

In the next chapter, we will discuss the techniques and implementations of cryptography, which is a critical factor in securing data at rest and in-transit.

Exercise

1. **Which of the following is a primary concern when enabling remote access to an organization's network?**

    a. Increased website traffic

    b. Unauthorized access and security threats

    c. Faster internet speeds

    d. Reducing file sizes

2. **What is the primary function of a VPN?**

   a. To increase internet speed

   b. To provide secure encrypted communication over an untrusted network

   c. To block advertisements on websites

   d. To replace antivirus software

3. **Which of the following is NOT typically considered a unified collaboration tool?**

   a. Microsoft Teams

   b. Zoom

   c. Adobe Photoshop

   d. Google Meet

4. **Which email protocol is primarily used for sending emails?**

   a. IMAP

   b. POP3

   c. SMTP

   d. FTP

5. **What is the primary objective of a phishing attack?**

   a. To improve network performance

   b. To steal sensitive information by deceiving users

   c. To update security software

   d. To increase search engine rankings

6. **Which of the following cloud-based platforms is widely used for document collaboration?**

   a. Google Drive

   b. VLC Media Player

   c. Adobe Premiere Pro

   d. WinRAR

7. **Which of the following is a key benefit of research collaboration in cybersecurity?**

   a. Increased individual workload

   b. Limited knowledge sharing

   c. Accelerated innovation and problem-solving

   d. Reduced access to global expertise

Answers

1. b
2. b
3. c
4. c
5. b
6. a
7. c

Join our book's Discord space

Join the book's Discord Workspace for Latest updates, Offers, Tech happenings around the world, New Release and Sessions with the Authors:

https://discord.bpbonline.com

CHAPTER 15

Implementing Cryptographic Techniques

Introduction

Cryptography is one of the most complicated fields of security expertise. Both at rest and in transit, cryptography is a vital component of data security. It is a science that comprises hiding data or altering it to make it unreadable. Message authorship, source verification, and delivery proof are all ensured via cryptography. Cryptography is concerned with confidentiality, integrity, and authentication, but not with availability. The CIA triumvirate is a basic security paradigm that includes secrecy, integrity, and availability, with cryptography addressing two of the triad's main pillars. It aids in the identification and prevention of data manipulation, deletion, and modification. Cryptography also provides non-repudiation by demonstrating a message's origin. Each of these ideas is examined in further depth in this chapter.

Structure

- Key stretching
- Hashing
- Digital signatures
- Perfect forward secrecy
- Encryption of data in transit

- Internet Protocol Security
- Securing data-in-memory
- Encryption of data at rest
- Symmetric algorithms
- Disk level encryption
- Block level encryption
- Record level encryption
- Steganography
- Digital rights management
- Applications
- Implementing cloud cryptography

Objectives

You will learn about cryptography methods, principles, and implementations that are used to safeguard data in the organization in this chapter. To secure private data, most firms use a variety of physical devices. External dangers are kept out of the network by these devices, which secure data. Data encryption guarantees that secret or private data is not read if one of an attacker's approaches succeeds and an organization's first line of defense is breached. The advantages of encryption include strength, transparency and flexibility.

Techniques

Various cryptographic algorithms are used depending on the demands of the company. Examining the context of the data and identifying which cryptographic approach to employ is the first step in selecting the proper cryptographic technique. Security experts should examine the data kind, sensitivity, value, and dangers to the data before deciding which approach to apply. Key stretching, hashing, digital signatures, message authentication, code signing, and pseudo-random number generation are some of the methods you will need to know. Data-in-transit encryption, data-at-rest encryption, and data-in-memory or processing are all examples of perfect forward secrecy.

Key stretching

Key stretching, also known as key strengthening, is a cryptographic approach that includes lengthening the time it takes to test each potential key to make a weak key stronger. The original key is passed into an algorithm to generate an upgraded key, which should be at least 128 bits in length to be effective. If key stretching is employed, an attacker must either attempt every conceivable combination of the improved key or a large number of plausible combinations of the original key. Because the attacker must calculate the stretching function for each guess in the attack, key stretching slows down the attacker. **Pretty Good Privacy (PGP), GNU Privacy Guard (GPG), Wi-Fi Protected Access (WPA),** and WPA2 are all systems that employ key stretching. **Password-Based Key Derivation Function 2 (PBKDF2),** bcrypt, and scrypt are some of the most widely used password key stretching algorithms.

Hashing

To generate a one-way message digest, the data is passed through a cryptographic procedure. The method utilized determines the size of the message digest. The data is represented by the message digest, which cannot be reversed to identify the original contents. The message digest may be used to verify data integrity since it is unique. A message is reduced to a hash value using a one-way hash algorithm. Message integrity is determined by comparing the sender's hash value to the receiver's hash value. The message has been tampered with if both the sender and recipient employed the same hash function but the resulting hash values are different. Hash functions do not prevent data change, but they do give a way to see whether the data has been altered, as shown in *Figure 15.1*:

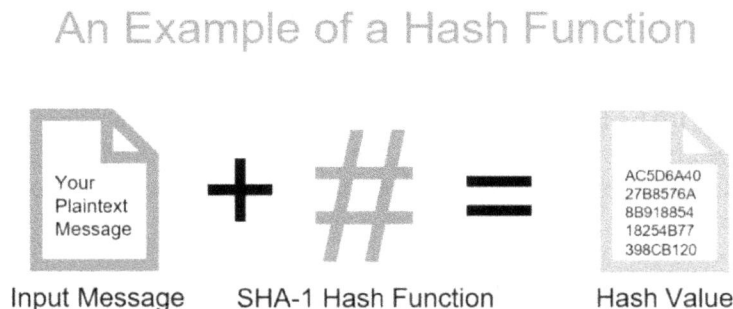

Figure 15.1: Hashing

There are certain restrictions to hash functions. If an attacker intercepts a message containing a hash value, the attacker may change the original message to construct a new incorrect message with a different hash value. If the attacker then sends the intended receiver a second faulty message, the intended recipient will have no means of recognizing that he has received an inaccurate message. When the recipient calculates the hash value, the incorrect message will seem to be legal since it was appended with the attacker's new hash value rather than the original message's hash value. To avoid this, the sender should provide a **message authentication code (MAC)** in the message. A keyed MAC is created by encrypting the hash function using a symmetric key method. The original message is not encrypted by the symmetric key. It is solely used to keep the hash value safe. The essential processes of a hash function are shown in *Figure 15.2*:

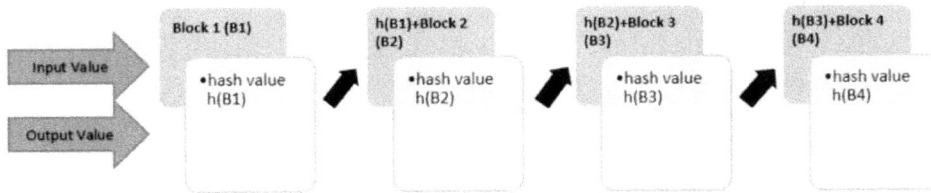

Figure 15.2: Process of a hash function

Collisions and rainbow table attacks are the two main hash function weaknesses. When a hash function gives the same hash value on several messages, it is known as a **collision**. When rainbow tables are used to reverse a hash by computing all possible hashes and finding the matching value, it is known as a **rainbow table attack**. Message digests may be used to compare multiple files to check whether they are similar down to the bit level since they are defined by the original contents. Data integrity has been compromised if a calculated message digest does not match the original message digest value. To guarantee that real passwords are not stolen, password hash values are often saved instead of actual passwords. It is always preferable to select the hashing function that utilizes a greater hash value when deciding which hashing algorithm to employ. The hash function should be used to determine a file's hash value. Let us say you have a document called contract. doc that you need to make sure is not changed in any manner. Use `md5sum contract.do`, this command will give you a hash value, which you should write down. Users should always use the `md5sum` command to recalculate the hash value when they require access to the file afterward. The file remains untouched if the value is the same as it was when it was first recorded. If it is not the same, the file has been altered. MD2/MD4/MD5/MD6, SHA/SHA-2/SHA-3, HAVAL, RIPEMD-160, and Tiger are some of the hash algorithms you should be aware of.

MD2/MD4/MD5/MD6

A 128-bit hash value is generated using the MD2 message-digest algorithm. It goes through 18 rounds of calculations. MD2 is still in use today, however, it is much slower than MD4, MD5, and MD6.

A 128-bit hash value is also generated using the MD4 algorithm. However, it only does three compute rounds. Despite the fact that MD4 is quicker than MD2, it has seen a considerable drop in usage due to the success of attacks against it.

The MD5 algorithm, like the previous MD algorithms, generates a 128-bit hash result. It goes through four rounds of calculations. It was established in response to problems with MD4, and it is more complicated than MD4. MD5 is not, however, collision-free. As a result, SSL certificates and digital signatures should not be utilized with it. Instead of MD5, the US government mandates the usage of SHA-2. However, when releasing software updates for commercial usage, many software providers disclose the MD5 hash value so that the consumers may check the product's integrity after downloading.

After conducting a variable number of calculations, the MD6 algorithm generates a variable hash value. Although it was initially proposed as a replacement for SHA-3, it was dropped due to early problems with differential attacks. Since then, MD6 has been re-released with this flaw patched. That release, however, was too late to be recognized as the SHA-3 standard by the **National Institute of Standards and Technology (NIST)**.

SHA/SHA-2/SHA-3

The **secure hash algorithm (SHA)** is a set of four algorithms developed by the NIST in the United States. After 80 rounds of calculations on 512-bit blocks, SHA-0 yields a 160-bit hash result. It was initially known as just SHA since there were no additional **family members**. This is because collisions were detected, SHA-0 was never particularly popular. After 80 rounds of calculations on 512-bit blocks, SHA-1 generates a 160-bit hash result, similar to SHA-0. The vulnerability in SHA-0 that left it vulnerable to assaults was fixed in SHA-1.

SHA-2 is a collection of hash functions, each with its own set of functional constraints. The SHA-2 family consists of the following members:

- **SHA-224**: After 64 rounds of calculations on 512-bit blocks, it generates a 224-bit hash value.

- **SHA-256**: After 64 rounds of calculations on 512-bit blocks, it generates a 256-bit hash value.

- **SHA-384**: After 80 rounds of calculations on 1,024-bit blocks, it generates a 384-bit hash value.

- **SHA-512**: After 80 rounds of calculations on 1,024-bit blocks, it generates a 512-bit hash result.

- **SHA-512/224**: After 80 rounds of calculations on 1,024-bit blocks, it generates a 224-bit hash value. The number 512 denotes the size of the internal state.

- **SHA-512/256**: After 80 rounds of calculations on 1,024-bit blocks, it generates a 256-bit hash value. The 512 identifier denotes the internal state size once again.

SHA-3, like SHA-2, is a hash function family. In May 2014, this standard was officially adopted. The size of the hash value ranges from 224 to 512 bits. By default, SHA-3 does 120 rounds of calculations. Keep in mind that today's SHA-1 and SHA-2 algorithms are still frequently utilized. SHA-3 was presented as an alternate hash function to the others, rather than being created because of a security issue in the two prior standards. For added security, hashing algorithms are often used with other cryptographic techniques. However, business managers should make sure that the algorithms used in tandem can deliver optimum security and performance. Implementing 3DES with SHA, for example, would give high security but worse performance than RC4 with MD5. Let us have a look at an example of hashing using SHA. Even though a package like 5.9.4-8-x86 64.rpm was obtained from an official repository, an administrator must check that the package has not been changed before installing it on a server. Before installing a package on a Linux computer, the administrator should run sha1sum and validate the hash of the package.

Digital signatures

A hash value encrypted with the sender's private key constitutes a digital signature. Authentication, non-repudiation, and integrity are all provided by a digital signature. A blind signature is a kind of digital signature in which the message's contents are hidden until it is signed, as shown in *Figure 15.3*:

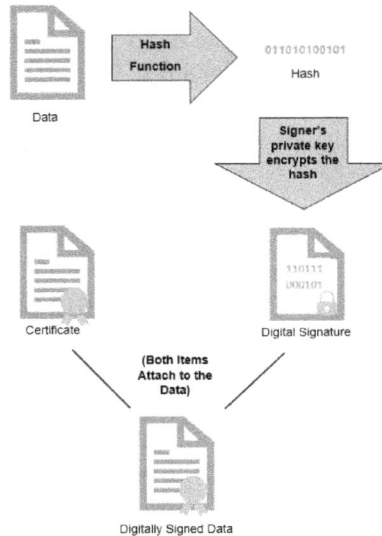

Figure 15.3: The process of creating a digital signature

The following is the procedure for establishing a digital signature:

1. For the data to be signed, the signer receives a hash value.

2. Using their private key, the signer encrypts the hash value.

3. The signer encrypts the material and encrypts a copy of their public key in a certificate before sending it to the recipient.

The following is the procedure for confirming the digital signature:

1. The data, encrypted hash, and certificate are separated by the receiver.

2. The receiver acquires the data's hash value.

3. Using the PKI, the receiver confirms that the public key is still valid.

4. Using the public key, the recipient decrypts the encrypted hash value.

5. The receiver compares the hash values of the two messages. The message has not been modified if the values are the same.

Digital signatures are created using public key cryptography. Users register their public keys with a **certification authority (CA)**, which then issues a certificate including the user's public key as well as the digital signature of the CA. The user's public key and validity period are coupled with the certificate issuer and digital signature algorithm identifier to create the digital signature. The **Digital Signature Standard (DSS)** is a federally mandated digital security standard that regulates the **Digital Security Algorithm (DSA)**. DSA creates a 160-bit message digest. For digital signatures, the US federal government mandates the use of DSA, **Rivest-Shamir-Adleman (RSA)**, or **Elliptic Curve DSA (ECDSA)**, as well as SHA. DSA is a slower version of RSA that only allows for digital signatures. Digital signatures, encryption, and secure symmetric key distribution are all provided by RSA. Keep the following things in mind while thinking about cryptography:

- Confidentiality is provided through encryption.

- Integrity is provided through hashing.

- Authentication, non-repudiation, and integrity are all provided via digital signatures.

- Authentication of messages.

In the same way that code signing provides message integrity and authenticity, a MAC may do the same. HMAC, CBC-MAC, and CMAC are the three kinds of MACs you should be aware of. A **Hash MAC (HMAC)** is a keyed-hash MAC that uses a symmetric key and a hash function. Data integrity and authentication are provided via HMAC. HMAC can be used with any of the previously listed hash functions, with HMAC prepended to the hash function name (for example, HMACSHA-1). The strength of HMAC is determined by the hash function's strength, as well as the size of the hash value and key. The output size of HMAC's hash value is the same as that of the underlying hash algorithm. HMAC may aid in lowering the hash function's collision rate. A block-cipher MAC that runs in CBC mode is known as a **Cipher Block Chaining MAC (CBC-MAC)**. Data integrity and authentication are provided via CBC-MAC. **Cipher-based MAC (CMAC)** is similar to CBC-MAC but has many superior mathematical functions. CMAC is authorized to work with AES and 3DES and overcomes several security concerns with CBC-MAC.

Signing of code

When code developers digitally sign executables and scripts, the user installing the code may be certain that it was written by the verified author. A cryptographic hash is used to sign the code, ensuring that it has not been tampered with or damaged. Code signing is often used for security in Java applets, ActiveX controls, and other active web and browser scripts. The signature is usually confirmed by a third party, such as VeriSign, as shown in *Figure 15.4*:

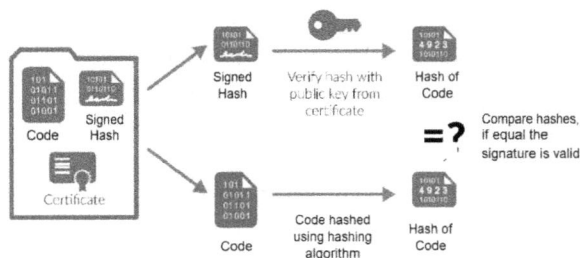

Figure 15.4: Code signing

Generation of pseudo-random numbers

A **pseudo-random number generator (PRNG)** employs an algorithm to create a series of integers that approximates the qualities of random numbers. This is because it is formed from a very narrow number of beginning values, the sequence is not random. Security experts should be able to see problems that might be remedied with a PRNG. A pseudo-random number should be created by Java at invocation if a business wants a system that generates a sequence of numbers with no clear mathematical progression for a Java-based, customer-facing website.

Perfect forward secrecy

Perfect forward secrecy (PFS) guarantees that a session key obtained from a collection of long-term keys cannot be compromised in the future if one of the long-term keys is compromised. The key cannot be used to generate any further keys. If the key was created with the help of another keying material, that keying material must not be utilized to create any further keys. Only the data protected by that single key may be accessed if a single key is compromised. PFS needs two requirements to function properly, which are as follows:

- Keys are never used again.
- No previously used keys are utilized to generate new keys.

Understanding when to use PFS is critical for any business. If a security audit reveals that certain encryption keys used to safeguard financial transactions with an organization's partners are too weak, the security administrator should use PFS across all VPN tunnels to guarantee that financial transactions are not jeopardized. PFS is most often associated with VPNs; however, it may also be found in web browsers, services, and apps.

Encryption of data in transit

When data is transported through a network or the Internet, it is safeguarded by transport encryption. Sniffing attacks on networks may be protected via transport encryption. In addition to securing data at rest, security experts should guarantee that data is safeguarded in transit. Consider a company that uses token and biometric authentication for all users, as well as secure administrator accounts, transaction logging, full-disk encryption, server virtualization, port security, and firewalls with ACLs, a NIPS, and secured access points. There is no security for data in transit with any of these options. To secure data in this context, transport encryption would be required. Secure communication protocols such as SSL/TLS, HTTP/HTTPS/SHTTP, SET, SSH, and IPsec should be utilized to enable this encryption.

SSL and TLS

Secure sockets layer (SSL) is an encryption, server, and client authentication, and message integrity protocol. It communicates with the application and transport layers, but it does not act inside them. Netscape created SSL in order to send confidential documents over the internet. SSL uses 40-bit encryption (SSL 2.0) or 128-bit encryption (SSL 3.0), although the 40-bit version is vulnerable to attacks due to its small key size. SSL enables a program to communicate across a network in an encrypted and authorized manner.

SSL 3.0 is the foundation for **transport layer security (TLS)** 1.0, however, it is more adaptable. TLS's fundamental objective is to provide data integrity and privacy between two interacting apps. When the data has to be encrypted while being transferred (in transit) through the media from one system to another, SSL and TLS are the most widely utilized protocols, as shown in *Figure 15.5*:

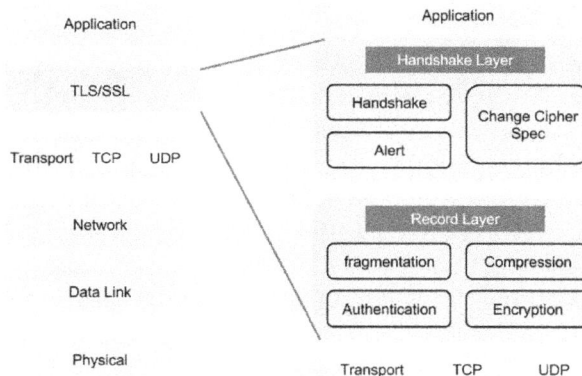

Figure 15.5: SSL and TLS

HTTP/HTTPS/SHTTP

The **Hypertext Transfer Protocol (HTTP)** is a web protocol for sending website data from a web server to a web client. This is because HTTP is a stateless protocol, a new connection is made with each new URL typed into the web browser, whether from the original user entry or by clicking a link on the page shown. **HTTP Secure (HTTPS)** is an HTTP implementation that uses the SSL or TLS protocol to create a secure connection using the server's digital certificate. SSL or TLS uses a secure channel to keep the session open. The https:// prefix is always included at the beginning of HTTPS webpages. **Secure HTTP (SHTTP)**, despite its similarity in name, safeguards HTTP transmission in a different way. Only a single communication message is encrypted using SHTTP, not the whole session (or conversation). SHTTP is less popular than HTTPS.

3-D secure and safeguard electronic transaction

Visa and MasterCard suggested **safeguard electronic transaction (SET)** to secure credit card transaction information over the Internet. It used asymmetric keys and X.509 certificates. It sent encrypted credit card information through a user's computer's electronic wallet. SET, on the other hand, would have needed complete cooperation from financial institutions, credit card users, wholesale and retail enterprises, and payment gateways in order to be completely implemented. It was never completely accepted. Instead of SET, Visa now pushes the 3-D secure standard. 3-D Secure is an XML-based technology that adds an extra layer of protection to credit and debit card transactions made online. Customers may get it under the label verified by Visa. MasterCard's implementation of 3-D Secure is known as **Secure Code**.

Internet Protocol Security

Internet Protocol Security (IPsec) is a set of protocols that creates a secure connection between two devices. VPNs often use IPsec as a security protocol. IPsec protects against traffic analysis by deciding on the methods to employ and implementing any cryptographic keys needed for IPsec. **Authentication Header (AH), Encapsulating Security Payload (ESP)**, and **Security Associations (SAs)** are all part of IPsec. Authentication and integrity are provided by AH, while authentication, integrity, and encryption are provided by ESP (confidentiality). SA is a configuration record for a device that needs to participate in IPsec communication. A **Security Parameter Index (SPI)** is a form of database that keeps track of the multiple SAs in use and guarantees that a device communicates with another device using the correct SA. As shown in *Figure 15.6*, each device has its own SPI:

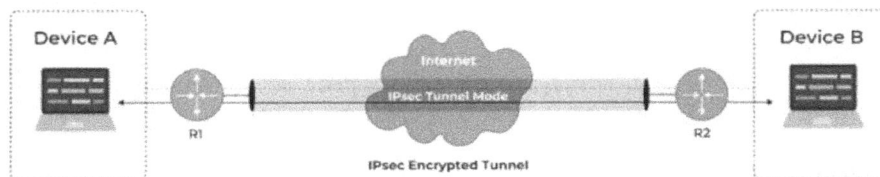

Figure 15.6: IPSec tunnel

IPsec may operate in one of the two modes, which is transport or tunnel. Only the message content is protected in the transport mode, but the payload, route, and header information are all protected in the tunnel mode. Both of these modes may be utilized for IPsec communication between gateways and hosts. Which hashing or encryption algorithm is employed is not determined by IPsec. The key exchange technique most widely used by IPsec is **Internet Key Exchange (IKE)**, which is a mix of **Oakley Key Determination Protocol (OAKLEY)** and **Internet Security Association and Key Management Protocol (ISAKMP)**. OAKLEY is a Diffie-Hellman-based key establishment mechanism that was replaced by IKE. The ISAKMP was created to create and manage SAs. Authentication and key exchange are provided via IKE with IPsec. Pre-shared keys, certificates, and public-key authentication are among the authentication methods used by IKE with IPsec. A PKI is required for the most secure implementations of pre-shared keys. However, if a pre-shared key is based on basic passwords, a PKI is not required.

Securing data-in-memory

In-memory processing is a method of processing data sets in which all data is handled in memory rather than on the hard disk. It expects that all data will be accessible in memory, rather than simply the most recently utilized data, as is typical with RAM or cache memory. As a consequence, company reporting and decision-making are expedited. Encrypting the data in RAM is required to secure this. The **Data-Protection API (DPAPI)** is a Windows feature that allows you to encrypt data using the user's login credentials. One of the most important considerations is where to keep the key since it is usually not a good idea to keep it in the same place as the data. **Software Guard Extensions (SGX)**, which comes as standard with Skylake and subsequent Intel processors, enables you to load a program into your processor, validate its status (remotely), and safeguard its execution. Everything that leaves the processor (that is, everything that is offloaded to RAM) is immediately encrypted by the CPU, ensuring security.

Encryption of data at rest

Data at rest refers to information that is physically stored in any digital format but is not in use. Databases, data warehouses, files, archives, tapes, offsite backups, mobile devices, and any other storage media may be used to store this information. Data encryption techniques are often used to secure data at rest. When converting plaintext to cipher text, computer algorithms apply sophisticated mathematical formulas to convert plaintext to cipher text. The key and the algorithm are the two most important parts of any encryption system. The two communicating parties utilize the same key in various encryption methods. Other encryption schemes include the use of distinct keys by the two communication parties, but the keys are connected. Symmetric algorithms, asymmetric algorithms, and hybrid ciphers are some of the encryption methods you will need to know about.

Symmetric algorithms

Symmetric algorithms rely on a private, or secret key that must be kept confidential between the two parties. A private key is required for each party pair. As a result, each user with whom they talk would need a separate secret key. Consider a scenario in which there are ten distinct users. To calculate the number of keys that would be needed in this example, you would use the following formula:

# of users' × (# of users − 1) / 2

In this example, you would calculate:

10 × (10 − 1) / 2, or 45 needed keys.

In this case, you would need to compute 10 (10 − 1) / 2, or 45 keys. The encryption key must be kept safe when using symmetric algorithms. The users must discover a safe out-of-band way for conveying the secret key, such as courier or direct physical contact, in order to get it. A session key is a sort of symmetric key that encrypts communications sent between two users during a communication session. Single-key, secret-key, private-key, and shared-key cryptography are all terms used to describe symmetric algorithms. Confidentiality is provided by symmetric systems, but not authentication or nonrepudiation. It's hard to tell where a message came from if both users utilize the same key. DES, AES, IDEA, Skipjack, Blowfish, Twofish, RC4/RC5/RC6, and CAST are symmetric algorithms. **Digital Encryption Standard (DES)** and **Triple DES (3DES)** are two types of encryption.

The DES employs a 64-bit key, with 8 bits dedicated to parity. As a result, DES's effective key length is 56 bits. A message is divided into 64-bit chunks using DES. Each block goes through sixteen rounds of transposition and substitution, resulting in a 64-bit cipher text block. 3DES and AES have largely replaced DES. In addition to the 56-bit DES key, DES-X is a version of DES that employs multiple 64-bit keys. The plaintext is XORed with the first 64-bit key, which is then encrypted using DES. The cipher is XORed with the second 64-bit key. Double-DES, a DES variant with a key length of 112 bits, is no longer in use. A security attack happened after it was published, reducing double-DES security to the same level as DES. 3DES, a variation of DES that uses three 56-bit keys to boost security, was created in response to the requirement to swiftly replace DES. Although 3DES is more resistant to assaults than DES, it is three times slower. 3DES was used as a stand-in for DES for a short time. Despite the fact that 3DES is still in use today, the NIST has chosen AES as the successor for DES.

Advanced Encryption Standard

Advanced Encryption Standard (AES) is the successor to the DES algorithm. The Rijndael algorithm is employed in the AES standard, despite the fact that AES is regarded as the standard. AES and Rijndael are frequently used interchangeably. The Rijndael algorithm uses three different block sizes, which are 128, 192, and 256 bits. Ten transformation rounds are performed on a 128-bit key with 128-bit block size. Twelve transformation rounds are performed on a 192-bit key with a 192-bit block size. Finally, 14 transformation rounds are performed on a 256-bit key with 256-bit block size. Rijndael uses three levels of transformations such as the nonlinear 737 layer, the key addition layer, and the linear-maxing layer. Rijndael architecture is basic, and its code is small, allowing it to run on a number of systems. It is the U.S. government's mandated algorithm for sensitive but unclassified material.

International Data Encryption Algorithm

The **International Data Encryption Algorithm (IDEA)** is a 64-bit block cipher. Each 64-bit block is broken down into 16 smaller ones. IDEA executes eight rounds of transformations on each of the 16 smaller blocks using a 128-bit key. IDEA is both quicker and more difficult to crack than DES. IDEA has been trademarked and licensed by Ascom, a Swiss corporation, although this algorithm is not as commonly utilized as DES or AES, as the patent expired in 2012. However, PGP makes use of IDEA.

Twofish

Twofish is a blowfish variant that employs 128-bit data blocks and keys of 128-, 192-, and 256-bit lengths. It has a total of 16 transformation rounds. Twofish, like blowfish, is not a patented product.

RC4/RC5/RC6

Ron Rivest has designed a total of six RC algorithms. RC1 was never released, RC2 was a 64-bit block cipher, and RC3 was cracked prior to its release. RC4, RC5, and RC6 are the primary RC implementations that a security expert should be familiar with. One of the most widely used stream ciphers is RC4, sometimes known as ARC4. SSL and WEP both utilize it. RC4 has a configurable key size of 40 to 2,048 bits and can perform up to 256 transformation rounds.

RC5 is a block cipher with a key size of up to 2,048 bits and 255 transformation rounds. The following block sizes are supported – 32, 64, and 128 bits. This is because of the many variables in RC5, the industry frequently refers to it as RC5-w/r/b, where w stands for block size, r for rounds, and b for the number of 8-bit bytes in the key. RC5-64/16/16, for example, implies a 64-bit word (or 128-bit data blocks), 16 transformation rounds, and a 16-byte (128-bit) key.

RC6 is a block cipher that employs the same key size, rounds, and block size as RC5. RC6 was initially intended to be an AES solution, but it was defeated by Rijndael in a competition. Asymmetric algorithms RC6 is quicker than RC5.

Asymmetric algorithms, often known as dual-key or public-key cryptography, use both a public and a private, or secret, key. Everyone has access to the public key, whereas only the owner has access to the private key. The message is encrypted using one of these keys and decrypted with the other. Even if the public key is known, finding a user's private key in asymmetric cryptography is almost hard, despite the fact that both keys are mathematically connected. The system, on the other hand, may be hacked if a user's private key is found. Confidentiality, integrity, authentication, and non-repudiation are all provided by asymmetric systems. It is feasible to determine where the communication originated since both users have one unique key that is part of the procedure. If an organization's main priority is secrecy, a message should be encrypted using the receiver's public key, which is known as a secure message format. If an organization's main concern is authentication, a message should be encrypted using the sender's private key, which is known as the open message format. When utilizing the open message format, anybody with the public key may decode the message. Diffie-Hellman, RSA, El Gamal, ECC, Knapsack, and zero knowledge proof are examples of asymmetric algorithms.

Diffie-Hellman

The key agreement procedure is overseen by Diffie-Hellman, and it operates as follows:

1. John and Sally decide to use Diffie-Hellman to converse via an encrypted channel.

2. John creates a private and public key, while Sally creates a private and public key.

3. John and Sally give each other their public keys.

4. A program on John's computer uses the Diffie-Hellman algorithm to combine John's private key and Sally's public key, and a program on Sally's computer uses the Diffie-Hellman method to combine Sally's private key and John's public key.

5. Using the asymmetric key agreement procedure, the same shared value is established for John and Sally, which in turn produces the identical symmetric key on each machine.

Diffie-Hellman enables safe key distribution but not secrecy, authentication, or non-repudiation with this method. Discrete logarithms are the subject of this algorithm. Unless an organization uses digital signatures or digital certificates for authentication at the start of the Diffie-Hellman process, Diffie-Hellman is vulnerable to man-in-the-middle attacks.

RSA

Ron Rivest, Adi Shamir, and Leonard Adleman created the most common asymmetric algorithm, RSA. Key exchange, encryption, and digital signatures are all possible with RSA. The difficulty of identifying prime factors of extremely big integers is the strength of the RSA method. RSA conducts one cycle of transformation with a key ranging from 1,024 to 4,096 bits. The algorithms for RSA-768 and RSA-704 have been factored in. If the prime numbers utilized by an RSA implementation factorize, the implementation is deemed breakable and should be avoided. The biggest RSA number is RSA-2048, which has a monetary reward of US$200,000 for successful factorization.

RSA encodes a DES or AES symmetric key for safe distribution as a key exchange mechanism. To offer encryption/decryption and digital signature verification/generation, RSA employs a one-way function. Encryption and digital signature verification are performed using the public key and the one-way function. Decryption and signature creation are performed using the private key and the one-way function. The one-way function is a trapdoor in RSA. The one-way function is known by the private key. The initial prime numbers may be determined using the private key. Finally, the private key understands how to decode the encrypted message using the one-way function. **Number field sieve (NFS),** a factoring technique, may be used to attack RSA.

El Gamal

El Gamal is a Diffie-Hellman algorithm-based asymmetric key algorithm. El Gamal, like Diffie-Hellman, works with discrete logarithms. El Gamal, on the other hand, can offer a key exchange, encryption, and digital signatures, while Diffie-Hellman can only be used for key agreement. Any key size may be utilized with El Gamal. A bigger key size, on the other hand, has a detrimental impact on performance. This is because El Gamal is the slowest asymmetric method, it is best to utilize a key size of at least 1,024 bits.

ECC

Secure key distribution, encryption, and digital signatures are all possible using **elliptic curve cryptography (ECC).** The size of the elliptic curve determines the problem's complexity. Despite the fact that ECC may utilize any key size, it can employ a much smaller key than RSA or any other asymmetric method while still providing equal security. As a result, ECC's principal advantage is a lower-key size, which means less storage and transmission is required. ECC keys are more efficient and secure than RSA keys of the same size.

Disk level encryption

Disk-level encryption encrypts a whole volume or disk, with the same key used for the entire disk or, in certain situations, a distinct key used for each partition or volume. A **Trusted Platform Module (TPM)** chip may also be used. Password protection, **digital rights management (DRM)**, and complete disk encryption are all provided by this chip, which is installed on the system's motherboard. It safeguards the keys used to encrypt the hard drives of the computer and offers integrity authentication for a secure boot route. This may help avoid data loss if the computer or hard drive is stolen. Because the TPM chip's key is necessary to access the hard drive, removing it makes decryption of the data on it difficult. Full disk encryption is an excellent way to prevent sensitive data from being stolen from laptops or other mobile devices. When considering disk encryption, keep the following qualities in mind:

- It encrypts a whole volume or disk.
- It employs a single encryption key per drive.
- It delays the boot and login process.
- It offers no encryption for data in transit.

Block level encryption

Block-level encryption is often used interchangeably with disk-level encryption, although it may also refer to the encryption of a disk partition or a file functioning as a virtual partition. When discussing different forms of encryption techniques, this phrase is also employed. In contrast to a stream cipher, which encrypts one bit at a time, a block cipher encrypts blocks of data at a time. File-level encryption is exactly what it sounds like, it encrypts files at the file level. Each file is encrypted and decrypted separately, and each file owner has a key.

Record level encryption

At the record level, storage encryption is also possible. In this situation, the option of which data to encrypt may be made, which has a substantial impact on both performance and security. Because a single key does not decode the whole disk or volume, this sort of encryption provides for greater granularity in who has the keys. Records should be encrypted in high-security contexts, such as those that store credit card information. The following entries in a database, for example, should trigger a red alert:

UserID	Address	Credit Card	Password
KaranSharma01	4, Rajpur Road, Dehradun	51XX-XXX-XXXX-9007	Pass007
NehaVerma02	F-15 Karol Bagh, New Delhi	12XX-XXX-XXXX-2547	17JAN2000

Table 15.1: *Unencrypted Database Records*

The passwords are saved in plain text format. When contemplating the use of file and record encryption, keep the following criteria in mind:

- It does not encrypt data while it is in transit.
- It only encrypts one file.
- It only utilizes one key per file, which slows down file opening.
- Encryption at the port level.

A network protocol analyzer may encrypt network data on selected ports to avoid network eavesdropping. Network encryption takes place at the protocol's network layer. Only while in transit is the network data encrypted. Network encryption is no longer in effect after the data has been received. When employing this encryption, you must consider the influence on performance.

Steganography

When a message is buried within another item, such as a photograph or document, it is known as steganography. It is critical in steganography that only those who are anticipating the message are aware that it exists. One approach to steganography is to use a concealing cipher. Digital watermarking is another kind of steganography. Digital watermarking is the process of embedding a logo or brand in papers, images, or other things. The watermarks serve as a deterrent to unlawful use of the content. Changing the least significant bit for each pixel in an image is the most popular method. Pixels are modified in this example in such a modest amount that the human eye cannot notice them. Cryptography is used by businesses in a variety of ways, depending on the demands of the company. Crypto modules, crypto processors, cryptographic service providers, DRM, watermarking, GPG, SSL/TLS, SSH, and S/MIME are just a few of the implementations that security professionals should be aware of.

Modules for cryptography

The phrase **crypto module** refers to the hardware, software, and firmware that implements cryptographic logic or operations. These courses may be evaluated and rated by a variety of organizations. The NIST uses the **Federal Information Processing Standard (FIPS)** Publication 140-2. The FIPS 140-2 standard specifies four degrees of security for such a module. The following is what FIPS 140-2 states regarding crypto modules:

- **Levels 1 and 2 of security**: The physical port(s) and logical interface(s) used for the input and output of plaintext cryptographic keys, cryptographic key components, authentication data, and CSPs in security levels 1 and 2 may be physically and logically shared with other cryptographic module ports and interfaces.

- **Security levels 3 and 4**: In security levels 3 and 4, the physical port(s) used for the input and output of plaintext cryptographic key components, authentication data, and CSPs must be physically separated from all other ports of the cryptographic module, or the logical interfaces used for the input and output of plaintext cryptographic key components, authentication data, and CSPs must be logically separated from all other interfaces using a trusted path, and plaintext cryptographic key components, authentication data, and C (for example, via a trusted path or directly attached cable).

Processors for cryptography

Encryption is the only purpose of crypto processors. To avoid tampering, they usually feature a number of physical safeguards. This principle has been implemented in a variety of ways. A processor on a smart card is an example of this. The processor receives encrypted program instructions and decrypts them to plain instructions, which are subsequently performed on the same chip where the decrypted instructions are kept inaccessibly.

The TPM on an endpoint device, which contains the RSA encryption keys unique to the host system for hardware authentication, is another example. The processors included in **Hardware Security Modules (HSMs)** are the final example.

Providers of cryptographic services

A **cryptographic service provider (CSP)** is a software library that runs on Windows and implements the Microsoft **CryptoAPI (CAPI)**. CSPs are cryptographic service modules that may be utilized by a variety of applications. CSPs are implemented as a sort of DLL with specific loading, and they use constraints. Microsoft must digitally sign all CSPs, and Windows must verify the signature when the CSP is loaded. After the CSP is loaded, Windows will check it on a regular basis for tampering, which might be caused by malicious software such as computer viruses or by the user attempting to get beyond limits (such as cryptographic key length) included into the CSP's code.

Digital rights management

Hardware manufacturers, publishers, copyright holders, and individuals utilize DRM to govern the usage of digital material. This often includes gadget controls. Copying is controlled by first-generation DRM software. Executing, viewing, copying, printing, and changing works or devices are all controlled by second-generation DRM. The **Digital Millennium Copyright Act (DMCA)** of 1998 in the United States imposes criminal penalties on anyone who makes technology accessible with the main goal of circumventing content protection systems. DRM comprises encryption and restrictive licensing agreements. Computer games and other software, documents, eBooks, films, music, and television are all protected by DRM. The DRM control of documents utilizing open, edit, print, or copy access limitations that are given on a permanent or temporary basis is the key focus in most corporate installations. Solutions that store protected data in a centralized or decentralized format may be employed. In the DRM implementation, encryption is utilized to safeguard data both at rest and in transit.

Watermarking

In steganography, digital watermarking is a technique. The process of embedding a logo or trademark in papers, images, or other things is known as **digital watermarking**. The watermark serves as a deterrent to unlawful use of the contents. GPG is a free software program that protects your privacy. PGP is closely connected to GPG. Both of these systems were created to safeguard electronic communications. PGP encrypts email over the Internet and employs various encryption methods depending on the organization's requirements. Based on the encryption techniques employed, PGP may guarantee secrecy, integrity, and authenticity. RSA key management is provided by PGP. The keys are managed by PGP via a web of trust. Instead of depending on a CA, people construct this network of trust by exchanging public keys. The public keys of all users are saved in a key ring file on each user's computer. Each user is given a degree of trust inside that file. Users on the Internet vouch for one another. User 1 may refer the other two users to each other if user 1 and user 2 have a trust connection and user 1 and user 3 have a trust relationship. Users may determine the amount of trust they want to attach to a user at the start, but they can adjust it later if circumstances change. However, if a user's private key is compromised in the PGP system, the user must contact everyone with whom they have shared their key to have it deleted from the key ring file.

Using IDEA, PGP delivers data encryption for secrecy. Other encryption techniques, on the other hand, maybe utilized. Data integrity is ensured by combining PGP and MD5. Authentication is provided using public certificates with PGP. GPG is a rewrite or update of PGP that employs AES encryption. Because the intention was to make it fully free, it does not employ the IDEA encryption algorithm. The OpenPGP Alliance keeps track of all algorithm data and makes it available to the public. Because AES is less expensive than IDEA and is regarded as more secure, GPG is a better alternative than PGP. GPG is also royalty-free since it isn't patented.

Although the core GPG software has a command-line interface, several vendors, such as KDE and Gnome for Linux and Aqua for macOS, have built front ends that give GPG a graphical user interface. GPG for Windows, Gnu Privacy Assistant, and GPG plug-ins for Windows Explorer and Outlook are all included in the Gpg4win software bundle.

Shell security

Secure Shell (SSH) is a program and protocol for remotely connecting to another computer over a secure tunnel. All communication between the two computers is encrypted across the secure channel when a session key is exchanged and the secure channel is created. SSH is a method of gaining remote access to equipment such as switches, routers, and servers. SSH is preferable over Telnet because Telnet's communication is not secure.

Secure Multipurpose Internet Mail Extensions

Multipurpose Internet Mail Extensions (MIME) is an Internet standard that enables non-text attachments, non-ASCII character sets, multiple-part message bodies, and non-ASCII header information to be sent over email. In today's world, a bulk of email is sent over SMTP in the MIME format. An email client may send an attachment with a header that describes the file type using MIME. This header, together with the file extension given in it, is used by the receiving system to identify the attachment type and open the associated program. When the user double-clicks the attachment, the computer will immediately run the necessary program. If no program is linked with that file type, the user may utilize the Open With option to choose an application, or a website may provide the required application. MIME can encrypt and digitally sign email messages and attachments using **Secure MIME (S/MIME)**. It follows the **Public Key Cryptography Standards (PKCS),** which are a set of PKCS created by the RSA algorithm's creators. S/MIME provides secrecy via encryption, integrity through hashing, authentication through public key certificates, and non-repudiation through message digests.

Implementations of cryptographic applications

For a business, cryptographic applications serve a variety of purposes. It is typically preferable to use encryption that is built into an operating system or program. This enables cryptography to be deployed invisibly, with little or no user involvement. When using the cryptographic features of any operating system or program, be sure you read and understand all vendor documentation. It's also crucial to maintain your operating system or application up to date with the most recent service packs, security patches, and hot fixes. Any cryptographic application that is implemented incorrectly might cause security difficulties for your company. This is particularly true in apps that deal with money or e-commerce. Designing your own cryptography algorithms, employing obsolete cryptographic approaches, or just partly applying standards are all things to avoid.

Balancing security and performance

While applying cryptographic methods may help your business become more secure, it is not a panacea for all challenges. Security specialists must be familiar with the data's confidentiality and integrity challenges. From key exchange through implementation to retirement, each algorithm used on a business must be correctly carried out. When implementing any algorithm, four factors must be considered, such as strength, performance, implementation practicality, and interoperability.

Strength

The size of the key used in an algorithm is frequently used to assess its strength. The algorithm's encryption is stronger when the key is longer. However, although utilizing longer keys might improve the algorithm's strength, it generally leads to poorer performance.

Performance

The key length and algorithm employed determine the method's performance. Symmetric algorithms are quicker than asymmetric algorithms, as previously stated.

Implementation possibilities

Proper planning and design of algorithm implementation guarantee that an algorithm can be executed for security professionals and the businesses they defend.

Interoperability

An algorithm's interoperability refers to its ability to work inside a company. Before trying to incorporate algorithms into their company, security professionals should investigate any known limits.

Block versus stream

If you want to adopt cryptography in your company, you need to think about the consequences. The parts that follow go over stream ciphers and block ciphers in more depth.

Ciphers in the stream

Stream-based ciphers employ keystream generators to execute encryption on a bit-by-bit basis. The plaintext bits are XORed with a bit stream generated by a keystream generator. The Ciphertext is the outcome of this XOR operation. Stream ciphers are used to encrypt video and audio streams. Synchronous stream-based encryption is based only on the key, while an asynchronous stream cipher is based on both the key and the plaintext. The key guarantees that the plaintext is XORed with a random bit stream.

Stream-based ciphers provide the following advantages:

- They are more often employed in hardware implementations since encryption happens on each bit.

- They utilize the same key for encryption and decryption.

- They are typically less expensive to build than block ciphers because they just require confusion rather than diffusion.

Cipher blocks

Block ciphers encrypt messages by dividing them into fixed-length chunks called blocks. A 1,024-bit message might be broken down into 16 blocks of 64 bits each. The algorithm formulae process each of the 16 blocks, resulting in a single block of encrypted text. The data will be padded if it is less than a full block. IDEA, Blowfish, RC5, and RC6 are examples of block ciphers.

The following are some of the benefits of block ciphers:

- Block cipher implementation is simpler than stream-based cipher implementation.

- Block ciphers are less vulnerable to security flaws in general.

- They're more commonly used in software implementations.

- Block ciphers utilize both confusion and diffusion, as well as a variety of modes such as ECB, CBC, CFB, and CTR.

- Modes are used in the implementations of DES and 3DES.

- DES Modes: DES is available in the following five different modes:

    o **Electronic Code Book (ECB)**

    o **Cipher Block Chaining (CBC)**

- o **Cipher Feedback (CFB)**
- o **Output Feedback (OFB)**
- o **Counter mode (CTR)**
- **3DES Modes**: 3DES is available in the following four different modes:
- **3DES-EEE3**: Each block of data is encrypted three times with distinct keys each time.
- **3DES-EDE3**: The first key encrypts the data, the second key decrypts it, and the third key encrypts it again.
- **3DES-EEE2**: Each block of data is encrypted with the first key, then with the second key, and then with the first key again.
- **3DES-EDE2**: Each data block is encrypted with the first key, decrypted with the second key, and then encrypted with the first key again.

Flaws or weaknesses that have been identified

When it comes to cryptographic algorithms, security experts must be aware of their shortcomings or weaknesses. The pros and limitations of symmetric and asymmetric algorithms are initially discussed in this section. Then we go through some of the attacks that may be made against cryptographic algorithms, as well as which algorithms are vulnerable to them. Keep in mind, however, that cryptanalysis evolves on a daily basis. Even the most advanced encryption algorithms have been cracked in the past. As a result, security experts should guarantee that their company's algorithms are maintained up to date and retired after a breach has happened.

Public key infrastructure

While the fundamentals of a PKI have been covered, an organization should also consider advanced PKI concepts such as wildcard, OCSP vs CRL, entity issuance, and key escrow. In addition to the fundamental aspects of **public key infrastructure (PKI),** organizations should explore advanced PKI concepts to enhance security and efficiency. Wildcard certificates simplify management by securing multiple subdomains under a single certificate, but they also pose security risks if compromised. **Online Certificate Status Protocol (OCSP)** vs. **Certificate Revocation Lists (CRL)** is a crucial consideration. OCSP provides real-time revocation status with lower overhead, while CRLs require periodic updates and distribution. Entity issuance involves defining strict policies for certificate provisioning, ensuring only authorized entities receive valid credentials. Key escrow plays a vital role in regulatory compliance and data recovery, allowing a trusted authority to securely store encryption keys for emergency access. Implementing these advanced PKI features strengthens trust, reduces operational risks, and ensures seamless cryptographic management within an enterprise.

Wildcard

A wildcard certificate is a public key certificate that can be used with a domain's multiple subdomains. The following are some of the benefits of using a wildcard certificate:

- A wildcard certificate can secure an unlimited number of subdomains.

- While wildcard certificates are more expensive than single certificates, they are often less expensive than purchasing individual certificates for each subdomain. In certain circumstances, an unlimited server license is available, allowing you to acquire only one wildcard certificate and use it on as many web servers as you need.

- Managing, deploying, and renewing a wildcard certificate is substantially simpler than managing, deploying, and renewing individual certificates for each subdomain.

However, there are several significant drawbacks to utilizing wildcard certificates, which are as follows:

- Some common mobile device operating systems do not understand the wildcard character (*) and, hence, cannot utilize a wildcard certificate.

- If one server in one subdomain is hacked, all servers in all subdomains that use the same wildcard certificate are affected.

Enterprises may have problems with wildcard certificates. If an administrator revokes an SSL certificate for a web server after a security breach, and the certificate is a wildcard certificate, all other servers using that certificate will begin to generate certificate problems. Let us look at a wildcard certificate deployment situation for a minute. A security auditor detects that the SSL certificate was granted to *.pearson.com*, indicating that a wildcard certificate was utilized, after connecting to a secure payment server at **https://payment. pearson.com**. The auditor also finds that a large number of internal development servers use the same certificate. If the USB flash drive containing the SSL certificate is subsequently found to be missing, all of the servers on which this wildcard certificate was installed will need new certificates. In this case, security specialists should install a fresh certificate on the most vulnerable server, which is most likely the *payment.pearson.com* server.

Applications

When a digital certificate is required by an application, suppliers employ the PKI standard to exchange keys through certificates. Before letting the certificate be used by the application, the browser utilizes the relevant keys and validates the trust pathways and revocation status.

Key escrow is the procedure of keeping keys with a third party in order to ensure that they can be decrypted. During investigations, this is most often employed to gather evidence. The process by which the administrator archives a key in a secure location is known as key recovery.

Certificate

The X.509 standard is met by an X.509 certificate. The following fields are included in an X.509 certificate:

- Subject
- Subject public key Info
- Public key algorithm
- Subject public key
- Issuer unique identifier
- Subject unique identifier
- Extensions
- Version
- Serial number
- Algorithm ID
- Issuer
- Validity

The following digital certificate classes were initially offered by VeriSign:

- **Class 1**: Intended for people and sent through email. Web browsers keep track of these certificates. There is no need to provide any true confirmation of identification.
- **Class 2**: For businesses that are required to produce confirmation of identification.
- **Class 3**: For servers and software signing, the issuing CA performs independent verification, identification, and authority checks.
- **Class 4**: For company-to-company Internet commercial transactions.
- **Class 5**: For the protection of commercial companies or government agencies.

Tokens

Tokens are small pieces of hardware that contain digital certificates and private keys. USB devices and smart cards are examples of implementations. *Figure 15.7* depicts an example of a USB token. Tokens play a crucial role in strong authentication by securely storing digital certificates and private keys, ensuring that sensitive cryptographic material remains protected from unauthorized access. These hardware-based security solutions come in various forms, including USB tokens, smart cards, and HSMs, each offering different levels of protection. USB tokens are compact, portable devices that connect directly to a computer, enabling secure authentication for VPN access, digital signatures, and encrypted email communication. Smart cards, often used in enterprise environments, require a card reader and provide multi-factor authentication when combined with a PIN. These tokens enhance security by preventing key extraction and mitigating phishing and credential theft risks. Their integration into PKI ensures robust identity verification and secure transactions.

Figure 15.7: USB token

Graph 15.7 pinning USB tokens

HTTPS websites can be impersonated by attackers using miss-issued or otherwise fraudulent certificates, thanks to public key pinning, which is delivered via an HTTP header. It sends the client (browser) a set of public keys, which should be the only ones trusted for connections to this domain. Public key pinning is a security technique that helps protect against man-in-the-middle attacks where fraudulent certificates might be used to impersonate a legitimate HTTPS website. By utilizing **HTTP Public Key Pinning (HPKP)**, a server sends a set of trusted public keys to the client's browser through an HTTP header, ensuring that only the specified keys are used for future connections. This prevents attackers from using fake or unauthorized certificates, as the browser will only accept certificates that match the pinned keys. However, it's crucial to manage key rotation carefully, as misconfiguration can lead to website inaccessibility. Additionally, pinning is increasingly being replaced by Certificate Transparency and Expect-CT headers for better security and ease of management. This layer of protection is particularly valuable for high-security websites, such as banking platforms and e-commerce sites, where the integrity of the connection is paramount.

Cryptocurrency or blockchain

Cryptography is also used in the implementation of cryptocurrencies, such as bitcoin. A mechanism known as blockchain is used by cryptocurrencies. A blockchain is a growing collection of documents, known as blocks that are connected and safeguarded using encryption. The majority of blockchain is administered via a peer-to-peer network that follows a protocol for verifying new blocks.

Blockchain is a system of recording information in a way that makes it difficult or impossible to change, hack, or cheat the system. Blockchain is essentially a digital ledger of transactions that is duplicated and distributed across the entire network of computer systems on the blockchain. Each block in the chain contains a number of transactions, and every time a new transaction occurs on the blockchain, a record of that transaction is added to every participant's ledger. The decentralized database managed by multiple participants is known as **distributed ledger technology (DLT)**. *Figure 15.8* depicts the blockchain process:

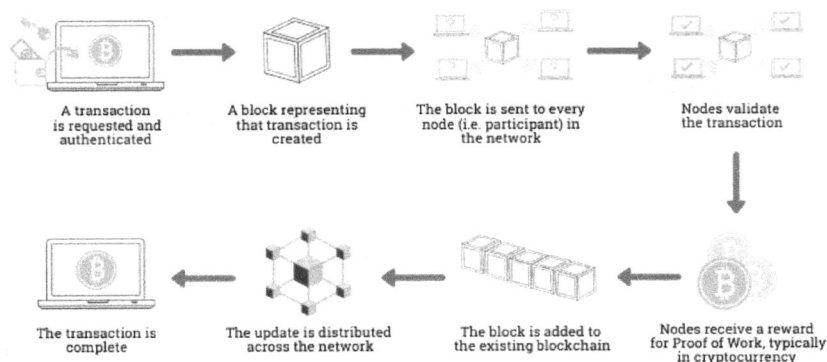

Figure 15.8: Blockchain methodology

Implementing cloud cryptography

The following are the use cases:

- **Use case 1:** Implementing and auditing encryption for data at rest

  Consider a scenario, a financial organization needs to encrypt sensitive customer data stored in a relational database to comply with regulatory requirements like GDPR and PCI DSS.

  Following are the practical implementation:

  - Set up the environment by installing a relational database (for example, PostgreSQL or MySQL) and populate the database with sample customer data.

  - Apply encryption using built-in encryption tools like enabling **Transparent Data Encryption (TDE)** if supported by the database, For MySQL, use InnoDB tablespaces with encryption enabled. Configure the master key and encrypt specific columns containing sensitive information like Social Security Numbers and credit card data. Implement custom encryption for specific columns using AES-256 and a cryptographic library such as PyCryptodome.

  - Assess encryption to verify the encryption implementation by attempting to access the data directly from disk using a hex editor. Use database audit logs to ensure encryption keys are handled securely and that unauthorized access attempts are detected.

    o   Validate compliance by performing a risk assessment using tools like Nessus to ensure the database encryption aligns with compliance frameworks. Document key rotation policies and backup encryption mechanisms.

Following are the commands:

```
# Generate AES-256 encryption key
openssl rand -base64 32 > encryption_key.txt

# Encrypt a sample file
openssl enc -aes-256-cbc -salt -in sensitive_data.txt -out
sensitive_data.enc -pass file:./encryption_key.txt
```

- **Use case 2:** Securing and assessing cloud infrastructure

Consider a scenario, a technology firm is migrating its workloads to a cloud platform (AWS) and must ensure robust security for its virtual machines, storage, and networks.

Following are the practical implementations:

    o   Configure secure infrastructure using AWS **identity and access management (IAM)** to create policies with the principle of least privilege. Enable encryption for S3 buckets using AWS **Key Management Service** (**KMS**).

    o   Set up **virtual private cloud (VPC)** by configuring secure infrastructure. For this set up a VPC with subnets for public-facing services and private back-end components. Use **network access control lists** (**NACLs**) to restrict traffic. Deploy EC2 instances with encrypted **Elastic Block Store (EBS)** volumes for data storage.

    o   Assess security configuration by conducting penetration testing on the cloud infrastructure using tools like Kali Linux. Simulate attacks on exposed services while adhering to AWS's penetration testing policy. Use AWS Trusted Advisor to evaluate security configurations and detect risks. Audit network traffic using VPC Flow Logs to identify unusual patterns.

    o   Validate cloud security by rereviewing AWS CloudTrail logs for unauthorized API calls or anomalous activity. Verify encryption at rest by checking S3 bucket configurations for KMS usage and ensuring no public access.

Following are the commands:

```
#Encrypt S3 Buckets:
aws s3api put-bucket-encryption --bucket example-bucket \
--server-side-encryption-configuration '{
    "Rules": [{
        "ApplyServerSideEncryptionByDefault": {
            "SSEAlgorithm": "aws:kms"
```

```
        }
    }]
}'
```

```
# Check EC2 Security Group Configuration
aws ec2 describe-security-groups --group-ids sg-123abc
```

- **Use case 3**: Implementing and evaluating blockchain for supply chain integrity

Consider the scenario, a logistics company wants to leverage blockchain to enhance the transparency and integrity of its supply chain.

Following are the practical implementation:

o Blockchain network setup using Ethereum to deploy a private blockchain network with tools like Ganache or Hyperledger Fabric. Create smart contracts to track the lifecycle of goods (e.g., manufacturing, shipping, delivery).

o Smart contract development is done by writing a smart contract in Solidity for tracking products. For example, a contract to update the status of goods at each checkpoint and smart contract deployed on the Ethereum blockchain.

o Evaluate blockchain security using tools like MythX to analyze smart contracts for vulnerabilities such as reentrancy or integer overflows and test the consensus mechanisms by simulating malicious nodes.

o Integration and assessment is done by developing a front-end dashboard that interacts with the blockchain using Web3.js or ethers.js. Then assessing blockchain performance is performed, including transaction latency and throughput, using tools like Caliper.

Following are the commands:

```
# Deploying a Smart Contract (Solidity):
pragma solidity ^0.8.0;

contract SupplyChain {
    struct Product {
        string name;
        string status;
    }

    mapping(uint => Product) public products;

    function updateStatus(uint productId, string memory
```

```
newStatus) public {
        products[productId].status = newStatus;
    }
}
```

```
# Compiling and Deploying the Contract:
```

Use Remix IDE or Hardhat to compile and deploy the smart contract on a test network like Rinkeby.

```
# Command for Ganache:
ganache-cli --port 8545 --networkId 5777
```

Following are the validation and practical assessment:

o   Confirm immutability by querying product records at different checkpoints.

o   Simulate double-spending attacks to ensure consensus resilience.

Implementing advanced cryptographic solutions

Secure multi-party computation (SMPC) for privacy-preserving ML is done by training an ML model on sensitive data distributed across multiple organizations (for example, hospitals and financial institutions) without revealing individual data points. This is crucial for collaborative research and data analysis while maintaining patient privacy or competitive advantage. Several hospitals want to jointly train a model to predict disease outbreaks but cannot share raw patient data due to privacy regulations (HIPAA). Each hospital encrypts its local data using homomorphic encryption. The encrypted data is then combined and processed using SMPC protocols. The final trained model can be generated without any individual hospital revealing their underlying patient information. Utilize a framework like secure **Multi-Party Computation Toolkit (MP-SPDZ)** or Sharemind. Implement a simple machine learning algorithm (for example, linear regression) using SMPC techniques. Experiment with different data distribution scenarios and observe the impact on accuracy and performance.

Post-quantum cryptography (PQC) for long-term data security protects long-term sensitive data (for example, government archives and digital assets) from the threat of quantum computers. Quantum computers could potentially break widely used public-key cryptography algorithms like RSA and ECC. A government agency needs to encrypt highly classified documents for decades to come. Implement encryption using post-quantum algorithms such as CRYSTALS-Kyber (for key exchange) and CRYSTALS-Dilithium (for digital signatures), which are considered resistant to attacks from both classical and quantum computers. Use libraries like **Open Quantum Safe (OQS)** to experiment with PQC algorithms. Implement a secure communication channel using a PQC-based key exchange protocol. Analyze the performance and resource consumption of different PQC algorithms compared to traditional public-key cryptography.

Analyze security requirements for various cryptographic techniques (for example, blockchain, PKI, SSL/TLS).

- **Analyzing security requirements for cryptographic techniques**: Cryptographic techniques are essential tools for securing digital information and communications. However, the effectiveness of these techniques depends heavily on a thorough analysis of security requirements. This analysis involves identifying the specific threats and vulnerabilities that the cryptographic system needs to address, as well as the desired security properties that the system should provide. Several key security requirements must be considered when analyzing cryptographic techniques:

    o **Confidentiality**: Ensures that only authorized parties can access and understand the information. This is achieved through encryption, which transforms data into an unreadable format unless the recipient has the appropriate decryption key.

    o **Integrity**: Guarantees that the information has not been tampered with or modified during transmission or storage. This is typically achieved through the use of hash functions and digital signatures.

    o **Authentication**: Verifies the identity of the sender or receiver of the information. This can be accomplished through various methods, such as digital certificates, passwords, and biometrics.

    o **Non-repudiation**: Prevents the sender of information from denying that they sent it. This is typically achieved through digital signatures, which create a unique cryptographic hash of the message that cannot be altered.

    o **Availability**: Ensures that the cryptographic system is accessible and functional when needed. This requires careful consideration of system reliability, fault tolerance, and disaster recovery mechanisms.

Security requirements for three prominent cryptographic techniques such as blockchain, PKI, and SSL/TLS:

- **Blockchain**: Blockchain is a DLT that provides a secure and transparent way to record transactions. The security requirements for blockchain systems include:

    o **Immutability**: Ensures that once a transaction is recorded on the blockchain, it cannot be altered or deleted. This is achieved through cryptographic hashing and consensus mechanisms.

    o **Transparency**: Allows anyone to view the transactions on the blockchain, while maintaining privacy for individual users. This is typically accomplished through pseudonymity, where users are identified by unique identifiers rather than their real names.

    o **Decentralization**: Distributes the ledger across multiple nodes, making it resistant to censorship and single points of failure.

o **Consensus**: Ensures that all nodes on the network agree on the state of the ledger. This is achieved through various consensus algorithms, such as **proof-of-work (PoW)** and **proof-of-stake (PoS).**

- **Public key infrastructure (PKI):** PKI is a system for managing digital certificates, which are used to verify the authenticity of entities (for example, individuals, organizations, and devices) and to encrypt and decrypt data. The security requirements for PKI systems include:

  o **Certificate Authority (CA) reliability**: Ensures that the CAs issuing certificates are trustworthy and follow strict security procedures.

  o **Key management**: Securely generates, stores, and distributes cryptographic keys.

  o **Certificate revocation**: Provides a mechanism for revoking compromised certificates, preventing unauthorized access.

  o **Time synchronization**: Maintains accurate time synchronization between different systems to ensure the validity of certificates.

- **Secure sockets layer (SSL) / transport layer security (TLS):** SSL/TLS is a cryptographic protocol that provides secure communication over computer networks. It is widely used to secure web traffic (HTTPS), but it can also be used for other applications, such as email and file transfer. The security requirements for SSL/TLS include:

  o **Confidentiality**: Encrypts the data transmitted between the client and server, preventing eavesdropping.

  o **Integrity**: Ensures that the data has not been tampered with during transmission.

  o **Authentication**: Verifies the identity of the server and, optionally, the client. This is typically achieved using digital certificates.

  o **Forward secrecy**: Ensures that if the server's long-term private key is compromised, past communication sessions remain secure.

Analyzing security requirements for cryptographic techniques requires a systematic approach. This typically involves the following steps:

1. **Identify the threat model**: Determine the potential threats and attacks that the system could face. This may include internal and external threats, such as malicious insiders, hackers, and nation-state actors.

2. **Define security objectives**: Specify the desired security properties that the system should provide, such as confidentiality, integrity, authentication, and non-repudiation.

3. **Select appropriate cryptographic techniques**: Choose the cryptographic algorithms and protocols that are best suited to meet the identified security requirements.

4. **Implement and test**: Implement the cryptographic system and conduct rigorous testing to ensure that it meets the specified security requirements.

5. **Monitor and maintain**: Continuously monitor the system for any vulnerabilities or threats and take appropriate action to maintain the system's security.

Conclusion

In this chapter, we discussed techniques for key stretching, hashing, digital signatures, and message authentication, including code signing and pseudo-random number generation. Related topics such as perfect forward secrecy, data-in-transit encryption, data-in-memory/processing, data-at-rest encryption, and steganography were also covered in this chapter. Cryptographic modules, processors, service providers, DRM, watermarking, GPG, SSL/TLS, SSH, S/MIME, cryptographic applications, and proper or improper implementations, stream versus block, PKI, cryptocurrency/blockchain, mobile device encryption considerations, and ECC were also discussed briefly.

In the next chapter, we will discuss authentication, authorization, and attestation, including identity verification and propagation of identity.

Exercise

1. **Which of the following is the primary purpose of key stretching?**

    a. To encrypt data with a stronger key

    b. To increase the length of encryption keys

    c. To make brute force attacks more difficult by applying additional computational work

    d. To securely transmit encryption keys over insecure channels

2. **What is the primary purpose of a cryptographic hash function?**

    a. To encrypt data for secure transmission

    b. To generate a fixed-length output from variable-length input

    c. To verify the integrity of encrypted data

    d. To store data securely in databases

3. **What is the primary use of a digital signature?**

    a. To provide encryption for data in transit

    b. To authenticate the sender and ensure data integrity

    c.   To ensure the data is only readable by the recipient

    d.   To verify the encryption algorithm used

4.   **Which of the following best describes Perfect Forward Secrecy (PFS)?**

    a.   A method to ensure data remains encrypted during storage

    b.   A cryptographic property ensuring session keys cannot be derived from long-term keys

    c.   A technique to validate digital signatures

    d.   A process for ensuring data integrity in transit

5.   **Which of the following is used to protect data during transmission over a network?**

    a.   Disk encryption

    b.   Public Key Infrastructure (PKI)

    c.   Encryption of data in transit

    d.   File-level encryption

6.   **What is the purpose of IPsec in network security?**

    a.   To enable encryption of data stored on hard drives

    b.   To ensure data is encrypted during transit over an IP network

    c.   To provide secure authentication of web servers

    d.   To protect passwords from brute-force attacks

7.   **Which of the following techniques is most commonly used to secure data-in-memory?**

    a.   Full disk encryption

    b.   Data masking

    c.   Secure memory management techniques and encryption

    d.   Public key cryptography

8.   **Which of the following is a technique to secure data when it is stored on a device?**

    a.   TLS encryption

    b.   End-to-end encryption

    c.   Encryption of data at rest

    d.   Hashing of files

9. **Which of the following is a characteristic of symmetric encryption algorithms?**

    a. The same key is used for both encryption and decryption

    b. Different keys are used for encryption and decryption

    c. They are slower than asymmetric algorithms

    d. They cannot be used for bulk data encryption

10. **Which type of encryption applies to an entire disk to secure all the data stored on it?**

    a. File-level encryption

    b. Block-level encryption

    c. Disk-level encryption

    d. Record-level encryption

11. **What is the main characteristic of block-level encryption?**

    a. It encrypts data at the file level

    b. It encrypts data in fixed-size blocks

    c. It encrypts individual records of data

    d. It provides encryption for network traffic

12. **What does record-level encryption protect?**

    a. The entire file

    b. Specific fields or records within a file

    c. The operating system

    d. Data in transit between servers

13. **What is the main purpose of steganography?**

    a. To encrypt data

    b. To hide data within other data

    c. To secure data in transit

    d. To generate cryptographic keys

Answers

1. c

2. b

3. b

4. b

5. c

6. b

7. c

8. c

9. a

10. c

11. b

12. b

13. b

Join our book's Discord space

Join the book's Discord Workspace for Latest updates, Offers, Tech happenings around the world, New Release and Sessions with the Authors:

https://discord.bpbonline.com

## CHAPTER 16

Identification, Authentication, and Authorization

Introduction

Identification of persons and devices, as well as determining the actions that a person or device is permitted to undertake, are at the heart of access control models. While this paradigm has stayed consistent since network computing's conception, the methodologies for conducting this key set of activities have developed tremendously and continue to do so.

While simple usernames and passwords have historically served as access control, in today's world, more complicated and secure approaches are fast developing. Not only are such primitive approaches no longer secure, but today's access credential systems value convenience above everything else. Single sign-on and federated access control are two techniques for making a system as user-friendly as possible. The newest authentication and authorization approaches and processes are discussed in this chapter.

Structure

In this chapter, we will cover the following topics:

- Authentication
- Authorization
- Attestation

- Identity propagation
- Federation
- Advanced authentication management strategies

Objective

This chapter covers certificate-based authentication, single sign-on, 802.1x, context-aware authentication, and push-based authentication. The objective of attestation, as well as OAuth, XACML, and SPML, are covered. SAML, OpenID, Shibboleth, and WAYF are all explored, as are identity proofing techniques, as well as the challenges and benefits of identity propagation. RADIUS, LDAP, and AD configurations are also covered.

Authentication

To get access to a resource, a user must verify their identity, provide the necessary credentials, and have the necessary permissions to execute the tasks they are completing. As a consequence, there are two distinct sections, which are as follows:

- **Identification**: A user identifies themselves to an access control system in the first phase.
- **Authentication**: The second stage comprises providing the appropriate credentials to authenticate a user's unique identity.

When seeking to differentiate between these two components, security professionals should remember that identification identifies the person, whereas authentication verifies the authenticity of the user's identity. Authentication is often accomplished by entering a user password at the time of login. The login method should validate the login when all of the input data has been submitted. The most prevalent types of user identification are user IDs or user accounts, account numbers, and **personal identity numbers (PINs)**, as illustrated in *Figure 16.1*:

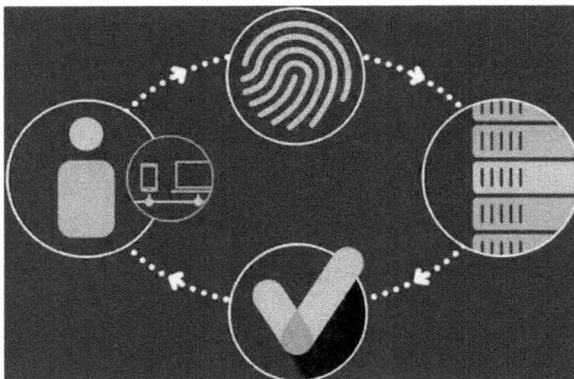

Figure 16.1: Authentication

Authentication factors

After the user identification mechanism has been developed, an organization must decide which authentication approach to employ. Authentication methods are divided into the following five categories:

- The knowledge of a person is employed as part of the authentication process.
- A person's possession is an aspect of ownership authentication.
- **Authentication factor**: A characteristic that distinguishes a person.
- The location of a person is utilized as a part of the authentication process.
- An authentication factor is a person's activity.

During authentication, a single-factor authentication ensures that a user provides at least one element from each of these categories. This may be shown by entering a username and password upon login. The user must provide two of the three factors when utilizing two-factor authentication. The two-factor authentication is shown by logging in using a username, password, and smart card. A user must provide three separate pieces of information when using three-factor authentication. Three-factor authentication entails using a username, password, smart card, and fingerprint to log in. For authentication to be considered strong, a user must provide components from at least two different categories. (It is important to note that the username is only identification and not an authentication factor.)

It is vital to note that a single-factor authentication is defined as the use of several authentication factors from the same category. When a user provides a login, password, and the user's mother's maiden name, single-factor authentication is used. In this situation, the user is still only providing information that a person is aware of.

Knowledge-based factors

The knowledge factor is based on a person's knowledge of a subject. For this sort of authentication, a Sort-I authentication factor is employed. Additional knowledge factors such as date of birth, mother's maiden name, key combination, or PIN may be used in addition to password authentication.

Ownership affecting factors

As previously stated, ownership factor authentication is a kind of authentication that is based on a person's possession of something. For this sort of authentication, a Form II authentication factor is employed. Some instances of ownership considerations are as follows:

- **Token devices**: A token device is a small device that transmits a one-time password to the authentication server. If the authentication method requires the use of a token device, the user must have the device on hand to authenticate. Despite sending a password to the authentication server, the token device is designated as a Type II authentication factor since its use necessitates device ownership. Due to the high cost of establishing a token device, it is often reserved for the most secure settings. Furthermore, owing to the battery life of the token device, challenges with token-based systems may arise.

- **Memory cards**: A valid user is given a memory card, which functions as a swipe card. The user's authentication information is stored on the card. When the card is swiped through a card reader, the information captured on the card is compared to the information input by the user. If the information is valid, the authentication server accepts the login. If the two do not match, authentication is denied. Because the card must be read by a card reader, each computer or access device must have its own card reader. In addition, the cards must be created and programmed. Both of these techniques add to the complexity and cost of the authentication process. The increased security it provides, however, is usually worth the added complexity and cost, which is a clear benefit of this method. The data on the memory cards, on the other hand, is not protected, which is a weakness that companies should be aware of before using this strategy. Memory cards are fairly easy to falsify.

- **Smart cards**: A smart card is similar to a memory card in that it accepts, stores, and transmits data, but it has a bigger storage capacity. Smart cards, also known as **Integrated Circuit Cards (ICCs)**, include embedded circuits similar to those used in bank or credit cards, as well as memory akin to memory cards. Smart cards are read using card readers. The authentication server, on the other hand, uses the data on a smart card without the requirement for user input. To protect against lost or stolen smart cards, most implementations require the user to input a secret PIN, meaning that the user is providing both Type I (PIN) and Type II (smart card) authentication factors.

Characteristics

As previously stated, characteristic factor authentication is authentication based on who a person is. For this sort of authentication, a Form III authentication factor is employed. Biometric technology is a kind of authentication that verifies a user's identification by using physiological or behavioral factors. Physiological features include any unique physical property of the user, such as the iris, retina, and fingerprints. Behavioral factors that measure a person's behaviors in a situation include voice patterns and data input characteristics.

Concepts of authentication that are not authentic

The following are some more authentication concepts that all security experts should be aware of:

- **Time-based one-time password method** (**TOTP**): This is a password-generating technique that generates a password using a shared secret and the current time. It is similar to HOTP, except that it utilizes an integer-based counter instead of the current time.

- **HMAC-based one-time password method** (**HOTP**): This method generates a password using a shared secret that is only used once. This is achieved by employing a synchronized incrementing counter on both the client and the server.

- **Single sign-on** (**SSO**): This functionality is accessible when an authentication system requires a user to authenticate just once in order to access all network resources.

Management of accounts and identity

Identity and account management are required for every authentication system. As a security professional, you must ensure that your organization has a system in place to handle the creation and distribution of access credentials or identities. If invalid accounts are allowed to be created and not terminated, security breaches will occur. Most firms set up a system to verify the identification and authentication method to ensure that user accounts are current. The following are a few questions that may be useful in the process:

- Is there a current, up-to-date, and approved list of permitted users and their permissions?

- Do you change your passwords at least once every 90 days or more often as needed?

- Is it true that inactive user accounts expire after a specific period of time?

As part of any identity management approach, users must be created, modified, and deleted from the access control system. When establishing an account, a new user should be prompted to produce an adequate photo identity and sign a disclaimer about password security. One-of-a-kind user accounts are required. There should be policies in place to standardize the structure of user accounts. For example, all user accounts should be called firstname.lastname or have another structure. This ensures that users inside an organization can determine the identification of a new user, which is helpful for communication.

Once created, user accounts should be maintained to ensure that they remain active. Inactive accounts should be automatically deleted after a predetermined period of inactivity, depending on business demands. A termination policy should also include procedures for deactivating or deleting all user accounts. The components of excellent account management are as follows:

- Establish a method for generating, issuing, and deleting user accounts that is methodical.

- Conduct frequent audits of user accounts.

- Create a system for keeping track of access authorizations.

- Regularly rescreen personnel in critical jobs.

- Ensure that user accounts are valid on a frequent basis.

Examining user accounts is a crucial component of account management. User accounts should be checked to see whether they adhere to the principle of least privilege (which is explained later in this chapter). User account assessments may be done on an enterprise-wide, system-wide, or application-by-application basis. The size of the company will have a significant influence on the technique employed. As part of their user account assessments, organizations should verify that all user accounts are active.

Password management

Password authentication is the most extensively used authentication technique today, as explained earlier in this chapter. Password types, on the other hand, may vary from one system to the next. You must be acquainted with the many types of passwords that may be used. The following are some password samples that you should be familiar with:

- **Standard word passwords**: This kind of password is made up of a single word with a mix of capital and lowercase letters, as the name implies. This password has the advantage of being easy to remember. However, this password type has the issue of being easy to crack or break for attackers, which might lead to a compromised account.

- **Combination passwords**: These are passwords made up of a few dictionary terms; usually two unrelated words. Like conventional word passwords, they may include capital and lowercase letters as well as numerals. This form of a password has the advantage of being more difficult to break than a standard word password. One disadvantage is that it may be difficult to remember.

- **Static passwords**: These are the passwords that are used every time you log in. Because the password is never updated, it provides only rudimentary security. **Peer-to-peer** (P2P) networks are the most prevalent.

- **Complex passwords**: When generating a complex password, a user must use a mix of upper- and lowercase letters, numerals, and special characters. Many businesses now demand this kind of password as part of their password rules. This password has the advantage of being very tough to crack. One disadvantage is that it is more difficult to remember and, in many cases, far more difficult to enter precisely.

- **Passphrases**: A long-phrase is required for this kind of password. Because the password is longer, it is easier to remember while also being much more difficult to break, which are both important advantages. Because it contains upper- and lowercase letters, numerals, and special characters, this kind of password may significantly improve authentication security.

- **Cognitive passwords**: A cognitive password is a piece of information that may be used to verify an individual's identity. This information is sent to the system by the user answering a series of questions about themselves, such as their favorite color, pet's name, mother's maiden name, and so on. The ability of customers to recollect this information is a benefit of this kind. The disadvantage is that someone who is closely familiar with the person's life (spouse, child, sibling, etc.) may also be able to provide this information.

- **One-time passwords (OTPs)**: A one-time password, also known as a dynamic password, is a one-time password that is used just once to log into an access control system. This password provides the highest level of protection since it is erased after one use.

- **Graphical passwords**: Also known as **Completely Automated Public Turing Test to Tell Computers and Humans Apart** (CAPTCHA) passwords, these use pictures to help with authentication. In one popular approach, a user must enter a string of characters that display in a visual. This method ensures that a human rather than a machine enters the password. Another common way involves the user selecting the appropriate graphic for his account from a library of photographs.

- **Numeric passwords**: These are passwords that are made up entirely of numbers. Keep in mind that the maximum number of digits you may use in a password is limited. The maximum number of potential passwords is 10,000, spanning from 0000 to 9999 if all passwords are four digits. Because the attacker will be aware of the alternatives, cracking user passwords will be much easier if they realize that only numbers are used.

Passwords, one-time passwords, token devices, and login phrases are all considered to be less secure than simple passwords. A corporation must establish password management policies after deciding on the kind of password to use. Password management considerations may include, but are not limited to the following:

- **Password life**: How long will a password be valid? In most businesses, passwords are good for 60 to 90 days.

- **Password history**: How long does a password have to be used before it may be reused? Most password rules only keep track of a certain number of previously used passwords.

- **Authentication period**: This indicates the length of time a user may be logged in without doing anything; if a user remains logged in for the specified amount of time without doing anything, they will be logged out instantly.

- **Password complexity**: This indicates the combination of upper- and lowercase letters, numerals, and special characters required by most firms.

- **Password length**: Most companies need passwords to be between eight and twelve characters long.

As part of password management, a system for upgrading passwords should be developed. Most companies provide a feature that allows customers' passwords to be automatically changed before they expire. In the event that users forget their passwords or the credentials are compromised, most firms should consider implementing a password reset procedure. A self-service password reset technique allows users to reset their passwords without the assistance of a help desk representative. Customers must call the support line for assistance in resetting their passwords using an assisted password reset process.

Other organizational rules, such as account lockout policies, might affect password reset processes. Businesses employ account lockout policies as a security strategy to protect themselves against password attacks. Organizations often set up account lockout policies that lock user accounts after a certain number of unsuccessful login attempts. If the user account has been shut out, the system administrator may need to unlock or re-enable it. Security experts should push businesses to require users to reset their passwords if their accounts have been locked. Most companies impose all password restrictions, including account lockout rules, at the enterprise level on the servers that govern the network.

Depending on which servers are used to run the company, security specialists must be aware of the security concerns that affect user accounts and password management. The two most popular server operating systems are Linux and Windows.

- UNIX/Linux passwords are saved in the **/etc/passwd** or **/etc/shadow** files. Because the **/etc/passwd** file is unencrypted and easily readable, all Linux servers should utilize the /etc/shadow file, which employs a hash to protect the passwords. The root user is a default account in Linux that has full administrative access to the system. If the root account is compromised, all passwords should be changed. The root account should be accessible only to system administrators, and root login should be done via a system console.

- For Windows Server 2003 and before, as well as all client versions of Windows in workgroups, the **Security Accounts Manager (SAM)** records user passwords in a hashed format. A password is kept in the form of a **LAN Manager (LM)** or **NT LAN Manager (NTLM)** hash. However, there are known security flaws with a SAM, especially with LM hashes, such as the ability to extract password hashes directly from the registry. You should follow all Microsoft-recommended security practices to protect this file. You should either rename or deactivate the default administrator account if you are in control of a Windows network. Make sure you give this account a password if you intend to maintain it. The default administrator account on a Windows server may have full access. Most versions of Windows may be configured to prohibit the creation and storing of valid LM hashes when a user changes her password. Although it was disabled by default in prior versions of Windows, this is the default option in Windows Vista and the following versions of Windows.

Physiological characteristics

In physiological systems, a biometric scanning device is used to examine particular information about a physiological trait. It is important to understand the following physiological biometric systems:

- **Fingerprint scan**: This form of scan examines a finger's ridges to determine whether they match. Minutiae matching, a kind of fingerprint scan that records bifurcations and other minute characteristics, is much smaller. Minutiae matching takes longer and takes up more capacity on the authentication server than ridge fingerprint scans. A fingerprint scanning system will be used and shared.

- **Finger scan**: This kind of scan only recovers certain fingerprint features. Because just a tiny percentage of the fingerprint information is needed, finger scans require less server space and processing time than other kinds of fingerprint scans.

- **Hand geometry scan**: This kind of scan is used to figure out the size, form, and other layout aspects of a user's hand, as well as bone length and finger length. Mechanical and image-edge detective systems are two forms of hand geometry systems. Hand geometry scanners use less server space and processing time than fingerprint or finger scans, regardless of which category is used.

    A hand topography scan records the hand's peaks and valleys as well as its shape. Hand topography scans are typically used in conjunction with hand geometry scans since they are not unique enough when used alone.

    Fingerprint and hand geometry technologies are combined in a palm or hand scan. It keeps track of the fingerprints on each finger as well as the hand's geometry.

- **Facial scan**: This kind of scan records data about your face, including bone structure, eye width, and forehead size. In this biometric method, eigenfeatures and eigenfaces are utilized.

- **Retina scan**: This kind of scan examines the pattern of blood vessels in the retina. Iris scanning is less intrusive than retina scanning.

- **Iris scan**: An iris scan examines the colored portion of the eye, as well as any rifts, corneas, or furrows. Iris scans have a better level of precision than other biometric scans.

- **Vascular scan**: This scan examines the user's vein pattern in their hand or face. While this process is a great option since it is non-invasive, depending on which system is utilized, physical harm to the hand or face may result in false rejections.

Behavior characteristics

In behavioral systems, a biometric scanning device is used to assess a person's behavior. It is important to understand the following behavioral biometric systems:

- **Signature dynamics**: This kind of technology tracks the speed, pressure, acceleration, and deceleration of the user's signature stroke. **Dynamic signature verification (DSV)** looks at the features of signatures as well as specific components of the signing process.

- **Keystroke dynamics**: This technology analyses a user's typing pattern as they type a password or another predetermined text. If the correct password or phrase is entered but the input pattern on the keyboard does not match the recorded value, the user will be denied access. In keystroke dynamics, flight time refers to the length of time it takes to migrate between keys. Dwell time refers to how long you keep a key pressed.

- **Voice pattern or print**: When a user pronounces particular words, this kind of technology analyses their voice pattern. When attempting to log in, the user will be asked to repeat the words in reverse order. If the pattern matches, authentication is allowed.

Biometrics considerations

Security experts should be familiar with the following terminology when it comes to biometrics:

- **Enrolment time**: This is the time it takes to acquire a sample for the biometric system. This technique has a number of stages that must be completed many times.

- **Methodology:** This is for obtaining biometric data from a sample of a user's physiological or behavioral traits is feature extraction.

- **Accuracy**: Accuracy is the most important aspect of biometric technologies. It has to do with the precision of the overall readings.

- **Throughput Rate**: This refers to how quickly a biometric system can scan and evaluate characteristics in order to allow or deny access. It is recommended that participants move at a rate of 6 to 10 per minute. A single user should be able to complete the procedure in 5 to 10 seconds.

- **Acceptability**: This relates to people's willingness to accept and follow the system.

- **False Rejection Rate (FRR):** This is a metric that indicates how many legitimate consumers the system would mistakenly reject. A Type I error is what it is called.

- **False Acceptance Rate (FAR):** This is a measure of how many invalid users will be wrongly accepted by the system. This is known as a Type II blunder. Type II mistakes are more hazardous than type I faults.

- **Crossover Error Rate (CER)**: This is the point at which FRR and FAR are equal. The most important metric is presented in percentages.

Security professionals sometimes utilize a Zephyr chart to evaluate biometric systems, which displays the relative strengths and weaknesses of biometric systems. However, you should consider the success of each biometric technique as well as user acceptance. When considering FAR, FRR, and CER, keep in mind that lower figures are preferable. FAR errors are more dangerous than FRR errors. Security specialists may use the CER for comparative analysis while aiding their company in determining which system to use. For example, voice print systems have a higher CER than iris scans, hand geometry, or fingerprints.

Multi-factor authentication

Combining information, characteristics, and behavioral elements may increase the security of an authentication system. When this is done, the phrase used is dual-factor or **multi-factor authentication** (**MFA**). MFA contains all three factors, while dual-factor authentication combines two authentication components (for example, a knowledge component and a behavioral factor). The following are a few examples:

- Dual-factor authentication, as illustrated in *Figure 16.2*, is a password (knowledge factor) and a one-time password (characteristic factor):

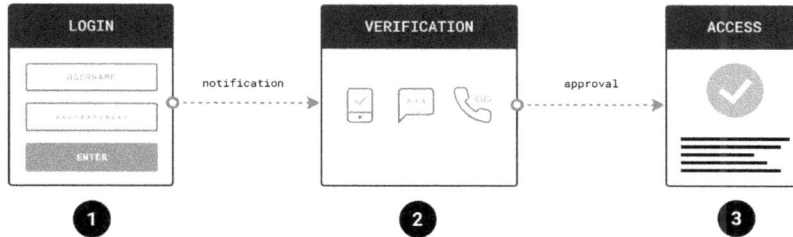

Figure 16.2: *Two factor authentication*

- Multi-factor, as presented in *Figure 16.3*, is PIN (knowledge factor), retina scan (characteristic factor), and signature dynamics (behavioral component):

Figure 16.3: *Multiple factor authentication*

Using certificates for authentication

When a system's authentication is based on certificates rather than passwords or PINs, the system's security is likely to be considerably enhanced. A digital certificate provides credentials to verify an entity's identity and links that identity to a public key, which is usually a user. At the very least, a digital certificate must contain the serial number, issuer, subject (owner), and public key. When employing certificate-based authentication, you will need to set up a **public key infrastructure** (**PKI**). A PKI consists of the systems, software, and communication protocols that distribute, manage, and control public key cryptography (PKI). A PKI issues digital certificates. Because it creates confidence within an environment, a PKI may certify that a public key is associated with an entity and verify that a public key is valid. Public keys are provided through digital certificates. In certain instances, trusting the certificates of another organization or vice versa may be essential. Cross-certification establishes confidence between **Certification Authorities** (**CAs**), enabling them to rely on other participants' digital certificates and public keys. Users may check each other's certificates when they are certified under different certification hierarchies. When a cross-certification trust relationship exists, a CA for one firm may be able to recognize digital certificates issued by a CA for another company. By using a SSO, you may save time and effort.

A user only has to enter his login credentials once to have access to all network resources in a SSO system. The Open Group Security Forum has defined a number of objectives for SSO systems. Some of the aims for a user sign-on interface and user account management are as follows:

- Regardless of the kind of authentication data handled, the user interface should be agnostic.

- Creating, deleting, and changing user accounts should all be available.

- With assistance, a user should be able to build a default user profile.

- The user interface should be independent of the platform and operating system.

The following are some of the advantages of using an SSO system:

- Users may create stronger passwords.

- User management and password administration are simpler.

- Getting to resources is a lot faster now.

- The user login procedure has been improved.

- Users only need to remember the login credentials for one system.

- Once a user has been granted system access via the initial SSO login, he has access to all resources to which he has been granted access.

- If a user's credentials are stolen, the attackers will have access to all of the user's resources.

While much of the discussion around SSO has focused on how it may be used for networks and domains, it can also be used for web-based services. **Enterprise access management** (**EAM**) provides access control management for web-based business applications. Support for a variety of authentication systems, as well as **role-based access control** (**RBAC**), are among its features. The web access control architecture in this example offers authentication and transmits attributes to a variety of applications through an HTTP header.

SSO entails a secondary authentication domain that depends on and trusts a primary domain to perform the following task:

Correctly assert the end user's identity and authentication credentials to the secondary domain for allowed usage by protecting the authentication credentials used to validate the end user's identity to the secondary domain.

Context-aware authentication

Context-aware or context-dependent access control is based on subject or object characteristics and environmental factors. These variables include things like location and time of the day. Assume that administrators have implemented a security policy that restricts users to logging in only at particular hours of the day from a specific workstation.

Push authentication

When a user accesses a protected resource, a notification is delivered to the user's device, which is often a smartphone, through a secure network. With push-based authentication, device possession becomes the main mode of authentication. To get access, the smartphone must be in the hands of someone who can reply correctly to a text message.

Authorization

After a person has been verified, resources must be made available to him or her. Authorization is the name of the process. Authorization necessitates the identification and authentication processes. Furthermore, standards for managing authorization functions have emerged in the form of OAuth, XACML, and SPML, as presented in *Figure 16.4*:

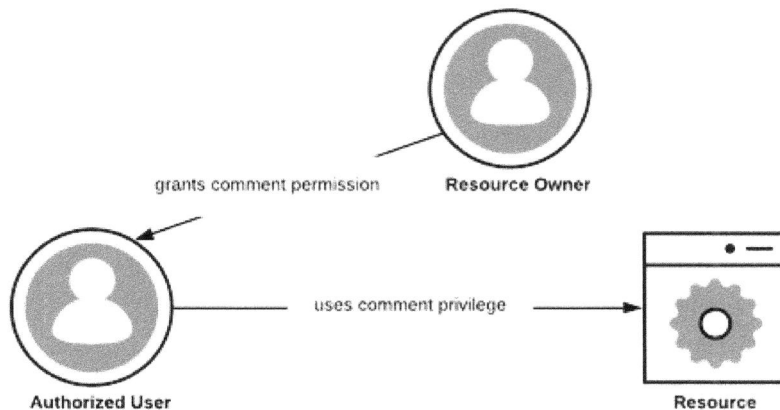

Figure 16.4: *Authorization*

Access control models

An access control model is a formal description of an organization's security policy, as presented in *Figure 16.5*. To make access control administration simpler, access control models are used to group things and themes. Subjects are entities that desire access to an object or data contained inside an object. Users, applications, and processes are among the topics covered. Objects are data-carrying or function-performing entities. Computers, databases, files, apps, directories, and fields are examples of objects. Secure items must not flow to objects with a lower category in a safe access control paradigm. Access control concepts and principles you should be aware of include discretionary access control, mandatory access control, RBAC, RBAC, content dependent access control, **access control matrix (ACM)**, and **access control list (ACL)**. *Figure 16.5* illustrates the access control models:

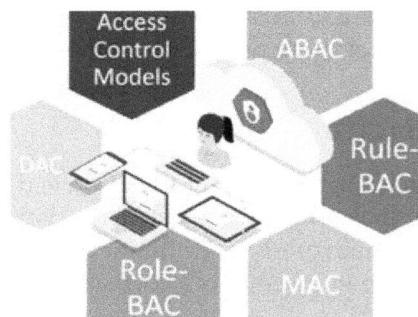

Figure 16.5: Access control models

Discretionary access control

Discretionary access control (DAC) is used by the item's owner to decide which subjects have access to the resource. DAC is often used in local and dynamic situations. Who has access is determined by the subject's identity, profile, or role. The DAC control is considered a **need-to-know** parameter. DAC may be an administrative burden since the data custodian or owner gives access credentials to users. Under DAC, a person's rights must be ended when he or she leaves an organization. DAC is a subset of identity-based access control, which is based on the user's identity or participation in a group. The subject's identity is checked against the object's ACL in DAC. The polar opposite of DAC is non-DAC. In non-DAC, access restrictions are established by a security administrator or another authority. The central authority selects which subjects have access to objects based on the organization's policy.

Mandatory access control

In required access control, subject approval is based on security labels (MAC). MAC is frequently referred to be limiting since it is based on a security label system. Under MAC, everything that is not expressly approved is banned. The category of a resource may only be changed by administrators. DAC is more flexible and extensible than MAC, despite MAC's superior security. This is because of the importance of security in MAC, labeling is required. Data classification reflects the sensitivity of the data. In a MAC system, a clearance is a privilege. Each subject and item is given a security or sensitivity designation. Security labels are presented in a logical order. Commercial businesses may be classified as private, proprietary, corporate, sensitive, or public in terms of security. Government or military groups may be classified as top secret, secret, confidential, or unclassified, depending on their level of security. When the clearance level of a person is compared to the security label of an item, MAC determines access decisions.

Role-based access control

Under RBAC, each subject is assigned to one or more roles. The roles are grouped in a hierarchical manner, and the roles define access control. RBAC may be used to simply assign minimal privileges to subjects. RBAC is used to implement different access control policies for bank tellers and loan officers. RBAC is less secure than the previously described access control systems since it is based on roles. RBAC is utilized in commercial applications since it is less expensive to build than the other varieties. It is a fantastic solution for firms with a high turnover rate. RBAC may effectively replace DAC and MAC since it allows you to specify and apply corporate security policies in a way that suits the organization's structure. There are four main techniques to regulate RBAC. There are no positions available in non-RBAC. Under limited RBAC, users are allocated to single application roles; however, some applications do not support RBAC and need identity-based access. In hybrid RBAC, each user is assigned to a single role that allows them access to several systems, but they may also be assigned to additional roles that provide them access to single systems. Users are allocated to a single role based on the organization's security policy, and organizational roles restrict access to systems.

Rules-based access control

Using rule-based access control, data permissions may be altered more often. This approach is used to construct a security policy by imposing global rules on all users. Profiles are used to manage access. Many routers and firewalls employ this kind of access control to identify which packet types are allowed on a network. Rules may be defined to enable or limit access based on the packet type, the port number used, the MAC address, and other factors.

Controlling access content-driven

Content-dependent access control makes access decisions based on an item's data. Depending on the policy and access restrictions in place with this kind of access control, the data that a user sees may vary. According to some security experts, another sort of access restriction is a limited user interface. A restricted user interface, such as a shell, is a software interface to an operating system that implements access control by limiting the system commands that are available. Another example is database views that are filtered depending on user or system criteria. Constrained user interfaces might be content or context-dependent, depending on how the administrator constrains the interface.

Access control matrix

An ACM is a table that contains a list of subjects, a list of objects, and a list of the actions that a subject may perform on each object. The subjects in the matrix are represented by the rows, while the objects are represented by the columns. A capabilities table or an ACL are common ways to create an ACL. The Capability table lists a subject's access rights to objects. A capability table is focused on the subject, and capability correlates to a subject's row in an ACM.

Access control lists

An ACL refers to a column in an item's ACM. An ACL is a list of all of a subject's access rights to a certain object. An ACL's focus is the object, as presented in *Figure 16.6*:

Figure 16.6: Access control lists

Access control policies

The way the users are identified and validated, as well as the level of access they have, are all specified in an access control policy. Organizations should develop access control rules to ensure that users' access control decisions are based on specified criteria. Access management will be difficult to assign, monitor, and administer if a business does not establish an access control policy. The default option is **no access**. During the authorization process, the default level of security for an organization's access control systems should be no access. This means that if a person or group has not been given certain rights, they will be unable to access the resource. Starting with no access and gradually increasing rights is the best security technique.

OAuth is an authorization standard that allows users to exchange private resources from one site with another without having to use passwords. It is often referred to as the **valet key** of the Internet. Unlike a valet key, which only enables the valet to park your car but not open the trunk, OAuth uses tokens to offer restricted access to a user's data when a client application requests it. These tokens are generated by an authorization server. The exact sequence of events changes based on how it is implemented. OAuth is a good option for authorization when one online application uses the API of another online application on behalf of the user. A good example is a Facebook-connected geolocation application. OAuth allows the geolocation application to get a Facebook access token without revealing the geolocation application's Facebook login information.

Attestation

Authorized parties may use attestation to detect changes to a user's system. It may also be used to verify a system for the correct software version or the presence of a particular piece of software. This function may be used to limit what a user can do in a certain situation. Consider the situation where you have a server that keeps credit card information for customers. According to the rules in place, approved users on allowed devices may only access the server if they are also running authorized software. In this situation, the following three goals must be fulfilled:

- Using authentication and authorization to identify authorized users will help the organization achieve these goals.

- Authorized computers are identified via authentication and authorization.

- Using attestation to identify programs that are allowed to execute.

Prior to granting access, attestation provides evidence about a target to an appraiser so that the target's policy compliance may be evaluated. Attestation has an impact on the operation of a **Trusted Platform Module** (**TPM**) chip. During the manufacturing process, an **Endorsement Key** (**EK**) pair is embedded in TPM chips. This key pair is specific to the chip and has been certified by a credible certifying organization. A pair of **Attestation Integrity Keys** (**AIK**) are also included. This key is generated and used to allow an application to do remote attestation of its integrity. Identity Proofing allows a third party to confirm that the software has not been modified.

Following the identification stage, identity proofing is the next step in the authentication process. One kind of identity proofing is the presentation of secret questions to which only the individual undertaking verification knows the answer. While the subject would still need to provide credentials such as a password, this additional step reduces the danger of a password being compromised.

Identity propagation

Identity propagation is the process of moving or distributing a user's or device's authenticated identity information from one part of a multitier system to another. Identity propagation is achievable because each component of the system normally performs its own authentication. Identity propagation may take place in a number of ways. Some systems, such as Microsoft's Active Directory, use a proprietary mechanism and tickets to propagate identities.

It is likely that not all system components support SSO (meaning a component can accept the identity token in its original format from the SSO server). A proprietary approach must be adjusted in this case to communicate in a manner that the third-party software understands. Assume the application service receives a request to visit an external third-party web application that is not SSO enabled. The application service redirects the user to the SSO server. The SSO server will now provide the authenticated identity information to the external application using an XML token rather than an SSO token.

Another protocol that performs identity propagation is the **Credential Security Support Provider** (**CredSSP**). In the Microsoft Remote Desktop Terminal services context, it is often used to provide network-layer authentication. Kerberos, TLS, and NTLM are just a few of the authentication and encryption protocols that might be utilized.

Federation

A federated identity is one that may be used across domains and organizations. When an organization enters a federation, it agrees to follow a set of common norms and standards. These rules and standards define how user authentication, authorization, and identity should be given and handled. Providing divergent authentication techniques with federated IDs has the lowest up-front development cost as compared to other alternatives, such as a PKI or attestation, as presented in *Figure 16.7*:

Figure 16.7: *Federated identity*

Federated identity management uses two major models to link firms inside the federation, which are as follows:

- **Model of cross-certification**: Each organization checks the credibility of every other institution in this paradigm. Trust is developed when organizations assess each other's standards. Due diligence requires each entity to investigate and certify that the other organizations meet or exceed requirements. The disadvantage of cross-certification is that it increases the number of trust links that must be managed.

- **Trusted third-party (or bridge) model**: Each organization follows a set of third-party standards under this strategy. Third-party manages all of the firms' verification, certification, and due diligence. This is usually the best option if a company has to have federated identity management agreements with a significant number of entities.

OpenID

The OpenID Foundation, a non-profit organization, has developed an open standard and decentralized protocol that allows users to be authenticated by specified websites. Sites that cooperate are referred to as **relying parties** (**RPs**). Users may connect to several websites using OpenID without having to re-register their information. A user selects an OpenID **identity provider** (**IdP**) and then uses that account to log in to any website that accepts OpenID authentication. While OpenID solves the same issue as SAML, it may be beneficial to an enterprise for the following reasons:

- It is easier to use than SAML, and it is widely utilized by companies like Google.

- When contrasted to SAML, however, OpenID has a few disadvantages:

- Each user must establish auto-discovery of the IdP using OpenID, although SAML offers better performance.

- With SAML, either the service provider or the IdP can start SSO, but with OpenID, only the service provider may start SSO.

In February 2014, **OpenID Connect** (**OIDC**), the third version of OpenID, was released. It is a layer of authentication developed on top of the OAuth 2.0 architecture. It is compatible with both native and mobile applications. It also outlines how papers should be signed and encrypted.

Advanced SSO methods for network authentication have been developed throughout time using various trust models. The following sections will teach you how to utilize the **Remote Access Dial-In User Service** (**RADIUS**), which allows you to centralize authentication for all network access devices. You will also learn about two network authentication protocols, **Lightweight Directory Access Protocol** (**LDAP**) and **Active Directory** (**AD**), which is a common service implementation.

RADIUS server configuration

Users must first be permitted before they may connect to the network in a number of ways. Users who connect to the network using dial-up remote access servers, VPN access servers, or **wireless access points** (**WAP**) may fall into this category, as illustrated in *Figure 16.8*:

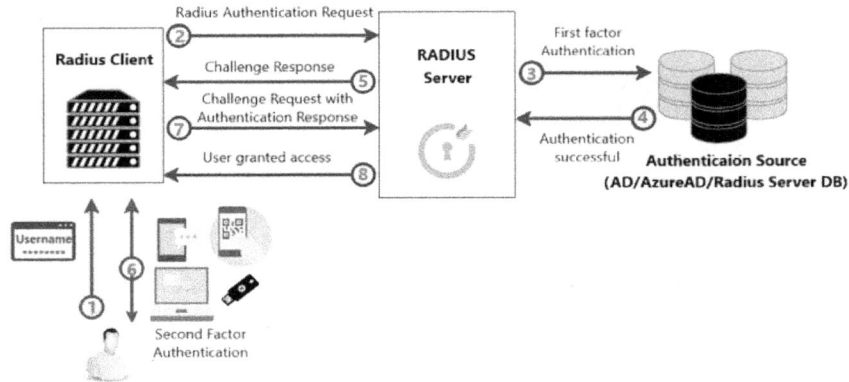

Figure 16.8: RADIUS server

Previously, each of the access devices had to perform the authentication operation locally. The administrators needed to ensure that all remote access rules and settings were consistent. When a password needed to be changed, it had to be done everywhere. RADIUS is a networking protocol that enables users to authenticate and authorize themselves remotely. Remote access, WAP, and VPN are clients of the RADIUS server, which can then be handled from a single, central location. Authentication and authorization are provided by the RADIUS server whenever they are requested. This provides a single location for managing the network's remote access rules and passwords. Another advantage of using these solutions is that the audit and access information (logs) are not kept on the access server.

RFC 2138 is the protocol that defines RADIUS. Its goal is to provide a three-part structure. The supplicant is the device that requests authentication. The authenticator is the device to which the supplicant is attempting to connect, and the RADIUS server is the authentication server (for example, an AP, switch, or remote access server). The device seeking access in RADIUS is not the RADIUS client. The authenticating server is the RADIUS server, and the authenticator is the RADIUS client (for example, an AP, switch, or remote access server).

In certain cases, a RADIUS server might be a client of another RADIUS server. In this case, the RADIUS server is acting as a proxy client for its RADIUS clients. The shared secret used to encrypt data between the network access device and the RADIUS server, as well as the fact that it only protects passwords and no other sensitive data like tunnel-group IDs or VLAN memberships, are all RADIUS security flaws. IPsec should be used to encrypt these communication paths since the shared secret offers inadequate security.

Lightweight Directory Access Protocol

A directory service is a database for managing information about network topics and objects. A traditional directory structure includes users, groups, systems, servers, client workstations, and so on, as presented in *Figure 16.9*. The directory service may be used by a broad variety of applications since it contains information about users and other network objects. A common directory service standard is **Lightweight Directory Access Protocol (LDAP)**, which is based on the older standard X.500. X.500 employs the **Directory Access Protocol (DAP)**. In X.500, the **Distinguished Name (DN)** describes the whole path to a record in the database. A **Relative Distinguishing Name (RDN)** in X.500 is the name of an entry that does not include the whole route. LDAP is a simpler protocol than X.500. The **Common Name (CN)**, **Domain Component (DC)**, and **Organizational Unit (OU)** characteristics are all available in LDAP in addition to DN and RDN. In a client/server design, LDAP uses TCP port 389 to communicate. If you need more protection, LDAP over SSL utilizes a TCP port. *Figure 16.9* illustrates the LDAP process:

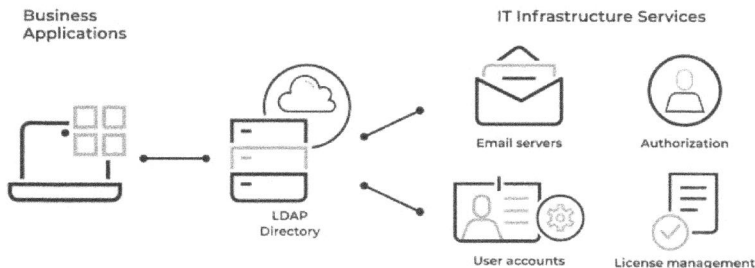

Figure 16.9: LDAP process

Active directory

Microsoft's version of LDAP, AD, separates directories into forests and trees. AD technologies are used to manage and organize everything in a company, including people and equipment. This is where security is implemented, and group policy aids in its effectiveness. AD is another example of an SSO scheme. The Kerberos and UNIX authentication and authorization schemes are used. This system authenticates a user once and then allows them to perform all actions and access all resources to which they have been given authorization without having to authenticate again. *Figure 16.10* illustrates the Active Directory flow:

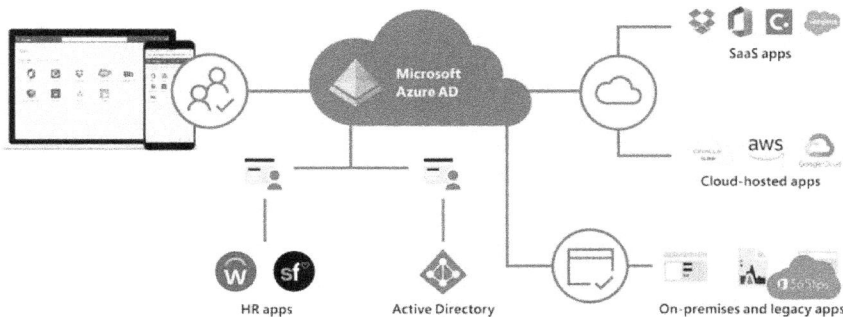

Figure 16.10: Active Directory flow

The stages involved in this method are shown in *Figure 16.11*:

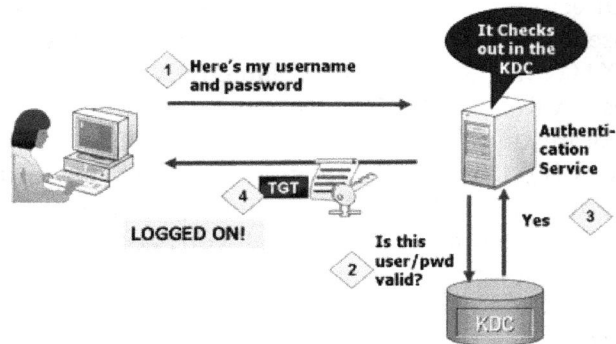

Figure 16.11: Kerberos protocol

The domain controller not only authenticates the user but also performs a variety of other tasks. The key distribution center runs the **Authorization Service (AS)**, which determines if a user has the right or permission to access a remote service or network resource (KDC).

When a user is authenticated, they are granted a ticket-granting ticket (when they connect to the network for the first time). This is then used to request session tickets, which are required to get access to resources. If they attempt to access a service or resource after that, they are redirected to the AS running on the KDC. When they produce their TGT, they are awarded a session, or service, a ticket for that resource. By providing the service ticket, which is signed by the KDC, the user allows access to the resource server. Because the resource server trusts the KDC, the user is granted access.

Advanced authentication management strategies

In today's rapidly evolving digital landscape, ensuring secure access to systems and data is more critical than ever. Advanced authentication, authorization, and identity management strategies play a pivotal role in protecting organizations from cyber threats, unauthorized access, and identity-related attacks. By implementing robust authentication mechanisms, enforcing granular authorization policies, and leveraging modern identity management frameworks, enterprises can enhance security, ensure compliance, and maintain seamless user experiences. This chapter explores cutting-edge techniques, emerging trends, and best practices for strengthening **identity and access management (IAM)** in modern digital ecosystems:

- **Use case 1**: Implementing MFA and risk-based access control

  Consider a scenario, a financial services organization, requires secure and dynamic access controls for its employees and clients accessing online services. To mitigate risks, the company implements MFA and risk-based access control.

In the financial services industry, securing access to sensitive customer data and transactions is paramount. Traditional password-based authentication methods are no longer sufficient to counter evolving cyber threats such as credential theft and account takeovers. To enhance security while maintaining a seamless user experience, organizations are adopting MFA and **risk-based access control** as part of their identity management strategy. By integrating MFA with a centralized IdP and leveraging adaptive authentication mechanisms, businesses can dynamically assess risk factors and enforce stronger security measures for high-risk access attempts. This use case explores the technical implementation of MFA and risk-based access control to fortify identity security and prevent unauthorized access. Following is the technical implementation:

o **MFA integration:**

  ▪ **Setup**: Deploy a centralized IdP such as Okta, Azure AD, or Duo Security. Integrate MFA mechanisms such as push notifications, biometrics, and **time-based one-time passwords (TOTP).**

  ▪ **Protocol**: Use protocols like OIDC or SAML to integrate MFA into applications.

o **Risk-based access control:**

  ▪ **Dynamic authentication**: Implement a risk engine that evaluates contextual factors such as geolocation, device health, and user behavior.

  ▪ **Adaptive decisions**: Configure access policies to escalate authentication requirements for high-risk scenarios, for example, logging in from an unrecognized IP address.

  ▪ **Define a rule**:

    Condition: Unusual login location.

    Action: Require additional biometric verification.

o **Testing and evaluation**:

  ▪ **Penetration testing**: Simulate credential theft and bypass attempts using tools like Hydra or Burp Suite.

  ▪ **Behavioral analysis**: Monitor user sessions and evaluate false positives/negatives in the risk engine.

o **Assessment:** To ensure the robustness of MFA and risk-based access control, it is essential to assess their effectiveness in real-world scenarios. Organizations must evaluate how well MFA mitigates phishing attacks and whether the risk engine introduces any operational overhead. Controlled phishing simulations help measure MFA's resilience against credential theft, while performance assessments analyze authentication latency introduced by dynamic risk evaluations. By systematically assessing these factors, financial institutions can fine-tune their security controls, balancing strong protection with seamless user experience. This assessment phase ensures that security mechanisms are both effective and efficient in safeguarding sensitive financial data.

- Evaluate the effectiveness of MFA against phishing attacks by conducting controlled simulations.

- Measure latency introduced by the risk engine during authentication flows.

- **Use case 2**: Implementing RBAC with identity federation

Consider a scenario, a multinational company operates hybrid environments across on-premises data centers and multiple cloud platforms. The company needs centralized identity management and granular authorization policies for diverse roles. In large multinational organizations operating across hybrid environments, managing user identities and access permissions efficiently is a critical challenge. **RBAC with identity federation** enables centralized identity management while ensuring seamless and secure access across on-premises and multi-cloud platforms. By leveraging identity federation tools such as AWS IAM Identity Center or Microsoft Azure AD, organizations can establish SSO and enforce granular authorization policies based on user roles. This use case explores the implementation of RBAC and identity federation to streamline access control, enhance security, and improve operational efficiency in complex IT ecosystems.

Following is the technical implementation:

- **Identity federation**:

  - Use identity federation tools like AWS IAM Identity Center (formerly AWS SSO) or Microsoft Azure AD to enable SSO across hybrid environments.

  - Configure trust relationships between on-premises **Active Directory (AD)** and cloud IdPs using SAML or ADFS.

- **RBAC implementation:** To ensure secure and efficient access management across a multinational organization's hybrid environment, RBAC must be implemented with a structured approach. RBAC enables organizations to assign permissions based on predefined roles, ensuring users have only the minimum necessary privileges required for their tasks. By defining hierarchical roles—such as Cloud Administrators with full management capabilities and developers with read-only access—organizations can enforce least privilege principles. Utilizing JSON-based access control policies further strengthens security by providing precise, policy-driven access enforcement. This implementation enhances operational control, reduces the risk of privilege escalation, and streamlines identity management across diverse IT environments.

- Define hierarchical roles with minimum necessary privileges for tasks. For instance, a **Cloud Administrator** can manage EC2 and S3, while a **developer** has read-only access.

- Use JSON-based access control policies to enforce least privilege:

```
{
    "Version": "2012-10-17",
    "Statement": [
        {
            "Effect": "Allow",
            "Action": ["s3:ListBucket"],
            "Resource": ["arn:aws:s3:::example-bucket"]
        }
    ]
}
```

o **Auditing and monitoring:** To maintain the integrity of RBAC with identity federation, continuous auditing and monitoring are essential. By enabling logging through services like AWS CloudTrail or Azure Activity Log, organizations can track user activities, detect anomalies, and ensure compliance with security policies. Proactive monitoring helps identify unauthorized privilege escalations or suspicious role changes in real time, reducing the risk of insider threats and external attacks. Configuring automated alerts further strengthens security by providing immediate notifications of potential breaches, enabling swift incident response and remediation. This approach ensures that access control policies remain effective and aligned with organizational security objectives.

  - Enable logging via AWS CloudTrail or Azure Activity Log to track user activities and detect anomalies.

  - Configure automated alerts for unauthorized privilege escalations or suspicious role changes.

o **Assessment:** To maintain the effectiveness of RBAC with identity federation, regular assessment and validation are crucial. Periodic access reviews help ensure that roles are appropriately assigned and that stale or unnecessary privileges are promptly revoked, minimizing security risks. Additionally, simulating insider threats by attempting privilege abuse provides a proactive approach to verifying that RBAC policies effectively prevent unauthorized access. These assessments not only strengthen compliance and security posture but also enhance the organization's ability to detect and mitigate potential threats before they can be exploited.

  - Conduct periodic access reviews to ensure roles are appropriately assigned and remove stale privileges.

- Simulate insider threats by attempting privilege abuse and verify RBAC rules prevent unauthorized access.

Following are the evaluation criteria:

o Effectiveness of SSO in reducing credential fatigue and improving user experience.

o Time-to-detect unauthorized access through real-time monitoring tools.

o Compliance with security standards like NIST SP 800-53 or ISO 27001.

o Address system vulnerabilities and security issues using advanced architectural techniques.

- **Use case 1:** Securing a microservices architecture with zero trust and service mesh

Consider a scenario, a tech startup has transitioned to a microservices architecture for its platform. As the system grows, the organization faces security challenges, particularly in managing communication between services, enforcing least privilege, and preventing lateral movement in case of a breach. The company decides to implement a **zero trust architecture (ZTA)** and integrate a service mesh to address these vulnerabilities.

Following are the technical implementation:

o **ZTA implementation**: In the context of modern distributed architectures, adopting a ZTA is crucial to safeguarding systems from internal and external threats. With the Zero Trust model, the principle of least privilege is paramount—each microservice, regardless of its location within the internal network, is treated as untrusted. All interactions between services must be authenticated and authorized to prevent unauthorized access. By implementing service identities with tools like Istio or Linkerd and leveraging **mutual TLS (mTLS)** for secure communication, organizations can enforce strict identity and authentication policies. To further enhance security, a policy engine like **Open Policy Agent (OPA)** allows for defining fine-grained access controls based on service identity, request origin, and contextual factors. This implementation strengthens access control and ensures that trust is never assumed but always verified.

- **Principle of least privilege**: Each microservice is treated as untrusted, even if it exists within the internal network. This means all interactions must be authenticated and authorized, regardless of their origin.

- **Identity and authentication**: Implement service identities using tools like **Istio** or **Linkerd** in the service mesh layer. Each microservice gets a unique identity for mTLS communication.

- **Policy enforcement**: Use a policy engine like OPA to define fine-grained access controls based on the identity of the service, the request's origin, and other contextual information.

o **Service mesh deployment:** In modern microservices architectures, securing communication and managing traffic between services is a key challenge. Service mesh deployment offers an effective solution by providing a dedicated layer for managing service-to-service interactions. By enabling mTLS across all microservices using Istio, organizations can ensure encrypted traffic and mutual authentication, verifying the identity of each service before any communication occurs. Additionally, Istio allows for the definition of strict traffic management and security policies, ensuring that sensitive services, such as user authentication can only interact with authorized components, like the user data service, while being isolated from other services, such as payment processing. This layered approach enhances both security and control within the microservices ecosystem.

- ▪ **mTLS for secure communication**: Enable mTLS across all microservices using Istio. This encrypts traffic between services and ensures that each service verifies the identity of the other.

- ▪ **Traffic management and security policies**: In Istio, define traffic policies that limit access between services. For instance, a service that handles user authentication might be restricted to only communicate with the user data service, and not with payment-related services.

o **Security monitoring and auditing:** Effective security monitoring and auditing are essential for detecting and responding to potential threats in a distributed microservices environment. By implementing distributed tracing tools like Jaeger or Zipkin, organizations can monitor service-to-service communication, identifying unusual patterns that may signal a compromised service. Additionally, integrating Prometheus and Grafana enables real-time collection and visualization of security metrics, allowing for proactive monitoring of system health and performance. By setting up alerts for traffic anomalies or violations of security policies, organizations can quickly respond to security incidents, ensuring continuous protection of critical services and data.

- ▪ **Distributed tracing**: Implement **Jaeger** or **Zipkin** for distributed tracing to monitor service-to-service communication. This can help identify anomalous communication patterns that might indicate a compromised service.

- ▪ **Alerting**: Set up Prometheus and Grafana for real-time security metrics. Alerts can be triggered based on traffic anomalies or violations of security policies.

o **Assessment and evaluation:** To ensure the resilience of a ZTA and service mesh deployment, assessment and evaluation are critical to identifying and mitigating vulnerabilities. Conducting penetration testing allows organizations to simulate real-world attacks, such as man-in-the-middle scenarios, to verify that mTLS is effectively protecting service communications. Additionally, utilizing tools like OWASP Threat Dragon for threat modeling enables teams to visualize potential risks and validate that zero trust principles, such as least privilege access and strict authentication—are consistently applied across the architecture. These assessments provide valuable insights to strengthen security and ensure the system remains robust against emerging threats.

- **Penetration testing**: Simulate attacks that exploit communication between microservices (for example, man-in-the-middle attacks) to ensure that mTLS is working effectively.

- **Threat modeling**: Use tools like **OWASP Threat Dragon** to conduct threat modeling exercises, ensuring that the Zero Trust principles are consistently enforced across the architecture.

- **Use case 2:** Securing a hybrid cloud environment with security automation and **infrastructure as code (IaC)**

Consider a scenario, a large enterprise is operating a hybrid cloud environment with workloads distributed across on-premises data centers and public cloud platforms like AWS and Azure. The company has experienced security incidents related to inconsistent configurations, misconfigurations, and manual interventions that exposed vulnerabilities in the cloud infrastructure. The company decides to implement security automation using IaC and continuous security monitoring to address these issues.

Following are the technical implementation:

o **IaC for consistent and secure deployments**:

Use **Terraform** or **AWS CloudFormation** to define and manage the infrastructure, including networks, servers, and security configurations. This ensures that all resources are provisioned according to best practices and security standards.

Implement security controls such as encryption, network isolation, and least privilege access within the IaC configuration.

To ensure data confidentiality and protection in cloud storage, IaC tools like Terraform can be used to configure secure resources. The following Terraform configuration defines an encrypted S3 bucket on AWS, ensuring that all data stored within the bucket is encrypted at rest. By enabling server-side encryption with the AES256 encryption algorithm, this setup provides an additional layer of security, safeguarding sensitive data from unauthorized access, even in the event of a breach. This configuration ensures that the S3 bucket is private and complies with best practices for securing cloud storage:

```
# Terraform configuration for an encrypted S3 bucket
  resource "aws_s3_bucket" "secure_bucket" {
```

```
      bucket = "my-secure-bucket"
      acl    = "private"

      server_side_encryption {
        enabled = true
        sse_algorithm = "AES256"
      }
    }
```

o   **Automated security testing and compliance**: To maintain a robust security posture and ensure compliance throughout the development and deployment lifecycle, automated security testing and compliance play a vital role in modern cloud environments. By integrating tools like Checkov or TerraScan into the CI/CD pipeline, organizations can automatically scan IaC for potential security vulnerabilities before deploying it to the cloud, ensuring that only secure configurations are implemented. Additionally, leveraging AWS Config and Azure Policy allows for continuous enforcement of compliance standards across hybrid cloud environments, automatically remediating non-compliant resources, such as instances running without encryption. This proactive approach helps mitigate security risks and ensures consistent adherence to regulatory and security requirements.

- Integrate **Checkov** or **TerraScan** into the CI/CD pipeline to scan the IaC code for security vulnerabilities before deploying it to the cloud.

- Use **AWS Config** and **Azure Policy** to enforce compliance across the hybrid cloud environment. Policies can be set to automatically remediate non-compliant resources, such as instances running without encryption.

o   **Continuous monitoring and threat detection:** Continuous monitoring and threat detection are fundamental to maintaining a proactive security posture in dynamic cloud and hybrid environments. By leveraging cloud-native security monitoring services like AWS GuardDuty, Azure Security Center, or Google Chronicle, organizations can continuously analyze logs for potential security threats, providing real-time insights into unusual activities. Additionally, implementing centralized logging with tools such as the **Elasticsearch, Logstash, and Kibana** (**ELK**) stack or Splunk enables the aggregation of logs from both on-premises and cloud environments, ensuring comprehensive visibility. This centralized approach helps identify vulnerabilities, detect threats early, and streamline incident response across diverse infrastructure.

- **Implement Cloud-native security monitoring**: Use services like **AWS GuardDuty**, **Azure Security Center**, or **Google Chronicle** to continuously monitor and analyze logs for security threats.

- **Centralized logging**: Use ELK stack or **Splunk** to aggregate logs from both on-premises and cloud environments. This enables visibility into the hybrid environment and helps identify vulnerabilities or threats.

o **Security automation for incident response:** In today's dynamic cloud environments, security automation for incident response plays a crucial role in swiftly detecting and mitigating security threats. By leveraging tools like AWS Lambda or Azure Functions, organizations can automate incident response workflows, enabling rapid remediation. For example, when a misconfigured security group with open inbound ports is detected, a Lambda function can automatically correct the configuration, reducing the risk of exposure. Additionally, using Terraform for state reconciliation ensures that infrastructure configurations remain consistent, automatically detecting and remediating any drift in real-time. This automated approach enhances security, improves response times, and minimizes human error during critical incidents.

- Automate incident response workflows using **AWS Lambda** or **Azure Functions**. For example, if a misconfigured security group is detected (such as open inbound ports), a Lambda function could automatically remediate the issue by applying the correct security group configuration.

- Use **Terraform** to enforce state reconciliation, ensuring that any drift in configurations is quickly detected and remediated automatically.

o **Assessment and evaluation:** Assessment and Evaluation are essential components of maintaining a strong security posture in cloud-based environments, especially when leveraging IaC for provisioning. Security posture reviews should be conducted periodically to ensure that IaC configurations are up to date and free from new vulnerabilities, such as deprecated encryption standards or insecure default settings. Additionally, automated penetration testing tools, like Prowler for AWS or Cloud-Ninja for Azure, can simulate attacks on the hybrid environment to identify configuration flaws or security weaknesses. These assessments help ensure that security is continuously reinforced as new infrastructure is provisioned, reducing the risk of misconfigurations and potential breaches.

- **Security posture review**: Conduct periodic security reviews of the IaC configurations to ensure that new vulnerabilities (for example, deprecated encryption standards) are not introduced during the infrastructure provisioning.

- **Automated penetration testing**: Simulate attacks on the hybrid environment using automated penetration testing tools like **Prowler** for AWS or **Cloud-Ninja** for Azure to identify configuration flaws or weaknesses.

These use cases show how advanced architectural techniques, such as zero trust combined with service meshes and security automation through IaC, can address system vulnerabilities and security issues. By automating security configurations, enforcing least privilege, and leveraging modern cloud-native security tools, organizations can mitigate security risks while maintaining flexibility and scalability in their IT environments.

Conclusion

This chapter discussed authentication, authorization, and attestation, including identity proofing and propagation as well as federation and trust models which identify persons and devices, as well as determine actions that a person or device is permitted to perform as the core of access control models.

In the next chapter, we will discuss incident response to help handle a data breach or cyberattack, including the way the organizations attempt to manage the consequences of the attack or breach (such as the incident). Ultimately, the goal is to effectively manage the incident so that the damage is limited and both recovery time and costs, as well as collateral damage such as brand reputation, are kept at a minimum.

Exercise

1. **What is the primary purpose of authentication in a security system?**

    a. To determine what resources a user can access

    b. To verify the identity of a user or system

    c. To grant permission to a user

    d. To store user credentials securely

2. **Which of the following best describes the process of authorization?**

    a. Confirming the identity of a user

    b. Defining what actions a user can perform on a resource

    c. Encrypting data for transmission

    d. Authenticating users with a password

3. **Which of the following best defines the concept of attestation in cybersecurity?**

    a. Verifying the accuracy of user credentials during authentication

    b. Verifying the security posture or configuration of a device or system

    c. Granting access to resources based on identity

    d. Propagating user identity across different systems

4. **What is the primary purpose of identity proofing in a digital identity verification process?**

   a. To authenticate a user using a password

   b. To verify that the user is the person they claim to be

   c. To assign roles and permissions to a user

   d. To propagate the user's identity to different services

5. **Which of the following describes identity propagation?**

   a. The process of verifying a user's identity

   b. The transfer of identity information across different systems or services

   c. The process of assigning roles based on user attributes

   d. The encryption of data during user authentication

6. **What is the main purpose of identity federation?**

   a. To grant users access to resources within their organization

   b. To allow a user to access resources across different systems or organizations using a single identity

   c. To manage encryption keys across different platforms

   d. To authenticate users via biometric data

7. **Which of the following is a key characteristic of a "hierarchical trust model"?**

   a. Trust is established through mutual agreement between peers

   b. Trust is established based on the reputation of individual users

   c. Trust is centralized with a single trusted authority at the top

   d. Trust is established through encryption standards

8. **Which of the following is a primary focus when evaluating AAA (Authentication, Authorization, and Accounting) management strategies?**

   a. Ensuring that passwords are stored securely

   b. Verifying that network traffic is encrypted

   c. Defining clear policies for user authentication, access control, and activity logging

   d. Optimizing server performance during user logins

Answers

1. b
2. b
3. b
4. b
5. b
6. b
7. c
8. c

Join our book's Discord space

Join the book's Discord Workspace for Latest updates, Offers, Tech happenings around the world, New Release and Sessions with the Authors:

https://discord.bpbonline.com

CHAPTER 17
Security Incidents and Response

Introduction

Security incident analysis involves an organization that should first capture the usual actions and performance of a system before determining if an event has happened. This serves as a benchmark against which all other activities are measured. To effectively determine when an event has happened, security professionals should ensure that the baseline is captured during periods of high and low activity. Additionally, they should collect baselines over time to ensure that the best overall baseline is achieved. Following that, the company must design policies that detail how security personnel should respond to incidents. A risk assessment allows an organization to identify the areas of risk and document the methods for dealing with those risks. Security personnel should keep up with current trends in order to spot unplanned problems. The security experts will have a plan to follow if incident response processes are documented. Security professionals should try to document and examine the evidence after an incident has been stopped. Systems should be restored to their operating form once the evidence has been documented. It may be required to seize an asset as part of a criminal investigation in specific instances. If this happens, the company must identify a substitute asset as soon as feasible. E-discovery, data breaches, incident detection and response, incident and emergency response, incident response support tools, issues affecting the severity of an event or breach, and post-incident response are all discussed in this chapter.

Structure

In this chapter, we will cover the following topics:

- Data breaches
- Incident detection and response
- Incident and emergency response
- Incident response support tools
- Severity of incident or breach
- Post-incident response
- Incident response
- Advanced forensic response strategies
- Analyze advanced threats

Data breach

Any situation in which information that is considered private or confidential is released to unauthorized people is referred to as a data breach. A plan must be in place for an organization to detect and respond to these situations appropriately. However, having an incident response plan is insufficient. An organization must also have trained staff who are familiar with the incident response strategy and possess the necessary abilities to respond to any incidents that may arise. An incident response team's ability to follow incident response procedures is critical. Depending on where you look, different procedures or phases of the incident response process may be included. For the CASP exam, you need to remember the following steps:

1. Detect the incident.
2. Respond to the incident.
3. Report the incident to the appropriate personnel.
4. Recover from the incident.
5. Remediate components to ensure that all traces of the incident have been removed.
6. Review the incident and document all findings.

If an incident remains unnoticed or unreported, the organization will not be able to intervene in the middle of it or prevent it from happening again. If a user claims that the mouse pointer on their workstation is moving and files are opening automatically, they should be directed to contact the incident response team for assistance. During the response, report, and recovery processes, the incident is really investigated. During the investigation, following suitable forensic and digital investigative protocols can help ensure that evidence is maintained.

Detection and collection

Finding the occurrence, securing the attacked system(s), and identifying the evidence are the initial steps in incident response. Reviewing audit logs, monitoring systems, assessing user complaints, and studying detection methods are all used to find proof. The system's status should be examined as part of this stage. At first, the investigators may be unaware of which evidence is crucial. It is always preferable to keep the evidence you may not need than to wish you had kept evidence you did not. This process also includes identifying the attacked system(s) (crime scene). The assault system is referred to as the crime scene in digital investigations. In some situations, the technology that was used to launch the attack can be regarded as a part of the crime scene. However, it is not always possible to entirely capture the attacker's systems. As a result, you should record any data that might be used to identify a specific system, such as IP addresses, users, and other identifiers. Evidence should be preserved and collected by security professionals. Making system pictures, implementing chain of custody, documenting the evidence, and collecting timestamps are all part of this process. Consider the sequence of volatility before gathering any proof.

Data analytics

Any data acquired as part of an incident response must be appropriately evaluated by a forensic investigator or a security professional with similar training. Depending on the amount of data that has to be processed, someone trained in big data analytics may be needed to assist with the study. The investigator must review and analyze the evidence after it has been preserved and collected. Any attributes, such as timestamps and identification properties, should be determined and documented while analyzing evidence. The entire occurrence should be reproduced and documented after the evidence has been thoroughly reviewed using scientific methodologies.

Mitigation

Mitigation refers to the prompt measures taken to stop a data breach in its tracks. Once an event has been discovered and evidence is being collected, security professionals must take the necessary steps to limit the incident's impact and isolate the critical infrastructure. Mitigation involves implementing immediate actions to contain the breach, such as disabling compromised accounts, blocking malicious IP addresses, or isolating affected systems. The goal is to prevent further exploitation while preserving evidence for investigation and legal proceedings. Effective mitigation strategies are essential to minimize the damage, prevent data loss, and ensure that the organization can resume normal operations as quickly as possible.

Minimize

Security experts should take necessary actions to mitigate the impact of a data breach as part of the mitigation process. In the majority of instances, this involves being open and responding to the data breach as soon as it occurs. It is just as critical to protect your organization's reputation as it is to protect its actual assets. As a result, businesses should ensure that their plan includes mechanisms for notifying the public of a data breach and mitigating the consequences.

Isolate

Isolating the compromised systems is a critical aspect of any data breach event response. Depending on the severity of the breach and the number of assets affected, it may be essential to temporarily cease some services in order to stop the current data breach or prevent future data breaches. The organization may just need to isolate a single system in some circumstances. Multiple systems that are involved in transactions may need to be segregated in other instances.

Recovery or reconstitution

Once a data breach has been prevented, the organization must recover the data and restore operations to as normal a state as feasible. While the goal is to fully restore a system, due to the nature of data backup and recovery and the data's availability, it is probable that not all data will be recovered. Some data may be lost if organizations are only able to restore data at a specific point in time. Organizations should make sure that their backup or recovery procedures are in place so that data may be recovered within the timeframes specified. Some firms, for example, may do transaction backups within an e-commerce database every hour, while others may do so every four hours. Senior management must be aware that some data may be unrecoverable, according to security professionals. It is important to remember that corporations must balance the risks with the expenses of countermeasures. The data owners should document the recovery processes for each system.

Response

Based on the analyses of a data breach, an enterprise should thoroughly evaluate the steps that may be taken to avoid a similar breach from occurring again. While the organization may not be able to implement all of the recommended preventative measures, it should at least adopt those that the risk analysis identifies as vital. Additionally, the enterprise should prioritize strengthening its security posture by investing in robust detection mechanisms and implementing layered defenses to mitigate potential vulnerabilities. Regular security audits, employee training, and updating security protocols are essential to ensure resilience against evolving threats. By adopting a proactive, risk-based approach, organizations can continuously enhance their cybersecurity strategies and reduce the likelihood of future breaches.

Disclosure

Once a data breach has been thoroughly recognized, security professionals should document all findings in a lessons-learned database to assist future personnel in grasping all elements of the breach. In addition, the incident response team and forensic investigators should present senior management with full disclosure reports. Senior management can then select how much information is shared with internal staff and the general public. Consider the case of a data breach that was not adequately disclosed due to a lack of incident response training. Assume a marketing department supervisor bought the most recent mobile device and linked it to the company's network. Through their email, the supervisor continued to download crucial marketing documents. The device was later misplaced while being transported to a conference. The supervisor alerted the company's help desk about the missing equipment, and a replacement was sent to them. The help desk ticket was closed at that point, indicating that the problem had been fixed. In reality, this situation should have been studied and analyzed to discover the best method to prevent a similar occurrence in the future. The first mobile device's disappearance was never addressed. Implementing remote wipe tools to delete company data from the original mobile device is one change you should consider.

Incident detection and response

An organization's security policy should include ensuring that systems are built to aid in incident response. It is critical to act quickly in the event of a security compromise. Actions should be guided by the six-step incident response method mentioned earlier. This is because the business may have the right controls in place to prevent an incident from escalating to the point where a security breach occurs, not all occurrences will result in a security breach. Internal and external violations, such as privacy policy violations, criminal acts, insider threats, and non-malicious threats or misconfigurations, should be understood by security professionals in order to appropriately build systems to aid in incident response. Finally, security experts should collaborate with management to implement system, audit, and security log collection and review in order to guarantee that incident response occurs as rapidly as feasible.

Internal and external violations

When it comes to security events and breaches, the perpetrators can be inside or external persons or groups. Furthermore, a security breach may result in the disclosure of external customer or internal employee information. Accounts connected with internal entities should be used to strictly limit system access. Depending on the demands of the account holder, different levels of access should be provided to these accounts. Users who require administrative-level access should be given both administrative-level and regular-level accounts. Administrative accounts should only be used to carry out administrative tasks. In general, users should utilize the account with the fewest privileges necessary to complete the task at hand. Any organization's normal procedure should include the monitoring of all accounts. Administrative accounts, on the other hand, should be monitored more closely than regular accounts. This is because insiders already have access to systems, and internal infractions are significantly easier to commit than external violations. These insiders have a level of information about the organization's internal workings, which offers them an advantage. Finally, users with administrator or higher-level accounts have the power to commit large-scale security breaches. Before they can even start an attack, outsiders must first gain credentials. When assessing internal and external infractions, security experts know how to distinguish between privacy policy violations, criminal actions, insider threats, and non-malicious threats or misconfigurations.

Privacy policy violations

Data privacy is strongly reliant on the security safeguards in place. While enterprises can provide security without ensuring data privacy, data privacy is impossible to achieve without proper security controls. A **privacy impact assessment** (**PIA**) is a risk assessment that identifies the hazards associated with the collection, usage, storage, and transmission of **personally identifiable information** (**PII**). This will establish whether suitable PII controls and protections have been put in place to avoid PII disclosure or compromise. Personnel, processes, technology, and gadgets should all be evaluated as part of the PIA. Any significant modification should be followed by a new PIA. Any contracted third parties with access to PII should be examined to verify that suitable controls are in place as part of preventing privacy policy violations. Third-party personnel should also be educated on the organization's policies and sign **non-disclosure agreements** (**NDAs**).

Criminal actions

When dealing with criminal event response, an organization must guarantee that the right steps are taken to move toward prosecution. If proper procedures are not followed, criminal prosecution may be avoided because the evidence may be challenged by the defense. When a criminal act is detected, involving law authorities as soon as possible is critical. The sequence of volatility and chain of custody are two aspects of evidence collection that must be examined.

Insider threats

One of the most serious worries for security workers should be insider threats. Insiders, as previously stated, have knowledge of and access to systems that outsiders do not, making it considerably easier for insiders to carry out or participate in an attack. To detect insider threats as they occur, an organization should establish the right event collection and log review policies.

Non-malicious threats or misconfigurations

Internal users can unwittingly contribute to the possibility of security breaches. These dangers are not malevolent in origin but can arise as a result of users' lack of understanding of how system changes can influence security. Examples of misconfigurations that can result in security breaches occurring and not being noticed should be covered in security awareness and training. For example, to complete an administrative operation, a user may temporarily disable **antivirus** (**AV**) software. If the user does not enable the AV software, the system is unwittingly exposed to infections. In this instance, a company should consider creating group policies or other means to ensure that AV software is enabled and running on a regular basis. Another option is to set AV software to restart automatically after a specified period of time has passed. System, audit, and security logs can be used to record and review user activity, allowing security experts to identify misconfigurations and adopt the relevant policies and controls.

Hunt teaming

Hunt teaming is a novel strategy for security that is offensive rather than defensive, as has been the case in the past with security teams. These groups collaborate to discover, detect, and comprehend advanced and determined threat agents. They are a significant financial investment for a company. They go after the assailants. To use a bank analogy, if a bank robber compromises a door in order to rob a bank, defensive measures would suggest getting a better door, but offensive tactics would suggest eliminating the bank robber. These cyber-hired firearms are yet another tool in the arsenal. Hunt teaming also refers to a set of strategies used by security employees to circumvent typical protection technology in order to track down other attackers who may have used similar techniques to carry out assaults that have already been detected, often by other firms. These methods aid in the detection of systems infected with advanced malware that avoids detection by traditional security technologies such as **Intrusion Detection/Prevention Systems** (**IDS/IPS**) or AV software. Security professionals could potentially get blacklisted from sites like DShield as part of hunt teaming. These blacklists would then be checked to current DNS entries to verify if the communication was taking place with known attackers on these blacklists. Hunt teaming can also be used to simulate previous assaults so that security personnel can gain a better understanding of the company's current vulnerabilities and learn how to fix and prevent future problems.

Heuristics and behavioral analytics

Heuristics are a type of algorithm used in virus detection, behavioral analysis, event detection, and other situations where patterns must be found in the middle of chaos. It is a method for ranking alternatives using search algorithms, and while it is not an exact science and is more of a guessing game, it has been found to approximate an accurate solution in many circumstances. It also contains a trial-and-error procedure for self-learning as it approaches the ultimate approximated result. Using this strategy, many IPS, IDS, and anti-malware systems with heuristics capability can commonly discover zero-day vulnerabilities.

Review system, audit, and security logs

Regular system events, such as operating system and service events, are recorded in system logs. Audit and security logs keep track of successful and unsuccessful efforts to conduct specified operations and need security professionals to configure the audited actions specifically. Policies for the collection, storage, and security of these logs should be established by organizations. The logs may usually be set up to send out warnings when particular occurrences take place. These logs must also be reviewed on a regular and methodical basis. Security personnel should also be taught how to use these data to detect incidents. It does not matter whether you have all the data in the world, if you do not have the right people to evaluate it. The amount of log data that needs to be evaluated for large organizations might be fairly considerable. As a result, a **security information event management** (SIEM) device, which provides an automated solution for evaluating events and determining where attention should be focused, may be implemented by an organization. Assume that an IDS detected an attempt to launch an attack from a remote IP address. After a week, the attacker had gained access to the network. It is very likely that no one was looking at the IDS event logs in this scenario. Consider another example of inadequate logging and review processes. Assume that a business was unaware that its internal financial systems had been hacked until the attacker made sensitive pieces of information public on multiple popular attacker websites. The company could not figure out when, how, or who carried out the attacks at first, so they rebuilt, restored, and updated the compromised database server to keep things running. If the organization is still unable to establish these details, it should examine its system configuration, audit, and security logs.

Incident and emergency response

Organizations must ensure that suitable response methods have been created in the event of an incident or an emergency. Security specialists should make sure that businesses consider the chain of custody, forensic examination of a compromised system, **continuity of operations plan** (COOP), and order of volatility as part of these processes.

Chain of custody

If your organization does not have trained personnel who understand the chain of custody and other digital forensic procedures, the organization should have a plan in place to bring in a trained forensic professional to ensure that evidence is properly collected. As part of understanding the chain of custody, security professionals should also understand evidence and surveillance, search, and seizure. You should ask who, what, when, where, and how questions at the start of any investigation. These questions can assist in gathering all of the information required for the chain of custody. The chain of custody identifies who was in charge of the evidence, who safeguarded it, and who obtained it. To properly prosecute a suspect, the chain of custody must be maintained. To maintain a correct chain of custody, evidence must be collected in compliance with predetermined processes and all applicable rules and regulations. The chain of custody's main goal is to ensure that evidence is admissible in court. Officers of the law place a premium on the investigations they perform. Early involvement of law enforcement can help ensure that the right chain of custody is followed during an investigation.

Evidence

Evidence must be relevant, legally permissible, credible, correctly identified, and stored in order to be admissible. Relevant means it must prove a material fact linked to the crime, such as that it proves a crime was done, that it can offer information detailing the incident, that it can provide information about the perpetrator's motives, or that it can verify what happened. The term **reliability** refers to the fact that it has not been tampered with or altered in any way. The term **preservation** refers to the fact that the evidence is neither damaged nor destroyed. Every piece of evidence must be labeled. When creating evidence tags, make sure to include the mode and means of transit as well as a detailed description of the evidence, including the quality, who received it, and who had access to it. An investigator must ensure that evidence adheres to the following five rules of evidence:

- Be authentic
- Be accurate
- Be complete
- Be convincing
- Be admissible

In addition, the investigator must be familiar with the various types of evidence available and how each one might be utilized in court. Surveillance, search, and seizure guidelines must be followed by investigators. Finally, investigators should be aware of the distinctions between media, software, network, and hardware or embedded device investigation. Even though digital evidence is more volatile than other types of evidence, it must nonetheless follow these five guidelines.

Surveillance, search, and seizure

Surveillance, search, and seizure are all crucial aspects of a criminal investigation. Surveillance is the act of watching someone's behavior, activities, or other changing information, which is usually about them. The act of looking for anything or information is known as searching. The act of seizing physical or digital components is known as a seizure. Physical and computer surveillance are the two types of surveillance used by investigators. When a person's actions are reported or filmed using cameras, direct observation, or **closed-circuit television** (**CCTV**), it is referred to as physical surveillance. When a person's actions are reported or collected using digital information, such as audit logs, this is known as **computer surveillance**. In most circumstances, a search warrant is required to actively explore a private site for evidence. A court must find probable cause that a crime has been committed before a search warrant can be issued. Corroboration of the presence of evidence must also be provided to the judge. The only time a search warrant is not required is in exigent circumstances, which are situations in which a search warrant is not required to prevent physical damage, evidence destruction, a suspect's escape, or any other improperly obstructing legitimate law enforcement efforts. When evidence is submitted in court, extreme conditions must be demonstrated. Evidence can only be seized if it is specifically specified as part of the search warrant unless the evidence is clearly visible. Only the evidence stated in the search warrant can be taken, and the search can only take place in the places listed on the warrant. Private organizations and people are exempt from search and seizure laws. Most companies inform their staff that any files maintained on company resources are considered the company's property. This is frequently included in any policy that has no expectation of privacy.

Forensic analysis of compromised system

Forensic analysis of a compromised system varies greatly depending on the type of system that needs analysis. Analysis can include media analysis, software analysis, network analysis, and hardware or embedded device analysis. In forensic analysis, investigators focus on identifying **indicators of compromise (IOCs)** such as malicious files, unusual network traffic, or system anomalies that could point to the nature and extent of the breach. They also use specialized tools and techniques to preserve evidence while ensuring that the integrity of the compromised system is maintained for further investigation or legal proceedings. Depending on the complexity of the compromise, a thorough examination may involve cross-referencing logs, analyzing memory dumps, and reviewing configurations across multiple layers of the compromised environment.

Media analysis

Investigators can perform many types of media analysis, depending on the media type. The following are some of the types of media analysis:

- **Disk imaging:** This involves creating an exact image of the contents of a hard drive.

- **Slack space analysis:** This involves analyzing the slack (marked as empty or reusable) space on a drive to see whether any old (marked for deletion) data can be retrieved.

- **Content analysis:** This involves analyzing the contents of a drive and gives a report detailing the types of data, by percentage.

- **Steganography analysis:** This involves analyzing the graphic files on a drive to see whether the files have been altered or to discover the encryption used on the file. Data can be hidden within graphic files.

Software analysis

Software analysis is a little harder to perform than media analysis because it often requires the input of an expert on software code. Software analysis techniques include the following:

- **Content analysis:** This involves analyzing the content of software, particularly malware, to determine the purpose for which the software was created.

- **Reverse engineering:** This involves retrieving the source code of a program to study how the program performs certain operations.

- **Author identification:** This involves attempting to determine the software's author.

- **Context analysis:** This involves analyzing the environment the software was found in to discover clues related to determining the risk.

Network analysis

Network analysis involves the use of networking tools to provide logs and activity for evidence. Network analysis techniques include the following:

- **Communications analysis:** This involves analyzing the communication over a network by capturing all or part of the communication and searching for particular types of activity.

- **Log analysis:** This involves analyzing network traffic logs.

- **Path tracing:** This involves tracing the path of a particular traffic packet or traffic type to discover the route used by the attacker.

Hardware or embedded device analysis

The use of tools and firmware included with devices to determine the actions done on and by a device is known as hardware or embedded device analysis. Depending on the device, several methodologies are utilized to assess the hardware or embedded device. In most circumstances, depending on the information requested, the device vendor can advise on the appropriate technique to utilize. Some of the common approaches utilized are log analysis, operating system analysis, and memory inspections.

Continuity of operations

Continuity planning entails determining the impact of a disaster and putting in place a workable recovery strategy for each function and system. Its main focus is on how to carry out organizational functions in the event of a disruption. COOP takes into account all aspects of a disaster's impact, including functions, systems, personnel, and facilities. It identifies and prioritizes the services that are required, with a focus on telecommunications and information technology. The COOP is usually included in a company's business continuity plan. COOP should include contingency plans for maintaining vital functions in a variety of situations. It should also include a management succession plan that outlines what to do if a senior executive is unable to carry out his or her responsibilities.

Disaster recovery

Recovery processes, personnel safety protocols, and restoration procedures are all part of the disaster recovery process. The focus of this chapter on incident response is on the restoration of information assets that have been lost as a result of an incident, as well as continuous access to information assets after an incident has occurred. Data backup formats and techniques, as well as methods of sustaining data access during disc failures, must all be understood by security professionals.

Incident response team

An organization must evaluate each individual's technical competence while forming an incident response team. Members of the team must be familiar with the company's security policy and have excellent communication skills. In addition, members should be trained in incident response and investigation. When an incident occurs, the team's first priority is to contain the attack and repair any damage that the incident has caused. When an incident is found, security isolation of the scene should begin immediately. Evidence must be kept safe, and the proper authorities must be notified. Access to the incident response plan should be granted to the incident response team. A list of authorities to call, team roles and duties, an internal contact list, processes for securing and preserving evidence, and a list of investigative experts who can be contacted for assistance should all be included in this plan. To guarantee that no procedures are missed, a step-by-step manual should be established for the incident response team to follow. All incident response actions should be documented after the incident response process has been initiated. Senior management and the appropriate authorities should be alerted quickly if the incident response team concludes that a crime has been committed.

Order of volatility

Before collecting any evidence, an organization should consider the order of volatility, which ensures that investigators collect evidence from the components that are most volatile first. The order of volatility is as follows:

- CPU, cache, and register content
- Routing table, ARP cache, process table, and kernel statistics
- Memory
- Temporary file system or swap space
- Data on hard disk

- Remotely logged data
- Data contained in archival media

You will need a tool that generates a bit-level duplicate of the system to create system images. To produce this bit-level replica, you must usually isolate the system and take it out of production. Make sure you keep two copies of the image. One copy of the image will be kept as proof, ensuring that it is undamaged and correct. During the examination and analysis, the other copy will be used. To ensure data integrity, message digests should be utilized. The system image is usually the most crucial piece of evidence, but it is not the only one you will need. Data saved in the cache, process tables, RAM, and the registry may also need to be captured. You should keep notes in a bound notebook when documenting a computer attack. It is also critical that you never take a page out of the notebook. Remember to enlist the help of specialists while conducting digital investigations to ensure that evidence is maintained and collected appropriately. Investigators usually put together a field kit to use during the investigation. Tags and labels, disassembly tools, and tamper-evident packaging could all be included in this kit. Commercial field kits are available, or you can put your own together based on your specific needs.

Incident response support tools

For the incident response process, security professionals must be skilled and comfortable using an array of analysis and detection tools. This section takes a look at some of these tools and the proper use of each, as follows:

- **dd** before any analysis is performed on the target disk in an investigation, a bit-level image of the disk should be made. Then the analysis should be done on that copy. This means that a forensic imaging utility should be part of your toolkit. There are many of these, and many of the forensic suites contain them. Moreover, many commercial forensic workstations have these utilities already loaded. The **dd** command is a UNIX/Linux command that is used to convert and copy files. The U.S. **Department of Defense** (**DoD**) created a fork (a variation) of this command called **dcfldd** that adds additional forensic functionality. By simply using **dd** with the proper parameters and using the correct syntax, you can make an image of a disk. Using **dcfldd** gives you the ability to also generate a hash of the source disk at the same time. For example, the following command reads 5 GB from the source drive and writes that information to a file called **mymage.dd.aa**. It also calculates the MD5 hash and the sha256 hash of the 5 GB chunk. It then reads the next 5 GB and names that **myimage.dd.ab**. The MD5 hashes are then stored in a file called **hashmd5.txt**, and the sha256 hashes are stored in a file called **hashsha.txt**. The block size for transferring has been set to 512 bytes, and in the event of read errors, **dcfldd** writes zeros.

- **Tcpdump** captures packets on Linux and UNIX platforms. A version for Windows, called WinDump, is also available. Using the **tcpdump** command is a matter of selecting the correct parameter to go with it. For example, the following command enables a capture (**-i**) on the Ethernet 0 interface, '**#sudo tcpdump**,' as illustrated in *figure 17.1*.

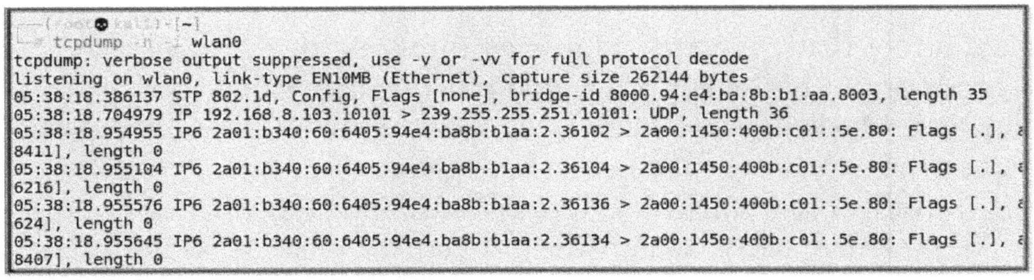

Figure 17.1: Tcpdump command

Figure 17.2 illustrates the packet captures from the network from specific wireless network interface.

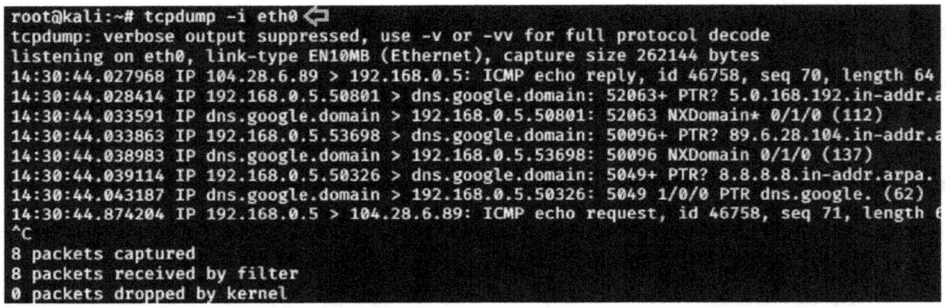

Figure 17.2: Capturing packets from specific network interface

- **Nbtstat** is used by Microsoft networks as an interface called **Network Basic Input/Output System** (**NetBIOS**) to resolve workstation names with IP addresses. The **nbtstat** command can be used to view NetBIOS information. **nbtstat -n** shows the NetBIOS names of the host that have been registered on the system; **nbtstat -c** displays the current contents of the NetBIOS name cache, which contains NetBIOS name to IP address mappings for other hosts on the network, as illustrated in *Figure 17.3*:

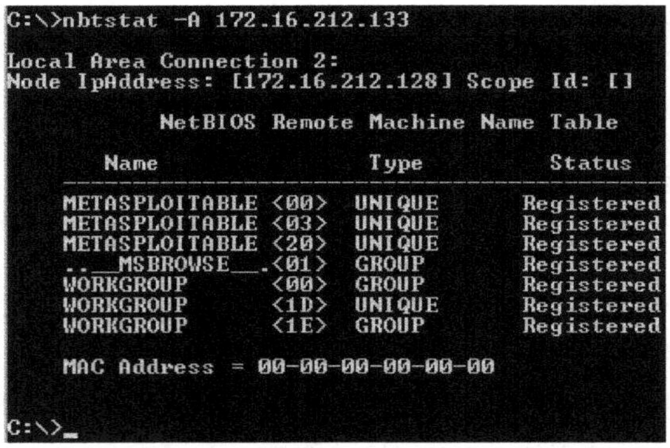

Figure 17.3: NetBIOS names of host registered on systems

- **Netstat** command is used to see what ports are listening on a TCP/IP-based system. The **-a** option is used to show all ports, and **/?** is used to show what other options are available. (The options differ based on the operating system you are using.) When executed with no switches, the command displays the current connections. **-a -all** shows both listening and non-listening sockets. The **-interfaces** option shows TCP connections as presented in *Figure 17.4*:

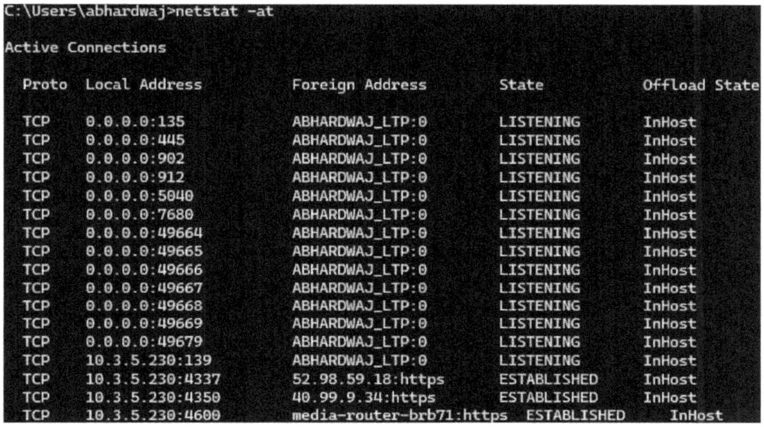

```
C:\Users\abhardwaj>netstat -at

Active Connections

  Proto  Local Address          Foreign Address        State           Offload State
  TCP    0.0.0.0:135            ABHARDWAJ_LTP:0        LISTENING       InHost
  TCP    0.0.0.0:445            ABHARDWAJ_LTP:0        LISTENING       InHost
  TCP    0.0.0.0:902            ABHARDWAJ_LTP:0        LISTENING       InHost
  TCP    0.0.0.0:912            ABHARDWAJ_LTP:0        LISTENING       InHost
  TCP    0.0.0.0:5040           ABHARDWAJ_LTP:0        LISTENING       InHost
  TCP    0.0.0.0:7680           ABHARDWAJ_LTP:0        LISTENING       InHost
  TCP    0.0.0.0:49664          ABHARDWAJ_LTP:0        LISTENING       InHost
  TCP    0.0.0.0:49665          ABHARDWAJ_LTP:0        LISTENING       InHost
  TCP    0.0.0.0:49666          ABHARDWAJ_LTP:0        LISTENING       InHost
  TCP    0.0.0.0:49667          ABHARDWAJ_LTP:0        LISTENING       InHost
  TCP    0.0.0.0:49668          ABHARDWAJ_LTP:0        LISTENING       InHost
  TCP    0.0.0.0:49669          ABHARDWAJ_LTP:0        LISTENING       InHost
  TCP    0.0.0.0:49679          ABHARDWAJ_LTP:0        LISTENING       InHost
  TCP    10.3.5.230:139         ABHARDWAJ_LTP:0        LISTENING       InHost
  TCP    10.3.5.230:4337        52.98.59.18:https      ESTABLISHED     InHost
  TCP    10.3.5.230:4350        40.99.9.34:https       ESTABLISHED     InHost
  TCP    10.3.5.230:4600        media-router-brb71:https  ESTABLISHED  InHost
```

Figure 17.4: Netstat TCP listening & non-listening sockets

Netstat -an listens to list all udp ports, as illustrated in *Figure 17.5*:

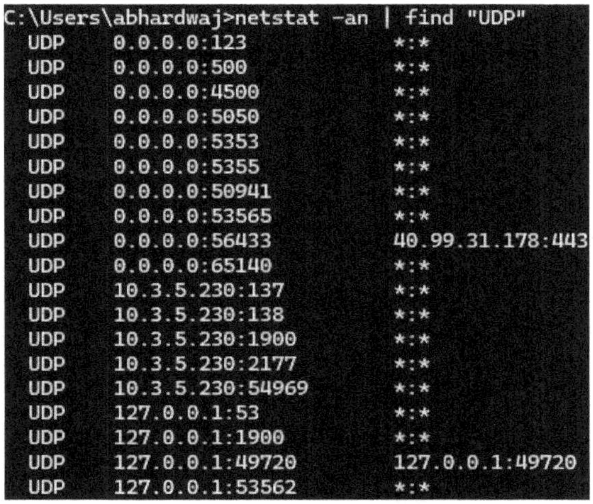

```
C:\Users\abhardwaj>netstat -an | find "UDP"
  UDP    0.0.0.0:123            *:*
  UDP    0.0.0.0:500            *:*
  UDP    0.0.0.0:4500           *:*
  UDP    0.0.0.0:5050           *:*
  UDP    0.0.0.0:5353           *:*
  UDP    0.0.0.0:5355           *:*
  UDP    0.0.0.0:50941          *:*
  UDP    0.0.0.0:53565          *:*
  UDP    0.0.0.0:56433          40.99.31.178:443
  UDP    0.0.0.0:65140          *:*
  UDP    10.3.5.230:137         *:*
  UDP    10.3.5.230:138         *:*
  UDP    10.3.5.230:1900        *:*
  UDP    10.3.5.230:2177        *:*
  UDP    10.3.5.230:54969       *:*
  UDP    127.0.0.1:53           *:*
  UDP    127.0.0.1:1900         *:*
  UDP    127.0.0.1:49720        127.0.0.1:49720
  UDP    127.0.0.1:53562        *:*
```

Figure 17.5: Netstat listening all UDP Ports

- **nc (Netcat)** is a command-line utility that can be used for many investigative operations, including port scanning, file transfers, and port listening. For example, the following command scans for ports 1 through 1,000 on the target at 192.168.1.2: **nc -v 192.168.1.2 1-1000** is presented in *Figure 17.6*:

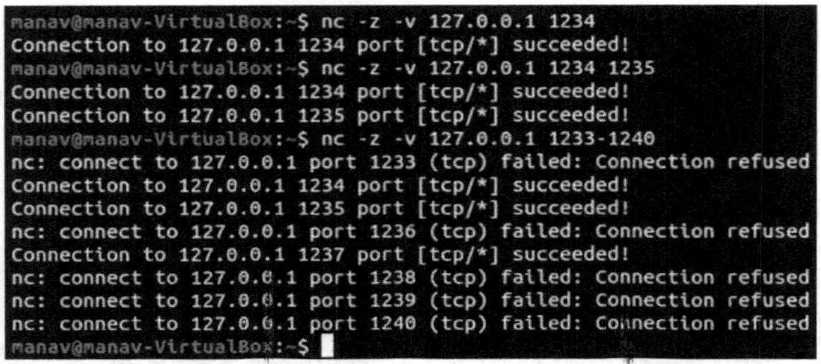

```
manav@manav-VirtualBox:~$ nc -z -v 127.0.0.1 1234
Connection to 127.0.0.1 1234 port [tcp/*] succeeded!
manav@manav-VirtualBox:~$ nc -z -v 127.0.0.1 1234 1235
Connection to 127.0.0.1 1234 port [tcp/*] succeeded!
Connection to 127.0.0.1 1235 port [tcp/*] succeeded!
manav@manav-VirtualBox:~$ nc -z -v 127.0.0.1 1233-1240
nc: connect to 127.0.0.1 port 1233 (tcp) failed: Connection refused
Connection to 127.0.0.1 1234 port [tcp/*] succeeded!
Connection to 127.0.0.1 1235 port [tcp/*] succeeded!
nc: connect to 127.0.0.1 port 1236 (tcp) failed: Connection refused
Connection to 127.0.0.1 1237 port [tcp/*] succeeded!
nc: connect to 127.0.0.1 port 1238 (tcp) failed: Connection refused
nc: connect to 127.0.0.1 port 1239 (tcp) failed: Connection refused
nc: connect to 127.0.0.1 port 1240 (tcp) failed: Connection refused
manav@manav-VirtualBox:~$
```

Figure 17.6: Using Netcat for post scanning

- **`memcopy`** is a controversial C+ function used to copy the bytes from the source memory location directly to the destination memory block. It is controversial because if the source and destination overlap, this function does not ensure that the original source bytes in the overlapping region are copied before being overwritten.
- **`tshark`** captures packets on Linux and UNIX platforms, much like **`tcpdump`**. It writes a file in pcap format, as Wireshark does. Whenever a scenario calls for working from the terminal interface rather than a GUI interface, this tool supports the same filter functions as Wireshark, and because it is a command-line tool, it can be scripted, as presented in *Figure 17.7*. The following are some examples of the filtering that can be done with **`tshark`**:

  `-i` to choose the interface on your machine

  `-a` for duration, which is in seconds

  `-w` to write the capture packets in the file

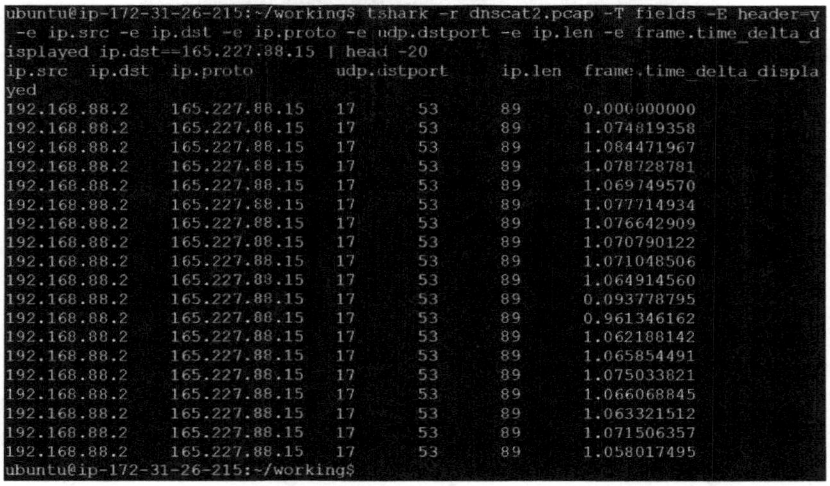

```
ubuntu@ip-172-31-26-215:~/working$ tshark -r dnscat2.pcap -T fields -E header=y
 -e ip.src -e ip.dst -e ip.proto -e udp.dstport -e ip.len -e frame.time_delta_d
isplayed ip.dst==165.227.88.15 | head -20
ip.src  ip.dst  ip.proto        udp.dstport     ip.len  frame.time_delta_displa
yed
192.168.88.2    165.227.88.15   17      53      89      0.000000000
192.168.88.2    165.227.88.15   17      53      89      1.074819358
192.168.88.2    165.227.88.15   17      53      89      1.084471967
192.168.88.2    165.227.88.15   17      53      89      1.078728781
192.168.88.2    165.227.88.15   17      53      89      1.069749570
192.168.88.2    165.227.88.15   17      53      89      1.077714934
192.168.88.2    165.227.88.15   17      53      89      1.076642909
192.168.88.2    165.227.88.15   17      53      89      1.070790122
192.168.88.2    165.227.88.15   17      53      89      1.071048506
192.168.88.2    165.227.88.15   17      53      89      1.064914560
192.168.88.2    165.227.88.15   17      53      89      0.093778795
192.168.88.2    165.227.88.15   17      53      89      0.961346162
192.168.88.2    165.227.88.15   17      53      89      1.062188142
192.168.88.2    165.227.88.15   17      53      89      1.065854491
192.168.88.2    165.227.88.15   17      53      89      1.075033821
192.168.88.2    165.227.88.15   17      53      89      1.066068845
192.168.88.2    165.227.88.15   17      53      89      1.063321512
192.168.88.2    165.227.88.15   17      53      89      1.071506357
192.168.88.2    165.227.88.15   17      53      89      1.058017495
ubuntu@ip-172-31-26-215:~/working$
```

Figure 17.7: Tshark commands

- **Foremost is a** digital forensic application that is used to recover lost or deleted files. Foremost it can recover files for hard disk, memory card, pen drive, and other modes of memory devices easily. It can also work on the image files that are being generated by any other application. It is a free command-line tool that is pre-installed in Kali Linux. This tool comes pre-installed in Kali Linux. Foremost is a very useful software that is used to recover the deleted files, if some files are deleted accidentally or, in any case, files are deleted. This tool works only if the data in the device is not overridden, which means that after deleting the files, no more data is added to the storage device. If the data is overridden, the chances of recovery are reduced, and data may get corrupted. This recovers files for Linux systems, using a process called file carving, which can recover image and data files from hard drives using ext3, FAT, and NTFS, and iPhones. *Figure 17.8* illustrates Foremost to recover data from mobile devices:

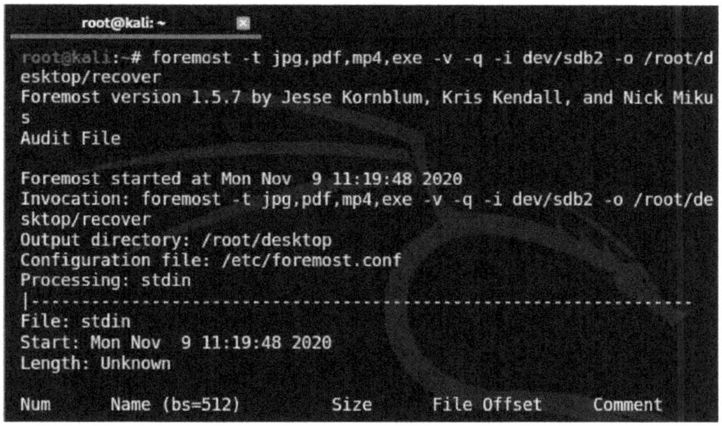

Figure 17.8: Foremost to recover data from mobile device

Severity of incident or breach

Each incident must be classified according to the magnitude of the incident and the types of data that have been compromised in order to effectively prioritize them. The scope of the incident is more than just how prevalent it is, and the factors to examine may be more diverse than you think. The following section goes through the factors that influence incident severity and prioritization.

Scope

The scale of the occurrence is determined by how prevalent it is. The extent of the event must be determined early on because it will determine the amount of resources to devote to it and, in most cases, the escalation procedures. The impact is likewise tied to the scope, in that as the scope expands, the impact expands as well.

Impact

The impact of an incident is directly related to the criticality of the resources involved. The **impact** of a security incident is closely tied to the **criticality of the resources** affected. When high-value or mission-critical assets, such as sensitive data, financial systems, or intellectual property, are compromised, the consequences can be far-reaching, potentially resulting in severe financial losses, reputational damage, and operational disruptions. Understanding the relative importance of different resources within an organization helps prioritize response efforts and allocate resources effectively to mitigate the impact of potential incidents. This approach ensures that the most critical assets are protected with the appropriate level of security and incident management.

System process criticality

Some assets are systems that offer access to information rather than the information itself. These systems or groupings of systems are referred to as critical systems when they give access to data that is necessary to continue doing business. While it is easier to value physical assets like servers, routers, switches, and other devices, their worth is greater than the hardware replacement cost in circumstances where these systems give access to important data or are necessary to continue a business-critical operation. The given value should be enhanced to reflect its relevance in giving data access or in allowing a critical operation to continue.

Cost

The value of the assets involved determines the economic impact of an incident. It can be difficult to determine those values, especially for intangible assets like plans, drawings, and recipes. Computers, facilities, materials, and staff are examples of tangible assets. Intellectual property, data, and corporate reputation are examples of intangible assets. The asset's value should be assessed in light of the asset owner's perspective. The following considerations can be used to determine an asset's value:

- Value to owner
- Work required to develop or obtain the asset
- Costs to maintain the asset
- Damage that would result if the asset were lost
- Cost that competitors would pay for asset
- Penalties that would result if the asset were lost

After determining the value of assets, you should determine the vulnerabilities and threats to each asset.

Downtime

One factor to consider is the amount of downtime that an incident could cause, as well as the time it will take to recover from the incident. You would have collected information about each asset that will help classify occurrences that affect each asset if you have built a proper business continuity strategy.

Legal ramifications

While the legal repercussions of a security incident can be costly to a business, the public relations harm can be even more costly if the organization is perceived by the general public to have mishandled the issue or been less than forthcoming about it. Furthermore, the impact is amplified when an organization operates in a regulated area such as the medical, financial, or retail sectors, which are subject to even stronger data restrictions (for example, HIPAA, GLBA, and PCI-DSS). In addition, organizations should ensure that law enforcement officials are involved in all investigations at the right time.

Post-incident response

When an incident has been wrapped up, there is still work to be done. While it is tempting to move on, you are not done until the paperwork is done, so let us talk about that follow-up work.

Root-cause analysis

In many circumstances, security professionals do not fully comprehend how or why an issue is occurring and simply want it to go away; later, even though they still do not know what happened, security professionals are relieved that it is gone. This also applies to attack vectors on occasion. Security experts may have thwarted an attack and possibly removed the attacker from the environment, but they may not have fully understood how the assault progressed and worked. In situations like this, you cannot just ignore the problem; otherwise, you risk falling victim to the same attack or device issue again. You must devote time to determining the fundamental source of the problem or attack.

Lessons learned

Almost every security incident teaches you something about the situation that necessitates improvements to your environment. Then, you must take corrective action to either address the new danger or make changes to address an identified vulnerability. A lessons-learned report should be the first document to be written. It briefly summarizes and discusses what is now known about the attack or the previously unknown environment. Shortly after the incident, a formal meeting should be held to compile this report. This report contains significant information that may be used to improve the organization's security posture. This report might answer questions such as the following:

- What went right, and what went wrong?
- How can we improve?
- What needs to be changed?
- What was the cost of the incident?

After-action report

The lessons-learned report may generate a number of changes that should be made. An after-action report drives the process of handling these changes. It leads to changes in other documents as well.

Change control process

A number of adjustments to the network infrastructure may be required. All of these modifications should go through the regular change control process, regardless of how necessary (or minor) they are. They should be presented to the change control board, where they will be scrutinized for unintended consequences and evaluated for proper integration into the current context. They should only be introduced after receiving approval. When time is of the essence, you might find it useful to construct a **rapid track** for evaluation in your change management system for changes like these.

Incident response

Consider a scenario, a leading e-commerce platform with a complex IT infrastructure, including machine learning-powered network security components like firewalls, **intrusion prevention systems (IPS)**, a **Security Information and Event Management (SIEM)** system, threat intelligence feeds, and a dedicated **Security Operations Center (SOC)** team. This environment faces various cyber threats, including DDoS attacks, data breaches, malware infections, and ransomware.

Incident response plan is that the organization establishes a comprehensive incident response plan, outlining roles, responsibilities, and procedures for handling security incidents. The plan includes:

Following is the incident detection:

- Machine learning algorithms within firewalls and IPS analyze network traffic patterns to detect anomalies and potential threats in real-time.
- SIEM correlates security logs from various sources, including firewalls, IPS, servers, and endpoints, to identify suspicious activities and potential threats.
- Threat intelligence feeds provide up-to-date information on emerging threats and vulnerabilities, enabling proactive threat hunting.

- The SOC team monitors alerts from these systems, analyzes threat intelligence, and investigates potential incidents.

Following are the **incident containment:**

- Upon detection of an incident, the SOC team isolates the affected systems or networks to prevent further damage.

- Network segmentation and micro-segmentation strategies are implemented to limit the blast radius of attacks.

- Automated response actions are triggered, such as blocking malicious IP addresses or disabling compromised accounts.

Following are the incident eradication:

- The root cause of the incident is identified and addressed.

- Malicious software is removed from affected systems.

- Systems are patched and updated with the latest security fixes.

Following are the incident recovery:

- Business operations are restored to normal as quickly as possible.

- Data is recovered from backups or alternative sources.

- Affected systems are brought back online with enhanced security measures.

Following is the business continuity plan, to ensure business continuity during major disruptions, the organization implements the following measures:

- **Disaster recovery site**: A secondary data center or cloud-based infrastructure is maintained to provide redundancy and enable rapid recovery in case of a major outage.

- **Data backup and recovery**: Regular backups of critical data are performed and stored off-site to facilitate rapid recovery in case of data loss.

- **Business impact analysis (BIA)**: A BIA is conducted to identify critical business functions and their dependencies, enabling prioritization of recovery efforts.

- **Crisis communication plan**: A plan is in place to communicate with customers, employees, and other stakeholders during and after a major incident.

Following is the regular testing and refinement; the incident response and business continuity plans are regularly tested and refined through tabletop exercises, simulations, and real-world incident response scenarios. The organization continuously monitors its security posture, adapts to evolving threats, and invests in advanced security technologies to improve its resilience. By implementing a robust incident response, recovery, and business continuity framework, the e-commerce platform can effectively mitigate the impact of cyberattacks, protect its critical assets, and maintain business operations during challenging times.

Advanced forensic response strategies

Forensic techniques are crucial for gathering evidence, identifying the root cause of an incident, and reconstructing the timeline of events. Forensic techniques provide crucial evidence that informs the advanced response strategy. For example, malware analysis can reveal the attack vector and identify other systems that may be compromised. Advanced response strategies, such as threat hunting and automated response actions, can help to contain and mitigate the impact of an incident, enabling faster and more effective forensic investigations. By integrating forensic techniques and advanced response strategies, organizations can achieve a higher level of security resilience, improve their ability to detect and respond to threats, and minimize the impact of cyberattacks. By implementing these advanced forensic and response strategies, the e-commerce portal can significantly enhance its ability to detect, investigate, and respond to cyber threats, protect its critical assets, and minimize the impact of security incidents on its business operations.

In the above-mentioned scenario, forensic techniques would be instrumental in:

- **Digital forensics:** Digital forensics plays a crucial role in investigating and understanding cyber incidents, enabling organizations to gather, preserve, and analyze evidence for legal or remedial purposes. The process begins with image acquisition, where forensic images of compromised systems are created to ensure the integrity of the data and prevent accidental evidence alteration. Malware analysis follows, focusing on identifying the functionality, origin, and attack vectors of malicious software through various techniques such as static and dynamic analysis, reverse engineering, and sandbox testing. Additionally, network traffic analysis helps pinpoint the attack's source, vectors, and exfiltrated data using methods like packet capture and protocol analysis. Finally, log analysis of system, application, and security logs is essential for tracking suspicious activity, understanding the actions of the attacker, and reconstructing the incident's timeline. Together, these forensic techniques provide a comprehensive view of an attack, facilitating both the containment and resolution of security incidents.

  o **Image acquisition:** Creating forensic images of compromised systems, including servers, workstations, and network devices. This ensures data integrity and prevents accidental alteration of evidence.

  o **Malware analysis:** Analyzing malicious software samples to determine their functionality, origin, and attack vectors. This can involve static and dynamic analysis techniques, reverse engineering, and sandbox analysis.

  o **Network traffic analysis:** Analyzing network traffic logs to identify the source of the attack, the attack vectors used, and the data exfiltrated. Techniques such as packet capture, protocol analysis, and IDS log analysis can be employed.

  o **Log analysis:** Analyzing system logs, application logs, and security logs to identify suspicious activity, track attacker actions, and reconstruct the timeline of the incident.

- **Data recovery:** Recovering deleted or encrypted data from compromised systems. This can involve data recovery tools, file system analysis, and specialized forensic techniques.

- **Evidence preservation**:
  - Chain of custody procedures are strictly followed to ensure the integrity and authenticity of evidence.

  - Evidence is properly documented, stored, and handled to maintain its admissibility in legal proceedings.

Advanced response strategies go beyond traditional incident response by leveraging automation, intelligence, and proactive measures. In this scenario, advanced response strategies would include:

- **Threat hunting:** Proactively searching for threats and vulnerabilities within the network environment. This involves utilizing threat intelligence feeds, analyzing network traffic for anomalies, and employing advanced security analytics tools.

- **Security orchestration, automation, and response (SOAR):** Automating repetitive tasks, such as threat intelligence gathering, incident triage, and response actions. This can significantly improve the speed and efficiency of incident response.

- **Artificial intelligence (AI) and machine learning (ML):** Leveraging AI and ML to detect and respond to threats in real-time. This includes using machine learning algorithms for anomaly detection, threat classification, and predicting future attacks.

- **Endpoint detection and response (EDR):** Deploying EDR solutions to monitor endpoint activity, detect malicious behavior, and respond to threats in real-time. EDR solutions can provide valuable insights into attacker **tactics, techniques, and procedures (TTPs).**

- **Cloud Security Posture Management (CSPM):** Continuously assessing and improving the security posture of the cloud environment, including identifying and mitigating misconfigurations, vulnerabilities, and threats.

Analyze advanced threats

The e-commerce portal, with its intricate infrastructure and reliance on sensitive data, demands a proactive approach to analyzing advanced malware and emerging threats, and implementing robust security controls. This requires a deep understanding of the evolving threat landscape and a continuous adaptation of security measures.

Advanced malware, such as ransomware, fileless malware, and **advanced persistent threats (APTs)**, poses significant challenges due to its sophisticated techniques, evasive tactics, and ability to bypass traditional security controls. Analyzing these threats requires a multi-layered approach:

- **Static analysis:** Examining malware samples without executing them. This involves analyzing the file structure, code, and metadata to identify suspicious patterns, strings, and functions. Tools like disassemblers, debuggers, and sandboxes can be used to analyze the malware's behavior in a controlled environment.

- **Dynamic analysis:** Observing the malware's behavior while it executes in a controlled environment, such as a virtual machine or sandbox. This allows security analysts to understand how the malware interacts with the system, communicates with command-and-control servers, and performs malicious activities.

- **Threat intelligence:** Leveraging threat intelligence feeds from reputable sources to gain insights into the latest malware trends, tactics, and techniques. This information can be used to identify potential threats, prioritize investigations, and develop effective countermeasures.

- **Reverse engineering:** Deeply analyzing the malware's code to understand its functionality, identify vulnerabilities, and develop mitigation strategies. This requires advanced skills in reverse engineering techniques, such as debugging, disassembly, and code analysis.

The cyber threat landscape is constantly evolving, with new threats and vulnerabilities emerging regularly. To effectively address these emerging threats, the e-commerce portal must:

- **Stay informed:** Continuously monitor industry news, security advisories, and research publications to stay informed about the latest threats and vulnerabilities.

- **Threat hunting:** Proactively search for threats and vulnerabilities within the network environment. This involves utilizing threat intelligence feeds, analyzing network traffic for anomalies, and employing advanced security analytics tools.

- **Vulnerability management:** Conduct regular vulnerability assessments and penetration tests to identify and remediate vulnerabilities in the environment.

- **Threat modeling:** Conduct threat modeling exercises to identify potential threats and vulnerabilities specific to the e-commerce platform. This helps prioritize risk mitigation efforts and focus on the most critical areas.

A multi-layered approach to security controls is essential to protect the e-commerce platform from advanced threats. This includes:

- **Network security:** Network security is a critical component of any organization's cybersecurity strategy, designed to protect against unauthorized access, data breaches, and malicious activities targeting the network infrastructure. Implementing **next-generation firewalls (NGFWs)** with advanced threat intelligence capabilities enhances the ability to detect and block malicious traffic in real-time. Complementing NGFWs, **intrusion detection and prevention systems (IDPS)** provide proactive defense by identifying and preventing network intrusions and other suspicious behaviors. To further minimize risk, network segmentation isolates critical systems, preventing malware from spreading across the entire network. Additionally, securing VPN and remote access connections with strong authentication and encryption ensures that remote users can access the network safely, without compromising sensitive data. Together, these measures form a robust security posture that defends against a wide range of network-based threats.

- o **Next-generation firewalls (NGFWs):** Implementing NGFWs with advanced threat intelligence capabilities to detect and block malicious traffic.

- o **Intrusion detection and prevention systems (IDPS):** Deploying IDS/IPS systems to detect and prevent network intrusions and other malicious activities.

- o **Network segmentation:** Implementing network segmentation to isolate critical systems and limit the spread of malware.

- o **VPN and remote access security:** Securing remote access connections using strong authentication and encryption.

- **Endpoint security:** Endpoint security is essential for protecting an organization's devices and systems from cyber threats that can originate from any point of entry, including workstations, laptops, and mobile devices. A critical component of endpoint security is EDR, which provides continuous monitoring of endpoint activity, enabling the detection of malicious behavior and real-time responses to mitigate threats. Additionally, AV and anti-malware solutions are deployed across all endpoints to proactively detect and prevent the execution of harmful software. To further enhance protection, organizations implement a **host-based intrusion detection system (HIDS)**, which monitors system activity for signs of suspicious behavior and potential breaches. Together, these measures create a robust defense layer that safeguards endpoints from evolving cyber threats.

- o **Endpoint detection and response (EDR):** Deploying EDR solutions to monitor endpoint activity, detect malicious behavior, and respond to threats in real-time.

- o **AV and anti-malware:** Implementing robust AV and anti-malware solutions on all endpoints.

- o **Host-based intrusion detection system (HIDS):** Deploying HIDS to monitor system activity for suspicious behavior.

- **Data security:** Data security is a critical aspect of any cybersecurity strategy, ensuring that sensitive information is protected from unauthorized access, loss, or theft. Data encryption is a foundational measure, safeguarding sensitive data both at rest and in transit, making it unreadable to unauthorized parties. **Data loss prevention (DLP)** solutions further enhance security by monitoring and preventing the unauthorized exfiltration of sensitive data. Additionally, implementing robust access control mechanisms ensures that only authorized individuals or systems have access to critical data and resources, minimizing the risk of insider threats and external breaches. Together, these strategies form a comprehensive approach to securing data across its entire lifecycle.

- o **Data encryption:** Encrypting sensitive data both at rest and in transit.

- o **Data loss prevention (DLP):** Implementing DLP solutions to prevent the exfiltration of sensitive data.

- o **Access control:** Implementing strong access controls to limit access to sensitive data and systems.

- **Identity and access management (IAM):** IAM is a fundamental component of an organization's security strategy, ensuring that only authorized users and systems can access critical resources. By implementing strong authentication mechanisms, such as **multi-factor authentication (MFA)**, organizations can significantly enhance security by requiring multiple forms of verification before granting access. Additionally, enforcing least privilege access controls ensures that users and systems are granted only the minimum permissions necessary for their tasks, reducing the potential impact of a compromised account. These IAM practices form the backbone of a robust security posture, helping to protect sensitive data and systems from unauthorized access and potential breaches.

  - o Implementing strong authentication mechanisms, such as MFA.

  - o Implementing least privilege access controls to minimize the impact of potential compromises.

- **Cloud security:** Cloud security is a critical component in protecting data and applications as organizations increasingly migrate to cloud environments. To strengthen Cloud Security, CSPM tools can be deployed to continuously assess and improve the security posture of cloud environments, identifying misconfigurations and vulnerabilities that may expose the system to risk. Additionally, implementing a **cloud access security broker (CASB)** enables organizations to monitor and control cloud usage across various platforms, ensuring compliance with security policies and protecting against unauthorized access or data leaks. Together, these solutions offer proactive, comprehensive protection for cloud infrastructure and applications.

  - o **Cloud security posture management (CSPM):** Implementing CSPM tools to continuously assess and improve the security posture of cloud environments.

  - o **Cloud access security broker (CASB):** Implementing a CASB to monitor and control cloud usage and enforce security policies.

- **Security information and event management:** SIEM systems are integral to modern cybersecurity frameworks, providing centralized visibility into an organization's security posture. By implementing a SIEM system, organizations can collect and analyze security logs from various sources, such as network devices, servers, and applications, to gain real-time insights into potential threats. Additionally, the use of machine learning algorithms within the SIEM helps to detect anomalous patterns and behaviors, enhancing the system's ability to identify emerging threats and prioritize alerts. This proactive approach enables security teams to quickly address vulnerabilities, reduce false positives, and respond to incidents more efficiently.

- o Implementing a SIEM system to collect and analyze security logs from various sources.

- o Utilizing machine learning algorithms within the SIEM to detect anomalies and prioritize alerts.

- **Security awareness training**: Providing regular security awareness training to employees to educate them about cyber threats and best practices for cybersecurity.

The e-commerce portal must continuously assess and improve its security posture to stay ahead of evolving threats. This includes:

- **Regular security assessments:** Conducting regular security assessments, including vulnerability assessments, penetration tests, and threat hunts.

- **Incident response testing:** Conducting regular incident response drills to test the effectiveness of the incident response plan.

- **Staying informed:** Staying informed about the latest threats, vulnerabilities, and security best practices through industry conferences, research publications, and security blogs.

- **Adapting to change:** Adapting security controls and strategies to address new and emerging threats.

By implementing a comprehensive approach to advanced malware analysis, threat intelligence, and security controls, the e-commerce portal can significantly enhance its cybersecurity posture, protect its critical assets, and ensure the continued operation of its business in the face of evolving cyber threats. This requires a proactive, adaptive, and data-driven approach to security, with a focus on continuous improvement and a commitment to staying ahead of the curve.

Conduct vulnerability and risk management assessments to maintain operational security.

Vulnerability and risk management assessments are crucial for maintaining operational security in today's complex and interconnected world. These assessments help organizations identify and address potential threats and weaknesses, ultimately minimizing the impact of security incidents. Vulnerability assessment is a systematic process of identifying and evaluating weaknesses in an organization's systems, applications, and processes. This involves scanning systems, networks, and applications to detect potential vulnerabilities, such as software flaws, misconfigurations, and weak passwords.

Following are the types of vulnerability assessments:

- **Vulnerability scanning:** Automated tools are used to scan systems for known vulnerabilities, such as missing patches, outdated software, and weak configurations.

- **Penetration testing:** Skilled security professionals attempt to exploit vulnerabilities to assess the organization's defenses and identify potential attack vectors.

- **Code reviews:** Manual or automated analysis of source code to identify vulnerabilities, such as buffer overflows, SQL injection, and cross-site scripting.

- **Social engineering tests:** Simulated phishing attacks and other social engineering techniques are used to assess employee awareness and susceptibility to social engineering attacks.

Once vulnerabilities have been identified, a risk assessment is conducted to determine the potential impact of each vulnerability. This involves evaluating the likelihood of exploitation and the potential consequences of a successful attack. Key Factors in Risk Assessment include:

- **Threat likelihood:** The probability of a threat occurring, based on factors such as the sophistication of attackers, the availability of exploit tools, and the organization's security posture.

- **Impact:** The potential consequences of a successful attack, such as data loss, financial loss, reputational damage, and disruption to business operations.

- **Vulnerability severity:** The severity of the vulnerability is based on factors such as the ease of exploitation and the potential impact.

Once risks have been identified and assessed, appropriate mitigation strategies can be implemented. These include:

- **Patching and updating:** Applying security patches and updates to address known vulnerabilities.

- **Configuration management:** Implementing and enforcing security configurations to harden systems and reduce the attack surface.

- **Access control:** Implementing strong access controls, such as MFA and least privilege access, to limit unauthorized access.

- **Security awareness training:** Educating employees about security threats and best practices to reduce the risk of social engineering attacks.

- **Incident response planning:** Developing and testing an incident response plan to minimize the impact of security incidents.

Vulnerability and risk management is an ongoing process. Organizations must continuously monitor their security posture, identify new threats and vulnerabilities, and update their risk mitigation strategies accordingly which involves Conducting regular vulnerability scans, penetration tests, and other security assessments. Monitoring threat intelligence feeds to stay informed about the latest threats and vulnerabilities. Implementing a SIEM system to collect and analyze security logs to identify and respond to security incidents. Regularly reviewing and updating risk assessments and mitigation strategies based on changes in the threat landscape and organizational needs. By conducting thorough vulnerability and risk management assessments and implementing appropriate mitigation strategies, organizations can significantly improve their security posture, reduce their exposure to cyber threats, and maintain operational security in today's challenging environment.

Conclusion

Security incident and response plans may also have weaknesses as a result of the lessons learned exercise. If this is the case, the plans need to be amended to reflect the necessary procedure adjustments. Then, once it is finished, double-check that both software and hard-copy versions of the plan have been updated so that everyone is working with the same data when the next event occurs. In this chapter, we discussed the organization's capacity to act quickly and address a wide range of security challenges based on well-planned incident response, a strong team, and suitable security technologies and processes. Damage, service outages, data theft, loss of reputation, and potential liabilities are all reduced as a result.

In the next chapter, we will look at adapting security when trying to meet the dynamic business needs for adhering to standards. This chapter will also discuss interoperability and resilience issues, relating to legacy, current systems, secure protocols and APIs.

Exercise

1. **Which of the following actions is most critical immediately after a data breach has been detected?**

   a. Start an internal investigation

   b. Notify all stakeholders and authorities

   c. Perform a system reboot

   d. Run antivirus software

2. **Which of the following is the primary function of a Security Information and Event Management (SIEM) system in incident detection?**

   a. Perform system backups

   b. Centralize and correlate security logs from multiple sources

   c. Encrypt data for secure storage

   d. Manage security awareness training programs

3. **Which of the following best describes the "Containment" phase in an incident response process?**

   a. Rebuilding systems from scratch

   b. Preventing further damage by isolating affected systems

   c. Identifying the root cause of the incident

   d. Reverting systems to their pre-incident state

4. **Which of the following tools is most commonly used for live memory analysis during an incident response investigation?**

   a. NetFlow

   b. FTK Imager

   c. Volatility

   d. Splunk

5. **What is the primary consideration when assessing the severity of an incident or breach?**

   a. The number of systems affected

   b. The financial cost of the incident

   c. The sensitivity and criticality of the compromised data

   d. The time taken to detect the incident

6. **Which of the following is a key activity during the post-incident response phase?**

   a. Reassessing network configurations

   b. Conducting a lessons-learned meeting

   c. Deploying new hardware

   d. Reconfiguring firewalls

7. **Which of the following strategies is most effective for ensuring business continuity during an incident?**

   a. Relying solely on a single data center

   b. Implementing a comprehensive disaster recovery and backup plan

   c. Disabling non-essential services

   d. Temporarily disconnecting from the internet

8. **What forensic technique is primarily used to recover data from a damaged or wiped disk?**

   a. File carving

   b. Network traffic analysis

   c. System snapshotting

   d. Volatile memory analysis

9. **Which of the following is most commonly used to analyze the behavior of unknown or advanced malware in a controlled environment?**

   a. Sandboxing

   b. IP filtering

   c. Encryption

   d. Data loss prevention (DLP)

Answers

1. b
2. b
3. b
4. c
5. c
6. b
7. b
8. a
9. a
10. a
11. a

Join our book's Discord space

Join the book's Discord Workspace for Latest updates, Offers, Tech happenings around the world, New Release and Sessions with the Authors:

https://discord.bpbonline.com

CHAPTER 18

Integrating Hosts, Networks, Storage, and Applications

Introduction

Organizations need to securely integrate hosts, storage, networks, and applications. It is the security practitioner's responsibility to ensure that appropriate security access controls are implemented and tested apart from several other steps. Effective integration requires a holistic approach, ensuring that all components function seamlessly while maintaining confidentiality, integrity, and availability. Security practitioners must assess vulnerabilities, enforce least privilege access, and implement robust authentication and encryption mechanisms. Regular security assessments, penetration testing, and compliance with industry standards help mitigate evolving cyber threats. Additionally, secure data transmission and storage practices must be enforced to protect sensitive information from unauthorized access. A well-defined security architecture aligns business objectives with risk management strategies, fostering a resilient and secure digital ecosystem. In addition to access controls, organizations must consider scalability and adaptability in their security designs, ensuring that systems can handle future growth and emerging threats. The integration of cloud-based storage and applications introduces new complexities, requiring robust encryption and identity management strategies. A proactive monitoring system is also essential to detect and respond to security incidents in real-time, minimizing potential damage. Finally, securing communication channels between disparate systems, whether on-premises or in the cloud, requires the use of secure protocols and the continuous evaluation of emerging technologies to stay ahead of evolving risks.

Structure

In this chapter, we will cover the following topics:

- Adapt security to meet business needs
- Interoperability issues
- Application requirement
- Open source
- Redundancy and high availability
- Data security considerations
- Resource provisioning and de-provisioning
- Applications
- Configuration management database
- Directory services

Objectives

After going through this chapter, you will be able to understand the following how to ensure a secure and efficient integration of hosts, networks, storage, and applications, organizations must continuously adapt security strategies to align with evolving business needs. Adhering to industry standards while addressing challenges related to competing or de facto standards is essential for maintaining compliance and interoperability. Security practitioners must consider resilience issues, especially when integrating legacy systems with modern applications, ensuring compatibility across various software types, standard data formats, protocols, and APIs. Effective security measures should encompass automation and orchestration of critical assets, redundancy for high availability, and a proactive approach to potential cyber threats. Data security plays a crucial role, requiring stringent controls for data remnants, aggregation, isolation, ownership, sovereignty, and volume management. Additionally, secure resource provisioning and de-provisioning, along with meticulous planning during mergers, acquisitions, and divestitures, help maintain security posture during organizational transitions. Network segmentation and delegation further enhance security by isolating critical components while maintaining controlled access. A well-defined logical and physical deployment diagram ensures clarity in security implementation across all relevant devices. Furthermore, secure storage integration demands rigorous privacy considerations, ensuring data confidentiality and integrity. Finally, integrating various applications, including CRM, ERP, CMDB, CMS, integration enablers, Directory Services, DNS, SOA, and ESB, requires robust security frameworks to facilitate seamless operation while safeguarding sensitive information.

Adapt security to meet business needs

The business demands of a company may vary, necessitating the deployment of security devices or controls in a new way of securing data flow. As a security professional, you should be able to assess business changes, determine how they influence security, and then implement the necessary controls. Security professionals should identify personal and private information to secure data during transfer. Once this data has been properly identified, the following analysis steps should occur:

1. Determine which applications and services access the information.

2. Document where the information is stored.

3. Document security controls to protect the stored information.

4. Determine how the information is transmitted.

5. Analyze whether authentication is used when accessing information. If it is, determine whether the authentication information is securely transmitted. If it is not, determine whether authentication can be used.

6. Analyze enterprise password policies, including password length, password complexity, and password expiration.

7. Determine whether encryption is used to transmit data. If it is, ensure that the level of encryption is appropriate and that the encryption algorithm is adequate. If it is not, determine whether encryption can be used.

8. Ensure that the encryption keys are protected.

To ensure the CIA of data throughout its life cycle, security practitioners should use the defense-in-depth philosophy. Applications and services should be examined to see whether better and more secure alternatives are available or if insufficient security measures are in place. To guarantee complete safety, data at rest may require encryption and proper **access control lists** (**ACLs**) to ensure that only authorized users have access. Secure protocols and encryption should be used for data transfer to prevent unauthorized users from intercepting and reading data. In the enterprise, the highest degree of authentication available should be applied. Password and account rules that are appropriate help defend against probable password attacks.

Finally, security professionals should guarantee that personal and private data is kept apart from other data, such as by storing it on separate physical servers or isolating it through **virtual LANs** (**VLANs**). On all devices, disable any superfluous services, protocols, and accounts. Based on vendor recommendations and releases, ensure that all firmware, operating systems, and applications are kept up to date.

When new technologies are implemented to meet the organization's changing business demands, security practitioners must be careful in ensuring that they understand all of the new technology's security implications and challenges. Deploying new technology without first doing a thorough security review might lead to security breaches that harm more than simply the newly installed technology. Keep in mind that changes are unavoidable. What will set you apart from other security experts is how you examine and plan for these developments.

Standards

The implementation of policies inside an organization is described by standards. They are tactical acts or rules, in the sense that they outline the processes required to accomplish security. Standards, like rules, should be evaluated and amended regularly. A governing body, such as the **National Institute of Standards and Technology** (**NIST**), normally establishes standards. Security experts must be conversant with the standards that have been created since companies require direction on how to secure their assets. Many organizations for standards have been established, including the NIST, the United States **Department of Defence** (**DOD**), and the **International Organization for Standardization** (**ISO**).

The United States DOD defines a certification and accreditation procedure for DOD information systems in DOD Instruction 8510.01. ISO collaborates with the **International Electrotechnical Commission** (**IEC**) to develop several information security standards. Other standards, such as those from the **European Union Agency for Network and Information Security** (**ENISA**), the **European Union** (**EU**), and the United States **National Security Agency** (**NSA**), may be needed by security experts. A company must examine the many standards accessible and implement the most advantageous recommendations based on the company's requirements. Open standards, conformity to standards, competing standards, a lack of standards, and de facto standards are briefly discussed in the following sections.

Open standards

The term open standard refers to standards that are available to the broader public. Without acquiring any rights to the standards or organizational membership, the general public can offer input on them and utilize them. Subject matter experts and industry specialists must assist in the establishment and upkeep of these standards.

Adherence to standards

Organizations might choose to follow just open standards or standards that are governed by a standards body. Depending on the industry, some organizations may choose to implement only certain elements of standards. Remember that each standard should be thoroughly reviewed and analyzed to see how its implementation will affect the company. If a company disregards well-established norms, it may face legal consequences. Failure to employ standards to drive your organization's security approach, particularly if others in your field do so, can have a severe negative impact on your company's image and position.

Competing standards

Competing standards are frequently enforced between rival companies. Microsoft, for example, frequently creates its authentication standards. Its standards are frequently based on an industry-standard with minor changes to suit Microsoft's needs. Linux, on the other hand, may adopt standards, but being an open-source operating system, changes may have been made along the road that may not entirely fit with the standards your company must follow. Always examine rival standards to see which one best meets your company's requirements.

Lack of standards

Standards have yet to be established in certain emerging technological domains. Do not let a lack of formal standards keep you from providing your company with the greatest security measures. If you can identify a similar technology that has formal standards, see if those standards apply to your solution. You could also wish to seek advice from specialists in the field (SMEs). A lack of standards does not exempt your company from taking all required precautions to safeguard personal and private information.

De facto standards

De facto standards are commonly accepted but not technically established standards. International standards groups adopt de jure standards, which are standards that are based on laws or regulations. De facto norms should be prioritized over de jure ones. If at all possible, your company should implement security policies that meet both de facto and de jure requirements. Consider the following scenario:

Assume that the major goal of a **chief information officer** (**CIO**) is to implement a system that supports the 802.11r standard, which will aid wireless VoIP devices in moving automobiles. The 802.11r standard, on the other hand, has not been fully certified. The products of the wireless vendor do support 802.11r as it is currently specified. The administrators have evaluated the product and found no security or compatibility concerns, but they are worried that the standard has not yet been finalized. The best course of action is to get the equipment right now, as long as the firmware can be upgraded to the final 802.11r standard.

Interoperability issues

When integrating solutions into a secure corporate architecture, security professionals must be aware of all potential interoperability difficulties with legacy systems/current systems, application needs, and in-house versus commercial versus adapted commercial apps. Interoperability issues also arise from differences in security protocols, authentication mechanisms, and encryption standards, which can create vulnerabilities if not properly aligned. Variations in data formats and communication protocols between heterogeneous systems may lead to compatibility challenges, requiring middleware solutions or API gateways for seamless integration. Regulatory and compliance mismatches across different systems, especially in multinational organizations, can further complicate interoperability efforts. The lack of standardized security controls across vendors may introduce security gaps, necessitating additional configuration, monitoring, and governance frameworks. Additionally, integrating cloud-based and on-premise solutions often presents synchronization challenges, requiring careful planning to ensure data consistency, access control, and threat detection across environments.

Legacy and current systems

Legacy systems are older technology, computers, or programs that provide a key role in the organization. Frequently, the vendor no longer maintains old systems, which means that no future technology, computer, or program upgrades will be supplied. Because of the security risks they pose, it is usually better to replace these systems as soon as feasible. However, due to the vital job they provide, these systems are occasionally required to be kept. Some guidelines when retaining legacy systems include the following:

- If possible, implement the legacy system in a protected network or **demilitarized zone (DMZ)**.
- Limit physical access to the legacy system to administrators.
- If possible, deploy the legacy application on a virtual computer.
- Employ ACLs to protect the data on the system.
- Deploy the highest-level authentication and encryption mechanisms possible.

The examples of legacy technologies that were highly popular decades ago, and are still in use today, are as follows:

- Mainframe computers running ancient applications
- Programming languages, such as COBOL
- Operating systems, such as MS-DOS, Windows 3.1, or XP
- Hardware, such as Apple IIGS machines or Intel 286 computers

There are a variety of reasons why businesses may decide not to upgrade legacy systems and instead continue to utilize them. The following are the primary reasons:

- Aside from the disadvantages of legacy systems, some businesses may want to keep them since they are still functional. Legacy technologies that have been tried and proven, are robust and reliable, and personnel have a high degree of technical knowledge.
- Upgrades and replacements are expensive, especially for complicated, organization-wide, critical technology. Furthermore, most firms have made significant investments in legacy technology. When the cost of maintenance is less than the cost of replacement, businesses may opt to keep legacy systems.

- It is possible that switching to a whole new technology may be too disruptive. Legacy technology plays an important function in a company, and a replacement may or may not be more dependable, secure, or speedier. As a result, the hazards associated with comprehensive replacement may jeopardize operations.

Consider the following scenario. Let us say a company has a historical **customer relationship management** (**CRM**) system that it has to keep. The application is only compatible with the Windows 2000 operating system, and the manufacturer no longer maintains it. The company might set up a **virtual machine** (**VM**) running Windows 2000 and migrate the application there. Users who want application access can utilize a remote desktop to connect to the VM and the application.

Let us have a look at a more complicated scenario. Assume that an administrator replaces servers whenever funds are available in the budget. The organization has used 20 servers and 50 PCs from five different manufacturers during the last few years. Increased mean time to failure of older servers, OS variations, patch availability, and the capacity to recover incompatible hardware are some of the management problems and hazards associated with this form of technology life cycle management.

Application requirements

Any installed program may demand hardware, software, or other requirements that the business does not have. However, thanks to recent developments in virtual technology, the company may use virtualization to create a VM that meets the application's requirements. For example, an application can demand a certain screen resolution or graphics driver that is not installed on any of the company's physical PCs. In this situation, the company might set up a VM with the necessary screen resolution or driver to ensure that the program runs well. Keep in mind that some apps may require operating system versions that are no longer accessible. You may opt to deploy a program in compatibility mode in current versions of Windows by utilizing the **Compatibility** tab of the application's executable file, as illustrated in *Figure 18.1*:

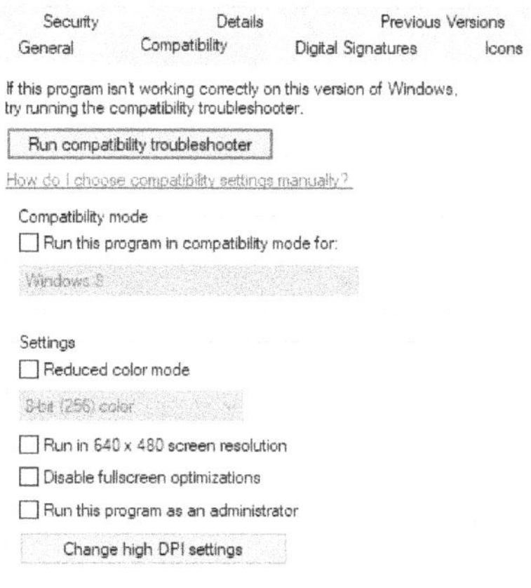

Figure 18.1: Compatibility tab software types

Software can be of several types, and each type has advantages and disadvantages. This section looks at the major types of software.

In-house developed

Applications can be built in-house or bought off the shelf. If developers have the requisite expertise, funding, and time, in-house-produced apps may be tailored to the firm. Commercial apps may give the organization customization possibilities. However, customization is typically limited. When a new application is required, businesses should thoroughly investigate their possibilities. Once an organization's requirements have been defined, it may compare them to all commercially available programs to see whether any of them will meet those requirements. Purchasing a commercial solution rather than developing one in-house is typically more cost-effective. However, each company must weigh the expenses of commercial applications against the expenditures of in-house development.

Commercial

Commercial software, often known as **commercial off-the-shelf** (**COTS**) software, is well-known and readily available. Information about vulnerabilities and possible attack patterns is commonly discussed among IT professionals. This implies that employing commercial software might expose the company to additional security vulnerabilities. In most circumstances, consumers do not have access to the source code, making it impossible to assess the security of commercial software programs.

Tailored commercial

Tailored commercial (or commercial customized) software is a new type of software that comes in modules that may be combined to create exactly the components that the business needs. It enables the company to customize it. Tailored commercial software offers a balance between fully custom-built and off-the-shelf solutions, allowing organizations to modify specific functionalities while benefiting from vendor support and updates. This approach reduces development time and cost compared to building software from scratch while still providing flexibility to meet unique business requirements. Integration with existing IT infrastructure is often smoother, as these solutions are designed with interoperability in mind. Security considerations remain crucial, as customization may introduce vulnerabilities that require thorough testing and regular patch management. Additionally, organizations must evaluate vendor lock-in risks, ensuring long-term compatibility and support for evolving business and regulatory needs.

Open source

Open-source software is free, but it comes with no assurances and limited support outside the user community's assistance. It necessitates a great deal of knowledge and ability to apply to a given business, but it also provides the most flexibility. Open-source software offers a wide range of benefits, including the ability to modify and customize the source code to fit specific business needs. It promotes transparency, allowing users to inspect and improve the software for enhanced security and performance. However, it often lacks formal vendor support, making it challenging for organizations without in-house expertise. Community-driven development can result in irregular updates or slower bug fixes, leaving users to manage their own security patches and updates. Additionally, integration with proprietary systems may pose compatibility challenges, requiring additional effort to ensure smooth operations across diverse technology environments. Despite these challenges, many organizations leverage open-source software for cost-effective solutions, particularly in environments where adaptability and innovation are key priorities.

Standard data formats

When integrating many apps in an organization, issues with data formats might develop. As shown by the filename extension, each program will have its own set of data formats unique to that software. Securing various data types is a difficulty. Some encryption methods work on some kinds but not on others. The **Trusted Data Format** (**TDF**), developed by Virtru, is one recent advancement in this field. TDF is essentially a content-containing protective wrapper. Your data are encrypted and **wrapped** into a TDF file, which connects with Virtru-enabled key stores to retain access privileges, whether you are transmitting an email message, an Excel document, or a kitten photo.

Protocols and APIs

Another barrier to interoperability is the usage of several protocols and **application program interfaces** (**APIs**). Both endpoints must support and comprehend the protocols in use when it comes to networking, storage, and authentication. To lower the attack surface, there should be an aim to reduce the number of protocols in use. Each protocol has its own set of flaws that must be addressed. There are a variety of API techniques available, including **Simple Object Access Protocol** (**SOAP**), **Representational State Transfer** (**REST**), and **JavaScript Object Notation** (**JSON**), and many businesses use all of them. Reducing the number of APIs in use should be a goal to limit the attack surface.

Resilience issues

When integrating technologies into safe enterprise architecture, security professionals must make sure that the result is an environment that can survive both in the short term and over time. Mission-critical operations, as well as the systems that enable the services and applications needed to keep the company running, must be robust. This section examines problems that affect availability.

Use of heterogeneous components

Heterogeneous components are systems that have many types of components. These components can be found within a system or in separate physical systems, such as when Windows and Linux computers must connect to complete a business process. A data warehouse, a repository of information from heterogeneous databases, is probably the greatest example of heterogeneous components. It allows multiple sources of data to not only be stored in one location, but also be organized in such a way that data redundancy is reduced (a process known as data normalization), and more sophisticated data mining tools to manipulate the data to discover previously unknown relationships. They provide greater security problems in addition to the benefits they bring.

Heterogeneous computing is another word for systems that have more than one type of processor or core. Such systems make use of the distinct qualities of the many components by assigning each one a job in which it excels. While this usually improves performance, it makes performance predictability a little more challenging. Because capacity planning relies on the ability to forecast performance under varying workloads, this can have a detrimental influence on resilience or lead to overcapacity.

Course of action automation or orchestration

While task automation has been used for some time (at least through scripts), orchestration takes it a step further by automating the whole workflow. One of the advantages of orchestration is the ability to program logic into the supporting systems, allowing them to react to changes in the environment. This can be a valuable tool for ensuring system resilience. To handle changing workflows, assets may be updated in real-time. For example, VMware vRealize is a virtual environment orchestration software that goes a step further by predicting workloads based on historical data.

Distribution of critical assets

Ensuring that key assets are not all situated in the same physical area is one method that can help improve resiliency. Collocating important assets exposes your company to the type of disaster that occurred at the Atlanta airport in 2017. The world's busiest airport stayed black for nearly 12 hours when a fire knocked out the primary and backup power systems (which were both located together). It is undeniable that distributing vital assets improves resilience.

Persistence and non-persistence of data

Persistent data is information that remains accessible after you close and restart an app or device. When an unexpected shutdown happens, non-persistent data is lost. The hibernation procedure that a laptop goes through when the battery runs out is one approach that has been used to safeguard non-persistent data. Another example is system images, which "store" all changes to a snapshot from time to time. Finally, database systems' journaling mechanism records changes to the database that are planned to be made (known as transactions) and saves them to disc before they are made. The transaction log is examined after a power outage to apply any un-applied transactions. When integrating new technologies, security experts must investigate and employ these diverse strategies to give the best possible level of protection for non-persistent data.

Redundancy and high availability

Fault tolerance permits a system to continue to function normally even if one or more of its components fail. Fault-tolerant drives and fault-tolerant drive adapters are used to provide fault tolerance for a hard disc system. The cost of fault tolerance, on the other hand, must be evaluated against the cost of a redundant device or hardware. If information system security capabilities are not fault-tolerant, attackers can get access to systems if the security mechanisms fail. The cost of implementing a fault-tolerant system should be weighed against the cost of an assault on the system under attack. While providing a fault-tolerant security method to protect public data may not be critical, providing a fault-tolerant security mechanism to safeguard confidential data is critical.

Availability refers to the ability to obtain data when it is required. Only those with a legitimate need for data should have access to it. The two basic scenarios in which availability is impacted are (1) when an attack disables or cripples a system and (2) when service is lost during and after disasters. Each system should be evaluated for its importance to the organization's operations. Controls should be implemented according to the criticality level of each system. The opposite of destruction or isolation is availability. Controls that can increase availability include fault-tolerant technology such as RAID or redundant locations.

The degree to which a new solution or system displays high availability, which is generally given by redundancy of internal components, network connections, or data sources, is perhaps the most visible effect on its resiliency. To take it a step further, some systems would need to be deployed in clusters to give the capacity to recover from the loss of an entire system. When the criticality of the operation that the system supports is stated, all new integrations should consider high-availability solutions and redundant components.

Assumed likelihood of attack

Risk analysis should be performed on all new integrations to identify the possibility and effect of various vulnerabilities and threats. Attacks can be prevented and their impact reduced when they are foreseen and measures are implemented. It is also crucial to examine the risk of new vulnerabilities arising from interactions between new and older systems.

Data security considerations

One of the most significant issues during integration is the security of the data processed by any new system. Every stage of the data life cycle must be considered for data security. This section highlights data security concerns during integration. In addition to the lifecycle considerations, ensuring that data is securely encrypted during both transit and storage is essential to prevent unauthorized access. It's also crucial to implement strict access controls and authentication mechanisms to limit who can view or modify sensitive data. Data masking and tokenization techniques should be employed when working with sensitive information to mitigate risks during testing and development. Moreover, compliance with data protection regulations such as GDPR or HIPAA must be continuously monitored throughout the integration process to avoid legal and financial repercussions. Finally, organizations should have clear data retention and deletion policies to securely dispose of data once it's no longer needed, reducing the risk of exposing outdated or irrelevant information.

Data remnants

When a computer or another resource is no longer in use, data remnants are that data that are left behind. An unauthorized user can access data leftovers if resources, particularly hard discs, are reused regularly. The best approach to safeguard this information is to use data encryption. Without the original encryption key, data that has been encrypted cannot be retrieved. Administrators must be aware of the types of data stored on physical discs to assess if data remains are an issue. The organization may not be concerned with data leftovers if the data stored on a disc is not private or secret.

If the data on the drive is secret or sensitive, however, the business should consider asset reuse and disposal rules. Residual data can be left behind after the data is wiped or removed from the storage medium. When an organization disposes of media, the data may be rebuilt, allowing unauthorized persons or organizations access to the information. Magnetic hard disc drives, solid-state drives, magnetic tapes, and optical media such as CDs and DVDs must all be considered by security professionals. When considering data reminisce, security professionals must understand the following countermeasures:

- **Clearing**: This includes removing data from the media so that the data cannot be reconstructed using normal file recovery techniques and tools. With this method, the data is recoverable only using special forensic techniques.

- **Purging**: Also referred to as sanitization, purging makes the data unreadable even with advanced forensic techniques. When this technique is used, data should be unrecoverable.

- **Destruction**: Destruction involves destroying the media on which the data resides. Overwriting is a destruction technique that writes data patterns over the entire media, thereby eliminating any trace data.

- **Degaussing**: Another destruction technique involves exposing the media to a powerful, alternating magnetic field to remove any previously written data and leave the media in a magnetically randomized (blank) state. Encryption scrambles the data on the media, thereby rendering it unreadable without the encryption key.

- **Physical destruction:** This involves physically breaking the media apart or chemically altering it. For magnetic media, physical destruction can also involve exposure to high temperatures.

Most of these countermeasures are effective against magnetic media. Solid-state drives, on the other hand, provide distinct issues since they cannot be rewritten. Sanitization instructions are provided by most solid-state drive manufacturers and can be used to wipe data from the device. These commands should be researched by security specialists to guarantee that they are effective. Erasing the cryptographic key is another option for these discs. To guarantee that the data is completely deleted, a combination of these procedures is frequently utilized. When adopting any cloud-based service for an enterprise, data reminiscence is also a factor to consider. Although it is difficult to establish whether data is effectively deleted, security specialists should be engaged in the negotiation of any contract with a cloud-based service to ensure that the contract includes data reminisce problems. When working with the cloud, data encryption is a wonderful technique to ensure that data reminiscence is not an issue.

Data aggregation

Data aggregation allows you to query data from numerous sources and aggregate it into a single report. On all of the domains and servers involved, the account used to access the data must have proper rights. In most situations, these sorts of installations include a dedicated server with a centralized data warehousing and mining system. Unwanted access to data is frequently the source of database security risks. The processes of aggregation and inference are two security vulnerabilities that occur in database management. Aggregation is the process of merging data from several sources. When a user does not have access to a group of data items but does have access to them individually or at least to some of them and can piece together the information to which he should not have access, this can constitute a security concern with databases. Inference refers to the process of putting together knowledge. The following two types of access measures can be put in place to help prevent access to inferable information:

- **Content-dependent access control**: Access is dependent on the sensitivity of the data using this sort of metric. A department manager, for example, may have access to the salaries of his or her employees but not to the salaries of employees in other departments. Increased processing overhead is the cost of this measure.

- **Context-dependent access control**: Access is dependent on various criteria using this sort of metric to help prevent inference. Location, time of day, and past access history are all elements that might influence access control.

Data isolation

In databases, data isolation prevents data corruption due to two concurrent activities. Using tenant IDs in the data labels, data isolation is used in cloud computing to guarantee that tenant data in a multi-tenant system is separated from other renters' data. In most cases, trusted login services are also utilized. Data isolation should be checked in each of these installations to ensure that data is not damaged. In most circumstances, a transaction rollback should be used to guarantee that appropriate recovery is possible.

Data ownership

While the majority of an organization's data is developed in-house, some of it is not. In many circumstances, businesses obtain data from others who create data similar to their own. These organizations may keep ownership of the information and simply license its usage. When integrated systems use such data, all duties associated with the data must be taken into account. **service-level agreements** (**SLAs**) should be observed if they stipulate certain sorts of data handling or protection. A data or information owner's primary task is to identify the categorization level of the information they own and to secure the data they are in charge of. This job grants or refuses data access permissions. The data owner, on the other hand, is typically not in charge of data access control implementation. The data owner's job is frequently performed by someone who has the best understanding of the data due to their affiliation with a certain business unit. A data owner should be assigned to each business unit. A human resources department employee, for example, has a superior understanding of human resources data than an accounting department person.

After the data owner has defined the information classification and controls, the data custodian applies them. The data custodian, on the other hand, does not require any understanding of the data beyond its classification levels, although the data owner normally does. Even though the data owner for human resources data should be a human resources manager, the data custodian for the data might be a member of the IT department.

Data sovereignty

Information that has been transformed to binary digital form and saved is governed by the laws of the jurisdiction in which it is stored. Data sovereignty is the term for this notion. When a company works on a worldwide scale, data sovereignty must be taken into account. It may have an impact on security concerns such as control selection, and it may eventually lead to a choice to centralize all data in the home nation. There is no such thing as a company that works in a vacuum. Laws, rules, and compliance requirements influence all businesses. Contracts, legislation, industry standards, and regulations must all be followed by organizations. Security personnel must be familiar with the rules and regulations of the nation or countries in which they work, as well as the industry in which they work. Many rules and regulations are constructed in such a way that specified activities are required. In certain circumstances, however, rules and regulations leave it up to the organization to figure out how to comply.

Both the United States and the EU have enacted rules and regulations that influence businesses operating inside their respective jurisdictions. While security professionals should endeavor to comprehend laws and regulations, they may lack the expertise and experience necessary to completely grasp these rules and regulations to defend their business. Security professionals should consult with legal counsel in certain situations to ensure legislative or regulatory compliance.

Data volume

Organizations should endeavor to keep their data storage to a minimum. A broader attack surface equals more data. Data retention rules should be established that require data to be destroyed when it is no longer useful to the company. Remember that the formulation of such policies should be guided by legal and regulatory requirements for the retention of data that is relevant to the industry in which the company operates.

Resources provisioning and de-provisioning

The flexibility to supply and de-provision resources as required is one of the advantages of many cloud installations. Users, servers, virtual devices, and applications may all be provisioned and de-provisioned. Your business may have an internal administrator who performs these activities, the cloud provider may handle these tasks, or you may have a hybrid solution where these tasks are shared between an internal administrator and cloud provider employees, depending on the deployment model employed. Remember that any solution that requires the cloud provider staff to offer provisioning and de-provisioning may not be suitable since those individuals may not be accessible to do any operations that you want right away.

Users

It is usually recommended to utilize an account template when provisioning (or establishing) user accounts to ensure that all of the relevant password policies, user rights, and other account settings are applied to the newly formed account. If you are going to de-provision a user account, you should first disable it. It may be hard to access files, directories, and other resources controlled by that user account once it has been destroyed. If an account is deactivated rather than destroyed, the administrator can re-enable it temporarily to provide access to the account's resources. A proper method for requesting the establishment, disablement, or deletion of user accounts should be adopted by an organization. Administrators should also keep an eye on the account used to ensure that accounts are still active.

Servers

Server provisioning and de-provisioning should be based on organizational requirements and performance metrics. Administrators must monitor existing server resource utilization to decide when a new server should be deployed. Procedures should be put in place whenever a pre-set threshold has been achieved to guarantee that fresh server resources are supplied. When such resources are no longer required, procedures for de-provisioning the servers should be in place. Monitoring is crucial once more.

Virtual devices

The host machine's resources are used by virtual devices. The RAM on a real system, for example, is shared among all virtual devices installed on that physical machine. When an organizational requirement arises, administrators should supply additional virtual devices. However, de-provisioning virtual devices when they are no longer needed is equally crucial to free up resources for other virtual devices.

Applications

Organizations frequently require a wide range of applications. It is critical to keep track of the licenses for any commercial software that is utilized. Administrators must be alerted so that licenses are not renewed when an organization no longer requires them or are renewed at a lesser level when the app demand is low.

Merger and acquisition considerations

The enterprise design must be addressed when companies combine, are purchased, or split. Each unique organization has its resources, infrastructure, and model in the case of mergers and acquisitions. As a security professional, you must guarantee that the architecture of two firms is properly examined before selecting how to integrate them. In the case of demergers, you will almost certainly have to assist in determining how to effectively distribute the resources. Data security should always be a top priority.

Network secure segmentation and delegation

An organization may need to segment its network for a variety of reasons, including improving network performance, protecting certain traffic, and so on. The employment of routers, switches, and firewalls is commonly used to segment a business network. A network administrator may choose to use switches to create VLANs or firewalls to create a DMZ. Whatever method you use to divide the network, make sure the interfaces connecting the segments are as safe as possible. This might entail shutting down ports, adopting MAC filtering, and employing other security measures. Separate physical trust zones can be implemented in a virtualized system. After the segments or zones have been formed, you may assign individual administrators to manage the various segments or zones.

Logical deployment diagram

Security professionals must be familiar with two types of enterprise deployment diagrams to pass the CASP exam: logical deployment diagrams and physical deployment diagrams. The architecture is depicted in a logical deployment diagram, which includes the domain architecture, which thus includes the current domain hierarchy, names, addressing scheme, server roles, and trust relationships. The details of physical communication links, such as cable length, grade, and wiring paths, servers, including computer name, IP address (if static), server role, and domain membership, device location, including printer, hub, switch, modem, router, or bridge, as well as proxy location, communication links and available bandwidth between sites, and the number of users, including mobile users, at each site, are all shown on a physical deployment diagram. In comparison to a physical diagram, a logical diagram often contains less information. While a logical diagram may frequently be created from a physical diagram, creating a physical diagram from a logical diagram is practically impossible. *Figure 18.2* shows an example of a logical network diagram:

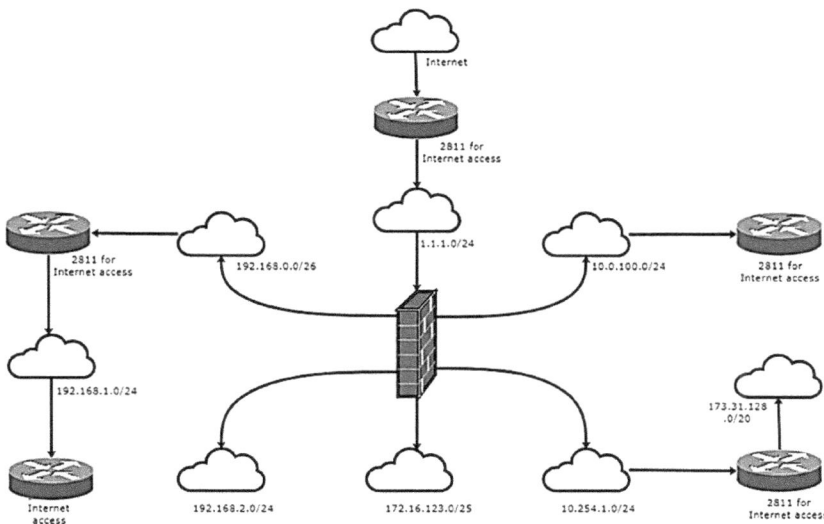

Figure 18.2: Logical network diagram

The logical diagram only depicts a handful of the network's servers, as well as the services they provide, their IP addresses, and DNS names. The arrows between the different servers represent the relationships between them. *Figure 18.3* shows an example of a physical network diagram; the cabling utilized, the devices on the network, the important information for each server, and the other connection information are all included in a physical network diagram, which provides more information than a logical one:

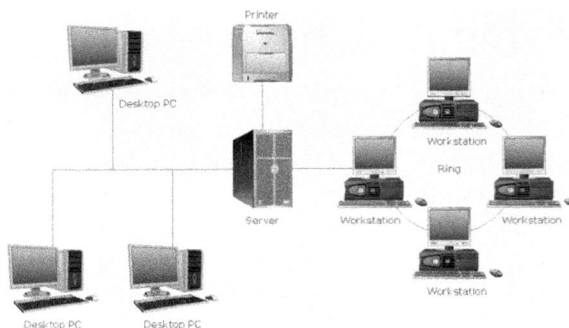

Figure 18.3: *Physical network diagram*

Storage security and privacy

To guarantee that security risks are considered when integrating storage systems into an organization, security practitioners should be included in the design and implementation. To guarantee that storage administrators prioritize the security of the storage solutions, security practitioners should ensure that an organization sets proper security policies for storage solutions. The following are some of the security considerations for storage integration:

- Limit physical access to the storage solution.
- Create a private network to manage the storage solution.
- Implement ACLs for all data, paths, subnets, and networks.
- Implement ACLs at the port level, if possible.
- Implement multi-factor authentication.

Enterprise application security

Enterprise application integration enablers guarantee that an enterprise's applications and services can communicate as needed. Understanding which enabler is required in a given circumstance or scenario and ensuring that the solution is delivered in the most secure manner feasible are the main issues for the CASP test. CRM, **enterprise resource planning (ERP)**, **governance, risk, and compliance (GRC)**, **enterprise service bus (ESB)**, **service-oriented architecture (SOA)**, Directory Services, **domain name system (DNS)**, **configuration management database (CMDB)**, and **content management systems (CMSs)** are some of the solutions you should be familiar with.

Customer relationship management

Customer relationship management (CRM) entails identifying customers and preserving all customer-related data, including contact information and information on any direct interactions with them. CRM security is critical to an organization's success. Access to the CRM system is often restricted to sales and marketing staff, as well as management. If remote access to the CRM system is essential, a VPN or equivalent solution should be used to safeguard the CRM data.

Enterprise resource planning

Data from product planning, product cost, manufacturing or service delivery, marketing/ sales, inventory management, shipping, payment, and any other company operations is collected, stored, managed, and interpreted by ERP. Personnel has access to an ERP system for reporting reasons. ERP should be installed on a secure internal network, sometimes known as a DMZ. When implementing ERP, you may encounter resistance from some departments that do not want to share their process data with other departments.

Configuration management database

A CMDB records the status of assets like goods, systems, software, facilities, and people at precise periods in time, as well as the relationships among them. CMDBs are commonly used as data warehouses by the IT department.

Content management system

From a central interface, a CMS publishes, edits, updates, organizes, deletes, and manages material. Users may readily discover material using this single interface. Users can easily access the most recent version of the material since modifications are made from a central place. Microsoft SharePoint is an example of a CMS.

Integration enablers

Enterprise application integration enablers guarantee that a company's applications and services can communicate when they are needed. These enablers include all of the services specified in this section.

Directory Services

Directory Services organizes, saves, and makes the information in a computer operating system's directory accessible. Users can access a resource using its name rather than its IP or MAC address with Directory Services. The majority of businesses set up an internal Directory Services server to handle all internal queries. To gather information on any resources that are not on the local company network, this internal server talks with a root server on a public network or with an externally facing server that is secured by a firewall or other security barriers. Directory Services include Active Directory, DNS, and LDAP, as illustrated in *Figure 18.4*:

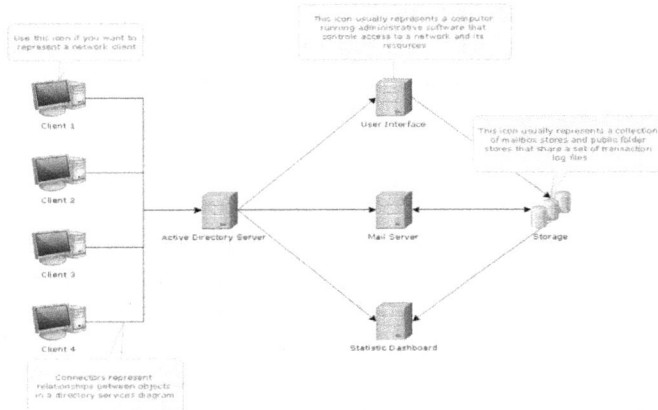

Figure 18.4: Active Directory Services

Domain name system

DNS is a hierarchical naming system for computers, services, and other resources that are connected to the Internet or a private network. To guarantee that a DNS server is authorized before the transfer of DNS information between the DNS server and the client, you should activate **Domain Name System Security Extensions (DNSSEC)**. **Transaction Signature (TSIG)** is a DNSSEC cryptographic method that allows a DNS server to update client resource entries automatically if their IP addresses or hostnames change. A DNS client's TSIG record is used to validate it. Internal DNS servers can be configured to only connect with root servers as a security precaution. When the internal DNS servers are configured to connect solely with the root servers, they are not allowed to contact any other external DNS servers, as shown in *Figure 18.5*:

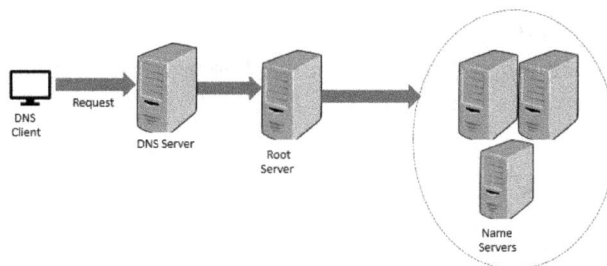

Figure 18.5: DNS Servers

The **Start of Authority (SOA)** includes information about the authoritative server for a DNS zone. The **time to live (TTL)** of a DNS record specifies how long it will last before it has to be renewed. When the TTL of a record expires, it is deleted from the DNS cache. To poison the DNS cache, you must add fake records to the DNS zone. Because the resource record is accessed less frequently with a longer TTL, it is less likely to be poisoned.

Let us have a look at a DNS-related security problem. Assume an IT administrator sets up new DNS name servers to host the company's MX records and resolve the public address of the webserver. Only server ACLs are used by the administrator to safeguard zone transfers between DNS servers. Any alternative DNS servers, on the other hand, would be vulnerable to the IP spoofing attacks.

Another situation is when a security team discovers that by asking the company's external DNS server, someone from outside the organisation has gotten critical information about the internal organization. The security manager should solve the problem by setting up a split DNS server, with the external DNS server containing only the information about domains that should be visible to the outside world and the internal DNS server maintaining authoritative records for internal systems.

Service-oriented architecture

Software is used to give application functionality as services to other applications in a SOA. A service is a single unit of functionality that is integrated to deliver all of the required capabilities; web services frequently overlap with this design, as presented in *Figure 18.6*:

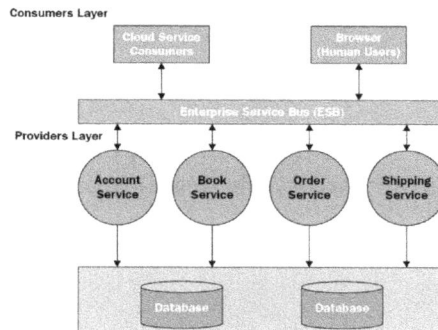

Figure 18.6: Service-oriented architecture

Consider the following SOA situation. Assume that a database team recommends installing an SOA-based system across the organization. The CIO chooses to seek advice from the security manager on the risks associated with this design. Two issues for the SOA system should be presented to the CIO by the security manager – SOA abstracts old systems like web services, which are frequently vulnerable to outside threats, and users and services are spread, typically across the Internet.

Enterprise service bus

In an SOA, planning and executing communication between mutually engaging software applications is called ESB. It enables the communication between SOAP, Java, .NET, and other applications. To facilitate communication with business partners, an ESB system is often implemented on a DMZ. ESB is the best option for offering safe software architecture that is event-driven and standards-based.

Conclusion

In this chapter, we discussed how organizations securely integrate hosts, storage, networks, and applications to meet changing business needs. The need to understand different security standards, interoperability issues, and the use of techniques to increase resilience has high priority. Designing a secure infrastructure (logical and physical) and integrating secure storage solutions within the enterprise were also discussed.

In the next chapter, we will discuss the security activities across the technology lifecycle, related to secure development and asset inventory, ensuring appropriate security controls are deployed.

Exercise

1. **Which of the following is the best method to ensure secure data flow between different systems?**

    a. Data compression

    b. Data encryption

    c. Data aggregation

    d. Data normalization

2. **In a secure data flow scenario, which component is primarily responsible for ensuring that data is only accessible to authorized users during transmission?**

    a. Firewall

    b. Encryption

    c. Compression

    d. Data tokenization

3. **What is the primary challenge in achieving interoperability between different systems in an organization?**

    a. Lack of user training

    b. Inconsistent data formats and protocols

    c. Insufficient hardware

    d. Overreliance on manual processes

4. **Which of the following can help resolve issues related to interoperability between legacy and modern systems?**

    a. Standardized APIs and protocols

    b. Use of proprietary software

c. High-bandwidth network connections

d. Enhanced end-user training

5. **What is the primary goal of network segmentation in a security context?**

    a. Improve network speed

    b. Isolate and protect critical systems

    c. Increase network bandwidth

    d. Simplify network architecture

6. **Which network security device is commonly used to enforce network segmentation?**

    a. Load balancer

    b. Router

    c. Firewall

    d. Switch

7. **Which design principle is crucial for creating a secure infrastructure?**

    a. Least privilege access

    b. High availability without redundancy

    c. Minimal data backup

    d. Centralized storage

8. **When designing secure infrastructure, what is the purpose of using a layered defense strategy?**

    a. To increase the complexity of system configuration

    b. To provide multiple points of security to reduce vulnerabilities

    c. To limit the need for security updates

    d. To optimize network traffic

9. **Which storage solution feature is critical for maintaining the confidentiality of sensitive data?**

    a. High-speed access

    b. Data encryption at rest

    c. Data replication

    d. Cloud-based backup

10. **What is a potential risk when integrating third-party storage solutions without proper security measures?**

    a. Reduced storage costs

    b. Loss of data integrity

    c. Enhanced access speeds

    d. Increased regulatory compliance

11. **What is a common challenge when integrating enterprise applications across different platforms?**

    a. Lack of cloud storage

    b. Incompatible data formats

    c. Excessive application updates

    d. Over-reliance on APIs

12. **Which technique can help ensure secure communication between integrated enterprise applications?**

    a. Using proprietary protocols

    b. Data encryption

    c. Simplifying data formats

    d. Increasing system redundancy

Answers

1. b
2. b
3. b
4. a
5. b
6. c
7. a
8. b
9. b
10. b
11. b
12. b

CHAPTER 19
Security Activities Across Technology Lifecycle

Introduction

When it comes to managing an enterprise's security, security practitioners must consider security throughout the whole technological life cycle. Security practitioners must ensure that the necessary security controls are installed as the company evolves as new devices and technologies are added, maintained, and removed. Understanding the systems and software development life cycles, adapting solutions to handle evolving risks, disruptive technologies, security trends, and asset management are all part of providing security across the technology life cycle.

Structure

In this chapter, we will cover the following topics:

- Systems development life cycle
- Asset disposal
- Adapt solutions
- Asset management

Objectives

The requirements for systems development, acquisition, testing and evaluation, commissioning/decommissioning, operating operations, asset disposal, and asset/object reuse are all covered in this chapter. Application security frameworks, software assurance, development methodologies, DevOps, secure coding standards, documentation, and validation and acceptance testing are all terms used to define software development. Emerging threats, disruptive technology, and security trends are discussed by adapt solutions. Asset management, inventory control, and related ideas are all part of asset management or inventory control.

Systems development life cycle

When a company defines new functionality that it must supply to consumers or internally, it must develop systems to deliver that functionality. Many judgments must be made, and those decisions must be made using a rational procedure. The **systems development life cycle** (**SDLC**) is the name for this procedure. The SDLC, rather than being a random method, offers clear and logical stages to guarantee that the system that emerges at the conclusion of the development process provides the expected functionality while maintaining an acceptable degree of security, as shown in *Figure 19.1*:

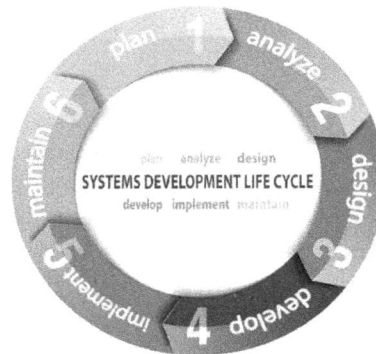

Figure 19.1: Systems development lifecycle

The steps in the SDLC are as follows:

1. **Initiate or plan**: The perception that new features or functions are needed or required in the company occurs during the start phase. This new feature might be an upgrade to an existing asset, or it could be the purchase or creation of a brand-new asset. Choosing whether to buy the product or develop it internally is part of the initial step. A company must also consider the solution's security needs at this point. The CIA's needs and concerns can be detailed in a preliminary risk assessment. It is critical to identify these difficulties early on so that these factors can drive the solution's procurement or development. The sooner security

requirements are identified in the SDLC, the more likely they are to be addressed effectively in the final product.

2. **Acquire or develop:** A set of actions in the SDLC's acquisition stage gives information to help decide whether to buy or build the solution. After that, the organization chooses a solution. The activities are designed to get answers to the following questions:

    a. What functions does the system need to perform?

    b. What potential risks to the CIA are exposed by the solution?

    c. What protection levels must be provided to satisfy legal and regulatory requirements?

    d. What tests are required to ensure that security concerns have been mitigated?

    e. How do various third-party solutions address these concerns?

    f. How do the security controls required by the solution affect other parts of the company's security policy?

    g. What metrics will be used to evaluate the success of the security controls?

   The answers to these questions should guide the questions during the acquisition step as well as the steps that follow this stage of the SDLC.

3. **Implement or design:** Before the system goes online, top management formally authorizes it during the implementation stage. The solution is next deployed in a real environment, which is known as the operation/maintenance stage but only when the company has accomplished both certification and accreditation. The process of certifying a solution's efficacy and security is known as certification. The management must give official approval to bring the solution into the production environment as part of the certification procedure. The security administrator would teach all users how to secure corporate information when using the new system, as well as how to spot social engineering threats, at this time.

4. **Operate or maintain:** When the system is turned on and started in the environment, the procedure does not finish there. It is crucial to establish a performance baseline so that ongoing monitoring can take place. The baseline guarantees that performance problems may be identified promptly. Any changes over time (for example, new features, solution patches, and so on) should be regularly monitored for their impact on the baseline. By establishing a systematic change management procedure, you can ensure that all modifications are authorized and recorded. Because any modifications might have an impact on both security and performance, it is important to pay close attention to the solution once any changes are made.

5. **Dispose:** Finally, when the solution has been deployed, vulnerability assessments and penetration testing can help identify any security or performance issues that

may have been caused by a change or occur as a result of a new threat. When the solution has served its purpose, the disposal stage involves removing it from the environment. When this occurs, an organization must consider certain issues, including the following:

a. Does removal or replacement of the solution introduce any security holes in the network?

b. How can the system be terminated in an orderly fashion so as not to disrupt business continuity?

c. How should any residual data left on any systems be removed?

d. How should any physical systems that were part of the solution be disposed of safely?

e. Are there any legal or regulatory issues that would guide the destruction of data?

You must know how to cover the SDLC from the beginning to the conclusion in order to pass the CASP test. Consider a corporation that wishes to increase earnings by cutting costs on non-core business operations. The IT manager requests clearance to move the company's email system to the cloud. Data life cycle concerns must be taken into account by the compliance officer. Data provisioning, data processing, data in transit, data at rest, and de-provisioning would represent the end-to-end data life cycle in this scenario.

Requirements

One of the tasks that occurs during the acquisition stage of the SDLC is the definition of system requirements. The purpose of this procedure is to guarantee that the system can execute all intended activities and that no resources are wasted on unnecessary functionality. Security needs are also established at this stage, which are driven by the needed functionality and the expected sensitivity of the data to be handled by the system. These criteria must be recognized early in the development process and included in the system design.

Acquisition

A system may be acquired rather than constructed in many circumstances, or a portion of a planned system may require acquisition. Before issuing any requests for bids, security specialists must be involved in determining the security criteria for the equipment to be procured when issuing some request for proposals or RFPs.

Test and evaluation

Several sorts of testing, including approaches to uncover both functional problems and security vulnerabilities, should take place throughout the test and assessment phase. The test data method is an auditing approach that determines the amount of system testing and identifies specific program logic that has not been tested. This approach assesses the behavior of the program in both cases by testing not only anticipated or legitimate input, but also incorrect and unexpected data. Assaults on the program should be made actively, including buffer overflows and **denial of service (DoS)** attacks.

Commissioning or decommissioning

The process of commissioning an asset is the process of integrating it into an organization, whereas the process of decommissioning an asset is the process of removing it from service. When an asset is put into production, it should be protected with the proper security measures. These security controls might be placed on the asset itself or on an enterprise asset like a firewall or router. When an asset is decommissioned, it is critical that the data held on the asset be safeguarded. Sometimes, an asset is retired temporarily, while at other times, it is permanently decommissioned. Regardless of the situation, it is critical to follow the right asset disposal and asset reuse policies to protect the organization's confidentiality, integrity, and availability. In most circumstances, you will need to back up all of the data on a decommissioned asset and make sure it is totally deleted before disposing of it. These rules should be reviewed and modified on a regular basis, especially when new assets or asset kinds are introduced to the company.

Consider the following scenario. Assume an **information security officer (ISO)** requests a security crew to go through the warehouse trash bin and gather abandoned PCs at random. Two outdated PCs and a faulty multi-function network printer are retrieved by the security team. The security team connects the two PCs' hard discs as well as the network printer to a computer with forensic tools. They are able to view the PDF files on the network printer hard drive, but not the data on the two older hard drives. The warehouse management should alter the hardware decommissioning processes as a result of this discovery to address the security problem.

Let us take a look at another scenario. Assume that a new vendor product has been purchased to replace an older one. Due to the present solution's near-end-of-life status and the lack of choices for prolonged support, there are significant timing restrictions. It has been stressed that only critical actions be completed for this project. You should test the new solution, migrate to the new solution, and then decommission the old system to strike a balance between security and time restrictions.

Operational activities

For example, an organization may have a policy in place that prevents the use of any wireless technology at the enterprise level. If a new device or technology requires wireless access, the organization will need to revisit the security policy to allow wireless access. However, the organization must ensure that the appropriate security controls are implemented when wireless access is added to the enterprise. Performing a security impact analysis involves examining the impact of the new functionality, application, or system on the organization's confidentiality, integrity, and availability. Operational activities are daily tasks performed with the use of a gadget or technology. All operational operations must be protected, and security controls must be checked on a regular basis to verify that they are still providing protection. While day-to-day operations are included, operational activities also involve the addition of new functionality, new applications, or entirely new systems to the infrastructure. Any new introduction, regardless of its nature, poses a risk to the company. As a result, security professionals must conduct a risk assessment and implement the necessary security measures to limit threats. An organization's security policy may be impacted by the addition of functionality, an application, or a system.

Finally, as noted several times throughout this book, security awareness and training are critical for ensuring the security of day-to-day operating activities. As new threats emerge, security awareness and training should be updated. Employees should go through this training when they first start working and at least once a year after that.

Monitoring

Once a system is up and running, it should be checked for security and performance problems. It is critical to establish a performance baseline so that ongoing monitoring can take place. The baseline guarantees that performance problems may be identified promptly. Any changes over time (for example, new features, solution patches, and so on) should be regularly monitored for their impact on the baseline. Significant changes may necessitate the construction of a new baseline in many circumstances, as the previous baseline may no longer be indicative of the current status quo. By establishing a formal change management process, you can ensure that all changes are approved and documented. Because any modifications might have an impact on both security and performance, it is important to pay close attention to the solution following any changes, as shown in *Figure 19.2*:

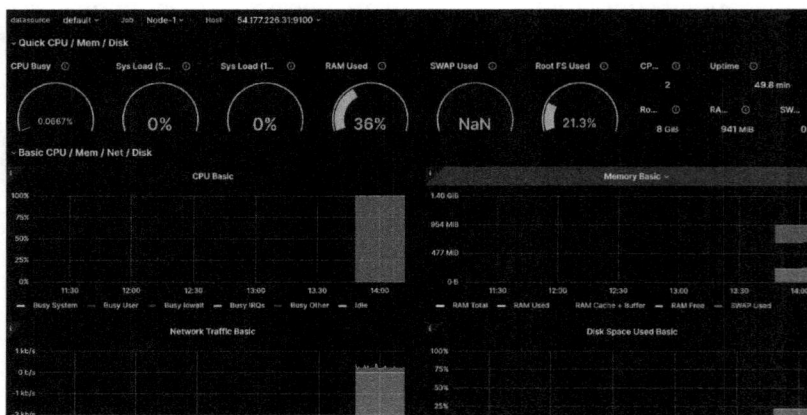

Figure 19.2: Dashboard for system monitoring

Finally, when the solution has been deployed, vulnerability assessments and penetration testing can help identify any security or performance issues that may have been caused by a change or occurred as a result of a new threat.

Maintenance

Patches, hotfixes, security updates, and service packs must all be maintained up to date for systems to function properly. Before releasing an update into production, it should be thoroughly tested in a lab setting. It is constantly vital to examine the security measures in place and to adopt any new controls when risks are found when maintenance is performed. Both hardware and software require maintenance, and both are equally critical in a maintenance strategy. Even if a device or a program is not utilized as frequently as others, it is still subject to timely updates. Hardware and software updates can frequently have unintended repercussions. Because the program interacts in a new way, a new application update may produce false positives on the corporate firewall. Ignoring a false positive (or turning off the warning) is not enough. Security professionals should do studies on issues like these to identify the best course of action. Another effect of an update might be that it introduces problems that cannot be fixed at the time of distribution. It may be essential to restore the hardware or software to its prior state in this situation. It is critical, however, that the update not be overlooked. A strategy should be put in place to guarantee that the update is deployed as soon as feasible.

It may be essential to reassign staff to guarantee that the issue is investigated and the update is re-deployed. Let us look at an example of maintenance and how it affects security. Let us say the **chief information security officer (CISO)** asks the IT manager who was responsible for the system upgrade after it causes considerable disruption. The IT manager says that because five separate persons have administrative access to the system, determining who is responsible is impossible. The IT manager should establish an enforceable change management system and allow user-level audits on all servers to boost responsibility and avoid this problem from recurring. Any maintenance program should contain documentation of all maintenance operations, including the person who performed the work, the type of work performed, the outcome of the work, and any issues that emerged, as well as issue resolution notes. This material will serve as a roadmap for the future.

Configuration and change management

Technology evolves, grows, and changes over time. Examples of changes that can occur include the following:

- Operating system configuration
- Software configuration
- Hardware configuration

Companies and their processes adapt and change as well, but change should be handled in a controlled manner to retain a shared sense of purpose. Change may be avoided from becoming a problem by following prescribed stages in a structured process. Keep in mind that change management collaborates with configuration management to guarantee that asset modifications do not accidentally compromise security. As a result, all modifications must be recorded, and all network diagrams, both logical and physical, must be updated on a regular basis to correctly represent the current configuration of each asset rather than the configuration two years ago. It should be a continuous activity to ensure that all change management policies are followed.

Consider the following scenario. Consider a corporation that has over 13,000 client PCs and 1,400 server machines. The IDS is sending many alarms to the security administrator about a probable virus spreading over the network via the Windows file sharing service. The security engineer feels that blocking the file-sharing service across the enterprise using **access control lists** (**ACLs**) on internal routers is the best course of action. To guarantee that the ACLs do not disrupt critical business operations, the company should convene an emergency change management meeting. In many circumstances, forming a change control board is advantageous. The tasks of the change control board can include the following:

- Ensuring that changes made are approved, tested, documented, and implemented correctly

- Meeting periodically to discuss change status accounting reports

- Maintaining responsibility for ensuring that changes made do not jeopardize the soundness of the verification system

Configuration management, while a subset of change management, focuses on bringing order to the chaos that can arise when different engineers and technicians have administrative access to the computers and devices that make the network run. It follows the same fundamental change management approach as before, but it may be even more important given the impact that competing changes might have on the network (in some cases instantaneously). Configuration management includes the following functions:

- Report the status of change processing.

- Document the functional and physical characteristics of each **configuration item** (**CI**).

- Perform information capture and version control.

- Control changes to the CIs and issue versions of CIs from the software library.

A software library is a regulated location available only to authorized users who are restricted to using an approved method in the context of configuration management. A CI is a discrete component of the system that is subject to its own configuration management mechanism. Configuration identification is the process of breaking down an operation into discrete CIs. The most important contribution of configuration management controls is ensuring that system modifications do not inadvertently compromise security.

Asset disposal

When an organization decides that an asset will no longer be utilized, it disposes of it. The business must guarantee that no data is left on the asset during disposal. Degaussing, which includes subjecting the media to a high alternating magnetic field, is the most dependable and secure method of extracting data from magnetic storage media, such as a magnetic hard drive. Degaussing clears the medium of all previously written data, leaving it magnetically randomized (blank). According to **Department of Defense** (**DoD**) Instruction 5220.22, functional hard discs should be rewritten three times before being discarded or reused.

According to NIST Special Publication, modern hard drives can resist traditional forensic recovery after a **single wiping pass** (**SP**). Keep in mind that encrypting data on a hard disc renders the data unrecoverable without the encryption key, assuming the encryption mechanism is not compromised. This is the most effective solution for data protection across all media types.

Assume a business intends to give 1,200 used computers to a local school. Some of the machines were previously utilized to store private research data in the company's vast research and development department. Data leftovers on donated devices should be a worry for the security administrator. If the company's data handling policy does not include a device sanitization clause, the best course of action for the security administrator is to postpone the donation until all storage media on the PCs has been sanitized. An organization should also make certain that an item is properly disposed of, in accordance with local, state, and federal rules and regulations.

Asset or object reuse

When a company intends to repurpose an asset, it should do a detailed examination of the asset's original and new uses. If the asset will be utilized in the same way, superfluous programs or services may merely need to be removed or disabled. It may, however, be essential to revert the asset to its factory settings. If the asset has a hard drive or another storage medium, it should be completely wiped of all data, particularly if it includes sensitive, private, or secret information.

Software development life cycle

The software development life cycle is a subset of the systems development life cycle, in that any system in development may (but is not required to) contain software development to support the solution. The software development life cycle's purpose is to create a predictable framework of methods for identifying and ensuring that all criteria for functionality, cost, dependability, and delivery schedule are satisfied in the final product. As shown in *Figure 19.3*, this section breaks down the processes in the software development life cycle and explains how each one contributes to the end objective; remember that the processes in the software development life cycle vary depending on the provider, and this is just one example:

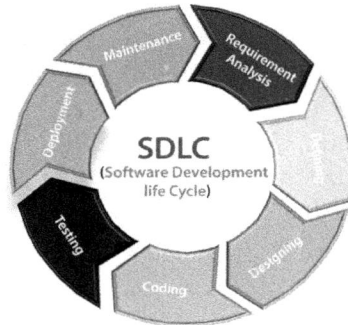

Figure 19.3: Software development lifecycle

The following sections flesh out the software development life cycle steps in detail:

1. Plan or initiate project
2. Gather requirements
3. Design
4. Develop
5. Test or validate
6. Release or maintain
7. Certify or accredit
8. Change management and configuration management or replacement

Plan or initiate project

The organization chooses to start a new software development project and formally plans it at the plan or initiate step of the software development life cycle. Security experts should be consulted in this phase to assess if the project's data needs to be protected and whether the application itself needs to be protected independently from the data it processes. Security specialists must examine the predicted outcomes of the new application to evaluate whether the resulting data is more valuable to the company and, as a result, requires more security. Any data processed by the program requires a value provided by its owner, as well as documentation of any unique regulatory or compliance requirements. Healthcare information, for example, is governed by various federal regulations and must be safeguarded. The classification of all input and output data for the application, as well as the required application controls to guarantee that the input and output data are safeguarded, should be documented. The sorts of networks utilized in data transmission must also be determined. All data sources must be scrutinized. Finally, the application's impact on organizational operations and culture must be evaluated.

Gather requirements

The functionality and security needs of the solution are identified during the gather requirements phase of the software development life cycle. These criteria might come from a variety of places, such as a competitive product evaluation for a commercial product or a user survey for an internal solution. These needs might originate from a direct request from a present customer in some situations. Organizations must assess possible weaknesses and threats from a security standpoint. When performing this assessment, keep in mind the software's intended function as well as the expected environment. Furthermore, the sensitivity of the data that the solution will create or manage must be evaluated. It could be beneficial to assign a privacy effect rating to the data in order to advise efforts to prevent the data from exposure.

Design

An organization produces a clear description of how the software will fulfill all functional and security goals throughout the design phase of the software development life cycle. It entails mapping the software's internal behavior and operations to specified criteria in order to detect those that have not been satisfied prior to installation and testing. Throughout this procedure, the application's state is determined at each stage of its operations. During each operation, the state of the application refers to its functional and security posture. As a result, all conceivable activities must be identified in order to guarantee that the program never becomes vulnerable or behaves in an unpredictable manner. This study also includes determining the attack surface. An attacker's attack surface defines what resources are available to them. At different stages of the application, the quantity of attack surface offered may fluctuate, but at no point should the attack surface provided contradict the security needs defined in the gather requirements stage.

Develop

The code or instructions that make the software work are written during the development phase. This phase is focused on ensuring that secure coding techniques are followed to the letter. Insecure coding techniques, such as the lack of input validation or data type checks, cause many software security concerns. These flaws must be identified via a code review that aims to anticipate all conceivable attack scenarios and their consequences for the code. Buffer overflows, injections, and other incorrect circumstances can occur if these problems are not identified.

Test or validate

Several sorts of testing should take place throughout the test or validate phase, including finding both functional and security concerns. The test data method is an auditing approach that determines the amount of system testing and identifies specific program logic that has not been tested. This approach assesses the behavior of the program in both cases by testing not only the anticipated or legitimate input, but also incorrect and unexpected data. An aggressive attempt at hacking the program should be performed, including buffer overflows and **denial-of-service** (**DoS**) attacks. Some types of testing performed at this time are as follows:

- **Verification testing**: Determines whether the original design specifications have been met

- **Validation testing**: Takes a higher-level view and determines whether the original purpose of the software has been achieved

Release or maintain

The introduction of the program into the live environment, as well as ongoing monitoring of its operation, are part of the release/maintenance phase. It is fairly uncommon to discover additional functional and security issues as the program begins to communicate with other network parts at this stage. In many circumstances, vulnerabilities in live settings are uncovered for which there is no current fix or patch. A zero-day vulnerability is what it is called. Supporting development employees should, ideally, find such flaws before those seeking to exploit them do.

Certify or accredit

The process of reviewing software for its security efficiency in relation to the customer's demands is known as certification. Ratings can obviously help, but they are not the only factor to consider. Management's official acknowledgment of the suitability of a system's overall security is known as accreditation. Provisional accreditation is granted for a certain period of time and it includes a list of needed adjustments to applications, systems, or accreditation paperwork. Full certification means that there are no adjustments that must be made. Once all of the revisions have been performed, assessed, and authorized by the certifying authority, provisional certification becomes full accreditation. While certification and accreditation are connected, they are not thought to be two separate phases in the same process.

Change and configuration management

Following the deployment of a solution in a live environment, more changes to the software will surely be required due to security concerns. The software may be changed in some circumstances to improve or expand its capabilities. Changes must be managed using a proper change and configuration management approach in any scenario. The goal of this procedure is to guarantee that any modifications to the source code's configuration and implementation are approved by the appropriate persons and carried out safely and rationally. This approach should always assure continuing operation in the live environment, and all modifications, including hardware and software changes, should be completely documented. It may be required to replace apps or systems entirely in some circumstances. While some errors may be rectified with additions or tweaks, some may necessitate a total replacement of the program.

Application security frameworks

Various frameworks have been designed to assist the secure development of apps to introduce some consistency to application security. These tools and frameworks help alleviate a lot of the tedium that comes with secure coding. These frameworks provide developers with structured guidelines and best practices for secure software development, reducing vulnerabilities in the application lifecycle. They often include pre-built security features, such as authentication mechanisms and encryption protocols, that streamline secure coding efforts. Many frameworks also offer automated security testing tools to detect vulnerabilities early in the development process, ensuring that security is integrated from the start. By standardizing security practices, application security frameworks help organizations comply with regulatory requirements and industry standards. Moreover, these frameworks often evolve to address emerging security threats, ensuring applications remain resilient in a constantly changing cybersecurity landscape.

Software assurance

Regardless of whether the software was built in-house or purchased commercially, security specialists must guarantee that the program is not only functional but also secure. There are two approaches to this audit the program's activities to see whether it conducts any insecure actions or evaluate it using a formal procedure.

Auditing and logging

Continuous auditing of the software's activities and regular examination of the audit data is a technique and a practice that should be continued once it has been introduced to the environment. Security flaws that may not have been obvious at the outset or that may have gone unnoticed until now can be found by monitoring audit logs. Furthermore, any modifications performed will be documented in the audit log, which can later be verified to ensure that no security vulnerabilities were introduced as a result of the change.

Risk analysis and mitigation

Risk management must be included in any software development since it is a continuous process. Risk analysis identifies potential hazards, whereas risk mitigation is taking efforts to mitigate the consequences of such risks. The following guidelines must be implemented by security experts while analyzing and mitigating software development risks:

- Integrate risk analysis and mitigation in the software development life cycle.
- Use qualitative, quantitative, and hybrid risk analysis approaches based on standardized risk analysis methods.
- Track and manage weaknesses that are discovered throughout risk assessment, change management, and continuous monitoring.

Since software frequently contains vulnerabilities that are not found until it is in use, security experts should make sure that a patch management procedure is established and deployed as needed to mitigate risk. Using a change control procedure, testing any patches, maintaining a functional backup, scheduling production downtime, and having a back-out strategy are all examples of this. Help desk workers and critical user groups should be alerted before any fixes are deployed. Patches should be applied to the least critical computers and devices first, progressing up the hierarchy until the most critical systems and devices are patched.

After mitigations have been implemented, they must be validated and confirmed, which is normally done as part of quality assurance and testing. Any risk mitigation that has been performed must be confirmed by a third party that is not the creator or owner of the system. Code signing should be promoted among developers to maintain code integrity, verify who wrote the code, and determine the code's purpose. Code-signing certificates are digital certificates that guarantee that a piece of code has not been tampered with. Organizations can identify if the code has been updated by someone other than the signer by signing it. Program signing is primarily concerned with running code rather than stored code. While code signing confirms code integrity, it does not ensure that a program is devoid of security flaws or that it will not execute unsafe or unmodified code.

Regression and acceptance testing

Regression and acceptability testing are required for any software updates or additions. Regression testing ensures that the program performs as expected. Regression testing identifies issues that may have been introduced inadvertently into a new build or release candidate. Acceptance testing ensures that the product performs as expected by the user. Acceptance testing is more formal and involves assessing the functioning of a product for users based on a user narrative.

Security impact of acquired software

Commercial software is frequently purchased, and businesses frequently contract with other firms to produce bespoke software. Security specialists must ensure that the business is aware of the security implications of any software it acquires. The four steps of the software acquisition process are as follows:

1. **Planning**: During this phase, the organization performs a needs assessment, develops the software requirements, creates the acquisition strategy, and develops evaluation criteria and plans.

2. **Contracting**: Once planning is completed, the organization creates an RFP or other supplier solicitation forms, evaluates the supplier proposals, and negotiates the final contract with the selected seller.

3. **Monitoring and accepting**: After a contract is in place, the organization establishes the contract work schedule, implements change control procedures, and reviews and accepts the software deliverables.

4. **Follow-on**: When the software is in place, the organization must sustain the software, including managing risks and changes. At some point, it may be necessary for the organization to de-commission the software.

Security professionals should be involved in the software assurance process. This process ensures that unintentional errors, malicious code, information theft, and unauthorized product changes or inserted agents are detected.

Web application security consortium

The **web application security consortium (WASC)** is a non-profit organization that promotes best practices for web-based apps, as well as a number of resources, tools, and information that businesses may use to create them. WASC keeps track of attacks and has compiled a list of the most common attack tactics. This list can help an organization stay on top of the most recent attack tactics and how pervasive they are. It can also help a business make the necessary adjustments to its online applications to prevent these sorts of attacks.

Open Web Application Security Project

Another organization that monitors assaults, especially web attacks, is the **Open Web Application Security Project (OWASP)**. OWASP keeps track of the top ten assaults on a regular basis. This organization also has monthly meetings in chapters all around the world, where they provide resources and tools like testing processes, code review stages, and development guidelines, as shown in *Figure 19.4*:

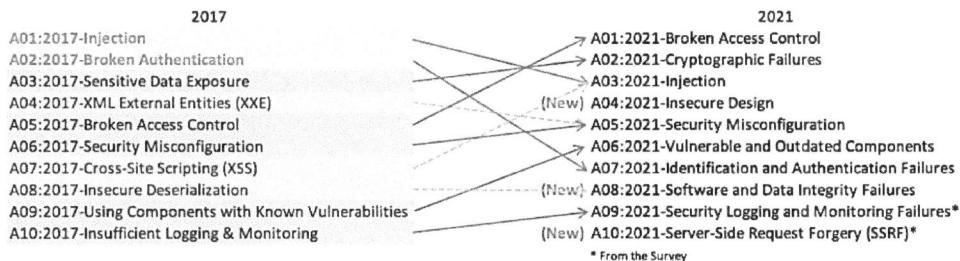

2017	2021
A01:2017-Injection	A01:2021-Broken Access Control
A02:2017-Broken Authentication	A02:2021-Cryptographic Failures
A03:2017-Sensitive Data Exposure	A03:2021-Injection
A04:2017-XML External Entities (XXE)	(New) A04:2021-Insecure Design
A05:2017-Broken Access Control	A05:2021-Security Misconfiguration
A06:2017-Security Misconfiguration	A06:2021-Vulnerable and Outdated Components
A07:2017-Cross-Site Scripting (XSS)	A07:2021-Identification and Authentication Failures
A08:2017-Insecure Deserialization	(New) A08:2021-Software and Data Integrity Failures
A09:2017-Using Components with Known Vulnerabilities	A09:2021-Security Logging and Monitoring Failures*
A10:2017-Insufficient Logging & Monitoring	(New) A10:2021-Server-Side Request Forgery (SSRF)*
	* From the Survey

Figure 19.4: *OWASP Top10 2021 vulnerabilities*

Figure 19.4 presents the top 10 Web application-related vulnerabilities for 2021, which presents the standard for reference to perform security tests on the following critical issues:

- A01:2021-Broken Access Control moved up from the fifth position to the category with the most serious web application security risk; the contributed data indicates that on average, 3.81% of applications tested had one or more **Common Weakness Enumerations (CWEs)** with more than 318k occurrences of CWEs in this risk category. The 34 CWEs mapped to Broken Access Control had more occurrences in applications than any other category.

- A02:2021-Cryptographic Failures shifted up one position to #2, previously known as A3:2017-Sensitive Data Exposure, which was a broad symptom rather than a root cause. The renewed name focuses on failures related to cryptography as it has been implicitly before. This category often leads to sensitive data exposure or system compromise.

- A03:2021-Injection slid down to the third position. 94% of the applications were tested for some form of injection with a max incidence rate of 19%, an average incidence rate of 3.37%, and the 33 CWEs mapped into this category have the second most occurrences in applications with 274k occurrences. Cross-site scripting is now part of this category in this edition.

- A04:2021-Insecure Design is a new category for 2021, with a focus on risks related to design flaws. If we genuinely want to "move left" as an industry, we need more threat modeling, secure design patterns and principles, and reference architectures. An insecure design cannot be fixed by a perfect implementation, as by definition, the needed security controls were never created to defend against specific attacks.

- A05:2021-Security Misconfiguration moved up from #6 in the previous edition; 90% of applications were tested for some form of misconfiguration, with an average incidence rate of 4.5%, and over 208k occurrences of CWEs mapped to this risk category. With more shifts into highly configurable software, it is not surprising to see this category move up. The former category for A4:2017-XML External Entities (XXE) is now part of this risk category.

- A06:2021-Vulnerable and Outdated Components was previously titled using components with known vulnerabilities and is #2 in the top 10 community survey, but also had enough data to make the top 10 via data analysis. This category moved up from #9 in 2017 and is a known issue that we struggle to test and assess risk. It is the only category not to have any **Common Vulnerability and Exposures (CVEs)** mapped to the included CWEs, so a default exploit and impact weights of 5.0 are factored into their scores.

- A07:2021-Identification and Authentication Failures was previously broken authentication and is sliding down from the second position, and now includes CWEs that are more related to identification failures. This category is still an integral part of the Top 10, but the increased availability of standardized frameworks seems to be helping.

- A08:2021-Software and Data Integrity Failures is a new category for 2021, focusing on making assumptions related to software updates, critical data, and CI/CD pipelines without verifying integrity. One of the highest weighted impacts from **Common Vulnerability and Exposures/Common Vulnerability Scoring System (CVE/CVSS)** data mapped to the 10 CWEs in this category. A8:2017-Insecure Deserialization is now a part of this larger category.

- A09:2021-Security Logging and Monitoring Failures was previously A10:2017-Insufficient Logging & Monitoring and is added to the top 10 community survey

(#3), moving up from #10 previously. This category is expanded to include more types of failures, is challenging to test for, and is not well represented in the CVE/CVSS data. However, failures in this category can directly impact visibility, incident alerting, and forensics.

- A10:2021-Server-Side Request Forgery is added from the top 10 community survey (#1). The data shows a relatively low incidence rate with above average testing coverage, along with above-average ratings for Exploit and Impact potential. This category represents the scenario where the security community members are telling us this is important, even though it is not illustrated in the data at this time.

ISO/IEC 27000

The 27034 standard was developed by the **International Organization for Standardization (ISO)** and the **International Electro-technical Commission (IEC)**, and it is part of the ISO/IEC 27000 family of standards. These guidelines help businesses include security in the creation and management of software systems. These recommendations apply not just to in-house application development, but also to the secure deployment and administration of third-party solutions in the company.

Web Services Security

For sharing structured data, web services commonly employ the **simple object access protocol (SOAP)** protocol definition. SOAP makes use of the **extensible markup language (XML)**, which is unsafe on its own. **Web Services Security (WS-Security, or WSS)** is a SOAP extension that allows web services to be secured. WS-Security describes three main mechanisms, as follows:

- How to sign SOAP messages to ensure integrity (and also nonrepudiation)
- How to encrypt SOAP messages to ensure confidentiality
- How to attach security tokens to ascertain the sender's identity

Forbidden coding techniques

While it would be impossible to cover every risky coding practice, there are a few techniques and strategies that you should avoid and be aware of, unless absolutely essential, an app should not do the following:

- Request enhanced rights.
- Allow access to parts of its app package with fewer restrictions.
- Connect to the internet in ways that are not essential.
- Keep an eye out for connections on non-essential network ports.
- Inadvertently listen for connections on public network interfaces.
- Unless the user directs otherwise, read or write files in publicly readable directories.

In addition, the following code-hardening approaches must be used:

- Add code to prevent integer overflows by validating inputs.
- To avoid buffer overflows, replace all unsafe string function calls with buffer size-aware ones.
- If at all possible, avoid giving data to interpreters. When using interpreters is inevitable, ensure that data is passed to the interpreters in a secure manner.
- Use parameterized **application programming interfaces** (**APIs**) to prevent command injection attacks in SQL queries (or manually quote the strings if parameterized APIs are unavailable).
- Use the POSIX system function sparingly.
- Set sensible settings for environment variables (PATH, USER, etc.) and do not base security choices on them.
- Fix problems that might lead to race situations and erroneous behavior (or worse).

Code quality

Another factor to consider when incorporating security into an application is code quality. Code quality is a phrase that is described in a variety of ways by various sources, but high-quality code includes the following characteristics:

- **Well-documented**: The code is self-explanatory, with comments outlining the code's purpose and functions.
- **Maintainable**: This is because the code is not overly complicated, anyone working with it does not need to grasp the entire context to make changes.
- **Effectiveness**: The code does not waste resources in order to complete the task.
- **Simplicity**: The code is simple to read and comprehend.
- Formatting has been refactored to be consistent and adhere to the language's coding norms.
- **Well-tested**: Critical issues are detected and fixed during testing to guarantee that the product performs as intended.
- **Longevity**: The code will be used for a long time.
- When the code is of high quality, it is considerably less likely to be hacked and is more likely to withstand assaults.

Code analyzers

Both automated tools and manual code review are used in code testing and analysis. The following sections look at some of the types of testing that code analysis could include, as shown in *Figure 19.5*:

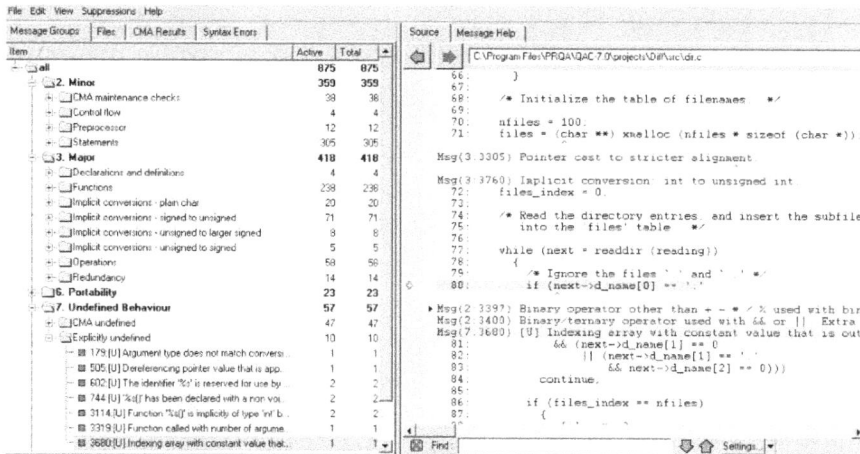

Figure 19.5: *Code analyser*

Fuzzing

In order to evaluate how an application behaves, fuzz testing entails inserting erroneous or unexpected input (also known as faults) into it. It is normally done with the help of a software program that automates the procedure. Environment variables, keyboard and mouse events, and API call sequences are all examples of inputs. The logic of the fuzzing process is depicted in *Figure 19.6*:

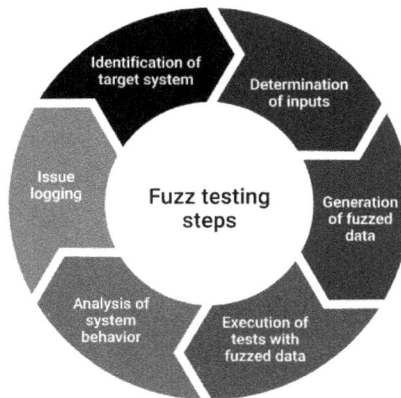

Figure 19.6: *Fuzzing process*

To determine the susceptibility to a fault injection attack, two of the following methods of fuzzing can be used:

- **Mutation fuzzing**: This type entails altering the current input values (blindly).

- **Generation-based fuzzing**: This method entails creating inputs from scratch based on a specification or format.

To enhance application security, it is essential to use fuzz testing to uncover potential flaws and prevent fault injection attacks, which could compromise the integrity of the system. In addition, adhering to proper coding practices and following effective project management procedures ensures that security considerations are integrated throughout the development process, reducing the likelihood of introducing vulnerabilities. Moreover, installing firewalls at the application level provides an additional layer of defense, helping to block malicious traffic and protect the application from unauthorized access or attacks.

Fuzzers are software tools that use a method called fuzzing to detect and exploit flaws in online applications. They work by inserting semi-random data into the program stack and then looking for problems. They are simple to use, but one of their drawbacks is that they are more likely to identify basic faults than the more sophisticated ones. JBroFuzz and WSFuzzer are two specialized tools recommended by OWASP, an organization dedicated to enhancing software security. WSFuzzer is primarily interested in HTTP-based SOAP services. A fuzzer could be used during the creation of a web application that will handle sensitive data, for example. The fuzzer will assist you in determining whether the program is processing error exceptions correctly.

Let us imagine you have a web application that is still being tested, and you find that if you input your credentials incorrectly on the login page, the software crashes, and you are greeted with a command prompt. If you wanted to explore the problem, you could use an online fuzzer to simulate the login screen. *Figure 19.7* depicts a fuzzer named Peach with a mutator named StringMutator that changes the input on a regular basis. Some input to the tool can even cause a crash. Peach confirms the error by duplicating it. It sends extra information to a log, which you may analyze to figure out which string value caused the crash, as shown in *Figure 19.7*:

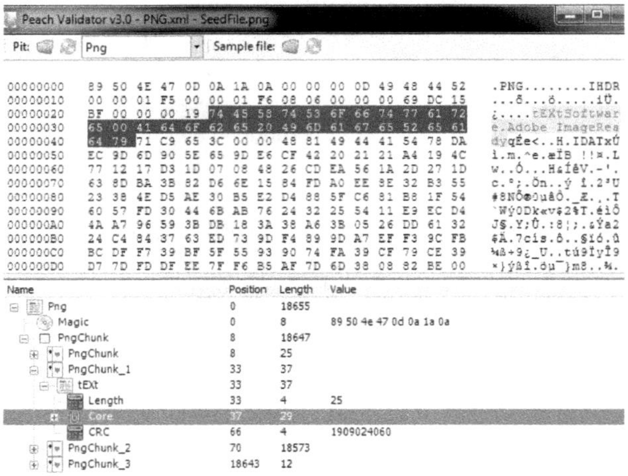

Figure 19.7: *Peach Fuzzer Output*

Microsoft SDL File/Regex Fuzzer consists of two components. The first is File Fuzzer, which creates random content in files, and the second is Regex Fuzzer, which tests regular expression-based routines. Although these tools are no longer accessible, Microsoft now offers a cloud-based fuzzing service. **Microsoft's Security Risk Detection (MSRD)** solution employs artificial intelligence to automate the reasoning process used by security professionals to uncover problems, as well as cloud-based scalability. The user is guided through the fuzzing process by Regex Fuzzer.

Static

Static testing is the process of evaluating or testing software while it is not in use. Code review is the most prevalent method of static analysis. The systematic analysis of the code for security and functional issues is known as code review. It can take many different forms, ranging from informal peer review to formal code review. There are two types of reviews as presented below.

- **Formal evaluation**: This is a very detailed, line-by-line inspection that is frequently done by numerous people across several phases. This is the most time-consuming sort of code review, but it is also the most effective in terms of detecting bugs.

- **Lightweight review**: Unlike a formal review, this style of code review is significantly more cursory. It is typically carried out as part of the development process. It can manifest itself in the following ways:

  o **Pair programming**: Two coders work side by side, constantly verifying each other's work.

  o **Email**: When time allows, the code is emailed to colleagues for them to evaluate.

  o **Over-the-shoulder**: Co-workers look over the code while the author explains why he or she did what they did.

  o **Tool-assisted**: The most efficient technique is to use automated testing tools.

While code review is most commonly performed on internal programs, it may also be necessary for other situations. Assume you are working with a third party to design a web application that will handle credit cards. Given the sensitive nature of the program, it is not uncommon for you to seek a code review to assess the product's security. Several tools should be utilized to test an application in many circumstances. For example, an online banking application that has had its source code updated should be subjected to both penetration testing and a code review of the important models to guarantee that no flaws exist.

Dynamic

Dynamic testing is the process of testing software while it is in use. This testing can be done manually or with the help of automated testing software. Dynamic testing can be approached in the following two ways:

- For websites and applications, **synthetic transaction monitoring**, a sort of proactive monitoring, is frequently favored. It gives visibility into the application's availability and performance, alerting users to any possible issues before they notice a change in the app's behavior. External agents are used to perform scripted transactions on an application. Synthetic transactions, for example, are used by Microsoft's System Centre Operations Manager to monitor databases, webpages, and TCP port utilization.

- **Real user monitoring (RUM)** is a sort of passive monitoring that records and analyses every transaction made by a user of an application or website. Unlike synthetic monitoring, which tries to glean performance insights by testing simulated interactions on a regular basis, RUM eliminates the guesswork by showing you exactly how your users interact with the app.

Misuse case testing

Misuse case testing, often known as negative testing, examines a program to ensure that it can manage unexpected behavior or invalid input. This testing is done to guarantee that an application does not crash and to improve the quality of the program by discovering its flaws. When organizations conduct misuse case testing, they should expect to identify issues. Testing for the following circumstances should be included in misuse testing:

- All required fields must be filled out.

- Fields that have a certain data type can only take data of that type.

- Fields with a character limit only accept data that falls within that limit; fields with a set data range only take data that falls within that range.

- Only valid data is accepted in fields.

Test coverage analysis

Test cases that are written against the application requirements specifications are used in test coverage analysis. To write the test cases, participants in this study do not need to see the code. Test groups relate to a fraction of the test cases that were run, passed, failed, and so on, after a document describing all of the test cases has been produced. Test coverage analysis is frequently done as part of unit testing by the application developer. Overall test coverage analysis is used by quality assurance organizations to show test metrics and coverage according to the test plan. To boost coverage, test coverage analysis generates more test cases. It aids developers in locating portions of an application that are not subjected to a set of test cases. It aids in the calculation of a quantitative measure of code coverage, which indirectly gauges the application or product's quality. One drawback of code coverage assessment is that it only tests what the code does not cover or what has not been developed. Furthermore, rather than looking at structures or functions that do not yet exist, this approach looks at those that do.

Interface testing

Interface testing determines whether the systems and components of an application communicate data and control to one another correctly. It checks to see if module interactions are performing properly and if errors are being handled correctly. Client interfaces, server interfaces, remote interfaces, **graphical user interfaces** (**GUIs**), APIs, external and internal interfaces, and physical interfaces should all be tested. GUI testing is using test cases to test a product's GUI to ensure that it fits its specifications. API testing entails testing APIs separately and as part of the end-to-end transactions performed during integration testing to see if they deliver the expected results.

Agile

Many of the processes that have been examined thus far are based on strict adherence to process-oriented paradigms. In many cases, the emphasis is on following procedural processes rather than reacting rapidly to changes and enhancing efficiency. Continuous feedback and cross-functional teamwork are increasingly important under the agile methodology. Agile aims to be agile enough to respond to unexpected situations throughout development. Less time is spent on upfront analysis, and greater emphasis is given to learning from the process and implementing real-time lessons acquired. Throughout the process, there is also increased interaction with the customer for the agile model, as shown in *Figure 19.8*:

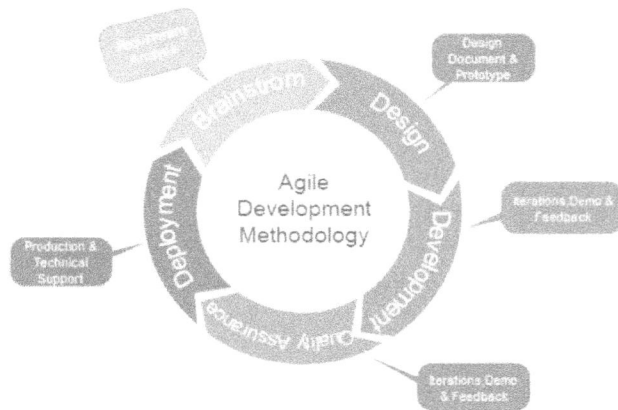

Figure 19.8: Agile model

DevOps

Traditionally, in the software development process, the three main actors **development (Dev)**, **quality assurance** (**QA**), and **operations** (**Ops**), performed their functions separately or in silos. As depicted in *Figure 19.9*, the work would flow in a linear pattern from development through quality assurance to operations:

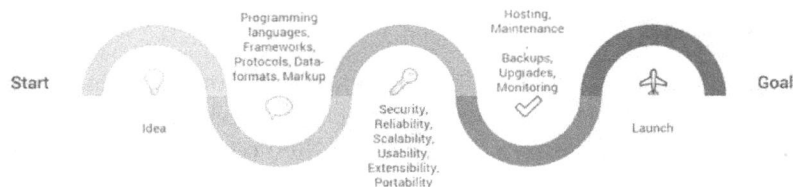

Figure 19.9: Traditional development

Due to a general lack of collaboration among the units, this frequently resulted in delays, finger-pointing, and many iterations through the linear cycle. Shorter development cycles, increased deployment frequency, and more reliable releases are all goals of DevOps, which are closely aligned with business goals. *Figure 19.10* depicts the DevOps paradigm, which encourages the three groups to collaborate throughout the development process:

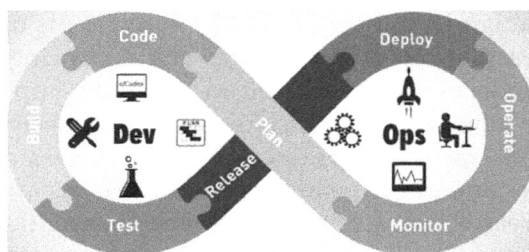

Figure 19.10: DevOps

Versioning

Versioning is an organizational concept that assigns a numbered system to software versions to help identify where they belong in the version history. Versioning ensures that developers are working with the most recent versions and that users are also using the most recent versions. There are several ways that can be applied. Changes in version numbers may introduce new features or fix bugs. A hierarchy is used to denote major and minor changes in a sequence-based versioning numbering system. *Figure 19.11* shows an example of this type of numbering; a major revision could be denoted by a change from 3.0 to 4.0, whereas minor version modifications are denoted by 4.6 to 4.7, and patches are denoted by 4.7.5 to 4.7.6:

Figure 19.11: Components of versioning

Other systems may be based on alphanumeric codes or the date of release.

Secure coding standards

Secure coding standards are methods that help limit an application's attack surface when followed throughout the software development life cycle. For common programming languages like C, C++, Java, and Perl, standards are produced through a community effort.

Documentation

Documentation is important during the development process to ensure optimal functionality and security. Many processes should be documented, resulting in multiple documents. The sections that follow look at some of these procedures and the documents that come from them.

Security requirements traceability matrix

A **security requirements traceability matrix** (**SRTM**) lists the security requirements that must be met by a new asset. In a grid, such as an Excel spreadsheet, the matrix maps the requirements to security controls and verification processes. The columns document the requirement identification number, description of the requirement, and source of the requirement, as well as the test goal and test verification technique for each row in the grid. It enables security professionals and developers to guarantee that all requirements are defined, implemented in the final design, and thoroughly tested. An SRTM would aid in determining whether the security requirements set at project inception are carried through to implementation with a sufficient level of certainty. Consider the following scenario. Assume a group of security engineers design a corporate network using regulatory and business guidelines. Based on their efforts and a thorough examination of the entire set of functional and performance criteria in the network design, the engineers create an SRTM. In this instance, the aim of an SRTM is to allow certifiers to verify that the network complies with applicable security criteria.

Requirements definition

A collection of functional and security requirements that must be met during the software development process is referred to as a requirements definition. It might be in a variety of formats. Contract style requirement lists, which are exactly what they sound like – lists of criteria, are one conventional approach of documenting needs. Another approach is to express these requirements using use cases, which are a set of scenarios that describe how the system should interact with a human user or another system in order to accomplish a given business goal.

System design document

The software is described in the **system design document** (**SDD**), which is frequently accompanied by an architectural diagram. It includes the following details:

- **Data design**: This sort of design explains the features and relationships between data objects that led to the selection of data structures.

- **Architecture design**: Data flow diagrams and transformation mapping are used to describe distinct boundaries between incoming and exiting data in this type of architecture. It incorporates information flow features into the program's structure. All interfaces, including internal and external program interfaces, as well as the design of the human interaction, are classified as interface design.

- **Procedural design**: This form of design uses graphical, tabular, and textual notations to represent procedural detail and organized programming concepts. It serves as a roadmap for implementation and serves as the foundation for all subsequent software engineering work.

Testing plans

A test plan is a document that outlines the test's scope (what it will test) as well as the precise actions that will take place throughout it. Test plans come in a variety of shapes and sizes, which are as follows:

- **Master plans**: For a project or product, this is a single high-level test plan that unifies all other test plans.

- **Test level-specific plans:** Test plan defines a test process at a lower level of testing, as follows:
    - Plan for unit testing
    - Pan for integration testing
    - System test strategy
    - Acceptance test strategy

- **Testing type-specific test plan**: This is a plan for a specific issue, such as performance or security testing. Create a test template to guarantee that all essential actions are completed and all relevant testing data is captured.

Validation and acceptance testing

Validation testing guarantees that a system fits the client's requirements, whereas acceptance testing ensures that the system is accepted by end-users. The implementation of a system that fits the client's criteria but is not accepted by the end-users will be considerably impeded. If a system fails to meet a client's needs, the client is likely to refuse to utilize it until the criteria are met. Before a system is formally given to a client, it should undergo validation testing. Acceptance testing should be carried out with a subset of users after validation testing has been finished. Validation and acceptance testing should be performed on more than simply systems. As a security professional, you must ensure that validation and acceptability testing are performed on any security controls deployed in your organization. There could be consequences for your business if you adopt a new security control that does not adequately guard against a recognized security issue. Employee morale will suffer if you deploy a security control that causes problems, delays, or any other user acceptance concerns. It is crucial to strike a balance between the two.

Unit testing

Software is usually created in bits, or as code modules, which are then put together to create the final output. In a method known as unit testing, each module should be tested separately. It is vital to have development employees conduct this testing, but using engineers who are not part of the team that built the code can ensure that the process is fair. This is an excellent illustration of the notion of job separation. Unit testing should include the following characteristics:

- The test results are included in the specifications.
- Out-of-range values and out-of-bounds circumstances should be checked during testing.
- Test output results that are correct should be generated and known ahead of time.
- Using live or actual field data in unit testing techniques is not encouraged.

Additional testing is recommended, including the following:

- **Integration testing**: This sort of testing evaluates how the modules interact and determines whether the functional and security requirements have been met.

  The advantages to this testing include the following:
  o Provides a systematic technique for assembling a system while uncovering errors.
  o Confirms assumptions that were made during unit testing.
  o Begins as soon as the relevant modules are available.
  o Verifies whether the software modules work in unity.

  The disadvantages include the following:
  o Locating faults is difficult.
  o Some interface links to be tested could be missed.
  o Starts only after all the modules are designed.
  o High-risk critical modules are not isolated and tested on priority.

- **User acceptance testing**: This sort of testing ensures that the software's functionality is satisfactory to the customer (internal or external).

The advantages to this testing include the following:

o   Satisfaction of the client is increased.

o   Criteria for quality are set early.

o   Improved communication between team and customer.

The only disadvantage is that this testing adds cost to the process.

- **Regression testing:** It is performed after modifications to the code have been done to check that the changes have not compromised functionality or security. Some of the benefits are as follows:

o   Improved change integration

o   Higher product quality

o   Detection of unfavorable consequences

The only drawback is the higher price, but it is well worth it.

- **Peer review**: Developers analyze each other's code for security vulnerabilities and code efficiency through peer review testing. It has the benefit of being more thorough than the automated procedures. The drawback is that it takes time.

Adapt solutions

Every day, new security dangers and trends arise. To keep the enterprise safe, organizations and the security professionals who work for them must adapt to new threats and grasp new security trends. An organization's security goal, on the other hand, rarely changes. Retail businesses are increasingly being targeted. Hackers breached security and stole sensitive client data, according to one company's public statement. Unfortunately, it appears that not every major shop was aware of the attack when it occurred, as a new victim appears almost monthly. As a result, banks and other financial institutions were required to provide their customers with new credit/debit cards. Retailers, their customers, and financial institutions were all impacted by these attacks. What might these businesses have done differently to avoid these attacks? When these types of attacks occur, perhaps more information should be shared within the retail business and among security professionals. Unless we discover some solutions, incidents like these will become the norm, and this is only one recent example of new challenges to which businesses must react. *Figure 19.12* depicts a common vulnerability cycle that is taught in many security seminars and explains the order in which the attackers exploit vulnerabilities over time:

Figure 19.12: *Vulnerability management lifecycle*

This vulnerability cycle tends to be followed by trends. A period in which human engagement and social engineering are common will be quickly followed by a period in which network attacks are common. As soon as a business adopts it, the attackers move on to the next phase of the cycle – services and servers. Organizations evolve with time, but so do adversaries. You must endeavor to stay one step ahead of the attackers as a security professional. You cannot relax once you have introduced a new security control or solution. Then you must conduct a study, keep an eye on your business, and identify the next threat or trend. One thing is certain – a security professional with genuine talents and a desire to learn and adapt will always have a job. An organization's understanding of emerging dangers is aided by threat intelligence. The organization will be better positioned to protect against new dangers once they are fully recognized. As a result, security professionals will be better prepared for the hazards to which they are exposed.

Addressing disruptive technologies

Disruptive technologies are those that are so innovative that they transform the way things are done and allow people to use technology in new ways. They are disruptive in the sense that they can alter the way a whole industry works. Self-driving automobiles, for example, will almost probably eliminate the need for chauffeurs. While disruptive technologies are usually innovative and forward-thinking, they are not necessarily safe. Security is not often a top priority while rushing to bring a breakthrough technology to market. As a result, many companies allow others to be on the cutting edge of technology. As we get closer to 2022, some of the disruptive technologies on the horizon will make the four-year upgrade cycle obsolete. Desktop upgrades will be done on a yearly basis. Phishing assaults are expected to increase by 25% in 2022, prompting security professionals to concentrate their efforts in the following areas:

- Ensuring perimeter security.
- Encryption in transit and at rest.

- **Bring-your-own-device** (**BYOD**) initiatives will promote **mobile device management** (**MDM**) solutions.

- Security-related usability difficulties will become less of an issue.

- There will be more cloud movement and adoption.

- Machine learning and artificial intelligence will be increasingly used to find new clients and customers.

- 5G wireless is expected to be at least 40 times faster than 4G and have at least four times the coverage.

Address security trends

By their very nature, trends are transient, and security trends are no exception. Some security visionaries predict the following in our future as we approach the 2020 decade:

Returning to the zero-trust paradigm: In the face of increasingly sophisticated threats, businesses will adopt a strongly defensive stance. Every privilege shall be granted to a user only when it is absolutely necessary. In the struggle to safeguard the **Internet of Things** (**IoT**), deception technologies will become more prevalent. This method floods the network, effectively preventing fraudsters from gaining access to a genuine set of user IDs. Deception technology warns IT when one of these forged credentials is hacked and utilized. In order to manage identities, behavioral analytics and artificial intelligence will be used as follows:

- The system will learn user habits and will be able to detect unusual behavior quickly. Robo hunters will be utilized as automated threat hunters, learning from their findings and taking appropriate action (for example, by isolating a bad packet or compromised device).

- Blockchain is a distributed network of computers that allows a digital log of transactions to be established and shared among participants. The blockchain ledger can identify and pinpoint dubious internet activities. This unchangeable ledger can also be used in court to show that data was retrieved or copied by an unauthorized person.

Asset management

Asset management and inventory control are crucial throughout the technology life cycle to ensure that assets are not stolen or lost, and that data on assets is not hacked. Inventory control and asset management are two topics that are intertwined. Asset management is keeping track of an organization's devices, while inventory control entails keeping track of and containing inventories. Asset management should be implemented by all organizations, while inventory control is not required by all organizations.

Device-tracking technologies

Device-tracking technologies enable enterprises to know the position of a device and, in many cases, retrieve the device. If the device cannot be retrieved, it may be necessary to erase the device to ensure that unauthorized users cannot access the device's data. You should emphasize to your organization as a security professional the importance of implementing device-tracking technologies and remote wiping capabilities.

Geolocation or global positioning system location

Geolocation, or the location of a device using the **global positioning system** (**GPS**), is one of the device-tracking technologies. If the necessary feature on the device is enabled, location and time information about an item can be tracked using this technology. The geolocation or GPS location capability on most mobile devices can be improved by connecting to Wi-Fi networks. A security professional must ensure that the company's mobile device security policy incorporates the use of GPS location functions as a requirement. Additionally, suitable credentials must be set up to allow workers to utilize the vendor's online device locating service. Finally, if the mobile devices hold confidential or private information, remote locking and wiping options should be properly examined.

Object tracking and containment technologies

Object tracking and containment systems are largely focused on keeping inventory within a designated region or location. Organizations can use object tracking systems to find out where their inventory is. When inventory leaves the perimeter of a predetermined place or area, containment technologies notify employees within the business. Object tracking and confinement systems are often utilized only for inventory assets worth more than a specific amount. For high-priced electrical gadgets and jewelry, for example, most retail stores use object containment methods. However, some firms, particularly in big warehouse environments, use these systems for all inventories. Geotagging or geo-fencing and **radio frequency identification** (**RFID**) are two technologies utilized in this area.

Geotagging or geo-fencing

Geotagging is the process of adding a GPS position to a video, photo, or other digital media. This function has recently gotten negative press since the attackers can use it to locate sensitive information, such as a person's home address. Geotagging, on the other hand, can be utilized by businesses to produce location-based news and media feeds. In the retail industry, it can assist customers in locating a store where a specific item is available. Geofencing is a method of defining geographic boundaries using GPS. A geofence is a virtual barrier that can trigger alerts when inventory enters or escapes. Geofencing is employed in a variety of industries, including retail, transportation, human resources, and law enforcement.

Radio frequency identification

To keep track of inventory, RFID chips and readers are used. The chips are placed on individual inventory items or pallets. To communicate with the chips, RFID readers are installed around the area. As part of the RFID communication, identification and location data are acquired. Organizations can tailor the information stored on an RFID chip to meet their specific requirements. **Active Reader/Passive Tag** (**ARPT**) and **Active Reader/ Active Tag** (**ARAT**) RFID systems can be used. The active reader in an ARPT system sends out signals and gets responses from passive tags. Active tags are woken up in an ARAT system by signals from the active reader. If RFID chips are within a particular range of RFID readers, they can be read-only.

Conclusion

This chapter covered the systems and software development lifecycle, including requirements, acquisition, testing and evaluation, commissioning/decommissioning, operational activities, asset disposal, and asset or object reuse. The chapter also discussed adapt solutions, emerging threats, disruptive technologies, and security trends. Asset management, including inventory control and associated concepts, was also discussed. This concludes the topics and chapters for this book that need to be studied for the **CompTIA Advanced Security Practitioner** (**CASP**) exam.

In the next few chapters, we will review some questions from the chapters discussed in this book. These questions and answers are simulations of questions that were asked in the CASP exam.

Exercise

1. **Which phase of the Software Development Life Cycle (SDLC) involves defining the project's objectives, scope, and requirements?**

   a. Design

   b. Implementation

   c. Planning

   d. Testing

2. **When adapting a solution to a new environment, which of the following is most important to consider?**

   a. Ensuring compatibility with hardware

   b. Ignoring the performance metrics

   c. Disregarding user requirements

   d. Focusing solely on cost reduction

3. **What is the primary purpose of asset management in IT security?**

   a. To track the hardware and software inventory

   b. To ensure high network bandwidth

   c. To improve the aesthetic design of applications

   d. To manage employee salaries

Answers

1. c
2. a
3. a

Join our book's Discord space

Join the book's Discord Workspace for Latest updates, Offers, Tech happenings around the world, New Release and Sessions with the Authors:

https://discord.bpbonline.com

CHAPTER 20

CASP+ Skill Assessment Exam-I

1. The security administrator is worried about possible SPIT attacks against the VoIP system. Which of the following security controls would most likely need to be implemented to detect this type of attack?

   a. SIP and SRTP traffic analysis

   b. QoS audit on Layer 3 devices

   c. IP and MAC filtering logs

   d. Email spam filter log

   Answer: a

2. A security administrator has been conducting a security assessment of company XYZ for the past two weeks. All of the penetration tests and other assessments have revealed zero flaws in the systems at company XYZ. However, company XYZ reports that it has been the victim of numerous security incidents in the past six months. In each of these incidents, the criminals have managed to exfiltrate large volumes of data from the secure servers at the company. Which of the following techniques should the investigation team consider in the next phase of their assessment in hopes of uncovering the attack vector that the criminals used?

   a. Vulnerability assessment

   b. Code review

    c.   Social engineering

    d.   Reverse engineering

Answer: c

3.   **A user reports that the workstation's mouse pointer is moving, and the files are opening automatically. Which of the following should the user perform?**

    a.   Unplug the network cable to avoid network activity.

    b.   Reboot the workstation to see if the problem occurs again.

    c.   Turn off the computer to avoid any more issues.

    d.   Contact the incident response team for direction.

Answer: d

4.   **Company A is purchasing Company B, and will import all of Company B's users into its authentication system. Company A uses 802.1x with a RADIUS server, while Company B uses a captive SSL portal with an LDAP backend. Which of the following is the BEST way to integrate these two networks?**

    a.   Enable RADIUS and endpoint security on Company B's network devices.

    b.   Enable LDAP authentication on Company A's network devices.

    c.   Enable LDAP/TLS authentication on Company A's network devices.

    d.   Enable 802.1x on Company B's network devices.

Answer: d

5.   **A bank has just outsourced the security department to a consulting firm, but retained the security architecture group. A few months into the contract, the bank discovers that the consulting firm has sub-contracted some of the security functions to another provider. Management is pressuring the sourcing manager to ensure that adequate protections are in place to insulate the bank from legal and service exposures. Which of the following is the most appropriate action to take?**

    a.   Directly establish another separate service contract with the sub-contractor to limit the risk exposure and legal implications.

    b.   Ensure the consulting firm has service agreements with the sub-contractor; if the agreement does not exist, exit the contract when possible.

    c.   Log in as a risk in the business risk register and pass the risk to the consulting firm for acceptance and responsibility.

    d.   Terminate the contract immediately and bring the security department in-house again to reduce legal and regulatory exposure.

Answer: b

6. A database hosting information assets with a computed CIA aggregate value of high. The database is located within a secured network zone where there is flow control between the client and the data center networks. Which of the following is the most likely threat?

   a. Inappropriate administrator access

   b. Malicious code

   c. Internal business fraud

   d. Regulatory compliance

   Answer: a

7. Which of the following activities could reduce the security benefits of mandatory vacations?

   a. Have a replacement employee run the same applications as the vacationing employee.

   b. Have a replacement employee perform tasks in a different order from the vacationing employee.

   c. Have a replacement employee perform the job from a different workstation than the vacationing employee.

   d. Have a replacement employee run several daily scripts developed by the vacationing employee.

   Answer: d

8. A firm's Chief Executive Officer (CEO) is concerned that its IT staff lacks the knowledge to identify complex vulnerabilities that may exist in the payment system being internally developed. The payment system being developed will be sold to several organizations and is in direct competition with another leading product. The CEO highlighted, in a risk management meeting, that code-based confidentiality is of utmost importance to allow the company to exceed the competition in terms of product reliability, stability, and performance. The CEO also highlighted that the company's reputation for security products is extremely important. Which of the following will provide the most thorough testing and satisfy the CEO's requirements?

   a. Use the security assurance team and development team to perform Grey box testing.

   b. Sign an NDA with a large consulting firm and use the firm to perform Black box testing.

c. Use the security assurance team and development team to perform Black box testing.

d. Sign an NDA with a small consulting firm and use the firm to perform Grey box testing.

Answer: d

9. **Which of the following are security components provided by an application security library or framework? (Select any three)**

a. Authorization database

b. Fault injection

c. Input validation

d. Secure logging

e. Directory services

f. Encryption and decryption

Answer: c, d, and f

10. **A security manager is concerned about performance and patch management, and, as a result, wants to implement a virtualization strategy to avoid potential future OS vulnerabilities in the host system. The IT manager wants a strategy that would provide the hypervisor with direct communications with the underlying physical hardware, allowing the hardware resources to be para-virtualized and delivered to the guest machines. Which of the following recommendations from the server administrator best meets the IT and security managers' requirements? (Select two)**

a. Nested virtualized hypervisors

b. Type 1 hypervisor

c. Hosted hypervisor with a three-layer software stack

d. Type 2 hypervisor

e. Bare metal hypervisor with a software stack of two layers

Answer: b and e

11. **An intruder was recently discovered inside the data center, a highly sensitive area. To gain access, the intruder circumvented numerous layers of physical and electronic security measures. Company leadership has asked for a thorough review of physical security controls to prevent this from happening again. Which of the following departments is the most heavily invested in rectifying the problem? (Select at least three)**

a. Facilities management

b. Human resources

    c. Research and development

    d. Programming

    e. Data center operations

    f. Marketing

    g. Information technology

Answer: a, e, and g

12. **A court order has ruled that your company must surrender all the emails sent and received by a certain employee for the past five years. After reviewing the backup systems, the IT administrator concludes that email backups are not kept that long. Which of the following policies must be reviewed to address future compliance?**

    a. Tape backup policies

    b. Offsite backup policies

    c. Data retention policies

    d. Data loss prevention policies

Answer: c

13. **An organization would like to allow employees to use their network username and password to access a third-party service. The company is using Active Directory Federated Services for its directory service. Which of the following should the company ensure is supported by the third party? (Select any two)**

    a. LDAPS

    b. SAML

    c. NTLM

    d. OAUTH

    e. Kerberos

Answer: b and e

14. **As a cost-saving measure, a company has instructed the security engineering team to allow all consumer devices to be able to access the network. They have asked for recommendations on what is needed to secure the enterprise, yet offer the most flexibility in terms of controlling applications, and stolen devices. Which of the following is best suited for the requirements?**

    a. MEAP with Enterprise Appstore

    b. Enterprise Appstore with client-side VPN software

   c. MEAP with TLS

   d. MEAP with MDM

Answer: d

15. **News outlets are beginning to report on many retail establishments that are experiencing payment card data breaches. The data exfiltration is enabled by malware on a compromised computer; after the initial exploit, network mapping and fingerprinting occur in preparation for further exploitation. Which of the following is the most effective solution to protect against unrecognized malware infections, reduce detection time, and minimize any damage that might be done?**

   a. Remove local admin permissions from all users and change anti-virus to a cloud-aware, push technology.

   b. Implement an application whitelist at all levels of the organization.

   c. Deploy a network-based heuristic IDS and configure all layer three switches to feed data to the IDS for more effective monitoring.

   d. Update router configuration to pass all network traffic through a new proxy server with advanced malware detection.

Answer: b

16. **Vikas, the Chief Executive Officer (CEO), was an Information security professor and a Subject Matter Expert for over 20 years. He has designed a network defense method that he says is significantly better than prominent international standards. He has recommended that the company use his cryptographic method. Which of the following methodologies should be adopted?**

   a. The company should develop an in-house solution and keep the algorithm a secret.

   b. The company should use the CEO's encryption scheme.

   c. The company should use a mixture of both systems to meet minimum standards.

   d. The company should use the method recommended by other respected information security organizations.

Answer: d

17. **Chief Executive Officer (CEO) of a company that allows telecommuting has challenged the Chief Security Officer's (CSO) request to harden the corporate network's perimeter. The CEO argues that the company cannot protect its employees at home, so the risk at work is no different. Which of the following BEST explains why this company should proceed with protecting its corporate network boundary?**

   a.   The corporate network is the only network that is audited by regulators and customers.

   b.   The aggregation of employees on a corporate network makes it a more valuable target for attackers.

   c.   Home networks are unknown to the attackers and less likely to be targeted directly.

   d.   Employees are more likely to be using personal computers for general web browsing when they are at home.

Answer: b

18. **An organization has decided to reduce labor costs by outsourcing back-office processing of credit applications to a provider located in another country. Data sovereignty and privacy concerns raised by the security team resulted in the third-party provider only accessing and processing the data via remote desktop sessions. To facilitate communications and improve productivity, staff at the third party have been provided with corporate email accounts that are only accessible via remote desktop sessions. Email forwarding is blocked and staff at the third party can only communicate with staff within the organization. Which of the following additional controls should be implemented to prevent data loss? (Select any three)**

   a.   Implement hashing of data in transit

   b.   Session recording and capture

   c.   Disable cross session cut and paste

   d.   Monitor approved credit accounts

   e.   User access audit reviews

   f.   Source IP whitelisting

Answer: c, e, and f

19. **An IT administrator has been tasked by the Chief Executive Officer with implementing security using a single device based on the following requirements:**

   i.   **Selective sandboxing of suspicious code to determine malicious intent.**

   ii.   **VoIP handling for SIP and H.323 connections.**

   iii. **Block potentially unwanted applications.**

Which of the following devices would best meet all of these requirements?

   a.   UTM

   b.   HIDS

    c. NIDS

    d. WAF

    e. HSM

Answer: a

20. **Chief Executive Officer (CEO) has asked the IT administrator to protect the externally facing web server from SQL injection attacks and ensure the backend database server is monitored for unusual behavior while enforcing rules to terminate unusual behavior. Which of the following would best meet the CEO's requirements?**

    a. WAF and DAM

    b. UTM and NIDS

    c. DAM and SIEM

    d. UTM and HSM

    e. WAF and SIEM

Answer: a

21. **Which of the following is the information owner responsible for?**

    a. Developing policies, standards, and baselines.

    b. Determining the proper classification levels for data within the system.

    c. Integrating security considerations into application and system purchasing decisions.

    d. Implementing and evaluating security controls by validating the integrity of the data.

Answer: b

22. **An administrator's company has recently had to reduce the number of Tier 3 help desk technicians available to support enterprise service requests. As a result, configuration standards have declined as administrators develop scripts to troubleshoot and fix customer issues. The administrator has observed that several default configurations have not been fixed through applied group policy or configured in the baseline. Which of the following controls should the administrator should recommend to the organization's security manager to prevent an authorized user from conducting internal reconnaissance on the organization's network? (Select any three)**

    a. Network file system

    b. Disable command execution

    c. Port security

    d. TLS

    e. Search engine reconnaissance

    f. NIDS

    g. BIOS security

    h. HIDS

    i. IDM

Answer: b, g, and i

23. **An extensible commercial software system was upgraded to the next minor release version to patch a security vulnerability. After the upgrade, an unauthorized intrusion into the system was detected. The software vendor is called in to troubleshoot the issue, and reports that all core components were updated properly. Which of the following has been overlooked in securing the system? (Select any two)**

    a. The company's IDS signatures were not updated.

    b. The company's custom code was not patched.

    c. The patch caused the system to revert to HTTP.

    d. The software patch was not cryptographically signed.

    e. The wrong version of the patch was used.

    f. Third-party plug-ins were not patched.

Answer: b and f

24. **A penetration tester is assessing a mobile banking application. Man-in-the-middle attempts via an HTTP intercepting proxy are failing with SSL errors. Which of the following controls has likely been implemented by the developers?**

    a. SSL certificate revocation

    b. SSL certificate pinning

    c. Mobile device root-kit detection

    d. Extended validation certificates

Answer: b

25. **A security administrator notices a recent increase in workstations becoming compromised by malware. Often, the malware is delivered via drive-by downloads, from malware-hosting websites, and is not being detected by the corporate antivirus. Which of the following solutions would provide the BEST protection for the company?**

a. Increase the frequency of antivirus downloads and install updates to all workstations.

b. Deploy a cloud-based content filter and enable the appropriate category to prevent further infections.

c. Deploy a NIPS to inspect and block all web traffic that may contain malware and exploits.

d. Deploy a web-based gateway antivirus server to intercept viruses before they enter the network.

Answer: b

26. **A Chief Information Security Officer (CISO) is approached by a business unit manager who heard a report on the radio this morning about an employee at a competing firm who shipped a VPN token overseas so a fake employee could log into the corporate VPN. The CISO asks what can be done to mitigate the risk of such an incident occurring within the organization. Which of the following is the most cost-effective way to mitigate such a risk?**

a. Require hardware tokens to be replaced every year.

b. Implement a biometric factor into the token response process.

c. Force passwords to be changed every 90 days.

d. Use PKI certificates as part of the VPN authentication process.

Answer: b

27. **The security administrator at a bank is receiving numerous reports that customers are unable to log in to the bank website. Upon further investigation, the security administrator discovers that the name associated with the bank website points to an unauthorized IP address. Which of the following solutions will most likely mitigate this type of attack?**

a. Security awareness and user training

b. Recursive DNS from the root servers

c. Configuring and deploying TSIG

d. Firewalls and IDS technologies

Answer: c

28. **A breach at a government agency resulted in the public release of top-secret information. The Chief Information Security Officer has tasked a group of security professionals to deploy a system that will protect against such breaches in the future. Which of the following can the government agency deploy to meet future security needs?**

    a.   DAC, which enforces no read-up; a DAC, which enforces no write-down; and a MAC, which uses an access matrix.

    b.   MAC, which enforces no write-up; a MAC, which enforces no read-down; and a DAC, which uses an ACL.

    c.   MAC, which enforces no read-up; a MAC, which enforces no write-down; and a DAC, which uses an access matrix.

    d.   DAC, which enforces no write-up; a DAC, which enforces no read-down; and a MAC, which uses an ACL.

Answer: c

29. **A corporate executive lost their smartphone while on an overseas business trip. The phone was equipped with file encryption and secured with a strong passphrase. The phone contained over 60 GB of proprietary data. Given this scenario, which of the following is the best course of action?**

    a.   File an insurance claim and assure the executive that the data is secure because it is encrypted.

    b.   Immediately implement a plan to remotely wipe all data from the device.

    c.   Have the executive change all passwords and issue the executive a new phone.

    d.   Execute a plan to remotely disable the device and report the loss to the police.

Answer: b

30. **A security incident happens three times a year on a company's web server, costing the company $1,500 in downtime, per occurrence. The web server is only for archival access and is scheduled to be decommissioned in five years. The cost of implementing software to prevent this incident would be $15,000 initially, plus $1,000 a year for maintenance. Which of the following is the most cost-effective manner to deal with this risk?**

    a.   Avoid the risk

    b.   Transfer the risk

    c.   Accept the risk

    d.   Mitigate the risk

Answer: d

31. **The company is about to upgrade a financial system through a third party, but wants to legally ensure that no sensitive information is compromised throughout the project. The project manager must also make sure that internal controls are set to mitigate the potential damage that one individual's actions may cause. Which of the following needs to be put in place to make certain both organizational requirements are met? (Select any two)**

    a. Separation of duties

    b. Forensic tasks

    c. MOU

    d. OLA

    e. NDA

    f. Job rotation

Answer: a and e

32. *The system shall implement measures to notify system administrators before a security incident occurs.* **Which of the following BEST restates the preceding statement to allow it to be implemented by a team of software developers?**

    a. The system shall cease processing data when certain configurable events occur.

    b. The system shall continue processing in the event of an error, and email the security administrator the error logs.

    c. The system shall halt on error.

    d. The system shall throw an error when specified incidents pass a configurable threshold.

Answer: d

33. **The Chief Executive Officer (CEO) of a corporation purchased the latest mobile device and wants to connect it to the internal network. The Chief Information Security Officer (CISO) was told to research and recommend how to secure this device. Which of the following should be implemented, keeping in mind that the CEO has stated that this access is required?**

    a. Mitigate and transfer

    b. Accept and transfer

    c. Transfer and avoid

    d. Avoid and mitigate

Answer: a

34. **As part of the testing phase in the SDLC, a software developer wants to verify that an application is properly handling user error exceptions. Which of the following is the best tool or process for the developer to use?**

    a. SRTM review

    b. Fuzzer

   c. Vulnerability assessment

   d. HTTP interceptor

Answer: b

35. **Juan is trying to perform a risk analysis of his network. He has chosen to use OCTAVE. What is OCTAVE primarily used for?**

   a. A language for vulnerability assessment

   b. A comprehensive risk assessment model

   c. A threat assessment tool

   d. An impact analysis tool

Answer: b

Explanation: OCTAVE, or operationally critical, threat, asset, and vulnerability evaluation, is a comprehensive risk assessment model. Answer option A is incorrect. OVAL or Open Vulnerability Assessment Language is the language for vulnerability assessment. Answer options C and D are incorrect. Threat assessment and impact analysis are both parts of OVAL, but only a part.

36. **Which of the following is a log that contains records of login/logout activity or other security-related events specified by the systems audit policy?**

   a. Process tracking

   b. Logon event

   c. Object manager

   d. Security log

Answer: d

Explanation: The Security log records events related to security, like valid and invalid logon attempts, or events related to resource usage, such as creating, opening, or deleting files. For example, when logon auditing is enabled, an event is recorded in the security log each time a user attempts to log on to the computer. Answer option B is incorrect. In computer security, a login or logon is the process by which individual access to a computer system is controlled by identifying and authorizing the user by referring to credentials presented by the user. Answer option C is incorrect. The object manager is a subsystem implemented as part of the Windows Executive, which manages Windows resources.

37. **Which of the following is a declarative access control policy language implemented in XML and a processing model, describing how to interpret the policies?**

a. SAML

b. SOAP

c. SPML

d. XACML

Answer: d

Explanation: XACML stands for extensible Access Control Markup Language. It is a declarative access control policy language implemented in XML and a processing model, describing how to interpret the policies. The latest version 2.0 was ratified by the OASIS standards organization on 1 February 2005. The planned version 3.0 will add generic attribute categories for the evaluation context and policy delegation profile (administrative policy profile).

Simple object access protocol (SOAP), is a protocol specification for exchanging structured information in the implementation of Web Services in computer networks; it relies on extensible Markup Language as its message format, and usually relies on other Applications Layer protocols for message negotiation and transmission. SOAP can form the foundation layer of a web services protocol stack, providing a basic messaging framework upon which web services can be built.

SPML is an XML-based framework developed by **Organization for the Advancement of Structured Information Standards (OASIS)**. It is used to exchange user, resource, and service provisioning information between cooperating organizations. SPML is the open standard for the integration and interoperation of service provisioning requests. It has a goal to allow organizations to securely and quickly set up user interfaces for Web applications and services, by letting enterprise platforms such as Web portals, application servers, and service centers produce provisioning requests within and across organizations. SPML is the open standard for the integration and interoperation of service provisioning requests. It has a goal to allow organizations to securely and quickly set up user interfaces for Web applications and services, by letting enterprise platforms such as Web portals, application servers, and service centers produce provisioning requests within and across organizations.

SAML is an XM-based standard for exchanging authentication and authorization data between security domains, that is, between an identity provider and a service provider. SAML is a product of the OASIS Security Services Technical Committee.

38. **Which of the following is the capability to correct flows in the existing functionality without affecting other components of the system?**

    a. Manageability

    b. Reliability

c. Maintainability

d. Availability

Answer: c

Explanation: The following are the reasons:

Availability: It is used to make certain that a service/resource is always accessible.

Manageability: It is the capability to manage the system for ensuring the constant health of the system concerning scalability, reliability, availability, performance, and security.

Maintainability: It is the capability to correct flows in the existing functionality without affecting the other components of the system.

Answer option B is incorrect. It is not a valid option.

39. **Fill in the blank with the appropriate word. _____ encryption protects a file as it travels over protocols, such as FTPS (SSL), SFTP (SSH), and HTTPS.**

    Answer: Transport

40. **Interceptor is a pseudo proxy server that performs HTTP diagnostics; which of the following features are provided by HTTP Interceptor? (Each correct answer represents a complete solution. Choose all that apply.)**

    a. It controls cookies being sent and received.

    b. It allows to browse anonymously by withholding the Referrer tag, and user agent.

    c. It can view each entire HTTP header.

    d. It debugs DOC, DOCX, and JPG files.

    Answer: a, b, and c

    Explanation: HTTP diagnostics is performed by the HTTP Interceptor, which is a pseudo proxy server, and it also facilitates viewing the two-way communication between the browser and the Internet. The various features of HTTP Interceptor are as follows:

    i. View each entire HTTP header.

    ii. Debug your PHP, ASP, CGI, or JavaScript and **htaccess** file.

    iii. Control Cookies being sent and received.

    iv. Find out what sort of URL redirection the site may be using.

    v. Browse anonymously by withholding the Referrer tag and user agent.

41. **Karan is concerned about internal security threats on the network he administers. He believes that he has taken every reasonable precaution against external threats but is concerned that he may have gaps in his internal security. Which of the following is the most likely internal threat?**

    a. Employees not following security policy

    b. Privilege Escalation

    c. SQL Injection

    d. Employees selling sensitive data

    Answer: a

    Explanation: Employees may disregard policies, such as policies limiting the use of USB devices or the ability to download programs from the Internet. This is the most pervasive internal security threat.

42. **Resource exhaustion includes all of the following except ....**

    a. Opening too many connections

    b. Allocating all system memory to a single application

    c. Overflowing a buffer with too much data

    d. Flooding a network with excessive packets

    Answer: c

    Explanation: Buffer overflow attacks are related to resource exhaustion but are not the same thing. The reason is that the buffer overflow is based on programmers not checking array bounds, rather than exhausting resources. Answer options A, B, and D are incorrect. All of these are examples of resource exhaustion.

43. **Which of the following security practices are included in the implementation phase of the Security Development Lifecycle (SDL)? (Select any two)**

    a. Establish design requirements

    b. Perform static analysis

    c. Use approved tools

    d. Execute incident response plan

    Answer: b and c

    Explanation: Security practices are performed during each phase of the **Security Development Lifecycle (SDL)** process.

44. **How many levels of threats are faced by the SAN?**

    a. 3

    b. 7

c. 2

d. 5

Answer: a

Explanation: The storage area network transfers and stores crucial data; often, this makes the storage area network vulnerable to risks. There are three different levels of threats faced by the SAN, which are as follows:

Level one: These types of threats are unintentional and may result in downtime and loss of revenue. However, administrators can prevent these threats.

Level two: These types of threats are simple malicious attacks that use existing equipment.

Level three: These types of threats are large-scale attacks and are difficult to prevent. These threats come from skilled attackers using uncommon equipment.

45. **Which of the following is a written document and is used in those cases where parties do not imply a legal commitment or in those situations where the parties are unable to create a legally enforceable agreement?**

   a. Patent law

   b. Memorandum of Understanding (MOU)

   c. Memorandum of Agreement (MOA)

   d. Certification and Accreditation (COA or CnA)

Answer: b

Explanation: A **Memorandum of Understanding (MOU)** is a document that defines a bilateral or multilateral agreement between two parties. This document specifies a convergence of will between the parties, representing a proposed common line of action. An MOU is generally used in those cases where parties do not imply a legal commitment or in those situations where the parties are unable to create a legally enforceable agreement. It is a proper substitute for a gentlemen's agreement.

46. **Which of the following statements are true about capability-based security?**

   a. It is a concept in the design of secure computing systems, which is one of the existing security models.

   b. It is a computer security model based on the Actor model of computation.

   c. It is a scheme used by some computers to control memory access.

   d. It is a concept in the design of secure computing systems.

Answer: d

Explanation: Capability-based security is a concept in the design of secure computing systems. A capability (known in some systems as a key) is a communicable, unforgivable token of authority. It refers to a value that references an object along with an associated set of access rights. A user program on the capability-based operating system must use a capability to access an object. Capability-based security refers to the principle of designing user programs such that they directly share capabilities according to the principle of least privilege, and to the operating system infrastructure necessary to make such transactions efficient and secure. Although most operating systems implement a facility that resembles capabilities, they typically do not provide enough support to allow for the exchange of capabilities among possibly mutually untrusting entities to be the primary means of granting and distributing access rights throughout the system. A capability-based system, in contrast, is designed with that goal in mind. Answer options B, C, and A are incorrect. These are not correct statements about capability-based security.

47. **A helpdesk manager at a financial company has received multiple reports from employees and customers that their phone calls sound metallic on the voice system. The helpdesk has been using VoIP lines encrypted from the handset to the PBX for several years. Which of the following should be done to address this issue in the future?**

    a. SIP session tagging and QoS

    b. A dedicated VLAN

    c. Lower encryption setting

    d. Traffic shaping

    Answer: b

48. **A new startup company with very limited funds wants to protect the organization from external threats by implementing some type of best-practice security controls across many hosts located in the application zone, the production zone, and the core network. The 50 hosts in the core network are a mixture of Windows and Linux-based systems, used by development staff to develop new applications. The single Windows host in the application zone is used exclusively by the production team to control software deployments into the production zone. There are 10 UNIX web application hosts in the production zone, which are publicly accessible. The development staff is required to install and remove various types of software from their hosts regularly, while the hosts in the zone rarely require any type of configuration changes. Which of the following, when implemented, would provide the best level of protection with the least amount of disruption to staff?**

a. NIPS in the production zone, HIPS in the application zone, and anti-virus/anti-malware across all Windows hosts.

b. NIPS in the production zone, NIDS in the application zone, HIPS in the core network, and anti-virus/anti-malware across all hosts.

c. HIPS in the production zone, NIPS in the application zone, and HIPS in the core network.

d. NIDS in the production zone, HIDS in the application zone, and anti-virus/anti-malware across all hosts.

Answer: a

49. **An administrator is reviewing the logs and sees the following entry:**

```
Message: Access denied with code 403 (phase 2). Pattern match "\
bunion\b.{1,100}?\bselect\b" at ARGS:$id. [data "union all select"]
[severity "CRITICAL"] [tag "WEB_ATTACK"] [tag "WASCTC/WASC-19"] [tag
"OWASP_TOP_10/A1"] [tag "OWASP_AppSensor/CIE1"] Action: Intercepted
(phase 2) Apache-Handler: php5-script
```

Which of the following attacks was being attempted?

a. Session hijacking

b. Cross-site script

c. SQL injection

d. Buffer overflow

Answer: c

50. **Scenario: A global financial institution experiences an unusual spike in network traffic originating from multiple geographic locations. Simultaneously, its DNS logs reveal a high volume of lookups for domains with randomized alphanumeric names. The security team also identifies a new, unauthorized scheduled task executing a PowerShell script with obfuscated commands.**

As a senior cybersecurity analyst, what is the most likely attack technique being employed, and what should be the primary focus of your investigation?

a. **Advanced Persistent Threat (APT) using Domain Fronting**: Investigate the use of legitimate cloud services to disguise malicious C2 traffic and analyze TLS fingerprinting data.

b. **Domain Generation Algorithm (DGA)-based Command and Control (C2) communication**: Focus on reverse engineering the domain patterns, correlating with endpoint PowerShell execution logs.

c. **Insider Threat leveraging DNS Tunneling for Exfiltration**: Prioritize monitoring DNS query volume for anomalies and correlate with privileged account activities.

d. **Supply Chain Attack deploying Fileless Malware**: Examine third-party integrations and memory-resident malicious scripts bypassing traditional defenses.

Answer: b .

Explanation: Domain Generation Algorithm (DGA)-based Command and Control (C2) communication: The combination of randomized DNS lookups, unauthorized scheduled PowerShell execution, and unusual traffic patterns suggests a botnet or malware using DGA for C2 communication. Investigating domain patterns and correlating them with PowerShell logs is critical.

Join our book's Discord space

Join the book's Discord Workspace for Latest updates, Offers, Tech happenings around the world, New Release and Sessions with the Authors:

https://discord.bpbonline.com

CHAPTER 21

CASP+ Skill Assessment Exam-II

1. A University uses a card transaction system that allows students to purchase goods using their student ID.

    Students can put money on their ID at terminals throughout the campus.

    The security administrator was notified that computer science students have been using the network to illegally put money on their cards.

    The administrator would like to attempt to reproduce what the students are doing. Which of the following is the best course of action?

    a. Notify the transaction system vendor of the security vulnerability that was discovered.

    b. Use a protocol analyzer to reverse engineer the transaction system's protocol.

    c. Contact the computer science students and threaten disciplinary action if they continue their actions.

    d. Install a NIDS in front of all the transaction system terminals.

    Answer: B

2. For a company to boost profits by implementing cost savings on non-core business activities, the IT manager has sought approval for the corporate email system to be hosted in the cloud. The compliance officer has been tasked with

ensuring that data lifecycle issues are taken into account. Which of the following best covers the data lifecycle end-to-end?

 a. Creation and secure destruction of mail accounts, emails, and calendar items

 b. Information classification, vendor selection, and the RFP process

 c. Data provisioning, processing, in transit, at rest, and de-provisioning

 d. Securing virtual environments, appliances, and equipment that handle email

Answer: C

3. **A security administrator at a Lab Company is required to implement a solution that will provide the highest level of confidentiality possible to all data on the lab network. The current infrastructure design includes the following:**

 i. **Two-factor token and biometric-based authentication for all users**

 ii. **Attributable administrator accounts**

 iii. **Logging of all transactions**

 iv. **Full disk encryption of all HDDs**

 v. **Finely granular access controls to all resources**

 vi. **Full virtualization of all servers**

 vii. **The use of LUN masking to segregate SAN data**

 viii. **Port security on all switches**

 The network is protected with a firewall implementing ACLs, a NIPS device, and secured wireless access points. Which of the following cryptographic improvements should be made to the current architecture to achieve the stated goals?

 a. PKI based authorization

 b. Transport encryption

 c. Data at rest encryption

 d. Code signing

Answer: B

4. **An organization has had six security incidents over the past year against their main web application. Each time the organization was able to determine the cause of the incident and restore operations within a few hours to a few days. Which of the following provides the most comprehensive method for reducing the time to recover?**

a. Create security metrics that provide information on response times and requirements to determine the best place to focus time and money.

b. Conduct a loss analysis to determine which systems to focus time and money on increasing security.

c. Implement a knowledge management process accessible to the help desk and finance departments to estimate cost and prioritize remediation.

d. Develop an incident response team, require training for incident remediation, and provide incident reporting and tracking metrics.

Answer: D

5. **A developer is coding the crypto routine of an application that will be installed on a standard headless and diskless server connected to a NAS housed in the data center.**

The developer has written the following six lines of code to add entropy to the routine:

   i. **If VIDEO input exists, use video data for entropy**

   ii. **If AUDIO input exists, use audio data for entropy**

   iii. **If MOUSE input exists, use mouse data for entropy**

   iv. **IF KEYBOARD input exists, use keyboard data for entropy**

   v. **IF IDE input exists, use IDE data for entropy**

   vi. **IF NETWORK input exists, use network data for entropy**

   Which of the following lines of code will result in the strongest seed when combined?

   a. 2 and 1

   b. 3 and 5

   c. 5 and 2

   d. 6 and 4

Answer: D

6. **Which of the following is the best place to contractually document security priorities, responsibilities, guarantees, and warranties when dealing with outsourcing providers?**

   a. NDA

   b. OLA

   c. MOU

   d. SLA

Answer: D

7. Company ABC is planning to outsource its Customer Relationship Management (CRM) systemand marketing/leads management to Company XYZ.

    Which of the following is the most important to be considered before going ahead with the service?

    a. Internal auditors have approved the outsourcing arrangement.

    b. Penetration testing can be performed on the externally facing web system.

    c. Ensure there are security controls within the contract and the right to audit.

    d. A physical site audit is performed on Company XYZ's management/ operation.

    Answer: C

8. A manager who was attending an all-day training session was overdue entering bonus and payroll information for subordinates. The manager felt the best way to get the changes entered while in training was to log into the payroll system, and then activate desktop sharing with a trusted subordinate. The manager granted the subordinate control of the desktop thereby giving the subordinate full access to the payroll system. The subordinate did not have the authorization to be in the payroll system. Another employee reported the incident to the security team. Which of the following would be the most appropriate method for dealing with this issue going forward?

    a. Provide targeted security awareness training and impose termination for repeat violators.

    b. Block desktop sharing and web conferencing applications and enable use only with approval.

    c. Actively monitor the data traffic for each employee using desktop sharing or web conferencing applications.

    d. Permanently block desktop sharing and web conferencing applications and do not allow their use at the company.

    Answer: A

9. Which of the following precautions should be taken to harden network devices in case of VMEscape?

    a. Database servers should be on the same virtual server as web servers in the DMZ network segment.

    b. Web servers should be on the same physical server as database servers in the network segment.

   c. Virtual servers should only be on the same physical server as others in their network segment.

   d. Physical servers should only be on the same WAN as other physical servers in their network.

Answer: C

10. **A production server has been compromised. Which of the following is the best way to preserve the non-volatile evidence?**

   a. Shut the server down and image the hard drive.

   b. Remove all power sources from the server.

   c. Install remote backup software and copy data to write-once media.

   d. Login remotely and perform a full backup of the server.

Answer: A

11. **A technician states that workstations that are on the network in location B are unable to validate certificates, while workstations that are on the main location A's network are having no issues. Which of the following methods allows a certificate to be validated by a single server that returns the validity of that certificate?**

   a. XACML

   b. OCSP

   c. ACL

   d. CRL

Answer: B

12. **A network engineer at Company ABC observes the following raw HTTP request:**

```
GET                      /disp_reports.php?SectionEntered=57&GroupEntered=-
1&report_type=alerts&to_date=01-01-0101&Run=
Run&UserEntered=dsmith&SessionID=5f04189bc&from_date=31-10-
2010&TypesEntered=1
HTTP/1.1
Host: test.example.net Accept: */*
Accept-Language: en Connection: close
Cookie: java14=1; java15=1; java16=1; js=1292192278001;
```

Which of the following should be the engineer's greatest concern?

   a. The HTTPS is not being enforced so the system is vulnerable.

   b. The numerical encoding on the session ID is limited to hexadecimal characters, making it susceptible to a brute force attack.

c. Sensitive data is transmitted in the URL.

d. The dates entered are outside a normal range, which may leave the system vulnerable to a denial of service attack.

Answer: C

13. **An administrator is assessing the potential risk impact on an accounting system and categorizes it as follows:**

Administrative Files = {(Confidentiality, Moderate), (Integrity, Moderate), (Availability, Low)}

Vendor Information = {(Confidentiality, Moderate), (Integrity, Low), (Availability, Low)}

Payroll Data = {(Confidentiality, High), (Integrity, Moderate), (Availability, Low)}

Which of the following is the aggregate risk impact on the accounting system?

a. {(Confidentiality, Moderate), (Integrity, Moderate), (Availability, Moderate)}

b. {(Confidentiality, High), (Integrity, Low), (Availability, Low)}

c. {(Confidentiality, High), (Integrity, Moderate), (Availability, Low)}

d. {(Confidentiality, Moderate), (Integrity, Moderate), (Availability, Low)}

Answer: C

14. **A company has purchased a new system, but security personnel is spending a great deal of time on system maintenance. A new third-party vendor has been selected to maintain and manage the company's system. Which of the following document types would need to be created before any work is performed?**

a. IOS

b. ISA

c. SLA

d. OLA

Answer: C

15. **A security manager has provided a Statement of Work (SOW) to an external penetration testing firm for a web application security test. The web application starts with a very simple HTML survey form with two components – a country selection dropdown list and a submit button. The penetration testers are required to provide their test cases for this survey form in advance. To adequately test the input validation of the survey form, which of the following tools would be the best tool for the technician to use?**

    a. HTTP interceptor

    b. Vulnerability scanner

    c. Port scanner

    d. Fuzzer

Answer: A

16. The IT department of a pharmaceutical research company is considering whether the company should allow or block access to social media websites during lunchtime. The company is considering the possibility of allowing access only through the company's guest wireless network, which is logically separated from the internal research network. The company prohibits the use of personal devices; therefore, such access will take place from company-owned laptops. Which of the following is the highest risk to the organization?

    a. Employee's professional reputation

    b. Intellectual property confidentiality loss

    c. Downloaded viruses on the company laptops

    d. Workstation compromise affecting the availability

Answer: B

17. A company currently does not use any type of authentication or authorization service for remote access. The new security policy states that all remote access must be locked down to only authorized personnel. The policy also dictates that only authorized external networks will be allowed to access certain internal resources. Which of the following would most likely need to be implemented and configured on the company's perimeter network to comply with the new security policy? (Select any two)

    a. VPN concentrator

    b. Firewall

    c. Proxy server

    d. WAP

    e. Layer 2 switch

Answer: A and B

18. The helpdesk is receiving multiple calls about slow and intermittent Internet access from the finance department. The network administrator reviews the tickets and compiles the following information for the security administrator:

Caller 1, IP 172.16.35.217, NETMASK 255.255.254.0

Caller 2, IP 172.16.35.53, NETMASK 255.255.254.0

Caller 3, IP 172.16.35.173, NETMASK 255.255.254.0

All callers are connected to the same switch and are routed by a router with five built-in interfaces. The upstream router interface's MAC is 00-01-42-32-ab-1a. The security administrator brings a laptop to the finance office, connects it to one of the wall jacks, starts up a network analyzer, and notices the following:

09:05:10.937590 arp (0:12:3f:f1:da:52)

09:05:15.934840 arp (0:12:3f:f1:da:52)

09:05:19.931482 arp (0:12:3f:f1:da:52)

Which of the following can the security administrator determine from the preceding information?

a. A man in the middle attack is underway – implementing static ARP entries is a possible solution.

b. An ARP flood attack targeted at the router is causing intermittent communication – implementing IPS is a possible solution.

c. The default gateway is being spoofed – implementing static routing with MD5 is a possible solution.

d. The router is being advertised on a separate network – router reconfiguration is a possible solution.

Answer: A

19. A certain script was recently altered by the author to meet certain security requirements, and needs to be executed on several critical servers. Which of the following describes the process of ensuring that the script being used was not altered by anyone other than the author?

a. Digital encryption

b. Digital signing

c. Password entropy

d. Code signing

Answer: D

20. A company that manufactures ASICs for use in an IDS wants to ensure that the ASICs' code is not prone to buffer and integer overflows. The ASIC technology is copyrighted and the confidentiality of the ASIC code design is exceptionally important. The company is required to conduct internal vulnerability testing as well as testing by a third party. Which of the following should be implemented in the SDLC to achieve these requirements?

a. Regression testing by the manufacturer and integration testing by the third party

b. User acceptance testing by the manufacturer and black-box testing by the third party

c. Defect testing by the manufacturer and user acceptance testing by the third party

d. White box unit testing by the manufacturer and black-box testing by the third party

Answer: D

21. **Which of the following attacks does Unicast Reverse Path Forwarding prevent?**

a. Man in the Middle

b. ARP poisoning

c. Broadcast storm

d. IP Spoofing

Answer: D

22. **A security administrator needs a secure computing solution to use for all of the company's security audit log storage, and to act as a central server to execute security functions from. Which of the following is the best option for the server in this scenario?**

a. A hardened Red Hat Enterprise Linux implementation running a software firewall

b. Windows 7 with a secure domain policy and smartcard-based authentication

c. A hardened bastion host permits all policies implemented in a software firewall

d. Solaris 10 with trusted extensions or SE Linux with a trusted policy

Answer: D

23. **Elaine is conducting an AAR after a hacker managed to breach the network security and steal data from the database server. Which of the following should not be part of the AAR?**

a. Getting input from multiple perspectives

b. Describe what happened

c. Remain unbiased

d. Assessing who is responsible for the breach

Answer: D

Explanation: Assessing blame is counter-productive. You do not want the blame to be part of the process of the AAR.

24. **Which of the following saves time and efforts in creating its programs and services by purchasing the products from a third-party vendor?**
    a. Collaboration platform
    b. End-to-end solution
    c. Change Management
    d. COTS product

Answer: D

Explanation: COTS stands for Commercial Off-The-Shelf products. These products save time and effort in creating their programs and services by purchasing these products from a third-party vendor. COTS products speed up and reduce the cost of system construction.

25. **Which of the following is the process of salvaging data from damaged, failed, corrupted, or inaccessible secondary storage media when it cannot be accessed normally?**
    a. Data handling
    b. Data recovery
    c. Data erasure
    d. Data breach

Answer: B

Explanation: Data recovery is the process of recovering data from damaged, failed, corrupted, or inaccessible secondary storage devices when it cannot be accessed normally. Often the data are being recovered from storage media like internal or external hard disk drives, **Solid-State Drives (SSD)**, USB drives, storage tapes, and other electronics. Recovery may be required due to physical damage to the storage device or logical damage to the file system that prevents it from being mounted by the host operating system. Answer options D, A, and C are incorrect. These are not valid op.

26. **Which of the following are the primary rules to apply RBAC-based delegation for a user on a network? Each correct answer represents a complete solution. Choose all that apply.**
    a. Authorization of Role
    b. Assignment of Roles

    c. Assignment of Permission

    d. Authorization of Permission

Answer: A, B, and D

Explanation: Role-based access control (or role-based security) is an approach to restricting system access to authorized users within an organization. In role-based access control, roles are created for various job functions. To perform certain operations, permissions are assigned to specific roles rather than individuals. Since users are not assigned permission directly, management of individual user rights becomes a matter of simply assigning appropriate roles to the user. There are three primary rules defined for RBAC, which are as follows:

- **Assignment of Roles**: A subject can exercise permission only if the subject has selected or been assigned a role.

- **Authorization of Role**: A subject's active role must be authorized for the subject. With rule 1, this rule ensures that users can take on only roles for which they are authorized.

- **Authorization of Permission**: A subject can exercise permission only if the permission is authorized for the subject's active role. With rules 1 and 2, this rule ensures that users can exercise only permissions for which they are authorized.

According to the requirements of an organization, additional constraints may be applied as well, and roles can be combined in a hierarchy where higher-level roles subsume permissions owned by sub-roles.

Answer option C is incorrect. In role-based access control, no permission is assigned to a user directly. Instead, permissions are assigned to a role and that role is assigned to the user.

27. **Fred is a network administrator for an insurance company. Lately, there has been an issue with the antivirus software not updating. What is the first thing Fred should do to solve the problem?**

    a. Devise a plan to solve the problem

    b. Clearly define the problem

    c. Try reasonable alternatives

    d. Consider probable causes

Answer: B

Explanation: The first step in problem-solving is always to clearly define the problem. You have to first be able to clearly define the problem before any other problem-solving steps can be taken.

Answer option C is incorrect. You cannot try reasonable alternatives until you define the problem. Answer option D is incorrect. Considering probable causes is an excellent idea once you have defined the problem. Answer option A is incorrect. You must first define the problem and then devise a plan before you have any chance of solving the problem.

28. **Which of the following are the benefits of public cloud computing? Each correct answer represents a complete solution. Choose any three.**

    a. Sensitive data

    b. Scalability

    c. Automation

    d. Elasticity

    Answer: B, C, and D

    Explanation: The following are the benefits of public cloud computing that you get with private cloud computing:

    • Reliability and predictability

    • Automation (self-healing and self-service)

    • Scalability

    • Elasticity

    Answer option A is incorrect. In public cloud computing, sensitive data is not secure since the sensitive data is shared beyond the corporate firewall.

29. **Mark wants to compress spreadsheets and PNG image files by using lossless data compression so that he can successfully recover original data whenever required. Which of the following compression techniques will Mark use? Each correct answer represents a complete solution. Choose any two.**

    a. Vector quantization

    b. Deflation

    c. Adaptive dictionary algorithm

    d. Color reduction

    Answer: B and C

    Explanation: To accomplish the task, Mark should use the following compression techniques:

    • Adaptive dictionary algorithm

    • Deflation

- Run-length encoding
- Entropy encoding

These techniques perform lossless data compression.

30. **Which of the following is the predicted elapsed time between inherent failures of a system during operation?**

    a. Mean time to recovery

    b. Mean time to repair

    c. Mean time between failures

    d. Mean downtime

    Answer: C

    Explanation: **Mean Time Between Failures (MTBF)** is the predicted elapsed time between inherent failures of a system during operation.

31. **Darryl is an administrator for a visualization company. He is concerned about security vulnerabilities associated with visualization. Which of the following are the most significant issues?**

    a. Privilege escalation from one VM to another

    b. The server drive crashing and bringing down all VMs

    c. Viruses moving from one VM to another

    d. Data from one VM being copied to another VM

    Answer: B

    Explanation: In a virtualized environment, any issues with the underlying drive affect all the VMs hosted on that drive.

32. **You work as a security administrator for uCertify Inc. You are conducting a security awareness campaign for the employees of the organization. What information will you provide to the employees about the security awareness program? Each correct answer represents a complete solution. Choose any three.**

    a. It improves awareness of the need to protect system resources.

    b. It improves the possibility for career advancement of the IT staff.

    c. It enhances the skills and knowledge so that the computer users can perform their jobs more securely.

    d. It constructs in-depth knowledge, as needed, to design, implement, or operate security programs for organizations and systems.

    Answer: A, C, and D

Explanation: The purpose of security awareness, training, and education is to increase security by implementing the following:

- Improving awareness of the need to protect system resources.

- Enhancing the skills and knowledge so that the computer users can perform their jobs more securely.

- Constructing in-depth knowledge, as needed, to design, implement, or operate security programs for organizations and systems.

- Making computer system users aware of their security responsibilities and teaching them correct practices, which helps users change their behavior.

It also supports individual accountability because, without the knowledge of the necessary security measures and how to use them, users cannot be truly accountable for their actions.

33. **Which of the following steps are involved in a generic cost-benefit analysis process? Each correct answer represents a complete solution. Choose any three.**

   a. Compile a list of key players

   b. Assess potential risks that may impact the solution

   c. Select measurement and collect all cost and benefits elements

   d. Establish alternative projects/programs

   Answer: A, C, and D

   Explanation: The following steps are involved in a generic cost-benefit analysis process:

   - Establish alternative projects/programs

   - Compile a list of key players

   - Select measurement and collect all cost and benefits elements

   - Predict the outcome of cost and benefits throughout the project

   - Put all effects of costs and benefits in dollars. Apply discount rate

   - Calculate the net present value of project options

   - Sensitivity analysis

   - Recommendation

   Answer option B is incorrect. It is not a valid step.

34. **John is setting up a public webserver. He has decided to place it in the DMZ. Which firewall should have the tightest restrictions?**

    a. On the web server itself

    b. Inner end of the DMZ

    c. Outer end of the DMZ

    d. The restrictions should be consistent

Answer: B

Explanation: The inner firewall is the one that protects the actual network from the outside world. Also, it is usually necessary to allow for more users to connect to the webserver than you allow into your actual network.

35. **Which of the following statements is true about Mean Time to Repair (MTTR)? Each correct answer represents a complete solution. Choose any three.**

    a. It is the total corrective maintenance time divided by the total number of corrective maintenance actions during a given period.

    b. It is the average time taken to repair a Configuration Item or IT Service after a failure.

    c. It represents the average time required to repair a failed component or device.

    d. It includes lead time for parts not readily available or other **Administrative or Logistic Downtime (ALDT)**.

Answer: A, B, and C

Explanation: Mean Time to Repair (MTTR) is the average time taken to repair a Configuration Item or IT Service after a failure. It represents the average time required to repair a failed component or device. Expressed mathematically, it is the total corrective maintenance time divided by the total number of corrective maintenance actions during a given period. It generally does not include lead time for parts not readily available or other **Administrative or Logistic Downtime (ALDT).** MTTR is often part of a maintenance contract, where a system whose MTTR is 24 hours is generally more valuable than for one of 7 days if the mean time between failures is equal because its Operational Availability is higher. MTTR is now and then incorrectly used to denote the Mean Time to Restore Service.

36. **A security administrator of a large private firm is researching and putting together a proposal to purchase an IPS. The specific IPS type has not been selected, and the security administrator needs to gather information from several vendors to determine a specific product. Which of the following documents would assist in choosing a specific brand and model?**

    a. RFC

    b. RTO

c. RFQ

d. RFI

Answer: D

37. **Within a large organization, the corporate security policy states that personal electronic devices are not allowed to be placed on the company network. There is considerable pressure from the company board to allow smartphones to connect and synchronize email and calendar items of board members and company executives. Which of the following options best balances the security and usability requirements of the executive management team?**

    a. Allow only the executive management team the ability to use personal devices on the company network, as they have important responsibilities and need convenient access.

    b. Review the security policy. Perform a risk evaluation of allowing devices that can be centrally managed, remotely disabled, and have device-level encryption of sensitive data.

    c. Stand firm on disallowing non-company assets from connecting to the network, as the assets may lead to undesirable security consequences, such as sensitive emails being leaked outside the company.

    d. Allow only certain devices that are known to have the ability to be centrally managed. Do not allow any other smartphones until the device is proven to be centrally managed.

    Answer: B

38. **An online banking application has had its source code updated and is soon to be re-launched. The underlying infrastructure has not been changed. To ensure that the application has an appropriate security posture, several security-related activities are required. Which of the following security activities should be performed to provide an appropriate level of security testing coverage? (Select any two)**

    a. Penetration test across the application with accounts of varying access levels (such as, non-authenticated, authenticated, and administrative users).

    b. Code review across critical modules to ensure that security defects, Trojans, and backdoors are not present.

    c. Vulnerability assessment across all of the online banking servers to ascertain host and container configuration lock-down and patch levels.

   d. Fingerprinting across all of the online banking servers to ascertain open ports and services.

   e. Black box code review across the entire code base to ensure that there are no security defects present.

   Answer: A and B

39. A small bank is introducing online banking to its customers through its new secured website. The firewall has three interfaces; one for the Internet connection, another for the DMZ, and the third for the internal network. Which of the following will provide the most protection from all likely attacks on the bank?

   a. Implement NIPS inline between the web server and the firewall.

   b. Implement a web application firewall inline between the web server and the firewall.

   c. Implement host intrusion prevention on all machines at the bank.

   d. Configure the firewall policy to only allow communication with the webserver using SSL.

   Answer: C

40. An employee was terminated and promptly escorted to their exit interview, after which the employee left the building. It was later discovered that this employee had started a consulting business using screenshots of their work at the company which included live customer data. This information had been removed through the use of a USB device. After this incident, it was determined a process review must be conducted to ensure this issue does not recur. Which of the following business areas should primarily be involved in this discussion? (Select any two)

   a. Database Administrator

   b. Human Resources

   c. Finance

   d. Network Administrator

   e. IT Management

   Answer: B and E

41. A company has decided to use the SDLC for the creation and production of a new information system. The security administrator is training all users on how to protect company information while using the new system, along with being able to recognize social engineering attacks. Senior Management must

also formally approve the system before it goes live. In which of the following phases would these security controls take place?

a. Operations and Maintenance

b. Implementation

c. Acquisition and Development

d. Initiation

Answer: B

42. Company ABC has recently completed the connection of its network to a national high-speed private research network. Local businesses in the area are seeking sponsorship from Company ABC to connect to the high-speed research network by directly connecting through Company ABC's network. Company ABC's Chief Information Officer (CIO) believes that this is an opportunity to increase revenues and visibility for the company, as well as promote research and development in the area. Which of the following must Company ABC require of its sponsored partners to document the technical security requirements of the connection?

a. SLA

b. ISA

c. NDA

d. BPA

Answer: B

43. A user logs into domain A using a PKI certificate on a smartcard protected by an 8-digit PIN. The credential is cached by the authenticating server in domain A. Later, the user attempts to access a resource in domain B. This initiates a request to the original authenticating server to somehow attest to the resource server in the second domain that the user is in fact who they claim to be. Which of the following is being described?

a. Authentication

b. Authorization

c. SAML

d. Kerberos

Answer: C

44. On Monday, the Chief Information Officer (CIO) of a state agency received an e-discovery request for the release of all emails sent and received by the agency's board of directors for the past five years. The CIO has contacted the

email administrator and asked the administrator to provide the requested information by the end of the day on Friday. Which of the following has the greatest impact on the ability to fulfill the e-discovery request?

a. Data retention policy

b. Backup software and hardware

c. Email encryption software

d. Data recovery procedures

Answer: A

45. An administrator is reviewing a recent security audit and determines that two users in finance also have access to the human resource data. One of those users fills in for any HR employees on vacation, and the other user only works in finance. Which of the following policies is being violated by the finance user according to the audit results?

a. Mandatory vacation

b. Non-disclosure

c. Job rotation

d. Least privilege

Answer: D

46. An IT administrator has installed new DNS name servers (Primary and Secondary), which are used to host the company MX records and resolve the web server's public address. To secure the zone transfer between the primary and secondary servers, the administrator uses only server ACLs. Which of the following attacks could the secondary DNS server still be susceptible to?

a. Email spamming

b. IP spoofing

c. Clickjacking

d. DNS replication

Answer: B

47. There has been a recent security breach that has led to the release of sensitive customer information. As part of improving security and reducing the disclosure of customer data, a training company has been employed to educate staff. Which of the following should be the primary focus of the privacy compliance training program?

a. Explain how customer data is gathered, used, disclosed, and managed.

b. Remind the staff of the company's data handling policy and have the staff sign an NDA.

c. Focus on explaining **how** and **why** the customer data is being collected.

d. Republish the data classification and the confidentiality policy.

Answer: A

48. **The sales staff at a software development company has received the following requirements from a customer:** *We need the system to notify us in advance of all software errors and report all outages.* **Which of the following best conveys these customer requirements to the software development team to understand and implement?**

a. The system shall send a status message to a network monitoring console every five seconds while in an error state and the system should email the administrator when the number of input errors exceeds five.

b. The system shall alert the administrator upon the loss of network communications and when error flags are thrown.

c. The system shall email the administrator when processing deviates from expected conditions and the system shall send a heartbeat message to a monitoring console every second while in normal operations.

d. The system shall email the administrator when an error condition is detected and a flag is thrown and the system shall send an email to the administrator when network communications are disrupted.

Answer: C

49. **A newly-hired Chief Information Security Officer (CISO) is faced with improving the security of a company with low morale and numerous disgruntled employees. After reviewing the situation for several weeks, the CISO publishes a more comprehensive security policy with associated standards. Which of the following issues could be addressed through the use of technical controls specified in the new security policy?**

a. Employees publish negative information and stories about company management on social network sites and blogs.

b. An employee remotely configures the email server at a relative's company during work hours.

    c.   Employees posting negative comments about the company from personal phones and PDAs.

    d.   External parties cloning some of the company's externally facing web pages and creating look-alike sites.

Answer: B

50. **When Company A and Company B merged, the network security administrator for Company A was tasked with joining the two networks. Which of the following should be done first?**

    a.   Implement a unified IPv6 addressing scheme on the entire network.

    b.   Conduct a penetration test of Company B's network.

    c.   Perform a vulnerability assessment on Company B's network.

    d.   Perform a peer code review on Company B's application.

Answer: C

Join our book's Discord space

Join the book's Discord Workspace for Latest updates, Offers, Tech happenings around the world, New Release and Sessions with the Authors:

https://discord.bpbonline.com

Index